'and we've had our ups and downs'

100 Years: Leeds United & Leeds City 1905-2005

David Saffer and Gary Shepherd

VERTICAL EDITIONS

First published in the United Kingdom in 2005 by
Vertical Editions, 7 Bell Busk, Skipton, North Yorkshire BD23 4DT

ISBN 1-904091-15-6

Cover design and typeset by HBA, York

Printed and bound by Cromwell Press, Trowbridge

CONTENTS

To my number one team...Deborah, Daniella, Abigail and Jake.

David Saffer

As this is my first statistical book I would like to dedicate it to my children Lee and Zoe. In addition, my parents Rosamund and Michael, and last but certainly not least my precious Mandy!

Gary Shepherd

FOREWORD

It's amazing to think that football in the city of Leeds began 100 years ago. When I first started playing football professionally for Celtic back in the late 1940s, I was not aware of the history of Leeds United. When Don Revie approached me in 1961 about joining the club, the only footballer that I had come across to play for Leeds was John Charles, who I played against when he was selected for Wales.

Don asked me to help save Leeds United from relegation to Division 3. The club was in a mess, motivation was low, the quality of players was poor, but through hard work, we achieved our objective on the final day of the season with a win at Newcastle United. My first full season at the club saw youngsters such as Gary Sprake, Paul Reaney, Norman Hunter gel with first team regulars like Billy Bremner and Jack Charlton as results picked up. We finished fifth, and then claimed the Division 2 title.

Nobody predicted success for us in Division 1, but we had a talented squad and the club's future was secure with the likes of Paul Madeley, Terry Cooper, Peter Lorimer and Eddie Gray in the youth team. Slowly we played our way into the title race and embarked on an FA Cup run. Ultimately, we lost the title on goal average and the FA Cup Final in extra-time, but nothing could detract from a remarkable campaign.

I was lucky enough to be awarded the Footballer of the Year award, and it is an honour I still cherish. My part in the history of the club covers just a small portion of the past 100 years when hundreds of footballers have graced the club and this book tells their story. I have known David for many years, he has written numerous books on Leeds United but this is his first complete history. Gary produced all the statistics for my biography, so I know that they will be comprehensive.

From good days to bad days, it's all here.

Bobby Collins
August 2005

INTRODUCTION

Football in the city of Leeds began during the 19th century but the road to a professional club would not take effect until 30 August 1904 when 50 people at the Griffin Hotel on Boar Lane were told, 'the time is ripe for a good association club in Leeds'. A resolution to form Leeds City was passed.

The new club's first competitive game finished 2-2 at Morley in the West Yorkshire League, while their first fixture at Elland Road saw Hull City win 2-0. Leeds City gained election to the Football League on 29 May 1905, and after a defeat in their Division 2 bow at Bradford City competed in the league until expulsion eight games into the 1919/20 season after allegations of illegal payments to players. City's final game was a 4-3 win at Wolves on 4 October 1919.

Leeds United surfaced from the ashes of the disgraced club. Voted into the Midland League the same month, following a 5-2 friendly win against Yorkshire Amateurs, United drew their opening league clash with Barnsley Reserves. Elected to the Football League Division 2 on 31 May 1920, United lost to Port Vale. Over the ensuing years, the team experienced ecstasy and heartache both domestically and in Europe, winning seven major honours including the Division 1 crown in 1968/69 and FA Cup in 1972.

'and we've had our ups and downs' tells the complete story of Leeds City and Leeds United to the end of the 2004/05 season. Covering 100 years of professional football in the city, every championship triumph, promotion, relegation, cup battle and tale of woe are recalled during a century of drama, mishap and adventure. Recalling the deeds of yesteryear stars such as Billy McLeod, Jim Baker, Ernie Hart, Willis Edwards, John Charles, Billy Bremner, Jack Charlton, Norman Hunter, Eddie Gray, Gordon Strachan, Lucas Radebe and Gary Kelly, the nostalgia is unrelenting.

Of course, we also recall the efforts of managers, including Herbert Chapman, Arthur Fairclough, Don Revie and Howard Wilkinson, and chairman such as Hilton Crowther and Harry Reynolds. All have contributed to club folklore during the era in which they served. Naturally, we are indebted to a number of people for making this publication possible. Grateful thanks are due to Leeds United legend Bobby Collins, *Yorkshire Post* Newspapers Ltd and Karl Waddicor at Vertical Editions.

Enjoy reminiscing

David Saffer and Gary Shepherd
August 2005

ROLL OF HONOUR

Division 1 champions	1968/69 1973/74 1991/92
Division 1 runners-up	1964/65 1965/66 1969/70 1970/71 1971/72
Division 2 champions	1923/24 1963/64 1989/90
Division 2 runners-up	1927/28 1931/32 1955/56
FA Cup winners	1971/72
FA Cup finalists	1964/65 1969/70 1972/73
Football League Cup winners	1967/68
Football League Cup finalists	1995/96
European Cup finalists	1974/75
European Cup Winners Cup finalists	1972/73
Inter-Cities Fairs Cup winners	1967/68 1970/71
Inter-Cities Fairs Cup finalists	1966/67
FA Charity Shield winners	1969/70 1992/93
FA Charity Shield finalists	1974/75
FA Youth Challenge Cup winners	1996/97

Leeds City's first season as a Football League club began inauspiciously with a 1-0 defeat at Bradford City in front of 15,000 spectators. Some 6,802 supporters attended the opening home encounter at Elland Road, which City lost 2-0 to West Bromwich Albion before Gilbert Gillies' charges gained their first league point with a 2-2 draw against Lincoln City, centre-forward Thomas Drain scoring the new club's first goals.

City finally settled down over the coming weeks following a victory at Leicester Fosse; Harry Singleton scoring the only goal of a tight encounter. Four triumphs followed in the next five matches, Fred Hargraves scoring five in victories against Hull City, Lincoln City, Barnsley and Grimsby Town. With new players coming in, inconsistency reigned with just one victory before the Christmas fixtures; Hargraves proving the deciding factor in a home clash against Glossop before Bradford completed a double over their West Yorkshire rivals with a 2-0 win in front of a season's best crowd at Elland Road of 22,000.

Prior to league status, City lost their sole preliminary FA Cup tie 3-1 to Rockingham Colliery but would fare better second time around. Making not only a home bow in the competition but also their first round debut, City trounced Morley 11-0 with Hargraves and Dickie Morris, City's first international player when he played for Wales against Scotland in 1906, notching four goals apiece. Hargraves once more showed his prowess with a crucial strike against Mexborough in a 3-1 second replay win. The sharpshooter earned a replay at Hull City in round three, before Leeds bowed out of the competition.

The turn of the year improved City's league fortunes. Defeating Blackpool and promotion bound Manchester United 3-0; City completed a first league double with a 4-1 win against Leicester. Although trailing behind runaway leaders Bristol City, centre-forward David Wilson immediately made his mark as a goal poacher. Opening the scoring in a 3-1 win against Burslem Port Vale, Wilson then notched eight in three consecutive games, including four in a 6-1 home win against Clapton Orient, City's biggest victory of the season. Wilson's strike at Glossop ended the league campaign on a high for skipper Dick Ray and manager Gillies as City encouragingly finished in sixth spot.

Hargraves led the way in the scoring charts with 19 league and cup goals, but top marksman in the league was Wilson with 13 goals in just 15 appearances. On a historic note, the club's first strip was blue and gold shirts with white shorts. Parnell missed only one of City's 44 league and cup matches and his spot kick in City's 2-1 win at Lincoln gave him the honour of scoring the club's first ever penalty. In a city renowned for rugby, football had begun to make its mark.

DIVISION TWO (FINAL LEAGUE POSITION - 6TH)
PLD 38 W 17 D 9 L 12 F 59 A 47 PTS 43

DATE	OPPONENTS	VENUE	SCORE	SCORERS	ATT.
02-Sep	BRADFORD CITY	AWAY	0 - 1		15,000
09-Sep	WEST BROMWICH ALBION	HOME	0 - 2		6,802
11-Sep	LINCOLN CITY	HOME	2 - 2	DRAIN 2	3,000
16-Sep	LEICESTER FOSSE	AWAY	1 - 0	SINGLETON	5,000
23-Sep	HULL CITY	HOME	3 - 1	MORRIS D 2 & HARGRAVES	13,654
30-Sep	LINCOLN CITY	AWAY	2 - 1	PARNELL (PEN) & HARGRAVES	3,000
14-Oct	BURSLEM PORT VALE	AWAY	0 - 2		1,500
21-Oct	BARNSLEY	HOME	3 - 2	MORRIS D, HARGRAVES & O. G. (STACEY)	12,000
11-Nov	GRIMSBY TOWN	HOME	3 - 0	HARGRAVES 2 & STRINGFELLOW	7,000
13-Nov	BURTON UNITED	AWAY	1 - 1	PARNELL	1,500
25-Nov	CHELSEA	HOME	0 - 0		20,000
02-Dec	GAINSBOROUGH TRINITY	AWAY	1 - 4	WATSON B	2,000
09-Dec	BRISTOL CITY	HOME	1 - 1	MORGAN	15,000
23-Dec	GLOSSOP	HOME	1 - 0	HARGRAVES	9,000
26-Dec	STOCKPORT COUNTY	AWAY	1 - 2	SINGLETON	5,000
30-Dec	BRADFORD CITY	HOME	0 - 2		22,000
01-Jan	BLACKPOOL	AWAY	3 - 0	MORRIS D, WILSON D & SINGLETON	3,000
06-Jan	WEST BROMWICH ALBION	AWAY	1 - 2	WILSON D	2,553
15-Jan	MANCHESTER UNITED	AWAY	3 - 0	WATSON B, WILSON D & SINGLETON	6,000
20-Jan	LEICESTER FOSSE	HOME	4 - 1	MURRAY D (PEN), DRAIN, WATSON B, HARGRAVES	8,000
27-Jan	HULL CITY	AWAY	0 - 0		10,000
03-Feb	BURNLEY	HOME	1 - 1	WATSON B	7,129
10-Feb	CHESTERFIELD TOWN	AWAY	2 - 0	MORRIS D & SINGLETON	4,000
17-Feb	BURSLEM PORT VALE	HOME	3 - 1	WILSON D, HARGRAVES & PARNELL	9,000
24-Feb	BARNSLEY	AWAY	0 - 3		5,000
27-Feb	CHESTERFIELD TOWN	HOME	3 - 0	WILSON D 2 & MURRAY D (PEN)	2,000
03-Mar	CLAPTON ORIENT	HOME	6 - 1	WILSON D 4, HARGRAVES & PARNELL	8,000
10-Mar	BURNLEY	AWAY	3 - 4	WILSON D 2 & SINGLETON	5,000
17-Mar	GRIMSBY TOWN	AWAY	1 - 1	MURRAY D	3,000
24-Mar	BURTON UNITED	HOME	2 - 1	WATSON B & SINGLETON	5,000
29-Mar	CLAPTON ORIENT	AWAY	0 - 0		1,000
31-Mar	CHELSEA	AWAY	0 - 4		15,000
07-Apr	GAINSBOROUGH TRINITY	HOME	1 - 0	HARGRAVES	12,000
13-Apr	STOCKPORT COUNTY	HOME	1 - 1	LAVERY	10,000
14-Apr	BRISTOL CITY	AWAY	0 - 2		12,000
16-Apr	BLACKPOOL	HOME	3 - 0	HARGRAVES 2 & WATSON B	10,000
21-Apr	MANCHESTER UNITED	HOME	1 - 3	LAVERY	10,000
28-Apr	GLOSSOP	AWAY	2 - 0	PARNELL & WILSON D	1,500

F. A. CUP

DATE	OPPONENTS	VENUE	SCORE	SCORERS	ATT.
07-Oct	MORLEY (P1)	HOME	11 - 0	HARGRAVES 4, WATSON B 2, MORRIS D 4 & PARNELL	3,000
28-Oct	MEXBOROUGH TOWN (P2)	HOME	1 - 1	HARGRAVES	4,000
02-Nov	MEXBOROUGH TOWN (P2R)	AWAY	1 - 1*	PARNELL	3,000
06-Nov	MEXBOROUGH TOWN (P22R)	HOME	3 - 1	WATSON B, MORRIS D & HARGRAVES	5,000
22-Nov	HULL CITY (P3)	AWAY	1 - 1	HARGRAVES	3,000
29-Nov	HULL CITY (P3R)	HOME	1 - 2	PARNELL	7,186

LEAGUE AND CUP
APPEARANCES

PLAYER	LEAGUE	F. A. CUP	TOTAL
BROMAGE	35	6	41
CLAY		1	1
DRAIN	9	1	10
FREEBOROUGH	2		2
GEORGE	5		5
HARGRAVES	28	6	34
HENDERSON	35	5	40
HOWARD	1		1
LAVERY	8		8
McDONALD J	25	6	31
MORGAN	35	6	41
MORRIS D	25	6	31
MORRIS J	9		9
MURRAY D	23		23
PARNELL	37	6	43
RAY	27	5	32
SINGLETON	37	6	43
STRINGFELLOW	13	3	16
SWIFT	1		1
WALKER F	15	3	18
WATSON B	30	6	36
WHITLEY	3		3
WILSON D	15		15

GOALSCORERS

PLAYER	LEAGUE	F. A. CUP	TOTAL
HARGRAVES	12	7	19
WILSON D	13		13
MORRIS D	5	5	10
WATSON B	6	3	9
PARNELL	5	3	8
SINGLETON	7		7
DRAIN	3		3
MURRAY D	3		3
LAVERY	2		2
MORGAN	1		1
STRINGFELLOW	1		1
OWN GOALS	1		1

LEEDS CITY ALSO PLAYED IN THE F. A. CUP IN 1904 - 05. IT WAS IN THE PRELIMINARY ROUND ONE ON SEPT. 17TH (AWAY) AT ROCKINGHAM COLLIERY. THE GAME WAS LOST 1 - 3 WITH MUSGRAVE SCORING. THE TEAM WAS MALLINSON, SKELDON, DIXON, MORRIS R., MORRIS J., TENNANT, HEFFRON, PAGE, MUSGRAVE, CUMMINGS & SIMPSON. (MORRIS J. IS THE SAME PLAYER WHO PLAYED IN 1905-06). THE ATTENDANCE WAS 1,000. LEEDS CITY ALSO PLAYED IN THE WEST YORKSHIRE LEAGUE (PLD 24 W 7 D 7 L 10 F 34 A 49 PTS 21) AND FINISHED 11TH

KEY :- PEN = PENALTY. * = AFTER EXTRA TIME. O. G. = OWN GOAL. P22R = PRELIMINARY ROUND 2 - SECOND REPLAY, PLD = PLAYED, W = WON, D = DRAWN, L = LOST, F = GOALS FOR, A = GOALS AGAINST, PTS = POINTS, SF = SEMI - FINAL, Fi = FINAL, R1-1 = ROUND 1 - FIRST LEG, R2 = ROUND 2, ATT = ATTENDANCE.

A derby crowd of 20,000 flocked to Elland Road for an opening day 2-2 draw against Bradford City. Leeds first win of the season came at the seventh attempt at Burton United and the 2-0 win was the first of three consecutive victories, including a 4-3 home triumph against Grimsby Town, John Lavery notching the winner. Lavery's third in as many games helped account for Burslem Port Vale, however in the next league encounter, tragedy struck the club when striker David Wilson died during a 1-0 home defeat to Burnley.

In a tough encounter Wilson left the field during the first half complaining of chest pains, but returned to the fray against medical advice when he heard two of his colleagues Harry Singleton and Lavery were struggling with knocks. Within minutes, Wilson departed and collapsed before reaching the dressing room. Despite efforts to revive him, 23-year-old Wilson died. His widow received the proceeds of a friendly against Hull City watched by 3,000 spectators

The defeat rocked City and formed part of a run of seven losses in eight games. The sole victory came at home against Clapton Orient, the winning strike in City's 3-2 win coming from Billy McLeod, heralding a career that would see the sharpshooter become the most prolific striker in the club's history. Whilst McLeod found his feet, Lavery kept the goals flowing, including a hat-trick in a club record 6-1 win against Stockport County. City's win however, was the only bright point in an appalling run of form.

The New Year brought no respite in League or FA Cup, reigning Division 2 champions Bristol City winning a first round tie with some comfort 4-1. McLeod grabbed City's consolation goal and his scoring exploits would be the focal point of the second part of the season that brought eight league wins. The sharpshooter's strikes came in five of the victories, including the only goal against Chesterfield and a brace in clashes against West Brom and Burton United. His third double of the season gained a point in the final game of the season as Leeds ended a disappointing campaign with a 2-2 draw at home against Hull City in front of just 7,000 followers; a stark contrast to the season's opener.

Finishing tenth, McLeod ended the campaign top scorer with 16 goals. Manager Gilbert Gillies will have been thankful for the improvement in form but alas, the season will always be notable for events off the field following the death of David 'Soldier' Wilson.

1906 - 1907

DIVISION TWO (FINAL LEAGUE POSITION - 10TH)
PLD 38 W 13 D 10 L 15 F 55 A 63 PTS 36

DATE	OPPONENTS	VENUE	SCORE	SCORERS	ATT.
01-Sep	BRADFORD CITY	HOME	1 - 1	LAVERY	20,000
08-Sep	WEST BROMWICH ALBION	AWAY	0 - 5		15,504
10-Sep	LINCOLN CITY	HOME	1 - 1	CUBBERLEY	5,000
15-Sep	LEICESTER FOSSE	HOME	1 - 1	JEFFERSON	11,000
22-Sep	NOTTINGHAM FOREST	AWAY	0 - 3		5,000
29-Sep	LINCOLN CITY	AWAY	1 - 1	JEFFERSON	4,000
06-Oct	BURTON UNITED	AWAY	2 - 0	LAVERY & WATSON B	3,000
13-Oct	GRIMSBY TOWN	HOME	4 - 3	WATSON B 2, MURRAY D (PEN) & LAVERY	10,000
20-Oct	BURSLEM PORT VALE	AWAY	2 - 1	LAVERY & PARNELL	4,000
27-Oct	BURNLEY	HOME	0 - 1		14,000
03-Nov	CHESTERFIELD TOWN	AWAY	0 - 1		3,000
10-Nov	BARNSLEY	AWAY	0 - 3		4,000
17-Nov	CHELSEA	HOME	0 - 1		8,000
24-Nov	WOLVERHAMPTON WANDERERS	AWAY	2 - 3	LAVERY & MURRAY D (PEN)	4,500
01-Dec	CLAPTON ORIENT	HOME	3 - 2	WATSON B, PARNELL & McLEOD	10,000
05-Dec	BLACKPOOL	AWAY	0 - 1		2,000
08-Dec	GAINSBOROUGH TRINITY	AWAY	0 - 1		3,000
15-Dec	STOCKPORT COUNTY	HOME	6 - 1	McLEOD, LAVERY 3 & WATSON B 2	8,000
22-Dec	HULL CITY	AWAY	1 - 2	LAVERY	10,000
29-Dec	BRADFORD CITY	AWAY	2 - 2	McLEOD & WILSON T	17,000
01-Jan	GLOSSOP	AWAY	0 - 2		1,000
05-Jan	WEST BROMWICH ALBION	HOME	3 - 2	McLEOD 2 & JEFFERSON	14,000
19-Jan	LEICESTER FOSSE	AWAY	2 - 2	McLEOD & KIRK	8,000
26-Jan	NOTTINGHAM FOREST	HOME	1 - 4	McLEOD	14,000
02-Feb	BLACKPOOL	HOME	1 - 1	JEFFERSON	7,000
09-Feb	BURTON UNITED	HOME	3 - 1	McLEOD 2 & PARNELL	7,000
16-Feb	GRIMSBY TOWN	AWAY	0 - 4		4,000
23-Feb	BURSLEM PORT VALE	HOME	2 - 0	PARNELL & WATSON B	7,000
02-Mar	BURNLEY	AWAY	2 - 1	HARWOOD & WILSON T	5,000
09-Mar	CHESTERFIELD TOWN	HOME	1 - 0	McLEOD	10,500
16-Mar	BARNSLEY	HOME	2 - 1	McLEOD & WATSON B	14,000
23-Mar	CHELSEA	AWAY	0 - 2		25,000
30-Mar	WOLVERHAMPTON WANDERERS	HOME	2 - 0	WATSON B & CUBBERLEY	15,000
01-Apr	GLOSSOP	HOME	1 - 4	O. G. (McEWAN)	8,000
06-Apr	CLAPTON ORIENT	AWAY	1 - 1	LAVERY	6,000
13-Apr	GAINSBOROUGH TRINITY	HOME	4 - 0	CUBBERLEY, LAVERY 2 & McLEOD	3,000
20-Apr	STOCKPORT COUNTY	AWAY	2 - 2	KENNEDY & McLEOD	3,000
27-Apr	HULL CITY	HOME	2 - 2	McLEOD 2	7,000
		F. A. CUP			
12-Jan	BRISTOL CITY (R1)	AWAY	1 - 4	McLEOD	14,000

LEAGUE AND CUP APPEARANCES

PLAYER	LEAGUE	F. A. CUP	TOTAL
BROMAGE	34	1	35
CLARK	24		24
CUBBERLEY	20		20
FREEBOROUGH	20		20
GEORGE	3		3
HARGRAVES	33	1	34
HARWOOD	1		1
HENDERSON	15		15
JEFFERSON	9	1	10
JOHNSON G	1		1
KENNEDY	35	1	36
KIRK	8	1	9
LAVERY	27	1	28
McLEOD	23	1	24
MORGAN	6		6
MORRIS J	1		1
MURRAY D	23	1	24
MURRAY W	8		8
PAGE	4		4
PARNELL	33		33
PICKARD	2		2
RAY	11	1	12
SINGLETON	8		8
WALKER F	11		11
WATSON B	28	1	29
WHITLEY	4		4
WILSON D	6		6
WILSON T	20	1	21

GOALSCORERS

PLAYER	LEAGUE	F. A. CUP	TOTAL
McLEOD	15	1	16
LAVERY	12		12
WATSON B	9		9
JEFFERSON	4		4
PARNELL	4		4
CUBBERLEY	3		3
MURRAY D	2		2
WILSON T	2		2
HARWOOD	1		1
KENNEDY	1		1
KIRK	1		1
OWN GOALS	1		1

Following two poor starts to a league campaign, City at last got off to a flyer with six wins in the opening 10 matches. Home form was especially impressive with five successive victories. An own goal settled the opening day's clash against Glossop, before a 5-2 win, including a goal from outside-left Fred Croot making only his third appearance, defeated Clapton Orient.

Billy McLeod had begun the season quietly but soon struck form with winning strikes against West Brom, Hull City and Lincoln City. Goals continued to flow for the prolific striker but triumphs dried up. By the end of March, City would claim just four wins in the 22 league games that followed the heady opening spell. McLeod scored in each match, including the opening goal during a 4-1 win against Grimsby Town and the clinching goal at Glossop to record City's only double of the season. However, the slide in form and drop down the league table resulted in decisive action from the board. Unimpressed with the team's progress they decided not to renew Gilbert Gillies' contract when it came up for renewal and appointed Frank Scott-Walford as City's new manager.

A couple of wins and draws in the closing six matches edged City into twelfth spot, but it could have been far worse as they finished just two points clear of third bottom club Grimsby Town. In the FA Cup, City failed to get past the first round and to compound a miserable season they suffered heavy defeats at champions-elect Bradford City 5-0, Lincoln City 5-0 and Derby County 6-1. The return with Bradford went the visitors way by a solitary goal in front of a record home attendance of 35,000 but City did avenge their heaviest defeat of the season against Derby in the return fixture at Elland Road with a 5-1 win, McLeod grabbing a brace.

McLeod once again took the scoring honours with 17 goals, all in the league. Finishing nine goals clear of Fred Parnell, McLeod's final goal in a 3-0 win against Stockport County was his first penalty for the club. City's centre-forward missed two Division 2 fixtures towards the end of the season, just one appearance behind centre-half Tom Hynds and two adrift of ever-present Croot, who made a tremendous impression in his debut season.

1907 - 1908

DIVISION TWO (FINAL LEAGUE POSITION - 12TH)
PLD 38 W 12 D 8 L 18 F 53 A 65 PTS 32

DATE	OPPONENTS	VENUE	SCORE	SCORERS	ATT.
02-Sep	GLOSSOP	HOME	2 - 1	LAVERY & O. G. (TUSTIN)	4,000
07-Sep	LEICESTER FOSSE	AWAY	2 - 2	WATSON B & McLEOD	10,000
09-Sep	CLAPTON ORIENT	HOME	5 - 2	WATSON B 2, CROOT & LAVERY 2	6,000
14-Sep	BLACKPOOL	AWAY	3 - 2	WATSON B, LAVERY & PARNELL	6,000
21-Sep	STOKE	AWAY	1 - 2	PARNELL	10,000
28-Sep	WEST BROMWICH ALBION	HOME	1 - 0	McLEOD	24,000
05-Oct	BRADFORD CITY	AWAY	0 - 5		27,000
12-Oct	HULL CITY	HOME	3 - 2	McLEOD 2 & WATSON B	15,000
19-Oct	DERBY COUNTY	AWAY	1 - 6	O. G. (ATKIN)	10,000
26-Oct	LINCOLN CITY	HOME	2 - 1	PARNELL & McLEOD	10,000
02-Nov	FULHAM	AWAY	0 - 2		20,000
09-Nov	BARNSLEY	HOME	1 - 1	McLEOD	11,000
16-Nov	CHESTERFIELD TOWN	AWAY	3 - 4	THOMAS 2 & PARNELL	4,000
23-Nov	BURNLEY	HOME	2 - 2	CROOT & McLEOD	7,000
30-Nov	OLDHAM ATHLETIC	AWAY	2 - 4	McLEOD & GEMMELL	8,000
14-Dec	GRIMSBY TOWN	HOME	4 - 1	McLEOD, CROOT 2 & MURRAY D (PEN)	5,000
21-Dec	WOLVERHAMPTON WANDERERS	AWAY	0 - 2		5,000
25-Dec	STOCKPORT COUNTY	AWAY	1 - 2	McLEOD	8,000
28-Dec	GAINSBOROUGH TRINITY	HOME	0 - 0		8,000
01-Jan	GLOSSOP	AWAY	2 - 0	CROOT & McLEOD	2,000
04-Jan	LEICESTER FOSSE	HOME	0 - 0		10,000
18-Jan	STOKE	HOME	0 - 1		10,000
25-Jan	WEST BROMWICH ALBION	AWAY	0 - 1		8,000
01-Feb	BRADFORD CITY	HOME	0 - 1		35,000
08-Feb	HULL CITY	AWAY	1 - 4	McLEOD	9,000
15-Feb	DERBY COUNTY	HOME	5 - 1	MURRAY D (PEN), CROOT, LAVERY & McLEOD 2	8,000
22-Feb	LINCOLN CITY	AWAY	0 - 5		1,000
29-Feb	FULHAM	HOME	0 - 1		10,000
07-Mar	BARNSLEY	AWAY	3 - 1	JEFFERSON, McLEOD & CROOT	5,000
14-Mar	CHESTERFIELD TOWN	HOME	0 - 0		6,000
21-Mar	BURNLEY	AWAY	0 - 1		7,000
28-Mar	OLDHAM ATHLETIC	HOME	1 - 2	PARNELL	15,000
04-Apr	CLAPTON ORIENT	AWAY	0 - 0		8,000
11-Apr	GRIMSBY TOWN	AWAY	0 - 2		6,000
17-Apr	STOCKPORT COUNTY	HOME	3 - 0	GEMMELL, McLEOD (PEN) & CROOT	12,000
18-Apr	WOLVERHAMPTON WANDERERS	HOME	3 - 1	PARNELL, GEMMELL & WATSON B	10,000
20-Apr	BLACKPOOL	HOME	1 - 1	LAVERY	7,000
22-Apr	GAINSBOROUGH TRINITY	AWAY	1 - 2	McLEOD	3,500

F. A. CUP

11-Jan	OLDHAM ATHLETIC (R1)	AWAY	1 - 2	PARNELL	14,000

LEAGUE AND CUP APPEARANCES

PLAYER	LEAGUE	F. A. CUP	TOTAL
BATES	3		3
BROMAGE	10		10
CROOT	38	1	39
CUBBERLEY	29	1	30
FREEBOROUGH	2		2
GEMMELL	16	1	17
HARGRAVES	2		2
HENDERSON	25		25
HYNDS	37	1	38
JEFFERSON	8		8
KAY	31	1	32
KENNEDY	8	1	9
LAVERY	21		21
McLEOD	36	1	37
MURRAY D	34	1	35
NAISBY	28	1	29
PARNELL	34	1	35
PICKARD	2		2
THOMAS	9	1	10
THORPE	9		9
TOMPKINS	11		11
WATSON B	25		25

GOALSCORERS

PLAYER	LEAGUE	F. A. CUP	TOTAL
McLEOD	17		17
CROOT	8		8
PARNELL	6	1	7
LAVERY	6		6
WATSON B	6		6
GEMMELL	3		3
MURRAY D	2		2
THOMAS	2		2
JEFFERSON	1		1
OWN GOALS	2		2

FOR EASE OF IDENTIFICATION WHERE TWO PLAYERS WITH THE SAME SURNAME HAVE PLAYED, EVERY EFFORT HAS BEEN MADE TO PERSONALISE THEM BY PUTTING THEIR INITIAL, EG :- HAMPSON J, HAMPSON Wm. OR HAMPSON Wa. THIS HAS BEEN UNDERTAKEN FOR LEEDS CITY AND LEEDS UNITED INDIVIDUALLY

Looking ahead to the new season, Frank Scott-Walford would have doubtless been hoping for a confident opening especially with the first five fixtures at Elland Road, although he would have been very disappointed that star striker Billy McLeod was unavailable for the first three matches.

Making an immediate impact in what would be his only season at the club was Tom Rodger with the only goal of the season's opener against promotion hopefuls Tottenham Hotspur in front of a bumper 20,000 crowd and the first goal in a 2-0 win against Hull City. McLeod though was soon back in the forward line and firing on all cylinders with a brace during a 2-0 win against Barnsley in his first game back in the side, but another double was mere consolation in a 5-2 defeat to Derby County.

McLeod's next goal in a 2-1 win against Stockport County, City's first win in four games, would herald a run of eight goals in as many games and six in consecutive matches, including crucial strikes against Birmingham and Fulham; the latter clash one of only two away victories all season. However, a 6-0 defeat at Oldham was the first of seven successive defeats running into the New Year, the worst series of losses in the club's fledgling history. With McLeod again injured, reserve striker Adam Bowman stepped in to end the drought against Blackpool, and two further strikes against Fulham and Chesterfield brought important victories that would ultimately push City clear of the bottom clubs. Bowman, like Rodger, would play just one season for the club, but making his mark at inside-forward was Scot Jimmy Gemmell.

Finishing second top scorer with eight goals behind McLeod on 17, the Glaswegian proved something of a lucky mascot as City won every match in which he scored. Amongst a number of notable performances were a brace in a 4-1 victory against Grimsby, the only goal in City's visit to the Humberside club and his only Leeds hat-trick in a 5-2 against Wolves; the first treble by a City player for two years.

City defeated Oldham after a replay in the FA Cup but lost out to West Ham in a second round clash. In Division 2, an eventual twelfth place finish, six points ahead of bottom side Blackpool was disappointing because with six games to go a top-six placing was not without hope. However, four defeats during the run in against sides not challenging for promotion sealed a mediocre position. One can only speculate where City would have finished had McLeod not missed 16 league games, a stark contrast to Fred Croot, who again made the most appearances, missing just one league match.

1908 - 1909

	DIVISION TWO (FINAL LEAGUE POSITION - 12TH)				
	PLD 38 W 14 D 7 L 17 F 43 A 53 PTS 35				
DATE	OPPONENTS	VENUE	SCORE	SCORERS	ATT.
05-Sep	TOTTENHAM HOTSPUR	HOME	1 - 0	RODGER	20,000
07-Sep	CLAPTON ORIENT	HOME	0 - 0		8,000
12-Sep	HULL CITY	HOME	2 - 0	RODGER & BOWMAN	12,000
14-Sep	BARNSLEY	HOME	2 - 0	McLEOD 2	8,000
19-Sep	DERBY COUNTY	HOME	2 - 5	McLEOD 2 (1 PEN)	20,000
26-Sep	BLACKPOOL	AWAY	0 - 1		5,000
03-Oct	CHESTERFIELD TOWN	AWAY	0 - 2		7,000
10-Oct	GLOSSOP	AWAY	0 - 0		4,000
17-Oct	STOCKPORT COUNTY	HOME	2 - 1	McLEOD & O. G. (MOLYNEUX)	8,500
24-Oct	WEST BROMWICH ALBION	AWAY	1 - 2	McLEOD	13,554
31-Oct	BIRMINGHAM	HOME	2 - 0	McLEOD & RODGER	15,000
07-Nov	GAINSBOROUGH TRINITY	AWAY	1 - 1	McLEOD	4,000
14-Nov	GRIMSBY TOWN	HOME	4 - 1	GEMMELL 2 & McLEOD 2	8,000
21-Nov	FULHAM	AWAY	1 - 0	McLEOD	18,000
28-Nov	BURNLEY	HOME	1 - 1	BOWMAN	14,000
12-Dec	WOLVERHAMPTON WANDERERS	HOME	5 - 2	McLEOD, GEMMELL 3 & GUY	14,000
19-Dec	OLDHAM ATHLETIC	AWAY	0 - 6		8,000
25-Dec	BOLTON WANDERERS	AWAY	0 - 2		19,400
26-Dec	BOLTON WANDERERS	HOME	1 - 2	JOYNES	15,000
01-Jan	BARNSLEY	AWAY	1 - 2	GUY	6,500
02-Jan	TOTTENHAM HOTSPUR	AWAY	0 - 3		16,000
09-Jan	HULL CITY	AWAY	1 - 4	McLEOD	7,000
23-Jan	DERBY COUNTY	AWAY	1 - 5	BOWMAN	7,000
30-Jan	BLACKPOOL	HOME	1 - 0	BOWMAN	8,000
13-Feb	GLOSSOP	HOME	3 - 1	CROOT, BURNETT & GEMMELL	10,000
20-Feb	STOCKPORT COUNTY	AWAY	0 - 1		6,000
27-Feb	WEST BROMWICH ALBION	HOME	1 - 1	McLEOD	12,000
13-Mar	GAINSBOROUGH TRINITY	HOME	0 - 2		7,000
20-Mar	GRIMSBY TOWN	AWAY	1 - 0	GEMMELL	5,500
27-Mar	FULHAM	HOME	2 - 0	BOWMAN & GUY	10,000
03-Apr	BURNLEY	AWAY	0 - 0		5,000
09-Apr	CHESTERFIELD TOWN	HOME	3 - 0	RODGER, GEMMELL & BOWMAN	10,000
10-Apr	BRADFORD PARK AVENUE	HOME	0 - 3		11,000
12-Apr	BIRMINGHAM	AWAY	0 - 1		3,000
13-Apr	CLAPTON ORIENT	AWAY	0 - 0		3,000
17-Apr	WOLVERHAMPTON WANDERERS	AWAY	1 - 2	McLEOD	7,000
24-Apr	OLDHAM ATHLETIC	HOME	3 - 0	BURNETT, CROOT & DOUGAL	4,500
27-Apr	BRADFORD PARK AVENUE	AWAY	0 - 2		6,000
	F. A. CUP				
16-Jan	OLDHAM ATHLETIC (R1)	AWAY	1 - 1	McLEOD	7,000
20-Jan	OLDHAM ATHLETIC (R1R)	HOME	2 - 0	McLEOD (PEN) & GUY	19,047
06-Feb	WEST HAM UNITED (R2)	HOME	1 - 1	BURNETT	31,471
11-Feb	WEST HAM UNITED (R2R) *	AWAY	1 - 2	BOWMAN	13,000

LEAGUE AND CUP APPEARANCES

PLAYER	LEAGUE	F. A. CUP	TOTAL
BATES	12		12
BOWMAN	15	1	16
BROMAGE	4		4
BURNETT	18	4	22
CROOT	37	4	41
CUBBERLEY	27	4	31
CUNNINGHAM T	1		1
DOUGAL	10		10
GEMMELL	28	4	32
GUY	18	4	22
HAMILTON J	21	4	25
JOYNES	15	1	16
KENNEDY	15		15
McALLISTER	32	4	36
McDONALD W	14		14
McLEOD	22	2	24
MORRIS T	9		9
MURRAY D	3		3
NAISBY	33	4	37
RODGER	25		25
WATSON J	28	4	32
WHITE	31	4	35

GOALSCORERS

PLAYER	LEAGUE	F. A. CUP	TOTAL
McLEOD	15	2	17
GEMMELL	8		8
BOWMAN	6	1	7
GUY	3	1	4
RODGER	4		4
BURNETT	2	1	3
CROOT	2		2
DOUGAL	1		1
JOYNES	1		1
OWN GOALS	1		1

KEY :- * = AFTER EXTRA TIME

15

City enjoyed their best opening day win since formation when they demolished Lincoln City 5-0 at Elland Road but optimism among supporters was summed up by a crowd 14,000 less than the previous season's opener when Tottenham came to town. Braces by Jimmy Gemmill and Billy Halligan plus a rare Tom Morris strike, one of only three in over 100 appearances by the centre-half, made it a day to remember.

In the absence of Billy McLeod through injury for all but two of the first 10 games, Halligan continued to deputise with some success, proving the hero in victories against Derby County and Birmingham. However, even with the return of McLeod, City's form was atrocious, gaining just four victories prior to Christmas. Nine defeats in 11 games plunged them down the table, but goals from McLeod and Hugh Roberts resulted in festive victories against Clapton Orient and Blackpool.

The New Year brought little respite for Frank Scott-Walford's side despite ringing the changes. Just one triumph in 13 games; 2-1 against relegation rivals Birmingham, Roberts and Fred Croot notching important goals, was grim as the run-in approached. McLeod was scoring goals and cometh the hour, City's mainstay in attack notched a brace in a 2-0 win at Clapton Orient and the winner in a 1-0 victory against Wolves during Easter fixtures.

Despite losses at Gainsborough Trinity and champions-elect Manchester City, McLeod's final goal of the campaign earned a 3-1 win at Grimsby Town, and a 1-1 draw at home to Leicester Fosse saw City finish seventeenth, three points clear of Grimsby Town and four clear of bottom-placed Birmingham, who both had to seek re-election. Three wins and a draw in the last six games saved embarrassment but it could easily have been worse.

Knocked out of the FA Cup at Sunderland, Elland Road staged a semi-final between Barnsley and Everton, but the hometown's efforts of 10 league wins all season was nothing to shout about. McLeod finished top scorer for a fourth consecutive season with 15 goals, whilst goalkeeper Harry Bromage, centre-half Stan Cubberley and Fred Croot made at least 35 league appearances.

1909 - 1910

DIVISION TWO (FINAL LEAGUE POSITION - 17TH)				
PLD 38 W 10 D 7 L 21 F 46 A 80 PTS 27				
DATE	OPPONENTS	VENUE	SCORE SCORERS	ATT.
01-Sep	LINCOLN CITY	HOME	5 - 0 GEMMELL 2, HALLIGAN 2 & MORRIS T	6,000
04-Sep	HULL CITY	AWAY	1 - 3 HALLIGAN	10,000
11-Sep	DERBY COUNTY	HOME	2 - 1 CROOT & HALLIGAN	12,000
18-Sep	STOCKPORT COUNTY	AWAY	0 - 0	7,000
25-Sep	GLOSSOP	HOME	1 - 2 McLEOD	12,000
02-Oct	BIRMINGHAM	AWAY	2 - 1 HALLIGAN 2	14,000
09-Oct	WEST BROMWICH ALBION	HOME	0 - 1	7,500
16-Oct	OLDHAM ATHLETIC	AWAY	1 - 2 HALLIGAN	10,000
23-Oct	BARNSLEY	HOME	0 - 7	8,000
30-Oct	FULHAM	AWAY	1 - 5 HALLIGAN	14,000
06-Nov	BURNLEY	HOME	1 - 0 HALLIGAN	7,000
13-Nov	BRADFORD PARK AVENUE	HOME	2 - 3 McLEOD 2	10,000
20-Nov	WOLVERHAMPTON WANDERERS	AWAY	0 - 5	5,500
27-Nov	GAINSBOROUGH TRINITY	HOME	0 - 0	3,000
04-Dec	GRIMSBY TOWN	AWAY	1 - 3 HALLIGAN	3,000
11-Dec	MANCHESTER CITY	HOME	1 - 3 McLEOD	5,000
18-Dec	LEICESTER FOSSE	AWAY	2 - 6 McLEOD & HALLIGAN	12,000
25-Dec	CLAPTON ORIENT	HOME	2 - 1 ROBERTS & McLEOD	6,000
27-Dec	BLACKPOOL	HOME	3 - 2 McLEOD & ROBERTS 2	10,000
28-Dec	LINCOLN CITY	AWAY	0 - 0	8,000
01-Jan	BLACKPOOL	AWAY	1 - 3 HALLIGAN	4,000
08-Jan	HULL CITY	HOME	1 - 1 GEMMELL	10,000
22-Jan	DERBY COUNTY	AWAY	0 - 1	7,000
05-Feb	GLOSSOP	AWAY	1 - 2 ROBERTS	1,000
12-Feb	BIRMINGHAM	HOME	2 - 1 ROBERTS & CROOT	10,000
26-Feb	OLDHAM ATHLETIC	HOME	3 - 5 McLEOD, MULHOLLAND & CROOT (PEN)	6,000
05-Mar	STOCKPORT COUNTY	HOME	0 - 2	5,000
07-Mar	WEST BROMWICH ALBION	AWAY	1 - 3 McLEOD	6,800
12-Mar	FULHAM	HOME	2 - 2 CROOT 2 (1 PEN)	4,000
17-Mar	BARNSLEY	AWAY	1 - 1 McLEOD	2,000
19-Mar	BURNLEY	AWAY	0 - 3	4,000
26-Mar	BRADFORD PARK AVENUE	AWAY	2 - 4 CROOT (PEN) & McLEOD	12,000
28-Mar	CLAPTON ORIENT	AWAY	2 - 0 McLEOD 2	7,000
02-Apr	WOLVERHAMPTON WANDERERS	HOME	1 - 0 McLEOD	5,000
09-Apr	GAINSBOROUGH TRINITY	AWAY	0 - 2	3,000
16-Apr	GRIMSBY TOWN	HOME	3 - 1 CROOT 2 (1 PEN) & McLEOD	5,000
23-Apr	MANCHESTER CITY	AWAY	0 - 3	15,000
30-Apr	LEICESTER FOSSE	HOME	1 - 1 DOUGAL	2,000
F. A. CUP				
15-Jan	SUNDERLAND (R1)	AWAY	0 - 1	18,000

LEAGUE AND CUP			
APPEARANCES			
PLAYER	LEAGUE	F. A. CUP	TOTAL
ACKERLEY	2		2
AFFLECK	25	1	26
ASTILL	1		1
BEREN	3		3
BRIDGETT	1		1
BROMAGE	35	1	36
BURNETT	2		2
CROOT	34	1	35
CUBBERLEY	35	1	36
DOUGAL	15		15
GEMMELL	23	1	24
HALLIGAN	24	1	25
HAMILTON E	3		3
HOGG	1		1
HORSLEY	20	1	21
JOYNES	7		7
McALLISTER	21	1	22
McLEOD	28	1	29
MORRIS T	24		24
MULHOLLAND	22		22
NAISBY	2		2
PICKARD	4		4
PRICE	8		8
ROBERTS	24	1	25
STOCKTON	3		3
TYLDESLEY	6	1	7
WATSON J	17		17
WHITE	28		28

GOALSCORERS			
PLAYER	LEAGUE	F. A. CUP	TOTAL
McLEOD	15		15
HALLIGAN	12		12
CROOT	8		8
ROBERTS	5		5
GEMMELL	3		3
MORRIS T	1		1
MULHOLLAND	1		1
DOUGAL	1		1

17

It is doubtful that Leeds could have dreamed up a shoddier beginning to a league campaign. Making their worst start to a season, five defeats in the opening six fixtures put Frank Scott-Walford's team firmly at the bottom of Division 2. However, Yorkshire teams are noted for grit and determination and to City's credit, the player's secured five wins over the next eight fixtures.

Billy McLeod grabbed his share of the headlines, but Billy Gillespie made the biggest impact. The slender inside-forward made his debut on the opening day of the season at Blackpool, a clash where fellow inside-forward and debutante Joseph Enright scored in a 2-1 defeat, prior to Gillespie notching his first City goal in a 1-1 draw at Birmingham. Seven strikes by the Irishman in as many games helped secure victories against Hull City, Bradford Park Avenue, Gainsborough Trinity and Stockport County.

A dip in form by City during early December was turned around in the Christmas fixtures with wins against Clapton Orient and Blackpool. Inside-right Tom Mulholland, who had only one goal to his credit since making his debut the previous term, grabbed the all-important goal at Orient. It would be the first of nine strikes for Mulholland over the remainder of the campaign, outstripping even McLeod's efforts.

The unlikely strike-force combined to see off Huddersfield Town and West Brom, before Mulholland struck against Fulham, Bradford and Bolton Wanderers during a four-game winning burst. A brace apiece accounted for Stockport County, before an Enright goal sealed a 1-0 win against Wolves at Elland Road in the final game of a disjointed season.

Finishing eleventh, endeavour and teamwork had seen City turn their season around, and similarly goals had been shared amongst a group of players. McLeod led the way with 14, ably supported by Enright, Gillespie and Mulholland. Fred Croot's efforts were also noteworthy, his eight strikes including five penalties, the most by any City player in a season. In the FA Cup, City lost to Brighton in round one.

The turnaround had been impressive and had much to do with Scott-Walford playing a reasonably unchanged team. Unlike the previous term when only three players made over 30 league appearances, the Leeds boss fielded nine players in at least 30 league matches. Left-back Alec Creighton was the only ever-present throughout the campaign with George Affleck and Enright missing just one encounter.

1910 - 1911

	DIVISION TWO (FINAL LEAGUE POSITION - 11TH)					
	PLD 38 W 15 D 7 L 16 F 58 A 56 PTS 37				
DATE	OPPONENTS	VENUE	SCORE	SCORERS	ATT.
03-Sep	BLACKPOOL	HOME	1 - 2	ENRIGHT	12,000
10-Sep	GLOSSOP	AWAY	1 - 2	ENRIGHT	8,000
17-Sep	LINCOLN CITY	HOME	0 - 1		8,000
24-Sep	HUDDERSFIELD TOWN	AWAY	2 - 3	CROOT (PEN) & McLEOD	7,500
01-Oct	BIRMINGHAM	HOME	1 - 1	GILLESPIE	8,000
08-Oct	WEST BROMWICH ALBION	AWAY	0 - 2		10,000
15-Oct	HULL CITY	HOME	1 - 0	GILLESPIE	8,000
22-Oct	FULHAM	AWAY	1 - 2	GILLESPIE	11,000
29-Oct	BRADFORD PARK AVENUE	HOME	2 - 0	McLEOD & GILLESPIE	13,000
05-Nov	BURNLEY	AWAY	1 - 4	McLEOD	8,000
12-Nov	GAINSBOROUGH TRINITY	HOME	4 - 0	ENRIGHT, GILLESPIE 2 & McLEOD	5,000
19-Nov	BOLTON WANDERERS	AWAY	0 - 3		10,000
26-Nov	STOCKPORT COUNTY	AWAY	4 - 0	GILLESPIE 2, McLEOD & BRIDGETT	4,000
03-Dec	DERBY COUNTY	HOME	3 - 2	MORRIS T & ROBERTS 2	10,000
10-Dec	BARNSLEY	AWAY	0 - 4		4,000
17-Dec	LEICESTER FOSSE	HOME	2 - 3	ENRIGHT & MORRIS T	5,000
24-Dec	WOLVERHAMPTON WANDERERS	AWAY	1 - 3	GILLESPIE	6,000
26-Dec	CHELSEA	HOME	3 - 3	ROBERTS, CROOT & McLEOD	18,000
27-Dec	CLAPTON ORIENT	HOME	1 - 0	MULHOLLAND	10,000
31-Dec	BLACKPOOL	AWAY	2 - 1	McLEOD & BRIDGETT	1,000
07-Jan	GLOSSOP	HOME	0 - 2		10,000
21-Jan	LINCOLN CITY	AWAY	1 - 1	ENRIGHT	5,000
28-Jan	HUDDERSFIELD TOWN	HOME	5 - 2	CROOT 2 (1 PEN), McLEOD 2 & MULHOLLAND	10,000
04-Feb	BIRMINGHAM	AWAY	1 - 2	McLEOD	15,000
11-Feb	WEST BROMWICH ALBION	HOME	3 - 1	McLEOD, MULHOLLAND & ENRIGHT	10,700
18-Feb	HULL CITY	AWAY	1 - 1	ENRIGHT	6,000
25-Feb	FULHAM	HOME	3 - 1	CROOT (PEN), ENRIGHT & MULHOLLAND	6,000
04-Mar	BRADFORD PARK AVENUE	AWAY	2 - 0	CROOT (PEN) & MULHOLLAND	12,000
18-Mar	GAINSBOROUGH TRINITY	AWAY	2 - 1	ENRIGHT & ROBERTS	4,000
25-Mar	BOLTON WANDERERS	HOME	1 - 0	MULHOLLAND	15,000
27-Mar	BURNLEY	HOME	0 - 0		5,500
01-Apr	STOCKPORT COUNTY	HOME	4 - 0	McLEOD 2 & MULHOLLAND 2	9,000
08-Apr	DERBY COUNTY	AWAY	2 - 2	CROOT (PEN) & MULHOLLAND	5,000
14-Apr	CHELSEA	AWAY	1 - 4	McLEOD	5,000
15-Apr	BARNSLEY	HOME	0 - 0		10,000
17-Apr	CLAPTON ORIENT	AWAY	0 - 1		6,000
22-Apr	LEICESTER FOSSE	AWAY	1 - 2	CROOT	5,000
29-Apr	WOLVERHAMPTON WANDERERS	HOME	1 - 0	ENRIGHT	6,000
	F. A. CUP				
14-Jan	BRIGHTON & HOVE ALBION (R1)	HOME	1 - 3	ROBERTS	18,270

LEAGUE AND CUP			
APPEARANCES			
PLAYER	LEAGUE	F. A. CUP	TOTAL
AFFLECK	37	1	38
BRIDGETT	8	1	9
BROMAGE	25	1	26
CREIGHTON	38	1	39
CROOT	30		30
CUBBERLEY	34	1	35
CUNNINGHAM G	3		3
ENRIGHT	37	1	38
FOLEY	4		4
GILLESPIE	18		18
HARKINS	31	1	32
HOGG	13		13
HORSLEY	9		9
KELLY	3		3
McLEOD	35	1	36
MORRIS T	36	1	37
MULHOLLAND	21	1	22
ROBERTS	35	1	36
WHITE	1		1

GOALSCORERS			
PLAYER	LEAGUE	F. A. CUP	TOTAL
McLEOD	14		14
ENRIGHT	10		10
GILLESPIE	9		9
MULHOLLAND	9		9
CROOT	8		8
ROBERTS	4	1	5
BRIDGETT	2		2
MORRIS T	2		2

EXCLUDES ANY DETAILS ON THE WEST RIDING SENIOR CUP (1910 - 1911 TO 1987 - 1988 AND 1991 - 1992 TO DATE AND THE YORKSHIRE & HUMBERSIDE CUP (1988 - 1989 TO 1990 - 1991)

Billy McLeod made a great start to the new campaign but City as a team did not replicate his form. A 0-0 draw against Chelsea was all they had to show for their efforts in the opening four fixtures but the coming games, especially at Elland Road, would show an improvement in form with four successive home wins. Joseph Enright and McLeod scored in victories against Bristol City and Huddersfield Town, whilst Tom Mulholland got in on the scoring act in encounters that City edged against Glossop and Barnsley.

Fred Croot, with three goals to his credit, struck home a spot kick to earn a point at local rivals Bradford Park Avenue, but it heralded a worrying run of five consecutive losses including five-goal defeats against future champions Derby County, Burnley and Wolves. During the festive period, an Enright brace accounted for Leicester Fosse and a draw was gleaned against Gainsborough Town, but 11 defeats in the opening half of the season was a worrying trend.

Overly reliant on home form, away victories at Grimsby Town and Huddersfield Town was welcome news. Mulholland strikes gained the points at Huddersfield and a first double of the season. Enright settled a home win against Blackpool, the first time City had won consecutive matches during the campaign. Unfortunately, it would be the only back-to-back triumphs all term.

The final 11 games of a troubled season would see City win just once, 4-3 at Barnsley, McLeod and Croot scoring a brace apiece and ensuring a second double. Croot's two spot kicks proved vital, the only time a City player would score two penalties in a game. The poor run of form meant that City were in a battle at the wrong end of the table and four draws in the final six matches, only 5,000 supporters attending the last home game against Wolves, was insufficient to edge them above Glossop. Finishing 19th was the club's worst ever finish and meant they would have to apply for re-election. The process proved successful but it resulted in a change of manager with Herbert Chapman taking the helm.

In the FA Cup, West Brom ended City's hopes in the second round, but the new boss was well aware that he would have his work cut out judging on the teams efforts during a miserable campaign. Outside-right Hugh Roberts scored Leeds' only cup goal in a 1-0 win against Glossop and was the only ever-present all season, with defenders George Affleck and Tom Morris missing just one clash. Again, McLeod led the scoring charts with 14 goals, closely followed by Enright and Mulholland.

1911 - 1912

DIVISION TWO (FINAL LEAGUE POSITION - 19TH)
PLD 38 W 10 D 8 L 20 F 50 A 78 PTS 28

DATE	OPPONENTS	VENUE	SCORE	SCORERS	ATT.
02-Sep	NOTTINGHAM FOREST	AWAY	1 - 2	McLEOD	10,000
04-Sep	BURNLEY	AWAY	2 - 4	McLEOD & ENRIGHT	15,000
09-Sep	CHELSEA	HOME	0 - 0		15,000
16-Sep	CLAPTON ORIENT	AWAY	1 - 2	McLEOD	13,000
23-Sep	BRISTOL CITY	HOME	3 - 1	CROOT, ENRIGHT & McLEOD	10,000
30-Sep	BIRMINGHAM	AWAY	3 - 4	ENRIGHT, ROBERTS & CROOT	10,000
07-Oct	HUDDERSFIELD TOWN	HOME	2 - 0	McLEOD & ENRIGHT	12,000
14-Oct	BLACKPOOL	AWAY	0 - 3		4,000
21-Oct	GLOSSOP	HOME	2 - 1	MULHOLLAND & CROOT	6,000
28-Oct	HULL CITY	AWAY	0 - 1		10,000
04-Nov	BARNSLEY	HOME	3 - 2	McLEOD & MULHOLLAND 2	12,000
11-Nov	BRADFORD PARK AVENUE	AWAY	1 - 1	CROOT (PEN)	13,000
18-Nov	FULHAM	HOME	0 - 2		8,000
25-Nov	DERBY COUNTY	AWAY	2 - 5	McLEOD & ROBERTS	12,000
04-Dec	GRIMSBY TOWN	HOME	1 - 2	McLEOD	3,000
09-Dec	BURNLEY	HOME	1 - 5	GILLESPIE (PEN)	10,000
16-Dec	WOLVERHAMPTON WANDERERS	AWAY	0 - 5		8,000
23-Dec	LEICESTER FOSSE	HOME	2 - 1	ENRIGHT 2	6,000
25-Dec	GAINSBOROUGH TRINITY	HOME	0 - 0		9,000
26-Dec	GAINSBOROUGH TRINITY	AWAY	1 - 2	MULHOLLAND	6,000
30-Dec	NOTTINGHAM FOREST	HOME	3 - 1	MULHOLLAND 2 & ENRIGHT	8,000
06-Jan	CHELSEA	AWAY	2 - 4	McLEOD & FOLEY	10,000
20-Jan	CLAPTON ORIENT	HOME	0 - 2		5,000
23-Jan	GRIMSBY TOWN	AWAY	2 - 1	JOHNSON S & ENRIGHT	3,000
27-Jan	BRISTOL CITY	AWAY	1 - 4	CROOT (PEN)	7,000
10-Feb	HUDDERSFIELD TOWN	AWAY	2 - 1	MULHOLLAND 2	8,000
17-Feb	BLACKPOOL	HOME	1 - 0	ENRIGHT	6,000
24-Feb	GLOSSOP	AWAY	1 - 2	MULHOLLAND	3,000
02-Mar	HULL CITY	HOME	0 - 0		8,000
16-Mar	BRADFORD PARK AVENUE	HOME	1 - 2	FOLEY	10,000
23-Mar	FULHAM	AWAY	2 - 7	ENRIGHT & MULHOLLAND	3,000
30-Mar	DERBY COUNTY	HOME	0 - 1		4,500
05-Apr	BIRMINGHAM	HOME	0 - 0		5,000
06-Apr	STOCKPORT COUNTY	HOME	1 - 1	ENRIGHT	4,000
11-Apr	BARNSLEY	AWAY	4 - 3	McLEOD 2 & CROOT 2 (2 PENS)	3,000
15-Apr	STOCKPORT COUNTY	AWAY	3 - 3	McLEOD 2 & MULHOLLAND	3,000
20-Apr	WOLVERHAMPTON WANDERERS	HOME	1 - 1	McLEOD	5,000
27-Apr	LEICESTER FOSSE	AWAY	1 - 2	ENRIGHT	10,000

F. A. CUP

DATE	OPPONENTS	VENUE	SCORE	SCORERS	ATT.
13-Jan	GLOSSOP (R1)	HOME	1 - 0	ROBERTS	21,000
03-Feb	WEST BROMWICH ALBION (R2)	HOME	0 - 1		21,320

LEAGUE AND CUP
APPEARANCES

PLAYER	LEAGUE	F. A. CUP	TOTAL
AFFLECK	37	2	39
BRIDGETT	3		3
CAMPBELL	1		1
CLARKIN	1		1
CREIGHTON	28	2	30
CROOT	32	2	34
CUBBERLEY	20		20
ENRIGHT	34	2	36
FOLEY	9	1	10
FORTUNE	1		1
GILLESPIE	6		6
HARKINS	32	2	34
HEANEY	2		2
HOGG	8		8
JOHNSON S	7		7
KELLY	1		1
McDANIEL	1		1
McLEOD	31	1	32
MORAN	24	2	26
MORRIS T	37	2	39
MULHOLLAND	35	2	37
MURPHY	18	1	19
REINHARDT	12	1	13
ROBERTS	38	2	40

GOALSCORERS

PLAYER	LEAGUE	F. A. CUP	TOTAL
McLEOD	14		14
ENRIGHT	12		12
MULHOLLAND	11		11
CROOT	7		7
ROBERTS	2	1	3
FOLEY	2		2
GILLESPIE	1		1
JOHNSON S	1		1

The appointment of Herbert Chapman was an inspired choice by the City board. Tactically astute, charismatic, a great motivator and innovative, Chapman successfully campaigned for Leeds' re-election to the Football League, and his tenure began well despite an opening 4-0 defeat at Fulham and 6-2 hammering at Hull City. Prior to December, City picked up six wins and remained unbeaten at Elland Road, the pick of results a 4-1 victory against Burnley and 4-0 triumph over Glossop.

Billy McLeod was in inspired form, scoring in both clashes, including his first City hat-trick against Glossop. With nine goals to his credit after a third of the season, Chapman realised that he had to build his team around City's goalscoring phenomenon. Whilst his charges went through an indifferent spell around the festive period, gaining no wins, the new boss signed Simpson Bainbridge and James Speirs, who led Bradford City to an FA Cup triumph in 1911, adding to close-season international signings Billy Scott and Evelyn Lintott.

With support from Fred Croot, results immediately improved. McLeod, Bainbridge and Croot scored in a 3-0 win at Blackpool on New Years Day and eight consecutive home victories followed during the remainder of the season. In an amazing sequence, City defeated Bradford Park Avenue, Leicester Fosse, Preston, Hull City, Clapton Orient, Bury, Nottingham Forest and Birmingham.

The series of results saw attendances soar, the Hull and Forest clashes attracting a gate of 20,000. McLeod was unstoppable, scoring the winner in both matches and grabbing his second hat-trick of the campaign against Bury. Notching 12 in nine games during the latter stages of the season, his final tally of 27 league goals was a club record by some distance as City finished sixth, a vast improvement on recent campaigns.

Scoring 70 goals, the highest to date, Chapman's signings had settled into the side. Inside-left Speirs in particular made a big impact, scoring 10 goals in just 20 appearances, including a brace against Clapton and Birmingham. With new players coming in, only five featured in more than 30 games, McLeod and centre-half Lintott ever-present.

Leeds went out of the FA Cup at the first round stage, but Elland Road staged a cup replay between Bradford City and Barnsley, however pandemonium reigned as officials failed to control a 45,000 crowd.

It had been a tremendous campaign as Chapman settled into the post, and on a historic note, Croot scored early season penalties against Barnsley, Wolves and Hull, taking his spot kick tally to 16, the most by any City player.

1912 - 1913

DIVISION TWO (FINAL LEAGUE POSITION - 6TH)
PLD 38 W 15 D 10 L 13 F 70 A 64 PTS 40

DATE	OPPONENTS	VENUE	SCORE	SCORERS	ATT.
07-Sep	FULHAM	AWAY	0 - 4		20,000
14-Sep	BARNSLEY	HOME	2 - 0	ROBERTSON & CROOT (PEN)	15,000
21-Sep	BRADFORD PARK AVENUE	AWAY	1 - 0	CUBBERLEY	18,000
28-Sep	WOLVERHAMPTON WANDERERS	HOME	2 - 2	McLEOD & CROOT (PEN)	20,000
05-Oct	LEICESTER FOSSE	AWAY	1 - 1	ROBERTSON	10,000
12-Oct	STOCKPORT COUNTY	HOME	2 - 1	McLEOD 2	15,000
19-Oct	PRESTON NORTH END	AWAY	2 - 3	McLEOD & ENRIGHT	9,000
26-Oct	BURNLEY	HOME	4 - 1	ROBERTSON 2, McLEOD & CUBBERLEY	10,000
02-Nov	HULL CITY	AWAY	2 - 6	McLEOD & CROOT (PEN)	10,000
09-Nov	GLOSSOP	HOME	4 - 0	McLEOD 3 & FOLEY	12,000
16-Nov	CLAPTON ORIENT	AWAY	0 - 2		10,000
23-Nov	LINCOLN CITY	HOME	2 - 2	ROBERTSON & LINTOTT	15,000
30-Nov	NOTTINGHAM FOREST	AWAY	2 - 1	ROBERTSON & ROBERTS	8,000
07-Dec	BRISTOL CITY	HOME	1 - 1	ROBERTSON	10,000
14-Dec	BIRMINGHAM	AWAY	2 - 2	McLEOD 2	21,000
21-Dec	HUDDERSFIELD TOWN	HOME	0 - 3		15,000
25-Dec	GRIMSBY TOWN	HOME	1 - 2	CUBBERLEY	15,000
26-Dec	BLACKPOOL	HOME	0 - 2		8,000
28-Dec	FULHAM	HOME	2 - 3	BAINBRIDGE & PRICE	10,000
01-Jan	BLACKPOOL	AWAY	3 - 0	CROOT, BAINBRIDGE & McLEOD	5,000
04-Jan	BARNSLEY	AWAY	0 - 2		5,000
18-Jan	BRADFORD PARK AVENUE	HOME	2 - 0	FOLEY & SPEIRS	10,000
25-Jan	WOLVERHAMPTON WANDERERS	AWAY	2 - 2	BAINBRIDGE & McLEOD	8,000
08-Feb	LEICESTER FOSSE	HOME	5 - 1	PRICE 2, SPEIRS, FENWICK & McLEOD	10,000
15-Feb	STOCKPORT COUNTY	AWAY	0 - 6		7,000
22-Feb	PRESTON NORTH END	HOME	5 - 1	AFFLECK (PEN), FENWICK 2, BAINBRIDGE & FOLEY	18,000
01-Mar	BURNLEY	AWAY	2 - 2	McLEOD & SPEIRS	12,000
08-Mar	HULL CITY	HOME	1 - 0	McLEOD	20,000
15-Mar	GLOSSOP	AWAY	1 - 2	McLEOD	2,000
21-Mar	GRIMSBY TOWN	AWAY	2 - 3	McLEOD 2	8,000
22-Mar	CLAPTON ORIENT	HOME	3 - 1	SPEIRS 2 & McLEOD	6,000
24-Mar	BURY	AWAY	1 - 1	McLEOD	10,000
25-Mar	BURY	HOME	4 - 2	McLEOD 3 & SPEIRS	17,000
29-Mar	LINCOLN CITY	AWAY	3 - 3	SPEIRS, McLEOD & CROOT	9,000
05-Apr	NOTTINGHAM FOREST	HOME	1 - 0	McLEOD	20,000
12-Apr	BRISTOL CITY	AWAY	1 - 1	SPEIRS	15,000
19-Apr	BIRMINGHAM	HOME	4 - 0	SPEIRS 2, McLEOD & FOLEY	8,000
26-Apr	HUDDERSFIELD TOWN	AWAY	0 - 1		8,000

F. A. CUP

DATE	OPPONENTS	VENUE	SCORE	SCORERS	ATT.
15-Jan	BURNLEY (R1)	HOME	2 - 3	McLEOD & FOLEY	13,109

LEAGUE AND CUP APPEARANCES

PLAYER	LEAGUE	F. A. CUP	TOTAL
AFFLECK	19	1	20
ALLAN	14	1	15
BAINBRIDGE	24	1	25
BRIDGETT	1		1
BROUGHTON	4		4
COPELAND	20		20
CROOT	32	1	33
CUBBERLEY	16		16
ENRIGHT	6		6
FENWICK	5		5
FERGUSON	17		17
FOLEY	36	1	37
GIBSON	5		5
HOGG	14	1	15
LAW	35	1	36
LINTOTT	38	1	39
McLEOD	38	1	39
MORAN	1		1
PRICE	12		12
ROBERTS	11		11
ROBERTSON	27	1	28
SCOTT	24		24
SPEIRS	19	1	20

GOALSCORERS

PLAYER	LEAGUE	F. A. CUP	TOTAL
McLEOD	27	1	28
SPEIRS	10		10
ROBERTSON	7		7
CROOT	5		5
FOLEY	4	1	5
BAINBRIDGE	4		4
CUBBERLEY	3		3
FENWICK	3		3
PRICE	3		3
AFFLECK	1		1
ENRIGHT	1		1
LINTOTT	1		1
ROBERTS	1		1

Looking to improve on the previous campaign, City got off to a flyer, winning six of the opening 10 encounters. Billy McLeod scored a brace in an opening day 3-0 win against Glossop and found the target against Bradford Park Avenue and Barnsley, both destined to be in the promotion shake-up. Also making his mark in all three encounters was Jimmy Speirs, who somewhat surprisingly outscored his prolific teammate, notching a brace against Wolves and the winner at home to Bury.

Confidence was high and it showed in a record-breaking display when Nottingham Forest were thumped 8-0; McLeod 4, Arthur Price 2, John Hampson and Speirs completing the rout at Elland Road. It was some performance, backed up in December with four consecutive victories, including a Christmas double against Fulham, the home clash attracting a gate of 30,000. McLeod scored in every game.

Pushing hard for promotion, City demonstrated their intentions with a 5-1 win against Stockport County in the first game of the New Year, but inexplicably three defeats followed. McLeod notched home hat-tricks in a 5-0 win against Wolves and 5-1 defeat of West Yorkshire neighbours Huddersfield Town, but these results were surrounded by inconsistency. The final nine games would bring four victories, three in the final four outings against Bristol City, Grimsby Town and Birmingham but it was too late. Only nine goals were scored in the run as McLeod's prolific form deserted him, although he did notch three, including winning strikes against Blackpool and Birmingham, but no one could fault his effort.

Scoring 28 league and cup goals, McLeod had enjoyed a phenomenal season as City finished fourth, two points adrift of runners up Bradford and third placed Arsenal. There was bitterness at the final standings because City had a superior goal average to both clubs and felt aggrieved by a failed appeal following a 3-1 defeat at Clapton Orient when Billy Scott claimed it was too dark to see the last two goals. The match kicked off at 4.30pm and the league fined Orient £25, but the result stood. That decision and a dip in mid-season form was all that separated Herbert Chapman's charges from top-flight football.

Scoring 76 goals, aside of McLeod's strikes, Spiers, Price and Hampson chipped in with twelve, ten and eight respectively. Leading the appearances ratings were ever-presents George Affleck and Mick Foley, closely followed by McLeod who missed one match. It had been a remarkable campaign with many highs, notably the 'Winter Wonderland' triumph against Forest. Finishing fourth would be City's highest ever finish.

1913 - 1914

DIVISION TWO (FINAL LEAGUE POSITION - 4TH)
PLD 38 W 20 D 7 L 11 F 76 A 46 PTS 47

DATE	OPPONENTS	VENUE	SCORE	SCORERS	ATT.
06-Sep	GLOSSOP	HOME	3 - 0	SPEIRS & McLEOD 2	8,000
13-Sep	STOCKPORT COUNTY	AWAY	1 - 2	McLEOD	10,000
20-Sep	BRADFORD PARK AVENUE	HOME	5 - 1	SPEIRS, PRICE, BAINBRIDGE 2 & McLEOD	23,000
27-Sep	NOTTS COUNTY	AWAY	0 - 4		12,000
04-Oct	LEICESTER FOSSE	HOME	2 - 1	BAINBRIDGE & PRICE	18,000
11-Oct	WOLVERHAMPTON WANDERERS	AWAY	3 - 1	SPEIRS 2 & SHARPE (PEN)	10,000
18-Oct	HULL CITY	HOME	1 - 2	SPEIRS	20,000
25-Oct	BARNSLEY	AWAY	4 - 1	SPEIRS 2, PRICE & McLEOD	12,000
01-Nov	BURY	HOME	2 - 1	PRICE & SPEIRS	20,000
08-Nov	HUDDERSFIELD TOWN	AWAY	1 - 1	TURNER	9,000
15-Nov	LINCOLN CITY	HOME	1 - 0	McLEOD	12,000
22-Nov	BLACKPOOL	AWAY	2 - 2	HAMPSON J & CROOT	5,000
29-Nov	NOTTINGHAM FOREST	HOME	8 - 0	McLEOD 4, PRICE 2, HAMPSON J & SPEIRS	14,000
06-Dec	WOOLWICH ARSENAL	AWAY	0 - 1		18,000
13-Dec	GRIMSBY TOWN	HOME	4 - 1	McLEOD 2, HAMPSON J & PRICE	10,000
20-Dec	BIRMINGHAM	AWAY	2 - 0	McLEOD & SHARPE	15,000
25-Dec	FULHAM	HOME	2 - 1	McLEOD & HAMPSON J	30,000
26-Dec	FULHAM	AWAY	1 - 0	McLEOD	25,000
27-Dec	GLOSSOP	AWAY	1 - 1	BAINBRIDGE	2,000
03-Jan	STOCKPORT COUNTY	HOME	5 - 1	SPEIRS, JACKSON 2, McLEOD & SHARPE	10,000
17-Jan	BRADFORD PARK AVENUE	AWAY	1 - 3	McLEOD	32,184
24-Jan	NOTTS COUNTY	HOME	2 - 4	SHARPE & HAMPSON J	25,000
07-Feb	LEICESTER FOSSE	AWAY	1 - 5	SPEIRS	4,000
14-Feb	WOLVERHAMPTON WANDERERS	HOME	5 - 0	McLEOD 3, SPEIRS & SHARPE	10,000
21-Feb	HULL CITY	AWAY	0 - 1		18,000
28-Feb	BARNSLEY	HOME	3 - 0	McLEOD & SHARPE 2 (1 PEN)	20,000
02-Mar	CLAPTON ORIENT	AWAY	1 - 3	HAMPSON J	7,000
07-Mar	BURY	AWAY	1 - 1	JACKSON	12,000
14-Mar	HUDDERSFIELD TOWN	HOME	5 - 1	HAMPSON J, McLEOD 3 & PRICE	14,000
21-Mar	LINCOLN CITY	AWAY	0 - 1		8,000
28-Mar	BLACKPOOL	HOME	2 - 1	McLEOD & HAMPSON J	12,000
04-Apr	NOTTINGHAM FOREST	AWAY	1 - 2	LAW	6,000
10-Apr	BRISTOL CITY	AWAY	1 - 1	McLEOD	20,000
11-Apr	WOOLWICH ARSENAL	HOME	0 - 0		25,000
13-Apr	BRISTOL CITY	HOME	1 - 0	TURNER	12,000
14-Apr	CLAPTON ORIENT	HOME	0 - 0		12,000
18-Apr	GRIMSBY TOWN	AWAY	1 - 0	PRICE	9,000
25-Apr	BIRMINGHAM	HOME	3 - 2	PRICE, McLEOD & O. G. (STUART)	10,000
	F. A. CUP				
10-Jan	GAINSBOROUGH TRINITY (R1)	HOME	4 - 2	JACKSON 2, LAW & McLEOD	14,000
31-Jan	WEST BROMWICH ALBION (R2)	HOME	0 - 2		29,733

LEAGUE AND CUP APPEARANCES

PLAYER	LEAGUE	F. A. CUP	TOTAL
AFFLECK	38	2	40
BAINBRIDGE	15	2	17
BLACKMAN	14		14
COPELAND	23	1	24
CROOT	10		10
DOUGHERTY	1		1
FOLEY	38	2	40
HAMPSON J	36	2	38
HOGG	36	2	38
JACKSON	22	2	24
JOHNSON J	1		1
LAMPH	1		1
LAW	35	2	37
LINTOTT	5	1	6
McLEOD	37	2	39
PEART	1		1
PRICE	35		35
SCOTT	2		2
SHARPE	35	2	37
SPEIRS	29	2	31
TURNER	4		4

GOALSCORERS

PLAYER	LEAGUE	F. A. CUP	TOTAL
McLEOD	27	1	28
SPEIRS	12		12
PRICE	10		10
HAMPSON J	8		8
SHARPE	7		7
JACKSON	3	2	5
BAINBRIDGE	4		4
LAW	1	1	2
TURNER	2		2
CROOT	1		1
OWN GOALS	1		1

25

For some years, the Leeds board had struggled under the financial strain of running a league club and pre-season, after on-going negotiations, accepted an offer from a local syndicate, headed by Mr Joseph Conner, President of the West Riding FA, to take over the club. The campaign began under the backdrop of war against the Kaiser's Germany. Predictions that the conflict would be over by Christmas were wrong, and the Football League curtailed professional football at the completion of the campaign.

Optimism was high at Elland Road, but from the opening game at Fulham, City struggled, losing the first four matches. Billy McLeod and Jimmy Speirs found their shooting boots to account for Derby County, Lincoln City and Grimsby Town but Herbert Chapman's charges were bereft of any sort of rhythm. Following a lean spell in November, City entered the festive period with a resounding 7-2 win against Leicester Fosse. Arthur Price grabbed a hat-trick, whilst Simpson Bainbridge and McLeod notched a brace apiece. Back-to-back 3-0 victories against Glossop on Christmas Day and Boxing Day, the trio scoring in the home fixture, brought festive joy and when McLeod set a new individual scoring record with five goals in City's 6-2 triumph against Hull City in January, hope returned, but it was a false dawn.

Successive four-game defeats and wins, the highpoint a 5-2 victory at Grimsby to complete a double, summed up City's season, which was sealed with six reverses during the run-in. A Price treble against Nottingham Forest in the penultimate home fixture of the season did little to raise spirits in front of a paltry attendance of 4,000, especially when a 5-1 drubbing at Leicester, a team City demolished earlier in the campaign, followed it. Finishing well adrift of champions Derby County, the end of the campaign could not come quickly enough for Leeds, but it was quickly forgotten as hostilities with Germany meant an end to peacetime football.

Finishing fifteenth and knocked out of the FA Cup in the second round, the only statistic of note to take from a disjointed season was the remarkable fact that McLeod, with 19 league and cup goals, finished top scorer for the ninth consecutive season. Price ended the campaign on 11 goals, former Great Britain gold medalist at the 1912 Olympic Games, Ivan Sharpe, notched 10, as did Speirs. On a historic note, in a century of football in the city of Leeds only Gordon Hodgson in 1937/38 has matched McLeod's five-goal performance against Hull.

Herbert Chapman used all his powers to change personnel in his line up, picking 26 players, just one short of the club's record in 1909/10. Five players made 30 plus appearances, George Law and Mick Foley missing just three league games. The suspension of league football on 3 July 1915 saw the sport take a backseat as war raged on Europe's battlefields.

DIVISION TWO (FINAL LEAGUE POSITION - 15TH)
PLD 38 W 14 D 4 L 20 F 65 A 64 PTS 32

DATE	OPPONENTS	VENUE	SCORE	SCORERS	ATT.
02-Sep	FULHAM	HOME	0 - 1		8,000
05-Sep	STOCKPORT COUNTY	AWAY	1 - 3	SHARPE	5,000
09-Sep	FULHAM	AWAY	0 - 1		5,000
12-Sep	HULL CITY	HOME	2 - 3	SPEIRS & JACKSON	8,000
19-Sep	BLACKPOOL	HOME	2 - 0	McLEOD & GOODWIN (PEN)	8,000
26-Sep	CLAPTON ORIENT	AWAY	0 - 2		9,000
03-Oct	ARSENAL	HOME	2 - 2	GOODWIN (PEN) & SPEIRS	10,000
10-Oct	DERBY COUNTY	AWAY	2 - 1	SPEIRS & McLEOD	5,000
17-Oct	LINCOLN CITY	HOME	3 - 1	McLEOD & SPEIRS 2	10,000
24-Oct	BIRMINGHAM	AWAY	3 - 6	SHARPE 2 & SPEIRS	8,000
31-Oct	GRIMSBY TOWN	HOME	5 - 0	McLEOD 2, SPEIRS, BAINBRIDGE & JACKSON	5,000
07-Nov	HUDDERSFIELD TOWN	AWAY	0 - 1		14,000
14-Nov	BRISTOL CITY	HOME	1 - 1	McLEOD	8,000
21-Nov	BURY	AWAY	0 - 0		6,000
28-Nov	PRESTON NORTH END	HOME	0 - 0		7,000
05-Dec	NOTTINGHAM FOREST	AWAY	1 - 3	SPEIRS	3,000
12-Dec	LEICESTER FOSSE	HOME	7 - 2	BAINBRIDGE 2, McLEOD 2 & PRICE 3	5,000
19-Dec	BARNSLEY	AWAY	1 - 2	SHARPE	3,000
25-Dec	GLOSSOP	AWAY	3 - 0	JACKSON 2 & McLEOD	1,000
26-Dec	GLOSSOP	HOME	3 - 0	BAINBRIDGE, PRICE & McLEOD	6,000
02-Jan	STOCKPORT COUNTY	HOME	1 - 3	SPEIRS	7,000
16-Jan	HULL CITY	AWAY	6 - 2	McLEOD 5 & SHARPE	5,000
23-Jan	BLACKPOOL	AWAY	0 - 1		6,000
03-Feb	CLAPTON ORIENT	HOME	0 - 1		4,000
06-Feb	ARSENAL	AWAY	0 - 2		10,000
13-Feb	DERBY COUNTY	HOME	3 - 5	EDMONDSON, SPEIRS & SHARPE	5,000
20-Feb	LINCOLN CITY	AWAY	1 - 0	EDMONDSON	4,000
27-Feb	BIRMINGHAM	HOME	2 - 0	JACKSON & PRICE	7,000
06-Mar	GRIMSBY TOWN	AWAY	5 - 2	EDMONDSON, JACKSON, SHARPE, GOODWIN & PRICE	4,000
13-Mar	HUDDERSFIELD TOWN	HOME	1 - 0	SHARPE	12,000
20-Mar	BRISTOL CITY	AWAY	0 - 1		5,000
27-Mar	BURY	HOME	2 - 1	McLEOD & PRICE	6,000
03-Apr	PRESTON NORTH END	AWAY	0 - 2		5,000
05-Apr	WOLVERHAMPTON WANDERERS	AWAY	1 - 5	McLEOD	15,000
06-Apr	WOLVERHAMPTON WANDERERS	HOME	2 - 3	McLEOD & PRICE	5,000
10-Apr	NOTTINGHAM FOREST	HOME	4 - 0	PRICE 3 & SHARPE	4,000
17-Apr	LEICESTER FOSSE	AWAY	1 - 5	JACKSON	3,000
24-Apr	BARNSLEY	HOME	0 - 2		5,000

F. A. CUP

DATE	OPPONENTS	VENUE	SCORE	SCORERS	ATT.
09-Jan	DERBY COUNTY (R1)	AWAY	2 - 1	McLEOD & SHARPE	9,417
30-Jan	QUEENS PARK RANGERS (R2)	AWAY	0 - 1		10,000

LEAGUE AND CUP
APPEARANCES

PLAYER	LEAGUE	F. A. CUP	TOTAL
AFFLECK	24	2	26
BAINBRIDGE	18	2	20
BLACKMAN	30	2	32
COPELAND	1		1
COWEN	2		2
CROOT	5		5
EDMONDSON	5		5
FOLEY	35	2	37
GOODWIN	19		19
GREEN	1		1
HAMPSON J	28	1	29
HOGG	24	2	26
JACKSON	32	2	34
LAMPH	2		2
LAW	35	2	37
LAWRENCE	6		6
McLEOD	31	2	33
McQUILLAN	20		20
PEART H	6	1	7
PRICE	24		24
RICHARDSON	2		2
ROTHWELL	1		1
SHARPE	26	2	28
SPEIRS	25	2	27
WAINWRIGHT	2		2
WALKER W	14		14

GOALSCORERS

PLAYER	LEAGUE	F. A. CUP	TOTAL
McLEOD	18	1	19
PRICE	11		11
SHARPE	9	1	10
SPEIRS	10		10
JACKSON	7		7
BAINBRIDGE	4		4
EDMONDSON	3		3
GOODWIN	3		3

The Government refused to comment on the Football League's decision to run regional tournaments. As players answered the country's call to enlist, a number of teams including Newcastle United, Sunderland and Middlesbrough refused to play on in the new amateur format, but Leeds City did and signed several North-East players, especially from Newcastle. There was no promotion or relegation, and players received expenses only, an issue that would cause the eventual demise of Leeds City.

Whilst a number of City stars received call up papers, others represented City or new clubs. Established Leeds players returning to action included George Affleck, Mick Foley, Arthur Price and Fred Croot. Guest players amongst the 34-man squad to turn out in City colours included Fred 'Fanny' Walden (Tottenham), Bill Bradley, Curtis Booth and Tom Bennett (Newcastle), Bob Hewison (Sunderland), Clem Stephenson (Aston Villa), Willie Wilson (Hearts) and Jack Peart (Barnsley).

Leeds centre-forward John Edmondson had scored three goals in a handful of appearances towards the end of the previous campaign and soon made his mark alongside Price in the post-league era as City won four of the opening five encounters. Both scored in a 3-1 win at Derby County, and found the target again in victories against Lincoln City and Hull City. The return fixtures with Derby and Hull brought more joy for the duo but with so many players out of position, high scores and inconsistency prevailed. Finishing tenth in the 26-match Principal Tournament, the pair made headlines when Price struck five in a 7-1 trouncing of Barnsley and Edmondson notched a hat-trick in a 4-1 win against Derby at Elland Road.

As the campaign concluded, Wilson, Stephenson and Peart entered the fray and immediately made their mark in the Midland Subsidiary Tournament. Comprising 10 games, Wilson scored the only goal against Rochdale as City claimed the first of seven victories. Stephenson notched a hat-trick in a 3-2 triumph against Bradford Park Avenue before Peart eclipsed the pair with four in a 6-4 win against Barnsley. Price earned a double over Park Avenue before opening the scoring in a 4-2 win against Bradford City to claim the title, Peart sealing victory with a penalty.

Price's 15 goals made him top scorer whilst Affleck, Foley and Walden were ever-presents throughout the campaign. Whether playing wartime football was morally correct was arguable but the sport was the national game. Between 1,000 and 10,000 spectators attended Elland Road fixtures, and notably within a year, football became a compulsory activity in the armed forces.

1915 - 1916

PRINCIPAL TOURNAMENT

DATE	OPPONENTS	VENUE	SCORE	SCORERS	ATT.
04-Sep	DERBY COUNTY	AWAY	3 - 1	EDMONDSON, BENNETT & PRICE	3,000
11-Sep	SHEFFIELD WEDNESDAY	HOME	2 - 1	PRICE & HAMPSON	8,000
18-Sep	BRADFORD PARK AVENUE	AWAY	3 - 4	BENNETT & EDMONDSON 2	10,000
25-Sep	LINCOLN CITY	HOME	2 - 1	EDMONSON & PRICE	6,000
02-Oct	HULL CITY	HOME	3 - 1	LAW, PRICE & EDMONDSON	7,000
09-Oct	NOTTINGHAM FOREST	AWAY	0 - 2		5,000
16-Oct	BARNSLEY	HOME	7 - 1	PRICE 5, EDMONDSON & BENNETT	7,000
23-Oct	LEICSTER FOSSE	AWAY	0 - 4		5,000
06-Nov	BRADFORD CITY	AWAY	0 - 3		5,000
13-Nov	HUDDERSFIELD TOWN	HOME	0 - 0		3,000
20-Nov	GRIMSBY TOWN	AWAY	0 - 0		4,000
27-Nov	NOTTS COUNTY	HOME	0 - 4		3,000
04-Dec	DERBY COUNTY	HOME	4 - 1	EDMONDSON 3 & WALDEN	1,000
11-Dec	SHEFFIELD WEDNESDAY	AWAY	0 - 0		3,000
18-Dec	BRADFORD PARK AVENUE	HOME	1 - 1	PRICE	4,000
25-Dec	LINCOLN CITY	AWAY	0 - 2		6,000
27-Dec	SHEFFIELD UNITED	HOME	2 - 3	BENNETT & BAINBRIDGE	6,000
01-Jan	HULL CITY	AWAY	3 - 0	FOLEY, EDMONDSON & PRICE (PEN)	3,000
08-Jan	NOTTINGHAM FOREST	HOME	1 - 0	BAINBRIDGE	5,000
15-Jan	BARNSLEY	AWAY	1 - 2	LAMPH	4,000
22-Jan	LEICSTER FOSSE	HOME	1 - 0	BAINBRIDGE	4,000
29-Jan	SHEFFIELD UNITED	AWAY	1 - 4	GOODWIN (PEN)	8,000
05-Feb	BRADFORD CITY	HOME	0 - 1		10,000
12-Feb	HUDDERSFIELD TOWN	AWAY	1 - 5	STEPHENSON C	6,000
19-Feb	GRIMSBY TOWN	HOME	3 - 1	PEART, SHARPE & STEPHENSON C	3,000
21-Apr	NOTTS COUNTY	AWAY	1 - 1	PRICE	3,000

SUBSIDIARY TOURNAMENT (NORTHERN DIVISION)

DATE	OPPONENTS	VENUE	SCORE	SCORERS	ATT.
04-Mar	ROCHDALE	AWAY	1 - 0	WILSON W	4,000
11-Mar	BRADFORD PARK AVENUE	HOME	3 - 2	STEPHENSON C 3	4,000
18-Mar	HUDDERSFIELD TOWN	AWAY	1 - 1	PRICE	5,000
25-Mar	BRADFORD CITY	HOME	0 - 1		3,000
01-Apr	BARNSLEY	AWAY	6 - 4	PEART 4, WALDEN & STEPHENSON C	3,000
08-Apr	ROCHDALE	HOME	3 - 1	WILSON W 2 & PEART	3,000
15-Apr	BRADFORD PARK AVENUE	AWAY	1 - 0	PRICE	4,000
22-Apr	HUDDERSFIELD TOWN	HOME	1 - 2	STEPHENSON C	5,000
24-Apr	BARNSLEY	HOME	1 - 0	STEPHENSON C	5,000
29-Apr	BRADFORD CITY	AWAY	4 - 2	PRICE, WILSON W, SHERWIN & PEART (PEN)	8,000

LEAGUE AND CUP

APPEARANCES

PLAYER	LEAGUE (PRINCIPAL)	LEAGUE (SUBSIDIARY)	TOTAL
AFFLECK / BAINBRIDGE	26 / 6	10 / 0	36 / 6
BENNETT / BOOTH	18 / 7	0 / 1	18 / 8
BRADLEY / COPELAND	11 / 15	0 / 10	11 / 25
COWEN / CROOT	1 / 13	0 / 0	1 / 13
DAVISON / DOWLING	0 / 1	1 / 0	1 / 1
DUNN / EDMONDSON	1 / 19	0 / 0	1 / 19
FOLEY / GOODWIN	26 / 4	10 / 0	36 / 4
HAMPSON J / HEWISON	19 / 2	7 / 9	26 / 11
HUGHES / JENNINGS	2 / 1	2 / 0	4 / 1
LAMPH / LAVERY	16 / 1	0 / 0	16 / 1
LAW / MALCOLM	22 / 1	0 / 0	22 / 1
PEART J / PRICE	3 / 22	7 / 10	10 / 32
ROBINSON S / SHARPE	1 / 1	2 / 1	3 / 2
SHERWIN / STEPHENSON C	0 / 3	1 / 9	1 / 12
WAINWRIGHT A / WALDEN	2 / 26	0 / 10	2 / 36
WALKER W / WILLIAMSON	15 / 0	10 / 1	25 / 1
WILSON W / WRIGGLESWORTH	0 / 1	9 / 0	9 / 1

GOALSCORERS

PLAYER	LEAGUE (PRINCIPAL)	LEAGUE (SUBSIDIARY)	TOTAL
PRICE	12	3	15
EDMONDSON	10		10
STEPHENSON C	2	6	8
PEART J	1	6	7
BENNETT	4		4
WILSON W		4	4
BAINBRIDGE	3		3
WALDEN	1	1	2
FOLEY	1		1
GOODWIN	1		1
HAMPSON J	1		1
LAMPH	1		1
LAW	1		1
SHARPE	1		1
SHERWIN		1	1

Herbert Chapman was earning a growing reputation in the game. One of his hardest tasks as manager was working with a constantly changing squad as players answered their country's call. City stalwarts to move on included George Affleck, Fred Croot and John Edmondson. Guests such as Levi Thorpe (Burnley), Tommy Mayson (Grimsby Town) and Billy Hampson (Newcastle), later to serve Leeds United as manager, joined the ranks, leaving just three Leeds players, Arthur Price, John Hampson and Charlie Copeland, from the first war campaign. With Clem Stephenson and Jack Peart remaining, Chapman had a settled squad and it paid dividends throughout a 30-match Principal Tournament.

The opening eight fixtures brought seven wins as City stamped their authority on the competition. Goals flowed from Peart, Price and Stephenson as opponents were swept aside during an amazing sequence of results. All three scored in City's 6-1 opening win at Grimsby Town. Stephenson notched a hat-trick in a 5-0 win against Notts County, Price grabbed four during a 5-0 triumph at Rotherham whilst Peart scored a hat-trick as Lincoln were defeated 5-2.

Defeats at Barnsley and Notts County were sandwiched between a tremendous spell of form that generated seven more wins before the New Year. Price drew plaudits during this spell with the only goal against Grimsby and a treble in a 4-1 win against Leicester Fosse. Stephenson and Peart scored a brace apiece in a 4-3 win against Chesterfield, whilst Mayson notched the only penalty of the season to defeat Bradford City 1-0 on Christmas Day.

With 15 wins in 20 games, the main wartime championship was in City's grasp but suddenly victories became harder to achieve. The final third of the season would yield just three as Chapman's title pretenders became draw specialists. Peart was by now the principle hitman in attack, scoring eight in the final six games. Braces against Nottingham Forest and Barnsley earned a draw and 3-0 win respectively, prior to a winning strike against Chesterfield in the penultimate game of the season. Fittingly, he also claimed City's final goal during a 2-2 draw at Sheffield United on the final day of the tournament as City took a deserved first 'major' honour.

Clearly elated, City failed to shine in the Subsidiary Tournament, finishing seventh but it did not detract from Chapman's first honour as a manager. Netting 76 goals in all, Peart led the way with 27, whilst Price scored 18 and Stephenson 14. Peart also made the most appearances along with Jim Stephenson.

MIDLAND SECTION PRINCIPAL TOURNAMENT - 1ST - PLD 30 W 18 D 10 L 2 F 68 A 29 PTS 46 &
MIDLAND SECTION SUBSIDIARY TOURNAMENT - 7TH - PLD 6 W 2 D 2 L 2 F 8 A 7 PTS 6

PRINCIPAL TOURNAMENT

DATE	OPPONENTS	VENUE	SCORE	SCORERS	ATT.
02-Sep	LEICESTER FOSSE	HOME	2 - 2	PRICE 2	3,000
09-Sep	GRIMSBY TOWN	AWAY	6 - 1	PEART 2, STEPHENSON C, THORPE, MAYSON & PRICE	4,000
16-Sep	NOTTS COUNTY	HOME	5 - 0	STEPHENSON C 3, MAYSON & PEART	3,000
23-Sep	ROTHERHAM COUNTY	AWAY	5 - 0	PRICE 4 & PEART	5,000
30-Sep	HUDDERSFIELD TOWN	HOME	1 - 0	PEART	8,000
07-Oct	LINCOLN CITY	AWAY	5 - 2	PEART 3, PATTINSON & STEPHENSON C	4,000
14-Oct	SHEFFIELD WEDNESDAY	HOME	1 - 0	STEPHENSON C	5,000
21-Oct	BRADFORD PARK AVENUE	AWAY	3 - 1	PRICE 2 & PEART	8,000
28-Oct	BIRMINGHAM	HOME	1 - 1	PEART	6,000
04-Nov	HULL CITY	AWAY	1 - 1	STEPHENSON C	4,000
11-Nov	NOTTINGHAM FOREST	HOME	3 - 1	PEART, SHERWIN & STEPHENSON C	5,000
18-Nov	BARNSLEY	AWAY	1 - 4	PEART	2,000
25-Nov	CHESTERFIELD	AWAY	4 - 3	PEART 2 & STEPHENSON C 2	4,000
02-Dec	SHEFFIELD UNITED	HOME	2 - 0	PRICE & STEPHENSON C	5,000
09-Dec	LEICESTER FOSSE	AWAY	4 - 1	PRICE 3 & THORPE	3,000
16-Dec	GRIMSBY TOWN	HOME	1 - 0	PRICE	3,000
23-Dec	NOTTS COUNTY	AWAY	0 - 1		500
25-Dec	BRADFORD CITY	HOME	1 - 0	MAYSON (PEN)	10,000
26-Dec	BRADFORD CITY	AWAY	3 - 0	STEPHENSON J, PEART & PRICE	11,000
30-Dec	ROTHERHAM COUNTY	HOME	2 - 0	MAYSON & HEWISON	4,000
06-Jan	HUDDERSFIELD TOWN	AWAY	1 - 1	TROTTER	7,000
13-Jan	LINCOLN CITY	HOME	3 - 1	PEART, PRICE & MOORE	2,000
20-Jan	SHEFFIELD WEDNESDAY	AWAY	2 - 2	STEPHENSON J & PEART	5,000
27-Jan	BRADFORD PARK AVENUE	HOME	0 - 0		6,000
03-Feb	BIRMINGHAM	AWAY	1 - 1	PEART	15,000
10-Feb	HULL CITY	HOME	1 - 1	PEART	2,000
17-Feb	NOTTINGHAM FOREST	AWAY	3 - 3	MOORE & PEART 2	3,000
24-Feb	BARNSLEY	HOME	3 - 0	PEART 2 & STEPHENSON C	6,000
03-Mar	CHESTERFIELD	HOME	1 - 0	PEART	4,000
10-Mar	SHEFFIELD UNITED	AWAY	2 - 2	PRICE & PEART	6,000

SUBSIDIARY TOURNAMENT

DATE	OPPONENTS	VENUE	SCORE	SCORERS	ATT.
17-Mar	BRADFORD PARK AVENUE	AWAY	1 - 1	PEART	6,000
24-Mar	HUDDERSFIELD TOWN	HOME	0 - 2		4,000
31-Mar	BRADFORD CITY	HOME	1 - 1	PRICE (PEN)	4,000
07-Apr	BRADFORD PARK AVENUE	HOME	0 - 2		3,000
09-Apr	HUDDERSFIELD TOWN	AWAY	1 - 0	STEPHENSON C	3,000
21-Apr	BRADFORD CITY	AWAY	5 - 1	MOORE 3, PEART & STEPHENSON C	3,000

LEAGUE AND CUP

APPEARANCES

PLAYER	LEAGUE (PRINCIPAL)	LEAGUE (SUBSIDIARY)	TOTAL
BARNSHAW / CAWLEY	1 / 0	0 / 2	1 / 2
CLIPSTONE / COPELAND	1 / 24	3 / 0	4 / 24
DAWSON / FEATHERS	4 / 1	0 / 0	4 / 1
HAMPSON J / HAMPSON T	14 / 2	0 / 6	14 / 8
HAMPSON Wm / HEWISON	16 / 25	6 / 6	22 / 31
HUDSON / HUDSPETH	11 / 0	0 / 1	11 / 1
JAMES / KAYE	1 / 1	0 / 0	1 / 1
McCREADIE / MAYSON	1 / 26	0 / 4	1 / 30
MOORE / PATTISON	7 / 1	5 / 0	12 / 1
PEART / PRICE	29 / 25	4 / 5	33 / 30
ROBINSON A / ROBINSON S	6 / 2	0 / 1	6 / 3
ROSE / SHERWIN	0 / 28	1 / 6	1 / 34
STEPHENSON C / STEPHENSON J	24 / 27	6 / 6	30 / 33
THORPE / TOMS	24 / 2	4 / 0	28 / 2
TROTTER / WALDEN	3 / 2	0 / 0	3 / 2
WALKER W	22	0	22 / 0

GOALSCORERS

PLAYER	LEAGUE (PRINCIPAL)	LEAGUE (SUBSIDIARY)	TOTAL
PEART	25	2	27
PRICE	17	1	18
STEPHENSON C	12	2	14
MOORE	2	3	5
MAYSON	4		4
STEPHENSON J	2		2
THORPE	2		2
HEWISON	1		1
PATTISON	1		1
SHERWIN	1		1
TROTTER	1		1

As a new season dawned, fresh players came into the squad. Loan players included Bob Hewison (Sunderland) and keeper Tommy Hampson (Accrington Stanley), one of five Hampson's to represent City during the campaign. City's strike force of Jack Peart, Arthur Price and Clem Stephenson was unaltered and the reigning champions took off where they left the previous season in the Principal Tournament.

In a change in format, City played 14 back-to-back clashes and quickly gained nine wins from 11 encounters. Peart found the target in nine of the matches as City claimed doubles over Sheffield Wednesday, Rotherham and Lincoln City. In a superb run of form, the sharpshooter scored the only goal in the season's opener against Wednesday and proved the difference against Birmingham. Price began brightly, notching a hat-trick in a 4-0 win against Bradford City before bagging a brace in a 4-0 canter at Grimsby.

Stephenson combined with Peart, Price and P Barrett to despatch Wednesday 5-0, but the biggest win of the season was reserved for a home clash against Rotherham, where goals from Peart 2, Price 2, Ernie Goodwin and Hewison gained a 6-0 victory. Chapman's team was in imperious form and immediately recovered from a defeat at Birmingham to claim seven successive victories, including doubles over Notts County, Barnsley and Huddersfield Town. Peart scored braces in a 4-2 win at Notts County and 4-3 victory at Barnsley before claiming a goal alongside Stephenson and Price as City defeated Huddersfield 3-1.

The run-in brought two reverses but could not stop Leeds claiming a second Principle title with victories over Leicester Fosse, Nottingham Forest and Bradford Park Avenue taking the doubles total to nine, a remarkable achievement. Finishing fifth in the Subsidiary Tournament meant little as City took on Lancashire champions Stoke City in an end of season play-off. Without Stephenson, called up to the army, Chapman brought in Billy Hibbert (Newcastle).

In the 'unofficial' championship matches, debutante Hibbert and Peart scored in a 2-0 win at Elland Road before losing the return 1-0 for a 2-1 aggregate win. Although not recognised in official league records Leeds City were League champions. Both legs attracted an attendance of 15,000 and the combined receipts of £913 benefited the National Footballer's War Fund. Fielding 32 players, Hewison, Billy Hampson, Harry Sherwin and Peart were ever-present in the Principal Tournament whilst Price missed one game. Peart top-scored with 21 goals, Price scored 18 and Stephenson 13.

1917 - 1918

MIDLAND SECTION PRINCIPAL TOURNAMENT - 1ST - PLD 28 W 23 D 1 L 4 F 75 A 23 PTS 47 &
MIDLAND SECTION SUBSIDIARY TOURNAMENT - 5TH - PLD 6 W 3 D 2 L 1 F 8 A 6 PTS 8

PRINCIPAL TOURNAMENT

DATE	OPPONENTS	VENUE	SCORE	SCORERS	ATT.
01-Sep	SHEFFIELD WEDNESDAY	AWAY	1 - 0	PEART	8,000
08-Sep	SHEFFIELD WEDNESDAY	HOME	5 - 0	PRICE 2, STEPHENSON C, PEART & BARRETT	6,000
15-Sep	BRADFORD CITY	AWAY	2 - 3	HAMPSON Wm., & STEPHENSON C	4,000
22-Sep	BRADFORD CITY	HOME	4 - 0	PEART & PRICE 3	4,000
29-Sep	ROTHERHAM COUNTY	AWAY	3 - 0	PEART, STEPHENSON C & SHERWIN	5,000
06-Oct	ROTHERHAM COUNTY	HOME	6 - 0	PRICE 2, PEART 2, GOODWIN & HEWISON	5,000
13-Oct	LINCOLN CITY	HOME	3 - 0	PEART, STEPHENSON C & ROBINSON S	4,000
20-Oct	LINCOLN CITY	AWAY	4 - 0	PEART, HEWISON, STEPHENSON J & MOORE	3,000
27-Oct	GRIMSBY TOWN	HOME	2 - 2	PEART 2	3,000
03-Nov	GRIMSBY TOWN	AWAY	4 - 0	ROBINSON S, PRICE 2 & SHERWIN	1,500
10-Nov	BIRMINGHAM	HOME	1 - 0	PEART	5,000
17-Nov	BIRMINGHAM	AWAY	1 - 3	CAWLEY	26,000
24-Nov	NOTTS COUNTY	HOME	2 - 0	GRANT & STEPHENSON C	2,000
01-Dec	NOTTS COUNTY	AWAY	4 - 2	PEART 2, PRICE & SHERWIN	3,000
08-Dec	BARNSLEY	AWAY	4 - 3	PEART 2, HAMPSON J & CAWLEY	1,400
15-Dec	BARNSLEY	HOME	2 - 1	PEART & HEWISON	3,500
25-Dec	HUDDERSFIELD TOWN	HOME	3 - 0	PRICE, SHERWIN (PEN) & HEWISON	5,000
26-Dec	HUDDERSFIELD TOWN	AWAY	3 - 1	STEPHENSON C, PEART & PRICE	4,000
05-Jan	HULL CITY	AWAY	2 - 0	PRICE & STEPHENSON C	3,000
12-Jan	HULL CITY	HOME	1 - 3	PRICE	2,000
19-Jan	LEICESTER FOSSE	AWAY	4 - 2	SHERWIN, STEPHENSON C & CAWLEY 2	3,000
26-Jan	LEICESTER FOSSE	HOME	4 - 0	PRICE, PEART, GOODWIN & STEPHENSON C	5,000
02-Feb	NOTTINGHAM FOREST	HOME	2 - 0	O.G. (WIGHTMAN) & BUCHAN	3,000
09-Feb	NOTTINGHAM FOREST	AWAY	1 - 0	PEART	3,000
16-Feb	BRADFORD PARK AVENUE	HOME	2 - 1	CAWLEY & STEPHENSON C	7,500
23-Feb	BRADFORD PARK AVENUE	AWAY	2 - 0	SHERWIN (PEN) & PEART	7,500
02-Mar	SHEFFIELD UNITED	AWAY	1 - 2	HEWISON	18,000
09-Mar	SHEFFIELD UNITED	HOME	2 - 0	CAWLEY & STEPHENSON C	15,000

SUBSIDIARY TOURNAMENT

16-Mar	HUDDERSFIELD TOWN	AWAY	2 - 4	PRICE & STEPHENSON C	6,500
23-Mar	HUDDERSFIELD TOWN	HOME	1 - 0	CAWLEY	6,000
30-Mar	BRADFORD PARK AVENUE	HOME	3 - 1	PRICE 2 & STEPHENSON C	1,000
06-Apr	BRADFORD PARK AVENUE	AWAY	2 - 1	WILSON A 2	7,000
13-Apr	BRADFORD CITY	HOME	0 - 0		3,000
20-Apr	BRADFORD CITY	AWAY	0 - 0		3,000

LEAGUE CHAMPIONSHIP PLAY - OFF (LEEDS CITY WON 2 - 1 ON AGGREGATE)

04-May	STOKE CITY	HOME	2 - 0	HIBBERT & PEART	15,000
11-May	STOKE CITY	AWAY	0 - 1		15,000

LEAGUE AND CUP

APPEARANCES

PLAYER	LEAGUE (PR.)	LEAGUE (SUB.)	LEAGUE (P-OFF)	TOTAL
ARKLE / BAINES	1 / 13	0 / 0	0 / 0	1 / 13
BARRETT / BUCHAN	5 / 1	2 / 0	0 / 0	7 / 1
CAWLEY / CHARD	18 / 1	6 / 0	2 / 0	26 / 1
CROOT / GOODWIN	0 / 7	1 / 0	0 / 2	1 / 9
GRANT / HAMPSON E	4 / 2	0 / 1	0 / 0	4 / 3
HAMPSON J / HAMPSON T	16 / 23	3 / 6	0 / 2	19 / 31
HAMPSON Wa / HAMPSON Wm	0 / 28	3 / 6	0 / 2	3 / 36
HEWISON / HIBBERT	28 / 0	6 / 0	2 / 2	36 / 2
KETTLE / KIRTON	0 / 1	1 / 0	0 / 0	1 / 1
LAMPH / MILLERSHIP	26 / 11	6 / 3	2 / 2	34 / 16
MOORE / PEART J	1 / 28	0 / 1	0 / 2	1 / 31
PRICE / ROBINSON A	27 / 2	6 / 0	2 / 0	35 / 2
ROBINSON S / RUTHERFORD W	8 / 0	0 / 1	0 / 0	8 / 1
SHERWIN / SPRATT	28 / 1	6 / 0	2 / 0	36 / 1
STEPHENSON C / STEPHENSON J	24 / 1	6 / 0	0 / 0	30 / 1
WALKER W / WILSON A	3 / 0	0 / 2	0 / 0	3 / 2

GOALSCORERS

PLAYER	LEAGUE (PR.)	LEAGUE (SUB.)	LEAGUE (P-OFF)	TOTAL
PEART J	20		1	21
PRICE	15	3		18
STEPHENSON C	11	2		13
CAWLEY	6	1		7
SHERWIN	6			6
HEWISON	5			5
GOODWIN	2			2
ROBINSON S	2			2
WILSON A		2		2
BARRETT	1			1
BUCHAN	1			1
GRANT	1			1
HAMPSON J	1			1
HAMPSON Wm	1			1
HIBBERT			1	1
MOORE	1			1
STEPHENSON J	1			1
OWN GOALS	1			1

33

During the final season of wartime football, Herbert Chapman again juggled players coming and going from Elland Road. Among a host of guest players in his 36-man squad, Tom Hall (Newcastle), Tom Cawley (Rotherham) and Albert McLachlan all made valuable contributions, whilst the likes of James Cartwright (Manchester City), James Hugall (Clapton Orient) and Harold Gough (Sheffield United) made a handful of starts. All however, kept football in mainstream society.

Two Leeds City players, Walter Cook and Willis Walker, shared goalkeeping duties, whilst Jack Peart and Arthur Price continued to lead the line. With so much disruption, continuing previous campaign success was going to be tough. Nevertheless, City made a solid start. Billy Hibbert picked up from his sensational debut in the championship play offs with a goal in City's opening day 4-1 win against Notts County. Another Hibbert strike earned a 3-1 victory against Birmingham, matches that also brought goals for Cawley.

Hibbert's penalty settled a 2-1 win at home to Rotherham, prior to a fixture that saw a cameo appearance by City legend Billy McLeod. A guest player with Bradford City during the conflict, McLeod scored in a 3-0 win but would only feature spasmodically during the season. Clem Stephenson also returned; notching a brace to defeat Lincoln City, but inconsistency around the festive period left City off the pace.

The second half of the campaign brought a double against Barnsley, City's third of the season. Peart returned to form with strikes in victories over Leicester Fosse, Nottingham Forest, Bradford Park Avenue, Sheffield United and Coventry City as City completed the Principal Tournament on a high. Finishing fourth, Chapman's team went one better in the Subsidiary Tournament, McLeod notching four goals, including a brace in City's 3-0 win at home to Bradford City, the final game before the cessation of war.

City's achievements during World War One are not recognised in 'official' league records but it was the most successful period of Leeds City's history. In all 84 players represented the club during the conflict. Top appearance makers were Arthur Price 120, Jack Peart, 107, John Hampson 92, Billy Hampson 91, Clem Stephenson 91 and Harry Sherwin 91. Top goalscorers were Jack Peart 71, Arthur Price 59 and Clem Stephenson 44.

One of the bloodiest periods in world history cost millions of lives and a number of Leeds City who took the 'Kings Shilling' paid the ultimate sacrifice. They included international stars Jimmy Speirs, killed in action in 1917, Evelyn Lintott, killed on the Somme on July 1 1916, Gerald Kirk, killed at Neuve Chapelle in 1915, and David Murray, killed in France in 1915. Numerous footballers were decorated including airman Joe Richmond, who received the French Medal Militaire.

1918 - 1919

MIDLAND SECTION PRINCIPAL TOURNAMENT - 4TH - PLD 30 W 17 D 4 L 9 F 53 A 38 PTS 38 &
MIDLAND SECTION SUBSIDIARY TOURNAMENT - 3RD - PLD 6 W 3 D 0 L 3 F 10 A 9 PTS 6

PRINCIPAL TOURNAMENT

DATE	OPPONENTS	VENUE	SCORE	SCORERS	ATT.
07-Sep	NOTTS COUNTY	HOME	4 - 1	PEART, CAWLEY 2 & HIBBERT	5,000
14-Sep	NOTTS COUNTY	AWAY	2 - 5	PRICE & PEART	7,000
21-Sep	BIRMINGHAM	HOME	3 - 1	HIBBERT, CAWLEY & HAMPSON E	3,000
28-Sep	BIRMINGHAM	AWAY	2 - 4	HIBBERT & PEART	14,000
05-Oct	ROTHERHAM COUNTY	HOME	2 - 1	PRICE & HIBBERT (PEN)	2,000
12-Oct	ROTHERHAM COUNTY	AWAY	3 - 0	SHERWIN, McLEOD & PEART	7,000
19-Oct	LINCOLN CITY	AWAY	0 - 1		4,000
26-Oct	LINCOLN CITY	HOME	2 - 0	STEPHENSON C 2	6,000
02-Nov	GRIMSBY TOWN	AWAY	2 - 0	STEPHENSON C & PEART	2,000
09-Nov	GRIMSBY TOWN	HOME	3 - 1	HIBBERT (PEN), PRICE & PEART	4,000
16-Nov	BRADFORD CITY	AWAY	1 - 3	PEART	8,000
23-Nov	BRADFORD CITY	HOME	2 - 1	HAMPSON J 2	7,500
30-Nov	SHEFFIELD WEDNESDAY	AWAY	2 - 0	HALL & PEART	10,000
07-Dec	SHEFFIELD WEDNESDAY	HOME	1 - 1	HALL	9,000
14-Dec	HULL CITY	HOME	0 - 0		5,000
21-Dec	HULL CITY	AWAY	1 - 2	PEART	4,500
25-Dec	HUDDERSFIELD TOWN	HOME	1 - 1	PRICE (PEN)	5,000
26-Dec	HUDDERSFIELD TOWN	AWAY	1 - 0	PRICE (PEN)	10,000
28-Dec	COVENTRY CITY	HOME	0 - 1		6,000
11-Jan	BARNSLEY	HOME	4 - 0	HALL, PRICE & STEPHENSON C 2	6,000
18-Jan	BARNSLEY	AWAY	1 - 0	HALL	7,000
25-Jan	LEICESTER FOSSE	HOME	4 - 2	STEPHENSON C, PRICE 2 & PEART	3,000
01-Feb	LEICESTER FOSSE	AWAY	0 - 0		4,000
08-Feb	NOTTINGHAM FOREST	AWAY	2 - 0	STEPHENSON C & PEART	10,000
15-Feb	NOTTINGHAM FOREST	HOME	0 - 4		11,000
22-Feb	BRADFORD PARK AVENUE	AWAY	3 - 1	PEART, STEPHENSON C & HALL	5,000
01-Mar	BRADFORD PARK AVENUE	HOME	2 - 5	HALL & STEPHENSON C	10,000
08-Mar	SHEFFIELD UNITED	HOME	2 - 1	PEART & HALL	8,000
15-Mar	SHEFFIELD UNITED	AWAY	0 - 1		22,000
22-Apr	COVENTRY CITY	AWAY	3 - 1	PEART, McLEOD & HALL (PEN)	9,000

SUBSIDIARY TOURNAMENT

DATE	OPPONENTS	VENUE	SCORE	SCORERS	ATT.
22-Mar	HUDDERSFIELD TOWN	HOME	3 - 0	PEART 2 & McLEOD	9,000
29-Mar	HUDDERSFIELD TOWN	AWAY	0 - 1		8,000
05-Apr	BRADFORD PARK AVENUE	AWAY	0 - 5		12,000
12-Apr	BRADFORD PARK AVENUE	HOME	3 - 1	McLEOD, STEPHENSON J & HALL	6,000
19-Apr	BRADFORD CITY	AWAY	1 - 2	BAINBRIDGE	16,000
26-Apr	BRADFORD CITY	HOME	3 - 0	McLEOD 2 & BAINBRIDGE	7,000

LEAGUE AND CUP

APPEARANCES

PLAYER	LEAGUE (PRINCIPAL)	LEAGUE (SUBSIDIARY)	TOTAL
BAINBRIDGE / BAVIN	1 / 1	4 / 0	5 / 1
CARTWRIGHT / CAWLEY	4 / 15	0 / 0	4 / 15
COOK / COPELAND	11 / 4	0 / 0	11 / 4
CURRIE / EDMONDSON	1 / 0	0 / 1	1 / 1
GOUGH / HALL	2 / 19	0 / 3	2 / 22
HAMPSON E / HAMPSON J	4 / 27	0 / 6	4 / 33
HAMPSON Wm / HEWISON	28 / 1	5 / 0	33 / 1
HIBBERT / HUGALL	14 / 1	0 / 0	14 / 1
LAMPH / LINFOOT	27 / 2	5 / 4	32 / 6
LOUNDS / McLACHLAN	3 / 18	3 / 6	6 / 24
McLEOD / MILLERSHIP	8 / 27	5 / 6	13 / 33
MOORE / PEART	1 / 29	0 / 4	1 / 33
PRICE / ROBERTS	23 / 1	0 / 0	23 / 1
ROBINSON S / RUTHERFORD A	3 / 3	0 / 0	3 / 3
SCOTT / SHERWIN	1 / 20	0 / 0	1 / 20
SMELT / STEPHENSON C	1 / 13	0 / 6	1 / 19
STEPHENSON J / SUTCLIFFE	0 / 0	2 / 2	2 / 2
VOYSEY / WALKER W	1 / 16	0 / 4	1 / 20

GOALSCORERS

PLAYER	LEAGUE (PRINCIPAL)	LEAGUE (SUBSIDIARY)	TOTAL
PEART J	14	2	16
HALL	8	1	9
STEPHENSON C	9		9
PRICE	8		8
McLEOD	2	4	6
HIBBERT	5		5
CAWLEY	3		3
BAINBRIDGE		2	2
HAMPSON J	2		2
HAMPSON E	1		1
SHERWIN	1		1
STEPHENSON J		1	1

As Herbert Chapman rebuilt his squad, Leeds City's darkest days began. Former full-back Charlie Copeland, dissatisfied with new contract terms, reported City to the Football League for making illegal payments to players during the war. 'Under the counter' payments to players other than normal expenses had been commonplace during the war but football authorities could no longer ignore it.

As investigations commenced, City began playing their Division 2 fixtures. Billy McLeod notched a brace in a 4-2 defeat at Blackpool. Another McLeod double and a strike by Clem Bainbridge brought a 3-0 victory at home to Coventry whilst John Edmondson notched the winner in a return fixture with Blackpool. By City's eighth game, at Wolves on Saturday 4 October 1919, club officials had been ordered to produce documents within 48 hours or face action. A McLeod hat-trick and Tom Lamph goal earned a 4-2 win, but it would be City's final game as club officials refused to present information for examination on the due deadline.

City's next fixture against South Shields was postponed and following a meeting, Football League administrators expelled Leeds City on 13 October. Supporters were stunned, the Lord Mayor of Leeds, Alderman Joseph Henry offered to run the club, but it was to no avail as Port Vale took over City's fixtures. Five club officials, including Chapman, received life bans and S. Whittham & Sons auctioned players at the Metropole Hotel, McLeod generating the highest fee of £1,250 from Notts County.

Chapman quit the game in December 1919, believing the FA Commission had harshly treated him. A manager at a munitions factory during the war, he claimed that he was not in the office when the alleged payments occurred. Suspended for a short time, Chapman successfully appealed against his suspension and went on to become one of the greatest managers of all time at Huddersfield Town and Arsenal.

Analysing the 15-year history of Leeds City, the name of Billy McLeod stands out. The first goalscoring hero for football followers in the city of Leeds, McLeod was top scorer in nine consecutive seasons and was the only player to make 300 appearances and score five goals in a game. Excluding the war years, McLeod's tally of 177 goals in 301 matches was remarkable, especially when you consider that the second top goal scorer and only other player to make over 200 appearances, Fred Croot, scored 39 goals in 227 games. Three other players made at least 150 appearances: George Affleck 191, Stan Cubberley 188 and Harry Bromage 152. An era was over but a new football club would soon rise from the ashes of Leeds City.

1919 - 1920

DIVISION TWO (FINAL LEAGUE POSITION - 13TH) $

LEEDS CITY PLD 8 W 4 D 2 L 2 F 17 A 10 PTS 10 & LEEDS CITY / PORT VALE PLD 42 W 16 D 8 L 18 F 59 A 62 PTS 40

DATE	OPPONENTS	VENUE	SCORE	SCORERS	ATT.
30-Aug	BLACKPOOL	AWAY	2 - 4	McLEOD 2	10,000
03-Sep	COVENTRY CITY	HOME	3 - 0	McLEOD 2 & BAINBRIDGE	8,000
06-Sep	BLACKPOOL	HOME	1 - 0	EDMONDSON	10,000
11-Sep	COVENTRY CITY	AWAY	4 - 0	McLEOD 2, EDMONDSON & BAINBRIDGE	12,000
13-Sep	HULL CITY	HOME	1 - 2	BAINBRIDGE	10,000
20-Sep	HULL CITY	AWAY	1 - 1	EDMONDSON	8,000
27-Sep	WOLVERHAMPTON WANDERERS	HOME	1 - 1	PRICE (PEN)	12,000
04-Oct	WOLVERHAMPTON WANDERERS	AWAY	4 - 2	LAMPH & McLEOD 3	15,000

$ = REMAINING 34 FIXTURES UNDERTAKEN BY PORT VALE AFTER LEEDS CITY WERE EXPELLED FROM THE FOOTBALL LEAGUE

LEAGUE AND CUP
APPEARANCES

PLAYER	LEAGUE	TOTAL
AFFLECK	2	2
BAINBRIDGE	7	7
EDMONDSON	6	6
FOLEY	5	5
GOODWIN	1	1
HAMPSON	7	7
HOPKINS	7	7
KIRTON	1	1
LAMPH	8	8
LOUNDS	8	8
McLEOD	8	8
MILLERSHIP	8	8
PRICE	7	7
SHORT	5	5
WALKER W	8	8

GOALSCORERS

PLAYER	LEAGUE	TOTAL
McLEOD	9	9
BAINBRIDGE	3	3
EDMONDSON	3	3
LAMPH	1	1
PRICE	1	1

Within hours of Leeds City's demise on 13 October 1919, devastated supporters held a meeting at Salem Central Hall in Leeds. Joe Henry Jr. was appointed chairman of a new club, Leeds United, and adverts for players appeared in the local press. Managed initially by former City player Dick Ray, United replaced Leeds City reserves in the Midland League on October 31 and moved back to Elland Road after Yorkshire Amateurs agreed to leave.

The key to eventual success however was the financial support and dedication of Huddersfield Town chairman Hilton Crowther. Disillusioned at local support for Town, rugby league being the main sport in the city, Crowther suggested moving Huddersfield 'lock, stock and barrel' to Elland Road. Many players and United's board agreed and a new name, Leeds Trinity, was discussed.

The Football League received Crowther's proposal and gave Huddersfield until 31 December to pay Crowther off. In a twist Huddersfield supporters, shocked at losing their team, demanded a right to buy Crowther's £25,000 stake. Crowther meanwhile was now United chairman, loaning £35,000 to be repaid when Division 1 status had been achieved and immediately appointed Arthur Fairclough manager. Fairclough and assistant Ray brought in new players whilst Crowther canvassed for votes to gain election to the Football League. With financial stability and the nucleus of a capable side assured, Leeds United polled the highest number of votes, 31, to gain Football League status on 31 May 1920.

Jim Baker was United's first captain and the club's first colours were blue and white striped shirts and white shorts. Although United lost their opening league fixture to Port Vale, a new era had dawned. Len Armitage scored against South Shields in a 2-1 defeat, a Merton Ellson brace secured a 3-1 win against Vale as did an Ernie Goldthorpe double, including a penalty, for a similar scoreline against Leicester City. By the end of September, United had withdrawn from the FA Cup, a decision agreed with the Football Association as Leeds were unwilling to compete in eight qualifying matches to reach the first round proper. Eugene O'Doherty's hat-trick accounted for Boothtown 5-2 and a Walter Butler treble secured a 7-0 victory against Leeds Steelworks in the qualifying rounds played before withdrawing. Centre-forward Robert Thompson notched a brace in United's highest league victory, 4-0 at home to Coventry City, and grabbed the club's first league hat-trick in a 3-0 win against Notts County.

Baker led by example and was vital in the centre of defence. He also scored his only goals for the club, winning penalties in tight games against Birmingham City 1-0 and Clapton Orient 2-1. Patchy performances throughout their inaugural Football League campaign saw United finish fourteenth but stability had been achieved and they had a promising average attendance of 16,000. Baker alongside Billy Down and Albert Duffield were ever present in Division 2 and Thompson finished the season top scorer with 12 goals.

DIVISION TWO (FINAL LEAGUE POSITION - 14TH)
PLD 42 W 14 D 10 L 18 F 40 A 45 PTS 38

DATE	OPPONENTS	VENUE	SCORE	SCORERS	ATT.
28-Aug	PORT VALE	AWAY	0 - 2		19,000
01-Sep	SOUTH SHIELDS	HOME	1 - 2	ARMITAGE	16,958
04-Sep	PORT VALE	HOME	3 - 1	BEST & ELLSON 2	15,000
08-Sep	SOUTH SHIELDS	AWAY	0 - 3		15,000
11-Sep	LEICESTER CITY	AWAY	1 - 1	ELLSON	16,000
18-Sep	LEICESTER CITY	HOME	3 - 1	ELLSON & GOLDTHORPE 2 (1 PEN)	11,000
25-Sep	BLACKPOOL	AWAY	0 - 1		8,000
02-Oct	BLACKPOOL	HOME	2 - 0	WALTON J & MASON G	10,000
09-Oct	SHEFFIELD WEDNESDAY	AWAY	0 - 2		20,000
16-Oct	SHEFFIELD WEDNESDAY	HOME	2 - 0	THOMPSON R & ELLSON	15,000
23-Oct	HULL CITY	AWAY	1 - 0	THOMPSON R	10,000
30-Oct	HULL CITY	HOME	1 - 1	ELLSON	20,000
06-Nov	STOKE CITY	AWAY	0 - 4		10,000
13-Nov	STOKE CITY	HOME	0 - 0		15,000
27-Nov	COVENTRY CITY	AWAY	1 - 1	LYON	18,000
01-Dec	COVENTRY CITY	HOME	4 - 0	THOMPSON R 2, ELLSON & MASON G	10,000
04-Dec	NOTTS COUNTY	AWAY	2 - 1	LYON 2	14,000
11-Dec	NOTTS COUNTY	HOME	3 - 0	THOMPSON R 3	12,000
18-Dec	BIRMINGHAM	AWAY	0 - 1		20,000
25-Dec	FULHAM	HOME	0 - 0		25,000
27-Dec	FULHAM	AWAY	0 - 1		30,000
01-Jan	BIRMINGHAM	HOME	1 - 0	BAKER J (PEN)	24,000
08-Jan	ROTHERHAM COUNTY	HOME	1 - 0	ELLSON	18,000
15-Jan	WOLVERHAMPTON WANDERERS	AWAY	0 - 3		20,000
22-Jan	WOLVERHAMPTON WANDERERS	HOME	3 - 0	THOMPSON R 2 & LYON	14,000
29-Jan	WEST HAM UNITED	HOME	1 - 2	THOMPSON R	15,000
05-Feb	WEST HAM UNITED	AWAY	0 - 3		23,000
12-Feb	STOCKPORT COUNTY	AWAY	1 - 3	THOMPSON R	9,000
19-Feb	STOCKPORT COUNTY	HOME	0 - 2		20,000
26-Feb	CLAPTON ORIENT	AWAY	0 - 1		17,000
05-Mar	CLAPTON ORIENT	HOME	2 - 1	MUSGROVE & BAKER J (PEN)	18,000
12-Mar	BURY	AWAY	1 - 1	HOWARTH	10,000
19-Mar	BURY	HOME	1 - 0	MUSGROVE	16,000
26-Mar	BRISTOL CITY	HOME	0 - 1		20,000
28-Mar	CARDIFF CITY	AWAY	0 - 1		30,000
29-Mar	CARDIFF CITY	HOME	1 - 2	HOWARTH	20,000
02-Apr	BRISTOL CITY	AWAY	0 - 0		24,000
09-Apr	BARNSLEY	HOME	0 - 0		13,000
16-Apr	BARNSLEY	AWAY	1 - 1	HOWARTH	12,000
23-Apr	NOTTINGHAM FOREST	HOME	1 - 1	HOWARTH	12,000
30-Apr	NOTTINGHAM FOREST	AWAY	0 - 1		8,000
07-May	ROTHERHAM COUNTY	AWAY	2 - 0	HOWARTH 2 (1 PEN)	10,000

F. A. CUP

DATE	OPPONENTS	VENUE	SCORE	SCORERS	ATT.
11-Sep	BOOTHTOWN (Q1)	HOME	5 - 2	ARMITAGE 2 & O'DOHERTY 3	1,500
25-Sep	LEEDS STEELWORKS (Q2) $	AWAY	7 - 0	BUTLER W 3, THOMPSON R, HART E, O'DOHERTY & WATERHOUSE	3,000

LEEDS WITHDREW FROM THE COMPETITION AFTER THE SECOND QUALIFYING ROUND

KEY :- $ = LEEDS STEELWORKS WERE DRAWN AT HOME BUT DECIDED TO PLAY AWAY

FOR EASE OF IDENTIFICATION WHERE TWO PLAYERS WITH THE SAME SURNAME HAVE PLAYED, EVERY EFFORT HAS BEEN MADE TO PERSONALISE THEM BY PUTTING THEIR INITIAL, EG :- WALLACE Ro., OR WALLACE Ra. THIS HAS BEEN UNDERTAKEN FOR LEEDS CITY AND LEEDS UNITED INDIVIDUALLY

LEAGUE AND CUP
APPEARANCES

PLAYER	LEAGUE	F. A. CUP	TOTAL
ARMITAGE	6	1	7
BAKER J	42		42
BEST	11		11
BOARDMAN	4		4
BROCK	6		6
BUTLER W	1	2	3
COOPE		2	2
COOPER G		2	2
DOWN	42		42
DUFFIELD	42		42
ELLSON	36		36
FREW	36		36
GOLDTHORPE	6		6
HART E	5	2	7
HILL	7	1	8
HOWARTH	11		11
JACKLIN		2	2
LAMPH	6		6
LYON	33		33
McGEE		1	1
MASON	35		35
MUSGROVE	36		36
O'DOHERTY		2	2
POWELL S	3		3
RODGERSON	3		3
SHARPE I	1		1
SMELT	1	1	2
STUART	1	2	3
THOMPSON R	23	2	25
TILLOTSON	2		2
WALTON J	41		41
WATERHOUSE		2	2
WOOD B	22		22

GOALSCORERS

PLAYER	LEAGUE	F. A. CUP	TOTAL
THOMPSON R	11	1	12
ELLSON	8		8
HOWARTH	6		6
LYON	4		4
O'DOHERTY		4	4
ARMITAGE	1	2	3
BUTLER W		3	3
BAKER J	2		2
GOLDTHORPE	2		2
MASON G	2		2
MUSGROVE	2		2
BEST	1		1
HART E		1	1
WALTON J	1		1
WATERHOUSE		1	1

Looking to build on their opening season Leeds faced Port Vale in the first game again. Centre-forward Tommy Howarth towards the backend of the previous campaign scored six goals in 11 games and opened his account in a 2-1 victory. Another Howarth strike brought a double over Vale prior to a brace in a 3-0 victory against Bristol City. More goals flowed during an impressive early-season spell for United, as Blackpool, Clapton Orient and South Shields were defeated.

Making a positive impression was teenage centre-back Ernie Hart, and alongside keeper Fred Walley, Harry Sherwin, Jim Moore and Ralph Coates, manager Arthur Fairclough was developing a promising squad. Howarth had scored half United's goals by January, but the side was lacking a cutting edge. Inconsistency was a problem and it carried on into the New Year; nine victories came in the opening half of the season, three would follow in the first 10 games of 1922.

During an unsettled spell, Swindon Town ended United's FA Cup first round hopes and Bill Poyntz made headlines when he became the first Leeds United player to be sent off in a 2-1 defeat at Bury, a week after scoring in a 2-0 win against the same outfit. Nine days on from his dismissal, United's reserve inside-forward experienced a rollercoaster of emotions when he scored a hat-trick in a 3-0 win at home against Leicester City only hours after getting married!

Fairclough needed to strengthen his forward line and responded with the signing of Jack Swan (Huddersfield Town). The left-footer delivered in 2-1 wins against Crystal Palace and Derby County before striking again with a hat-trick in an impressive 5-2 win at home to Coventry City, Len Armitage grabbing the other two goals. The clash came just before Easter and began a fine unbeaten run with four victories in seven games as United moved into the top half of the table. The duo earned a draw at Barnsley before a Swan brace engineered a 4-0 victory in the return fixture as Leeds secured a double over their South Yorkshire rivals.

Poyntz also scored against the Tykes and opened the scoring in a 2-0 win against Fulham. Armitage's strike in the return clash with the Londoners earned a win but it would be United's last as two draws in the final three games brought an encouraging eighth place finish. Skipper Jim Baker was the only ever-present and Howarth top scored with 13 goals.

1921 - 1922

DIVISION TWO (FINAL LEAGUE POSITION - 8TH)
PLD 42 W 16 D 13 L 13 F 48 A 38 PTS 45

DATE	OPPONENTS	VENUE	SCORE	SCORERS	ATT.
27-Aug	PORT VALE	HOME	2 - 1	HOWARTH & WALTON J	18,000
29-Aug	BRISTOL CITY	AWAY	0 - 0		16,000
03-Sep	PORT VALE	AWAY	1 - 0	HOWARTH	18,000
05-Sep	BRISTOL CITY	HOME	3 - 0	HOWARTH 2 & MOORE J	18,000
10-Sep	BLACKPOOL	HOME	0 - 0		18,000
17-Sep	BLACKPOOL	AWAY	3 - 1	HOWARTH, WOOD B & MASON G	15,000
24-Sep	CLAPTON ORIENT	HOME	2 - 0	WOOD B & HOWARTH	20,000
01-Oct	CLAPTON ORIENT	AWAY	2 - 4	HOWARTH (PEN) & MOORE J	20,000
08-Oct	SOUTH SHIELDS	HOME	0 - 0		20,000
15-Oct	SOUTH SHIELDS	AWAY	1 - 0	HOWARTH	15,000
22-Oct	STOKE CITY	HOME	1 - 2	HOWARTH	10,000
29-Oct	STOKE CITY	AWAY	0 - 3		15,000
05-Nov	BRADFORD PARK AVENUE	HOME	3 - 0	HOWARTH (PEN), ARMITAGE & MASON G	18,000
12-Nov	BRADFORD PARK AVENUE	AWAY	1 - 0	HOWARTH	20,000
19-Nov	HULL CITY	AWAY	0 - 1		12,800
26-Nov	HULL CITY	HOME	0 - 2		20,000
03-Dec	NOTTS COUNTY	AWAY	1 - 4	HOWARTH	12,000
10-Dec	NOTTS COUNTY	HOME	1 - 1	MOORE J	16,000
17-Dec	CRYSTAL PALACE	HOME	0 - 0		10,000
24-Dec	CRYSTAL PALACE	AWAY	2 - 1	SWAN J & MOORE J	10,000
26-Dec	SHEFFIELD WEDNESDAY	HOME	1 - 1	SWAN J	20,540
27-Dec	SHEFFIELD WEDNESDAY	AWAY	1 - 2	HOWARTH	25,000
31-Dec	ROTHERHAM COUNTY	HOME	0 - 2		12,000
14-Jan	ROTHERHAM COUNTY	AWAY	0 - 1		6,000
21-Jan	WEST HAM UNITED	HOME	0 - 0		7,000
28-Jan	WEST HAM UNITED	AWAY	1 - 1	ARMITAGE	20,000
04-Feb	BURY	HOME	2 - 0	ARMITAGE & POYNTZ	5,000
11-Feb	BURY	AWAY	1 - 2	ARMITAGE	10,000
20-Feb	LEICESTER CITY	HOME	3 - 0	POYNTZ 3	5,000
25-Feb	LEICESTER CITY	AWAY	0 - 0		14,000
04-Mar	DERBY COUNTY	HOME	2 - 1	SWAN J 2	12,000
11-Mar	DERBY COUNTY	AWAY	0 - 2		9,000
18-Mar	COVENTRY CITY	AWAY	0 - 1		15,000
25-Mar	COVENTRY CITY	HOME	5 - 2	ARMITAGE 2 & SWAN J 3	10,000
01-Apr	BARNSLEY	AWAY	2 - 2	SWAN J & ARMITAGE	12,660
08-Apr	BARNSLEY	HOME	4 - 0	SWAN J 2, O. G. (GITTINS) & POYNTZ	10,000
14-Apr	FULHAM	HOME	2 - 0	POYNTZ & COATES	20,000
15-Apr	WOLVERHAMPTON WANDERERS	AWAY	0 - 0		10,000
17-Apr	FULHAM	AWAY	1 - 0	ARMITAGE	20,000
22-Apr	WOLVERHAMPTON WANDERERS	HOME	0 - 0		7,000
29-Apr	NOTTINGHAM FOREST	AWAY	0 - 1		16,000
06-May	NOTTINGHAM FOREST	HOME	0 - 0		10,000

F. A. CUP

DATE	OPPONENTS	VENUE	SCORE	SCORERS	ATT.
07-Jan	SWINDON TOWN (R1)	AWAY	1 - 2	SWAN J	16,000

LEAGUE AND CUP
APPEARANCES

PLAYER	LEAGUE	F. A. CUP	TOTAL
ARMITAGE	31	1	32
BAKER J	42	1	43
CLARK W	10		10
COATES	20		20
DOWN	1		1
DUFFIELD	37	1	38
ELLSON	1		1
FREW	23		23
GASCOIGNE	6		6
HART E	32		32
HOWARTH	28	1	29
JACKLIN	3		3
MASON G	17	1	18
MOORE J	27	1	28
POTTS Jo.	1		1
POWELL S	2		2
POYNTZ	15		15
ROBSON W	3		3
RODGERSON	24	1	25
SHERWIN	28	1	29
SWAN J	22	1	23
WALTON J	17	1	18
WHALLEY	38	1	39
WOOD B	34		34

GOALSCORERS

PLAYER	LEAGUE	F. A. CUP	TOTAL
HOWARTH	13		13
SWAN J	10	1	11
ARMITAGE	8		8
POYNTZ	6		6
MOORE J	4		4
MASON G	2		2
WOOD B	2		2
COATES	1		1
WALTON J	1		1
OWN GOALS	1		1

In just two seasons United had consolidated their place in Division 2. The defence had a solid foundation in front of keeper Fred Walley. Both full backs Bert Duffield and Jimmy Frew were consistent and in Ernie Hart and Jim Baker, United had a formidable central defensive unit. The biggest problem was in attack and manager Arthur Fairclough strengthened his attacking options with the signing of Joe Harris (Bristol City).

Jack Swan scored in a 1-1 draw in the season's opener against Blackpool and struck in a 1-0 win at Southampton. Harris settled the return with the Saints before consecutive strikes against West Yorkshire neighbours Bradford City resulted in a second double of the season. It was certainly an encouraging start by the left-winger but just five wins in the opening 12 games demonstrated the club's inconsistency and Fairclough reacted by investing £750 for Percy Whipp (Sunderland).

Whipp responded with a debut hat-trick in a 3-1 win against West Ham and sparked a run that would yield eight victories in 13 games with just one defeat. The stylish inside-forward was at the heart of everything and raced ahead in the scoring charts with a further seven goals over the next two months. His efforts included the opening goal in a 2-0 victory against South Shields, a crucial strike that defeated Coventry City, a Christmas Day goal to earn a draw at Bury and consecutive braces against Port Vale over the New Year for an impressive United double.

Unfortunately, just when hopes of a promotion charge looked on, a dreadful run brought nine matches without a win, although Swan did rediscover his scoring touch with goals in draws against Barnsley and Hull City. Whipp inspired a victory at last with the first of United's goals in a 4-1 win at home to Crystal Palace and the last in a 2-0 home victory over Rotherham. Three wins in the final games of the season pushed United up to seventh spot, but it could have been far better had it not been for the winter dip in form. Nevertheless, Leeds had a settled team and finishing just one point off fourth place in the table and six adrift of champions Notts County augured well for the coming season.

Whipp led the way with 16 goals, but United's strength lay in defence where Walley and Baker were ever-present, whilst Duffield and Hart missed just one game. For Leeds skipper Baker it had been an incredible demonstration of consistency, playing in the club's opening 126 league matches.

DIVISION TWO (FINAL LEAGUE POSITION - 7TH)
PLD 42 W 18 D 11 L 13 F 43 A 36 PTS 47

DATE	OPPONENTS	VENUE	SCORE	SCORERS	ATT.
26-Aug	BLACKPOOL	HOME	1 - 1	SWAN J	18,000
28-Aug	SOUTHAMPTON	AWAY	1 - 0	SWAN J	16,000
02-Sep	BLACKPOOL	AWAY	0 - 1		15,000
04-Sep	SOUTHAMPTON	HOME	1 - 0	HARRIS J	6,000
09-Sep	STOCKPORT COUNTY	HOME	2 - 0	WALTON J & ARMITAGE	12,000
16-Sep	STOCKPORT COUNTY	AWAY	1 - 2	ARMITAGE	14,000
23-Sep	BRADFORD CITY	HOME	1 - 0	HARRIS J	20,000
30-Sep	BRADFORD CITY	AWAY	2 - 0	SWAN J & HARRIS J	22,000
07-Oct	CLAPTON ORIENT	AWAY	0 - 3		14,000
14-Oct	CLAPTON ORIENT	HOME	0 - 0		15,000
21-Oct	LEICESTER CITY	HOME	0 - 0		12,000
28-Oct	LEICESTER CITY	AWAY	1 - 2	HARRIS J	20,000
04-Nov	WEST HAM UNITED	HOME	3 - 1	WHIPP 3 (1 PEN)	12,000
11-Nov	WEST HAM UNITED	AWAY	0 - 0		14,000
18-Nov	SOUTH SHIELDS	HOME	0 - 1		12,000
25-Nov	SOUTH SHIELDS	AWAY	2 - 0	WHIPP & POYNTZ	18,000
02-Dec	WOLVERHAMPTON WANDERERS	HOME	1 - 0	WALTON J	14,000
09-Dec	WOLVERHAMPTON WANDERERS	AWAY	1 - 0	HART E	16,000
16-Dec	COVENTRY CITY	AWAY	2 - 1	RICHMOND 2	12,000
23-Dec	COVENTRY CITY	HOME	1 - 0	WHIPP	10,000
25-Dec	BURY	AWAY	1 - 1	WHIPP	20,000
26-Dec	BURY	HOME	0 - 0		27,000
30-Dec	PORT VALE	AWAY	2 - 1	WHIPP 2	8,000
06-Jan	PORT VALE	HOME	2 - 1	WHIPP 2	15,000
20-Jan	MANCHESTER UNITED	AWAY	0 - 0		25,000
27-Jan	MANCHESTER UNITED	HOME	0 - 1		25,000
10-Feb	BARNSLEY	AWAY	0 - 1		11,000
17-Feb	SHEFFIELD WEDNESDAY	HOME	0 - 0		14,000
24-Feb	BARNSLEY	HOME	1 - 1	SWAN J	8,000
03-Mar	HULL CITY	HOME	2 - 2	SWAN J 2	12,000
10-Mar	HULL CITY	AWAY	1 - 3	SWAN J	14,000
17-Mar	CRYSTAL PALACE	AWAY	0 - 1		15,000
19-Mar	SHEFFIELD WEDNESDAY	AWAY	1 - 3	POWELL S	11,000
24-Mar	CRYSTAL PALACE	HOME	4 - 1	WHIPP, SWAN J, POWELL S & SHERWIN	8,000
30-Mar	ROTHERHAM COUNTY	HOME	2 - 0	POWELL S & WHIPP	12,000
31-Mar	FULHAM	AWAY	0 - 3		16,000
02-Apr	ROTHERHAM COUNTY	AWAY	1 - 3	HARRIS J (PEN)	10,000
07-Apr	FULHAM	HOME	1 - 1	WHIPP	10,000
14-Apr	NOTTS COUNTY	AWAY	0 - 1		10,000
21-Apr	NOTTS COUNTY	HOME	3 - 0	WHIPP 2 & POWELL S	8,000
28-Apr	DERBY COUNTY	AWAY	1 - 0	NOBLE	5,000
05-May	DERBY COUNTY	HOME	1 - 0	POWELL S (PEN)	4,000

F. A. CUP

DATE	OPPONENTS	VENUE	SCORE	SCORERS	ATT.
13-Jan	PORTSMOUTH (R1)	AWAY	0 - 0		26,046
17-Jan	PORTSMOUTH (R1R)	HOME	3 - 1	WHIPP, ARMITAGE & SWAN J	21,240
03-Feb	BOLTON WANDERERS (R2)	AWAY	1 - 3	SWAN J	43,389

LEAGUE AND CUP APPEARANCES

PLAYER	LEAGUE	F. A. CUP	TOTAL
ARMAND	7		7
ARMITAGE	11	3	14
BAKER J	42	3	45
BELL T	1		1
CLARK W	3		3
COATES	1		1
DARK	3		3
DUFFIELD	41	3	44
FREW	33	3	36
GASCOIGNE	11		11
HARRIS J	39	3	42
HART E	41	3	44
HOWARTH	6		6
MASON G	13		13
NOBLE	28	3	31
POTTS Jo.	9		9
POWELL S	12		12
POYNTZ	14		14
RICHMOND	5		5
ROBSON W	7		7
SHERWIN	28	3	31
SMITH L	2		2
SWAN J	23	2	25
WALTON J	11	1	12
WHALLEY	42	3	45
WHIPP	29	3	32

GOALSCORERS

PLAYER	LEAGUE	F. A. CUP	TOTAL
WHIPP	15	1	16
SWAN J	8	2	10
HARRIS J	5		5
POWELL S	5		5
ARMITAGE	2	1	3
RICHMOND	2		2
WALTON J	2		2
HART E	1		1
NOBLE	1		1
POYNTZ	1		1
SHERWIN	1		1

Pre-season, assistant manager Dick Ray became boss at Doncaster Rovers. Fairclough replaced Ray with Blackpool manager Bill Norman. Tipped for promotion, Fairclough's charges started poorly, winning only one of the first six matches. Winger Alan Noble scored in a 1-1 draw at Stoke City and a 3-0 win against Crystal Palace but Fairclough required changes and introducing keeper Billy Down and striker Jack Swan heralded nine wins in 10 games, seven consecutively, to send Leeds top by the end of November.

Since election to the Football League, United had operated on a tight budget and Fairclough allowed reserves to flourish. Centre-forward Joe Richmond, with two first team goals to his credit, had been in the first team since the Stoke clash and immediately benefited from Swan's inclusion. Swan's brace won a tight battle at Hull City 2-1 before Richmond scored a hat-trick in the return fixture for an impressive 5-2 win. Richmond and Harris accounted for Clapton Orient in back-to-back clashes before Richmond scored again in a third successive 1-0 win to defeat Port Vale. With confidence high, Richmond and Swan scored in a 3-0 win against Vale prior to Percy Whipp completing a 'magnificent seven' triumphs with a 1-0 victory against Bradford City. Pole position came when Swan and Richmond notched a brace in wins against Barnsley.

United's road to the top had been based on hard work but suddenly three successive defeats asked questions of Fairclough's team. However, a Richmond double earned a 2-2 result at Oldham Athletic on Christmas Day, a clash when left-back Bill Menzies made his United debut, prior to a five-star Boxing Day performance when two goals apiece from Swan and Whipp, and another Richmond strike, completed a 5-0 win against the Lancastrians. Any festive cheer soon disappeared with a defeat at South Shields and after an exciting FA Cup run, Aston Villa, in front of the largest crowd United players had played before, dashed Yorkshire hopes of a third round upset.

Back in the league, Leeds quickly found form with a six-match winning streak. Swan strikes accounted for Sheffield Wednesday and Bristol City, whilst another reserve, inside-forward John Armand, scored in wins against Coventry City and South Shields. Ernie Hart's only goal of the campaign defeated Southampton before Swan and Harris scored in the return fixture for a 3-0 win. With promotion looming, two wins in nine games, including five draws, threatened United's ambitions however, Swan, Richmond and Harris had scored goals throughout the season and in the penultimate home game, in front of 22,500 fans, the trio combined for a 4-0 win against Stockport County to clinch promotion as Bury fell at Barnsley.

Five days later, Walter Coates late winner at Elland Road against Nelson, combined with Derby County's 3-0 defeat at Leicester, settled the Division 2 championship, Leeds United's first honour. Harris was the only player to make at least 40 league appearances, missing one encounter, whilst Swan topped the scoring charts with 18 goals. Individual honours aside United's success was achieved by team effort. At last, the city of Leeds would now host top-flight football.

DIVISION TWO (FINAL LEAGUE POSITION - 1ST)
PLD 42 W 21 D 12 L 9 F 61 A 35 PTS 54

DATE	OPPONENTS	VENUE	SCORE	SCORERS	ATT.
25-Aug	STOKE CITY	AWAY	1 - 1	NOBLE	12,000
27-Aug	CRYSTAL PALACE	HOME	3 - 0	FULLAM, NOBLE & WHIPP	10,000
01-Sep	STOKE CITY	HOME	0 - 0		12,900
05-Sep	CRYSTAL PALACE	AWAY	1 - 1	WHIPP	8,000
08-Sep	LEICESTER CITY	AWAY	0 - 2		18,000
15-Sep	LEICESTER CITY	HOME	1 - 2	SWAN J	15,000
22-Sep	HULL CITY	AWAY	2 - 1	SWAN J 2	11,500
29-Sep	HULL CITY	HOME	5 - 2	RICHMOND 3, SWAN J & HARRIS J	12,000
06-Oct	CLAPTON ORIENT	AWAY	1 - 0	RICHMOND	25,000
13-Oct	CLAPTON ORIENT	HOME	1 - 0	HARRIS J	15,000
20-Oct	PORT VALE	AWAY	1 - 0	RICHMOND	10,000
27-Oct	PORT VALE	HOME	3 - 0	SWAN J 2 & RICHMOND	12,000
03-Nov	BRADFORD CITY	HOME	1 - 0	WHIPP	17,000
10-Nov	BRADFORD CITY	AWAY	0 - 0		25,000
17-Nov	BARNSLEY	HOME	3 - 1	SWAN J 2 & WHIPP	12,000
24-Nov	BARNSLEY	AWAY	3 - 1	HARRIS J & RICHMOND 2	12,000
01-Dec	MANCHESTER UNITED	HOME	0 - 0		20,000
08-Dec	MANCHESTER UNITED	AWAY	1 - 3	WHIPP	30,000
15-Dec	BURY	HOME	1 - 2	WHIPP (PEN)	17,000
22-Dec	BURY	AWAY	0 - 3		10,000
25-Dec	OLDHAM ATHLETIC	AWAY	2 - 2	RICHMOND 2	17,000
26-Dec	OLDHAM ATHLETIC	HOME	5 - 0	SWAN J 2, RICHMOND & WHIPP 2	12,000
05-Jan	SOUTH SHIELDS	AWAY	0 - 2		10,000
19-Jan	SHEFFIELD WEDNESDAY	AWAY	0 - 0		18,000
26-Jan	SHEFFIELD WEDNESDAY	HOME	1 - 0	SWAN J	15,000
09-Feb	COVENTRY CITY	HOME	3 - 1	ARMAND, RICHMOND & HARRIS J	11,239
16-Feb	BRISTOL CITY	AWAY	1 - 0	SWAN J	14,000
27-Feb	SOUTH SHIELDS	HOME	2 - 1	WHIPP & ARMAND	8,000
01-Mar	SOUTHAMPTON	AWAY	1 - 0	HART E	8,000
08-Mar	SOUTHAMPTON	HOME	3 - 0	O. G. (SHELLEY), SWAN J & HARRIS J	15,000
10-Mar	COVENTRY CITY	AWAY	1 - 2	SHERWIN	6,000
15-Mar	FULHAM	HOME	3 - 0	SWAN J 2 & COATES	18,000
19-Mar	BRISTOL CITY	HOME	0 - 0		8,000
22-Mar	FULHAM	AWAY	2 - 0	FULLAM & WHIPP	17,000
29-Mar	BLACKPOOL	HOME	0 - 0		25,000
05-Apr	BLACKPOOL	AWAY	1 - 1	RICHMOND	14,000
12-Apr	DERBY COUNTY	HOME	1 - 1	WHIPP	20,000
18-Apr	STOCKPORT COUNTY	AWAY	1 - 1	RICHMOND	15,000
19-Apr	DERBY COUNTY	AWAY	0 - 2		21,622
21-Apr	STOCKPORT COUNTY	HOME	4 - 0	SWAN J 2, RICHMOND & HARRIS J	22,500
26-Apr	NELSON	HOME	1 - 0	COATES	20,000
03-May	NELSON	AWAY	1 - 3	SWAN J	10,000

F. A. CUP

DATE	OPPONENTS	VENUE	SCORE	SCORERS	ATT.
12-Jan	STOKE CITY (R1)	HOME	1 - 0	WHIPP	26,574
02-Feb	WEST HAM UNITED (R2)	AWAY	1 - 1	COATES	30,123
06-Feb	WEST HAM UNITED (R2R)	HOME	1 - 0	HARRIS J	31,071
23-Feb	ASTON VILLA (R3)	AWAY	0 - 3		51,238

LEAGUE AND CUP
APPEARANCES

PLAYER	LEAGUE	F. A. CUP	TOTAL
ALLEN Ja.	2		2
ARMAND	7	1	8
BAKER J	36	4	40
BAKER L	10		10
BELL A	1		1
COATES	18	3	21
DOWN	32	4	36
DUFFIELD	38	4	42
FREW	4		4
FULLAM	7		7
GASCOIGNE	3		3
HARRIS J	41	4	45
HART E	29	4	33
JOHNSON B	3		3
LAMBERT	1		1
MASON B	10		10
MENZIES	17	1	18
NOBLE	21		21
POWELL S	4		4
RICHMOND	34	4	38
SHERWIN	30	4	34
SMITH L	9		9
SPEAK	23	3	26
SWAN J	36	4	40
WHALLEY	7		7
WHIPP	39	4	43

GOALSCORERS

PLAYER	LEAGUE	F. A. CUP	TOTAL
SWAN J	18		18
RICHMOND	15		15
WHIPP	11	1	12
HARRIS J	6	1	7
COATES	2	1	3
ARMAND	2		2
FULLAM	2		2
NOBLE	2		2
HART E	1		1
SHERWIN	1		1
OWN GOALS	1		1

During the close season, Major Albert Braithwaite replaced Hilton Crowther as Chairman. Crowther remained on the board until his death in 1957 and his investment of time, money and leadership were paramount in Leeds United's formative years. Limited finances meant the club's debut campaign in Division 1 would be hard graft as Arthur Fairclough had to rely on the players that had gained promotion but 33,722 supporters flocked to the opening game at Elland Road against Sunderland.

Jack Swan earned a 1-1 draw, a result matched when Notts County visited. A brace from the popular striker inspired United's first top-flight victory, a 4-0 win against Preston North End, a clash that saw Jack Thom and Joe Harris open their season's account. Thom settled a home clash against Everton before a dip in form, though a club record 41,800 watched United draw with Huddersfield, Swan scoring for Leeds.

Three consecutive wins against Tottenham Hotspur, Blackburn Rovers and West Ham kept optimism high but reality soon filtered through with just one more victory coming before the New Year. The triumph was special, 6-0 against Aston Villa, with all the goals coming in a first half bonanza on Christmas Day. Percy Whipp scored a hat-trick, Swan a brace and Ernie Hart fired home to send supporters into raptures but the News Year would bring little joy as three victories in 15 games meant United faced a relegation battle. Percy Whipp and Sam Powell earned a 4-1 win against Preston North End, but Leeds' 4-1 victory against Liverpool was more meaningful as three new arrivals were destined to become legends.

Inside-left Russell Wainscoat followed up a debut strike in a 4-1 defeat at Newcastle United with a strike against Liverpool. Another player on target was centre-forward Tom Jennings, who would go on to re-write the club's scoring records. Finally, making his debut was right-half Willis Edwards. Whether the trio's arrival proved the decisive factor in the club's survival is debatable, but there was an immediate improvement in results as Leeds finished above the relegation zone.

The final seven games brought four defeats, however Jennings scored the only goal against Bury before notching the winner against Bolton in the next outing, Wainscoat scoring United's opening goal in a 2-1 win. Whipp's goal in the final home fixture secured the club's Division 1 status to everyone's relief. Harris was the only ever-present throughout the league campaign, whilst Bill Menzies played 40 games. Swan, who lost his place in the side to Jennings, finished top scorer on 11 goals.

1924 - 1925

DIVISION ONE (FINAL LEAGUE POSITION - 18TH)
PLD 42 W 11 D 12 L 19 F 46 A 59 PTS 34

DATE	OPPONENTS	VENUE	SCORE	SCORERS	ATT.
30-Aug	SUNDERLAND	HOME	1 - 1	SWAN J	33,722
01-Sep	NOTTS COUNTY	AWAY	0 - 1		16,000
06-Sep	CARDIFF CITY	AWAY	0 - 3		30,000
10-Sep	NOTTS COUNTY	HOME	1 - 1	SWAN J	18,000
13-Sep	PRESTON NORTH END	HOME	4 - 0	SWAN J 2, THOM & HARRIS J	20,000
17-Sep	EVERTON	HOME	1 - 0	THOM	22,000
20-Sep	BURNLEY	AWAY	1 - 1	THOM	23,000
27-Sep	HUDDERSFIELD TOWN	HOME	1 - 1	SWAN J	41,800
04-Oct	BIRMINGHAM	HOME	0 - 1		24,000
11-Oct	WEST BROMWICH ALBION	AWAY	1 - 3	ROBSON C	21,332
18-Oct	TOTTENHAM HOTSPUR	HOME	1 - 0	WHIPP	23,000
25-Oct	BLACKBURN ROVERS	AWAY	3 - 2	ROBSON C 2 & SWAN J	20,000
01-Nov	WEST HAM UNITED	HOME	2 - 1	RICHMOND (PEN) & SWAN J	17,000
08-Nov	SHEFFIELD UNITED	AWAY	1 - 1	SWAN J	30,000
15-Nov	NEWCASTLE UNITED	HOME	1 - 1	WHIPP	30,000
22-Nov	LIVERPOOL	AWAY	0 - 1		20,000
29-Nov	NOTTINGHAM FOREST	HOME	1 - 1	ROBSON C	20,000
06-Dec	BURY	AWAY	0 - 1		15,000
13-Dec	MANCHESTER CITY	HOME	0 - 3		15,000
20-Dec	ARSENAL	AWAY	1 - 6	WHIPP	30,000
25-Dec	ASTON VILLA	HOME	6 - 0	WHIPP 3, SWAN J 2 & HART E	24,000
26-Dec	ASTON VILLA	AWAY	1 - 2	SWAN J	50,000
27-Dec	SUNDERLAND	AWAY	1 - 2	RICHMOND	18,000
03-Jan	CARDIFF CITY	HOME	0 - 0		19,000
17-Jan	PRESTON NORTH END	AWAY	4 - 1	WHIPP 2 & POWELL S 2	15,000
24-Jan	BURNLEY	HOME	0 - 2		15,000
31-Jan	HUDDERSFIELD TOWN	AWAY	0 - 2		12,000
07-Feb	BIRMINGHAM	AWAY	0 - 0		20,000
14-Feb	WEST BROMWICH ALBION	HOME	0 - 1		18,500
28-Feb	BLACKBURN ROVERS	HOME	1 - 1	NOBLE	17,000
07-Mar	WEST HAM UNITED	AWAY	0 - 0		15,000
09-Mar	TOTTENHAM HOTSPUR	AWAY	1 - 2	ARMAND	12,000
14-Mar	SHEFFIELD UNITED	HOME	1 - 1	HARRIS J	25,000
21-Mar	NEWCASTLE UNITED	AWAY	1 - 4	WAINSCOAT	15,000
28-Mar	LIVERPOOL	HOME	4 - 1	WAINSCOAT, ARMAND, HARRIS J & JENNINGS	25,000
04-Apr	NOTTINGHAM FOREST	AWAY	0 - 4		5,000
10-Apr	BOLTON WANDERERS	AWAY	0 - 1		25,000
11-Apr	BURY	HOME	1 - 0	JENNINGS	25,000
14-Apr	BOLTON WANDERERS	HOME	2 - 1	WAINSCOAT & JENNINGS	30,000
18-Apr	MANCHESTER CITY	AWAY	2 - 4	WAINSCOAT & WHIPP	14,000
25-Apr	ARSENAL	HOME	1 - 0	WHIPP	20,000
02-May	EVERTON	AWAY	0 - 1		10,000

F. A. CUP

DATE	OPPONENTS	VENUE	SCORE	SCORERS	ATT.
10-Jan	LIVERPOOL (R1)	AWAY	0 - 3		39,000

LEAGUE AND CUP
APPEARANCES

PLAYER	LEAGUE	F. A. CUP	TOTAL
ARMAND	14	1	15
ATKINSON	13		13
BAKER J	29		29
BAKER L	1		1
CLARK J	3		3
COATES	8		8
DOWN	21	1	22
DUFFIELD	39		39
DUXBURY	3		3
EDWARDS Wi.	9		9
GRAVER	3		3
HARRIS J	42	1	43
HART E	37	1	38
JENNINGS	10		10
JOHNSON B	6		6
MARTIN J	2		2
MASON B	5		5
MENZIES	40	1	41
MOORE B	6		6
NOBLE	11		11
POWELL S	7		7
RICHMOND	17		17
ROBSON C	17	1	18
RUSSELL	9		9
SHERWIN	12	1	13
SMITH L	15	1	16
SPEAK	5	1	6
SWAN J	27	1	28
THOM	7		7
WAINSCOAT	9		9
WHIPP	35	1	36

GOALSCORERS

PLAYER	LEAGUE	F. A. CUP	TOTAL
SWAN J	11		11
WHIPP	10		10
ROBSON C	4		4
WAINSCOAT	4		4
HARRIS J	3		3
JENNINGS	3		3
THOM	3		3
ARMAND	2		2
POWELL S	2		2
RICHMOND	2		2
HART E	1		1
NOBLE	1		1

Having survived relegation, Arthur Fairclough strengthened his squad by adding right-winger Bobby Turnbull, full-back Jim Allen, centre-back Tom Townsley and goalkeeper Bill Johnson to his squad. With Russell Wainscoat, Willis Edwards and Tom Jennings establishing themselves, four stalwarts would depart during the season; skipper Jim Baker, Bert Duffield, Jack Swan and Joe Harris.

Fairclough's reshaped team made a promising start, winning five and drawing two of the opening 10 fixtures. Leading the line was Jennings, scoring in victories against Bolton Wanderers 2-1, Leicester City 3-1, Newcastle United 2-0, West Ham 5-2 and Manchester United 2-0. The crackshot marksman also scored a brace in a 2-2 against Aston Villa, but it was not a one-man team. Wainscoat was impressive, matching Jennings brace against the Londoners, before scoring in a 1-1 draw at Liverpool.

United's confidence was soaring but drained away during an appalling 13-match run before the New Year that yielded a solitary 1-0 win at home to Cardiff City, Turnbull striking the all-important goal. Nine defeats, including a 4-0 drubbing at home against Huddersfield Town and a 6-3 Boxing Day reverse at Burnley, sent Leeds tumbling towards the relegation zone. During a worrying period Jennings struggled in front of goal and Wainscoat was sidelined through injury, but January brought some cheer via reserve striker John Armand, who struck five goals in defeats against Manchester City, Tottenham Hotspur and Burnley. Calm and collected, Armand scored successive penalties in wins against Sunderland 3-1 and Notts County 2-1, and another reserve, Wilf Chadwick, in Turnbull's brief absence, scored the only goal to defeat Leicester City.

With self-belief returning Jennings scored eight goals in five games, including a first Leeds hat-trick in a 4-2 win at home to Arsenal; the only success of another poor run. Within weeks, Jimmy Potts took over in goal and Wainscoat returned with a goal in a 3-1 defeat against Huddersfield that heralded a five-game spell, which generated wins against Bury, Blackburn Rovers and Sheffield United. Safety seemed assured but four April defeats culminated in a 2-1 loss at relegation rivals Manchester City, which meant City needed a draw to survive even if Leeds and Burnley won final fixtures. United fortunately had the edge on Burnley via goal average but could not afford to slip up against Tottenham.

Needing a hero, Jennings notched a brace, and with Turnbull and Percy Whipp also scoring, safety was assured. In the end, Burnley won and City lost 3-2 to Newcastle United, so joined Notts County in Division 2, but it had been mighty close. In a troubled season, Middlesbrough hammered Leeds 5-1 in the FA Cup, Jock McClelland scoring all five goals. Despite the difficulties, Jennings had fulfilled his potential, the only ever-present and top scorer with 26 goals. United was also in the spotlight when Edwards made his international debut against Wales. The first Leeds United player to represent England, Edwards became the 500th England player, in what was, one way and another, a memorable season.

1925 - 1926

DIVISION ONE (FINAL LEAGUE POSITION - 19TH)
PLD 42 W 14 D 8 L 20 F 64 A 76 PTS 36

DATE	OPPONENTS	VENUE	SCORE	SCORERS	ATT.
29-Aug	NOTTS COUNTY	AWAY	0 - 1		18,155
31-Aug	BOLTON WANDERERS	HOME	2 - 1	JENNINGS & HARRIS J	24,188
05-Sep	ASTON VILLA	HOME	2 - 2	JENNINGS 2	29,501
07-Sep	BOLTON WANDERERS	AWAY	0 - 1		23,343
12-Sep	LEICESTER CITY	AWAY	3 - 1	JENNINGS & TURNBULL 2	23,592
16-Sep	NEWCASTLE UNITED	HOME	2 - 0	JENNINGS & JACKSON B	21,291
19-Sep	WEST HAM UNITED	HOME	5 - 2	WHIPP, JENNINGS 2 & WAINSCOAT 2	16,433
26-Sep	ARSENAL	AWAY	1 - 4	WAINSCOAT	32,531
03-Oct	MANCHESTER UNITED	HOME	2 - 0	JENNINGS & WAINSCOAT	26,265
10-Oct	LIVERPOOL	AWAY	1 - 1	WAINSCOAT	30,088
17-Oct	HUDDERSFIELD TOWN	HOME	0 - 4		33,008
24-Oct	EVERTON	AWAY	2 - 4	JENNINGS & WAINSCOAT	28,660
31-Oct	BURY	HOME	2 - 3	HART E & JACKSON B	15,008
07-Nov	BLACKBURN ROVERS	AWAY	2 - 2	HART E & JENNINGS	9,190
14-Nov	CARDIFF CITY	HOME	1 - 0	TURNBULL	19,360
21-Nov	SHEFFIELD UNITED	AWAY	0 - 2		22,327
28-Nov	WEST BROMWICH ALBION	HOME	0 - 1		14,774
05-Dec	BIRMINGHAM	AWAY	1 - 2	JENNINGS	13,435
12-Dec	MANCHESTER CITY	HOME	3 - 4	ARMAND 2 (1 PEN) & CHADWICK	18,762
19-Dec	TOTTENHAM HOTSPUR	AWAY	2 - 3	ARMAND 2 (1 PEN)	19,200
25-Dec	BURNLEY	HOME	2 - 2	TURNBULL & WHIPP	23,325
26-Dec	BURNLEY	AWAY	3 - 6	WHIPP, ARMAND & JENNINGS	22,207
01-Jan	SUNDERLAND	AWAY	3 - 1	ARMAND (PEN), TOWNSLEY & JENNINGS	29,527
02-Jan	NOTTS COUNTY	HOME	2 - 1	ARMAND (PEN) & WHIPP	14,615
23-Jan	LEICESTER CITY	HOME	1 - 0	CHADWICK	19,569
30-Jan	WEST HAM UNITED	AWAY	2 - 4	JENNINGS 2	17,246
03-Feb	ASTON VILLA	AWAY	1 - 3	JENNINGS	11,573
06-Feb	ARSENAL	HOME	4 - 2	JENNINGS 3 & CHADWICK	26,239
13-Feb	MANCHESTER UNITED	AWAY	1 - 2	JENNINGS	29,584
20-Feb	LIVERPOOL	HOME	1 - 1	JENNINGS	24,158
27-Feb	HUDDERSFIELD TOWN	AWAY	1 - 3	WAINSCOAT	26,248
06-Mar	EVERTON	HOME	1 - 1	WAINSCOAT	18,163
13-Mar	BURY	AWAY	2 - 0	ARMAND & JENNINGS	15,226
20-Mar	BLACKBURN ROVERS	HOME	2 - 1	FELL & ARMAND	22,419
27-Mar	CARDIFF CITY	AWAY	0 - 0		18,300
03-Apr	SHEFFIELD UNITED	HOME	2 - 0	JENNINGS & TURNBULL	26,262
05-Apr	NEWCASTLE UNITED	AWAY	0 - 3		16,666
06-Apr	SUNDERLAND	HOME	0 - 2		27,345
10-Apr	WEST BROMWICH ALBION	AWAY	0 - 3		11,358
17-Apr	BIRMINGHAM	HOME	0 - 0		12,186
27-Apr	MANCHESTER CITY	AWAY	1 - 2	JENNINGS	43,475
01-May	TOTTENHAM HOTSPUR	HOME	4 - 1	TURNBULL, JENNINGS 2 & WHIPP	16,158

F. A. CUP

DATE	OPPONENTS	VENUE	SCORE	SCORERS	ATT.
09-Jan	MIDDLESBROUGH (R3)	AWAY	1 - 5	ARMAND (PEN)	29,000

LEAGUE AND CUP
APPEARANCES

PLAYER	LEAGUE	F. A. CUP	TOTAL
ALLAN Ji.	35	1	36
ARMAND	17	1	18
ATKINSON	23	1	24
BAKER J	9		9
CHADWICK	14		14
DUFFIELD	6		6
EDWARDS Wi.	40	1	41
FELL	7		7
HARRIS J	4		4
HART E	26		26
JACKSON B	30	1	31
JENNINGS	42	1	43
JOHNSON B	29	1	30
KIRKPATRICK	7		7
MEARS	1		1
MENZIES	35	1	36
POTTS Ji.	12		12
REED	1		1
ROBERTS	1		1
SISSONS	6		6
SMITH L	6		6
THORNTON	1		1
TOWNSLEY	21	1	22
TURNBULL	37	1	38
WAINSCOAT	25		25
WHIPP	27	1	28

GOALSCORERS

PLAYER	LEAGUE	F. A. CUP	TOTAL
JENNINGS	26		26
ARMAND	9	1	10
WAINSCOAT	8		8
TURNBULL	6		6
WHIPP	5		5
CHADWICK	3		3
HART E	2		2
JACKSON B	2		2
FELL	1		1
HARRIS J	1		1
TOWNSLEY	1		1

After three relegation battles, United not surprisingly were one of the favourites for demotion and illustrated the viewpoint with two draws from four encounters. Tom Jennings however began the season in a rich vein of form and opened his account in a 2-2 at Manchester United. Further strikes claimed a 1-0 win against Derby County and contributed to a 3-1 victory over Aston Villa, but nothing could prepare fans for Jennings goal-scoring exploits over the coming weeks after a 1-0 defeat at Sheffield United.

Quite simply, Jennings re-wrote every record at Leeds United and almost eight decades on, two still stand! Jennings club-record haul totalled 19 goals in nine games, including one penalty, and amazingly 11 came in consecutive wins at home to Arsenal 4-1 (3), at Liverpool 4-2 (4) and at home to Blackburn 4-1 (4). A fourth hat-trick accounted for Bury 4-1. Legendary striker John Charles scored five hat-tricks and 42 league goals in 1953/54, but Jennings three-game total and three consecutive hat-trick milestones still stand at Elland Road, and nationally his treble achievement has only been matched by Liverpool's Jack Balmer in 1947.

One can only speculate what supporters thought, but his escapades came at a time when for all his prowess, the defence was leaking goals at an alarming rate. Following the Bury victory in November, only one win would follow in the next 18 games, culminating in a 6-2 drubbing at Sunderland, Russell Wainscoat scoring a brace. The run included 12 defeats as relegation appeared a certainty. Fairclough had altered his defence with the enforced season-long absence of Ernie Hart, who would make just five appearances. Harry Roberts and George Reed stepped up from the reserves, and new skipper Jimmy Potts performed heroically in goal, but for all Fairclough's permutations, defeats continued.

Jennings battled away in attack, scoring the lions share of goals, and in a desperate bid to escape relegation, the Leeds manager signed winger Tom Mitchell (Newcastle United) and set a club record with the £5,600 purchase of inside-forward John White (Hearts). The losing streak did end with victories against West Brom 3-1 and Birmingham 2-1, Jennings scoring in both clashes, but it was to no avail. In the final home clash of the season, Wainscoat scored four in a 6-3 win against West Ham. A 1-0 defeat at Sheffield Wednesday confirmed an end to top-flight football as Leeds joined West Brom in Division 2.

For Fairclough and assistant Bill Norman, relegation ended their tenure, a sad finale for Fairclough in particular who had guided Leeds to a first honour and left behind tremendous talent in Jennings, White, Wainscoat, Edwards and Hart. Despite relegation, the season is remembered for Jennings outstanding achievements at the highest level, scoring 37 goals, over half the team's total. Missing only one match, only Potts and Tom Townsley were ever-present but all thoughts quickly focused on bouncing back from Division 2.

1926 - 1927

DIVISION ONE (FINAL LEAGUE POSITION - 21ST)
PLD 42 W 11 D 8 L 23 F 69 A 88 PTS 30

DATE	OPPONENTS	VENUE	SCORE	SCORERS	ATT.
28-Aug	BOLTON WANDERERS	HOME	2 - 5	WAINSCOAT & TURNBULL	23,699
30-Aug	CARDIFF CITY	HOME	0 - 0		14,242
04-Sep	MANCHESTER UNITED	AWAY	2 - 2	JENNINGS & WAINSCOAT (PEN)	26,338
06-Sep	CARDIFF CITY	AWAY	1 - 3	WHIPP	13,653
11-Sep	DERBY COUNTY	HOME	1 - 0	JENNINGS	17,411
15-Sep	ASTON VILLA	HOME	3 - 1	ARMAND, SISSONS & JENNINGS	13,792
18-Sep	SHEFFIELD UNITED	AWAY	0 - 1		19,940
25-Sep	ARSENAL	HOME	4 - 1	JENNINGS 3 & WAINSCOAT	20,544
02-Oct	LIVERPOOL	AWAY	4 - 2	JENNINGS 4	30,942
09-Oct	BLACKBURN ROVERS	HOME	4 - 1	JENNINGS 4	16,304
16-Oct	LEICESTER CITY	AWAY	2 - 3	JENNINGS 2 (1 PEN)	27,753
23-Oct	EVERTON	HOME	1 - 3	JENNINGS	24,867
30-Oct	HUDDERSFIELD TOWN	AWAY	1 - 4	JENNINGS	29,679
06-Nov	SUNDERLAND	HOME	2 - 2	JENNINGS & DUGGAN	15,667
13-Nov	WEST BROMWICH ALBION	AWAY	4 - 2	MITCHELL T 2, WHIPP & ARMAND	10,269
20-Nov	BURY	HOME	4 - 1	JENNINGS 3 & MITCHELL T	18,332
27-Nov	BIRMINGHAM	AWAY	0 - 2		19,707
04-Dec	TOTTENHAM HOTSPUR	HOME	1 - 1	ARMAND	24,470
11-Dec	WEST HAM UNITED	AWAY	2 - 3	ARMAND & MENZIES	20,924
18-Dec	SHEFFIELD WEDNESDAY	HOME	4 - 1	EDWARDS WI., JENNINGS, MITCHELL T & WHIPP	20,722
27-Dec	NEWCASTLE UNITED	HOME	1 - 2	JENNINGS	48,590
28-Dec	ASTON VILLA	AWAY	1 - 5	ARMAND	43,963
01-Jan	NEWCASTLE UNITED	AWAY	0 - 1		51,343
15-Jan	BOLTON WANDERERS	AWAY	0 - 3		19,149
22-Jan	MANCHESTER UNITED	HOME	2 - 3	JENNINGS 2 (1 PEN)	16,816
05-Feb	SHEFFIELD UNITED	HOME	1 - 1	JENNINGS	18,348
12-Feb	ARSENAL	AWAY	0 - 1		25,961
19-Feb	DERBY COUNTY	AWAY	0 - 1		14,597
23-Feb	LIVERPOOL	HOME	0 - 0		13,776
26-Feb	BLACKBURN ROVERS	AWAY	1 - 4	WHITE J	16,149
05-Mar	LEICESTER CITY	HOME	1 - 1	JENNINGS	21,420
12-Mar	EVERTON	AWAY	1 - 2	JENNINGS	57,440
19-Mar	HUDDERSFIELD TOWN	HOME	1 - 1	TURNBULL	36,364
26-Mar	SUNDERLAND	AWAY	2 - 6	WAINSCOAT 2	12,288
02-Apr	WEST BROMWICH ALBION	HOME	3 - 1	JENNINGS 2 & WAINSCOAT	20,176
09-Apr	BURY	AWAY	2 - 4	WAINSCOAT & JENNINGS	12,489
15-Apr	BURNLEY	AWAY	2 - 3	TURNBULL & JENNINGS	21,099
16-Apr	BIRMINGHAM	HOME	2 - 1	TURNBULL & JENNINGS	18,703
19-Apr	BURNLEY	HOME	0 - 2		18,740
23-Apr	TOTTENHAM HOTSPUR	AWAY	1 - 4	JENNINGS	17,745
30-Apr	WEST HAM UNITED	HOME	6 - 3	TURNBULL, WHITE J & WAINSCOAT 4	10,997
07-May	SHEFFIELD WEDNESDAY	AWAY	0 - 1		12,027

F. A. CUP

DATE	OPPONENTS	VENUE	SCORE	SCORERS	ATT.
08-Jan	SUNDERLAND (R3)	HOME	3 - 2	JENNINGS 2 (1 PEN) & DUGGAN	31,000
29-Jan	BOLTON WANDERERS (R4)	HOME	0 - 0		42,694
02-Feb	BOLTON WANDERERS (R4R)	AWAY	0 - 3		46,686

LEAGUE AND CUP
APPEARANCES

PLAYER	LEAGUE	F. A. CUP	TOTAL
ALLAN Ji	22	1	23
ARMAND	18	2	20
ATKINSON	11		11
CHADWICK	2		2
DUGGAN	8	1	9
EDWARDS WI.	37	3	40
FELL	6		6
HART E	5		5
JACKSON B	8		8
JENNINGS	41	3	44
KIRKPATRICK	3		3
MEARS	1	1	2
MENZIES	30	2	32
MITCHELL T	23	3	26
POTTS Ji.	42	3	45
REED	22	3	25
ROBERTS	34	3	37
ROBINSON D	4		4
SISSONS	16	1	17
TOWNSLEY	42	3	45
TURNBULL	31	1	32
WAINSCOAT	25	2	27
WHIPP	15		15
WHITE J	16	1	17

GOALSCORERS

PLAYER	LEAGUE	F. A. CUP	TOTAL
JENNINGS	35	2	37
WAINSCOAT	11		11
ARMAND	5		5
TURNBULL	5		5
MITCHELL T	4		4
WHIPP	3		3
DUGGAN	1	1	2
WHITE J	2		2
EDWARDS WI.	1		1
MENZIES	1		1
SISSONS	1		1

Following a taste of top-flight football Leeds United directors were keen to return quickly. Wanting an individual who could quickly fit in and had experience, United's board appointed former Leeds City captain Dick Ray. It was an inspired choice as Ray knew United intimately, having served as a committee member, secretary and assistant manager prior to Arthur Fairclough's appointment. He had also now cut his managerial teeth at Doncaster Rovers where he must have created a record by signing four brothers; Tom, Harry, Joe and Frank Keetley. Ray's first signing at Elland Road was another Keetley brother, 21-year-old Charlie, who would go on to become a prolific goal poacher for the club.

Russell Wainscoat struck the first goal in a 5-1 win on the opening day of the season against South Shields. Tom Mitchell, Tom Jennings and a John White brace completed the scoring, and the coming weeks would see further success with a number of sparkling performances as Nottingham Forest 4-0, Swansea Town 5-0 and Reading 6-2 were put to the sword. Jennings and Bobby Turnbull scored in each clash, whilst White notched a brace in the latter two.

Despite these impressive wins, Ray's side was inconsistent, losing six of the opening 17 games but following the last, a 2-1 defeat at Clapton Orient, a scintillating run of seven consecutive victories instigated a drive for promotion. Jennings scored four in a 5-0 win against Chelsea and a brace against Stoke City 5-1 and Port Vale 3-0. Wainscoat struck at Bristol City 2-1 and against Port Vale in home and away wins, before Keetley, who scored seven in a 10-1 Central League win against Bolton Wanderers, made an explosive first team start with a debut strike in a 3-0 win against South Shields and one of United's four goals at Southampton.

White had scored a brace against the Saints and teamed up with Keetley to gain a draw at Nottingham Forest. Keetley was in inspired form, scoring all three in a 3-2 win at home to Bristol City. Ray's team was on track and overcame a three-match dip in form that yielded only a 1-1 draw at Swansea, to record nine wins in 11 games, five consecutively, against Oldham, Notts County, Reading, Blackpool and West Brom. The Oldham game saw Keetley shine at centre-forward with Jennings sidelined for the run-in, scoring the only goal of the match. A hat-trick in a 6-0 win against County and winner against Reading underlined his talent, which he further demonstrated with a brace in a 3-0 win over Wolves. Another treble in an amazing spell, against Clapton Orient, and brace in a win at Chelsea clinched promotion.

A defeat in the penultimate match to Manchester City, who knocked United out of the FA Cup, cost the title, but Leeds deservedly finished runners-up. Scoring 98 league goals, Jennings with 21, White 21, Wainscoat 18 and Keetley 18 terrorised defences. Jennings total came in 27 games while Keetley's arrived in just 16 matches, both remarkable rates. Tom Townsley, George Reed and Mitchell were ever-present as Ray's team reclaimed top-flight status.

1927 - 1928

DIVISION TWO (FINAL LEAGUE POSITION - 2ND)
PLD 42 W 25 D 7 L 10 F 98 A 49 PTS 57

DATE	OPPONENTS	VENUE	SCORE	SCORERS	ATT.
27-Aug	SOUTH SHIELDS	AWAY	5 - 1	WAINSCOAT, MITCHELL T, WHITE J 2 & JENNINGS	9,826
29-Aug	BARNSLEY	HOME	2 - 2	WHITE J & JENNINGS	21,219
03-Sep	SOUTHAMPTON	HOME	2 - 0	WAINSCOAT 2	19,479
10-Sep	NOTTINGHAM FOREST	HOME	4 - 0	TURNBULL, JENNINGS, WAINSCOAT & MITCHELL T	19,478
17-Sep	MANCHESTER CITY	AWAY	1 - 2	JENNINGS	40,931
24-Sep	HULL CITY	HOME	2 - 0	JENNINGS & WAINSCOAT	21,943
26-Sep	BARNSLEY	AWAY	1 - 2	MITCHELL T	13,038
01-Oct	PRESTON NORTH END	AWAY	1 - 5	WHITE J	16,966
08-Oct	SWANSEA TOWN	HOME	5 - 0	JENNINGS 2 (1 PEN), TURNBULL & WHITE J 2	18,697
15-Oct	FULHAM	AWAY	1 - 1	WHITE J	16,704
22-Oct	GRIMSBY TOWN	AWAY	2 - 3	JENNINGS & WAINSCOAT	11,909
29-Oct	OLDHAM ATHLETIC	HOME	1 - 0	MITCHELL T	17,615
05-Nov	NOTTS COUNTY	AWAY	2 - 2	JENNINGS 2	9,866
12-Nov	READING	HOME	6 - 2	WAINSCOAT, TURNBULL 2, WHITE J 2 & JENNINGS	17,257
19-Nov	BLACKPOOL	AWAY	2 - 0	MITCHELL T 2	9,008
26-Nov	WEST BROMWICH ALBION	HOME	1 - 2	TOWNSLEY	23,690
03-Dec	CLAPTON ORIENT	AWAY	1 - 2	MITCHELL T	12,838
10-Dec	CHELSEA	HOME	5 - 0	JENNINGS 4 & WHITE J	22,059
17-Dec	BRISTOL CITY	AWAY	2 - 1	WAINSCOAT & WHITE J	18,326
24-Dec	STOKE CITY	HOME	5 - 1	JENNINGS 2, WHITE J, TURNBULL & HART E	12,889
26-Dec	PORT VALE	AWAY	2 - 1	WAINSCOAT & WHITE J	18,869
27-Dec	PORT VALE	HOME	3 - 0	WAINSCOAT & JENNINGS 2	32,275
31-Dec	SOUTH SHIELDS	HOME	3 - 0	TURNBULL, WAINSCOAT & KEETLEY	12,752
07-Jan	SOUTHAMPTON	AWAY	4 - 1	WHITE J 2, WAINSCOAT & KEETLEY	13,966
21-Jan	NOTTINGHAM FOREST	AWAY	2 - 2	WHITE J & KEETLEY	13,133
28-Jan	BRISTOL CITY	HOME	3 - 2	KEETLEY 3	15,534
04-Feb	HULL CITY	AWAY	1 - 3	JENNINGS	12,502
11-Feb	PRESTON NORTH END	HOME	2 - 4	WAINSCOAT 2	24,276
18-Feb	SWANSEA TOWN	AWAY	1 - 1	JENNINGS	13,444
25-Feb	FULHAM	HOME	2 - 1	WHITE J & WAINSCOAT	17,358
03-Mar	GRIMSBY TOWN	HOME	0 - 0		23,567
10-Mar	OLDHAM ATHLETIC	AWAY	1 - 0	KEETLEY	22,029
17-Mar	NOTTS COUNTY	HOME	6 - 0	KEETLEY 3, TURNBULL, ARMAND & WHITE J	17,643
24-Mar	READING	AWAY	1 - 0	KEETLEY	13,098
31-Mar	BLACKPOOL	HOME	4 - 0	WAINSCOAT 2, MITCHELL T & ARMAND	19,630
07-Apr	WEST BROMWICH ALBION	AWAY	1 - 0	TURNBULL	23,644
09-Apr	WOLVERHAMPTON WANDERERS	AWAY	0 - 0		25,251
10-Apr	WOLVERHAMPTON WANDERERS	HOME	3 - 0	KEETLEY 2 & WHITE J	29,821
14-Apr	CLAPTON ORIENT	HOME	4 - 0	KEETLEY 3 & WHITE J	22,884
21-Apr	CHELSEA	AWAY	3 - 2	KEETLEY 2 & WHITE J	47,562
25-Apr	MANCHESTER CITY	HOME	0 - 1		48,470
05-May	STOKE CITY	AWAY	1 - 5	WAINSCOAT	12,401
			F. A. CUP		
14-Jan	MANCHESTER CITY (R3)	AWAY	0 - 1		50,473

LEAGUE AND CUP APPEARANCES

PLAYER	LEAGUE	F. A. CUP	TOTAL
ALLAN Ji.	13		13
ARMAND	2		2
ATKINSON	5		5
BAKER A	2		2
COUTTS	1		1
EDWARDS Wi.	32	1	33
HART E	30	1	31
JENNINGS	26	1	27
JOHNSON B	4		4
KEETLEY	16		16
MENZIES	33	1	34
MITCHELL T	42	1	43
POTTS Ji.	38	1	39
REED	42	1	43
ROBERTS	7		7
ROBINSON D	1		1
SISSONS	8		8
STACEY	2		2
TOWNSLEY	42	1	43
TURNBULL	34	1	35
WAINSCOAT	41	1	42
WHITE J	41	1	42

GOALSCORERS

PLAYER	LEAGUE	F. A. CUP	TOTAL
JENNINGS	21		21
WHITE J	21		21
KEETLEY	18		18
WAINSCOAT	18		18
MITCHELL T	8		8
TURNBULL	8		8
ARMAND	2		2
HART E	1		1
TOWNSLEY	1		1

Back in the big-time, Dick Ray made no new signings but his charges surprised opponents by winning eight of their opening 12 encounters. Charlie Keetley blasted an opening day hat-trick in a 4-1 thrashing of Aston Villa, Russell Wainscoat completing the rout. Keetley followed up with a brace in a thrilling 4-4 draw at Leicester City and a goal in Leeds' 3-2 victory against Manchester United before being sidelined through injury for two months.

Any concerns Ray had over Keetley's absence was dispelled by Wainscoat's form. Notching 11 goals during this spell, including five in consecutive matches, memorable displays included a brace to despatch Bury 3-1, United's goal in a 1-1 draw at Liverpool and the winner at Merseyside neighbours Everton. As a bonus, Tom Jennings was back, scoring a brace in a 4-1 win against West Ham and the winner in a 2-1 victory over Burnley. Another injury however would worryingly sideline Jennings for three months.

Fortunately, Keetley was back in the firing line and marked his return with a goal in an exciting 4-3 win against Derby County and the only goal of a tight encounter at Blackburn. United's encouraging start though was beginning to wane and apart from a Christmas Day victory against Cardiff City, Keetley, John White and Ernie Hart scoring, there would be little reason for festive cheer. Two new signings had made debuts, but Tom Cochrane and George Milburn would not make their mark until future seasons.

Knocked out of the FA Cup by Huddersfield Town at the fourth round stage, Keetley was the main source of inspiration and opened the New Year with a hat-trick as Leeds thrillingly edged past Leicester City 4-3 before scoring in a 2-1 win against Manchester United to record a double; Hart claiming the winner. However, three wins in 10 games, including another Keetley treble in a 3-1 win against Everton, would see any semblance of a top-six finish vanish, which was confirmed following five defeats in the last six games.

Finishing thirteenth, the backend of the season was very different from the opening shots. The campaign had generated impressive wins, but had been blighted by heavy defeats, and bizarrely Ray's dream partnership of Keetley and Jennings for five games, resulted in no victories nor goals for either player. Indeed, United claimed two draws and suffered the campaign's heaviest defeats against Huddersfield 6-1, West Ham 8-2 and Burnley 5-0.

On the bright side, Willis Edwards 12th cap brought him the ultimate honour when he captained England (v Ireland), the first Leeds United player to do so and in his next international against Wales, Edwards lined up alongside Hart; the first time two Leeds players had represented England together. In a season of contrasting fortunes, Ray kept a settled team with four players missing three league games, though no one was ever-present. Two players reached double figures in the scoring charts. Keetley led the way for the first time with 22 goals.

DIVISION ONE (FINAL LEAGUE POSITION - 13TH)
PLD 42 W 16 D 9 L 17 F 71 A 84 PTS 41

DATE	OPPONENTS	VENUE	SCORE	SCORERS	ATT.
25-Aug	ASTON VILLA	HOME	4 - 1	KEETLEY 3 & WAINSCOAT	26,588
27-Aug	BURY	HOME	3 - 1	ARMAND & WAINSCOAT 2	18,354
01-Sep	LEICESTER CITY	AWAY	4 - 4	KEETLEY 2, TURNBULL & ARMAND	27,507
08-Sep	MANCHESTER UNITED	HOME	3 - 2	WAINSCOAT, KEETLEY & ARMAND	28,723
15-Sep	HUDDERSFIELD TOWN	AWAY	1 - 6	WAINSCOAT (PEN)	39,869
22-Sep	LIVERPOOL	AWAY	1 - 1	WAINSCOAT	37,417
29-Sep	WEST HAM UNITED	HOME	4 - 1	JENNINGS 2, WAINSCOAT & WHITE J	29,423
06-Oct	NEWCASTLE UNITED	AWAY	2 - 3	WAINSCOAT & JENNINGS	39,166
13-Oct	BURNLEY	HOME	2 - 1	WHITE J & JENNINGS	29,565
20-Oct	MANCHESTER CITY	HOME	4 - 1	WHITE J 3 & WAINSCOAT	32,866
27-Oct	EVERTON	AWAY	1 - 0	WAINSCOAT	41,504
03-Nov	PORTSMOUTH	HOME	3 - 2	WAINSCOAT, JENNINGS & WHITE J	29,022
10-Nov	BOLTON WANDERERS	AWAY	1 - 4	TURNBULL	16,308
17-Nov	SHEFFIELD WEDNESDAY	HOME	0 - 2		25,519
24-Nov	DERBY COUNTY	AWAY	4 - 3	WHITE J, KEETLEY, MITCHELL T & WAINSCOAT	16,601
01-Dec	SUNDERLAND	HOME	0 - 3		30,082
08-Dec	BLACKBURN ROVERS	AWAY	1 - 0	KEETLEY	17,333
15-Dec	ARSENAL	HOME	1 - 1	KEETLEY	20,293
22-Dec	BIRMINGHAM	AWAY	1 - 5	TURNBULL	16,057
25-Dec	CARDIFF CITY	HOME	3 - 0	KEETLEY, WHITE J & HART E	28,188
26-Dec	CARDIFF CITY	AWAY	1 - 2	TURNBULL	20,409
29-Dec	ASTON VILLA	AWAY	0 - 1		31,565
01-Jan	BURY	AWAY	2 - 2	TURNBULL & WAINSCOAT	21,696
05-Jan	LEICESTER CITY	HOME	4 - 3	KEETLEY 3 & TURNBULL	18,870
19-Jan	MANCHESTER UNITED	AWAY	2 - 1	KEETLEY & HART E	21,995
02-Feb	LIVERPOOL	HOME	2 - 2	O. G. (DONE) & JENNINGS	18,780
09-Feb	WEST HAM UNITED	AWAY	2 - 8	WAINSCOAT & JENNINGS	18,055
16-Feb	NEWCASTLE UNITED	HOME	0 - 0		16,036
23-Feb	BURNLEY	AWAY	0 - 5		13,506
02-Mar	MANCHESTER CITY	AWAY	0 - 3		33,921
09-Mar	EVERTON	HOME	3 - 1	KEETLEY 3	22,459
16-Mar	PORTSMOUTH	AWAY	2 - 0	MITCHELL T & WAINSCOAT	17,700
30-Mar	SHEFFIELD WEDNESDAY	AWAY	2 - 4	WAINSCOAT & KEETLEY	30,655
01-Apr	SHEFFIELD UNITED	AWAY	1 - 1	KEETLEY	20,400
02-Apr	SHEFFIELD UNITED	HOME	2 - 0	JENNINGS & WHITE J	20,119
06-Apr	DERBY COUNTY	HOME	1 - 1	MITCHELL T	19,985
13-Apr	SUNDERLAND	AWAY	1 - 2	KEETLEY	12,208
20-Apr	BLACKBURN ROVERS	HOME	0 - 1		17,201
27-Apr	ARSENAL	AWAY	0 - 1		21,465
29-Apr	BOLTON WANDERERS	HOME	2 - 2	WAINSCOAT 2	12,877
01-May	HUDDERSFIELD TOWN	HOME	1 - 2	JENNINGS	17,291
04-May	BIRMINGHAM	HOME	0 - 1		8,151

F. A. CUP

DATE	OPPONENTS	VENUE	SCORE	SCORERS	ATT.
12-Jan	EXETER CITY (R3)	AWAY	2 - 2	KEETLEY & MENZIES	13,500
16-Jan	EXETER CITY (R3R)	HOME	5 - 1	WAINSCOAT, REED, COCHRANE T, KEETLEY & O. G. (LOWTON)	23,000
26-Jan	HUDDERSFIELD TOWN (R4)	AWAY	0 - 3		53,700

LEAGUE AND CUP APPEARANCES

PLAYER	LEAGUE	F. A. CUP	TOTAL
ARMAND	9		9
BUCK	8		8
COCHRANE T	11	2	13
EDWARDS Wi.	29	3	32
FIRTH	1		1
GRIBBEN	3		3
HART E	35	3	38
JENNINGS	17		17
KEETLEY	29	3	32
LONGDEN	3		3
McNESTRY	3		3
MENZIES	38	3	41
MILBURN G	5		5
MITCHELL T	30	1	31
POTTS Ji.	39	2	41
REED	39	3	42
ROBERTS	6		6
STACEY	6		6
TOWNSLEY	38	3	41
TURNBULL	39	3	42
UNDERWOOD	1		1
WAINSCOAT	39	3	42
WHITE J	28	3	31
WILSON G	3		3
WILSON J	3	1	4

GOALSCORERS

PLAYER	LEAGUE	F. A. CUP	TOTAL
KEETLEY	20	2	22
WAINSCOAT	18	1	19
JENNINGS	9		9
WHITE J	9		9
TURNBULL	6		6
ARMAND	3		3
MITCHELL T	3		3
HART E	2		2
COCHRANE T		1	1
MENZIES		1	1
REED		1	1
OWN GOALS	1	1	2

Manager Dick Ray began the new term with no major changes but had one headache with the enforced absence of Charlie Keetley for much of the season. However, Tom Jennings was back, though not as sharp, and waiting in the wings was inside-forward Eric Longden and centre-forward Dave Mangnall. Another Milburn, Jim would fill in for much of the campaign with Bill Menzies injured.

In a poor start, a 4-1 win against Aston Villa was all United had to show from the opening skirmishes. Right-back Harry Roberts became the first United player to score two penalties in a match but bizarrely they would be his only goals for the club. Suddenly, eight wins in nine games set the campaign alight, which was surprising with Keetley injured and Jennings unavailable for four games. Leading the way with six goals was Russell Wainscoat as United despatched in successive games Everton, Sheffield Wednesday, Portsmouth, Burnley, Sunderland, Bolton Wanderers and Birmingham. Also contributing was Mangnall, scoring six goals in six games. His efforts included a brace at Sunderland and the winner at Bolton. The trio were also on target in a 6-0 mauling against Grimsby, however, as in previous seasons, a poor run followed, with five successive defeats.

With Jennings returning by December and Longden given an extended run-out, results improved. Both scored a brace in a 5-2 win against Newcastle United, Wainscoat completing the scoring, and though not totally fit, Jennings rediscovered his touch over the New Year with 10 goals in nine games, before another injury sidelined him for the season. A natural in front of goal, highlights included braces in a 2-0 win against Arsenal, a 4-3 victory at Aston Villa and 3-0 triumph at Burnley.

Jennings was also on target in a 5-0 mauling of Sunderland and an 8-1 FA Cup thumping of Crystal Palace, a club record that still stands. On a landmark day, Wainscoat notched a hat-trick while John White bagged a brace. Jennings scored Leeds' goal in the fourth round but was on the wrong end of a 4-1 thumping at West Ham. Wainscoat in particular was in impressive form and went on to notch important strikes in draws against Sheffield United and Liverpool, but talk during the run-in centred on one player with Jennings sidelined, Keetley.

Leading the line, Keetley inspired a run that generated four wins in April. Scoring 10 goals in eight appearances, the hitman earned a draw in his first game back at Middlesbrough before notching a hat-trick against Sheffield Wednesday and contributing to victories against Blackburn Rovers, Manchester City and Manchester United. Finishing with a flourish, Leeds ended the season fifth, a position not bettered for three decades. As for the record FA Cup score, it became an elusive mark until Don Revie's stars defeated Spora Luxembourg 9-0 in 1967. Whilst Wainscoat led the way in appearances and goalscoring, the deadly duo of Jennings and Keetley had contributed in short bursts.

1929 - 1930

DIVISION ONE (FINAL LEAGUE POSITION - 5TH)
PLD 42 W 20 D 6 L 16 F 79 A 63 PTS 46

DATE	OPPONENTS	VENUE	SCORE	SCORERS	ATT.
31-Aug	ARSENAL	AWAY	0 - 4		41,855
07-Sep	ASTON VILLA	HOME	4 - 1	ROBERTS 2 (2 PENS), LONGDEN & JENNINGS	23,649
11-Sep	EVERTON	AWAY	1 - 1	TURNBULL	24,098
14-Sep	HUDDERSFIELD TOWN	AWAY	0 - 1		28,287
16-Sep	EVERTON	HOME	2 - 1	WAINSCOAT & JENNINGS	16,667
21-Sep	SHEFFIELD WEDNESDAY	AWAY	2 - 1	TURNBULL & WAINSCOAT	21,353
23-Sep	PORTSMOUTH	HOME	1 - 0	WHITE J	14,027
28-Sep	BURNLEY	HOME	3 - 0	WAINSCOAT, HART E & WHITE J	26,676
05-Oct	SUNDERLAND	AWAY	4 - 1	MANGNALL 2, WAINSCOAT & TURNBULL	23,503
12-Oct	BOLTON WANDERERS	HOME	2 - 1	TURNBULL & MANGNALL	29,749
19-Oct	BIRMINGHAM	HOME	1 - 0	TURNBULL	20,067
26-Oct	LEICESTER CITY	AWAY	2 - 2	MITCHELL T & MANGNALL	27,242
02-Nov	GRIMSBY TOWN	HOME	6 - 0	WHITE J, WAINSCOAT 2, TURNBULL, MANGNALL & REED	24,013
09-Nov	SHEFFIELD UNITED	AWAY	2 - 3	TURNBULL & MANGNALL	25,359
16-Nov	WEST HAM UNITED	HOME	1 - 3	WAINSCOAT	18,582
23-Nov	LIVERPOOL	AWAY	0 - 1		30,643
30-Nov	MIDDLESBROUGH	HOME	1 - 2	REED	19,508
07-Dec	BLACKBURN ROVERS	AWAY	1 - 2	MITCHELL T	13,504
14-Dec	NEWCASTLE UNITED	HOME	5 - 2	WAINSCOAT, LONGDEN 2 & JENNINGS 2	21,097
21-Dec	MANCHESTER UNITED	AWAY	1 - 3	LONGDEN	15,054
25-Dec	DERBY COUNTY	HOME	2 - 1	LONGDEN & WAINSCOAT	25,360
26-Dec	DERBY COUNTY	AWAY	0 - 3		30,307
28-Dec	ARSENAL	HOME	2 - 0	JENNINGS 2	29,167
04-Jan	ASTON VILLA	AWAY	4 - 3	JENNINGS 2, WHITE J & WAINSCOAT	32,476
18-Jan	HUDDERSFIELD TOWN	HOME	0 - 1		40,789
01-Feb	BURNLEY	AWAY	3 - 0	DUGGAN & JENNINGS 2	12,505
08-Feb	SUNDERLAND	HOME	5 - 0	COCHRANE T, WAINSCOAT 2, JENNINGS & LONGDEN	22,377
15-Feb	BOLTON WANDERERS	AWAY	2 - 4	JENNINGS & DUGGAN	18,104
22-Feb	BIRMINGHAM	AWAY	0 - 1		17,703
01-Mar	LEICESTER CITY	HOME	1 - 2	JENNINGS	18,486
08-Mar	GRIMSBY TOWN	AWAY	2 - 1	FIRTH & JENNINGS	16,591
15-Mar	SHEFFIELD UNITED	HOME	2 - 2	TURNBULL & WAINSCOAT	7,569
22-Mar	WEST HAM UNITED	AWAY	0 - 3		18,351
29-Mar	LIVERPOOL	HOME	1 - 1	WAINSCOAT	14,178
05-Apr	MIDDLESBROUGH	AWAY	1 - 1	KEETLEY	14,136
09-Apr	SHEFFIELD WEDNESDAY	HOME	3 - 0	KEETLEY 3	3,950
12-Apr	BLACKBURN ROVERS	HOME	4 - 2	LONGDEN, KEETLEY, HART E & MITCHELL T	15,451
19-Apr	NEWCASTLE UNITED	AWAY	1 - 2	KEETLEY	23,066
21-Apr	MANCHESTER CITY	AWAY	1 - 4	KEETLEY	23,578
22-Apr	MANCHESTER CITY	HOME	3 - 2	TURNBULL, KEETLEY & WAINSCOAT	16,636
26-Apr	MANCHESTER UNITED	HOME	3 - 1	KEETLEY 2 & FIRTH	10,596
03-May	PORTSMOUTH	AWAY	0 - 0		13,925
			F. A. CUP		
11-Jan	CRYSTAL PALACE (R3)	HOME	8 - 1	TURNBULL, WHITE J 2, JENNINGS 2 & WAINSCOAT 3	31,418
25-Jan	WEST HAM UNITED (R4)	AWAY	1 - 4	JENNINGS	31,000

LEAGUE AND CUP
APPEARANCES

PLAYER	LEAGUE	F. A. CUP	TOTAL
COCHRANE T	10		10
DUGGAN	6		6
EDWARDS Wi.	39	2	41
FIRTH	6		6
FURNESS	3		3
HART E	30	2	32
JENNINGS	23	2	25
JOHNSON B	26		26
KEETLEY	9		9
LONGDEN	23		23
MANGNALL	9		9
MENZIES	14		14
MILBURN G	1		1
MILBURN Ja.	38	2	40
MITCHELL T	33	2	35
POTTS Ji.	16	2	18
REED	37	2	39
ROBERTS	31	2	33
STACEY	3		3
TOWNSLEY	9		9
TURNBULL	35	2	37
UNDERWOOD	4		4
WAINSCOAT	40	2	42
WHITE J	17	2	19

GOALSCORERS

PLAYER	LEAGUE	F. A. CUP	TOTAL
WAINSCOAT	15	3	18
JENNINGS	14	3	17
KEETLEY	10		10
TURNBULL	9	1	10
LONGDEN	7		7
MANGNALL	6		6
WHITE J	4	2	6
MITCHELL T	3		3
DUGGAN	2		2
FIRTH	2		2
HART E	2		2
REED	2		2
ROBERTS	2		2
COCHRANE T	1		1

There was genuine belief that Leeds United could challenge at the top of Division 1, despite during the close season, John White returning to Hearts and George Reed suffering a long-term knee injury. Reed's absence saw Wilf Copping's introduction into the half-back line. The Edwards-Hart-Copping partnership would make forwards shudder over the coming years.

Dick Ray's charges had every reason to be confident, but started inconsistently. Keetley inspired a 4-2 win against Manchester City with a hat-trick and opened the scoring in a 4-2 victory against Blackburn Rovers, a match that saw Billy Furness score. The youngster added a brace along with Keetley in a 7-3 hammering of Blackpool, the only time United have scored seven goals away from home, but Keetley was absent when bizarrely, Leeds' next win, a 7-0 demolition against Middlesbrough; Harry Duggan, Russell Wainscoat and Jennings notching a brace apiece, followed four defeats.

One of Ray's biggest problems was replacing key players when out for brief spells. The squad was not strong enough, funds were limited and it showed in results. By the time of Keetley's return in December, United had gained no wins, and were thankful for four quick-fire victories, including festive wins against Manchester United and a double over Birmingham. Furness scored in all three, but the honours went to Bobby Turnbull with a hat-trick in a 5-0 win against their Pennine rivals. His only United treble, Mick Jones matched Turnbull's feat in 1972. Keetley also scored at Birmingham in a 3-1 Boxing Day win, but injury would curtail his appearances. With Keetley out, Tom Jennings expected a recall, but Ray gave Arthur Hydes his bow, signalling the end of Jennings career at Elland Road.

Disappointment followed in the FA Cup after exciting wins over Huddersfield Town and Newcastle United, but a shock defeat at Exeter City ended hopes of a first quarter-final appearance. In the league, the New Year brought no respite, the first win not arriving until March when Turnbull's penalty earned a 1-0 win against Newcastle United, another spot kick edged Leeds towards a 3-0 victory against West Ham. During the key Easter fixtures, Copping's only goal of the campaign earned a draw at Sheffield United, a Keetley brace set United up for a 4-0 win over their Yorkshire neighbours in the return but 2-0 defeats at Bolton and Aston Villa meant Ray's team were staring at relegation with just one game to go.

Leeds had to defeat Derby County, and did 3-1, Keetley notching a brace, but a late Blackpool equaliser against Manchester City gave the Seasiders the point required to send United down to Division 2 by just one point. It was tough luck on Ray's team as Blackpool had conceded 125 goals and somehow survived. Copping was the only ever-present of a season to forget, whilst Keetley top scored. As for the first goal-scoring hero at Leeds United, Jennings, his goals to games ratio (117 in 174 appearances) stacks up against every striker to follow his path.

DIVISION ONE (FINAL LEAGUE POSITION - 21ST)
PLD 42 W 12 D 7 L 23 F 68 A 81 PTS 31

DATE	OPPONENTS	VENUE	SCORE	SCORERS	ATT.
30-Aug	PORTSMOUTH	HOME	2 - 2	TURNBULL & KEETLEY	15,900
03-Sep	DERBY COUNTY	AWAY	1 - 4	WAINSCOAT	13,924
06-Sep	ARSENAL	AWAY	1 - 3	FURNESS	40,828
08-Sep	MANCHESTER CITY	HOME	4 - 2	COCHRANE T & KEETLEY 3 (1 PEN)	12,295
13-Sep	BLACKBURN ROVERS	HOME	4 - 2	KEETLEY, DUGGAN, FURNESS & WAINSCOAT	11,837
17-Sep	MANCHESTER CITY	AWAY	0 - 1		17,051
20-Sep	BLACKPOOL	AWAY	7 - 3	FURNESS 2, COCHRANE T 2, KEETLEY 2 (1 PEN) & TURNBULL	25,473
27-Sep	HUDDERSFIELD TOWN	HOME	1 - 2	WAINSCOAT	30,625
04-Oct	SUNDERLAND	HOME	0 - 3		16,378
11-Oct	LEICESTER CITY	AWAY	0 - 4		19,405
18-Oct	LIVERPOOL	AWAY	0 - 2		25,637
25-Oct	MIDDLESBROUGH	HOME	7 - 0	MITCHELL T, DUGGAN 2, WAINSCOAT 2 & JENNINGS 2	18,116
01-Nov	NEWCASTLE UNITED	AWAY	1 - 4	JENNINGS	13,534
08-Nov	SHEFFIELD WEDNESDAY	HOME	2 - 3	JENNINGS & HART E	22,040
15-Nov	WEST HAM UNITED	AWAY	1 - 1	WAINSCOAT	16,612
22-Nov	CHELSEA	HOME	2 - 3	WAINSCOAT & DUGGAN	13,602
29-Nov	GRIMSBY TOWN	AWAY	0 - 2		6,783
06-Dec	BOLTON WANDERERS	HOME	3 - 1	TURNBULL, WAINSCOAT & KEETLEY	7,595
13-Dec	ASTON VILLA	AWAY	3 - 4	TURNBULL & KEETLEY 2	26,272
20-Dec	MANCHESTER UNITED	HOME	5 - 0	WAINSCOAT, TURNBULL 3 & FURNESS	11,282
25-Dec	BIRMINGHAM	AWAY	1 - 0	FURNESS	24,991
26-Dec	BIRMINGHAM	HOME	3 - 1	KEETLEY & FURNESS 2	12,381
27-Dec	PORTSMOUTH	AWAY	1 - 1	KEETLEY	18,530
01-Jan	MANCHESTER UNITED	AWAY	0 - 0		9,875
17-Jan	BLACKBURN ROVERS	AWAY	1 - 3	HYDES	11,975
28-Jan	BLACKPOOL	HOME	2 - 2	HART E & TURNBULL	7,750
31-Jan	HUDDERSFIELD TOWN	AWAY	0 - 3		13,044
07-Feb	SUNDERLAND	AWAY	0 - 4		25,765
18-Feb	LEICESTER CITY	HOME	1 - 3	DUGGAN	5,572
21-Feb	LIVERPOOL	HOME	1 - 2	WAINSCOAT	15,570
28-Feb	MIDDLESBROUGH	AWAY	0 - 5		15,707
07-Mar	NEWCASTLE UNITED	HOME	1 - 0	TURNBULL (PEN)	6,845
11-Mar	ARSENAL	HOME	1 - 2	TURNBULL (PEN)	12,212
14-Mar	SHEFFIELD WEDNESDAY	AWAY	1 - 2	WAINSCOAT	14,562
21-Mar	WEST HAM UNITED	HOME	3 - 0	TURNBULL (PEN) & ALDERSON 2	11,611
28-Mar	CHELSEA	AWAY	0 - 1		25,446
04-Apr	GRIMSBY TOWN	HOME	0 - 0		14,951
06-Apr	SHEFFIELD UNITED	AWAY	1 - 1	COPPING	12,948
07-Apr	SHEFFIELD UNITED	HOME	4 - 0	KEETLEY 2, O. G. (THORPE) & WAINSCOAT	13,315
11-Apr	BOLTON WANDERERS	AWAY	0 - 2		15,438
18-Apr	ASTON VILLA	HOME	0 - 2		10,388
02-May	DERBY COUNTY	HOME	3 - 1	KEETLEY 2 & GREEN	11,190
			F. A. CUP		
10-Jan	HUDDERSFIELD TOWN (R3)	HOME	2 - 0	HYDES & FURNESS	41,103
24-Jan	NEWCASTLE UNITED (R4)	HOME	4 - 1	FURNESS, WAINSCOAT 2 & MITCHELL T	40,261
14-Feb	EXETER CITY (R5)	AWAY	1 - 3	MITCHELL T	19,130

LEAGUE AND CUP
APPEARANCES

PLAYER	LEAGUE	F. A. CUP	TOTAL
ALDERSON	4		4
BROWN V	1		1
COCHRANE T	28		28
COPPING	42	3	45
DANSKIN	1		1
DUGGAN	12		12
EDWARDS Wi.	40	3	43
FIRTH	2		2
FURNESS	37	3	40
GREEN	3		3
HART E	36	3	39
HORNBY	10		10
HYDES	2	2	4
JENNINGS	8		8
JOHNSON B	4		4
KEETLEY	29	1	30
LONGDEN	2		2
MENZIES	13		13
MILBURN G	22	3	25
MILBURN Ja.	41	3	44
MITCHELL T	14	3	17
POTTS Ji.	38	3	41
ROBERTS	5		5
TOWNSLEY	7		7
TURNBULL	27	3	30
UNDERWOOD	1		1
WAINSCOAT	33	3	36

GOALSCORERS

PLAYER	LEAGUE	F. A. CUP	TOTAL
KEETLEY	16		16
WAINSCOAT	12	2	14
TURNBULL	11		11
FURNESS	8	2	10
DUGGAN	5		5
JENNINGS	4		4
COCHRANE T	3		3
MITCHELL T	1	2	3
ALDERSON	2		2
HART E	2		2
HYDES	1	1	2
COPPING	1		1
GREEN	1		1
OWN GOALS	1		1

Determined to bounce back again at the first attempt, manager Dick Ray knew he had one of the best squads in the Division. His half-back combination of Edwards-Hart-Copping was the best in the league by far and in Charlie Keetley, winger Tom Cochrane, and inside-forwards Billy Furness and Joe Firth, Ray had plenty of firepower. Keeper Stan Moore was the only addition to the squad. Off the field, Eric Clarke replaced Major Braithwaite as chairman and early in the season two stalwarts moved on, Russell Wainscoat and Tom Mitchell. Both had served the club with distinction.

Winning their opening two away games and losing the first two home fixtures was not quite what the Leeds manager had planned, but United quickly set their stall out with an unbeaten 15-match run starting with a 1-1 draw at Notts County and 3-2 victory at Millwall; Keetley, Furness and Cochrane scoring. Inspired, Ray's team embarked on a club-record nine consecutive victories defeating Bristol City 2-0, Oldham Athletic 5-0, Bury 4-1, Wolves 2-1, Charlton Athletic 1-0, Stoke City 2-0, Manchester United 5-2, Preston North End 4-1 and Burnley 5-0.

Keetley led the way with eight goals, including a hat-trick against Oldham and the winner in the clash with Wolves, but supporting was Firth with braces against Manchester United, Preston and Burnley. Furness also made his mark, beginning an eight-match scoring spree at Molineux. Carrying on beyond the winning streak, Furness grabbed goals in 3-3 draws against Chesterfield and Nottingham Forest, matches in which Keetley scored back-to-back braces. A Harry Green strike accounted for Tottenham Hotspur before the unbeaten run finally ended at Southampton. Bradford Park Avenue inflicted a Christmas Day defeat but Leeds bounced back on Boxing Day against their West Yorkshire neighbours, Keetley notching a brace in a 3-2 win.

Despite exiting the FA Cup immediately against Queens Park Rangers, promotion was the major objective. Keetley was in terrific form, scoring in wins over Swansea Town and Barnsley, but suddenly in February, goals dried up. United were indebted to Firth for winning strikes against Bristol City and Bury, before opening the scoring in a 2-0 win against Charlton Athletic. With promotion in sight, Leeds were ahead of the pack alongside Wolves and defeated Stoke City 4-3 in an exciting encounter, but nerves suddenly began to affect Ray's team.

Two wins in 10 games leading up to and beyond Easter cost the title, the latter an edgy 1-0 victory at home to Southampton in the penultimate game of the season, Keetley scoring the crucial goal. A 2-0 defeat in the last match against Port Vale in front of 9,588 supporters at Elland Road was disappointing, but the runners-up spot was already secure. Jack Milburn was the only ever-present, Cochrane missed one whilst Copping missed two games of the league campaign. Mission accomplished, Keetley led the way with 23 goals, backed up superbly by Firth and Furness.

1931 - 1932

DIVISION TWO (FINAL LEAGUE POSITION - 2ND)
PLD 42 W 22 D 10 L 10 F 78 A 54 PTS 54

DATE	OPPONENTS	VENUE	SCORE	SCORERS	ATT.
29-Aug	SWANSEA TOWN	AWAY	2 - 0	FIRTH & GREEN	16,175
31-Aug	PORT VALE	AWAY	2 - 1	WAINSCOAT & GREEN	16,874
05-Sep	BARNSLEY	HOME	0 - 1		13,078
07-Sep	MILLWALL	HOME	0 - 1		8,388
12-Sep	NOTTS COUNTY	AWAY	1 - 1	COCHRANE T	12,630
14-Sep	MILLWALL	AWAY	3 - 2	KEETLEY, FURNESS & COCHRANE T	11,844
19-Sep	PLYMOUTH ARGYLE	HOME	0 - 0		10,782
26-Sep	BRISTOL CITY	AWAY	2 - 0	FURNESS & KEETLEY	9,157
03-Oct	OLDHAM ATHLETIC	HOME	5 - 0	KEETLEY 3 & COCHRANE T 2	12,336
10-Oct	BURY	AWAY	4 - 1	FIRTH, DUGGAN, HART E & KEETLEY	16,353
17-Oct	WOLVERHAMPTON WANDERERS	HOME	2 - 1	FURNESS & KEETLEY	13,825
24-Oct	CHARLTON ATHLETIC	AWAY	1 - 0	FURNESS	11,303
31-Oct	STOKE CITY	HOME	2 - 0	COCHRANE T & FURNESS	15,524
07-Nov	MANCHESTER UNITED	AWAY	5 - 2	DUGGAN, FIRTH 2, KEETLEY & FURNESS	9,512
14-Nov	PRESTON NORTH END	HOME	4 - 1	FIRTH 2, FURNESS & KEETLEY	15,439
21-Nov	BURNLEY	AWAY	5 - 0	COCHRANE T 2, FURNESS & FIRTH 2	12,767
28-Nov	CHESTERFIELD	HOME	3 - 3	KEETLEY 2 & FURNESS	13,483
05-Dec	NOTTINGHAM FOREST	AWAY	3 - 3	KEETLEY 2 & FURNESS	12,214
12-Dec	TOTTENHAM HOTSPUR	HOME	1 - 0	GREEN	15,689
19-Dec	SOUTHAMPTON	AWAY	1 - 2	DUGGAN	11,736
25-Dec	BRADFORD PARK AVENUE	AWAY	0 - 3		32,421
26-Dec	BRADFORD PARK AVENUE	HOME	3 - 2	DUGGAN & KEETLEY 2	34,005
02-Jan	SWANSEA TOWN	HOME	3 - 2	KEETLEY, FIRTH & DANSKIN	12,885
16-Jan	BARNSLEY	AWAY	2 - 0	KEETLEY & FIRTH	9,136
23-Jan	NOTTS COUNTY	HOME	2 - 2	KEETLEY 2	14,562
30-Jan	PLYMOUTH ARGYLE	AWAY	2 - 3	FIRTH & HYDES	28,426
06-Feb	BRISTOL CITY	HOME	1 - 0	FIRTH	10,677
13-Feb	OLDHAM ATHLETIC	AWAY	1 - 2	KEETLEY	6,496
20-Feb	BURY	HOME	1 - 0	FIRTH	13,748
27-Feb	WOLVERHAMPTON WANDERERS	AWAY	1 - 1	COCHRANE T	34,520
05-Mar	CHARLTON ATHLETIC	HOME	2 - 0	FIRTH & KEETLEY	11,092
12-Mar	STOKE CITY	AWAY	4 - 3	BENNETT 2, KEETLEY & HORNBY	17,981
19-Mar	MANCHESTER UNITED	HOME	1 - 4	BENNETT	13,644
26-Mar	PRESTON NORTH END	AWAY	0 - 0		12,151
28-Mar	BRADFORD CITY	AWAY	1 - 4	BENNETT	22,354
29-Mar	BRADFORD CITY	HOME	1 - 1	HYDES	18,277
02-Apr	BURNLEY	HOME	3 - 1	COCHRANE T, FURNESS & HYDES	13,037
09-Apr	CHESTERFIELD	AWAY	1 - 1	DUGGAN	11,992
16-Apr	NOTTINGHAM FOREST	HOME	1 - 1	MILBURN Ja. (PEN)	12,195
23-Apr	TOTTENHAM HOTSPUR	AWAY	1 - 3	FURNESS	17,285
30-Apr	SOUTHAMPTON	HOME	1 - 0	KEETLEY	13,401
07-May	PORT VALE	HOME	0 - 2		9,588
09-Jan	QUEENS PARK RANGERS (R3)	AWAY	1 - 3	MILBURN Ja. (PEN)	41,097

LEAGUE AND CUP APPEARANCES

PLAYER	LEAGUE	F. A. CUP	TOTAL
BENNETT	10	1	11
COCHRANE T	41	1	42
COPPING	40	1	41
DANSKIN	4	1	5
DUGGAN	35	1	36
EDWARDS Wi.	28	1	29
FIRTH	33	1	34
FURNESS	25		25
GREEN	9		9
HART E	38		38
HORNBY	11		11
HYDES	8		8
KEETLEY	37	1	38
MAHON	2		2
MENZIES	28	1	29
MILBURN G	12		12
MILBURN Ja.	42	1	43
MOORE S	10	1	11
NEAL	2		2
POTTS Ji.	32		32
STACEY	9		9
TURNBULL	1		1
WAINSCOAT	3		3
WILKINSON	2		2

GOALSCORERS

PLAYER	LEAGUE	F. A. CUP	TOTAL
KEETLEY	23		23
FIRTH	14		14
FURNESS	12		12
COCHRANE T	9		9
DUGGAN	5		5
BENNETT	4		4
GREEN	3		3
HYDES	3		3
MILBURN Ja.	1	1	2
DANSKIN	1		1
HART E	1		1
HORNBY	1		1
WAINSCOAT	1		1

Playing top-flight football was welcome, but promotion had come at a cost because revenue was down, which meant Dick Ray would have no new faces in his side. Nevertheless, defensively Leeds would be hard to break down with their half-back trio, and the Milburn brothers, Jack and George, about to forge a partnership at full-back. Also, Ray now had two new internationals in his ranks with Wilf Copping and Billy Furness receiving full England honours.

After defeats in the opening two games, United began to settle down and put together an impressive 14-match unbeaten run. Charlie Keetley missed the opening encounters but immediately got back into the old routine with five goals in as many games, including a brace in a 3-2 win against Sheffield Wednesday and the decisive strike at West Brom. Indeed, Keetley, after his opening to the season, was unfortunate not to add his name to the list of internationals at the club when selected as a Football League reserve during the autumn for a clash in Belfast, but injury would curtail his campaign.

Making his mark on the first team was Arthur Hydes. Though not as prolific as Keetley, Hydes was a clinical striker and after opening his account in a 2-1 victory against Manchester City, Hydes helped overcome Wolves before notching a brace during a 2-0 win against Chelsea. Keetley was back in the side by December, inspiring a fine run with the winner at Middlesbrough, a goal in a 4-3 winning thriller against Bolton Wanderers and both goals in an outstanding 2-1 win at champions-elect Arsenal on Boxing Day. The next day a record 56,796 crowd packed Elland Road to witness an exciting 0-0 draw against the Gunners.

A 5-1 defeat at Derby County ended the year on a dampener, which unfortunately carried on into the New Year, although Leeds did reach the fifth round of the FA Cup, accounting for Newcastle United with a Hydes hat-trick at St James' Park, and Tranmere, before losing at Everton 2-0 in front of a 58,000 crowd. In the league, one victory in 12 games ended any hopes of a top-four finish, the only triumph against Liverpool. Leeds' 5-0 win at Elland Road included a goal by Harry Duggan, who scored in Leeds' 1-0 win at Anfield earlier in the season, completing a rare double against the Reds, the first of only three in the club's history.

Easter finally brought some cheer and the end of an abysmal run with a sensational 6-1 victory against Newcastle United and back-to-back 1-0 wins against Everton; Hydes and Duggan grabbing the goals. Finishing eighth was a commendable effort in their first season back in the big time. Both Milburn brothers were ever-present along with Furness, whilst Hart, Copping and top scorer Hydes, with 20 goals, missed three games.

1932 - 1933

DIVISION ONE (FINAL LEAGUE POSITION - 8TH)
PLD 42 W 15 D 14 L 13 F 59 A 62 PTS 44

DATE	OPPONENTS	VENUE	SCORE	SCORERS	ATT.
27-Aug	DERBY COUNTY	HOME	0 - 2		16,344
29-Aug	BLACKPOOL	AWAY	1 - 2	ROPER	20,313
03-Sep	BLACKBURN ROVERS	AWAY	1 - 1	COCHRANE T	13,010
05-Sep	BLACKPOOL	HOME	3 - 1	KEETLEY, COPPING & FURNESS	9,171
10-Sep	HUDDERSFIELD TOWN	HOME	1 - 1	KEETLEY	23,882
17-Sep	SHEFFIELD WEDNESDAY	HOME	3 - 2	KEETLEY 2 & DUGGAN	17,977
24-Sep	WEST BROMWICH ALBION	AWAY	1 - 0	KEETLEY	26,497
01-Oct	BIRMINGHAM	HOME	1 - 1	DUGGAN	14,193
08-Oct	SUNDERLAND	AWAY	0 - 0		9,651
15-Oct	MANCHESTER CITY	HOME	2 - 1	HYDES & MILBURN Ja. (PEN)	16,898
22-Oct	SHEFFIELD UNITED	AWAY	0 - 0		13,842
29-Oct	WOLVERHAMPTON WANDERERS	HOME	2 - 0	O'GRADY H & HYDES	11,486
05-Nov	LIVERPOOL	AWAY	1 - 0	DUGGAN	25,464
12-Nov	LEICESTER CITY	HOME	1 - 1	HYDES	12,426
19-Nov	PORTSMOUTH	AWAY	3 - 3	MILBURN Ja. (PEN), FURNESS & COCHRANE T	17,579
26-Nov	CHELSEA	HOME	2 - 0	HYDES 2	19,709
03-Dec	NEWCASTLE UNITED	AWAY	1 - 3	HYDES	20,965
10-Dec	ASTON VILLA	HOME	1 - 1	HYDES	23,794
17-Dec	MIDDLESBROUGH	AWAY	1 - 0	KEETLEY	9,341
24-Dec	BOLTON WANDERERS	HOME	4 - 3	HYDES 2, KEETLEY & FURNESS	15,804
26-Dec	ARSENAL	AWAY	2 - 1	KEETLEY 2	55,876
27-Dec	ARSENAL	HOME	0 - 0		56,796
31-Dec	DERBY COUNTY	AWAY	1 - 5	KEETLEY	13,375
07-Jan	BLACKBURN ROVERS	HOME	3 - 1	FURNESS, KEETLEY & MAHON	14,043
21-Jan	HUDDERSFIELD TOWN	AWAY	2 - 2	O'GRADY H & FURNESS	18,619
04-Feb	WEST BROMWICH ALBION	HOME	1 - 1	HYDES	19,696
08-Feb	SHEFFIELD WEDNESDAY	AWAY	0 - 2		9,585
11-Feb	BIRMINGHAM	AWAY	1 - 2	HYDES	22,157
22-Feb	SUNDERLAND	HOME	2 - 3	HYDES & DUGGAN	7,971
04-Mar	SHEFFIELD UNITED	HOME	1 - 3	HYDES	13,448
11-Mar	WOLVERHAMPTON WANDERERS	AWAY	3 - 3	KEETLEY 3	24,901
18-Mar	LIVERPOOL	HOME	5 - 0	O. G. (BRADSHAW), MAHON 2, HYDES & DUGGAN	12,268
25-Mar	LEICESTER CITY	AWAY	1 - 3	FURNESS	13,669
01-Apr	PORTSMOUTH	HOME	0 - 1		9,839
05-Apr	MANCHESTER CITY	AWAY	0 - 0		16,789
08-Apr	CHELSEA	AWAY	0 - 6		31,095
15-Apr	NEWCASTLE UNITED	HOME	6 - 1	FOWLER A 2, MAHON 2, COPPING & HYDES	14,967
17-Apr	EVERTON	AWAY	1 - 0	HYDES	21,265
18-Apr	EVERTON	HOME	1 - 0	DUGGAN	19,663
22-Apr	ASTON VILLA	AWAY	0 - 0		21,238
29-Apr	MIDDLESBROUGH	HOME	0 - 1		9,006
06-May	BOLTON WANDERERS	AWAY	0 - 5		10,048

F. A. CUP

DATE	OPPONENTS	VENUE	SCORE	SCORERS	ATT.
14-Jan	NEWCASTLE UNITED (R3)	AWAY	3 - 0	HYDES 3	47,554
28-Jan	TRANMERE ROVERS (R4)	AWAY	0 - 0		16,417
01-Feb	TRANMERE ROVERS (R4R)	HOME	4 - 0	MILBURN Ja. (PEN), MAHON, COCHRANE T & HYDES	25,000
18-Feb	EVERTON (R5)	AWAY	0 - 2		58,073

LEAGUE AND CUP APPEARANCES

PLAYER	LEAGUE	F. A. CUP	TOTAL
COCHRANE T	30	4	34
COPPING	39	4	43
DUGGAN	28	1	29
EDWARDS Wi.	23	4	27
FIRTH	5		5
FOWLER A	6		6
FURNESS	42	4	46
GREEN	5		5
HART E	39	4	43
HORNBY	3		3
HYDES	39	4	43
KEETLEY	24	3	27
MAHON	22	3	25
MILBURN G	42	4	46
MILBURN Ja.	42	4	46
MOORE S	12		12
NEAL	3		3
O'GRADY H	8	1	9
POTTS Ji.	30	4	34
ROPER	1		1
STACEY	19		19

GOALSCORERS

PLAYER	LEAGUE	F. A. CUP	TOTAL
HYDES	16	4	20
KEETLEY	14		14
DUGGAN	6		6
FURNESS	6		6
MAHON	5	1	6
COCHRANE T	2	1	3
MILBURN Ja.	2	1	3
COPPING	2		2
FOWLER A	2		2
O'GRADY H	2		2
ROPER	1		1
OWN GOALS	1		1

During the close season, in a boardroom change, former Leeds City vice-chairman Alf Masser, who was a key player in United's election to the Football League, succeeded Eric Clarke as chairman. Dick Ray signed teenager Bert Sproston, who would go on to represent England, whilst Stan Moore was given an opportunity to shine in goal.

Leeds began the season brightly, winning six of their opening 10 matches. Arthur Hydes led the line due to Charlie Keetley's absence through injury, and the stand-in striker impressed, scoring four goals in a 5-2 victory against Middlesbrough, the final goal in a 3-0 win over Newcastle United and a brace in a 3-0 triumph against West Brom. Injured for a short period, reserve centre-forward Alan Fowler stepped in to settle clashes against Sheffield Wednesday, Manchester City and Portsmouth.

By Hydes return, Keetley was fit and the duo teamed up to shoot down Stoke City, but it would be the only win in a worrying 11-game spell until the final game of December when a Hydes hat-trick and strike by Billy Furness brought a welcome 4-0 win against Blackburn Rovers. Distressingly for United, an injury to Hydes at Newcastle would sideline him for the season. Shorn of Edwards in defence, and both Hydes and Keetley in attack, Ray adapted with a threadbare squad, but centre-half Charlie Turner, inside-forward Harry Roper, half-back Joe Firth and outside-right John Mahon battled away. After four months of frustration, February brought a purple patch with four successive wins as Ray's team edged away from relegation, and at the fore were Ray's bit-part players. A Mahon brace began the renaissance with a 3-0 win against West Brom, Furness accounted for Birmingham while Firth struck twice in three days as Leeds overcame Manchester City and Sheffield Wednesday. A defeat at Portsmouth was quickly overcome with comfortable home wins against Sunderland and Liverpool.

Harry Duggan, playing as an emergency centre-forward, was the star of both games. Liverpool may not have been a force, but Duggan bagged a brace in a 5-1 victory, he also scored during a 4-3 defeat at Anfield earlier in the season which gave him the distinction of scoring both home and away during a league campaign for the second year in succession. He is still the only player to do so in the club's history. Duggan continued to plunder goals, notching a brace against Everton. Another double was one of four on a red-letter day when Leeds set a club record for a league game; defeating Leicester City 8-0, Mahon, Firth and Furness the other scorers.

Safe from relegation, it was fitting that Firth scored in United's final triumphs of the season against Stoke City and Chelsea. Finishing ninth, Moore was the only ever-present, whilst Jim Milburn, Furness and Tom Cochrane missed one game. Despite playing only 19 games, Hydes top scored with 16 goals. Ray's endeavours were justly rewarded when he was appointed the first manager of a Football League XI, his team drawing 2-2 against the Scottish League at Ibrox in 1934.

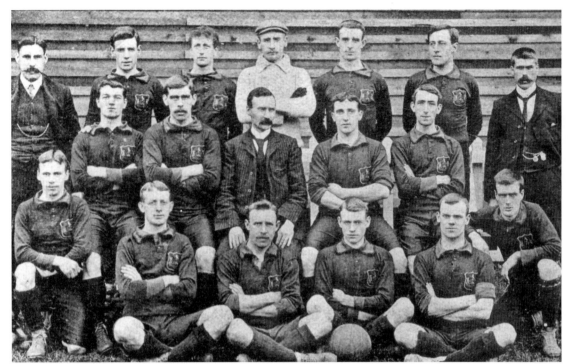

Leeds City 1905-06

Leeds City 1908-09

Leeds United 1920-21

Leeds United 1923-24

Leeds United 1927-28

Russell Wainscoat 1928

Ernie Hart 1931   *Tom Jennings 1928*   *Willis Edwards 1928*   *Gordon Hodgson 1938*

Leeds United 1949-50

Leeds v Sheffield United 1950

Leeds United 1955-56.

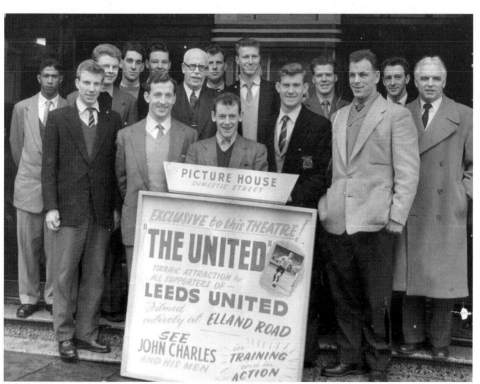

1957 Leeds players promote a film of the team shown at a local cinema.

1957 Don Revie and John Charles at Charles' last game before departing for Juventus.

Don Revie signs for Leeds United in 1958.

Leeds United 1961-62.

Bobby Collins and co. 1965.

Bremner scores in the 1965 FA Cup Final against Liverpool.

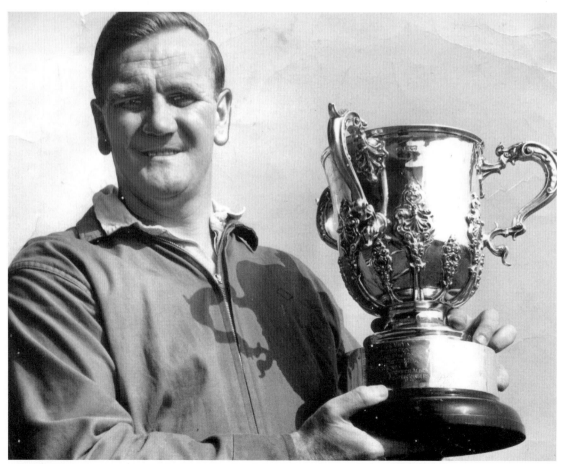

Don Revie displays the League Cup after victory over Arsenal in the 1968 final.

1933 - 1934

	DIVISION ONE (FINAL LEAGUE POSITION - 9TH)				
	PLD 42 W 17 D 8 L 17 F 75 A 66 PTS 42				
DATE	OPPONENTS	VENUE	SCORE	SCORERS	ATT.
26-Aug	BLACKBURN ROVERS	AWAY	2 - 4	HYDES & COCHRANE T	10,130
28-Aug	MIDDLESBROUGH	HOME	5 - 2	HYDES 4 & ROPER	10,896
02-Sep	NEWCASTLE UNITED	HOME	3 - 0	MILBURN Ja. (PEN), COCHRANE T & HYDES	17,721
09-Sep	HUDDERSFIELD TOWN	AWAY	0 - 0		18,976
16-Sep	DERBY COUNTY	AWAY	1 - 3	HYDES	16,584
23-Sep	WEST BROMWICH ALBION	HOME	3 - 0	HYDES 2 & O. G. (SHAW)	17,364
30-Sep	BIRMINGHAM	AWAY	0 - 4		21,566
07-Oct	SHEFFIELD WEDNESDAY	HOME	2 - 1	FOWLER A 2	16,165
14-Oct	MANCHESTER CITY	AWAY	1 - 0	FOWLER A	22,413
21-Oct	PORTSMOUTH	HOME	1 - 0	FOWLER A	18,255
28-Oct	SUNDERLAND	AWAY	2 - 4	FOWLER A & KEETLEY	14,578
04-Nov	ASTON VILLA	HOME	2 - 4	HORNBY & FURNESS (PEN)	20,148
11-Nov	LIVERPOOL	AWAY	3 - 4	HYDES, FOWLER A & DUGGAN	26,181
18-Nov	TOTTENHAM HOTSPUR	HOME	0 - 0		19,681
25-Nov	LEICESTER CITY	AWAY	2 - 2	DUGGAN & HYDES	14,022
02-Dec	STOKE CITY	HOME	2 - 0	KEETLEY & HYDES	12,601
09-Dec	SHEFFIELD UNITED	AWAY	1 - 2	FURNESS	11,113
16-Dec	WOLVERHAMPTON WANDERERS	HOME	3 - 3	KEETLEY 2 & DUGGAN	11,013
23-Dec	CHELSEA	AWAY	1 - 1	KEETLEY	18,157
25-Dec	ARSENAL	HOME	0 - 1		33,192
26-Dec	ARSENAL	AWAY	0 - 2		22,817
30-Dec	BLACKBURN ROVERS	HOME	4 - 0	HYDES 3 & FURNESS	10,722
01-Jan	MIDDLESBROUGH	AWAY	1 - 2	HYDES	16,071
06-Jan	NEWCASTLE UNITED	AWAY	0 - 2		21,587
20-Jan	HUDDERSFIELD TOWN	HOME	1 - 1	MILBURN Ja. (PEN)	24,957
31-Jan	DERBY COUNTY	HOME	0 - 2		11,790
03-Feb	WEST BROMWICH ALBION	AWAY	3 - 0	ROPER & MAHON 2	13,343
10-Feb	BIRMINGHAM	HOME	1 - 0	FURNESS	14,753
24-Feb	MANCHESTER CITY	HOME	3 - 1	FIRTH, MAHON & FURNESS	15,761
26-Feb	SHEFFIELD WEDNESDAY	AWAY	2 - 0	FIRTH & KEETLEY	6,546
07-Mar	PORTSMOUTH	AWAY	1 - 2	COPPING	10,568
10-Mar	SUNDERLAND	HOME	3 - 1	COCHRANE T, DUGGAN & FURNESS	7,333
24-Mar	LIVERPOOL	HOME	5 - 1	MAHON, FIRTH 2 & DUGGAN 2	12,907
30-Mar	EVERTON	HOME	2 - 2	DUGGAN 2	19,951
31-Mar	TOTTENHAM HOTSPUR	AWAY	1 - 5	KEETLEY	29,574
02-Apr	EVERTON	AWAY	0 - 2		25,624
07-Apr	LEICESTER CITY	HOME	8 - 0	DUGGAN 2, MAHON 2, FURNESS 2 & FIRTH 2	11,871
14-Apr	STOKE CITY	AWAY	2 - 1	DUGGAN & FIRTH	16,262
21-Apr	SHEFFIELD UNITED	HOME	1 - 1	O. G. (HOLMES)	10,815
28-Apr	WOLVERHAMPTON WANDERERS	AWAY	0 - 2		5,571
30-Apr	ASTON VILLA	AWAY	0 - 3		9,849
05-May	CHELSEA	HOME	3 - 1	MAHON, FIRTH & COCHRANE T	6,092
	F. A. CUP				
13-Jan	PRESTON NORTH END (R3)	HOME	0 - 1		29,158

LEAGUE AND CUP APPEARANCES			
PLAYER	LEAGUE	F. A. CUP	TOTAL
COCHRANE T	41	1	42
COPPING	38	1	39
DUGGAN	33	1	34
EDWARDS Wi.	15		15
FIRTH	18	1	19
FOWLER A	9		9
FURNESS	41	1	42
GREEN	2		2
HART E	33	1	34
HORNBY	19	1	20
HYDES	19		19
KEETLEY	15	1	16
MAHON	18		18
MILBURN G	37	1	38
MILBURN Ja.	41	1	42
MOORE S	42	1	43
NEAL	1		1
ROPER	14		14
SPROSTON	5		5
STACEY	12		12
TURNER C	8		8
WILKINSON	1		1

GOALSCORERS			
PLAYER	LEAGUE	F. A. CUP	TOTAL
HYDES	16		16
DUGGAN	11		11
FIRTH	8		8
FURNESS	8		8
KEETLEY	7		7
MAHON	7		7
FOWLER A	6		6
COCHRANE T	4		4
MILBURN Ja.	2		2
ROPER	2		2
COPPING	1		1
HORNBY	1		1
OWN GOALS	2		2

The close season brought heartache for Leeds United fans when cult hero Wilf Copping joined Arsenal in an astounding £6,000 deal and within months of the new campaign, Charlie Keetley departed. Keetley's absence was forgivable due to injuries over recent seasons, but Copping's departure brought resentment from home supporters as United struggled from the outset. An 8-1 defeat at Stoke City and 6-3 reverse at West Brom in opening away games was a dreadful start, but it didn't help manager Dick Ray that George Milburn and Willis Edwards accrued injuries within four games.

One player returning from a spell out was striker Arthur Hydes, and he celebrated by scoring in a 2-0 defeat of Everton before notching braces in resounding wins against Chelsea 5-2 and Derby County 4-2. For all his efforts and those of Furness, who scored in all three clashes, and Harry Duggan who struck two goals in a 3-3 draw against Preston North End, results went against Leeds, and were compounded by an injury to Ernie Hart at Stamford Bridge.

The festive period brought little joy for Leeds with back-to-back defeats by Manchester City, but the year ended on a high when goals from Hydes and John Mahon clinched a 3-3 draw with Middlesbrough. In the first game of the New Year, Hydes scored a hat-trick in an emphatic 5-1 win against Blackburn Rovers and followed it up with a brace to overcome Bradford Park Avenue 4-1 as Leeds gained a confidence boosting FA Cup win. Despite going out to Norwich City in a fourth round replay, United's next outing saw Milburn, Edwards and Hart strengthen the defence.

Defeats followed at Liverpool and Huddersfield Town, but the coming weeks would bring important 3-1 victories against Portsmouth and Grimsby. Hydes was on target in both matches, and scored a brace along with Eric Stephenson in a thrilling 4-4 draw at Everton. Pressure though was mounting on Ray, who resigned from his £1,000 a year job following a traumatic 7-1 defeat at Chelsea and 3-0 loss at Sunderland.

United appointed Billy Hampson, who played for Leeds City during the war, as manager, and despite a loss against Leicester City, Hampson cajoled his charges to their most consistent form of the campaign, winning three and drawing two of the final six games. Billy Furness was the hero with seven goals, including both in a 2-1 win at Derby County and strikes in 1-1 draws against Aston Villa and Birmingham. Safety was achieved in the final two games, which brought victories against Preston 2-0; Duggan and Hydes scoring, and Tottenham 4-3; Furness 2, Hydes and Hart finding the net.

It had been a difficult campaign for everyone connected with the club. Eventually finishing eighteenth, some 20 points adrift of champions Arsenal; where Copping had been an immediate hit. Jim Milburn and Tom Cochrane missed one match, whilst Hydes top scored for the third consecutive season with 25 goals. Dick Ray served Leeds City and Leeds United with distinction and seven decades on a number of his side's records still stand, but it was time to rebuild.

1934 - 1935

DIVISION ONE (FINAL LEAGUE POSITION - 18TH)
PLD 42 W 13 D 12 L 17 F 75 A 92 PTS 38

DATE	OPPONENTS	VENUE	SCORE	SCORERS	ATT.
25-Aug	MIDDLESBROUGH	HOME	2 - 4	MILLS F 2	15,949
27-Aug	STOKE CITY	AWAY	1 - 8	HORNBY	24,568
01-Sep	BLACKBURN ROVERS	AWAY	1 - 1	MILBURN Ja. (PEN)	12,316
03-Sep	STOKE CITY	HOME	4 - 2	COCHRANE T, MAHON, FURNESS & DUGGAN	8,932
08-Sep	ARSENAL	HOME	1 - 1	FURNESS	29,447
15-Sep	PORTSMOUTH	AWAY	0 - 0		17,470
22-Sep	LIVERPOOL	HOME	0 - 3		10,877
29-Sep	HUDDERSFIELD TOWN	HOME	2 - 0	DUGGAN 2	12,298
06-Oct	WEST BROMWICH ALBION	AWAY	3 - 6	MILBURN Ja. (PEN), DUGGAN & MAHON	15,843
13-Oct	SHEFFIELD WEDNESDAY	HOME	0 - 0		16,860
20-Oct	EVERTON	HOME	2 - 0	HYDES & FURNESS	16,731
27-Oct	GRIMSBY TOWN	AWAY	2 - 3	HYDES 2	10,940
03-Nov	CHELSEA	HOME	5 - 2	O. G. (McAULAY), FURNESS, HYDES 2 & MAHON	13,295
10-Nov	WOLVERHAMPTON WANDERERS	AWAY	2 - 1	MILBURN Ja. (PEN) & MAHON	13,602
17-Nov	SUNDERLAND	HOME	2 - 4	DUGGAN & FURNESS	24,141
24-Nov	LEICESTER CITY	AWAY	0 - 1		12,785
01-Dec	DERBY COUNTY	HOME	4 - 2	FURNESS 2 & HYDES 2	16,565
08-Dec	ASTON VILLA	AWAY	1 - 1	HYDES	31,682
15-Dec	PRESTON NORTH END	HOME	3 - 3	HORNBY & DUGGAN 2	13,342
22-Dec	TOTTENHAM HOTSPUR	AWAY	1 - 1	FURNESS	23,662
25-Dec	MANCHESTER CITY	HOME	1 - 2	MILBURN Ja. (PEN)	24,810
26-Dec	MANCHESTER CITY	AWAY	0 - 3		51,387
29-Dec	MIDDLESBROUGH	AWAY	3 - 3	HYDES 2 & MAHON	15,615
05-Jan	BLACKBURN ROVERS	HOME	5 - 1	HYDES 3, FIRTH & FURNESS	13,832
19-Jan	ARSENAL	AWAY	0 - 3		37,026
02-Feb	LIVERPOOL	AWAY	2 - 4	HYDES 2	21,201
09-Feb	HUDDERSFIELD TOWN	AWAY	1 - 3	MAHON	18,413
20-Feb	WEST BROMWICH ALBION	HOME	4 - 1	MILBURN Ja. (PEN), MAHON 2 & DUGGAN	7,408
23-Feb	SHEFFIELD WEDNESDAY	AWAY	0 - 1		19,591
02-Mar	PORTSMOUTH	HOME	3 - 1	HYDES 2 & MILBURN G	13,450
06-Mar	EVERTON	AWAY	4 - 4	HYDES 2 & STEPHENSON 2	10,441
09-Mar	GRIMSBY TOWN	HOME	3 - 1	O. G. (HODGSON), HYDES & MILBURN Ja. (PEN)	15,458
16-Mar	CHELSEA	AWAY	1 - 7	KELLY Ja.	35,698
23-Mar	WOLVERHAMPTON WANDERERS	HOME	1 - 1	HORNBY	9,001
30-Mar	SUNDERLAND	AWAY	0 - 3		19,118
06-Apr	LEICESTER CITY	HOME	0 - 2		12,086
13-Apr	DERBY COUNTY	AWAY	2 - 1	FURNESS 2	11,041
19-Apr	BIRMINGHAM	HOME	1 - 1	FURNESS	14,786
20-Apr	ASTON VILLA	HOME	1 - 1	FURNESS	16,234
22-Apr	BIRMINGHAM	AWAY	1 - 3	FURNESS	18,008
27-Apr	PRESTON NORTH END	AWAY	2 - 0	DUGGAN & HYDES	11,758
04-May	TOTTENHAM HOTSPUR	HOME	4 - 3	FURNESS 2, HYDES & HART E	7,668

F. A. CUP

DATE	OPPONENTS	VENUE	SCORE	SCORERS	ATT.
12-Jan	BRADFORD PARK AVENUE (R3)	HOME	4 - 1	HYDES 2, FURNESS & MAHON	35,444
26-Jan	NORWICH CITY (R4)	AWAY	3 - 3	MAHON, DUGGAN & COCHRANE T	13,710
30-Jan	NORWICH CITY (R4R)	HOME	1 - 2	HYDES	27,269

LEAGUE AND CUP APPEARANCES

PLAYER	LEAGUE	F. A. CUP	TOTAL
ABEL	1		1
COCHRANE T	41	3	44
DANIELS	1		1
DUGGAN	35	2	37
EDWARDS Wi.	28	2	30
FIRTH	7	1	8
FURNESS	34	2	36
HART E	27	1	28
HORNBY	34		34
HYDES	30	3	33
KEETLEY	1		1
KELLY Ja.	10	1	11
KELLY Jo.	2		2
McDOUGALL	11	3	14
MAHON	32	3	35
MILBURN G	17		17
MILBURN Ja.	41	3	44
MILLS F	16		16
MOORE S	14	3	17
NEAL	9	3	12
ROPER	3		3
SAVAGE	27		27
SPROSTON	25	3	28
STEPHENSON	4		4
TURNER C	5		5
WILCOCKSON	4		4
WORSLEY	3		3

GOALSCORERS

PLAYER	LEAGUE	F. A. CUP	TOTAL
HYDES	22	3	25
FURNESS	16	1	17
DUGGAN	9	1	10
MAHON	8	2	10
MILBURN Ja.	6		6
HORNBY	3		3
COCHRANE T	1	1	2
MILLS F	2		2
STEPHENSON	2		2
FIRTH	1		1
HART E	1		1
KELLY Ja.	1		1
MILBURN G	1		1
OWN GOALS	2		2

Manager Billy Hampson turned to experience for his first season at the helm. Building from the back, Hampson signed veteran keeper and former England international Albert McInroy, centre-half Jock McDougall and striker Jack Kelly. McDougall's arrival signalled the end to Ernie Hart's career at Elland Road, though it was the start for youngster Bert Sproston, replacing George Milburn at full-back. Hart, a stalwart down the years, and Bill Menzies were the only members of the Division 2 title and promotion winning squads.

Hampson's reshaped defence took time to settle as Leeds lost four of the opening six games. To pep up his attack, Hampson brought in experienced forward George Brown, but it took time for the Brown-Kelly partnership to gel. Kelly opened his account during a draw against Arsenal and struck in a win at Grimsby. Slowly results improved, and Leeds were indebted to full-back Jim Milburn's expertise from the spot kick, which began a fine run that brought one defeat in 13 games.

Milburn slotted home four penalties in five games. The first defeated Liverpool, before three consecutive spot kicks gained draws against Huddersfield Town, West Brom and Middlesbrough. With confidence restored, Brown and Kelly notched a brace apiece to despatch Aston Villa 4-2 and found the target again in a 5-2 victory against Bolton Wanderers. Brown also accounted for Derby County in a tight encounter, but the best performance came against Sheffield Wednesday. Leeds' 7-2 win proved the best of the season, with Harry Duggan claiming the headlines with a hat-trick.

The festive period brought a dip in form, but Brown, Kelly and a Milburn spot kick ensured a positive result against Stoke City, which then carried into early February. Brown struck against Chelsea in a 2-0 win and grabbed an FA Cup brace during a 3-2 win at home to Bury. However, following a 2-1 league win against Huddersfield Town, Brown and Kelly scoring, a 3-1 FA Cup defeat at Sheffield United preceded five defeats in six games when both McDougall and Edwards were absent.

The run-in saw Milburn slot home his ninth spot kick to defeat Portsmouth, whilst Arthur Hydes made a belated contribution on his first team return with goals against Wolves and Manchester City, before Brown and Kelly combined to see off Everton and Sunderland. A 5-0 loss at Preston and a draw at Arsenal meant an eleventh place finish, which was a satisfactory conclusion to a campaign that had started in such disarray.

Sproston and Tom Cochrane missed two games, one ahead of Milburn and Edwards. Brown's 20 goals made him top scorer; Kelly notched 16. The season's hero though was Milburn. Despatching a club record number of penalties in a season, Milburn was the first player to score three spot kicks in successive matches, a feat matched only by Johnny Giles and Gordon Strachan. By his retirement, of Milburn's 30 goals for Leeds, 29 were penalties!

DIVISION ONE (FINAL LEAGUE POSITION - 11TH)
PLD 42 W 15 D 11 L 16 F 66 A 64 PTS 41

DATE	OPPONENTS	VENUE	SCORE	SCORERS	ATT.
31-Aug	STOKE CITY	AWAY	1 - 3	MILBURN Ja. (PEN)	22,552
04-Sep	BIRMINGHAM	HOME	0 - 0		13,271
07-Sep	BLACKBURN ROVERS	HOME	1 - 4	HYDES	14,514
11-Sep	BIRMINGHAM	AWAY	0 - 2		14,298
14-Sep	CHELSEA	AWAY	0 - 1		35,720
18-Sep	ARSENAL	HOME	1 - 1	KELLY Ja.	24,283
21-Sep	LIVERPOOL	HOME	1 - 0	MILBURN Ja. (PEN)	17,931
28-Sep	GRIMSBY TOWN	AWAY	1 - 0	KELLY Ja.	11,236
05-Oct	HUDDERSFIELD TOWN	HOME	2 - 2	MILBURN Ja. (PEN) & BROWN G	33,224
12-Oct	WEST BROMWICH ALBION	HOME	1 - 1	MILBURN Ja. (PEN)	21,657
19-Oct	MIDDLESBROUGH	AWAY	1 - 1	MILBURN Ja. (PEN)	12,256
26-Oct	ASTON VILLA	HOME	4 - 2	BROWN G 2 & KELLY Ja. 2	19,358
02-Nov	WOLVERHAMPTON WANDERERS	AWAY	0 - 3		22,243
09-Nov	SHEFFIELD WEDNESDAY	HOME	7 - 2	KELLY Ja., COCHRANE T, DUGGAN 3, EDWARDS Wi. & MILBURN Ja. (PEN)	19,897
16-Nov	PORTSMOUTH	AWAY	2 - 2	DUGGAN & FURNESS	15,120
23-Nov	BOLTON WANDERERS	HOME	5 - 2	DUGGAN, BROWN G 2, KELLY Ja. & FURNESS	22,973
30-Nov	BRENTFORD	AWAY	2 - 2	COCHRANE T & BROWN G	23,914
07-Dec	DERBY COUNTY	HOME	1 - 0	BROWN G	21,331
14-Dec	EVERTON	AWAY	0 - 0		28,901
21-Dec	PRESTON NORTH END	HOME	0 - 1		17,749
26-Dec	SUNDERLAND	AWAY	1 - 2	MILBURN Ja. (PEN)	25,296
28-Dec	STOKE CITY	HOME	4 - 1	BROWN G 2, KELLY Ja. & MILBURN Ja. (PEN)	18,621
04-Jan	BLACKBURN ROVERS	AWAY	3 - 0	DUGGAN, BROWN G & KELLY Ja.	13,110
18-Jan	CHELSEA	HOME	2 - 0	BROWN G & FURNESS	18,999
01-Feb	GRIMSBY TOWN	HOME	1 - 2	O. G. (HODGSON)	24,212
08-Feb	HUDDERSFIELD TOWN	AWAY	2 - 1	KELLY Ja. & BROWN G	20,862
19-Feb	WEST BROMWICH ALBION	AWAY	2 - 3	FURNESS & STEPHENSON	7,939
22-Feb	MIDDLESBROUGH	HOME	0 - 1		21,055
29-Feb	SHEFFIELD WEDNESDAY	AWAY	0 - 3		6,316
07-Mar	BRENTFORD	HOME	1 - 2	BROWN G	10,509
14-Mar	ASTON VILLA	AWAY	3 - 3	FURNESS, BROWN G & KELLY Ja.	37,382
18-Mar	LIVERPOOL	AWAY	1 - 2	BROWN G	16,210
21-Mar	PORTSMOUTH	HOME	1 - 0	MILBURN Ja. (PEN)	13,031
28-Mar	BOLTON WANDERERS	AWAY	0 - 3		21,289
04-Apr	WOLVERHAMPTON WANDERERS	HOME	2 - 0	HYDES & KELLY Ja.	10,754
10-Apr	MANCHESTER CITY	AWAY	3 - 1	HYDES 2 & KELLY Ja.	17,175
11-Apr	DERBY COUNTY	AWAY	1 - 2	KELLY Ja.	15,585
13-Apr	MANCHESTER CITY	HOME	1 - 1	FURNESS	38,773
18-Apr	EVERTON	HOME	3 - 1	KELLY Ja. & BROWN G 2	13,738
22-Apr	SUNDERLAND	HOME	3 - 0	BROWN G (PEN), KELLY Ja. & COCHRANE T	16,682
25-Apr	PRESTON NORTH END	AWAY	0 - 5		10,927
02-May	ARSENAL	AWAY	2 - 2	FURNESS (PEN) & HYDES	25,920

F. A. CUP

DATE	OPPONENTS	VENUE	SCORE	SCORERS	ATT.
11-Jan	WOLVERHAMPTON WANDERERS (R3)	AWAY	1 - 1	McDOUGALL	39,176
15-Jan	WOLVERHAMPTON WANDERERS (R3R)	HOME	3 - 1	KELLY Ja., COCHRANE T & DUGGAN	35,637
28-Jan	BURY (R4)	HOME	3 - 2	BROWN G 2 & DUGGAN	19,633
15-Feb	SHEFFIELD UNITED (R5)	AWAY	1 - 3	FURNESS	68,287

LEAGUE AND CUP APPEARANCES

PLAYER	LEAGUE	F. A. CUP	TOTAL
ARMES	7	1	8
BROWN G	33	4	37
BROWNE B	25	4	29
CARR	2		2
COCHRANE T	40	4	44
DUGGAN	29	3	32
EDWARDS Wi.	39	4	43
FURNESS	34	4	38
HARGREAVES	2		2
HART E	4		4
HORNBY	11		11
HYDES	10		10
KANE	10		10
KELLY Ja.	34	4	38
KELLY Jo.	2		2
MAHON	4		4
MAKINSON	3		3
McDOUGALL	29	4	33
McINROY	41	4	45
MILBURN G	5		5
MILBURN Ja.	39	4	43
NEAL	5		5
SAVAGE	1		1
SPROSTON	40	4	44
STEPHENSON	10		10
TURNER J	3		3

GOALSCORERS

PLAYER	LEAGUE	F. A. CUP	TOTAL
BROWN G	18	2	20
KELLY Ja.	15	1	16
MILBURN Ja.	9		9
DUGGAN	6	2	8
FURNESS	7	1	8
HYDES	5		5
COCHRANE T	3	1	4
EDWARDS Wi.	1		1
McDOUGALL		1	1
STEPHENSON	1		1
OWN GOALS	1		1

In a busy close season the previous campaign's top sharpshooter, George Brown, and two consistent performers of recent seasons, Tom Cochrane and Harry Duggan, departed. Billy Hampson's side made an abysmal start, losing seven of their 10 opening matches, the only successes coming against Charlton Athletic and Liverpool. The last defeat, 2-1 at Birmingham, saw a scoring return for Arthur Hydes.

The coming weeks would encouragingly see an improvement in results with new arrival, winger Arthur Buckley, impressing. Hydes was also at the fore backed up by inside-forwards Eric Stephenson and John Thomson. Hydes, Stephenson and Thomson scored in a 3-0 win against Everton before contributing to four victories, three consecutively against Preston North End, Sheffield Wednesday and Manchester United. Hydes notched all the goals against Preston and Sheffield; the win at Hillsborough, Leeds' sole away victory all season, whilst Stephenson and Thomson shot down the Red Devils.

Hydes opened the scoring in a 5-0 Christmas Day romp against Middlesbrough, but it would be Leeds' only victory in the festive period. Buckley and John Ainsley made sure the New Year began with a bang against Stoke City, whilst Hydes and Billy Furness accounted for Grimsby Town. Hydes' strike however, was his last scoring contribution of his Leeds career due to injury. Out of the FA Cup, following a 4-0 drubbing at Chelsea, one of three defeats during the season by the Londoners, a rare Willis Edwards strike and an own goal brought a 2-1 win over Huddersfield Town, but the result would be the prelude to six defeats in eight matches.

With the loss of Hydes, and in desperate need of a striker, Hampson pulled a masterstroke with the purchase of veteran centre-forward Gordon Hodgson. A prolific striker for Liverpool, the 33-year old arrived at Elland Road for £1,500 with Leeds heading for relegation. Hodgson's opening six games yielded one point, including a debut goal in a 7-1 defeat at Everton and one of Leeds' goals in a 4-3 loss to Arsenal. Of the remaining seven games, five were at Elland Road; fortuitous as United's away record would be the worst in club history. Hodgson and Stephenson engineered a 3-1 win against West Brom and 2-0 triumph over Derby County. Sandwiched between, Leeds gained their only draw of a dreadful season on the road at relegation rivals Manchester United.

Following consecutive defeats to Wolves, two games remained. Under intense pressure, Furness returned and rose to the challenge, scoring in victories against Sunderland 3-0 and Portsmouth 3-1. These games would be his last for Leeds and a fitting finale. Other scorers included Milburn, with penalties in both games, and Hodgson against Sunderland to ensure safety, but only just. Stepping in for the final game was Tom Holley, who would serve the club diligently, and in a tortuous season, only four players made 30 appearances, Milburn leading the way, whilst Hydes with 11 goals in 19 games, top scored for a fourth time in five seasons.

1936 - 1937

DIVISION ONE (FINAL LEAGUE POSITION - 19TH)
PLD 42 W 15 D 4 L 23 F 60 A 80 PTS 34

DATE	OPPONENTS	VENUE	SCORE	SCORERS	ATT.
29-Aug	CHELSEA	HOME	2 - 3	MILBURN Ja. 2 (1 PEN)	19,379
02-Sep	MANCHESTER CITY	AWAY	0 - 4		24,726
05-Sep	STOKE CITY	AWAY	1 - 2	STEPHENSON	19,193
09-Sep	MANCHESTER CITY	HOME	1 - 1	HARGREAVES	13,933
12-Sep	CHARLTON ATHLETIC	HOME	2 - 0	EDWARDS Wi. & BROWN G	13,789
16-Sep	PORTSMOUTH	AWAY	0 - 3		12,222
19-Sep	GRIMSBY TOWN	AWAY	1 - 4	O. G. (BETMEAD)	11,217
26-Sep	LIVERPOOL	HOME	2 - 0	FURNESS & HARGREAVES	16,861
03-Oct	HUDDERSFIELD TOWN	AWAY	0 - 3		18,654
10-Oct	BIRMINGHAM	AWAY	1 - 2	HYDES	23,833
17-Oct	EVERTON	HOME	3 - 0	THOMSON, STEPHENSON & HYDES	16,861
24-Oct	BOLTON WANDERERS	AWAY	1 - 2	THOMSON	20,411
31-Oct	BRENTFORD	HOME	3 - 1	ARMES, STEPHENSON & HYDES	21,498
07-Nov	ARSENAL	AWAY	1 - 4	THOMSON	32,535
14-Nov	PRESTON NORTH END	HOME	1 - 0	HYDES	15,651
21-Nov	SHEFFIELD WEDNESDAY	AWAY	2 - 1	HYDES 2	18,411
28-Nov	MANCHESTER UNITED	HOME	2 - 1	STEPHENSON & THOMSON	17,610
05-Dec	DERBY COUNTY	AWAY	3 - 5	BUCKLEY A 2 & HYDES	15,557
19-Dec	SUNDERLAND	AWAY	1 - 2	AINSLEY	23,633
25-Dec	MIDDLESBROUGH	HOME	5 - 0	HYDES, O. G. (ROSS), AINSLEY 2 & BUCKLEY A	30,647
26-Dec	CHELSEA	AWAY	1 - 2	HYDES	27,761
28-Dec	MIDDLESBROUGH	AWAY	2 - 4	HYDES & POWELL A	14,191
02-Jan	STOKE CITY	HOME	2 - 1	BUCKLEY A & AINSLEY	13,506
09-Jan	CHARLTON ATHLETIC	AWAY	0 - 1		26,760
23-Jan	GRIMSBY TOWN	HOME	2 - 0	HYDES & FURNESS	11,752
30-Jan	LIVERPOOL	AWAY	0 - 3		11,252
06-Feb	HUDDERSFIELD TOWN	HOME	2 - 1	EDWARDS Wi. & O. G. (MOUNTFORD)	28,930
13-Feb	BIRMINGHAM	HOME	0 - 2		13,674
27-Feb	BOLTON WANDERERS	HOME	2 - 2	EDWARDS Wi. & FURNESS	15,090
03-Mar	EVERTON	AWAY	1 - 7	HODGSON G	17,064
06-Mar	BRENTFORD	AWAY	1 - 4	POWELL A	16,588
13-Mar	ARSENAL	HOME	3 - 4	THOMSON, HODGSON G & BUCKLEY A	25,148
20-Mar	PRESTON NORTH END	AWAY	0 - 1		18,050
27-Mar	SHEFFIELD WEDNESDAY	HOME	1 - 1	AINSLEY	20,776
29-Mar	WEST BROMWICH ALBION	AWAY	0 - 3		31,247
30-Mar	WEST BROMWICH ALBION	HOME	3 - 1	HODGSON G 2 & STEPHENSON	16,016
03-Apr	MANCHESTER UNITED	AWAY	0 - 0		34,429
10-Apr	DERBY COUNTY	HOME	2 - 0	STEPHENSON & HODGSON G	20,228
17-Apr	WOLVERHAMPTON WANDERERS	AWAY	0 - 3		13,688
21-Apr	WOLVERHAMPTON WANDERERS	HOME	0 - 1		14,220
24-Apr	SUNDERLAND	HOME	3 - 0	FURNESS, HODGSON G & MILBURN Ja. (PEN)	22,234
01-May	PORTSMOUTH	HOME	3 - 1	FURNESS, KELLY Ja. & MILBURN Ja. (PEN)	15,034
	F. A. CUP				
16-Jan	CHELSEA (R3)	AWAY	0 - 4		34,589

LEAGUE AND CUP APPEARANCES

PLAYER	LEAGUE	F. A. CUP	TOTAL
AINSLEY	13	1	14
ARMES	20		20
BROWN G	4		4
BROWNE B	16		16
BUCKLEY A	30	1	31
COCHRANE T	2		2
DUGGAN	1		1
EDWARDS Wi.	35	1	36
FURNESS	27		27
GADSBY	1		1
HARGREAVES	10		10
HODGSON G	13		13
HOLLEY	7		7
HYDES	19	1	20
KANE	27	1	28
KELLY Ja.	10		10
McDOUGALL	12		12
McINROY	26		26
MAKINSON	5		5
MILBURN G	16	1	17
MILBURN Ja.	38		38
MILLS F	31	1	32
POWELL A	11	1	12
SAVAGE	16	1	17
SPROSTON	23	1	24
STEPHENSON	22		22
THOMSON	16		16
TRAINOR	2	1	3
TURNER J	9		9

GOALSCORERS

PLAYER	LEAGUE	F. A. CUP	TOTAL
HYDES	11		11
HODGSON G	6		6
STEPHENSON	6		6
AINSLEY	5		5
BUCKLEY A	5		5
FURNESS	5		5
THOMSON	5		5
MILBURN Ja.	4		4
EDWARDS Wi.	3		3
HARGREAVES	2		2
POWELL A	2		2
ARMES	1		1
BROWN G	1		1
KELLY Ja.	1		1
OWN GOALS	3		3

Manager Billy Hampson decided to build for the future as teenager Aubrey Powell, James Mackinson and Ken Gadsby joined Eric Stephenson, Tom Holley and Bert Sproston, now an England international, in the first team squad. Seasoned campaigners Jock McDougall, Albert McInroy, Billy Furness and George Milburn ended associations with the club, whilst Jack Kelly moved on during the season. Willis Edwards joined the coaching team at Elland Road as Ernest Pullan replaced Alf Masser as chairman.

The experience of Jack Milburn and Gordon Hodgson was very much in evidence as Hampson's youthful team made a fine start, winning four games in the opening weeks of the campaign, three in succession at home against Portsmouth 3-1, Huddersfield Town 2-1 and Liverpool 2-0. Hodgson, George Ainsley and Sammy Armes contributed with goals, and Ainsley carried on his good form with the winner against Birmingham before a Hodgson brace set Leeds on the way to a 4-2 win at Leicester City.

Further strikes by Hodgson gained draws against Derby County and Bolton Wanderers as the festive period approached, and December proved a month of joy for United fans, and Stephenson in particular. The young inside-left hit top-form after netting his opening goal of the campaign in a 4-1 defeat at Arsenal. Scoring his first hat-trick in a 4-3 against Sunderland, Hodgson notched the other goal and struck in a 1-1 draw at Brentford. Stephenson, who made his England debut during the season, scored in a 2-1 win against Manchester City and 5-3 Christmas Day victory over Middlesbrough. The triumph sent Leeds into second spot for the first time in their history but the lofty position behind pacesetters Brentford would last only 48 hours after a 2-0 loss against Middlesbrough in the return.

The New Year started badly with one victory in January at Huddersfield Town and results got steadily worse, despite a burst of seven goals in four games from goal-machine Hodgson, including all four Leeds goals in a 4-4 draw with Everton. Hodgson scored the only goal to gain a win against West Brom, but it would be the only triumph in 11 games before an own goal brought a win at Stoke City during the Easter programme. Title ambitions had long since vanished, and Irishman Jim Twomey, who gained his first Northern Ireland cap whilst still a reserve, replaced Reg Savage in goal. The final home games brought victories over Stoke and Brentford, whose title aspirations had also floundered.

Hodgson ended the season at Elland Road on a high with a hat-trick against the Londoners, and followed up with a goal in a 6-2 thumping at Manchester City. Portsmouth avoided relegation when they trounced Leeds 4-0 in the season's final game. Overcoming a mid-season dip in form, finishing ninth was commendable after the trauma of the previous campaign. Milburn was ever-present, whilst Makinson missed two games; Hodgson top scored with 26 goals.

1937 - 1938

DIVISION ONE (FINAL LEAGUE POSITION - 9TH)
PLD 42 W 14 D 15 L 13 F 64 A 69 PTS 43

DATE	OPPONENTS	VENUE	SCORE	SCORERS	ATT.
28-Aug	CHARLTON ATHLETIC	AWAY	1 - 1	HODGSON G	30,979
01-Sep	CHELSEA	HOME	2 - 0	ARMES & O. G. (BARBER)	18,858
04-Sep	PRESTON NORTH END	HOME	0 - 0		22,513
08-Sep	CHELSEA	AWAY	1 - 4	HODGSON G	17,300
11-Sep	GRIMSBY TOWN	AWAY	1 - 1	HODGSON G	9,328
15-Sep	PORTSMOUTH	HOME	3 - 1	HODGSON G 2 & AINSLEY	12,579
18-Sep	HUDDERSFIELD TOWN	HOME	2 - 1	MILBURN Ja. (PEN) & ARMES	33,200
25-Sep	LIVERPOOL	HOME	2 - 0	ARMES & AINSLEY	21,477
02-Oct	WEST BROMWICH ALBION	AWAY	1 - 2	MILBURN Ja. (PEN)	25,609
09-Oct	BIRMINGHAM	HOME	1 - 0	AINSLEY	20,698
16-Oct	EVERTON	AWAY	1 - 1	ARMES	26,035
23-Oct	WOLVERHAMPTON WANDERERS	HOME	1 - 2	BUCKLEY A	13,304
30-Oct	LEICESTER CITY	AWAY	4 - 2	HODGSON G 2, MILBURN Ja. (PEN) & BUCKLEY A	18,833
06-Nov	BLACKPOOL	HOME	1 - 1	BUCKLEY A	18,438
13-Nov	DERBY COUNTY	AWAY	2 - 2	THOMSON & HODGSON G	15,966
20-Nov	BOLTON WANDERERS	HOME	1 - 1	HODGSON G	23,687
27-Nov	ARSENAL	AWAY	1 - 4	STEPHENSON	34,350
04-Dec	SUNDERLAND	HOME	4 - 3	STEPHENSON 3 & HODGSON G	15,349
11-Dec	BRENTFORD	AWAY	1 - 1	HODGSON G	18,184
18-Dec	MANCHESTER CITY	HOME	2 - 1	STEPHENSON & BUCKLEY A	22,144
25-Dec	MIDDLESBROUGH	HOME	5 - 3	HODGSON G 2, BUCKLEY A, STEPHENSON & THOMSON	37,020
27-Dec	MIDDLESBROUGH	AWAY	0 - 2		34,640
01-Jan	CHARLTON ATHLETIC	HOME	2 - 2	STEPHENSON & BUCKLEY A	26,433
15-Jan	PRESTON NORTH END	AWAY	1 - 3	THOMSON	14,032
26-Jan	GRIMSBY TOWN	HOME	1 - 1	BUCKLEY A	10,512
29-Jan	HUDDERSFIELD TOWN	AWAY	3 - 0	ARMES, BUCKLEY A & THOMSON	16,677
05-Feb	LIVERPOOL	AWAY	1 - 1	HODGSON G	34,468
12-Feb	WEST BROMWICH ALBION	HOME	1 - 0	HODGSON G	21,819
19-Feb	BIRMINGHAM	AWAY	2 - 3	HODGSON G & THOMSON	20,403
26-Feb	EVERTON	HOME	4 - 4	HODGSON G 4	23,497
05-Mar	WOLVERHAMPTON WANDERERS	AWAY	1 - 1	SPROSTON	38,849
12-Mar	LEICESTER CITY	HOME	0 - 2		19,839
19-Mar	BLACKPOOL	AWAY	2 - 5	AINSLEY & HODGSON G	18,029
26-Mar	DERBY COUNTY	HOME	0 - 2		19,911
02-Apr	BOLTON WANDERERS	AWAY	0 - 0		18,492
09-Apr	ARSENAL	HOME	0 - 1		29,365
16-Apr	SUNDERLAND	AWAY	0 - 0		21,450
18-Apr	STOKE CITY	AWAY	1 - 0	O. G. (MOULD)	25,114
19-Apr	STOKE CITY	HOME	2 - 1	AINSLEY & STEPHENSON	17,896
23-Apr	BRENTFORD	HOME	4 - 0	HODGSON G 3 & AINSLEY	17,840
30-Apr	MANCHESTER CITY	AWAY	2 - 6	HODGSON G & BUCKLEY A	26,732
07-May	PORTSMOUTH	AWAY	0 - 4		29,571

F. A. CUP

DATE	OPPONENTS	VENUE	SCORE	SCORERS	ATT.
08-Jan	CHESTER (R3)	HOME	3 - 1	ARMES, BUCKLEY A & AINSLEY	37,155
22-Jan	CHARLTON ATHLETIC (R4)	AWAY	1 - 2	HODGSON G	50,516

LEAGUE AND CUP APPEARANCES

PLAYER	LEAGUE	F. A. CUP	TOTAL
AINSLEY	26	2	28
ARMES	39	2	41
BROWNE B	31		31
BUCKLEY A	35	2	37
COCHRANE D	1		1
EDWARDS Wi.	3		3
FRANCIS C	1		1
GOLDBERG	3		3
HARGREAVES	7		7
HODGSON G	36	2	38
HOLLEY	24		24
KANE	14	2	16
KELLY D	4		4
KELLY Ja.	5		5
MAKINSON	40	2	42
MILBURN Ja.	42	2	44
MILLS F	12	2	14
SAVAGE	32	2	34
SPROSTON	37	2	39
STEPHENSON	38	2	40
THOMSON	19		19
TRAINOR	1		1
TURNER J	2		2
TWOMEY	10		10

GOALSCORERS

PLAYER	LEAGUE	F. A. CUP	TOTAL
HODGSON G	25	1	26
BUCKLEY A	9	1	10
STEPHENSON	8		8
AINSLEY	6	1	7
ARMES	5	1	6
THOMSON	5		5
MILBURN Ja.	3		3
SPROSTON	1		1
OWN GOALS	2		2

No additions came into the Leeds United squad during the close season, but Billy Hampson moved Ken Gadsby to left-back following the near Football League record transfer of Bert Sproston to Tottenham Hotspur for £9,500. Jack Milburn switched to right-back. For the first time in seven years, Leeds opened a campaign with two consecutive wins. Gordon Hodgson opened the scoring in a 2-1 win against Preston North End; Arthur Buckley struck the winner and scored again in a 2-0 victory against Birmingham.

Hodgson was soon back on the score sheet in three consecutive games including the only goal at Huddersfield Town, but nothing could prepare supporters for events at Elland Road on October 1 when Hodgson scored five goals against Leicester City in an 8-2 victory. The only United player to score five goals in a match, numerous strikers have totalled more than Hodgson, and 11 have enjoyed four-goal performances, but no-one has equalled Hodgson's feat. Indeed, 67 years on, Billy McLeod of Leeds City is the only professional footballer in the city to match Hodgson's achievement. United's other scorers on this historic day were David Cochrane, Jack Hargreaves and Milburn.

The mercurial Cochrane, beginning his Leeds career, would illuminate matches with his skills, whilst Milburn was in his final league season at the club. A stalwart; Milburn's penalty would be his last goal for United and there could be no more fitting game. Hargreaves would prove to be an efficient ally for Hodgson during the season. The win galvanised Leeds, and five victories in seven games, including consecutive wins against defending champions Arsenal 3-2, Brentford 3-2 and Blackpool 2-1, shot United up the table. The victory at Highbury was sealed by an Eric Stephenson brace and Buckley strike, while Hodgson struck in the other two games. Disappointingly, no more wins would be forthcoming until New Years Eve when Hodgson and Cochrane sent supporters home happy following a 2-1 win over Charlton Athletic.

The FA Cup campaign ended at the fourth round stage and the poor form finally receded when Arsenal visited Elland Road in March. During an amazing turn of fortunes, goals by Stephenson, Aubrey Powell, Hodgson and Hargreaves earned a 4-2 win and a first double over The Gunners. It was a game also memorable for the return of legendary half-back Wilf Copping, who made his 'second' home debut against his former club.

Hargreaves and Cochrane settled 1-0 victories and further doubles over Brentford and Blackpool, before the Easter fixtures ended on a high with wins against Huddersfield Town and Aston Villa, Hodgson scoring his final goal of the season against Town and Hargreaves doing likewise against Villa. Finishing thirteenth was again disappointing after the early season form. Keeper Twomey missed three league matches, whilst Hodgson top scored with 21 goals but it is his record-breaking efforts against Leicester that are linked to this campaign.

1938 - 1939

DIVISION ONE (FINAL LEAGUE POSITION - 13TH)
PLD 42 W 16 D 9 L 17 F 59 A 67 PTS 41

DATE	OPPONENTS	VENUE	SCORE	SCORERS	ATT.
27-Aug	PRESTON NORTH END	HOME	2 - 1	HODGSON G & BUCKLEY A	19,255
31-Aug	BIRMINGHAM	HOME	2 - 0	AINSLEY & BUCKLEY A	13,578
03-Sep	CHARLTON ATHLETIC	AWAY	0 - 2		30,383
05-Sep	STOKE CITY	AWAY	1 - 1	HODGSON G	16,052
10-Sep	BOLTON WANDERERS	HOME	1 - 2	HODGSON G	20,381
17-Sep	HUDDERSFIELD TOWN	AWAY	1 - 0	HODGSON G	19,793
24-Sep	LIVERPOOL	AWAY	0 - 3		32,197
01-Oct	LEICESTER CITY	HOME	8 - 2	HODGSON G 5, COCHRANE D, MILBURN Ja. (PEN) & HARGREAVES	15,001
08-Oct	MIDDLESBROUGH	AWAY	2 - 1	ARMES & HODGSON G	23,009
15-Oct	WOLVERHAMPTON WANDERERS	HOME	1 - 0	THOMSON	25,860
22-Oct	EVERTON	AWAY	0 - 4		30,747
29-Oct	PORTSMOUTH	HOME	2 - 2	AINSLEY & O. G. (ROWE)	18,055
05-Nov	ARSENAL	AWAY	3 - 2	STEPHENSON 2 & BUCKLEY A	39,092
12-Nov	BRENTFORD	HOME	3 - 2	HODGSON G 2 & BUCKLEY A	22,555
19-Nov	BLACKPOOL	AWAY	2 - 1	HODGSON G & HARGREAVES	16,612
26-Nov	DERBY COUNTY	HOME	1 - 4	BUCKLEY A	34,158
03-Dec	GRIMSBY TOWN	AWAY	2 - 3	ARMES & POWELL A	11,202
10-Dec	SUNDERLAND	HOME	3 - 3	AINSLEY, HARGREAVES & POWELL A	20,853
17-Dec	ASTON VILLA	AWAY	1 - 2	HARGREAVES	28,990
24-Dec	PRESTON NORTH END	AWAY	0 - 2		18,424
26-Dec	CHELSEA	HOME	1 - 1	EDWARDS Wi.	27,586
27-Dec	CHELSEA	AWAY	2 - 2	HODGSON G & STEPHENSON	32,692
31-Dec	CHARLTON ATHLETIC	HOME	2 - 1	HODGSON G & COCHRANE D	18,774
14-Jan	BOLTON WANDERERS	AWAY	2 - 2	HODGSON G & O. G. (GOSLIN)	14,893
28-Jan	LIVERPOOL	HOME	1 - 1	HODGSON G	13,679
04-Feb	LEICESTER CITY	AWAY	0 - 2		12,618
11-Feb	MIDDLESBROUGH	HOME	0 - 1		18,273
18-Feb	WOLVERHAMPTON WANDERERS	AWAY	1 - 4	SUTHERLAND	31,977
25-Feb	EVERTON	HOME	1 - 2	AINSLEY	21,728
08-Mar	PORTSMOUTH	AWAY	0 - 2		14,469
11-Mar	ARSENAL	HOME	4 - 2	STEPHENSON (PEN), POWELL A, HODGSON G & HARGREAVES	22,160
18-Mar	BRENTFORD	AWAY	1 - 0	HARGREAVES	21,480
25-Mar	BLACKPOOL	HOME	1 - 0	COCHRANE D	21,818
01-Apr	DERBY COUNTY	AWAY	0 - 1		11,278
07-Apr	MANCHESTER UNITED	AWAY	0 - 0		35,564
08-Apr	GRIMSBY TOWN	HOME	0 - 1		19,700
10-Apr	MANCHESTER UNITED	HOME	3 - 1	AINSLEY, HODGSON G & BUCKLEY A	13,771
15-Apr	SUNDERLAND	AWAY	1 - 2	AINSLEY	10,913
19-Apr	HUDDERSFIELD TOWN	HOME	2 - 1	HODGSON G & POWELL A	12,006
22-Apr	ASTON VILLA	HOME	2 - 0	HARGREAVES 2	14,241
29-Apr	BIRMINGHAM	AWAY	0 - 4		12,522
06-May	STOKE CITY	HOME	0 - 0		12,048

F. A. CUP

DATE	OPPONENTS	VENUE	SCORE	SCORERS	ATT.
17-Jan	BOURNEMOUTH (R3)	HOME	3 - 1	STEPHENSON, HARGREAVES & COCHRANE D	10,114
21-Jan	HUDDERSFIELD TOWN (R4)	HOME	2 - 4	HODGSON G & COCHRANE D	43,702

LEAGUE AND CUP APPEARANCES

PLAYER	LEAGUE	F. A. CUP	TOTAL
AINSLEY	20		20
ARMES	13		13
BROWNE B	16		16
BUCKLEY A	16		16
COCHRANE D	27	2	29
COPPING	12		12
DUNDERDALE	3		3
EDWARDS Wi.	20	2	22
GADSBY	37	2	39
GOLDBERG	16		16
HAMPSON	2		2
HARGREAVES	26	2	28
HENRY	2		2
HODGSON G	32	2	34
HOLLEY	37	2	39
KANE	5		5
MAKINSON	20		20
MILBURN Ja.	22	2	24
MILLS F	8		8
PARRY	6	2	8
POWELL A	28	2	30
SAVAGE	3	2	5
SCAIFE	9		9
STEPHENSON	34	2	36
SUTHERLAND	3		3
THOMSON	6		6
TWOMEY	39		39

GOALSCORERS

PLAYER	LEAGUE	F. A. CUP	TOTAL
HODGSON G	20	1	21
HARGREAVES	8	1	9
AINSLEY	6		6
BUCKLEY A	6		6
COCHRANE D	3	2	5
STEPHENSON	4	1	5
POWELL A	4		4
ARMES	2		2
EDWARDS Wi.	1		1
MILBURN Ja.	1		1
SUTHERLAND	1		1
THOMSON	1		1
OWN GOALS	2		2

LEEDS UNITED ALSO PLAYED IN A LEAGUE JUBILEE FUND MATCH AT HOME TO HUDDERSFIELD TOWN ON AUG. 20TH 1938. THE GAME ENDED 1 - 1 (0 - 1) - MILBURN Ja. (PEN) WITH THE ATTENDANCE BEING 7,352. THE TEAM WAS TWOMEY, MILBURN Ja., GADSBY, EDWARDS, HOLLEY, MAKINSON, ARMES, AINSLEY, HODGSON, STEPHENSON & BUCKLEY

The Division 1 campaign was only three games old when the dark clouds of war settled over Britain. One player had joined the club during the close season, Norman Wharton, and the former York City keeper played in two matches, both 1-0 defeats, following a 0-0 draw on the opening day against Preston North End. The Preston clash was memorable because striker George Ainsley replaced Jim Twomey in goal due to injury and held the visitors at bay for an hour. Germany had invaded Poland when Leeds faced Sheffield United in what would be the last professional game at Elland Road for some years to come. Leeds sitting bottom of the table became irrelevant when Neville Chamberlain declared that Britain was at war the following morning.

As in the previous conflict, league football was postponed and player contracts were suspended with many awaiting call up papers. Leeds United took part in a number of friendly games, the first a 3-2 defeat at Halifax Town. The only friendly to take place at Elland Road saw Leeds draw 2-2 with Grimsby Town before competitive football returned in the form of 10 regional leagues. As in the Great War, most teams competed. Leeds played in the North-East division. With Elland Road requisitioned by the war office for administrative work, United officials were entitled to use offices two hours a week on Saturday's.

In the new format, over 220 players would represent the club. Against a backdrop of sentries on duty and fans with gas masks, Leeds made a flying start, winning their opening four encounters. Gordon Hodgson scored in all four clashes, notching a brace in a 3-0 win against Bradford City, before strikes earned wins over Hull City, Darlington and Hartlepools United. Call-ups made consistency impossible, and following draws with York City and Huddersfield Town, Leeds won their only festive fixture 3-1 against Middlesbrough. United's final goal was struck by Gerry Henry, who also claimed Leeds' goal at York.

Due to a severe winter, only one game took place in January before action resumed in March. Leeds defeated Darlington 3-2, Henry notching the winner, before David Cochrane scored a brace in United's biggest win of the campaign, 5-2 against Bradford Park Avenue. Another Cochrane brace and Henry strike accounted for Hull City prior to a 3-1 defeat at home to Newcastle. Finishing fifth, Henry would become United's most prolific goalscorer during the war years.

In the League War Cup, Alf Stephens scored a hat-trick in a 6-3 win against Sheffield Wednesday. Leeds won 8-6 over the two legs before going down to Sunderland in the next round. Among numerous players to appear, Jim Makinson missed two games, whilst Hodgson and Cochrane top scored with seven goals.

1939 - 1940

REGIONAL LEAGUE NORTH - EAST DIVISION (FINAL LEAGUE POSITION 5TH) - PLD 18 W 9 D 3 L 6 F 36 A 27 PTS 21

DIVISION ONE

DATE	OPPONENTS	VENUE	SCORE	SCORERS	ATT.
26-Aug	PRESTON NORTH END	HOME	0 - 0		20,491
30-Aug	CHARLTON ATHLETIC	HOME	0 - 1		12,049
02-Sep	SHEFFIELD UNITED	HOME	0 - 1		9,779

REGIONAL LEAGUE NORTH - EAST DIVISION

DATE	OPPONENTS	VENUE	SCORE	SCORERS	ATT.
28-Oct	BRADFORD CITY	HOME	3 - 0	HODGSON G 2 & BROWN	3,000
04-Nov	HULL CITY	AWAY	3 - 0	POWELL A, HODGSON G & McGRAW	3,000
11-Nov	DARLINGTON	AWAY	3 - 1	McGRAW, HODGSON G & BROWN	5,727
18-Nov	HARTLEPOOLS UNITED	HOME	2 - 1	HOLLEY & HODGSON G	4,000
25-Nov	YORK CITY	AWAY	1 - 1	HENRY	4,000
02-Dec	HUDDERSFIELD TOWN	HOME	0 - 0		4,000
09-Dec	BRADFORD PARK AVENUE	AWAY	1 - 3	HODGSON G (PEN)	4,000
23-Dec	MIDDLESBROUGH	HOME	3 - 1	COCHRANE D, POWELL A & HENRY	5,000
06-Jan	NEWCASTLE UNITED	AWAY	0 - 3		6,000
09-Mar	DARLINGTON	HOME	3 - 2	COCHRANE D, STEPHENSON (PEN), & HENRY	4,000
16-Mar	HARTLEPOOLS UNITED	AWAY	1 - 2	STEPHENS J	1,500
23-Mar	YORK CITY	HOME	3 - 1	SHORT 2 & POWELL A	3,000
30-Mar	HUDDERSFIELD TOWN	AWAY	1 - 2	SHORT	5,833
06-Apr	BRADFORD PARK AVENUE	HOME	5 - 2	POWELL A, McGRAW, STEPHENS A & COCHRANE D 2	3,000
13-Apr	MIDDLESBROUGH	AWAY	1 - 1	STEPHENS A	1,000
25-May	HALIFAX TOWN	AWAY	2 - 3	HENRY 2	600
01-Jun	HULL CITY	HOME	3 - 1	HENRY & COCHRANE D 2	500
08-Jun	NEWCASTLE UNITED	HOME	1 - 3	COCHRANE D	200

LEAGUE WAR CUP

DATE	OPPONENTS	VENUE	SCORE	SCORERS	ATT.
20-Apr	SHEFFIELD WEDNESDAY	HOME	6 - 3	THOMPSON, STEPHENS A 3 & HARGREAVES 2	8,065
27-Apr	SHEFFIELD WEDNESDAY	AWAY	2 - 3	POWELL A & HODGSON G	9,506
04-May	SUNDERLAND	AWAY	0 - 0		11,226
11-May	SUNDERLAND	HOME	0 - 1		9,000

THE MATCHES AGAINST BRADFORD CITY (AWAY) AND HALIFAX TOWN (HOME) WERE NOT PLAYED IN THE REGIONAL LEAGUE NORTH - EAST DIVISION

LEEDS UNITED ALSO PLAYED IN A LEAGUE JUBILEE FUND MATCH AWAY TO HUDDERSFIELD TOWN ON AUG. 19TH 1939. THE GAME ENDED 0 - 5   (0 - 2) WITH THE ATTENDANCE BEING 4,630. THE TEAM WAS TWOMEY, GOLDEBERG, GADSBY, EDWARDS, HOLLEY, COPPING, COCHRANE, AINSLEY, DUNDERDALE, STEPHENSON & BUCKLEY

LEAGUE AND CUP
APPEARANCES

PLAYER	LEAGUE	REG. LEAGUE	LG. WAR CUP	TOTAL
AINSLEY	2		1	3
BROWN		8		8
BROWNE B	3	3		6
BUCKLEY A	2	1		3
COCHRANE D	3	10	3	16
COPPING	3	3		6
DUNDERDALE	1			1
EDWARDS Wi.		2	2	4
GADSBY	3	14	4	21
GOLDBERG	2	12	3	17
HARGREAVES	1	6	4	11
HENRY		14	1	15
HODGSON G	1	10	2	13
HOLLEY	2	13	3	18
KANE	1			1
LEE		9	4	13
McGRAW		12	1	13
MAKINSON		16	3	19
MILBURN Ja.		6	1	7
MILBURN Ji.	1	1		2
MURGATROYD		3		3
POWELL A	2	12	2	16
SAXON		1		1
SHORT		7		7
STEPHENS A		2	3	5
STEPHENS J		4		4
STEPHENSON	3	5	3	11
SWINDIN		9		9
THOMPSON		15	4	19
TWOMEY	1			1
WHARTON	2			2

GOALSCORERS

PLAYER	LEAGUE	REG. LEAGUE	LG. WAR CUP	TOTAL
COCHRANE D		7		7
HODGSON G		6	1	7
HENRY		6		6
POWELL A		4	1	5
STEPHENS A		2	3	5
McGRAW		3		3
SHORT		3		3
BROWN		2		2
HARGREAVES			2	2
HOLLEY		1		1
STEPHENS J		1		1
STEPHENSON		1		1
THOMPSON			1	1

As war raged in Europe, the summer months saw France fall after the evacuation from Dunkirk beaches and by the close season, the Battle of Britain was underway. To help morale back home, 38 players would take to the field for Leeds United during a campaign which was split into two regional leagues.

The opening three months yielded two wins, 5-2 at home to Huddersfield Town, John Short scoring two goals, and 6-3 at Bradford City, Gordon Hodgson notching a hat-trick. Aubrey Powell and Short grabbed United's other goals in a fine performance. Jack Milburn returned for a spell and with his usual proficiency scored a penalty in a 1-1 draw at Huddersfield.

Playing in front of crowds totalling around 3,000, due to crowd restrictions, the City result gave the team confidence and with a semi-settled side, four consecutive home victories came Leeds' way in November. Len Townsend and Eric Stephenson struck to defeat Middlesbrough 2-1, before the pair scored again as Leeds ran up their biggest win of the season, 6-0 against Bradford City. Other scorers were Milburn (pen), Hodgson and Johnny Mahon. Townsend was on fire and added two more goals in 3-2 victories against Hull City and Newcastle United.

The festive fixtures brought a Christmas Day win over Bradford Park Avenue at Elland Road, Townsend scoring the winner before notching a brace during a 4-2 win against Chesterfield in the opening New Year game. The return ended in a 3-2 defeat, but the result could have been worse as Leeds keeper Alex Lee played outfield after picking up an injury. John Daniels replaced Lee and performed admirably. As for Lee, the emergency centre-forward scored twice! Daniels would feature prominently over the remaining war years. Townsend signed off in style for Leeds with a hat-trick against Halifax in a League War Cup clash.

The run-in brought United's most consistent form with an unbeaten six-game spell including wins against Sheffield Wednesday, Rochdale, Doncaster Rovers and Sheffield United. Jack Hargeaves returned to the side for a clash against Wednesday and began a mini-scoring spree that would yield six goals. The end to United's season came within a three-day period against Middlesbrough. A 2-2 draw saw Leeds crash out of the League War Cup 4-2 on aggregate before a 3-2 defeat brought a fifteenth place finish. Jim Makinson was the only ever present, whilst Townsend led the scoring charts with 14 goals in 12 games.

1940 - 1941

NORTH REGIONAL LEAGUE (FINAL LEAGUE POSITION 15TH)
PLD 30 W 13 D 8 L 9 F 62 A 54 PTS 34

DATE	OPPONENTS	VENUE	SCORE	SCORERS	ATT.
31-Aug	BRADFORD CITY	HOME	2 - 2	STEPHENSON & SUTHERLAND	3,000
07-Sep	NEWCASTLE UNITED	AWAY	0 - 1		4,000
14-Sep	HUDDERSFIELD TOWN	HOME	5 - 2	SHORT 2, HODGSON G, O. G. (YOUNG) & POWELL A	3,000
21-Sep	MANCHESTER CITY	HOME	0 - 0		5,000
28-Sep	EVERTON	AWAY	1 - 5	BAIRD	3,000
05-Oct	HUDDERSFIELD TOWN	AWAY	1 - 1	MILBURN Ja. (PEN)	3,368
12-Oct	ROTHERHAM UNITED	AWAY	0 - 0		4,208
19-Oct	BRADFORD CITY	AWAY	6 - 3	HODGSON G 3, POWELL A 2 & SHORT	3,000
02-Nov	BARNSLEY	AWAY	0 - 3		1,244
09-Nov	MIDDLESBROUGH	HOME	2 - 1	TOWNSEND & STEPHENSON	2,000
16-Nov	BRADFORD CITY	HOME	6 - 0	MILBURN Ja. (PEN), MAHON, STEPHENSON, TOWNSEND 2 & HODGSON G	2,500
23-Nov	HULL CITY	HOME	3 - 2	TOWNSEND 2 & MAHON	3,000
30-Nov	NEWCASTLE UNITED	HOME	3 - 2	TOWNSEND 2 & STEPHENSON	3,000
07-Dec	BURNLEY	HOME	1 - 1	HARGREAVES	3,000
14-Dec	CHESTERFIELD	AWAY	0 - 3		1,000
21-Dec	HALIFAX TOWN	AWAY	2 - 2	McGRAW & TOWNSEND	3,000
25-Dec	BRADFORD PARK AVENUE	HOME	2 - 1	HODGSON G & TOWNSEND	4,500
28-Dec	CHESTERFIELD	HOME	1 - 2	SHORT	4,000
04-Jan	CHESTERFIELD *	AWAY	4 - 2	TOWNSEND 2, HENRY & STEPHENSON	2,000
11-Jan	CHESTERFIELD *	HOME	2 - 3	LEE 2	5,000
18-Jan	HULL CITY	AWAY	1 - 4	McGRAW	1,500
22-Mar	SHEFFIELD WEDNESDAY	HOME	3 - 2	HARGREAVES, MAKINSON & BURDITT	1,500
29-Mar	ROCHDALE	AWAY	3 - 2	BURDITT, AINSLEY & MAKINSON	800
05-Apr	DONCASTER ROVERS	AWAY	4 - 1	HENRY, EDWARDS & HARGREAVES 2	4,000
12-Apr	MANCHESTER CITY	AWAY	1 - 1	HARGREAVES	3,000
14-Apr	BURY	HOME	2 - 2	HENRY & HARGREAVES	2,400
26-Apr	SHEFFIELD UNITED	HOME	2 - 0	HARGREAVES & BURDITT	2,000
03-May	NEWCASTLE UNITED	AWAY	2 - 3	SHORT 2	2,000
10-May	HUDDERSFIELD TOWN *	HOME	1 - 0	POWELL A	4,000
17-May	MIDDLESBROUGH *	AWAY	2 - 3	MILBURN Ji. (PEN) & SHORT	3,000

LEAGUE WAR CUP

DATE	OPPONENTS	VENUE	SCORE	SCORERS	ATT.
15-Feb	HALIFAX TOWN	AWAY	3 - 2	TOWNSEND 3	4,000
01-Mar	HALIFAX TOWN	HOME	2 - 2	HODGSON G & EDWARDS	5,000
08-Mar	MIDDLESBROUGH	AWAY	0 - 2		9,000
15-Mar	MIDDLESBROUGH	HOME	2 - 2	HENRY & MILBURN Ja.	5,000

MATCHES MARKED * WERE ALSO IN THE WEST RIDING CUP AND COUNTED TOWARDS THE FINAL LEAGUE POSITION WHICH WAS DECIDED ON GOAL AVERAGE ONLY. LEEDS UNITED'S AVERAGE OF 1.148 GAVE THEM 15TH PLACE IN A LEAGUE WITH SIXTEEN TEAMS

LEAGUE AND CUP APPEARANCES

PLAYER	REG. LEAGUE	LG. WAR CUP	TOTAL
AINSLEY / BAIRD	3 / 2	0 / 0	3 / 2
BAKER / BROWN	1 / 1	0 / 0	1 / 1
BURDITT / COPPING	8 / 10	1 / 4	9 / 14
DANIELS / DEMPSEY	9 / 3	0 / 0	9 / 3
EDWARDS / FARRAGE	16 / 2	3 / 1	19 / 3
GADSBY / GOLDBERG	23 / 1	2 / 0	25 /1
GOSLING / HARGREAVES	3 / 14	0 / 3	3 / 17
HEATON / HENRY	2 / 14	0 / 3	2 / 17
HODGSON G / HODGSON J	17 / 1	4 / 0	21 /1
HOLLEY / HOULDERSHAW R	21 / 4	4 / 0	25 / 4
HOWITT / JACKETT	4 / 1	0 / 0	4 / 1
LEE / McGRAW	20 / 9	4 / 1	24 / 10
McTAVISH / MAHON	1 / 6	0 / 0	1 / 6
MAKINSON / MEENS	30 / 1	4 / 0	34 / 1
MILBURN Ja. / MILBURN Ji.	21 / 9	4 / 0	25 / 9
POWELL A / SHORT	13 / 12	1 / 0	14 / 12
SPIKE / STACEY	1 / 1	0 / 0	1 / 1
STEPHENSON / SUTHERLAND	23 / 2	4 / 0	27 / 2
THOMPSON / TOWNSEND	10 / 11	0 / 1	10 / 12

GOALSCORERS

PLAYER	REG. LEAGUE	LG. WAR CUP	TOTAL
TOWNSEND	11	3	14
HARGREAVES	7		7
HODGSON G	6	1	7
SHORT	7		7
STEPHENSON	5		5
HENRY	3	1	4
POWELL A	4		4
BURDITT	3		3
MILBURN Ja.	2	1	3
EDWARDS	1	1	2
LEE	2		2
McGRAW	2		2
MAHON	2		2
MAKINSON	2		2
AINSLEY	1		1
BAIRD	1		1
MILBURN Ji.	1		1
SUTHERLAND	1		1
OWN GOALS	1		1

A new season brought a new format for competitive football as divisional league sides took part in two championships, the first finishing at Christmas, a pivotal moment in the war as USA forces joined Allied efforts following Japan's attack on Pearl Harbour.

On the field, 53 players, 21 unregistered, represented Leeds United so it was not too surprising that Leeds struggled from the outset. It could not have been easy for manager Billy Hampson as he mixed and matched his team, but Gerry Henry did give Leeds a winning start at home to York City with a brace. Thereafter there were only fleeting moments of success. Henry found the target in all but one of the few wins that United did achieve, scoring against Gateshead 5-1, Bradford Park Avenue 4-0, Newcastle United 5-2, Bradford City 4-2 and Huddersfield Town 2-1. The latter fixture, which took place on Christmas Day, was watched by 6,000 spectators; the biggest Elland Road gate of the season.

Among numerous defeats, the heaviest came on visits to Sunderland 6-1, Bradford Park Avenue 6-0 and Bradford City 5-0. Leeds finished 26th overall when their results were compared with other divisional leagues. Henry with 15 goals scored almost half United's goals, including four against Newcastle and featured in every game alongside Aubrey Powell and Jim Makinson.

In the second championship, again Leeds managed to win seven games, but like 29 teams competing in other divisional leagues, failed to complete their 18 fixtures so had no final league position. A number of games doubled up for the League War Cup qualifying tournament and Combined Counties Cup. Again, Henry led the attack with verve, striking a hat-trick in a 5-1 win against Lincoln City, a brace during a 5-0 mauling over Rochdale and four in United's biggest victory of the season, 6-1 against Doncaster Rovers; Arnold Knight and George Ainsley completing the rout.

As with the previous tournament, there was a sprinkling of heavy losses, the worst at Halifax Town 6-1 and Huddersfield Town 5-1. Among the many guest players to entertain supporters were Reg Attwell (West Ham), Eric Litchfield (Newcastle United), Johnny Shafto (Liverpool) and Duncan McClure (Hearts). Goalkeeper Tom Daniels played in all 17 fixtures, whilst Henry top scored with 13 goals, giving him an impressive season's total of 28 from 33 appearances.

1941 - 1942

FIRST CHAMPIONSHIP

DATE	OPPONENTS	VENUE	SCORE	SCORERS	ATT.
30-Aug	YORK CITY	HOME	2 - 0	HENRY 2	3,000
06-Sep	YORK CITY	AWAY	0 - 1		4,000
13-Sep	GATESHEAD	AWAY	2 - 3	HENRY & SHORT	4,000
20-Sep	GATESHEAD	HOME	5 - 1	HENRY 2, SHORT 2 & HARGREAVES	2,500
27-Sep	SUNDERLAND	HOME	1 - 2	SHORT	3,000
04-Oct	SUNDERLAND	AWAY	1 - 6	STEPHENSON	10,000
11-Oct	BRADFORD PARK AVENUE	AWAY	0 - 6		3,000
18-Oct	BRADFORD PARK AVENUE	HOME	4 - 0	HARGREAVES, HENRY, ADAM & POWELL A	2,000
25-Oct	CHESTERFIELD	AWAY	0 - 3		1,500
01-Nov	CHESTERFIELD	HOME	2 - 2	HENRY & HARGREAVES	3,000
08-Nov	MIDDLESBROUGH	HOME	2 - 3	HARGREAVES 2	2,000
15-Nov	MIDDLESBROUGH	AWAY	2 - 1	POWELL A & HARGREAVES	4,000
22-Nov	NEWCASTLE UNITED	AWAY	2 - 4	HARGREAVES & SHANKS (PEN)	4,500
29-Nov	NEWCASTLE UNITED	HOME	5 - 2	HARGREAVES & HENRY 4	3,000
06-Dec	BRADFORD CITY	HOME	4 - 2	O. G. (GREGORY), HENRY, POWELL A & LITCHFIELD	1,500
13-Dec	BRADFORD CITY	AWAY	0 - 5		2,000
20-Dec	HUDDERSFIELD TOWN	AWAY	2 - 4	HENRY 2	2,063
25-Dec	HUDDERSFIELD TOWN	HOME	2 - 1	HENRY & McGRAW	6,000

SECOND CHAMPIONSHIP

DATE	OPPONENTS	VENUE	SCORE	SCORERS	ATT.
27-Dec	ROTHERHAM UNITED +	AWAY	1 - 3	POWELL A	3,606
03-Jan	LINCOLN CITY +	HOME	5 - 1	HENRY 3, TURNER & MILBURN Ja. (PEN)	3,000
10-Jan	ROCHDALE +	AWAY	0 - 2		2,000
17-Jan	ROCHDALE +	HOME	5 - 0	KNIGHT 2, ADAM & HENRY 2	3,000
14-Feb	BARNSLEY +	HOME	3 - 2	ADAM 2 & HENRY	2,500
21-Feb	BLACKBURN ROVERS +	AWAY	0 - 1		1,000
28-Feb	BLACKBURN ROVERS	HOME	0 - 1		5,200
14-Mar	DONCASTER ROVERS +	HOME	6 - 1	KNIGHT, AINSLEY & HENRY 4	3,000
21-Mar	BARNSLEY +	AWAY	2 - 3	POWELL A & O. G. (HARPER)	4,500
28-Mar	DONCASTER ROVERS +	AWAY	0 - 1		1,225
04-Apr	SHEFFIELD WEDNESDAY	HOME	1 - 2	McGRAW	3,000
06-Apr	HALIFAX TOWN *	AWAY	1 - 6	ASQUITH	2,000
11-Apr	HALIFAX TOWN *	HOME	3 - 1	HENRY, HOLLEY & AINSLEY	2,000
18-Apr	HUDDERSFIELD TOWN *	AWAY	1 - 5	HENRY	1,636
25-Apr	MIDDLESBROUGH *	AWAY	3 - 2	ADAM, O. G. (HEPPLEWHITE) & MILBURN Ji. (PEN)	2,500
02-May	CHESTERFIELD *	HOME	1 - 0	HENRY	2,000
09-May	MIDDLESBROUGH *	HOME	1 - 2	ADAM	2,000

MATCHES MARKED + WERE IN THE LEAGUE WAR CUP QUALIFYING COMPETITION. MATCHES MARKED * WERE IN THE COMBINED COUNTIES CUP. ALL CUP GAMES COUNTED TOWARDS THE LEAGUE. THE FIRST CHAMPIONSIP CONSISTED OF 38 TEAMS. THE SECOND CHAMPIONSHIP PROVIDED A TABLE OF 22 WHILST A FURTHER 29 TEAMS - LEEDS UNITED AMONGST THEM - FAILED TO QUALIFY BECAUSE THEY HAD PLAYED FEWER THAN 18 GAMES

LEAGUE AND CUP APPEARANCES

PLAYER	FIRST LEAGUE	SECOND LEAGUE	TOTAL
ADAM / AINSLEY / ASQUITH	11 / 0 / 0	12 / 9 / 2	23 / 9 / 2
ATTWELL / BRATLEY / BROWN	0 / 1 / 2	1 / 1 / 0	1 / 2 / 2
BURTON / BUSH / CLARKE	0 / 0 / 0	1 / 4 / 1	1 / 4 / 1
COPPING / DANIELS / EASTHAM	7 / 11 / 0	4 / 17 / 3	11 / 28 / 3
FOWLER / GADSBY / GOLDBERG	12 / 1 / 2	2 / 4 / 1	14 / 5 / 3
HADDOW / HARGREAVES / HARVEY	6 / 13 / 1	0 / 6 / 0	6 / 19 / 1
HEATON / HENRY / HOLLEY	2 / 18 / 11	0 / 15 / 11	2 / 33 / 22
KEEPING / KIDD / KNIGHT	2 / 0 / 4	0 / 1 / 9	2 / 1 / 13
LEE / LITCHFIELD / LIVINGSTONE	8 / 12 / 2	0 / 3 / 0	8 / 15 / 2
McCLURE / McGRAW / MADDISON	0 / 2 / 1	3 / 8 / 0	3 / 10 / 1
MAKINSON / MILBURN Ja. / MILBURN Ji.	18 / 0 / 3	15 / 4 / 11	33 / 4 / 14
MURGATROYD / POWELL A / RAMSDEN	3 / 18 / 0	0 / 13 / 8	3 / 31 / 8
RAMSLEY / SCAIFE / SELLAR R	2 / 0 / 0	0 / 1 / 1	2 / 1 / 1
SHAFTO J / SHANKS / SHORT	0 / 6 / 5	1 / 0 / 1	1 / 6 / 6
SPIKE / SPINK / STANTON	5 / 1 / 3	0 / 0 / 0	5 / 1 / 3
STEPHENSON / TAYLOR / TURNER	4 / 0 / 0	0 / 3 / 2	4 / 3 / 2
VICKERS / WARBURTON / WATSON	0 / 0 / 1	5 / 2 / 0	5 / 2 / 1
WESLEY J / WILLIAMS W	0 / 0	1 / 1	1 / 1

GOALSCORERS

PLAYER	FIRST LEAGUE	SECOND LEAGUE	TOTAL
HENRY	15	13	28
HARGREAVES	8		8
ADAM	1	5	6
POWELL A	3	2	5
SHORT	4		4
KNIGHT		3	3
AINSLEY		2	2
McGRAW	1	1	2
ASQUITH		1	1
HOLLEY		1	1
LITCHFIELD	1		1
MILBURN Ja.		1	1
MILBURN Ji.		1	1
SHANKS	1		1
STEPHENSON	1		1
TURNER		1	1
OWN GOALS	1	2	3

Adopting an identical format to the previous season, home supporters got used to seeing different line-ups every game. In excess of 70 players appeared during the two championships. Guests came and went, arriving from around the country on the morning of a match on many occasions. It was an administrative nightmare for club officials, but keeping the game functional was seen as paramount to morale and though Leeds struggled, thousands of people up and down the country enjoyed the entertainment.

Those local to Aldershot were spoiled for choice, at one time accommodating the England half back-line of Cliff Britton, Stan Cullis and Joe Mercer. Wartime cup finals attracted huge Wembley attendances and as well as domestic football in England and Scotland, international matches took place, with the likes of Stanley Matthews, Denis Compton and Tommy Lawton showing their paces. Former Leeds United star Bert Sproston and future Leeds boss Raich Carter also appeared for England, whilst Scotland fielded renowned players such as Bill Shankly, Matt Busby, Bobby Flavell and Archie Macauley.

New signings at Elland Road included Albert Wakefield, Frank Butterworth and Dennis Kirby, but with so much disruption, United claimed just three wins and four draws during the first 18-match championship. Losing the opening four fixtures, Wakefield opened the scoring in an exciting 5-3 win at Newcastle United, John Short notched a brace, Eddie Rutherford and John Brown also scored. Only five players from the victory featured for Leeds in the return match seven days later, such was the frequency of weekly team changes. It showed as a different looking XI lost 7-1 to Newcastle!

Aubrey Powell and Short struck braces in a 6-0 canter against Doncaster Rovers, whilst Gerry Henry opened the scoring in a 2-1 win against York City as Leeds finished 43rd in the Northern section. Powell and keeper John Daniels featured in every game of the championship, whilst Wakefield, who notched a brace in the final game; a 3-3 at home to Huddersfield Town, led the scoring with seven goals.

The second championship began with five defeats, the last 9-0 at Newcastle. Fortune though, favoured Leeds in the next clash. Fielding eight of the same players, United claimed a 7-2 win. Powell struck four goals, Ainsley hit two and Henry completed Leeds' biggest win of the season. Three defeats and a draw followed before Leeds enjoyed a consistent spell, claiming four wins in the remaining six clashes.

A brace apiece by Wakefield and Henry earned consecutive 3-2 wins against Middlesbrough but the most bizarre game took place at Newcastle. Four goals down with 20 minutes remaining, Leeds staged the greatest comeback in their history, winning 5-4 with goals from Short, Powell 2, Rutherford and Tom Williams. For Williams it would be his only Leeds appearance, but a notable one. Following a 2-0 win over Bradford Park Avenue in the return, Powell scored United's final goal of the campaign in a 5-2 defeat. Arnold Knight missed only one match, whilst Powell top scored with 10 goals.

FOOTBALL LEAGUE NORTHERN SECTION (1ST. CHAMPIONSHIP - FINAL LGE. POS. 43RD & 2ND. CHAMPIONSHIP - FINAL LGE. POS. 47TH)

FIRST - PLD 18 W 3 D 4 L 11 F 28 A 45 PTS 10 & SECOND - PLD 16 W 5 D 1 L 10 F 32 A 50 PTS 11

FIRST CHAMPIONSHIP

DATE	OPPONENTS	VENUE	SCORE	SCORERS	ATT.
29-Aug	MIDDLESBROUGH	HOME	0 - 1		3,000
05-Sep	MIDDLESBROUGH	AWAY	0 - 2		3,500
12-Sep	GATESHEAD	AWAY	1 - 3	SHORT	3,000
19-Sep	GATESHEAD	HOME	1 - 2	POWELL A	3,000
26-Sep	NEWCASTLE UNITED	AWAY	5 - 3	WAKEFIELD, SHORT 2, RUTHERFORD & BROWN	6,000
03-Oct	NEWCASTLE UNITED	HOME	1 - 7	POWELL A	3,000
10-Oct	DONCASTER ROVERS	HOME	6 - 0	POWELL A 2, SHORT 2, RUTHERFORD & WAKEFIELD	3,000
17-Oct	DONCASTER ROVERS	AWAY	2 - 2	HARGREAVES & HENRY (PEN)	2,000
24-Oct	SUNDERLAND	HOME	1 - 2	WAKEFIELD	4,000
31-Oct	SUNDERLAND	AWAY	1 - 4	POWELL A	3,000
07-Nov	BRADFORD PARK AVENUE	HOME	1 - 1	POWELL A	3,000
14-Nov	BRADFORD PARK AVENUE	AWAY	0 - 1		4,465
21-Nov	YORK CITY	HOME	2 - 1	HENRY & HOULDERSHAW R	4,000
28-Nov	YORK CITY	AWAY	1 - 3	WAKEFIELD	5,000
05-Dec	HALIFAX TOWN	HOME	1 - 1	WAKEFIELD	1,000
12-Dec	HALIFAX TOWN	AWAY	1 - 5	FALLAIZE	4,000
19-Dec	HUDDERSFIELD TOWN	AWAY	1 - 4	HENRY	2,286
25-Dec	HUDDERSFIELD TOWN	HOME	3 - 3	WAKEFIELD 2 & HENRY	4,000

SECOND CHAMPIONSHIP

DATE	OPPONENTS	VENUE	SCORE	SCORERS	ATT.
26-Dec	BARNSLEY + $	AWAY	1 - 2	RUTHERFORD	6,000
02-Jan	BARNSLEY +	HOME	1 - 3	POWELL A	2,000
09-Jan	HUDDERSFIELD TOWN +	HOME	2 - 4	POWELL A & HOULDERSHAW R	1,000
16-Jan	HUDDERSFIELD TOWN +	AWAY	1 - 4	POWELL A	1,179
23-Jan	NEWCASTLE UNITED +	AWAY	0 - 9		7,000
30-Jan	NEWCASTLE UNITED +	HOME	7 - 2	POWELL A 4, HENRY & AINSLEY 2	2,000
06-Feb	BRADFORD PARK AVENUE +	AWAY	1 - 2	HENRY	4,500
13-Feb	BRADFORD PARK AVENUE +	HOME	2 - 2	RUTHERFORD & HENRY	3,000
20-Feb	BRADFORD CITY +	AWAY	0 - 1		4,287
27-Feb	BRADFORD CITY +	HOME	1 - 5	RUTHERFORD	3,000
06-Mar	MIDDLESBROUGH *	HOME	3 - 2	WAKEFIELD 2 & HOULDERSHAW R	2,000
13-Mar	MIDDLESBROUGH *	AWAY	3 - 2	LAWN & HENRY 2	2,500
20-Mar	NEWCASTLE UNITED	HOME	1 - 3	SHORT	2,500
27-Mar	NEWCASTLE UNITED	AWAY	5 - 4	SHORT, POWELL A 2, RUTHERFORD & WILLIAMS	8,000
03-Apr	BRADFORD PARK AVENUE *	HOME	2 - 0	SMITH & MILBURN Ji.	3,000
10-Apr	BRADFORD PARK AVENUE *	AWAY	2 - 5	ARGUE & POWELL A	3,908

MATCHES MARKED + WERE IN THE LEAGUE WAR CUP QUALIFYING COMPETITION. MATCHES MARKED * WERE IN THE COMBINED COUNTIES CUP. ALL CUP GAMES COUNTED TOWARDS THE LEAGUE. THE FIRST CHAMPIONSIP CONSISTED OF 48 TEAMS. THE SECOND CHAMPIONSHIP PROVIDED A TABLE OF 54. IN THE LEAGUE CUP 32 TEAMS QUALIFIED FOR THE KNOCK - OUT COMPETITION. LEEDS UNITED WERE AMONGST THE 22 NON - QUALIFIERS
$ = MATCH ABANDONED AFTER 66 MINUTES BUT RESULT STOOD

LEAGUE AND CUP
APPEARANCES

PLAYER	FIRST LEAGUE	SECOND LEAGUE	TOTAL
AINSLEY / ANSON / ARGUE / BEDFORD	6 / 1 / 0 / 0	6 / 0 / 4 / 1	12 / 1 / 4 / 1
BINNS / BOKAS / BOYES / BROWN	0 / 0 / 0 / 3	2 / 1 / 2 / 0	2 / 1 / 2 / 3
BUSH / BUTTERWORTH / CAMPBELL / CLUTTERBUCK	2 / 11 / 1 / 1	0 / 11 / 0 / 0	2 / 22 / 1 / 1
DAINTY / DANIELS / D'ARCY / DUNN	0 / 18 / 1 / 0	1 / 14 / 0 / 1	1 / 32 / 1 / 1
EASTHAM / EDWARDS / FALLAIZE / FOWLER	3 / 0 / 1 / 3	0 / 1 / 2 / 0	3 / 1 / 3 / 3
GADSBY / GOLDBERG / HARGREAVES / HARPER	4 / 1 / 1 / 1	3 / 0 / 0 / 2	7 / 1 / 1 / 3
HARRIS / HARSTON / HENRY / HICK	0 / 2 / 14 / 0	2 / 0 / 13 / 1	2 / 2 / 27 / 1
HOLLEY / HOULDERSHAW H / HOULDERSHAW R / JONES	9 / 2 / 7 / 2	1 / 0 / 6 / 0	10 / 2 / 13 / 2
JONES B ('W H') / KINGHORN / KIRBY / KNIGHT	0 / 2 / 1 / 11	2 / 0 / 0 / 15	2 / 2 / 1 / 26
LAWN / LIMBERT / McGRAW	0 / 1 / 9	2 / 2 / 10	2 / 3 / 19
McINNES / MARSHALL / MILBURN Ja. / MILBURN Ji.	3 / 1 / 4 / 6	0 / 0 / 2 / 4	3 / 1 / 6 / 10
MOSS / O'FARRELL / PATTERSON / POWELL A	4 / 1 / 3 / 18	4 / 0 / 0 / 14	8 / 1 / 3 / 32
POXON / PYKE / RHODES / ROBBINS H	4 / 0 / 0 / 1	0 / 1 / 4 / 0	4 / 1 / 4 / 1
RUTHERFORD / SCAIFE / SHORT / SIMPSON	8 / 1 / 4 / 2	12 / 0 / 4 / 0	20 / 1 / 8 / 2
SMITH / STURROCK / TAYLOR / TAYLOR W	0 / 2 / 2 / 0	2 / 0 / 0 / 2	2 / 2 / 2 / 2
TINDALL / VICKERS / WAKEFIELD / WARREN	1 / 1 / 11 / 2	0 / 0 / 10 / 5	1 / 1 / 21 / 7
WHEELER / WHITTLE / WILCOX / WILDON	0 / 0 / 0 / 0	1 / 1 / 2 / 1	1 / 1 / 2 / 1
WILKINSON / WILLIAMS T / WOOFINDEN	0 / 0 / 1	1 / 1 / 0	1 / 1 / 1

GOALSCORERS

PLAYER	FIRST LEAGUE	SECOND LEAGUE	TOTAL
POWELL A	6	10	16
HENRY	4	5	9
WAKEFIELD	7	2	9
SHORT	5	2	7
RUTHERFORD	2	4	6
HOULDERSHAW R	1	2	3
AINSLEY		2	2
ARGUE		1	1
BROWN	1		1
FALLAIZE	1		1
HARGREAVES	1		1
LAWN		1	1
MILBURN Ji.		1	1
SMITH		1	1
WILLIAMS T		1	1

Billy Hampson looked ahead to the new campaign but his charges could barely make a worse start. Losing the opening clash at Sunderland 7-1, United followed up with consecutive 5-1 home defeats to Sunderland and Bradford City. The defeat at Roker Park saw the final appearance of Albert Wakefield, who scored Leeds' consolation goal. His replacement Walter Boyes slotted into the side and took on the responsibility of taking penalties. Having scored Leeds' sole effort against Bradford City, his spot kick and a Gerry Henry brace earned United a draw in the return against their West Yorkshire neighbours.

Suddenly confidence returned, and for Henry in particular, who went on a sensational scoring spree, notching 12 goals in 10 consecutive games. Henry is the only United player to score in 10 successive first team games, and during his purple patch, Leeds would suffer only one defeat, another mauling, this time at Bradford Park Avenue 6-1. However, Henry was on song, helping United to victories against Middlesbrough and Gateshead, and a brace in a 3-1 win at York City.

The home clash with Gateshead brought a 5-2 win, when Jack Tremmeling, who scored Leeds' consolation in Sunderland's five-goal win at Elland Road, scored a hat-trick. These would be Tremmeling's only appearances, his two-game stay was not without memories. Leeds' other scorer at York was Arnold Knight, without a goal the previous season, but he would enjoy further goal success, hitting the winner in the York return and the opening goal in United's most comprehensive victory, 4-0 against Halifax Town. Both Frank Butterworth and Henry missed two games, whilst Henry top scored with 12 goals. Finishing 27th qualified Leeds for the League War Cup again, but Sheffield United won 3-2 on aggregate in the first round.

In the second championship, Leeds fared better in terms of wins, claiming eight, seven consecutively at home, but away form let them down badly with only one victory to boast. Leeds even endured an 8-1 defeat at York City, having beaten them 2-1 seven days earlier. Finishing 35th overall, whilst Henry was not as prolific, a number of players struck form during brief spells, including George Antonio (Stoke City), John Davie (Brighton & Hove Albion) and Boyes.

Antonio was first to shine as Leeds overcame Bradford Park Avenue, Barnsley and Huddersfield. Boyes was also on target against Town, prior to sealing victory against Bradford City, whilst Davie entered the fray at the back end of the season. Notching two goals on his debut at Chesterfield, Davie scored in the final games against Halifax Town. In excess of 60 players represented Leeds, including Maurice Lindley in a 1-0 win against Sheffield United, a clash that attracted a 15,000 gate, the biggest Elland Road crowd since the hostilities began. In time, Lindley would return as Don Revie's assistant manager. Henry missed just one game, whilst Antonio top scored with five goals.

1943 - 1944

FIRST CHAMPIONSHIP

DATE	OPPONENTS	VENUE	SCORE	SCORERS	ATT.
28-Aug	SUNDERLAND	AWAY	1 - 7	WAKEFIELD	4,000
04-Sep	SUNDERLAND	HOME	1 - 5	TREMMELLING	4,000
11-Sep	BRADFORD CITY	HOME	1 - 5	BOYES (PEN)	2,000
18-Sep	BRADFORD CITY	AWAY	3 - 3	HENRY 2 & BOYES (PEN)	6,000
25-Sep	MIDDLESBROUGH	HOME	3 - 0	STEVENS, JAMESON & HENRY	3,000
02-Oct	MIDDLESBROUGH	AWAY	3 - 3	POWELL A, HENRY & SHORT	3,000
09-Oct	GATESHEAD	HOME	5 - 2	HENRY, TREMELLING 3 & BOYES	3,000
16-Oct	GATESHEAD	AWAY	4 - 3	SHORT, HENRY & POWELL A 2	3,000
23-Oct	DONCASTER ROVERS	AWAY	3 - 3	KNIGHT 2 & HENRY	8,264
30-Oct	DONCASTER ROVERS	HOME	2 - 2	HENRY (PEN) & FALLAIZE	5,000
06-Nov	BRADFORD PARK AVENUE	AWAY	1 - 6	HENRY	5,301
13-Nov	BRADFORD PARK AVENUE	HOME	2 - 2	HENRY & HINDLE	6,000
20-Nov	YORK CITY	AWAY	3 - 1	HENRY 2 & KNIGHT	4,708
27-Nov	YORK CITY	HOME	1 - 0	KNIGHT	4,000
04-Dec	HALIFAX TOWN	AWAY	1 - 2	BROWN	3,000
11-Dec	HALIFAX TOWN	HOME	4 - 0	KNIGHT, BOYES, DORLING & HINDLE (PEN)	4,000
18-Dec	HUDDERSFIELD TOWN	HOME	0 - 3		5,000
25-Dec	HUDDERSFIELD TOWN	AWAY	0 - 3		7,792

SECOND CHAMPIONSHIP

DATE	OPPONENTS	VENUE	SCORE	SCORERS	ATT.
26-Dec	BRADFORD PARK AVENUE *	AWAY	1 - 2	POWELL A	13,186
01-Jan	BRADFORD PARK AVENUE *	HOME	3 - 1	HINDLE, POWELL A & ANTONIO	7,200
08-Jan	BARNSLEY *	HOME	2 - 0	ANTONIO & HENRY	7,000
15-Jan	BARNSLEY *	AWAY	2 - 3	HENRY 2	4,347
22-Jan	HUDDERSFIELD TOWN *	AWAY	1 - 4	HINDLE	1,810
29-Jan	HUDDERSFIELD TOWN *	HOME	2 - 0	BOYES & ANTONIO	8,000
05-Feb	BRADFORD CITY *	AWAY	3 - 3	ANTONIO 2 & BOYES	4,800
12-Feb	BRADFORD CITY *	HOME	2 - 0	HINDLE & BOYES	8,000
19-Feb	YORK CITY *	HOME	2 - 1	MAHON & HENRY	7,000
26-Feb	YORK CITY *	AWAY	1 - 8	KNIGHT	5,176
04-Mar	SHEFFIELD UNITED $	AWAY	1 - 3	BOYES	12,000
11-Mar	SHEFFIELD UNITED $	HOME	1 - 0	DAVIES	15,000
18-Mar	DERBY COUNTY	AWAY	2 - 2	CURRY 2	6,000
01-Apr	CHESTERFIELD +	AWAY	3 - 1	DAVIE 2 & GADSBY	1,000
08-Apr	CHESTERFIELD +	HOME	1 - 0	STEELE	4,500
10-Apr	ROTHERHAM UNITED	AWAY	3 - 5	TATTON, POWELL A & SHORT	8,000
15-Apr	HALIFAX TOWN +	HOME	2 - 2	TATTON & DAVIE	6,000
22-Apr	HALIFAX TOWN +	AWAY	2 - 5	STEELE & DAVIE	4,000

MATCHES MARKED + WERE IN THE COMBINED COUNTIES CUP. MATCHES MARKED * WERE IN THE LEAGUE WAR CUP QUALIFYING COMPETITION. MATCHES MARKED $ WERE IN THE LEAGUE WAR CUP KNOCK - OUT COMPETITION WHICH WAS ON A TWO - LEGGED BASIS. ALL CUP GAMES COUNTED TOWARDS THE LEAGUE. THE FIRST CHAMPIONSIP CONSISTED OF 50 TEAMS. THE SECOND CHAMPIONSHIP ALSO PROVIDED A FINAL TABLE OF 50 TEAMS. LEEDS UNITED WERE AMONGST THE 32 QUALIFIERS FROM THE LEAGUE WAR CUP'S INITIAL STAGES BUT WERE ELIMINATED ON AGGREGATE IN THE FIRST ROUND OF THE KNOCK - OUT STAGE

LEAGUE AND CUP

APPEARANCES

PLAYER	FIRST LEAGUE	SECOND LEAGUE	TOTAL
AINSLEY / ANTONIO / ATTWELL / BOWEN	1 / 0 / 1 / 1	0 / 10 / 0 / 0	1 / 10 / 1 / 1
BOYES / BROWN J / BUTTERWORTH / CHALLINOR	15 / 1 / 16 / 5	13 / 0 / 16 / 9	28 / 1 / 32 / 14
CORBETT / CURRY / DANIELS / DAVIE	0 / 0 / 9 / 0	1 / 1 / 16 / 5	1 / 1 / 25 / 5
DAVIES / DEWIS / DORLING / DUTCHMAN	0 / 1 / 1 / 0	6 / 1 / 3 / 1	6 / 2 / 4 / 1
FALLAIZE / FARRELL / GADSBY / GALLEY	2 / 0 / 7 / 3	0 / 1 / 3 / 1	2 / 1 / 10 / 4
GLOVER / GOLDBERG / GOODBURN / HENRY	1 / 1 / 0 / 16	0 / 3 / 1 / 17	1 / 4 / 1 / 33
HINDLE / HIRST / HODGSON J / HOLLEY	14 / 1 / 0 / 1	11 / 0 / 1 / 2	25 / 1 / 1 / 3
HOULDERSHAW H / JAMESON / JONES / JORDAN	1 / 1 / 3 / 1	0 / 0 / 0 / 0	1 / 1 / 3 / 1
KIRBY / KIRTON / KNIGHT / LAWN	3 / 4 / 10 / 1	0 / 2 / 8 / 0	3 / 6 / 18 / 1
LINDLEY / McGRAW / McKELLAR / MAHON	0 / 9 / 1 / 1	1 / 9 / 0 / 4	1 / 18 / 1 / 5
MAKINSON / MILBURN G / MILBURN Ja. / MILBURN Ji.	10 / 0 / 0 / 4	7 / 3 / 5 / 3	17 / 3 / 5 / 7
MOULE / O'NEILL / PADGETT / PATON	1 / 1 / 1 / 1	1 / 0 / 0 / 0	2 / 1 / 1 / 1
POLAND / POWELL A / RHODES / RODGERS	9 / 11 / 2 / 2	1 / 11 / 0 / 0	10 / 22 / 2 / 2
ROSIER / SHARP / SHORT / STEELE	0 / 1 / 3 / 0	3 / 0 / 2 / 2	3 / 1 / 5 / 2
STEVENS / STOKES / TATTON / THOMPSON	1 / 5 / 1 / 2	0 / 0 / 4 / 1	1 / 5 / 5 / 3
TREMELLING / WAKEFIELD / WALKER / WARD	2 / 1 / 2 / 1	0 / 0 / 0 / 3	2 / 1 / 2 / 4
WILCOCKS / WILLIAMS C E / WRIGHT / YEOMANSON	2 / 0 / 3 / 0	0 / 1 / 0 / 5	2 / 1 / 3 / 5

GOALSCORERS

PLAYER	FIRST LEAGUE	SECOND LEAGUE	TOTAL
HENRY	12	4	16
BOYES	4	4	8
KNIGHT	5	1	6
POWELL A	3	3	6
ANTONIO		5	5
HINDLE	2	3	5
DAVIE		4	4
TREMELLING	4		4
SHORT	2	1	3
CURRY		2	2
STEELE		2	2
TATTON		2	2
BROWN J	1		1
DAVIES		1	1
DORLING	1		1
FALLAIZE	1		1
GADSBY		1	1
JAMESON	1		1
MAHON		1	1
STEVENS	1		1
WAKEFIELD	1		1

During the close season, at last, a feeling that war was ending emerged with the Allied invasion of Normandy. Attendances increased when Leeds embarked on what would be the last season of two-championship football. Again, a poor start wrecked any chance of an assault on honours although United did enjoy an unbeaten run of eight games that yielded seven wins, of which five were consecutive.

Tom Hindle netted goals in victories against Middlesbrough 4-2, Hull City 5-2, Newcastle United 4-2, Bradford City 6-2 and 4-1, and Hartlepools United 6-2. George Ainsley scored hat-tricks both home and away against Bradford City, whilst John Short notched a treble against Hartlepools United. During the run-in, three defeats were quickly forgotten, as in the space of four days. Leeds claimed a double over York City. Gerry Henry fired home a hat-trick in a 3-1 win at Elland Road, before in the final game of the championship, Hindle notched a treble in a 6-3 mauling. Finishing 22nd, Frank Butterworth and Hindle missed one match, Hindle top scored with 11 goals.

In the second championship, Hindle blasted another treble in an opening 9-1 annihilation of Bradford City; Leeds' biggest win of the war period, before adding a brace in wins over York City 5-0, Hull City 6-1 and Preston North End 3-1. Not to be outdone, Henry notched a brace in the Hull clash and added a hat-trick in an exciting 4-3 win against Sheffield Wednesday; Hindle struck the other goal. Inconsistency had dogged Leeds throughout the regional tournaments and it meant a 32nd place finish and no place in the knockout tournament.

Hindle led the way in appearances, missing only the last match, a 6-1 defeat at Chesterfield, and edged Henry in the scoring stakes, totalling 15 goals. His season's effort of 26 strikes was six better than Henry. Within two weeks of the season's end, peace was announced in Europe.

Several Leeds United players paid the ultimate price in World War 2. Robert Montgomery was reported killed in 1944, Eric Stephenson achieved the rank of major before losing his life in Burma in September 1944, while Leslie Thompson was killed in 1945. Alan Fowler was a sergeant in France when he lost his life in July 1944, and guest players during the war years, Tom Farrage and Harry Goslin also died. Many other players saw action abroad, including Tom Holley and Jim Milburn in India, Aubrey Powell in Belgium, Albert Wakefield in Italy and Wilf Copping in the North African campaign. Alex Lee received the Air Force medal and United's future club president, the Earl of Harewood, was a prisoner in Colditz.

1944 - 1945

FOOTBALL LEAGUE NORTHERN SECTION (1ST. CHAMPIONSHIP - FINAL LGE. POS. 22ND & 2ND. CHAMPIONSHIP - FINAL LGE. POS. 32ND)

FIRST - PLD 18 W 9 D 2 L 7 F 53 A 42 PTS 20 & SECOND - PLD 22 W 9 D 3 L 10 F 53 A 55 PTS 21

FIRST CHAMPIONSHIP

DATE	OPPONENTS	VENUE	SCORE	SCORERS	ATT.
26-Aug	BRADFORD PARK AVENUE	AWAY	3 - 4	MILBURN Ja. (PEN), HENRY & SUTHERLAND	8,416
02-Sep	BRADFORD PARK AVENUE	HOME	3 - 3	MILBURN Ja. (PEN), YEOMANSON & SUTHERLAND	6,000
09-Sep	SUNDERLAND	HOME	0 - 1		8,000
16-Sep	SUNDERLAND	AWAY	1 - 5	MAHON	8,000
23-Sep	MIDDLESBROUGH	AWAY	2 - 3	AINSLEY 2	4,500
30-Sep	MIDDLESBROUGH	HOME	4 - 2	MAHON 2, HINDLE & COYNE	8,000
07-Oct	HULL CITY	HOME	5 - 2	COYNE 2, MAHON, HINDLE & HENRY	8,000
14-Oct	HULL CITY	AWAY	0 - 0		5,000
21-Oct	NEWCASTLE UNITED	HOME	2 - 1	COYNE 2	8,000
28-Oct	NEWCASTLE UNITED	AWAY	4 - 2	HINDLE, MAHON, SHORT & AINSLEY	25,000
04-Nov	BRADFORD CITY	AWAY	6 - 2	HINDLE 2, AINSLEY 3 & COYNE	6,657
11-Nov	BRADFORD CITY	HOME	4 - 1	AINSLEY 3 & HINDLE	8,760
18-Nov	HARTLEPOOLS UNITED	HOME	6 - 2	SHORT 3, HINDLE 2 & AINSLEY	9,000
25-Nov	HARTLEPOOLS UNITED	AWAY	0 - 3		4,940
02-Dec	HUDDERSFIELD TOWN	AWAY	2 - 4	HENRY & MOULE	7,880
09-Dec	HUDDERSFIELD TOWN	HOME	2 - 3	HENRY & MOULE	14,000
16-Dec	YORK CITY	HOME	3 - 1	HENRY 3	5,000
23-Dec	YORK CITY	AWAY	6 - 3	HINDLE 3, SHORT 2 & MOULE	4,871

SECOND CHAMPIONSHIP

DATE	OPPONENTS	VENUE	SCORE	SCORERS	ATT.
26-Dec	BRADFORD CITY +	HOME	9 - 1	HINDLE 3, SHORT 2, HENRY, MAHON, BURBANKS & WEAVER (PEN)	3,500
30-Dec	BRADFORD CITY +	AWAY	2 - 6	MAHON & HENRY	7,672
06-Jan	BARNSLEY +	HOME	0 - 1		12,000
13-Jan	BARNSLEY +	AWAY	0 - 5		6,989
20-Jan	YORK CITY +	AWAY	5 - 0	MOULE, DUNDERDALE 2 & HINDLE 2	1,000
27-Jan	YORK CITY +	HOME	4 - 3	MOULE, HENRY, HINDLE & BURBANKS	6,000
03-Feb	HULL CITY +	HOME	6 - 1	COYNE, HINDLE 2, HENRY 2 & WEAVER (PEN)	8,000
10-Feb	HULL CITY +	AWAY	1 - 1	CAMPBELL	4,000
17-Feb	BRADFORD PARK AVENUE +	AWAY	2 - 5	HINDLE & HENRY	10,198
24-Feb	BRADFORD PARK AVENUE +	HOME	0 - 2		15,000
03-Mar	SHEFFIELD WEDNESDAY	HOME	4 - 3	HENRY 3 & HINDLE	7,000
10-Mar	PRESTON NORTH END	HOME	3 - 1	HINDLE 2 & COYNE	8,500
17-Mar	SHEFFIELD WEDNESDAY	AWAY	1 - 1	HENRY	7,000
24-Mar	GRIMSBY TOWN	HOME	1 - 1	KNIGHT	7,000
02-Apr	CHESTERFIELD	HOME	0 - 2		6,500
09-Apr	GRIMSBY TOWN	AWAY	0 - 3		6,000
14-Apr	HULL CITY	HOME	6 - 2	HENRY 2, HINDLE 2, COYNE & MOULE	2,000
21-Apr	BARNSLEY	AWAY	3 - 1	KNIGHT 2 & O. G. (HARTSON)	3,380
28-Apr	BARNSLEY	HOME	1 - 3	MOULE	4,000
05-May	SHEFFIELD UNITED	AWAY	0 - 6		4,000
12-May	SHEFFIELD UNITED	HOME	4 - 1	MILBURN Jl., HINDLE, WARD & HENRY	4,000
21-May	CHESTERFIELD	AWAY	1 - 6	MORTON	4,000

MATCHES MARKED + WERE IN THE LEAGUE WAR CUP QUALIFYING COMPETITION WHICH ALSO COUNTED TOWARDS THE LEAGUE AND IN WHICH LEEDS UNITED FAILED TO FINISH IN THE TOP 32 TO QUALIFY FOR THE KNOCK - OUT COMPETITION. THE FIRST CHAMPIONSHIP CONSISTED OF 54 TEAMS AND THE SECOND CHAMPIONSHIP 60

LEAGUE AND CUP

APPEARANCES

PLAYER	FIRST LEAGUE	SECOND LEAGUE	TOTAL
AINSLEY / BEAN / BIRCH	10 / 0 / 1	0 / 1 / 0	10 / 1 / 1
BOKAS / BOOTH / BURBANKS	0 / 2 / 7	4 / 0 / 5	4 / 2 / 12
BUTTERWORTH / BYROM / CALVERLEY	17 / 4 / 2	19 / 0 / 0	36 / 4 / 2
CAMPBELL / CHERRY / COYNE	6 / 0 / 12	13 / 1 / 17	19 / 1 / 29
CROOKES / DANIELS / DOWNING	0 / 16 / 0	3 / 11 / 1	3 / 27 / 1
DUNDERDALE / DUTCHMAN / DUTHOIT	0 / 1 / 0	4 / 0 / 4	4 / 1 / 4
FEARNLEY / FORDE / GADSBY	0 / 0 / 6	6 / 2 / 7	6 / 2 / 13
GLEAVE / GLOVER / GOLDBERG	0 / 0 / 0	2 / 1 / 2	2 / 1 / 2
HARDAKER / HARGREAVES / HARPER	2 / 0 / 0	0 / 1 / 1	2 / 1 / 1
HENRY / HINDLE / HODGSON	14 / 17 / 2	17 / 21 / 0	31 / 38 / 2
HOULDERSHAW R / HOWE / HULBERT	0 / 2 / 0	5 / 0 / 1	5 / 2 / 1
JAMES / KIRBY / KNIGHT	1 / 5 / 9	0 / 0 / 10	1 / 5 / 19
McGRAW / MAHON / MILBURN Ja.	8 / 14 / 5	5 / 8 / 9	13 / 22 / 14
MILBURN Jl. / MORTON / MOULE	0 / 0 / 4	1 / 1 / 12	1 / 1 / 16
NORMANTON / PATON / PICKERING	0 / 0 / 2	2 / 4 / 0	2 / 4 / 2
POWELL A / RUECROFT / SHARPLES	0 / 0 / 1	1 / 2 / 0	1 / 2 / 1
SHORT / SHOTTON / STEPHENS J	5 / 0 / 0	4 / 5 / 1	9 / 5 / 1
SUTHERLAND / TWOMEY / WARD	3 / 0 / 0	0 / 5 / 1	3 / 5 / 1
WEAVER / YEOMANSON	11 / 9	16 / 6	27 / 15

GOALSCORERS

PLAYER	FIRST LEAGUE	SECOND LEAGUE	TOTAL
HINDLE	11	15	26
HENRY	7	13	20
AINSLEY	10		10
COYNE	6	3	9
SHORT	6	2	8
MAHON	5	2	7
MOULE	3	4	7
KNIGHT		3	3
BURBANKS		2	2
DUNDERDALE		2	2
MILBURN Ja.	2		2
SUTHERLAND	2		2
WEAVER		2	2
CAMPBELL		1	1
MILBURN Jl.		1	1
MORTON		1	1
WARD		1	1
YEOMANSON	1		1
OWN GOALS		1	1

87

The conflict in Europe may have been officially over but many players would not return for months and numerous grounds were in desperate need of repair. With this in mind, the Football League decided to play regional football for one more season but they did resurrect the FA Cup. Leeds United competed in the Northern Section playing back-to-back encounters in a 22-club league. Again, guest players were utilised.

The opening games brought no joy for United followers. Losing the first five games, there was relief when Dennis Grainger and Gerry Henry scored in a 2-0 win at Everton to open Leeds' account for the season. Henry struck the winner against Preston North End for a 2-1 victory, but each game was followed by heavy defeats, at Bolton Wanderers 6-0 and Preston 8-2. John Short notched the winning goal in a 3-2 win at Burnley and John Dutchman sealed a 4-2 triumph at home to Sunderland, however this latter win was sandwiched between more woe following visits to Manchester United 6-1 and Sunderland 5-1. Leaking goals would unfortunately be the story of Leeds' season.

Dennis Grainger scored Leeds' consolation goal at Sunderland as he did in a 6-2 loss against Sheffield United but he did bring some festive joy when striking the only goal of a Christmas Day clash against Middlesbrough. Bottom of the table, the New Year brought little reprieve for Billy Hampson's charges.

Ainsley had missed the opening two months of the season, but despite United's poor form, had scored on a regular basis and would hit a purple patch during January and early February, scoring in seven consecutive games, including goals in Leeds' forlorn attempt to make progress in the FA Cup. Drawn against Middlesbrough in the third round, Ainsley scored in a thrilling 4-4 draw at Elland Road, before notching a consolation strike in a 7-2 replay defeat, when astonishingly Boro scored all their goals in the first half.

Leeds did manage one victory in this spell, 3-0 against Liverpool, when Henry's brace completed the scoring, but it would herald an 11-match winless spell. The remainder of the season was a drawn out affair of on-going disappointment, the lowest point of a campaign to forget coming when Bradford Park Avenue annihilated Leeds 9-4 prior to a 5-1 loss at Manchester City. Ainsley scored a brace at United's West Yorkshire rivals and repeated his efforts in the final game of the season at Elland Road, but this time he had the satisfaction of completing a 3-2 win against Bradford Park Avenue.

Winning only three games in the second half of the season, a tortuous 42-match campaign was finally over as Leeds finished bottom of the table. United's record of 9 wins, 7 draws and 26 defeats was abysmal. Keeper John Hodgson made the most appearances, missing six games, whilst Ainsley top scored with 22.

1945 - 1946

FOOTBALL LEAGUE - NORTHERN SECTION (FINAL LEAGUE POSITION - 22ND)

PLD 42 W 9 D 7 L 26 F 66 A 118 PTS 25

DATE	OPPONENTS	VENUE	SCORE	SCORERS	ATT.
25-Aug	CHESTERFIELD	AWAY	1 - 3	HINDLE	7,229
01-Sep	CHESTERFIELD	HOME	1 - 3	SHORT	7,339
08-Sep	BARNSLEY	HOME	1 - 2	POWELL A	8,561
13-Sep	STOKE CITY	AWAY	1 - 2	HINDLE	6,882
15-Sep	BARNSLEY	AWAY	2 - 3	HENRY & HINDLE	10,055
22-Sep	EVERTON	AWAY	2 - 0	GRAINGER D & HENRY	19,711
29-Sep	EVERTON	HOME	2 - 3	SHORT & HINDLE	13,541
06-Oct	BOLTON WANDERERS	HOME	2 - 1	GRAINGER D & HINDLE	11,836
13-Oct	BOLTON WANDERERS	AWAY	0 - 6		17,770
20-Oct	PRESTON NORTH END	HOME	2 - 1	DUTCHMAN & HENRY	11,782
27-Oct	PRESTON NORTH END	AWAY	2 - 8	CHEW & HENRY	12,344
03-Nov	BURNLEY	HOME	1 - 2	AINSLEY	11,387
10-Nov	BURNLEY	AWAY	3 - 2	AINSLEY, HENRY & SHORT	6,925
17-Nov	MANCHESTER UNITED	HOME	3 - 3	AINSLEY, SHORT & HENRY	12,013
24-Nov	MANCHESTER UNITED	AWAY	1 - 6	O . G . (WHALLEY)	21,312
01-Dec	SUNDERLAND	HOME	4 - 2	AINSLEY, GRAINGER D, O. G . (STELLING) & DUTCHMAN	9,509
08-Dec	SUNDERLAND	AWAY	1 - 5	GRAINGER D	10,106
15-Dec	SHEFFIELD UNITED	HOME	2 - 4	STEPHENS J & HENRY	10,401
22-Dec	SHEFFIELD UNITED	AWAY	2 - 6	AINSLEY & GRAINGER D	14,926
25-Dec	MIDDLESBROUGH	HOME	1 - 0	GRAINGER D	12,217
26-Dec	MIDDLESBROUGH	AWAY	1 - 4	AINSLEY	23,019
29-Dec	STOKE CITY	HOME	0 - 0		22,219
12-Jan	BLACKPOOL	HOME	1 - 2	AINSLEY	14,372
19-Jan	BLACKPOOL	AWAY	2 - 4	AINSLEY 2	8,734
26-Jan	GRIMSBY TOWN	AWAY	2 - 3	AINSLEY & HENRY	10,105
02-Feb	LIVERPOOL	HOME	3 - 0	HENRY 2 (1 PEN) & AINSLEY	11,881
09-Feb	BURY	HOME	3 - 3	HINDLE 2 & AINSLEY (PEN)	13,474
16-Feb	BURY	AWAY	1 - 3	GRAINGER D	8,623
23-Feb	BLACKBURN ROVERS	AWAY	0 - 0		6,048
02-Mar	BLACKBURN ROVERS	HOME	1 - 4	AINSLEY (PEN)	10,752
09-Mar	GRIMSBY TOWN	HOME	2 - 2	HENRY & HEATON	8,000
16-Mar	BRADFORD PARK AVENUE	AWAY	4 - 9	AINSLEY 2, McGRAW & GRAINGER D	11,302
23-Mar	MANCHESTER CITY	AWAY	1 - 5	HEATON	20,000
30-Mar	MANCHESTER CITY	HOME	1 - 3	PRICE	10,000
06-Apr	NEWCASTLE UNITED	HOME	0 - 3		14,000
10-Apr	LIVERPOOL	AWAY	1 - 1	GRAINGER D	10,620
13-Apr	NEWCASTLE UNITED	AWAY	1 - 1	AINSLEY	25,000
20-Apr	HUDDERSFIELD TOWN	HOME	3 - 2	O. G. (BRIGGS), POWELL A & HEATON	15,000
22-Apr	SHEFFIELD WEDNESDAY	HOME	0 - 1		14,000
23-Apr	SHEFFIELD WEDNESDAY	AWAY	0 - 2		14,000
27-Apr	HUDDERSFIELD TOWN	AWAY	2 - 3	AINSLEY 2	4,622
01-May	BRADFORD PARK AVENUE	HOME	3 - 2	HINDLE & AINSLEY 2	10,000

F. A. CUP

DATE	OPPONENTS	VENUE	SCORE	SCORERS	ATT.
05-Jan	MIDDLESBROUGH (R3-1)	HOME	4 - 4	HENRY, AINSLEY, O. G. (HARDWICK) & SHORT	18,000
09-Jan	MIDDLESBROUGH (R3-2) $	AWAY	2 - 7	GRAINGER D & AINSLEY	23,878

LEAGUE AND CUP
APPEARANCES

PLAYER	LEAGUE	F. A. CUP	TOTAL
AINSLEY / ALBERRY	28 / 1	2 / 0	30 / 1
BARTON / BATEY	4 / 8		4 / 8
BLAIR / BROWNE	1 / 4		1 / 4
BUCKLEY / BURBANKS	1 / 2		1 / 2
BUTTERWORTH F / CHEW	18 / 6	2 / 0	20 / 6
COLLIER / COYNE	2 / 24	0 / 2	2 / 26
CROOKES / DUFFY	1 / 15		1 / 15
DUTCHMAN / DUTHOIT	3 / 17	0 / 2	3 / 19
FEARNLEY / GADSBY	4 / 6	0 / 2	4 / 8
GLACKIN / GOLDBERG	1 / 7		1 / 7
GRAINGER D / HEATON	35 / 19	2 / 0	37 / 19
HENRY / HINDLE	30 / 33	2 / 2	32 / 35
HODGSON J / HOLLEY	36 / 28	2 / 1	38 / 29
HUDSON / ICETON	7 / 2		7 / 2
JONES E / JONES S	1 / 11		1 / 11
KNIGHT / LAIDMAN	6 / 3		6 / 3
LAKING / McGRAW	1 / 5		1 / 5
MILBURN Ja. / MILBURN Ji.	3 / 10		3 / 10
MOULE / OLIVER	3 / 1		3 / 1
PARKER / POGSON	2 / 1		2 / 1
POPE / POWELL A	1 / 12		1 / 12
PRICE / SHORT	21 / 11	1 / 2	22 / 13
SKIDMORE / SMITH	2 / 11		2 / 11
STEPHENS A / STEPHENS J	1 / 11		1 / 11
WALKER / WESTLAKE	1 / 1		1 / 1

GOALSCORERS

PLAYER	LEAGUE	F. A. CUP	TOTAL
AINSLEY	20	2	22
HENRY	11	1	12
GRAINGER D	9	1	10
HINDLE	8		8
SHORT	4	1	5
HEATON	3		3
DUTCHMAN	2		2
POWELL A	2		2
CHEW	1		1
McGRAW	1		1
PRICE	1		1
STEPHENS J	1		1
OWN GOALS	3	1	4

KEY :- $ = LEEDS LOST 6 - 11 ON AGGREGATE

If Leeds United supporters thought the previous campaign was calamitous they were in for a shock. With limited funds, manager Billy Hampson added Con Martin (Glentoran) and Harry Clarke (Darlington) to his squad consisting of ageing stars of the late 1930s such as Tom Holley, David Cochrane, George Ainsley and Aubrey Powell, and promising players like Gerry Henry and John Short, who had made their mark in war games. On paper, Hampson's squad seemed a good blend, but in reality, it would prove a disaster following an opening day 3-2 defeat at Preston North End; Dennis Grainger scoring Leeds' goals.

Initially there was optimism when Leeds thumped Bolton Wanderers 4-0; Short netting a brace, and Huddersfield Town 5-0; Ainsley notching a hat-trick, before edging a win against Grimsby Town courtesy of a Powell strike in consecutive home games. However, heavy defeats were plentiful, notably at Stoke City 5-2, Charlton Athletic 5-0 and Portsmouth 4-1. Powell kept the points coming at Elland Road with goals in victories against Everton 2-1 and Blackpool 4-2 but these would be the last triumphs of the year.

Cochrane earned a draw against Brentford and Sunderland, and scored Leeds' third goal on Christmas Day for a point at home to Middlesbrough. Another scorer for United in the 3-3 draw was Jim Milburn, younger brother of Jack and George. Wounded in Belgium, Jim recovered to continue his Leeds playing career and remarkably, the war years meant that when he played in the opening game of the season, 10 years had elapsed since joining the club. Jim is the club's only player to have his first two appearances separated by seven years!

Leeds' festive period ended with 3-0 defeats against Middlesbrough and Preston. Thereafter the season deteriorated. Hammered 6-2 at Sheffield United, West Brom finished United's FA Cup hopes before Henry and Cochrane conjured a 2-1 win against Chelsea on January 18, a match that would prove to be United's last win of the campaign. In April, former legend Willis Edwards replaced Hampson as manager, but Edwards only managed to improve the player's fitness, not overall results.

The last 17 games would yield two draws with relegation confirmed before the season's conclusion when Everton officially ended Leeds' tenure in Division 1 with a 4-1 defeat, Powell scoring Leeds' final top-flight goal. Finishing 15 points from safety, unwanted records galore were created; least points (18), most defeats (30) and least wins (6). It was a season to forget at Elland Road as Leeds endured their worst season since formation. Tom Holley played in 39 games; Cochrane appeared in 38 whilst Ainsley top scored with 12 goals.

1946 - 1947

DATE	OPPONENTS	VENUE	SCORE	SCORERS	ATT.

DIVISION ONE (FINAL LEAGUE POSITION - 22ND)
PLD 42 W 6 D 6 L 30 F 45 A 90 PTS 18

DATE	OPPONENTS	VENUE	SCORE	SCORERS	ATT.
31-Aug	PRESTON NORTH END	AWAY	2 - 3	GRAINGER D 2	25,311
04-Sep	CHARLTON ATHLETIC	HOME	0 - 2		22,857
07-Sep	SHEFFIELD UNITED	HOME	2 - 2	POWELL A & HENRY	28,543
14-Sep	CHELSEA	AWAY	0 - 3		57,184
16-Sep	STOKE CITY	AWAY	2 - 5	AINSLEY 2	21,141
21-Sep	BOLTON WANDERERS	HOME	4 - 0	COCHRANE D, AINSLEY & SHORT 2	25,739
25-Sep	CHARLTON ATHLETIC	AWAY	0 - 5		16,488
28-Sep	LIVERPOOL	AWAY	0 - 2		51,042
05-Oct	HUDDERSFIELD TOWN	HOME	5 - 0	AINSLEY 3, POWELL A & SHORT	30,622
12-Oct	GRIMSBY TOWN	HOME	1 - 0	POWELL A	28,877
19-Oct	WOLVERHAMPTON WANDERERS	AWAY	0 - 1		40,113
26-Oct	BLACKBURN ROVERS	HOME	0 - 1		28,683
02-Nov	PORTSMOUTH	AWAY	1 - 4	AINSLEY	25,984
09-Nov	EVERTON	HOME	2 - 1	POWELL A & SHORT	22,992
16-Nov	ARSENAL	AWAY	2 - 4	AINSLEY 2	36,377
23-Nov	BLACKPOOL	HOME	4 - 2	POWELL A 2, AINSLEY & GRAINGER D	25,829
30-Nov	BRENTFORD	AWAY	1 - 1	COCHRANE D	20,352
07-Dec	SUNDERLAND	HOME	1 - 1	COCHRANE D	25,784
14-Dec	ASTON VILLA	AWAY	1 - 2	POWELL A	29,410
21-Dec	DERBY COUNTY	HOME	1 - 2	HENRY (PEN)	21,320
25-Dec	MIDDLESBROUGH	HOME	3 - 3	MILBURN JI., SHORT & COCHRANE D	28,742
26-Dec	MIDDLESBROUGH	AWAY	0 - 3		45,336
28-Dec	PRESTON NORTH END	HOME	0 - 3		33,433
04-Jan	SHEFFIELD UNITED	AWAY	2 - 6	COCHRANE D & AINSLEY	31,947
18-Jan	CHELSEA	HOME	2 - 1	HENRY (PEN) & COCHRANE D	37,884
01-Feb	LIVERPOOL	HOME	1 - 2	GRAINGER D	25,430
03-Feb	BOLTON WANDERERS	AWAY	0 - 2		6,278
22-Feb	WOLVERHAMPTON WANDERERS	HOME	0 - 1		30,313
01-Mar	BLACKBURN ROVERS	AWAY	0 - 1		28,371
22-Mar	ARSENAL	HOME	1 - 1	GRAINGER D	32,190
29-Mar	BLACKPOOL	AWAY	0 - 3		14,501
05-Apr	BRENTFORD	HOME	1 - 2	HENRY (PEN)	23,962
07-Apr	MANCHESTER UNITED	AWAY	1 - 3	COCHRANE D	41,912
08-Apr	MANCHESTER UNITED	HOME	0 - 2		15,528
12-Apr	SUNDERLAND	AWAY	0 - 1		30,429
19-Apr	ASTON VILLA	HOME	1 - 1	CLARKE H	22,291
26-Apr	DERBY COUNTY	AWAY	1 - 2	POWELL A	10,994
03-May	STOKE CITY	HOME	1 - 2	SHORT	21,714
10-May	HUDDERSFIELD TOWN	AWAY	0 - 1		20,596
17-May	GRIMSBY TOWN	AWAY	1 - 4	SHORT	10,795
24-May	PORTSMOUTH	HOME	0 - 1		14,097
26-May	EVERTON	AWAY	1 - 4	POWELL A	21,001

F. A. CUP

DATE	OPPONENTS	VENUE	SCORE	SCORERS	ATT.
11-Jan	WEST BROMWICH ALBION (R3)	AWAY	1 - 2	AINSLEY	31,007

LEAGUE AND CUP APPEARANCES

PLAYER	LEAGUE	F. A. CUP	TOTAL
AINSLEY	28	1	29
BANNISTER	23		23
BATEY	8		8
BROWNE B	19		19
BROWNING	1		1
CLARKE H	14		14
COCHRANE D	38	1	39
FEARNLEY	9		9
GADSBY	16	1	17
GOLDBERG	12		12
GRAINGER D	32	1	33
HEATON	14		14
HENRY	36	1	37
HINDLE	11		11
HODGKINSON	1		1
HODGSON J	19		19
HOLLEY	39	1	40
KANE	1		1
MARTIN C	8	1	9
MILBURN JI.	36	1	37
POWELL A	34	1	35
PRICE	6		6
SHORT	32	1	33
TWOMEY	14	1	15
WILLINGHAM	11		11

GOALSCORERS

PLAYER	LEAGUE	F. A. CUP	TOTAL
AINSLEY	11	1	12
POWELL A	9		9
COCHRANE D	7		7
SHORT	7		7
GRAINGER D	5		5
HENRY	4		4
CLARKE H	1		1
MILBURN JI.	1		1

In the clear out that followed relegation during the close season and early months of Leeds' first Division 2 campaign for 16 years, numerous players including strikers George Ainsley and Gerry Henry departed. Ainsley did score two goals in an opening day 3-1 win against Leicester City, but was immediately out of the frame following a 3-0 defeat at Barnsley. Manager Willis Edwards' new signing Albert Wakefield, a guest player during the conflict, made a fine start at centre-forward with the winning goal against Southampton on his league debut and notched a brace as Leeds quickly gained revenge over Barnsley with a 4-1 win at Elland Road.

Inside-forward Aubrey Powell was soon into his stride with a hat-trick in a 5-0 win against Plymouth Argyle and a brace to despatch Coventry City. Attendances had quickly risen with improved results over the first seven games but a crowd of over 37,000 went home disappointed after a 1-0 defeat at the hands of Birmingham in the next home fixture. The loss would become the norm as winter set in, culminating in a 6-1 defeat at Luton Town.

Despite reduced attendances, there was the occasional spark of encouragement from Leeds' strike-force, Wakefield notching a brace in a West Yorkshire derby win over Bradford Park Avenue and Powell matching his teammate in a 2-1 defeat of Millwall, but in the main, Leeds' form was poor. Edwards signed half-back Jim Bullions but following Leeds' exit from the FA Cup after a 4-0 thumping at Blackpool, the Leeds boss reinforced his ranks with the purchase of inside-forward Ken Chisholm. Results immediately improved. Wakefield inspired wins against Newcastle United and Coventry, before Chisholm set the seal on a 3-1 win against West Brom and a 4-0 victory over Cardiff City.

Inconsistency was still dominating results however, but in a season of transition, Edwards captured the signature of half-back Jim McCabe, who would win full honours for Ireland within months of his move to Elland Road. McCabe would prove to be the most enduring of his purchases. Although never quite in danger of relegation, emphatic home wins against Chesterfield 3-0 and Bury 5-1 ended a difficult campaign in style as Leeds finished eighteenth, their lowest placing since formation.

Wakefield, who scored a hat-trick in the Bury clash, top scored with 21 goals, whilst Powell, who notched 10 goals, made the most appearances. Edwards improved fitness levels, but decided to step down to a coaching role, before serving as a scout during the 1950s. Sam Bolton had replaced Eric Clarke as chairman during the season and decided to bring an experienced manager to the club in the shape of Major Frank Buckley, a charismatic personality who had enjoyed tremendous success, especially at Wolves.

1947 - 1948

DIVISION TWO (FINAL LEAGUE POSITION - 18TH)				
PLD 42 W 14 D 8 L 20 F 62 A 72 PTS 36				
DATE	OPPONENTS	VENUE	SCORE SCORERS	ATT.
23-Aug	LEICESTER CITY	HOME	3 - 1 SHORT & AINSLEY 2	26,519
27-Aug	BARNSLEY	AWAY	0 - 3	23,440
30-Aug	SOUTHAMPTON	AWAY	2 - 1 O . G . (SMITH) & WAKEFIELD	21,023
03-Sep	BARNSLEY	HOME	4 - 1 WAKEFIELD 2, SHORT & COCHRANE D	36,501
06-Sep	FULHAM	AWAY	2 - 3 SHORT & WAKEFIELD	26,247
10-Sep	PLYMOUTH ARGYLE	HOME	5 - 0 SHORT, POWELL A 3 & HEATON (PEN)	29,396
13-Sep	COVENTRY CITY	HOME	2 - 1 POWELL A 2	30,462
17-Sep	PLYMOUTH ARGYLE	AWAY	0 - 1	21,126
20-Sep	NEWCASTLE UNITED	AWAY	2 - 4 WAKEFIELD & COCHRANE D	57,275
27-Sep	BIRMINGHAM CITY	HOME	0 - 1	37,135
04-Oct	WEST BROMWICH ALBION	AWAY	2 - 3 HEATON & WAKEFIELD	30,479
11-Oct	DONCASTER ROVERS	HOME	0 - 0	34,775
18-Oct	NOTTINGHAM FOREST	AWAY	0 - 1	22,380
25-Oct	BRADFORD PARK AVENUE	HOME	2 - 0 WAKEFIELD 2	31,532
01-Nov	CARDIFF CITY	AWAY	0 - 0	36,851
08-Nov	SHEFFIELD WEDNESDAY	HOME	2 - 2 WAKEFIELD 2	32,547
15-Nov	TOTTENHAM HOTSPUR	AWAY	1 - 3 COCHRANE D (PEN)	41,563
22-Nov	MILLWALL	HOME	2 - 1 POWELL A 2	24,160
29-Nov	CHESTERFIELD	AWAY	0 - 3	15,501
06-Dec	WEST HAM UNITED	HOME	2 - 1 SHORT & MARTIN C	21,866
13-Dec	BURY	AWAY	1 - 1 WAKEFIELD	13,104
20-Dec	LEICESTER CITY	AWAY	0 - 2	22,252
26-Dec	LUTON TOWN	HOME	0 - 2	28,597
27-Dec	LUTON TOWN	AWAY	1 - 6 COCHRANE D	16,964
03-Jan	SOUTHAMPTON	HOME	0 - 0	23,794
17-Jan	FULHAM	HOME	0 - 1	29,640
24-Jan	NEWCASTLE UNITED	HOME	3 - 1 COCHRANE D & WAKEFIELD 2	30,367
31-Jan	COVENTRY CITY	AWAY	2 - 1 WAKEFIELD 2	22,269
14-Feb	BIRMINGHAM CITY	AWAY	1 - 5 CHISHOLM	39,955
21-Feb	WEST BROMWICH ALBION	HOME	3 - 1 HINDLE, O. G. (PEMBERTON) & CHISHOLM	22,333
28-Feb	DONCASTER ROVERS	AWAY	0 - 3	26,569
06-Mar	NOTTINGHAM FOREST	HOME	2 - 2 POWELL A & WAKEFIELD	27,018
13-Mar	BRADFORD PARK AVENUE	AWAY	1 - 3 POWELL A	21,060
20-Mar	CARDIFF CITY	HOME	4 - 0 CHISHOLM 2, POWELL A & SHORT	34,276
26-Mar	BRENTFORD	AWAY	0 - 3	30,538
27-Mar	SHEFFIELD WEDNESDAY	AWAY	1 - 3 SHORT	38,736
29-Mar	BRENTFORD	HOME	1 - 1 BANNISTER (PEN)	26,775
03-Apr	TOTTENHAM HOTSPUR	HOME	1 - 3 WAKEFIELD	24,891
10-Apr	MILLWALL	AWAY	1 - 1 CHISHOLM	21,426
17-Apr	CHESTERFIELD	HOME	3 - 0 HINDLE, CHISHOLM & WAKEFIELD	28,794
24-Apr	WEST HAM UNITED	AWAY	1 - 2 CHISHOLM	13,594
01-May	BURY	HOME	5 - 1 WAKEFIELD 3 & COCHRANE D 2	17,573
		F. A. CUP		
10-Jan	BLACKPOOL (R3)	AWAY	0 - 4	28,500

LEAGUE AND CUP			
APPEARANCES			
PLAYER	LEAGUE	F. A. CUP	TOTAL
AINSLEY	2		2
BANNISTER	8		8
BULLIONS	24	1	25
CHISHOLM	17		17
COCHRANE D	38	1	39
DUNN	15		15
FEARNLEY	6		6
GADSBY	24	1	25
GRAINGER D	5		5
HEATON	24		24
HENRY	6		6
HINDLE	21	1	22
HODGKINSON	1		1
HODGSON J	1		1
HOLLEY	23	1	24
INGHAM	1		1
KIRBY	8		8
McCABE	10		10
MARTIN C	35	1	36
MILBURN JI.	34	1	35
MORTON	1		1
POWELL A	39	1	40
SHORT	21		21
TWOMEY	35	1	36
WAKEFIELD	37	1	38
WILLINGHAM	24	1	25
WINDLE	2		2

GOALSCORERS			
PLAYER	LEAGUE	F. A. CUP	TOTAL
WAKEFIELD	21		21
POWELL A	10		10
CHISHOLM	7		7
COCHRANE D	7		7
SHORT	7		7
AINSLEY	2		2
HEATON	2		2
HINDLE	2		2
BANNISTER	1		1
MARTIN C	1		1
OWN GOALS	2		2

Major Frank Buckley's arrival resulted in national headlines and he quickly took control on and off the park. Needing to raise finances to rebuild his squad, early casualties were Aubrey Powell and Con Martin. An eccentric, Buckley employed state-of-the-art training techniques such as a 'kicking machine' to sharpen his player's skills. Buckley was a strict disciplinarian and ahead of his time in terms of coaching practices. His players endured arduous training sessions in a bid to reach peak fitness.

Despite his meticulous pre-season preparations, Leeds lost their opening encounter 6-2 at Leicester City. Ken Chisholm scored a consolation, before striking in consecutive wins against Luton Town 2-0, Brentford 3-1 and Coventry City 4-1. Full-back Jim Milburn, who switched flanks to accommodate Jimmy Dunn at right-back, notched a penalty in the win against Brentford and would strike again when Leeds defeated Lincoln City 3-1 and Grimsby Town 6-3 but these would be the only triumphs in a 15-match run.

Convinced his team's inconsistency was partly down to his player's inability to pick out the club strip, Buckley changed Leeds' blue and gold halved shirts to old gold shirts with blue sleeves. Impatient, the Leeds boss continued to reconstruct his mid-table team in spite of being in the middle of a season. The Grimsby clash saw centre-forward Len Browning and wing-half Tommy Burden score. Both would feature prominently in coming seasons, although current form was dire. December generated one win against Leicester but all festive joy was lost with a double defeat to West Ham.

The New Year began badly as Newport County inflicted an embarrassing 3-1 home defeat on Leeds in the FA Cup. Browning was combining well with Albert Wakefield and Chisholm, and found the target in another 4-1 defeat against Coventry. More changes followed as Chisholm, Tom Hindle and John Short made way for Eddie McMorran, Billy Heaton, Ray Iggleden, Billy Rudd and keeper Harry Searson.

At last, results picked up with five home wins and the new-boys contributed. McMorran scored the only goal against Blackburn Rovers; Browning accounted for Chesterfield and struck a brace in four-goal wins against Bradford Park Avenue and Barnsley, whilst Iggleden claimed the points against Nottingham Forest. The final seven games brought a solitary victory against Plymouth Argyle, Browning scoring the winner as Leeds finished two points clear of relegation.

As for other fixtures, a goalless draw at Blackburn did not grab headlines, but marked the debut of a prodigious teenage talent. 16-year-old John Charles bow signalled the end of skipper Tom Holley's career at Elland Road. Holley would become a respected journalist with the *Evening Post* and write many column inches about his successor. Finishing fifteenth, United had endured a difficult season, but Buckley had the makings of a good squad. Milburn was the only ever-present, whilst Browning top-scored with 14 goals.

1948 - 1949

DIVISION TWO (FINAL LEAGUE POSITION - 15TH)				
PLD 42 W 12 D 13 L 17 F 55 A 63 PTS 37				

DATE	OPPONENTS	VENUE	SCORE SCORERS	ATT.
21-Aug	LEICESTER CITY	AWAY	2 - 6	CHISHOLM & SHORT	34,937
25-Aug	BRENTFORD	HOME	0 - 0		26,625
28-Aug	LUTON TOWN	HOME	2 - 0	CHISHOLM 2	25,463
01-Sep	BRENTFORD	AWAY	3 - 1	MILBURN Ji. (PEN), SHORT & CHISHOLM	19,212
04-Sep	COVENTRY CITY	HOME	4 - 1	CHISHOLM 2 & SHORT 2	29,557
08-Sep	TOTTENHAM HOTSPUR	HOME	0 - 0		37,640
11-Sep	SHEFFIELD WEDNESDAY	AWAY	1 - 3	COCHRANE D	31,735
13-Sep	TOTTENHAM HOTSPUR	AWAY	2 - 2	MILBURN Ji. & COCHRANE D	33,793
18-Sep	LINCOLN CITY	HOME	3 - 1	WAKEFIELD, MILBURN Ji. (PEN) & COCHRANE D	33,963
25-Sep	CHESTERFIELD	AWAY	1 - 3	WAKEFIELD	15,150
02-Oct	WEST BROMWICH ALBION	HOME	1 - 3	MARSH	33,706
09-Oct	BRADFORD PARK AVENUE	AWAY	1 - 1	CHISHOLM	25,587
16-Oct	SOUTHAMPTON	HOME	1 - 1	COCHRANE D	34,959
23-Oct	BARNSLEY	AWAY	1 - 1	BROWNING	26,010
30-Oct	GRIMSBY TOWN	HOME	6 - 3	BURDEN 2, MILBURN Ji. (PEN), HEATON, CHISHOLM & BROWNING	33,581
06-Nov	NOTTINGHAM FOREST	AWAY	0 - 0		24,237
13-Nov	FULHAM	HOME	1 - 1	BROWNING	26,240
20-Nov	PLYMOUTH ARGYLE	AWAY	1 - 2	HEATON	24,752
04-Dec	CARDIFF CITY	AWAY	1 - 2	BROWNING	31,973
11-Dec	QUEENS PARK RANGERS	HOME	1 - 2	BURDEN	26,420
18-Dec	LEICESTER CITY	HOME	3 - 1	HEATON 2 & CHISHOLM	22,600
25-Dec	WEST HAM UNITED	AWAY	2 - 3	HOLLEY & BROWNING	20,660
26-Dec	WEST HAM UNITED	HOME	1 - 3	CHISHOLM	32,577
01-Jan	LUTON TOWN	AWAY	0 - 0		15,310
15-Jan	COVENTRY CITY	AWAY	1 - 4	BROWNING	23,670
22-Jan	SHEFFIELD WEDNESDAY	HOME	1 - 1	COCHRANE D	42,053
29-Jan	BLACKBURN ROVERS	HOME	1 - 0	McMORRAN	32,963
05-Feb	LINCOLN CITY	AWAY	0 - 0		18,060
12-Feb	BURY	HOME	0 - 1		27,063
19-Feb	CHESTERFIELD	HOME	1 - 0	BROWNING	29,362
05-Mar	BRADFORD PARK AVENUE	HOME	4 - 2	BROWNING 2, IGGLEDEN & COCHRANE D	22,477
12-Mar	SOUTHAMPTON	AWAY	1 - 2	O. G. (WEBBER)	25,736
19-Mar	BARNSLEY	HOME	4 - 1	MOSS, McMORRAN & BROWNING 2	29,701
26-Mar	GRIMSBY TOWN	AWAY	1 - 5	BROWNING	15,848
02-Apr	NOTTINGHAM FOREST	HOME	1 - 0	IGGLEDEN	23,932
06-Apr	WEST BROMWICH ALBION	AWAY	0 - 1		28,662
09-Apr	FULHAM	AWAY	0 - 1		23,961
16-Apr	PLYMOUTH ARGYLE	HOME	1 - 0	BROWNING	24,326
18-Apr	BURY	AWAY	1 - 3	McMORRAN	15,305
23-Apr	BLACKBURN ROVERS	AWAY	0 - 0		18,873
30-Apr	CARDIFF CITY	HOME	0 - 0		19,945
07-May	QUEENS PARK RANGERS	AWAY	0 - 2		16,730

F. A. CUP				
08-Jan	NEWPORT COUNTY (R3)	HOME	1 - 3	BROWNING	31,500

LEAGUE AND CUP

APPEARANCES

PLAYER	LEAGUE	F. A. CUP	TOTAL
BANNISTER	5		5
BROWNING	24	1	25
BULLIONS	10	1	11
BURDEN	35	1	36
CHARLES	3		3
CHISHOLM	23		23
COCHRANE D	37	1	38
DEPEAR	4	1	5
DUNN	37	1	38
EDWARDS Wa.	2		2
FEARNLEY	13	1	14
HEATON	21	1	22
HINDLE	11		11
HOLLEY	32		32
IGGLEDEN	16		16
INGHAM	1		1
LOMAS	1		1
McADAM	20		20
McCABE	37	1	38
McMORRAN	12		12
MARSH	4	1	5
MARTIN C	4		4
MILBURN Ji.	42	1	43
MOSS	8		8
RUDD	12		12
SEARSON	18		18
SHORT	7		7
TWOMEY	10		10
WAKEFIELD	12		12
WILLIAMS J	1		1

GOALSCORERS

PLAYER	LEAGUE	F. A. CUP	TOTAL
BROWNING	13	1	14
CHISHOLM	10		10
COCHRANE D	6		6
HEATON	4		4
MILBURN Ji.	4		4
SHORT	4		4
BURDEN	3		3
McMORRAN	3		3
IGGLEDEN	2		2
WAKEFIELD	2		2
HOLLEY	1		1
MARSH	1		1
MOSS	1		1
OWN GOALS	1		1

A busy close season at Elland Road brought more tinkering with the first-team pool by Major Frank Buckley. Harold Williams, who starred for Newport County in a shock FA Cup win at Leeds the previous term, joined the ranks, whilst keeper Jim Twomey departed and Frank Dudley traded clubs with Albert Wakefield. Sensing an upturn 31,000 fans attended Leeds' opening clash at home to Queens Park Rangers, where Jim Milburn earned a draw with a penalty, but the initial weeks of United's campaign were disappointing, only one victory coming in 11 games, Len Browning notching the winner at Sheffield United.

Undeterred, Browning and Dudley, in particular, reversed Leeds' fortunes with three consecutive wins. United's strikers saw off Cardiff City before Dudley grabbed the headlines with winning goals against Blackburn Rovers and Brentford. Williams by now had scored his first goal for Leeds in a 1-1 draw with Sheffield Wednesday, before his future Welsh international teammate John Charles, making an impression at centre-half, scored Leeds' winning goal during a 2-1 victory at Plymouth Argyle with a penalty in Milburn's absence. Charles' Leeds goal against Argyle would be the first of many.

The Argyle win in November galvanised Leeds, and set them on a 19-match streak that would go well into the New Year with just a 2-0 loss at Bury prior to Christmas. Although not scoring at will, Browning, Dudley, Williams, David Cochrane and Ray Iggleden all contributed. The run also saw the debut of tough-tackling wing-half Eric Kerfoot to bolster the defensive midfield in Jim McCabe's absence.

The festive period in particular, heralded rich dividends, yielding consecutive league victories against Barnsley, Swansea Town, Tottenham Hotspur, Southampton, Coventry City and Luton Town. The pick was a sensational 3-0 win against champions-elect Tottenham, strikes by Cochrane and Iggleden accounting for the North London giants in front of a capacity home crowd of 50,476.

Leeds' best run since the successful 1931/32 promotion campaign galvanised supporters and was enhanced by an exciting FA Cup run. Making an impression was Williams and the tricky flyer was on target in Leeds' 5-2 romp at Carlisle United, before netting against powerful Division 1 outfit Bolton Wanderers. Given no chance in the replay, Buckley's charges caused a sensational cup shock by winning a thrilling match after extra-time 3-2, Dudley the hero with a second cup brace.

A home draw against Cardiff City attracted 53,000 to Elland Road. Williams, Cochrane and Iggleden secured a comfortable 3-1 win. Cup fever gripped the city during the build up to United's first FA Cup quarter-final clash. Thousands joined a 62,000 Highbury crowd as Leeds went down 1-0 at Arsenal, the top-flight team hanging on in the closing minutes. Unsurprisingly, the loss brought a dip in form, but three wins in the final five games against Grimsby Town, Blackburn and Bury earned a fifth place finish. In a memorable campaign, Charles, Searson, and Burden were ever-present, whilst in a season of few goals Dudley top-scored with 16.

1949 - 1950

DIVISION TWO (FINAL LEAGUE POSITION - 5TH)				
PLD 42 W 17 D 13 L 12 F 54 A 45 PTS 47				
DATE	OPPONENTS	VENUE	SCORE SCORERS	ATT.
20-Aug	QUEENS PARK RANGERS	HOME	1 - 1 MILBURN Ji. (PEN)	31,589
22-Aug	WEST HAM UNITED	AWAY	1 - 3 RUDD	24,728
27-Aug	PRESTON NORTH END	AWAY	1 - 1 BURDEN	31,378
31-Aug	WEST HAM UNITED	HOME	2 - 2 COCHRANE D & DUDLEY	29,732
03-Sep	SWANSEA TOWN	HOME	1 - 2 DUDLEY	29,767
05-Sep	SHEFFIELD UNITED	AWAY	1 - 0 BROWNING	22,126
10-Sep	TOTTENHAM HOTSPUR	AWAY	0 - 2	48,274
14-Sep	SHEFFIELD UNITED	HOME	0 - 1	23,199
17-Sep	SOUTHAMPTON	AWAY	1 - 2 HARRISON P	23,214
24-Sep	COVENTRY CITY	HOME	3 - 3 McMORRAN, DUDLEY & COCHRANE D	22,590
01-Oct	LUTON TOWN	AWAY	0 - 1	15,291
08-Oct	CARDIFF CITY	HOME	2 - 0 DUDLEY & BROWNING	25,523
15-Oct	BLACKBURN ROVERS	AWAY	1 - 0 DUDLEY	22,038
22-Oct	BRENTFORD	HOME	1 - 0 DUDLEY	27,342
29-Oct	HULL CITY	AWAY	0 - 1	47,638
05-Nov	SHEFFIELD WEDNESDAY	HOME	1 - 1 WILLIAMS H	33,733
12-Nov	PLYMOUTH ARGYLE	AWAY	2 - 1 FROST & CHARLES (PEN)	21,923
19-Nov	CHESTERFIELD	HOME	0 - 0	24,409
26-Nov	BRADFORD PARK AVENUE	AWAY	2 - 1 DUDLEY & FROST	18,401
03-Dec	LEICESTER CITY	HOME	1 - 1 HARRISON P	26,768
10-Dec	BURY	AWAY	0 - 2	13,381
17-Dec	QUEENS PARK RANGERS	AWAY	1 - 1 DUDLEY	13,256
24-Dec	PRESTON NORTH END	HOME	3 - 1 BROWNING, DUDLEY & O. G. (QUIGLEY)	41,303
26-Dec	BARNSLEY	AWAY	1 - 1 MILBURN Ji.	27,017
27-Dec	BARNSLEY	HOME	1 - 0 WILLIAMS H	47,817
31-Dec	SWANSEA TOWN	AWAY	2 - 1 WILLIAMS H & BROWNING	23,192
14-Jan	TOTTENHAM HOTSPUR	HOME	3 - 0 COCHRANE D 2 & IGGLEDEN	50,476
21-Jan	SOUTHAMPTON	HOME	1 - 0 WILLIAMS H	38,646
04-Feb	COVENTRY CITY	AWAY	4 - 0 WILLIAMS H 2, IGGLEDEN & BROWNING	22,990
18-Feb	LUTON TOWN	HOME	2 - 1 BROWNING & IGGLEDEN	37,263
25-Feb	CARDIFF CITY	AWAY	0 - 1	28,423
11-Mar	BRENTFORD	AWAY	0 - 0	22,231
18-Mar	HULL CITY	HOME	3 - 0 WILLIAMS H, McMORRAN & MILBURN Ji. (PEN)	49,465
25-Mar	SHEFFIELD WEDNESDAY	AWAY	2 - 5 BROWNING & WILLIAMS H	50,485
01-Apr	BRADFORD PARK AVENUE	HOME	0 - 0	31,062
07-Apr	GRIMSBY TOWN	AWAY	0 - 2	22,511
08-Apr	LEICESTER CITY	AWAY	1 - 1 McMORRAN	33,881
10-Apr	GRIMSBY TOWN	HOME	1 - 0 MILBURN Ji. (PEN)	17,991
15-Apr	PLYMOUTH ARGYLE	HOME	1 - 1 WILLIAMS H	24,132
22-Apr	CHESTERFIELD	AWAY	1 - 3 DUDLEY	11,346
26-Apr	BLACKBURN ROVERS	HOME	2 - 1 DUNN & WILLIAMS H	12,538
29-Apr	BURY	HOME	4 - 1 DUDLEY 2, MOSS & COCHRANE D	8,913

F. A. CUP				
07-Jan	CARLISLE UNITED (R3)	AWAY	5 - 2 BROWNING, DUDLEY 2, WILLIAMS H & COCHRANE D	22,832
28-Jan	BOLTON WANDERERS (R4)	HOME	1 - 1 WILLIAMS H	51,488
01-Feb	BOLTON WANDERERS (R4R) *	AWAY	3 - 2 DUDLEY 2 & BROWNING	29,440
11-Feb	CARDIFF CITY (R5)	HOME	3 - 1 WILLIAMS H, COCHRANE D & IGGLEDEN	53,099
04-Mar	ARSENAL (R6)	AWAY	0 - 1	62,573

LEAGUE AND CUP

APPEARANCES

PLAYER	LEAGUE	F. A. CUP	TOTAL
BANNISTER	8		8
BROWNING	29	5	34
BULLIONS	1		1
BURDEN	42	5	47
CASEY To.	4		4
CHARLES	42	5	47
COCHRANE D	29	5	34
DUDLEY	38	5	43
DUNN	40	5	45
FROST	9		9
HARRISON P	4		4
HARRISON R	2		2
HILTON	1		1
IGGLEDEN	16	3	19
INGHAM	1		1
KERFOOT	9		9
McADAM	4		4
McCABE	27	5	32
McMORRAN	26	2	28
MILBURN Ji.	36	5	41
MOSS	8		8
RUDD	6		6
SEARSON	42	5	47
TAYLOR F	3		3
WILKINS	3		3
WILLIAMS H	32	5	37

GOALSCORERS

PLAYER	LEAGUE	F. A. CUP	TOTAL
DUDLEY	12	4	16
WILLIAMS H	10	3	13
BROWNING	7	2	9
COCHRANE D	5	2	7
IGGLEDEN	3	1	4
MILBURN Ji.	4		4
McMORRAN	3		3
FROST	2		2
HARRISON P	2		2
BURDEN	1		1
CHARLES	1		1
DUNN	1		1
MOSS	1		1
RUDD	1		1
OWN GOALS	1		1

KEY :- * = AFTER EXTRA TIME

One of the pre-season promotion favourites, Buckley's solid-looking team had a question mark over whether the attack had sufficient cutting edge but his charges began the campaign in fine style winning three of their opening four encounters. Frank Dudley's brace at home to Doncaster Rovers inspired a 3-1 win in front of over 40,000 spectators, before Harold Williams and skipper Tommy Burden earned a hard-fought 2-1 victory at Brentford. Len Browning, who also scored in the Rovers triumph, found the net again to settle a 1-0 win against Coventry City, but his next meaningful strike would not come until the end of September after a poor run with a 2-1 victory against Luton Town.

Struggling for rhythm, it would take another dozen matches for Leeds to double their 'win' total. Dudley marked the occasion with a hat-trick in a 5-1 rout against Leicester City, Williams and Burden also scoring. The Leeds skipper notched again to complete a 3-0 win over Birmingham City at the start of December prior to a thrilling 4-4 draw at Doncaster when Peter Harrison netted twice for United. Also finding the mark were Dudley and Browning. Dudley sent Leeds fans home happy in the festive build-up with the winner against Brentford, but the inconsistency that had afflicted Buckley's team to date returned at West Ham on Christmas Day with a 3-1 loss before Leeds' topsy-turvy season got back on track with a 2-0 Boxing Day win against the Hammers.

Browning's brace acted as a catalyst and finally kick-started United's season with six league wins in seven games. The powerful centre-forward plundered a hat-trick to crush Southampton 5-3 before notching winning strikes against Sheffield United and Luton Town. Another scorer against the Hatters was Ernie Stevenson, a mid-term exchange signing from the Saints; Dudley moving in the opposite direction, and the inside-left would complete Leeds' whirlwind run of form with the only goal at Bury. United's FA Cup sojourn did not hit the previous season's dizzy heights, Manchester United ending Leeds hopes with a thumping 4-0 win at Old Trafford, and any hopes of a late promotion charge were dashed when Buckley's team suffered four defeats, the worst a 4-1 drubbing at title-contenders Manchester City.

The Maine Road clash however, was significant in that Buckley played his colossus of a defender John Charles for the first time as an emergency centre-forward with Browning injured. The change came in an unbeaten seven-match spell during the run-in and included six victories. Charles was a natural, notching a brace in a 3-0 win over Hull City and the winner against Grimsby Town in his three games leading the line. Also playing the emergency striking role was Burden who scored two in a four-game stint to defeat Leicester 2-1, whilst Ray Iggleden struck opening goals in 2-0 wins against Cardiff City and Swansea Town, a match that saw a scoring return from Browning. His strike made him top marksman with 20 goals but it had been a frustrating campaign. Stalwart defender Jim Milburn was the only ever-present.

1950 - 1951

DIVISION TWO (FINAL LEAGUE POSITION - 5TH)

PLD 42 W 20 D 8 L 14 F 63 A 55 PTS 48

DATE	OPPONENTS	VENUE	SCORE	SCORERS	ATT.
19-Aug	DONCASTER ROVERS	HOME	3 - 1	DUDLEY 2 & BROWNING	40,208
21-Aug	COVENTRY CITY	AWAY	0 - 1		30,213
26-Aug	BRENTFORD	AWAY	2 - 1	WILLIAMS H & BURDEN	20,381
30-Aug	COVENTRY CITY	HOME	1 - 0	BROWNING	28,938
02-Sep	BLACKBURN ROVERS	HOME	0 - 1		32,799
07-Sep	SWANSEA TOWN	AWAY	2 - 4	DUDLEY & BROWNING	19,501
09-Sep	SOUTHAMPTON	AWAY	0 - 2		25,806
16-Sep	BARNSLEY	HOME	2 - 2	BROWNING & WILLIAMS H	37,633
23-Sep	SHEFFIELD UNITED	AWAY	2 - 2	DUDLEY & HUGHES C	28,872
30-Sep	LUTON TOWN	HOME	2 - 1	DUDLEY & BROWNING	21,209
07-Oct	BURY	HOME	1 - 1	WILLIAMS H	28,859
14-Oct	PRESTON NORTH END	AWAY	0 - 2		35,578
21-Oct	CHESTERFIELD	HOME	2 - 0	BROWNING & IGGLEDEN	23,032
28-Oct	QUEENS PARK RANGERS	AWAY	0 - 3		15,935
04-Nov	MANCHESTER CITY	HOME	1 - 1	DUDLEY	30,764
11-Nov	LEICESTER CITY	AWAY	5 - 1	BURDEN, DUDLEY 3 & WILLIAMS H	26,573
18-Nov	NOTTS COUNTY	HOME	0 - 1		29,728
25-Nov	GRIMSBY TOWN	AWAY	2 - 2	BROWNING 2	15,561
02-Dec	BIRMINGHAM CITY	HOME	3 - 0	MILBURN JI., BROWNING & BURDEN	23,355
09-Dec	CARDIFF CITY	AWAY	0 - 1		23,716
16-Dec	DONCASTER ROVERS	AWAY	4 - 4	HARRISON P 2, DUDLEY & BROWNING	16,745
23-Dec	BRENTFORD	HOME	1 - 0	DUDLEY	19,839
25-Dec	WEST HAM UNITED	AWAY	1 - 3	HARRISON P	19,519
26-Dec	WEST HAM UNITED	HOME	2 - 0	BROWNING 2	33,162
13-Jan	SOUTHAMPTON	HOME	5 - 3	WILLIAMS H, BROWNING 3 & BURDEN	29,253
20-Jan	BARNSLEY	AWAY	2 - 1	MILBURN JI. (PEN) & O. G. (GLOVER)	21,967
03-Feb	SHEFFIELD UNITED	HOME	1 - 0	BROWNING	28,438
10-Feb	BLACKBURN ROVERS	AWAY	1 - 2	HARRISON P	25,496
17-Feb	LUTON TOWN	AWAY	3 - 2	IGGLEDEN, STEVENSON E & BROWNING	13,323
24-Feb	BURY	AWAY	1 - 0	STEVENSON E	13,517
03-Mar	PRESTON NORTH END	HOME	0 - 3		42,114
10-Mar	CHESTERFIELD	AWAY	0 - 1		9,856
17-Mar	QUEENS PARK RANGERS	HOME	2 - 2	MILBURN JI. & BROWNING	18,094
23-Mar	HULL CITY	AWAY	0 - 2		46,701
24-Mar	MANCHESTER CITY	AWAY	1 - 4	HARRISON P	35,149
26-Mar	HULL CITY	HOME	3 - 0	CHARLES 2 & STEVENSON E	27,887
31-Mar	LEICESTER CITY	HOME	2 - 1	BURDEN 2	14,397
07-Apr	NOTTS COUNTY	AWAY	0 - 0		23,466
14-Apr	GRIMSBY TOWN	HOME	1 - 0	CHARLES	15,524
21-Apr	BIRMINGHAM CITY	AWAY	1 - 0	STEVENSON E	23,809
28-Apr	CARDIFF CITY	HOME	2 - 0	IGGLEDEN & O. G. (HOLLYMAN)	14,765
05-May	SWANSEA TOWN	HOME	2 - 0	IGGLEDEN & BROWNING	11,213

F. A. CUP

DATE	OPPONENTS	VENUE	SCORE	SCORERS	ATT.
06-Jan	MIDDLESBROUGH (R3)	HOME	1 - 0	BROWNING	45,583
27-Jan	MANCHESTER UNITED (R4)	AWAY	0 - 4		55,434

LEAGUE AND CUP
APPEARANCES

PLAYER	LEAGUE	F. A. CUP	TOTAL
BROWNING	34	2	36
BURDEN	39	2	41
CHARLES	34	2	36
COCHRANE D	2		2
DUDLEY	26	2	28
DUNN	40	2	42
FROST	1		1
HAIR	2		2
HARRISON P	30	2	32
HUGHES C	11		11
IGGLEDEN	23	1	24
KERFOOT	31		31
KIRK	9		9
McCABE	28	2	30
McNEISH	1		1
MILBURN JI.	42	2	44
MILLER	9	1	10
MOSS	7		7
SCOTT	17		17
SEARSON	25	2	27
STEVENSON E	13		13
VICKERS	2		2
WILLIAMS H	36	2	38

GOALSCORERS

PLAYER	LEAGUE	F. A. CUP	TOTAL
BROWNING	19	1	20
DUDLEY	11		11
BURDEN	6		6
HARRISON P	5		5
WILLIAMS H	5		5
IGGLEDEN	4		4
STEVENSON E	4		4
CHARLES	3		3
MILBURN JI.	3		3
HUGHES C	1		1
OWN GOALS	2		2

LEEDS ALSO PLAYED IN TWO FESTIVAL OF BRITAIN MATCHES :- 1) - MAY 9TH 1951 VS. RAPID VIENNA AT HOME 2 - 2 (1 - 0) - ATTENDANCE 18,000. THE GOALSCORERS WERE IGGLEDEN & HUGHES. THE TEAM WAS SEARSON, DUNN, MILBURN JI., McCABE, KIRK, BURDEN, HARRISON, IGGLEDEN, CHARLES, HUGHES & WILLIAMS. 2) - MAY 14TH 1951 VS. F. C. HAARLEM AT HOME 2 - 0 (1 - 0) - ATTENDANCE WAS 9,362. THE GOALSCORERS WERE MILLER & HARRISON. THE TEAM WAS SCOTT, ROSS, HAIR, KERFOOT, CHARLES, BURDEN, HARRISON, MILLER, BROWNING, HUGHES & WILLIAMS

Although promotion candidates, for all Len Browning and Ray Iggleden's endeavour, Major Frank Buckley's attack, was not prolific, and with John Charles on National Service, Buckley's options in attack and defence was limited. Starting with Roy Kirk at centre-half, Browning earned a draw against Brentford, before scoring a brace in Leeds' 3-2 victory against Sheffield Wednesday, but three wins in 12 games was not promotion form. In need of inspiration, Iggledon scored back-to-back braces in a 4-2 defeat at Rotherham and a 3-1 win against Sheffield United. A consolation strike by Iggleden in a 3-1 reverse at Barnsley coincided with Buckley, somewhat surprisingly, accepting an offer from Sheffield United for Browning, resulting in a search for a centre-forward.

Suddenly, Leeds claimed four consecutive wins. Iggleden extended his scoring spree to six games in victories against Hull City 2-0, Blackburn Rovers 3-2 and Queens Park Rangers 3-0, and immediately making an impact in attack was Frank Fidler, after Buckley discarded Ron Barritt. Following a debut strike at Blackburn and a goal against Rangers, Fidler made it three in three outings with an opening goal at Notts County, Eric Kerfoot grabbing the winner for a 2-1 win. Combining with Iggleden, the pair found the target in a 2-1 victory at Bury. Six wins in eight games was impressive and with Charles back from duty and Grenville Hair settled at left-back, confidence was high, but the festive build up would yield just two draws.

Christmas Day though, would bring an upturn in fortunes as Iggleden and Mills secured a 2-1 triumph at Leicester City and a Fidler brace ensured no Boxing Day blues in the return with Leicester. Unfortunately, for Fidler, a goal and an injury in a 1-1 draw with Southampton would mean a spell out, but for Leeds, the New Year would bring glad tidings with one reverse before March. With Fidler out, Buckley weighed up his options. Charles stayed in defence, whilst Jim Milburn slotted in as emergency striker, and again, Buckley's eye for a partnership brought immediate dividends when, following Iggleden's brace in a 2-1 win at Sheffield Wednesday, Iggledon and Milburn secured home wins against West Ham 3-1 and Rotherham 3-0.

Notching Leeds' second goal against the Hammers was Kirk, who bizarrely kick started another cup campaign with both goals in United's 2-0 win at Rochdale. Milburn and Iggleden earned a fourth round victory against Bradford City before the second 50,000 plus gate at Elland Road in three weeks witnessed an enthralling 1-1 draw with Chelsea, Milburn scoring Leeds' goal. The replay at Stamford Bridge attracted a near 61,000 crowd, Kirk playing at centre-forward and scoring in another 1-1 draw, but the replay saw the Londoners romp to a 5-1 win.

FA Cup elimination brought patchy form and more striker changes with Milburn, Barritt, Kirk, Charles and Fidler wearing the number nine shirt as the final months of the season yielded five home wins in 12 games. Don Mills strikes accounted for Barnsley and Bury, Iggleden settled a tight encounter with Blackburn, Barritt notched his only goal against Notts County and Fidler set the seal on superb home form with a 3-1 win against Coventry City. In a season of change, sixth place was creditable. Iggleden missed one game and top scored with 20 goals.

1951 - 1952

DIVISION TWO (FINAL LEAGUE POSITION - 6TH)

PLD 42 W 18 D 11 L 13 F 59 A 57 PTS 47

DATE	OPPONENTS	VENUE	SCORE	SCORERS	ATT.
18-Aug	BRENTFORD	HOME	1 - 1	BROWNING	20,268
22-Aug	BIRMINGHAM CITY	AWAY	1 - 1	STEVENSON E	17,081
25-Aug	DONCASTER ROVERS	AWAY	0 - 2		22,222
29-Aug	BIRMINGHAM CITY	HOME	1 - 1	IGGLEDEN	15,098
01-Sep	EVERTON	HOME	1 - 2	MILLER	16,873
08-Sep	SOUTHAMPTON	AWAY	0 - 0		19,682
12-Sep	CARDIFF CITY	HOME	2 - 1	HUGHES C & MILBURN Ji.	12,860
15-Sep	SHEFFIELD WEDNESDAY	HOME	3 - 2	BROWNING 2 & TYRER	20,016
22-Sep	WEST HAM UNITED	AWAY	0 - 2		19,464
29-Sep	ROTHERHAM UNITED	AWAY	2 - 4	IGGLEDEN 2	21,352
06-Oct	SHEFFIELD UNITED	HOME	3 - 1	IGGLEDEN 2 & MILLS Do.	26,915
13-Oct	BARNSLEY	AWAY	1 - 3	IGGLEDEN	15,565
20-Oct	HULL CITY	HOME	2 - 0	IGGLEDEN & HARRISON P	24,656
27-Oct	BLACKBURN ROVERS	AWAY	3 - 2	HARRISON P, FIDLER & IGGLEDEN	20,631
03-Nov	QUEENS PARK RANGERS	HOME	3 - 0	IGGLEDEN, FIDLER & WILLIAMS H	22,875
10-Nov	NOTTS COUNTY	AWAY	2 - 1	FIDLER & KERFOOT	25,307
17-Nov	LUTON TOWN	HOME	1 - 1	IGGLEDEN	27,405
24-Nov	BURY	AWAY	2 - 1	FIDLER & IGGLEDEN	11,836
01-Dec	SWANSEA TOWN	HOME	1 - 1	MILLS Do.	26,235
08-Dec	COVENTRY CITY	AWAY	2 - 4	WILLIAMS H & KERFOOT	14,621
15-Dec	BRENTFORD	AWAY	1 - 2	MILLS Do.	17,957
22-Dec	DONCASTER ROVERS	HOME	0 - 0		21,793
25-Dec	LEICESTER CITY	AWAY	2 - 1	IGGLEDEN & MILLS Do.	24,498
26-Dec	LEICESTER CITY	HOME	2 - 1	FIDLER 2	29,422
29-Dec	EVERTON	AWAY	0 - 2		37,616
05-Jan	SOUTHAMPTON	HOME	1 - 1	FIDLER	25,319
19-Jan	SHEFFIELD WEDNESDAY	AWAY	2 - 1	IGGLEDEN 2	42,354
26-Jan	WEST HAM UNITED	HOME	3 - 1	MILBURN Ji., KIRK & IGGLEDEN	32,297
09-Feb	ROTHERHAM UNITED	HOME	3 - 0	STEWART J, MILBURN Ji. & IGGLEDEN	47,985
16-Feb	SHEFFIELD UNITED	AWAY	0 - 3		36,265
01-Mar	BARNSLEY	HOME	1 - 0	MILLS Do.	32,221
08-Mar	HULL CITY	AWAY	2 - 3	STEWART J & WILLIAMS H	28,767
15-Mar	BLACKBURN ROVERS	HOME	1 - 0	IGGLEDEN	29,226
22-Mar	QUEENS PARK RANGERS	AWAY	0 - 0		15,195
29-Mar	NOTTS COUNTY	HOME	1 - 0	BARRITT	12,867
05-Apr	LUTON TOWN	AWAY	1 - 2	IGGLEDEN	11,460
11-Apr	NOTTINGHAM FOREST	AWAY	1 - 1	WILLIAMS H	28,808
12-Apr	BURY	HOME	2 - 1	MILLS Do. 2	23,004
14-Apr	NOTTINGHAM FOREST	HOME	0 - 0		26,511
19-Apr	SWANSEA TOWN	AWAY	1 - 4	WILLIAMS H	18,206
26-Apr	COVENTRY CITY	HOME	3 - 1	O. G. (DORMAN), KERFOOT & FIDLER	16,322
03-May	CARDIFF CITY	AWAY	1 - 3	IGGLEDEN	45,925

F. A. CUP

DATE	OPPONENTS	VENUE	SCORE	SCORERS	ATT.
12-Jan	ROCHDALE (R3)	AWAY	2 - 0	KIRK 2	21,475
02-Feb	BRADFORD CITY (R4)	HOME	2 - 0	MILBURN Ji. & IGGLEDEN	50,645
23-Feb	CHELSEA (R5)	HOME	1 - 1	MILBURN Ji.	52,328
27-Feb	CHELSEA (R5R) *	AWAY	1 - 1	KIRK	60,851
03-Mar	CHELSEA (R52R) +	NEUTRAL	1 - 5	MILLS Do.	30,504

LEAGUE AND CUP

APPEARANCES

PLAYER	LEAGUE	F. A. CUP	TOTAL
BARRITT	6		6
BROWNING	9		9
BURDEN	40	5	45
CHARLES	18	5	23
DUNN	36	5	41
FIDLER	17	1	18
FINLAY	1		1
HAIR	27	5	32
HARRISON P	31		31
HUDSON	4		4
HUGHES C	10	2	12
IGGLEDEN	41	5	46
KERFOOT	34	5	39
KIRK	25	5	30
McCABE	14		14
MILBURN Ji.	17	2	19
MILLER	4		4
MILLS Do.	25	3	28
MOLLATT	4		4
ROSS	5		5
SCOTT	12		12
SEARSON	19	5	24
STEVENSON E	3		3
STEWART J	7	2	9
TAYLOR J	11		11
TYRER	5		5
WILLIAMS H	37	5	42

GOALSCORERS

PLAYER	LEAGUE	F. A. CUP	TOTAL
IGGLEDEN	19	1	20
FIDLER	8		8
MILLS Do.	7	1	8
MILBURN Ji.	3	2	5
WILLIAMS H	5		5
KIRK	1	3	4
BROWNING	3		3
KERFOOT	3		3
HARRISON P	2		2
STEWART J	2		2
BARRITT	1		1
HUGHES C	1		1
MILLER	1		1
STEVENSON E	1		1
TYRER	1		1
OWN GOALS	1		1

KEY :- + = PLAYED AT VILLA PARK, BIRMINGHAM. * = AFTER EXTRA TIME

Leeds United began the season with high hopes, but Major Frank Buckley was desperate for a prolific leader of the line. In the opening 12 games Don Mills, Frank Fidler, Barry Smith and Ken Hastie all failed to shine at centre-forward; the quartet netting four goals. Just two victories against Bury and Fulham confirmed Buckley's view that the time was right to move John Charles from centre-half to centre-forward. With Jim McCabe taking over at centre-half and new signings Albert Nightingale and George Meek charged with creating opportunities, Buckley's decision would have a stunning effect and change the course of Charles' career.

A complete natural, Charles plundered 14 goals in nine games. His opening strike came in a 4-1 win against Barnsley, before he scored all Leeds' goals in a five-match spell against Lincoln City 1-1, Hull City 3-1, Blackburn Rovers 1-1, Everton 2-2 and Brentford 3-2. Against his hometown team Swansea Town, Charles notched a brace as Leeds claimed a 5-1 win; Nightingale and Ray Iggleden completing the rout, whilst another strike claimed a 2-1 win over Huddersfield Town.

Following Leeds' opening goal in a 2-2 draw against Luton Town, Charles struck again in an early FA Cup exit at Brentford before claiming a third hat-trick of the season to destroy Rotherham 4-0. Somewhat unfairly, sportswriters dubbed the club 'Charles United' but their summation was difficult to argue against due to his impact. Back-to-back braces quickly came against West Ham 3-2 and Leicester City 3-3, taking his tally to an amazing 24 goals in just 17 games.

One win during a seven-game lean spell ended any hopes of a late surge for promotion but it was unrealistic to expect Leeds' rookie striker to keep on scoring at the rate he had set. Buckley's latest signing's, Nightingale and Meek, were certainly impressing and finding the net on occasion. Meek notched a brace to defeat Lincoln 2-1 while Nightingale scored both during a 2-2 draw at Southampton. However, there was no denying that the man of moment, now a full Welsh international, was Charles, and after a couple of games out through injury Charles returned with a goal in a 3-2 loss at Swansea, before completing a remarkable opening season as a striker with two more goals in an exciting 3-3 draw at Brentford.

Under 13,000 home supporters witnessed the ending of Leeds' campaign as Tommy Burden and Eric Kerfoot struck to defeat Nottingham Forest before a Kerfoot strike earned a draw with Doncaster, a clash that saw the debut of rookie defender Jack Charlton. Leeds' tenth place finish would be the end for Major Buckley. His tenure brought stability, but not the promotion he craved. Buckley's legacy was the basis of a team ready to challenge for promotion, but above all, Buckley discovered the prodigious talent of Charles and his long-term replacement at centre-half, Charlton. John Scott, Jimmy Dunn and Burden played in every game, whilst Grenville Hair and Charles missed just two games. Charles top scored with 27 goals, the highest total since Tom Jennings struck 37 in 1926/27.

1952 - 1953

				DIVISION TWO (FINAL LEAGUE POSITION - 10TH)	
				PLD 42 W 14 D 15 L 13 F 71 A 63 PTS 43	
DATE	OPPONENTS	VENUE	SCORE	SCORERS	ATT.
23-Aug	HUDDERSFIELD TOWN	AWAY	0 - 1		35,230
28-Aug	BURY	AWAY	2 - 2	IGGLEDEN & LANGLEY	12,274
30-Aug	PLYMOUTH ARGYLE	HOME	1 - 1	O. G. (RUNDLE)	25,067
03-Sep	BURY	HOME	2 - 0	IGGLEDEN & LANGLEY	14,623
06-Sep	ROTHERHAM UNITED	AWAY	1 - 3	IGGLEDEN	14,900
10-Sep	BIRMINGHAM CITY	HOME	0 - 1		14,133
13-Sep	FULHAM	HOME	2 - 0	SMITH B & MILLS Do.	18,371
17-Sep	BIRMINGHAM CITY	AWAY	2 - 2	HASTIE 2	18,371
20-Sep	WEST HAM UNITED	AWAY	2 - 2	IGGLEDEN & TYRER	22,437
24-Sep	SOUTHAMPTON	HOME	1 - 1	IGGLEDEN	13,299
27-Sep	LEICESTER CITY	HOME	0 - 1		19,724
04-Oct	NOTTS COUNTY	AWAY	2 - 3	IGGLEDEN & O. G. (SOUTHWELL)	22,836
11-Oct	SHEFFIELD UNITED	AWAY	1 - 2	NIGHTINGALE	33,683
18-Oct	BARNSLEY	HOME	4 - 1	NIGHTINGALE 2, CHARLES & MILLS Do.	22,155
25-Oct	LINCOLN CITY	AWAY	1 - 1	CHARLES	15,491
01-Nov	HULL CITY	HOME	3 - 1	CHARLES 3	25,538
08-Nov	BLACKBURN ROVERS	AWAY	1 - 1	CHARLES	22,510
22-Nov	EVERTON	AWAY	2 - 2	CHARLES 2	28,664
29-Nov	BRENTFORD	HOME	3 - 2	CHARLES 3	16,077
06-Dec	DONCASTER ROVERS	AWAY	0 - 0		15,744
13-Dec	SWANSEA TOWN	HOME	5 - 1	CHARLES 2 (1 PEN), NIGHTINGALE & IGGLEDEN 2	21,065
20-Dec	HUDDERSFIELD TOWN	HOME	2 - 1	IGGLEDEN & CHARLES	34,365
26-Dec	LUTON TOWN	AWAY	0 - 2		19,480
27-Dec	LUTON TOWN	HOME	2 - 2	CHARLES & LANGLEY	31,634
03-Jan	PLYMOUTH ARGYLE	AWAY	1 - 0	IGGLEDEN	22,146
17-Jan	ROTHERHAM UNITED	HOME	4 - 0	CHARLES 3 & NIGHTINGALE	24,048
24-Jan	FULHAM	AWAY	1 - 2	TYRER	21,210
07-Feb	WEST HAM UNITED	HOME	3 - 2	IGGLEDEN & CHARLES 2	17,680
14-Feb	LEICESTER CITY	AWAY	3 - 3	MEEK & CHARLES 2	21,754
21-Feb	NOTTS COUNTY	HOME	3 - 1	BURDEN, IGGLEDEN & McCALL	22,922
28-Feb	SHEFFIELD UNITED	HOME	0 - 3		39,858
07-Mar	BARNSLEY	AWAY	2 - 2	CHARLES & McCALL	11,536
14-Mar	LINCOLN CITY	HOME	2 - 1	MEEK 2	18,293
21-Mar	HULL CITY	AWAY	0 - 1		25,387
28-Mar	BLACKBURN ROVERS	HOME	0 - 3		10,644
04-Apr	NOTTINGHAM FOREST	AWAY	1 - 2	NIGHTINGALE	18,734
06-Apr	SOUTHAMPTON	AWAY	2 - 2	NIGHTINGALE 2	17,704
11-Apr	EVERTON	HOME	2 - 0	FORREST & MEEK	15,363
16-Apr	SWANSEA TOWN	AWAY	2 - 3	MEEK & CHARLES	21,262
18-Apr	BRENTFORD	AWAY	3 - 3	CHARLES 2 & FORREST	12,783
22-Apr	NOTTINGHAM FOREST	HOME	2 - 1	BURDEN & KERFOOT	11,497
25-Apr	DONCASTER ROVERS	HOME	1 - 1	KERFOOT	12,715
			F. A. CUP		
10-Jan	BRENTFORD (R3)	AWAY	1 - 2	CHARLES	26,570

LEAGUE AND CUP

APPEARANCES

PLAYER	LEAGUE	F. A. CUP	TOTAL
BURDEN	42	1	43
CHARLES	40	1	41
CHARLTON	1		1
DUNN	42	1	43
FIDLER	5		5
FORREST	6		6
HAIR	40	1	41
HASTIE	4		4
IGGLEDEN	38	1	39
KERFOOT	39	1	40
LANGLEY	9		9
MARSDEN	7		7
McCABE	22	1	23
McCALL	16		16
MEEK	28	1	29
MILLS Do.	9		9
MOLLATT	3		3
NIGHTINGALE	26	1	27
SCOTT	42	1	43
SMITH B	2		2
STEWART J	2		2
TYRER	21	1	22
WILLIAMS H	18		18

GOALSCORERS

PLAYER	LEAGUE	F. A. CUP	TOTAL
CHARLES	26	1	27
IGGLEDEN	12		12
NIGHTINGALE	8		8
MEEK	5		5
LANGLEY	3		3
BURDEN	2		2
FORREST	2		2
HASTIE	2		2
KERFOOT	2		2
McCALL	2		2
MILLS Do.	2		2
TYRER	2		2
SMITH B	1		1
OWN GOALS	2		2

The close season was a busy period at Elland Road with the arrival of new manager Raich Carter and rumours suggesting that John Charles may be sold for more than the £34,000 British record fee Sheffield Wednesday paid for Jackie Sewell. Carter quickly quashed suggestions of Charles' departure and began the new campaign with the same line-up as his predecessor in addition to the introduction of a fit-again Harold Williams and another winger, new signing Eddie Burbanks, with George Meek unavailable due to National Service.

In a quite astounding opening, Charles thundered home seven goals in Leeds' first two fixtures. Scoring from all angles with head and either foot, Charles notched four in a 6-0 rout against Notts County and a hat-trick in a 4-2 win over Rotherham United. By 10 games, the Welsh phenomenon had 15 goals to his credit, including braces in a 3-2 win against Swansea Town and a 3-1 victory at Fulham. Although goals were flying in for Leeds, a concern was the number of goals being conceded. By the halfway point of the league campaign only three more victories had been claimed following wins against Derby County 3-1; Charles notching a brace, Doncaster Rovers 3-1; courtesy of a Nightingale hat-trick, and Oldham Athletic; Bobby Forrest and Nightingale scoring.

Far too many games were being frittered away, despite Carter bringing centre-back Jack Marsden in for Jim McCabe. High scoring draws included thrillers at Birmingham City 3-3, Bristol Rovers 3-3; Forrest scoring a hat-trick, and Bury 4-4. Charles notched his third treble of the season in the latter clash, and added another prior to Christmas in Leeds' 4-2 win at Rotherham, but this victory would be the only win throughout December, Nottingham Forest claiming a double in the festive games.

Carter stated his desire for Leeds to be attractive and his charges were entertaining. However, when the opening New Year fixtures included a 7-1 thumping of Leicester City; Iggledon scoring a hat-trick, and a 5-2 rout against Lincoln City; Charles grabbing a treble, sandwiched between a 4-0 loss at Stoke City and 5-2 defeat at West Ham, consistency for promotion was impossible. Ten more goals would come Charles' way in as many games during the run-in, including a brace against Brentford 4-0 and Luton Town 2-1, but Leeds' five wins would bring a tenth place finish.

Scoring 89 goals would be the club's highest total since 1927/28 when Dick Ray's charges claimed promotion with 98 goals, however Ray's team only conceded 49 goals compared to the current crop's 81. Both Grenville Hair and Eric Kerfoot were ever-present, but the campaign was all about one extra-ordinary footballer as Charles plundered 42 league goals. His mark of 43 goals in total was the highest since Tom Jennings exploits in 1926/27, and together with five hat-tricks in a campaign, are still club records half a century on. Charles along with Charlie Keetley is also one of only two players to score three hat-tricks for Leeds United in a season.

1953 - 1954

DIVISION TWO (FINAL LEAGUE POSITION - 10TH)				
PLD 42 W 15 D 13 L 14 F 89 A 81 PTS 43				
DATE	OPPONENTS	VENUE	SCORE SCORERS	ATT.
19-Aug	NOTTS COUNTY	HOME	6 - 0	CHARLES 4, WILLIAMS H & NIGHTINGALE	18,432
22-Aug	ROTHERHAM UNITED	HOME	4 - 2	CHARLES 3 & NIGHTINGALE	24,309
27-Aug	SWANSEA TOWN	AWAY	3 - 4	CHARLES, NIGHTINGALE & BURBANKS	26,408
29-Aug	LEICESTER CITY	AWAY	0 - 5		21,984
02-Sep	SWANSEA TOWN	HOME	3 - 2	NIGHTINGALE & CHARLES 2	20,949
05-Sep	STOKE CITY	HOME	1 - 1	CHARLES	27,571
07-Sep	PLYMOUTH ARGYLE	AWAY	1 - 1	CHARLES	20,356
12-Sep	FULHAM	AWAY	3 - 1	CHARLES 2 & WILLIAMS H	26,044
16-Sep	PLYMOUTH ARGYLE	HOME	1 - 1	WILLIAMS H	20,621
19-Sep	WEST HAM UNITED	HOME	1 - 2	CHARLES	28,635
26-Sep	LINCOLN CITY	AWAY	0 - 2		17,979
03-Oct	BIRMINGHAM CITY	AWAY	3 - 3	CHARLES, IGGLEDEN & KERFOOT	26,434
10-Oct	BRISTOL ROVERS	HOME	3 - 3	FORREST 3	19,386
17-Oct	BRENTFORD	AWAY	1 - 2	CHARLES	18,329
24-Oct	DERBY COUNTY	HOME	3 - 1	CHARLES 2 & NIGHTINGALE	26,430
31-Oct	BLACKBURN ROVERS	AWAY	2 - 2	WILLIAMS H & NIGHTINGALE	25,272
07-Nov	DONCASTER ROVERS	HOME	3 - 1	NIGHTINGALE 3	26,830
14-Nov	BURY	AWAY	4 - 4	CHARLES 3 & NIGHTINGALE	11,915
21-Nov	OLDHAM ATHLETIC	HOME	2 - 1	FORREST & NIGHTINGALE	26,747
28-Nov	EVERTON	AWAY	1 - 2	CHARLES	55,970
05-Dec	HULL CITY	HOME	0 - 0		21,070
12-Dec	NOTTS COUNTY	AWAY	0 - 2		17,552
19-Dec	ROTHERHAM UNITED	AWAY	4 - 2	CHARLES 3 (1 PEN) & IGGLEDEN	13,145
25-Dec	NOTTINGHAM FOREST	AWAY	2 - 5	NIGHTINGALE & CHARLES	19,725
26-Dec	NOTTINGHAM FOREST	HOME	0 - 2		22,135
02-Jan	LEICESTER CITY	HOME	7 - 1	IGGLEDEN 3, WILLIAMS H, CHARLES, NIGHTINGALE & TYRER	21,532
16-Jan	STOKE CITY	AWAY	0 - 4		26,794
23-Jan	FULHAM	HOME	1 - 2	CHARLES	20,170
06-Feb	WEST HAM UNITED	AWAY	2 - 5	IGGLEDEN & McCALL	15,585
13-Feb	LINCOLN CITY	HOME	5 - 2	CHARLES 3, IGGLEDEN & NIGHTINGALE	15,325
20-Feb	BIRMINGHAM CITY	HOME	1 - 1	BURDEN	22,803
27-Feb	BRISTOL ROVERS	AWAY	1 - 1	NIGHTINGALE	26,846
06-Mar	BRENTFORD	HOME	4 - 0	CHARLES 2, NIGHTINGALE & WILLIAMS H	16,501
13-Mar	DERBY COUNTY	AWAY	2 - 0	FORREST 2	12,773
20-Mar	BLACKBURN ROVERS	HOME	3 - 2	McCALL, NIGHTINGALE & CHARLES (PEN)	24,915
27-Mar	OLDHAM ATHLETIC	AWAY	2 - 4	WILLIAMS H & CHARLES	18,067
03-Apr	EVERTON	HOME	3 - 1	WILLIAMS H, FORREST & KERFOOT	22,581
10-Apr	DONCASTER ROVERS	AWAY	0 - 0		12,472
16-Apr	LUTON TOWN	AWAY	1 - 1	CHARLES	16,129
17-Apr	BURY	HOME	3 - 4	CHARLES 2 (1 PEN) & FORREST	17,156
19-Apr	LUTON TOWN	HOME	2 - 1	CHARLES 2 (1 PEN)	13,930
24-Apr	HULL CITY	AWAY	1 - 1	CHARLES	18,619
F. A. CUP				
09-Jan	TOTTENHAM HOTSPUR (R3)	HOME	3 - 3	IGGLEDEN, CHARLES & O. G. (RAMSEY)	41,645
13-Jan	TOTTENHAM HOTSPUR (R3R)	AWAY	0 - 1		35,023

LEAGUE AND CUP			
APPEARANCES			
PLAYER	LEAGUE	F. A. CUP	TOTAL
BURBANKS	13		13
BURDEN	40	2	42
CHARLES	39	2	41
DAVIES	1		1
DAWSON	1		1
DUNN	41	2	43
FLYNN P	1		1
FORREST	10		10
HAIR	42	2	44
IGGLEDEN	31	2	33
KERFOOT	42	2	44
MARSDEN	28	2	30
McCABE	14		14
McCALL	18		18
MOLLATT	5		5
NIGHTINGALE	39	2	41
SCOTT	26	2	28
TYRER	13	2	15
WEBB	2		2
WHEATLEY	6		6
WILLIAMS H	37	2	39
WILLIS	3		3
WOOD R	10		10

GOALSCORERS			
PLAYER	LEAGUE	F. A. CUP	TOTAL
CHARLES	42	1	43
NIGHTINGALE	17		17
FORREST	8		8
IGGLEDEN	7	1	8
WILLIAMS H	8		8
KERFOOT	2		2
McCALL	2		2
BURBANKS	1		1
BURDEN	1		1
TYRER	1		1
OWN GOALS		1	1

John Charles was fast becoming the hottest property in British football but Raich Carter had a dilemma because for all Charles' success in attack, the defence was leaking goals. During the close season, Carter signed Harold Brook (Sheffield United) and began the campaign with the pair in attack. Following a 2-0 win at Hull City, Brook and Charles scoring, Leeds leaked 16 goals in five consecutive defeats, including losses to Rotherham United 4-2 and 3-0, and Bury 5-3. Carter had to act.

Defensive stalwart Jim McCabe had departed during the close season, now Tommy Burden would move on. Needing to change his formation, Carter controversially moved his main striker into defence alongside new skipper Eric Kerfoot, and partnered pre-season signing Harold Brook with Bobby Forrest in attack, whilst youngster Keith Ripley filled Kerfoot's wing-half role. United's highly rated star, desperate for top-flight soccer, handed in a written transfer request, and immediately suitors enquired. Arsenal and Cardiff City were ready to bid but United chairman Sam Bolton rejected Charles request. With the club's talisman going nowhere, Carter's reshaped team put together a superb run of one loss, 5-1 at Bristol Rovers, when Charles briefly moved back to centre-forward, in 17 matches. Winning 10 games in 12 matches, Leeds were genuine promotion contenders. Though not prolific in goal terms, Albert Nightingale with 11 goals, hit a rich vein of form during the run, scoring a hat-trick in a 5-2 win against Swansea Town, the winning strike during a 2-1 win at Ipswich Town, and braces in 2-1 wins at Notts County and Blackburn Rovers. Forrest claimed the only goal against Stoke City and Birmingham City, and struck the winner in a 2-1 win against West Ham, whilst Brook notched a brace in a 4-2 win at Derby County. All three scored in a 3-0 home win over Hull City.

It was a remarkable turnaround for Leeds, who had a new goalkeeper in close season signing Roy Wood, impressing with each game. The Blackburn win saw Leeds go joint-top whilst the Hull victory put Carter's charges a point ahead of Stoke, however a disastrous run at the turn of the year saw Leeds slip off the pace in the league. They also crashed out of the FA Cup following a 4-0 drubbing at lowly Torquay United. Just three wins registered in 10 games, including two scrappy home 1-0 triumphs against Bury and Derby, was not promotion material, but of greater concern for Carter was that only once did Leeds score more than one goal, a brace apiece from Brook and Vickers securing a 4-1 over Ipswich Town.

The onset of spring, however, brought seven victories in the final 10 games; Brook scoring in seven, and included five in the final five games against Notts County, Luton Town, Liverpool, Blackburn and Fulham but it was insufficient. Finishing one point adrift of Birmingham, Luton and Rotherham, Carter's team had agonisingly missed out. Defenders Jimmy Dunn and Grenville Hair were ever-present, while Charles missed two games. Brook edged the scoring ranks with 16 goals, Nightingale scored 13 and Charles grabbed 12, including five penalties. Missing promotion was a crushing disappointment for Carter's team but more concerning, club officials were fully aware that Charles could not be held back much longer from Division 1 football. A successful promotion campaign was now a necessity for United to keep their major asset.

DIVISION TWO (FINAL LEAGUE POSITION - 4TH)

PLD 42 W 23 D 7 L 12 F 70 A 53 PTS 53

DATE	OPPONENTS	VENUE	SCORE	SCORERS	ATT.
21-Aug	HULL CITY	AWAY	2 - 0	BROOK & CHARLES	32,071
25-Aug	ROTHERHAM UNITED	HOME	2 - 4	CHARLES 2	25,021
28-Aug	LINCOLN CITY	HOME	2 - 3	TONER & VICKERS	22,326
30-Aug	ROTHERHAM UNITED	AWAY	0 - 3		17,799
04-Sep	BURY	AWAY	3 - 5	McCALL, CHARLES & O . G . (MAY)	15,357
08-Sep	STOKE CITY	HOME	0 - 1		20,295
11-Sep	SWANSEA TOWN	HOME	5 - 2	NIGHTINGALE 3, KERFOOT & BROOK	20,040
13-Sep	STOKE CITY	AWAY	1 - 0	FORREST	19,311
18-Sep	NOTTINGHAM FOREST	HOME	1 - 1	FORREST	22,402
25-Sep	IPSWICH TOWN	AWAY	2 - 1	WILLIAMS H & NIGHTINGALE	16,716
02-Oct	BIRMINGHAM CITY	HOME	1 - 0	FORREST	21,200
09-Oct	DERBY COUNTY	AWAY	4 - 2	BROOK 2 & McCALL 2	20,214
16-Oct	WEST HAM UNITED	HOME	2 - 1	RIPLEY & FORREST	21,074
23-Oct	BRISTOL ROVERS	AWAY	1 - 5	BROOK	24,568
30-Oct	PLYMOUTH ARGYLE	HOME	3 - 2	WILLIAMS H, NIGHTINGALE & McCALL	20,613
06-Nov	PORT VALE	AWAY	1 - 0	NIGHTINGALE	16,062
13-Nov	DONCASTER ROVERS	HOME	1 - 0	RIPLEY	15,757
20-Nov	NOTTS COUNTY	AWAY	2 - 1	NIGHTINGALE 2	14,519
27-Nov	LIVERPOOL	HOME	2 - 2	FORREST & CHARLES (PEN)	22,263
04-Dec	BLACKBURN ROVERS	AWAY	2 - 1	NIGHTINGALE 2	26,187
11-Dec	FULHAM	HOME	1 - 1	CHARLES	30,714
18-Dec	HULL CITY	HOME	3 - 0	BROOK, NIGHTINGALE & FORREST	23,991
25-Dec	MIDDLESBROUGH	HOME	1 - 1	FORREST	26,344
27-Dec	MIDDLESBROUGH	AWAY	0 - 1		45,271
01-Jan	LINCOLN CITY	AWAY	0 - 2		12,231
15-Jan	BURY	HOME	1 - 0	LYDON	8,954
22-Jan	SWANSEA TOWN	AWAY	0 - 2		19,637
05-Feb	NOTTINGHAM FOREST	AWAY	1 - 1	CHARLES	14,074
12-Feb	IPSWICH TOWN	HOME	4 - 1	BROOK 2 & VICKERS 2	12,038
26-Feb	DERBY COUNTY	HOME	1 - 0	CHARLES (PEN)	16,994
02-Mar	BIRMINGHAM CITY	AWAY	0 - 2		10,774
05-Mar	WEST HAM UNITED	AWAY	1 - 2	FORREST	19,664
12-Mar	BRISTOL ROVERS	HOME	2 - 0	BROOK & FORREST	16,922
19-Mar	PLYMOUTH ARGYLE	AWAY	1 - 3	BROOK	19,968
26-Mar	PORT VALE	HOME	3 - 0	HENDERSON J, RIPLEY & CHARLES (PEN)	8,831
02-Apr	DONCASTER ROVERS	AWAY	1 - 0	BROOK	12,740
08-Apr	LUTON TOWN	AWAY	0 - 0		25,775
09-Apr	NOTTS COUNTY	HOME	2 - 0	BROOK & NIGHTINGALE	24,564
11-Apr	LUTON TOWN	HOME	4 - 0	BROOK, CHARLES 2 (2 PENS) & HENDERSON J	29,583
16-Apr	LIVERPOOL	AWAY	2 - 2	MEEK & BROOK	34,950
23-Apr	BLACKBURN ROVERS	HOME	2 - 0	BROOK 2	39,208
30-Apr	FULHAM	AWAY	3 - 1	O. G. (SMITH), HENDERSON J & NIGHTINGALE	21,400

F. A. CUP

DATE	OPPONENTS	VENUE	SCORE	SCORERS	ATT.
08-Jan	TORQUAY UNITED (R3)	HOME	2 - 2	KERFOOT & CHARLES	28,150
12-Jan	TORQUAY UNITED (R3R)	AWAY	0 - 4		11,426

LEAGUE AND CUP

APPEARANCES

PLAYER	LEAGUE	F. A. CUP	TOTAL
BROOK	37	2	39
BURDEN	5		5
CHARLES	40	2	42
CHARLTON	1		1
DUNN	42	2	44
FORREST	25		25
GIBSON	12		12
HAIR	42	2	44
HENDERSON J	9		9
IGGLEDEN	4		4
KERFOOT	39	2	41
LYDON	4		4
McCALL	28	2	30
MARSDEN	7	2	9
MEEK	10		10
MOLLATT	5		5
NIGHTINGALE	38	2	40
RIPLEY	25	2	27
SCOTT	14		14
TONER	7		7
VICKERS	7		7
WEBB	1		1
WILLIAMS H	32	2	34
WOOD R	28	2	30

GOALSCORERS

PLAYER	LEAGUE	F. A. CUP	TOTAL
BROOK	16		16
NIGHTINGALE	13		13
CHARLES	11	1	12
FORREST	9		9
McCALL	4		4
HENDERSON J	3		3
RIPLEY	3		3
VICKERS	3		3
KERFOOT	1	1	2
WILLIAMS H	2		2
LYDON	1		1
MEEK	1		1
TONER	1		1
OWN GOALS	2		2

Expectations were high for a promotion charge, which was a major factor in Raich Carter turning down the opportunity of a return to former club Derby County as manager during the close season. Carter began the campaign with John Charles in defence and Harold Brook leading the attack, and his charges got off to a flyer with four victories in the opening six games against Bury, Middlesbrough, Bristol City and Hull City. However, the coming weeks would bring inconsistent form and little cutting edge.

With Archie Gibson sidelined, Jack Charlton grasped his opportunity at centre-back in a 4-1 win against Rotherham United, Keith Ripley scoring a hat-trick, but home form alone could not sustain a promotion campaign. A 3-0 win against Nottingham Forest, Charles notching his first goal of the season, preceded a 4-0 defeat at Sheffield Wednesday, convincing Carter to revert his powerhouse to centre-forward.

A third of the season gone and struggling for goals, Charles led the line in a 4-1 loss at Bristol Rovers, but the Welshman quickly showed his ability, scoring nine goals in six games, including strikes in victories against Stoke City, Liverpool, Doncaster Rovers and Blackburn Rovers. The festive games saw a Christmas Eve humdinger at Middlesbrough that Leeds lost 5-3, followed by a win against Notts County, Brook scoring the decisive goal. After a 2-1 defeat at County, Brook proved the hero with the winner against Bristol City on New Years Eve.

Inconsistency, however, continued well into March. Knocked out of the FA Cup at home by Cardiff City, United had scored 10 goals in eight games, including just one victory, 2-1 against Sheffield Wednesday. They had also suffered a first home defeat in 34 matches to Blackburn, a remarkable sequence going back to September 1954. Few pundits backed Leeds for success, despite Charles' proficiency in front of goal. Leeds were hampered by the absence of Albert Nightingale and George Meek bar a handful of games since October, however the duo returned for the final nine matches.

Immediately, United's fluency returned with a 4-2 win against Plymouth Argyle; Brook, Nightingale and a Charles brace securing the points. Brook and Charles accounted for Fulham, before completing a superb Easter programme and a double to boot over the Londoners with a thumping 6-1 triumph at Elland Road, Charles notching a treble. Back on song, Leeds' return to Division 1 was sealed with five victories to snatch the runners-up spot behind Sheffield Wednesday.

It was incredibly close though, and included three crucial games. Firstly, the last home game against promotion rivals Bristol Rovers, who had a two-point advantage, when Leeds came from behind to win 2-1 with goals from Charles and Overfield. This priceless victory over Rovers placed them second for the first time on goal average. Then, after a 2-0 midweek win at Rotherham, Nightingale notching a brace, Leeds went into the last match at Hull City knowing a victory would seal promotion. Charles grabbed two goals in a 4-1 win.

Nine years after relegation, Leeds United's fourth promotion since formation had again, bizarrely, come in a leap year. Finishing third in the annual vote for Footballer of the Year was an extraordinary achievement by Charles, who struck 29 league goals in his 41 games, 28 coming in 29 matches at centre-forward, including a dozen in the final nine games. Roy Wood, Jimmy Dunn and Eric Kerfoot were the only ever-presents.

1955 - 1956

DIVISION TWO (FINAL LEAGUE POSITION - 2ND)

PLD 42 W 23 D 6 L 13 F 80 A 60 PTS 52

DATE	OPPONENTS	VENUE	SCORE	SCORERS	ATT.
20-Aug	BARNSLEY	AWAY	1 - 2	BROOK	19,341
22-Aug	BURY	HOME	1 - 0	HENDERSON J	19,722
27-Aug	MIDDLESBROUGH	HOME	2 - 0	NIGHTINGALE & BROOK	22,535
30-Aug	BURY	AWAY	0 - 1		11,674
03-Sep	BRISTOL CITY	AWAY	1 - 0	FORREST	31,060
05-Sep	HULL CITY	HOME	1 - 0	RIPLEY	17,524
10-Sep	WEST HAM UNITED	HOME	3 - 3	RIPLEY, NIGHTINGALE & MEEK	21,855
17-Sep	PORT VALE	AWAY	0 - 2		21,348
24-Sep	ROTHERHAM UNITED	HOME	4 - 1	NIGHTINGALE & RIPLEY 3	23,763
01-Oct	SWANSEA TOWN	AWAY	1 - 1	BROOK	29,477
08-Oct	NOTTINGHAM FOREST	HOME	3 - 0	RIPLEY, BROOK & CHARLES	21,272
15-Oct	SHEFFIELD WEDNESDAY	AWAY	0 - 4		27,640
22-Oct	LINCOLN CITY	HOME	1 - 0	OVERFIELD	17,378
29-Oct	BRISTOL ROVERS	AWAY	1 - 4	BROOK	24,575
05-Nov	STOKE CITY	HOME	1 - 0	CHARLES	21,261
12-Nov	PLYMOUTH ARGYLE	AWAY	3 - 4	O. G. (ROBERTSON), WILLIAMS H & CHARLES	19,122
19-Nov	LIVERPOOL	HOME	4 - 2	OVERFIELD, CHARLES 2 & BROOK	22,596
26-Nov	LEICESTER CITY	AWAY	2 - 5	CHARLES 2 (2 PENS)	30,196
03-Dec	DONCASTER ROVERS	HOME	3 - 0	HUTCHINSON, CHARLES & OVERFIELD	21,769
10-Dec	BLACKBURN ROVERS	AWAY	3 - 2	OVERFIELD & CHARLES 2 (1 PEN)	18,898
17-Dec	BARNSLEY	HOME	3 - 1	HUTCINSON 2 & WILLIAMS H	23,493
24-Dec	MIDDLESBROUGH	AWAY	3 - 5	HUTCHINSON, CHARLES & VICKERS	19,416
26-Dec	NOTTS COUNTY	HOME	1 - 0	BROOK	24,869
27-Dec	NOTTS COUNTY	AWAY	1 - 2	CHARLES	23,910
31-Dec	BRISTOL CITY	HOME	2 - 1	HUTCHINSON & BROOK	31,751
14-Jan	WEST HAM UNITED	AWAY	1 - 1	CHARLES	20,000
21-Jan	PORT VALE	HOME	1 - 1	BROOK	23,680
11-Feb	SWANSEA TOWN	HOME	2 - 2	CHARLES (PEN) & NIGHTINGALE	20,089
25-Feb	SHEFFIELD WEDNESDAY	HOME	2 - 1	CHARLES & FORREST	43,268
28-Feb	LIVERPOOL	AWAY	0 - 1		21,068
03-Mar	LINCOLN CITY	AWAY	1 - 1	CHARLES (PEN)	13,713
10-Mar	BLACKBURN ROVERS	HOME	1 - 2	CHARLES	28,380
17-Mar	STOKE CITY	AWAY	1 - 2	BROOK	22,784
24-Mar	PLYMOUTH ARGYLE	HOME	4 - 2	BROOK, NIGHTINGALE & CHARLES 2	12,348
30-Mar	FULHAM	AWAY	2 - 1	BROOK & CHARLES	25,459
31-Mar	NOTTINGHAM FOREST	AWAY	0 - 2		19,448
02-Apr	FULHAM	HOME	6 - 1	CHARLES 3, NIGHTINGALE 2 & BROOK	20,115
07-Apr	LEICESTER CITY	HOME	4 - 0	OVERFIELD, BROOK & CHARLES 2 (1 PEN)	26,408
14-Apr	DONCASTER ROVERS	AWAY	2 - 1	CHARLES & NIGHTINGALE	18,404
21-Apr	BRISTOL ROVERS	HOME	2 - 1	CHARLES & OVERFIELD	49,274
23-Apr	ROTHERHAM UNITED	AWAY	2 - 0	NIGHTINGALE 2	20,013
28-Apr	HULL CITY	AWAY	4 - 1	CHARLES 2 (1 PEN) & BROOK 2	31,123
		F. A. CUP			
07-Jan	CARDIFF CITY (R3)	HOME	1 - 2	BROOK	39,406

LEAGUE AND CUP
APPEARANCES

PLAYER	LEAGUE	F.A. CUP	TOTAL
ASHALL	6		6
BROOK	32	1	33
CHARLES	41	1	42
CHARLTON	34	1	35
DUNN	42	1	43
FORREST	12		12
GIBSON	27	1	28
HAIR	34	1	35
HENDERSON J	6		6
HUTCHINSON	11		11
KERFOOT	42	1	43
MARSDEN	2		2
MEEK	26		26
NIGHTINGALE	26		26
OVERFIELD	30	1	31
RIPLEY	19		19
VICKERS	11	1	12
WILLIAMS H	19	1	20
WOOD R	42	1	43

GOALSCORERS

PLAYER	LEAGUE	F.A. CUP	TOTAL
CHARLES	29		29
BROOK	16	1	17
NIGHTINGALE	10		10
OVERFIELD	6		6
RIPLEY	6		6
HUTCHINSON	5		5
FORREST	2		2
WILLIAMS H	2		2
HENDERSON J	1		1
MEEK	1		1
VICKERS	1		1
OWN GOALS	1		1

Back in Division 1, stalwarts such as Jimmy Dunn, Grenville Hair and Eric Kerfoot could test themselves against the likes of Nat Lofthouse, Tom Finney and Stan Matthews but the main talking point for fans and pundits was how John Charles would perform against star defenders such as Harry Johnson, Duncan Edwards and Billy Wright. The answer in his debut season of top-flight football came swiftly and decisively with a goal in an opening day 5-1 win against Everton, though 34-year-old Harold Brook claimed the day's headlines with a 21-minute treble after Jack Overfield had begun the scoring spree inside three minutes. Tragically, a knee injury sustained by Albert Nightingale would end his career.

Fearing nobody, and offering a threat through wingmen George Meek and Overfield, Carter's charges tore into unsuspecting opponents. Claiming a further six wins in the opening 10 games, the Welsh sharpshooter notched nine goals. Charles was unstoppable. A brace accounted for Charlton Athletic before the Charles-Brook partnership combined to shoot down the South Londoners again, Bolton Wanderers and Manchester City. Further Charles strikes defeated Wolves and Aston Villa.

The Villa clash came four days after a fire destroyed the West Stand, resulting in £100,000 damage to dressing rooms, club offices, medical equipment and players records. The club launched an appeal for changing facilities and equipment but on the field, Leeds played on. Charles was a hit, but with Brook picking up an injury and Carter having to rotate Jack Charlton and Jack Marsden, Leeds stumbled.

Finding a replacement for Brook was troublesome. Andy Ripley and Bobby Forrest struggled before Frank McKenna immediately scored a brace against Newcastle United to get Leeds back to winning ways, Charles notching Leeds' other goal in a 3-2 win. A Charles hat-trick sent Sheffield Wednesday home with nothing, before braces earned a 3-3 draw with Arsenal and a 4-1 victory over Portsmouth.

The festive games brought hard earned draws at Blackpool and Chelsea, either side of a 5-0 Christmas Day romp against the Seasiders. However, the New Year would be anything but joyous following a second successive third round FA Cup home loss to Cardiff City, and a 5-3 defeat at Bolton. The remainder of the campaign would generate four wins from 15 games, with Charles on target in each triumph. Although a worrying dip in form, Leeds suffered only one drubbing, 6-2 at Birmingham City. Notching both goals against City, Charles plundered Leeds' second goal against Cardiff to gain revenge for the cup defeat, a brace in a 5-2 triumph at Portsmouth, a treble at Sheffield Wednesday and a brace in the final game of the season at home to Sunderland; captained by future Leeds boss Don Revie.

It was a remarkable exhibition in the art of scoring goals by Charles. Top scorer for a fourth time in five campaigns with 39 goals, Charles' trebles took him to a club-record 11 hat-tricks. The Leeds board though realised that they could no longer hang on to their prize asset and accepted a world record bid of £65,000 from Italian giants Juventus, using the money to rebuild the West Stand. Utilising 17 players, no fewer than five were ever-present, Roy Wood, Dunn, Hair, Kerfoot and Overfield.

1956 - 1957

	DIVISION ONE (FINAL LEAGUE POSITION - 8TH)				
	PLD 42 W 15 D 14 L 13 F 72 A 63 PTS 44				
DATE	OPPONENTS	VENUE	SCORE	SCORERS	ATT.
18-Aug	EVERTON	HOME	5 - 1	OVERFIELD, CHARLES & BROOK 3	31,379
23-Aug	CHARLTON ATHLETIC	AWAY	2 - 1	CHARLES 2	23,299
25-Aug	TOTTENHAM HOTSPUR	AWAY	1 - 5	RIPLEY	51,212
29-Aug	CHARLTON ATHLETIC	HOME	4 - 0	FORREST 2, CHARLES & BROOK	34,444
01-Sep	CHELSEA	HOME	0 - 0		38,679
05-Sep	MANCHESTER CITY	AWAY	0 - 1		34,185
08-Sep	BOLTON WANDERERS	HOME	3 - 2	MEEK, CHARLES & BROOK	40,010
12-Sep	MANCHESTER CITY	HOME	2 - 0	CHARLES & BROOK	35,068
15-Sep	WOLVERHAMPTON WANDERERS	AWAY	2 - 1	CHARLES 2	40,824
22-Sep	ASTON VILLA	HOME	1 - 0	CHARLES	35,388
29-Sep	LUTON TOWN	AWAY	2 - 2	CHARLES 2	20,949
06-Oct	CARDIFF CITY	AWAY	1 - 4	FORREST	38,333
13-Oct	BIRMINGHAM CITY	HOME	1 - 1	RIPLEY	34,460
20-Oct	BURNLEY	AWAY	0 - 0		26,440
27-Oct	PRESTON NORTH END	HOME	1 - 2	O. G. (WILSON)	36,571
03-Nov	NEWCASTLE UNITED	AWAY	3 - 2	McKENNA 2 & CHARLES	49,034
10-Nov	SHEFFIELD WEDNESDAY	HOME	3 - 1	CHARLES 3	31,857
17-Nov	MANCHESTER UNITED	AWAY	2 - 3	McKENNA & CHARLES (PEN)	52,401
24-Nov	ARSENAL	HOME	3 - 3	CHARLES 2 & FORREST	39,113
01-Dec	WEST BROMWICH ALBION	AWAY	0 - 0		29,000
08-Dec	PORTSMOUTH	HOME	4 - 1	CHARLES 2 & RIPLEY 2	29,866
15-Dec	EVERTON	AWAY	1 - 2	RIPLEY	33,765
25-Dec	BLACKPOOL	AWAY	1 - 1	BROOK	20,517
26-Dec	BLACKPOOL	HOME	5 - 0	BROOK 3 & CHARLES 2	22,689
29-Dec	CHELSEA	AWAY	1 - 1	O. G. (ARMSTRONG)	43,860
12-Jan	BOLTON WANDERERS	AWAY	3 - 5	CHARLES 2 & MEEK	25,705
19-Jan	WOLVERHAMPTON WANDERERS	HOME	0 - 0		32,910
02-Feb	ASTON VILLA	AWAY	1 - 1	FORREST	39,432
09-Feb	LUTON TOWN	HOME	1 - 2	CHARLES	25,646
16-Feb	CARDIFF CITY	HOME	3 - 0	McKENNA, CHARLES & FORREST	21,695
23-Feb	PRESTON NORTH END	AWAY	0 - 3		14,036
02-Mar	TOTTENHAM HOTSPUR	HOME	1 - 1	CHARLES	33,895
09-Mar	PORTSMOUTH	AWAY	5 - 2	CHARLES 2, CROWE 2 & MEEK	23,596
11-Mar	BURNLEY	HOME	1 - 1	CHARLES	31,956
16-Mar	NEWCASTLE UNITED	HOME	0 - 0		32,541
26-Mar	SHEFFIELD WEDNESDAY	AWAY	3 - 2	CHARLES 3	33,205
30-Mar	MANCHESTER UNITED	HOME	1 - 2	CHARLES	47,216
06-Apr	ARSENAL	AWAY	0 - 1		40,388
13-Apr	WEST BROMWICH ALBION	HOME	0 - 0		20,905
19-Apr	SUNDERLAND	AWAY	0 - 2		56,551
20-Apr	BIRMINGHAM CITY	AWAY	2 - 6	CHARLES 2	30,642
22-Apr	SUNDERLAND	HOME	3 - 1	CHARLES 2 & BROOK	29,328
	F. A. CUP				
05-Jan	CARDIFF CITY (R3)	HOME	1 - 2	CHARLES	34,459

LEAGUE AND CUP
APPEARANCES

PLAYER	LEAGUE	F. A. CUP	TOTAL
BROOK	24	1	25
CHARLES	40	1	41
CHARLTON	21	1	22
CROWE	13		13
DUNN	42	1	43
FORREST	27	1	28
GIBSON	40	1	41
HAIR	42	1	43
KERFOOT	42	1	43
McKENNA	6		6
MARSDEN	21		21
MEEK	40	1	41
NIGHTINGALE	1		1
O'BRIEN	8		8
OVERFIELD	42	1	43
RIPLEY	11		11
WOOD R	42	1	43

GOALSCORERS

PLAYER	LEAGUE	F. A. CUP	TOTAL
CHARLES	38	1	39
BROOK	11		11
FORREST	6		6
RIPLEY	5		5
McKENNA	4		4
MEEK	3		3
CROWE	2		2
OVERFIELD	1		1
OWN GOALS	2		2

Without John Charles, scoring goals was going to be a major problem for Raich Carter's team. A replacement would face unfair comparison, and the task was quickly apparent following opening defeats at Blackpool and Aston Villa. Undeterred, Hugh Baird, a £12,000 purchase and prolific scorer from Airdrie, got on with the challenge and struck five goals during four victories in the first 10 matches. Baird set Leeds on their way to a 2-1 win against Leicester City, notched a brace in a 4-0 victory against Villa, the winning goal against Bolton Wanderers and another opener in a 2-1 win against Sunderland.

Baird was doing his best, and following Leeds' goal in a draw against Wolves, the Scot scored the opener in a 2-1 victory at Portsmouth. The winning goal came from veteran striker Harold Brook, but this would be his final goal for United. Results in the opening third of the season had gone reasonably well, but with Baird accounting for almost half Leeds' total, Carter had to make changes. Bringing Bobby Forrest back into the fray initially failed to achieve the desired effect during a dreadful run that yielded just two wins in a dozen games, including successive defeats against Tottenham Hotspur, Preston North End, Sheffield Wednesday, Manchester City and Burnley. The only solace in the build up to Christmas came with back-to-back home wins against Newcastle United 3-0 and Blackpool 2-1, Forrest scoring in both games.

With Grenville Hair and Jimmy Dunn sidelined for a period, Carter had patched up his side, whilst slowly building for the future. New arrivals, Noel Peyton (Shamrock Rovers) and Wilbur Cush (Glenavon), replaced Brook and Keith Ripley, while Cush marked his third home game with the opening strike against the Seasiders. The New Year bizarrley brought a third consecutive 2-1 FA Cup defeat at home to Cardiff City, however, Carter had more concerns with Leeds' perilous form in the league. Fourteen defeats to date meant an immediate improvement was necessary, and Baird would provide the inspiration. Beginning the New Year with goals in hard-earned draws against Manchester United and Nottingham Forest, Baird's brace at relegation-bound Portsmouth brought a welcome 2-0 win.

Three consecutive defeats in early March generated a few relegation nerves, but finding their most consistent form of the season, five wins in the final nine fixtures edged Carter's team to safety in seventeenth place. George Meek led the way with goals in home wins against Arsenal and Burnley, before two 1-0 victories over Everton during the Easter fixtures; Baird and Forrest notching vital strikes, completed Leeds' fight for survival. Fittingly, Baird signed off his only full season at Elland Road with a goal in a 2-1 triumph at Newcastle on the final day of the season.

A disappointing campaign, but it came as something of a shock when the board decided against renewing Carter's contract, instead appointing Bill Lambton to the post, initially on a part-time basis. A fitness fanatic, Carter brought Lambton to Elland Road as trainer-coach for Bob Roxburgh, now physiotherapist. Eric Kerfoot was the only ever-present; keeper Roy Wood missed one game. Baird to his credit scored 20 goals, the only player to reach double figures.

1957 - 1958

DIVISION ONE (FINAL LEAGUE POSITION - 17TH)

PLD 42 W 14 D 9 L 19 F 51 A 63 PTS 37

DATE	OPPONENTS	VENUE	SCORE	SCORERS	ATT.
24-Aug	BLACKPOOL	AWAY	0 - 3		26,700
26-Aug	ASTON VILLA	AWAY	0 - 2		25,693
31-Aug	LEICESTER CITY	HOME	2 - 1	BAIRD H (PEN) & OVERFIELD	26,660
04-Sep	ASTON VILLA	HOME	4 - 0	BAIRD H 2, O'BRIEN & BROOK	22,685
07-Sep	MANCHESTER UNITED	AWAY	0 - 5		50,842
11-Sep	LUTON TOWN	HOME	0 - 2		21,972
14-Sep	NOTTINGHAM FOREST	HOME	1 - 2	OVERFIELD	25,566
18-Sep	LUTON TOWN	AWAY	1 - 1	OVERFIELD	16,887
21-Sep	BOLTON WANDERERS	HOME	2 - 1	MEEK & BAIRD H	18,379
25-Sep	SUNDERLAND	HOME	2 - 1	BAIRD H & GIBSON	17,600
28-Sep	ARSENAL	AWAY	1 - 2	BROOK	39,538
05-Oct	WOLVERHAMPTON WANDERERS	HOME	1 - 1	BAIRD H	28,635
12-Oct	PORTSMOUTH	AWAY	2 - 1	BAIRD H & BROOK	23,534
19-Oct	WEST BROMWICH ALBION	HOME	1 - 1	FORREST	24,614
26-Oct	TOTTENHAM HOTSPUR	AWAY	0 - 2		33,860
02-Nov	PRESTON NORTH END	HOME	2 - 3	BAIRD H 2 (2 PENS)	23,832
09-Nov	SHEFFIELD WEDNESDAY	AWAY	2 - 3	RIPLEY & FORREST	21,469
16-Nov	MANCHESTER CITY	HOME	2 - 4	KERFOOT & BAIRD H	23,855
23-Nov	BURNLEY	AWAY	1 - 3	BAIRD H (PEN)	24,144
30-Nov	BIRMINGHAM CITY	HOME	1 - 1	CUSH	21,358
07-Dec	CHELSEA	AWAY	1 - 2	BAIRD H	17,038
14-Dec	NEWCASTLE UNITED	HOME	3 - 0	FORREST, CROWE & OVERFIELD	23,363
21-Dec	BLACKPOOL	HOME	2 - 1	CUSH & FORREST	32,411
26-Dec	SUNDERLAND	AWAY	1 - 2	CROWE	34,875
28-Dec	LEICESTER CITY	AWAY	0 - 3		31,747
11-Jan	MANCHESTER UNITED	HOME	1 - 1	BAIRD H	39,401
18-Jan	NOTTINGHAM FOREST	AWAY	1 - 1	BAIRD H	23,368
01-Feb	BOLTON WANDERERS	AWAY	2 - 0	FORREST & CUSH	18,558
19-Feb	WOLVERHAMPTON WANDERERS	AWAY	2 - 3	PEYTON & FORREST	35,527
22-Feb	PORTSMOUTH	HOME	2 - 0	BAIRD H 2	26,713
08-Mar	TOTTENHAM HOTSPUR	HOME	1 - 2	BAIRD H	23,429
12-Mar	WEST BROMWICH ALBION	AWAY	0 - 1		16,412
15-Mar	PRESTON NORTH END	AWAY	0 - 3		21,353
19-Mar	ARSENAL	HOME	2 - 0	MEEK & PEYTON	25,948
22-Mar	BURNLEY	HOME	1 - 0	MEEK	24,994
29-Mar	MANCHESTER CITY	AWAY	0 - 1		21,962
04-Apr	EVERTON	AWAY	1 - 0	BAIRD H	32,679
05-Apr	SHEFFIELD WEDNESDAY	HOME	2 - 2	MEEK & BAIRD H	26,212
07-Apr	EVERTON	HOME	1 - 0	FORREST	25,188
12-Apr	BIRMINGHAM CITY	AWAY	1 - 1	O'BRIEN	23,112
19-Apr	CHELSEA	HOME	0 - 0		20,515
26-Apr	NEWCASTLE UNITED	AWAY	2 - 1	BAIRD H & O'BRIEN	32,594
	F. A. CUP				
04-Jan	CARDIFF CITY (R3)	HOME	1 - 2	FORREST	30,374

LEAGUE AND CUP

APPEARANCES

PLAYER	LEAGUE	F. A. CUP	TOTAL
ASHALL	9		9
BAIRD H	39		39
BROOK	9		9
CHARLTON	40	1	41
CROWE	19	1	20
CUSH	21	1	22
DUNN	35	1	36
FORREST	24	1	25
FRANCIS G	1		1
GIBSON	25	1	26
HAIR	34	1	35
KERFOOT	42	1	43
MARSDEN	4		4
MEEK	40	1	41
NIMMO	1		1
O'BRIEN	19		19
OVERFIELD	36	1	37
PEYTON	11		11
RIPLEY	12		12
WOOD R	41	1	42

GOALSCORERS

PLAYER	LEAGUE	F. A. CUP	TOTAL
BAIRD H	20		20
FORREST	7	1	8
MEEK	4		4
OVERFIELD	4		4
BROOK	3		3
CUSH	3		3
O'BRIEN	3		3
CROWE	2		2
PEYTON	2		2
GIBSON	1		1
KERFOOT	1		1
RIPLEY	1		1

New boss Bill Lambton introduced innovative ideas during pre-season, including trampolining sessions for suppleness. On the field however, little changed in first team fortunes, and the new boss wasted no time in changing his squad following one win in the opening nine games, Hugh Baird and Jack Overfield securing the points against Preston North End. Baird's strike proved his last for Leeds and would move on along with Bobby Forest as Bill Lambton freshened his side.

Recalling Chris Crowe, who appeared briefly in the past two seasons, Lambton's first signing, was Billy Humphries (Ards), and the Irish winger's debut at home to Arsenal brought a welcome 2-1 win, Crowe and Overfield scoring. Disappointingly, it heralded another poor run of two wins in eight games; Overfield notching the winner in an exciting 3-2 win against Tottenham Hotspur.

With reinforcements needed, Lambton went back into the transfer market and purchased striker Alan Shackleton from Burnley, who made a scoring debut at Manchester United and struck a hat-trick in a 4-2 win at Blackburn Rovers, the first by a Leeds player since John Charles' days. The result renewed confidence and coincided with the arrival of a player that would change the history of Leeds United. Veteran playmaker and inside-forward Don Revie had made his name at a number of clubs, including Manchester City, who he inspired to an FA Cup triumph in 1956.

Lambton paid £12,000 to Sunderland for Revie's services and the former England International and Footballer of the Year played his part as Leeds claimed victories against Newcastle United, West Ham and Nottingham Forest. Crowe was enjoying a hot-streak, notching six goals in seven games including a penalty against the Hammers, the only goal against Forest and another spot kick in a Boxing Day win at league leaders West Brom. Six points behind the Midlanders, Lambton signed a full contract but the New Year would begin disastrously on and off the pitch.

A run of seven defeats in 10 encounters included a 5-1 battering at Luton Town in the FA Cup and a 6-2 drubbing at Wolves in the league. Revie took over the captaincy from Wilbur Cush, who believed it hindered his form. Dressing room discontent was rife and following a 'clear the air' meeting between Lambton, the players and chairman Sam Bolton, Lambton resigned. Lambton's tenure was disappointing on the field, but his legacy would be the purchase of Revie.

With a possible relegation battle looming, Bolton put Bob Roxborough in charge temporarily. Scoring goals was Leeds' biggest headache, despite Shackleton's best efforts; two strikes defeating Leicester City and Everton. Slowly, results began to pick up. Ted Burgin replaced Roy Wood in goal, and Shackleton was at the fore in the final nine games, hitting the target in five victories, including a second hat-trick of the season at Nottingham Forest, and the only goal in the final game of the season at home to West Ham. Finishing fifteenth, Jack Charlton made 40 appearances and scored his first goal for the club in a 2-1 win against Blackburn Rovers, whilst Shackleton top scored with 17 goals.

1958 - 1959

DATE	OPPONENTS	VENUE	SCORE	SCORERS	ATT.
23-Aug	BOLTON WANDERERS	AWAY	0 - 4		25,922
26-Aug	LUTON TOWN	HOME	1 - 1	CROWE (PEN)	25,498
30-Aug	BURNLEY	HOME	1 - 1	FORREST	22,739
03-Sep	LUTON TOWN	AWAY	1 - 1	BAIRD H	13,497
06-Sep	PRESTON NORTH END	AWAY	2 - 1	BAIRD H (PEN) & OVERFIELD	22,765
10-Sep	BIRMINGHAM CITY	HOME	0 - 0		25,228
13-Sep	LEICESTER CITY	HOME	1 - 1	MEEK	23,487
17-Sep	BIRMINGHAM CITY	AWAY	1 - 4	FORREST	24,068
20-Sep	EVERTON	AWAY	2 - 3	CUSH & CROWE	31,105
27-Sep	ARSENAL	HOME	2 - 1	CROWE (PEN) & OVERFIELD	33,961
04-Oct	MANCHESTER CITY	AWAY	1 - 2	O. G. (LEIVERS)	31,989
11-Oct	PORTSMOUTH	AWAY	0 - 2		22,570
18-Oct	ASTON VILLA	HOME	0 - 0		21,088
25-Oct	TOTTENHAM HOTSPUR	AWAY	3 - 2	CUSH, O'BRIEN & OVERFIELD	38,691
01-Nov	MANCHESTER UNITED	HOME	1 - 2	SHACKLETON	48,574
08-Nov	CHELSEA	AWAY	0 - 2		33,357
15-Nov	BLACKPOOL	HOME	1 - 1	CROWE	29,252
22-Nov	BLACKBURN ROVERS	AWAY	4 - 2	SHACKLETON 3 & HUMPHRIES	28,727
29-Nov	NEWCASTLE UNITED	HOME	3 - 2	OVERFIELD, CROWE & O. G. (SCOTT)	23,732
06-Dec	WEST HAM UNITED	AWAY	3 - 2	CROWE (PEN), OVERFIELD & O. G. (BOND)	22,022
13-Dec	NOTTINGHAM FOREST	HOME	1 - 0	CROWE	26,341
20-Dec	BOLTON WANDERERS	HOME	3 - 4	CROWE (PEN), GIBSON & SHACKLETON	28,534
26-Dec	WEST BROMWICH ALBION	AWAY	2 - 1	HUMPHRIES & CROWE (PEN)	34,878
27-Dec	WEST BROMWICH ALBION	HOME	0 - 1		44,929
03-Jan	BURNLEY	AWAY	1 - 3	SHACKLETON	26,013
17-Jan	PRESTON NORTH END	HOME	1 - 3	REVIE	22,043
31-Jan	LEICESTER CITY	AWAY	1 - 0	SHACKLETON	23,376
07-Feb	EVERTON	HOME	1 - 0	SHACKLETON	18,200
14-Feb	WOLVERHAMPTON WANDERERS	AWAY	2 - 6	SHACKLETON & OVERFIELD	26,790
21-Feb	MANCHESTER CITY	HOME	0 - 4		18,515
24-Feb	ARSENAL	AWAY	0 - 1		30,034
28-Feb	PORTSMOUTH	HOME	1 - 1	CUSH	14,900
07-Mar	ASTON VILLA	AWAY	1 - 2	OVERFIELD	27,631
14-Mar	TOTTENHAM HOTSPUR	HOME	3 - 1	CROWE, SHACKLETON & OVERFIELD	17,010
21-Mar	MANCHESTER UNITED	AWAY	0 - 4		45,473
28-Mar	CHELSEA	HOME	4 - 0	O'BRIEN 2, SHACKLETON & CROWE	16,676
31-Mar	WOLVERHAMPTON WANDERERS	HOME	1 - 3	CROWE	35,819
04-Apr	BLACKPOOL	AWAY	0 - 3		14,089
11-Apr	BLACKBURN ROVERS	HOME	2 - 1	SHACKLETON & CHARLTON	15,232
18-Apr	NEWCASTLE UNITED	AWAY	2 - 2	REVIE & PEYTON	19,321
22-Apr	NOTTINGHAM FOREST	AWAY	3 - 0	SHACKLETON 3	18,650
25-Apr	WEST HAM UNITED	HOME	1 - 0	SHACKLETON	11,257
	F. A. CUP				
10-Jan	LUTON TOWN (R3)	AWAY	1 - 5	SHACKLETON	18,354

LEAGUE AND CUP

APPEARANCES

PLAYER	LEAGUE	F. A. CUP	TOTAL
ASHALL	32	1	33
BAIRD H	6		6
BURGIN	16		16
CHARLTON	39	1	40
CROWE	35	1	36
CUSH	36	1	37
DUNN	10		10
FORREST	15		15
GIBSON	31	1	32
HAIR	37	1	38
HUMPHRIES	23	1	24
KEMP	1		1
KERFOOT	16		16
KILFORD	1		1
McCONNELL	6		6
MARSDEN	2		2
MEEK	18		18
MITCHELL R	4		4
O'BRIEN	17		17
OVERFIELD	35	1	36
PEYTON	8		8
REVIE	20	1	21
SHACKLETON	28	1	29
WOOD R	26	1	27

GOALSCORERS

PLAYER	LEAGUE	F. A. CUP	TOTAL
SHACKLETON	16	1	17
CROWE	12		12
OVERFIELD	8		8
CUSH	3		3
O'BRIEN	3		3
BAIRD H	2		2
FORREST	2		2
HUMPHRIES	2		2
REVIE	2		2
CHARLTON	1		1
GIBSON	1		1
MEEK	1		1
PEYTON	1		1
OWN GOALS	3		3

During another frenetic close season, Frank Taylor became Leeds United's fourth manager of the decade as a wind of change began at Elland Road. Veteran defender Jimmy Dunn severed links with the club and goalkeeper Roy Wood announced his retirement. Following opening 3-2 defeats against Burnley and Leicester City, Taylor transformed his team with inside-forward Bobby Cameron (Rangers) reinforcing the line up, but surprisingly United's principal striker Alan Shackleton, joined Everton, while Willie Humphries returned to Ards.

Skipper Don Revie opened his own and Leeds' account for the season in a 1-0 win at Luton Town, before Chris Crowe notched braces in 2-1 victories over West Ham and Chelsea. Sandwiched between these triumphs was a 6-0 trouncing at Manchester United. Entering the transfer market again, Lambert signed centre-forward John McCole from Bradford City for £10,000, but his entry coincided with a dreadful 14-match run that yielded only a 3-2 victory against Arsenal; Peyton and McCole sealing a hard-fought win, and topsy-turvy 3-3 draws against Everton, Blackpool and Manchester City.

Deep in relegation trouble, bizarrely winger Jack Overfield earned a welcome triumph at title contenders Burnley, before McCole, with eight goals to his credit, began a scoring blitz, striking 10 goals in seven league and cup games at the turn of the year. Notching consecutive braces against high-flying Tottenham Hotspur in a 4-2 Boxing Day defeat at Elland Road, McCole stunned Tottenham followers during a sensational 4-1 win at White Hart Lane in the final game of the decade.

The New Year saw FA Cup interests end at Aston Villa before successive three-goal victories against West Ham and Chelsea, McCole scoring in both clashes. Whilst not making excuses, Taylor played various youngsters for brief spells with injuries to numerous players. One teenager to make his bow at Stamford Bridge was 18-year-old Billy Bremner, a youngster destined to be at the forefront of the club's greatest era. A willing partner to Revie, Bremner scored his first Leeds goal in a 3-3 draw against Birmingham City in front of Elland Road's lowest gate since the 1945/46 campaign. The clash is the only game both scored for Leeds, Revie notching two goals.

McCole's fifth brace of the season coupled with strikes by Bremner and Noel Peyton, secured a 4-3 win against Manchester City but with Easter fixtures coming up, survival was questionable. Chris Crowe by now had departed to Blackburn Rovers for £25,000, while Taylor invested in Manchester United defender Freddie Goodwin. Following defeats against Wolves and Sheffield Wednesday, Jack Charlton renewed hope with goals in victories against Bolton Wanderers and Preston North End, but two further losses proved disastrous. McCole's winner in the final game against Nottingham Forest proved meaningless, Forest finishing one point and a place above Leeds, who dropped into Division 2 after three seasons of top-flight football. Charlton again led the appearances chart, missing one game, whilst McCole scored 23 goals.

1959 - 1960

DIVISION ONE (FINAL LEAGUE POSITION - 21ST)

PLD 42 W 12 D 10 L 20 F 65 A 92 PTS 34

DATE	OPPONENTS	VENUE	SCORE	SCORERS	ATT.
22-Aug	BURNLEY	HOME	2 - 3	CHARLTON & CUSH (PEN)	20,233
26-Aug	LEICESTER CITY	AWAY	2 - 3	CROWE & CUSH	24,790
29-Aug	LUTON TOWN	AWAY	1 - 0	REVIE	15,822
02-Sep	LEICESTER CITY	HOME	1 - 1	CROWE	18,384
05-Sep	WEST HAM UNITED	AWAY	2 - 1	CROWE 2 (1 PEN)	27,777
09-Sep	MANCHESTER UNITED	AWAY	0 - 6		48,619
12-Sep	CHELSEA	HOME	2 - 1	CROWE 2	17,011
16-Sep	MANCHESTER UNITED	HOME	2 - 2	CUSH & CROWE	34,048
19-Sep	WEST BROMWICH ALBION	AWAY	0 - 3		26,364
26-Sep	NEWCASTLE UNITED	HOME	2 - 3	McCOLE & REVIE	28,306
03-Oct	BIRMINGHAM CITY	AWAY	0 - 2		25,301
10-Oct	EVERTON	HOME	3 - 3	CROWE (PEN), FRANCIS G & McCOLE	19,122
17-Oct	BLACKPOOL	AWAY	3 - 3	McCOLE 2 & FRANCIS G	22,301
24-Oct	BLACKBURN ROVERS	HOME	0 - 1		17,159
31-Oct	BOLTON WANDERERS	AWAY	1 - 1	McCOLE	20,183
07-Nov	ARSENAL	HOME	3 - 2	PEYTON 2 & McCOLE	21,617
14-Nov	WOLVERHAMPTON WANDERERS	AWAY	2 - 4	CROWE & PEYTON	21,546
21-Nov	SHEFFIELD WEDNESDAY	HOME	1 - 3	McCOLE	21,260
28-Nov	NOTTINGHAM FOREST	AWAY	1 - 4	REVIE	21,366
05-Dec	FULHAM	HOME	1 - 4	McCOLE	18,846
12-Dec	MANCHESTER CITY	AWAY	3 - 3	REVIE, CROWE & GIBSON	19,715
19-Dec	BURNLEY	AWAY	1 - 0	OVERFIELD	17,398
26-Dec	TOTTENHAM HOTSPUR	HOME	2 - 4	McCOLE 2	36,037
28-Dec	TOTTENHAM HOTSPUR	AWAY	4 - 1	McCOLE 2, CAMERON & MEEK	54,170
02-Jan	LUTON TOWN	HOME	1 - 1	McCOLE	19,921
16-Jan	WEST HAM UNITED	HOME	3 - 0	CROWE, McCOLE & MEEK	15,284
23-Jan	CHELSEA	AWAY	3 - 1	McCOLE 2 & PEYTON	18,963
06-Feb	WEST BROMWICH ALBION	HOME	1 - 4	McCOLE (PEN)	23,729
13-Feb	NEWCASTLE UNITED	AWAY	1 - 2	REVIE	16,148
27-Feb	FULHAM	AWAY	0 - 5		23,355
05-Mar	BLACKPOOL	HOME	2 - 4	McCOLE & MEEK	23,127
09-Mar	BIRMINGHAM CITY	HOME	3 - 3	REVIE 2 & BREMNER	8,557
19-Mar	MANCHESTER CITY	HOME	4 - 3	McCOLE 2 (2 PENS), BREMNER & PEYTON	32,545
26-Mar	ARSENAL	AWAY	1 - 1	GIBSON	19,597
02-Apr	WOLVERHAMPTON WANDERERS	HOME	0 - 3		29,492
09-Apr	SHEFFIELD WEDNESDAY	AWAY	0 - 1		27,073
16-Apr	BOLTON WANDERERS	HOME	1 - 0	CHARLTON	19,272
18-Apr	PRESTON NORTH END	AWAY	1 - 1	GIBSON	15,879
19-Apr	PRESTON NORTH END	HOME	2 - 1	CHARLTON & FRANCIS G	23,764
23-Apr	EVERTON	AWAY	0 - 1		37,885
27-Apr	BLACKBURN ROVERS	AWAY	2 - 3	MEEK & McCOLE	19,295
30-Apr	NOTTINGHAM FOREST	HOME	1 - 0	McCOLE (PEN)	11,699

F. A. CUP

09-Jan	ASTON VILLA (R3)	AWAY	1 - 2	McCOLE	43,421

LEAGUE AND CUP
APPEARANCES

PLAYER	LEAGUE	F. A. CUP	TOTAL
ASHALL	38	1	39
BREMNER	11		11
BURGIN	32		32
CALDWELL T	10		10
CAMERON	21	1	22
CHARLTON	41	1	42
CROWE	28	1	29
CUSH	30	1	31
FRANCIS G	12		12
GIBSON	34	1	35
GOODWIN	10		10
HAIR	32	1	33
HUMPHREYS	3		3
HUMPHRIES	2		2
KILFORD	4		4
McCOLE	33	1	34
McCONNELL	8		8
MEEK	33	1	34
OVERFIELD	16		16
PEYTON	20	1	21
REVIE	35		35
SHACKLETON	2		2
WOOD R	7	1	8

GOALSCORERS

PLAYER	LEAGUE	F. A. CUP	TOTAL
McCOLE	22	1	23
CROWE	11		11
REVIE	7		7
PEYTON	5		5
MEEK	4		4
CHARLTON	3		3
CUSH	3		3
FRANCIS G	3		3
GIBSON	3		3
BREMNER	2		2
CAMERON	1		1
OVERFIELD	1		1

In a summer clear out, Frank Taylor attempted to build a squad capable of challenging for promotion. Recruits included wing-half Eric Smith (Celtic) and winger Colin Grainger (Sunderland), whilst Jack Overfield, George Meek and Wilbur Cush moved on. With finances stretched and an eye on the future, Taylor boosted the scouting set-up; by the start of the new season, 50 youngsters from local districts had been recruited. Many failed to make the grade but a number would become legends in years to come.

Taylor's new-look team began poorly, winning three matches in the opening two months against Rotherham United, Southampton and Leyton Orient. Skipper Don Revie gained a win at Orient, while teenager John Hawksby immediately impressed with goals against Rotherham and in a 4-4 humdinger at Bristol Rovers. John McCole scored in both clashes and United's first black player, Gerry Francis, scored in a 3-2 win at Sunderland and a 2-1 victory against Plymouth Argyle. But four defeats in five games, Grainger scoring the winner against Charlton Athletic, piled pressure on the Leeds boss.

Leeds competed in the inaugural League Cup competition, McCole scoring at Blackpool and Chesterfield before notching a goal in a thrilling 5-4 defeat at Southampton. Recovering from 4-0 behind to level, the Saints clinched victory in the last minute. Among United scorers in a 4-0 win against Chesterfield was Billy Bremner, fast becoming a regular in the first team despite bouts of homesickness and along with McCole, inspired an unbeaten eight-match league run throughout December and January. Sustaining only a defeat in the FA Cup at Sheffield Wednesday, Leeds climbed the table with five victories.

The return to form began with 3-2 wins at Lincoln City and Derby County, McCole and Bremner scoring in both games, before McCole opened the scoring in a 3-1 win at Rotherham on New Years Eve. The first of three successive wins, Francis scored a brace in a 3-0 win against Southampton, and McCole grabbed the only goal at Huddersfield Town. However, with declining crowds, injuries and loss of form afflicting the club, results dipped and six defeats in eight games ended Taylor's reign at Elland Road.

By now, 33-year-old Revie had passed the captaincy to Freddie Goodwin, believing he was an unlucky skipper, and looking ahead, applied for the manager's post at Bournemouth. Needing a reference, director Harry Reynolds penned a letter, but realised Revie was the person Leeds needed despite a lack of managerial experience. His fellow directors agreed and the greatest period in the club's history began, although Revie's opening to management was not impressive.

Following a 2-1 defeat to Sheffield United, Leeds gained one victory in seven games, a 7-0 romp against Lincoln City in the penultimate home clash; United's biggest victory for seven years. Goalscorers in the brightest moment of a gruelling season were McCole with a brace, Bremner, Willie Bell, Noel Peyton, Peter McConnell and an own goal. Finishing fourteenth, Jack Charlton, who scored braces against Scunthorpe United and Swansea Town in the run-in, notched his only penalty for Leeds against Scunthorpe and led the way for a third term with 46 appearances. McCole scored 23 goals, including both in the final home game of a gruelling season, a match that eclipsed the previous season's low gate against Birmingham City.

1960 - 1961

DIVISION TWO (FINAL LEAGUE POSITION - 14TH)

PLD 42 W 14 D 10 L 18 F 75 A 83 PTS 38

DATE	OPPONENTS	VENUE	SCORE	SCORERS	ATT.
20-Aug	LIVERPOOL	AWAY	0 - 2		43,041
24-Aug	BRISTOL ROVERS	HOME	1 - 1	McCOLE	11,330
27-Aug	ROTHERHAM UNITED	HOME	2 - 0	HAWKSBY & McCOLE	16,480
29-Aug	BRISTOL ROVERS	AWAY	4 - 4	HAWKSBY. GRAINGER C, PEYTON & McCOLE	18,864
03-Sep	SOUTHAMPTON	AWAY	4 - 2	GRAINGER C, CAMERON, FRANCIS G & McCOLE	21,862
07-Sep	LEYTON ORIENT	HOME	1 - 3	CAMERON	17,363
10-Sep	HUDDERSFIELD TOWN	HOME	1 - 4	CAMERON (PEN)	22,146
14-Sep	LEYTON ORIENT	AWAY	1 - 0	REVIE	8,505
17-Sep	MIDDLESBROUGH	HOME	4 - 4	O. G. (STONEHOUSE), GOODWIN, CAMERON (PEN) & McCOLE	17,799
24-Sep	BRIGHTON & HOVE ALBION	AWAY	1 - 2	McCOLE	16,276
01-Oct	IPSWICH TOWN	HOME	2 - 5	McCOLE 2	13,502
08-Oct	SUNDERLAND	AWAY	3 - 2	PEYTON, FRANCIS G & McCOLE	22,296
15-Oct	PLYMOUTH ARGYLE	HOME	2 - 1	GRAINGER C & FRANCIS G	12,229
22-Oct	NORWICH CITY	AWAY	2 - 3	BREMNER 2	18,970
29-Oct	CHARLTON ATHLETIC	HOME	1 - 0	GRAINGER C	14,014
05-Nov	SHEFFIELD UNITED	AWAY	2 - 3	CAMERON (PEN) & FRANCIS G	17,565
12-Nov	STOKE CITY	HOME	0 - 1		13,486
19-Nov	SWANSEA TOWN	AWAY	2 - 3	McCOLE & CAMERON	11,140
03-Dec	LINCOLN CITY	AWAY	3 - 2	McCOLE, BREMNER & PEYTON	5,678
10-Dec	PORTSMOUTH	HOME	0 - 0		9,421
17-Dec	LIVERPOOL	HOME	2 - 2	MURRAY & BREMNER	11,929
24-Dec	DERBY COUNTY	AWAY	3 - 2	McCOLE & BREMNER 2	15,185
27-Dec	DERBY COUNTY	HOME	3 - 3	McCOLE, MURRAY & CHARLTON	18,517
31-Dec	ROTHERHAM UNITED	AWAY	3 - 1	McCOLE, O. G (LAMBERT) & O. G. (WATERHOUSE)	12,557
14-Jan	SOUTHAMPTON	HOME	3 - 0	CAMERON & FRANCIS G 2	14,039
21-Jan	HUDDERSFIELD TOWN	AWAY	1 - 0	McCOLE	18,938
04-Feb	MIDDLESBROUGH	AWAY	0 - 3		16,593
10-Feb	BRIGHTON & HOVE ALBION	HOME	3 - 2	McCOLE, CHARLTON & GOODWIN	12,598
18-Feb	IPSWICH TOWN	AWAY	0 - 4		13,125
25-Feb	SUNDERLAND	HOME	2 - 4	SMITH E & BREMNER	15,136
04-Mar	PLYMOUTH ARGYLE	AWAY	1 - 3	GRAINGER C	14,878
08-Mar	LUTON TOWN	HOME	1 - 2	CAMERON (PEN)	9,995
11-Mar	NORWICH CITY	HOME	1 - 0	SMITH E	11,294
18-Mar	PORTSMOUTH	AWAY	1 - 3	CHARLTON	16,230
25-Mar	SHEFFIELD UNITED	HOME	1 - 2	O. G. (SHAW)	13,688
01-Apr	LUTON TOWN	AWAY	1 - 1	BREMNER	11,137
03-Apr	SCUNTHORPE UNITED	AWAY	2 - 3	CHARLTON 2 (1 PEN)	8,725
08-Apr	SWANSEA TOWN	HOME	2 - 2	CHARLTON 2	11,862
15-Apr	STOKE CITY	AWAY	0 - 0		7,130
22-Apr	LINCOLN CITY	HOME	7 - 0	McCOLE 2 (1 PEN), BELL W, PEYTON, McCONNELL, BREMNER & O. G. (DRYSDALE)	8,432
25-Apr	SCUNTHORPE UNITED	HOME	2 - 2	McCOLE 2	6,975
29-Apr	CHARLTON ATHLETIC	AWAY	0 - 2		9,081

F. A. CUP

DATE	OPPONENTS	VENUE	SCORE	SCORERS	ATT.
07-Jan	SHEFFIELD WEDNESDAY (R3)	AWAY	0 - 2		36,225

LEAGUE CUP

DATE	OPPONENTS	VENUE	SCORE	SCORERS	ATT.
28-Sep	BLACKPOOL (R2)	HOME	0 - 0		13,064
05-Oct	BLACKPOOL (R2R) *	AWAY	3 - 1	REVIE, McCOLE & GRAINGER C	9,614
23-Nov	CHESTERFIELD (R3)	AWAY	4 - 0	McCOLE, CAMERON (PEN), BREMNER & PEYTON	2,021
05-Dec	SOUTHAMPTON (R4)	AWAY	4 - 5	PEYTON, McCOLE, CHARLTON & CAMERON (PEN)	13,448

LEAGUE AND CUP

APPEARANCES

PLAYER	LEAGUE	F. A. CUP	LEAGUE CUP	TOTAL
ASHALL	4			4
BELL W	5			5
BREMNER	31	1	2	34
BURGIN	10		1	11
CALDWELL T	10		2	12
CAMERON	30	1	4	35
CARLING	4		1	5
CHARLTON	41	1	4	46
FITZGERALD	8			8
FRANCIS G	31	1	3	35
GOODWIN	36	1	4	41
GRAINGER C	33	1	3	37
HAIR	39	1	4	44
HAWKSBY	7			7
HUMPHREYS	28	1	2	31
JOHANNESON	5			5
JONES A	20	1	2	23
KILFORD	10			10
McCOLE	35	1	4	40
McCONNELL	11			11
McGUGAN	1			1
MARTIN G			1	1
MURRAY	7			7
PEYTON	23		3	26
REVIE	14		3	17
SMITH E	18	1		19
WRIGHT R	1		1	2

GOALSCORERS

PLAYER	LEAGUE	F. A. CUP	LEAGUE CUP	TOTAL
McCOLE	20		3	23
BREMNER	9		1	10
CAMERON	8		2	10
CHARLTON	7		1	8
FRANCIS G	6			6
GRAINGER C	5		1	6
PEYTON	4		2	6
GOODWIN	2			2
HAWKSBY	2			2
MURRAY	2			2
REVIE	1		1	2
SMITH E	2			2
BELL W	1			1
McCONNELL	1			1
OWN GOALS	5			5

KEY :- * = AFTER EXTRA TIME

119

With limited funds, the close season saw Preston winger Derek Mayers join promising youngsters in the first team including Scot, Willie Bell and South African, Albert Johanneson. Off the field, Don Revie completed his backroom staff with the arrival of coach Syd Owen, trainer Les Cocker and scout Maurice Lindley. Revie's inaugural season as boss began with wins over Charlton Athletic and Brighton, Billy Bremner scoring in both clashes. However, a 3-1 win against Stoke City, Bremner again scoring, was the only victory in the next 10 games and included heavy defeats at Liverpool and Bristol Rovers.

The past 12 months had seen Alan Humphreys and Terry Carling replace Ted Burgin in goal. The Rovers result saw former Scottish international keeper Tommy Younger arrive in a bid to stem the flow of goals. Initially, Leeds gained draws against Plymouth Argyle, Southampton and Leyton Orient before Bremner and Jack Charlton, playing as emergency centre-forward following an injury to McCole (who notched four goals in a League Cup clash against Brentford), inspired wins over Huddersfield Town, Middlesbrough and Walsall. Another Bremner strike gained a win against Liverpool but with Leeds in the relegation zone, these were troubled times at Elland Road.

At board level, Harry Reynolds succeeded Sam Bolton as chairman, but the New Year brought further grief. Out of both cups, Division Three football was a distinct possibility for the first time following numerous defeats through January and February. Eric Smith claimed a sole win against Sunderland but the purchase of striker Billy McAdams (Bolton) made little impact. Although, Revie was aware of talent in the junior ranks, survival was paramount. Bottom of the table and heavily in debt, backed by Reynolds, Revie signed three experienced players in March; left-back Cliff Mason (Sheffield United), centre-forward Ian Lawson (Burnley) and veteran playmaker Bobby Collins (Everton).

The most expensive purchase at £25,000, Collins signing was viewed as risky but Revie's hunch proved inspirational. Fearless and a born-leader, Collins scored in a winning debut against Swansea Town. Despite a loss at Southampton, a match that saw teenage keeper Gary Sprake make a dramatic bow when Younger fell ill on the day, Collins never-say-die spirit brought the best from teammates. Grinding out six draws and three wins against Luton Town; Bremner notching a brace, Middlesbrough; Grenville Hair scoring his only league goal in 443 league appearances, and at Newcastle United; Johanneson, scoring the opening goal, edged Leeds clear of the relegation zone. Finishing nineteenth was Leeds' worst finish to date but marked a major turning point in the club's history.

Skipper Freddie Goodwin missed one game, whilst Bremner and Charlton top scored with 12 goals apiece in a remarkable campaign on and off the pitch. The season saw Revie's retirement as a player, but as manager, Reynolds believed totally in him. Revie had changed the club strip to the all-white of Real Madrid and enhanced the youth policy. He insisted on the best travel and conditions for his players, despite the club being £150,000 in debt. A remarkable man, behind the scenes, Reynolds made everyone feel important, whether player's wives, ground staff, cleaners or tea ladies. On the pitch, if Revie wanted a player, Reynolds ensured it happened.

DIVISION TWO (FINAL LEAGUE POSITION - 19TH)

PLD 42 W 12 D 12 L 18 F 50 A 61 PTS 36

DATE	OPPONENTS	VENUE	SCORE	SCORERS	ATT.
19-Aug	CHARLTON ATHLETIC	HOME	1 - 0	BREMNER	12,916
22-Aug	BRIGHTON & HOVE ALBION	AWAY	3 - 1	PEYTON, BREMNER & MAYERS	22,744
26-Aug	LIVERPOOL	AWAY	0 - 5		42,450
30-Aug	BRIGHTON & HOVE ALBION	HOME	1 - 1	BREMNER	12,642
02-Sep	ROTHERHAM UNITED	HOME	1 - 3	McCOLE	12,610
06-Sep	NORWICH CITY	AWAY	0 - 2		26,860
09-Sep	SUNDERLAND	AWAY	1 - 2	McCOLE	30,737
16-Sep	STOKE CITY	HOME	3 - 1	McCOLE, BREMNER & PEYTON	9,578
20-Sep	NORWICH CITY	HOME	0 - 1		10,948
23-Sep	BRISTOL ROVERS	AWAY	0 - 4		13,676
30-Sep	PRESTON NORTH END	HOME	1 - 2	CHARLTON	9,360
07-Oct	PLYMOUTH ARGYLE	AWAY	1 - 1	McCONNELL	10,144
14-Oct	HUDDERSFIELD TOWN	HOME	1 - 0	CHARLTON	19,162
21-Oct	SWANSEA TOWN	AWAY	1 - 2	McCONNELL	11,091
28-Oct	SOUTHAMPTON	HOME	1 - 1	McCONNELL	10,145
04-Nov	LUTON TOWN	AWAY	2 - 3	REVIE & BREMNER (PEN)	10,341
11-Nov	LEYTON ORIENT	HOME	0 - 0		7,967
18-Nov	MIDDLESBROUGH	AWAY	3 - 1	MAYERS, BREMNER & CHARLTON	10,758
25-Nov	WALSALL	HOME	4 - 1	CHARLTON 2, BREMNER (PEN) & PEYTON	10,999
02-Dec	DERBY COUNTY	AWAY	3 - 3	PEYTON, MAYERS & BELL W	16,408
16-Dec	CHARLTON ATHLETIC	AWAY	1 - 3	BREMNER (PEN)	9,459
23-Dec	LIVERPOOL	HOME	1 - 0	BREMNER	17,214
26-Dec	SCUNTHORPE UNITED	HOME	1 - 4	CHARLTON	19,481
12-Jan	ROTHERHAM UNITED	AWAY	1 - 2	McADAMS	6,207
20-Jan	SUNDERLAND	HOME	1 - 0	SMITH E	17,763
27-Jan	NEWCASTLE UNITED	HOME	0 - 1		17,120
03-Feb	STOKE CITY	AWAY	1 - 2	PEYTON	21,935
10-Feb	BRISTOL ROVERS	HOME	0 - 0		9,108
20-Feb	SCUNTHORPE UNITED	AWAY	1 - 2	MAYERS (PEN)	9,186
24-Feb	PLYMOUTH ARGYLE	HOME	2 - 3	CHARLTON & MAYERS	8,554
03-Mar	HUDDERSFIELD TOWN	AWAY	1 - 2	CHARLTON	16,799
10-Mar	SWANSEA TOWN	HOME	2 - 0	COLLINS & McADAMS	17,314
17-Mar	SOUTHAMPTON	AWAY	1 - 4	LAWSON	11,924
24-Mar	LUTON TOWN	HOME	2 - 1	BREMNER 2	13,078
31-Mar	LEYTON ORIENT	AWAY	0 - 0		13,290
07-Apr	MIDDLESBROUGH	HOME	2 - 0	HAIR & O. G. (GATES)	16,116
09-Apr	PRESTON NORTH END	AWAY	1 - 1	O. G. (CUNNINGHAM)	10,492
14-Apr	WALSALL	AWAY	1 - 1	JOHANNESON	9,005
20-Apr	BURY	AWAY	1 - 1	CHARLTON	11,313
21-Apr	DERBY COUNTY	HOME	0 - 0		11,922
24-Apr	BURY	HOME	0 - 0		21,482
28-Apr	NEWCASTLE UNITED	AWAY	3 - 0	JOHANNESON, McADAMS & O. G. (KEITH)	21,708

F. A. CUP

DATE	OPPONENTS	VENUE	SCORE	SCORERS	ATT.
06-Jan	DERBY COUNTY (R3)	HOME	2 - 2	PEYTON & CHARLTON	27,089
10-Jan	DERBY COUNTY (R3R)	AWAY	1 - 3	McADAMS	28,168

LEAGUE CUP

DATE	OPPONENTS	VENUE	SCORE	SCORERS	ATT.
13-Sep	BRENTFORD (R2)	HOME	4 - 1	McCOLE 4	4,517
04-Oct	HUDDERSFIELD TOWN (R3)	HOME	3 - 2	BREMNER (PEN), CHARLTON & McCONNELL	10,023
12-Dec	ROTHERHAM UNITED (R4)	AWAY	1 - 1	CHARLTON	10,899
15-Jan	ROTHERHAM UNITED (R4R)	HOME	1 - 2	JOHANNESON (PEN)	6,385

LEAGUE AND CUP

APPEARANCES

PLAYER	LEAGUE	F. A. CUP	LEAGUE CUP	TOTAL
ADDY			1	1
BELL W	23	2	3	28
BREMNER	39	2	4	45
CAMERON	7			7
CARLING	1			1
CASEY Te.	3		1	4
CHARLTON	34	2	3	39
COLLINS	11			11
FRANCIS G	4			4
GOODWIN	41	2	4	47
HAIR	38	2	3	43
HAWKSBY	25		4	29
HUMPHREYS	9		1	10
JOHANNESON	13		1	14
JONES A	5		1	6
KILFORD	6		2	8
LAWSON	11			11
McADAMS	11	2		13
McCOLE	10		1	11
McCONNELL	23	2	3	28
MASON C	11			11
MAYERS	20	2	2	24
PEYTON	37	2	4	43
REVIE	7			7
SMITH E	41	2	3	46
SPRAKE	1			1
YOUNGER	31	2	3	36

GOALSCORERS

PLAYER	LEAGUE	F. A. CUP	LEAGUE CUP	TOTAL
BREMNER	11		1	12
CHARLTON	9	1	2	12
McCOLE	3		4	7
PEYTON	5	1		6
MAYERS	5			5
McADAMS	3	1		4
McCONNELL	3		1	4
JOHANNESON	2		1	3
BELL W	1			1
COLLINS	1			1
HAIR	1			1
LAWSON	1			1
REVIE	1			1
SMITH E	1			1
OWN GOALS	3			3

An injection of capital saw Don Revie develop his squad. Among new arrivals, most attention surrounded John Charles' return from Juventus for a record £53,000 fee, but the former legend would soon join Roma at a profit for £70,000. Airdrie striker Jim Storrie's £15,650 purchase was less newsworthy but would have more immediate impact, while departures included Billy McAdams, Derek Mayers and Bobby Cameron.

Storrie made his mark with a debut goal in a 1-0 win at Stoke City on the opening day and struck, along with Charles and Albert Johanneson, as Leeds went down 4-3 to Rotherham United. However, though Billy Bremner edged a win against Sunderland, an uninspiring start resulted in Revie blooding four promising youngsters at Swansea Town. Gary Sprake (for only his second match), Paul Reaney, Norman Hunter and striker Rodney Johnson shone in a 2-0 triumph, Johnson and Bremner scoring.

Sprake, Reaney and Hunter would quickly become first team regulars, while fans saw 15-year-old Peter Lorimer, dubbed the 'Cannonball Kid' due to his shooting power, make his bow against Southampton. Revie's rookies helped Leeds climb the table and making an impression was Johanneson. Blessed with blistering pace, the 'Black Flash' overcame racist taunts from fans and opposing players with mesmerising performances, and backed up Storrie in the scoring stakes, notching goals against Chelsea, Newcastle United, Norwich City and Plymouth Argyle at Elland Road. Storrie was the most prolific striker however, and scored his first Leeds hat-trick in a 6-1 win against Plymouth Argyle.

Although out of the League Cup, following an early exit at Blackburn Rovers, Revie's team was taking shape around the indomitable Bobby Collins, and Don Weston's arrival further strengthened a forward line fast becoming one of the most feared in the division. Weston opened his scoring account spectacularly with a hat-trick in Leeds' 3-1 win against Stoke City, but the December clash would be the penultimate game before a winter freeze necessitated a halt to professional football for two months. Come March, Weston opened the scoring in another 3-1 win over Derby County; Storrie and Charlton also finding the net.

Although Nottingham Forest ended Leeds' FA Cup interests, in the league a Storrie brace accounted for Walsall, whilst a Collins double saw off Grimsby Town. Bremner was also on target in a 3-0 win against Grimsby, the first of five victories in six games as Leeds defeated Scunthorpe United, Preston North End, and Charlton Athletic in an Easter double. The winning burst continued when Ian Lawson scored a brace at Scunthorpe, while Storrie struck a hat-trick versus Cardiff City and a double against Luton Town.

Suddenly, Revie's team were potential promotion candidates behind Stoke City, Chelsea and Sunderland, but three consecutive defeats in May ended any chance of a late charge. Nevertheless, a 5-0 win against Swansea rounded off a promising season with so much talent making giant strides. Both Collins and Johanneson missed three games, whilst in a remarkable effort Storrie top scored with 27 goals. Two players, Tom Jennings and Charles, have bettered his 25 league goals whilst three decades on, in addition to Jennings and Charles, only Lorimer and Lee Chapman have accumulated more goals in a season.

DIVISION TWO (FINAL LEAGUE POSITION - 5TH)

PLD 42 W 19 D 10 L 13 F 79 A 53 PTS 48

DATE	OPPONENTS	VENUE	SCORE	SCORERS	ATT.
18-Aug	STOKE CITY	AWAY	1 - 0	STORRIE	27,118
22-Aug	ROTHERHAM UNITED	HOME	3 - 4	STORRIE, CHARLES & JOHANNESON	14,119
25-Aug	SUNDERLAND	HOME	1 - 0	BREMNER	17,753
28-Aug	ROTHERHAM UNITED	AWAY	1 - 2	CHARLES	19,508
01-Sep	HUDDERSFIELD TOWN	AWAY	1 - 1	CHARLES	34,946
05-Sep	BURY	HOME	1 - 2	BREMNER	28,313
08-Sep	SWANSEA TOWN	AWAY	2 - 0	JOHNSON R & BREMNER	17,696
15-Sep	CHELSEA	HOME	2 - 0	JOHANNESON 2	27,520
18-Sep	BURY	AWAY	1 - 3	STORRIE	18,876
22-Sep	LUTON TOWN	AWAY	2 - 2	STORRIE & COLLINS	8,958
29-Sep	SOUTHAMPTON	HOME	1 - 1	STORRIE	25,408
06-Oct	MIDDLESBROUGH	HOME	2 - 3	HUNTER & BREMNER	28,222
13-Oct	DERBY COUNTY	AWAY	0 - 0		14,246
20-Oct	NEWCASTLE UNITED	HOME	1 - 0	JOHANNESON	23,386
27-Oct	WALSALL	AWAY	1 - 1	JOHANNESON	7,353
03-Nov	NORWICH CITY	HOME	3 - 0	STORRIE, BELL W & JOHANNESON	15,919
10-Nov	GRIMSBY TOWN	AWAY	1 - 1	STORRIE	9,183
17-Nov	PLYMOUTH ARGYLE	HOME	6 - 1	JOHANNESON, STORRIE 3, COLLINS & BREMNER	15,301
24-Nov	PRESTON NORTH END	AWAY	1 - 4	BELL W	13,145
01-Dec	PORTSMOUTH	HOME	3 - 3	STORRIE, COLLINS & JOHANNESON	15,519
08-Dec	CARDIFF CITY	AWAY	0 - 0		11,334
15-Dec	STOKE CITY	HOME	3 - 1	WESTON 3	19,331
22-Dec	SUNDERLAND	AWAY	1 - 2	BREMNER	40,252
02-Mar	DERBY COUNTY	HOME	3 - 1	WESTON, STORRIE & CHARLTON (PEN)	22,912
09-Mar	NEWCASTLE UNITED	AWAY	1 - 1	STORRIE	29,570
13-Mar	WALSALL	HOME	3 - 0	JOHANNESON & STORRIE 2	17,077
23-Mar	NORWICH CITY	AWAY	2 - 3	COLLINS & JOHANNESON	26,154
30-Mar	GRIMSBY TOWN	HOME	3 - 0	BREMNER & COLLINS 2	13,938
03-Apr	SCUNTHORPE UNITED	HOME	1 - 0	BREMNER	15,783
06-Apr	PLYMOUTH ARGYLE	AWAY	1 - 3	STORRIE	8,992
13-Apr	PRESTON NORTH END	HOME	4 - 1	BREMNER 2, STORRIE & COLLINS	16,016
15-Apr	CHARLTON ATHLETIC	AWAY	2 - 1	CHARLTON & HUNTER	13,538
16-Apr	CHARLTON ATHLETIC	HOME	4 - 1	WESTON, HENDERSON T, JOHANNESON & STORRIE	24,646
20-Apr	PORTSMOUTH	AWAY	0 - 3		7,773
23-Apr	SCUNTHORPE UNITED	AWAY	2 - 0	LAWSON 2	7,794
27-Apr	CARDIFF CITY	HOME	3 - 0	STORRIE 3	19,752
30-Apr	CHELSEA	AWAY	2 - 2	LAWSON 2	24,387
04-May	LUTON TOWN	HOME	3 - 0	STORRIE 2 & WESTON	23,781
06-May	MIDDLESBROUGH	AWAY	1 - 2	JOHANNESON	17,365
11-May	HUDDERSFIELD TOWN	HOME	0 - 1		28,501
15-May	SOUTHAMPTON	AWAY	1 - 3	WESTON	11,619
18-May	SWANSEA TOWN	HOME	5 - 0	STORRIE 2, LAWSON, COLLINS & JOHANNESON	11,314

F. A. CUP

DATE	OPPONENTS	VENUE	SCORE	SCORERS	ATT.
06-Mar	STOKE CITY (R3)	HOME	3 - 1	COLLINS, REANEY & HAIR	36,873
16-Mar	MIDDLESBROUGH (R4)	AWAY	2 - 0	STORRIE & JOHANNESON	39,672
19-Mar	NOTTINGHAM FOREST (R5)	AWAY	0 - 3		36,392

LEAGUE CUP

DATE	OPPONENTS	VENUE	SCORE	SCORERS	ATT.
26-Sep	CRYSTAL PALACE (R2)	HOME	2 - 1	CHARLTON & STORRIE	7,274
17-Oct	BLACKBURN ROVERS (R3)	AWAY	0 - 4		7,680

LEAGUE AND CUP

APPEARANCES

PLAYER	LEAGUE	F. A. CUP	LEAGUE CUP	TOTAL
ADDY	2		1	3
BELL W	32	3	1	36
BREMNER	24			24
CHARLES	11			11
CHARLTON	38	3	1	42
COLLINS	41	3		44
GOODWIN	8			8
GREENHOFF J	2			2
HAIR	26	3	1	30
HALLETT			1	1
HAWKSBY	5		2	7
HENDERSON T	20	3		23
HUNTER	36	3	2	41
JOHANNESON	41	3		44
JOHNSON R	4		2	6
LAWSON	6		2	8
LORIMER	1			1
MASON C	20		2	22
PEYTON	6		2	8
REANEY	35	3	1	39
SMITH E	6			6
SPRAKE	33	3	2	38
STORRIE	38	3	2	43
WESTON	15	3		18
WILLIAMSON	3			3
WRIGHT B	3			3
YOUNGER	6			6

GOALSCORERS

PLAYER	LEAGUE	F. A. CUP	LEAGUE CUP	TOTAL
STORRIE	25	1	1	27
JOHANNESON	13	1		14
BREMNER	10			10
COLLINS	8	1		9
WESTON	7			7
LAWSON	5			5
CHARLES	3			3
CHARLTON	2		1	3
BELL W	2			2
HUNTER	2			2
HAIR		1		1
HENDERSON T	1			1
JOHNSON R	1			1
REANEY		1		1

With Don Revie's youth policy flourishing Leeds United were amongst the pre-season favourites. Joining his talented youngsters in the first team following an opening win against Rotherham United, Don Weston scoring, was 22-year-old Irish international Johnny Giles (Manchester United). After a comfortable victory over Bury, Revie's team lost 3-2 at Manchester City, but it heralded an unbeaten 20-game run, the best since 1927/28, including consecutive victories against Norwich City, Northampton Town, Scunthorpe United, Middlesbrough and Huddersfield Town. Skipper Bobby Collins and Weston scored in three clashes.

A 4-1 win at Southampton, Ian Lawson notching a brace, was Leeds' ninth win in 15 games and a 2-0 triumph at Grimsby Town took Revie's charges top. With the halfback partnership of Bremner-Charlton-Hunter playing with assurance, Leeds had the look of winners, but the key was Collins, constantly encouraging his teammates. Approaching the season's halfway point, winger Albert Johanneson scored in consecutive wins against Leyton Orient, Swansea Town and Plymouth Argyle, but a 2-1 victory at Bury prior to Christmas was the prelude to a dip in form. Sunderland ended Leeds' unbeaten run with a 2-0 victory, in turn opening up the promotion battle. A point ahead of Sunderland and Preston North End, promotion outsiders were Charlton Athletic and Manchester City.

The Sunderland loss was part of a nine-match spell that yielded two wins, including one over rivals Manchester City. The run saw Leeds interests end in both cup competitions, however promotion was the major target and with Jim Storrie sidelined, Revie signed Alan Peacock (Middlesbrough). It proved an inspired decision. The former England international made a scoring debut in a 2-2 draw at Norwich and added balance to the side but a 2-0 defeat at Preston saw Leeds slip to second spot, ahead of the Deepdale club on goal average, but it would be the last reverse as Leeds rediscovered their form in the final 10 games.

The renaissance began at home with a 3-1 win against Southampton, Lawson, Collins and Johanneson scoring. Further 3-1 wins against Middlesbrough and Grimsby sent Leeds top prior to three Easter games in four days. Arranging overnight stops, Revie's planning paid dividends with a hard-fought win at Newcastle United, Giles scoring, before picking up a point at Derby County. Following a days rest, Johanneson struck a brilliant winner in the return with Newcastle. Needing four points for promotion, Giles and Weston secured a 2-1 win against Leyton Orient before a Peacock brace and a Giles strike sealed top-flight football. With Sunderland and Southampton drawing, two points separated Leeds from the title and 40 years on from their last championship triumph, they duly claimed the crown, courtesy of a Peacock brace in the final match at Charlton Athletic.

Among numerous records, United's 63 points total was the highest by a Division 2 club since World War 2. Leeds completed a season unbeaten at home for the first time, while eight consecutive away wins and 10 unbeaten away matches set new standards. Norman Hunter was the only ever-present in the league, Sprake, Reaney and Collins missed one match, Giles two and Bremner three. Weston and Johanneson notched 13 league goals apiece, while Peacock scored eight in 14 games.

1963 - 1964

DIVISION TWO (FINAL LEAGUE POSITION - 1ST)				
PLD 42 W 24 D 15 L 3 F 71 A 34 PTS 63				
DATE	OPPONENTS	VENUE	SCORE SCORERS	ATT.
28-Aug	ROTHERHAM UNITED	HOME	1 - 0 WESTON	22,517
31-Aug	BURY	HOME	3 - 0 COLLINS, STORRIE & JOHANNESON	26,041
03-Sep	ROTHERHAM UNITED	AWAY	2 - 2 CHARLTON & JOHANNESON	14,178
07-Sep	MANCHESTER CITY	AWAY	2 - 3 LAWSON & JOHANNESON	29,186
11-Sep	PORTSMOUTH	HOME	3 - 1 STORRIE, WESTON & BREMNER	24,926
14-Sep	SWINDON TOWN	HOME	0 - 0	33,301
18-Sep	PORTSMOUTH	AWAY	1 - 1 HENDERSON T	12,569
21-Sep	CARDIFF CITY	AWAY	0 - 0	16,117
28-Sep	NORWICH CITY	HOME	4 - 2 WESTON 2, JOHANNESON & COLLINS (PEN)	22,804
01-Oct	NORTHAMPTON TOWN	AWAY	3 - 0 LAWSON, WESTON & COLLINS	15,079
05-Oct	SCUNTHORPE UNITED	AWAY	1 - 0 LAWSON	10,793
09-Oct	MIDDLESBROUGH	HOME	2 - 0 HUNTER & COLLINS	36,919
12-Oct	HUDDERSFIELD TOWN	AWAY	2 - 0 GILES & WESTON	31,220
19-Oct	DERBY COUNTY	HOME	2 - 2 CHARLTON & WESTON	29,864
26-Oct	SOUTHAMPTON	AWAY	4 - 1 LAWSON 2, GILES & JOHANNESON	18,036
02-Nov	CHARLTON ATHLETIC	HOME	1 - 1 CHARLTON	32,344
09-Nov	GRIMSBY TOWN	AWAY	2 - 0 LAWSON & WESTON	12,194
16-Nov	PRESTON NORTH END	HOME	1 - 1 JOHANNESON	33,841
23-Nov	LEYTON ORIENT	AWAY	2 - 0 COLLINS & JOHANNESON	12,072
30-Nov	SWANSEA TOWN	HOME	2 - 1 JOHANNESON & BELL W	21,870
07-Dec	PLYMOUTH ARGYLE	AWAY	1 - 0 JOHANNESON	9,918
14-Dec	NORTHAMPTON TOWN	HOME	0 - 0	21,108
21-Dec	BURY	AWAY	2 - 1 WESTON & LAWSON	7,453
26-Dec	SUNDERLAND	HOME	1 - 1 LAWSON	41,167
28-Dec	SUNDERLAND	AWAY	0 - 2	55,046
11-Jan	MANCHESTER CITY	HOME	1 - 0 WESTON	33,737
18-Jan	SWINDON TOWN	AWAY	2 - 2 GILES & HUNTER	19,015
01-Feb	CARDIFF CITY	HOME	1 - 1 JOHANNESON	28,039
08-Feb	NORWICH CITY	AWAY	2 - 2 WESTON & PEACOCK	20,843
15-Feb	SCUNTHORPE UNITED	HOME	1 - 0 JOHANNESON	28,868
22-Feb	HUDDERSFIELD TOWN	HOME	1 - 1 STORRIE	36,439
03-Mar	PRESTON NORTH END	AWAY	0 - 2	35,612
07-Mar	SOUTHAMPTON	HOME	3 - 1 LAWSON, COLLINS & JOHANNESON	24,077
14-Mar	MIDDLESBROUGH	AWAY	3 - 1 LAWSON, PEACOCK & GILES	15,986
21-Mar	GRIMSBY TOWN	HOME	3 - 1 LAWSON, BREMNER & PEACOCK	25,351
27-Mar	NEWCASTLE UNITED	AWAY	1 - 0 GILES	55,038
28-Mar	DERBY COUNTY	AWAY	1 - 1 PEACOCK	16,757
30-Mar	NEWCASTLE UNITED	HOME	2 - 1 WESTON & JOHANNESON	40,105
04-Apr	LEYTON ORIENT	HOME	2 - 1 GILES & WESTON	30,920
11-Apr	SWANSEA TOWN	AWAY	3 - 0 PEACOCK 2 & GILES	14,321
18-Apr	PLYMOUTH ARGYLE	HOME	1 - 1 BELL W	34,725
25-Apr	CHARLTON ATHLETIC	AWAY	2 - 0 PEACOCK 2	21,323
F. A. CUP				
04-Jan	CARDIFF CITY (R3)	AWAY	1 - 0 BREMNER	13,932
25-Jan	EVERTON (R4)	HOME	1 - 1 LAWSON	48,197
28-Jan	EVERTON (R4R)	AWAY	0 - 2	66,167
LEAGUE CUP				
25-Sep	MANSFIELD TOWN (R2)	HOME	5 - 1 LAWSON 2, BELL W & JOHANNESON 2	8,493
22-Oct	SWANSEA TOWN (R3)	HOME	2 - 0 LAWSON & STORRIE	10,769
27-Nov	MANCHESTER CITY (R4)	AWAY	1 - 3 WESTON	10,584

LEAGUE AND CUP

APPEARANCES

PLAYER	LEAGUE	F. A. CUP	LEAGUE CUP	TOTAL
BELL W	35	3	3	41
BREMNER	39	3	1	43
CHARLTON	25		2	27
COLLINS	41	2	1	44
COOPER T	2			2
GILES	40	3	2	45
GOODWIN	12	1	1	14
GREENHOFF J	2		1	3
HAIR	8		2	10
HAWKSBY		1	1	2
HENDERSON T	2	3	2	7
HUNTER	42	3	2	47
JOHANNESON	37	2	2	41
LAWSON	24	3	2	29
LORIMER			1	1
MADELEY	4	2		6
PEACOCK	14			14
REANEY	41	3	2	46
SMITH E			1	1
SPRAKE	41	3	3	47
STORRIE	15		2	17
WESTON	35	1	2	38
WILLIAMSON	1			1
WRIGHT B	2			2

GOALSCORERS

PLAYER	LEAGUE	F. A. CUP	LEAGUE CUP	TOTAL
JOHANNESON	13		2	15
LAWSON	11	1	3	15
WESTON	13		1	14
PEACOCK	8			8
GILES	7			7
COLLINS	6			6
STORRIE	3		1	4
BELL W	2		1	3
BREMNER	2	1		3
CHARLTON	3			3
HUNTER	2			2
HENDERSON T	1			1

During a hectic close season, Eric Smith and Grenville Hair departed, whilst *FA News* published a list of clubs with the worst disciplinary record from the previous campaign and Leeds United headed it. Accusations of 'dirty play' and 'over-professionalism' began to afflict the club even though the bulk of offenders were juniors and reserves, not first team players, but the damage was done. Nevertheless, Leeds won opening clashes against Aston Villa, Liverpool and Wolves.

Though four of the next seven games ended in defeat, the heaviest at Blackpool by 4-0, consecutive victories against Stoke City, Tottenham Hotspur, Burnley, Sheffield United, Everton, Arsenal and Birmingham City moved Leeds among the pacesetters. Jim Storrie scored in four of the clashes, whilst Willie Bell notched winners at Burnley and Everton, a clash that saw Sandy Brown dismissed within two minutes for a foul on Bell prior to the referee taking both sides off to cool down.

Despite a loss at West Ham, wins against West Brom, league leaders Manchester United; Collins striking the only goal, Aston Villa and Wolves meant Leeds were joint leaders at Christmas before reaching the summit after a 2-1 win over Sunderland in the New Year; Norman Hunter scoring a rare goal. Leeds now led the way, but a sole victory at Arsenal amongst six unbeaten league games meant a three-way title race with Manchester United and Chelsea.

During the run, Revie's team had moved into the FA Cup semi-finals for the first time after defeating Southport, Everton, Shrewsbury and Crystal Palace. The Everton clash was a classic before Leeds, watched by some 66,000 spectators, came through 2-1 in a replay at Goodison Park, Weston scoring the winner. At Selhurst Park, second half goals earned a 3-0 win, Alan Peacock notching a brace. The semi-final clash at Hillsborough against Manchester United was a punishing encounter but the replay was a different spectacle, Billy Bremner's late winner securing a titanic victory.

Chasing the double, Leeds drew with Fulham before demolishing Burnley 5-1 and Everton 4-1, Johanneson scoring in both fixtures. Further wins came against West Ham, Stoke City and West Brom. Eighteen league games unbeaten but consecutive Easter defeats against Manchester United and Sheffield Wednesday dented Leeds' challenge. In spite of victories over Wednesday and Sheffield United, Matt Busby's team was in control. Leeds recovered from a three-goal deficit to draw 3-3 at Birmingham in the final game but the title went to Old Trafford. Leeds had enjoyed their best ever league campaign and finished with the highest number of points by a Division 1 runner-up, but Revie's charges had lost out on goal average by 0.686 of a goal.

Five days later Leeds walked out at Wembley for a first FA Cup final, but it was not to be. In a dour match, the game sprang into action during extra-time after Roger Hunt scored. Leeds equalised with a classic Bremner strike but Liverpool claimed the trophy with an Ian St John header. Collins capped a remarkable season by becoming the club's first player to receive the prestigious Football Writers Player of the Year award. Hunter made 51 appearances, Storrie top scored with 19 goals.

1964 - 1965

DIVISION ONE (FINAL LEAGUE POSITION - 2ND)

PLD 42 W 26 D 9 L 7 F 83 A 52 PTS 61

DATE	OPPONENTS	VENUE	SCORE	SCORERS	ATT.
22-Aug	ASTON VILLA	AWAY	2 - 1	JOHANNESON & CHARLTON	28,000
26-Aug	LIVERPOOL	HOME	4 - 2	O.G. (YEATS), WESTON, BREMNER & GILES	36,005
29-Aug	WOLVERHAMPTON WANDERERS	HOME	3 - 2	STORRIE 2 & CHARLTON	34,538
02-Sep	LIVERPOOL	AWAY	1 - 2	COLLINS	52,548
05-Sep	SUNDERLAND	AWAY	3 - 3	STORRIE, BELL W & JOHANNESON	48,858
07-Sep	BLACKPOOL	AWAY	0 - 4		26,310
12-Sep	LEICESTER CITY	HOME	3 - 2	BREMNER 2 (1 PEN) & JOHANNESON	32,300
16-Sep	BLACKPOOL	HOME	3 - 0	COLLINS 2 & HUNTER	35,973
19-Sep	CHELSEA	AWAY	0 - 2		38,006
26-Sep	NOTTINGHAM FOREST	HOME	1 - 2	STORRIE	32,776
30-Sep	FULHAM	HOME	2 - 2	STORRIE 2	31,260
10-Oct	STOKE CITY	AWAY	3 - 2	STORRIE 2 & GREENHOFF J	27,561
17-Oct	TOTTENHAM HOTSPUR	HOME	3 - 1	BELFITT, GILES & BELL W (PEN)	41,464
24-Oct	BURNLEY	AWAY	1 - 0	BELL W	24,329
31-Oct	SHEFFIELD UNITED	HOME	4 - 1	COLLINS, STORRIE, JOHANNESON & BELFITT	33,357
07-Nov	EVERTON	AWAY	1 - 0	BELL W	43,605
11-Nov	ARSENAL	HOME	3 - 1	CHARLTON, BELFITT & STORRIE	38,620
14-Nov	BIRMINGHAM CITY	HOME	4 - 1	STORRIE, CHARLTON, COLLINS & GILES (PEN)	32,030
21-Nov	WEST HAM UNITED	AWAY	1 - 3	BELFITT	28,150
28-Nov	WEST BROMWICH ALBION	HOME	1 - 0	JOHNSON R	29,553
05-Dec	MANCHESTER UNITED	AWAY	1 - 0	COLLINS	53,374
12-Dec	ASTON VILLA	HOME	1 - 0	JOHANNESON	27,339
19-Dec	WOLVERHAMPTON WANDERERS	AWAY	1 - 0	JOHNSON R	17,126
26-Dec	BLACKBURN ROVERS	HOME	1 - 1	STORRIE	45,341
28-Dec	BLACKBURN ROVERS	AWAY	2 - 0	STORRIE & JOHANNESON	24,511
02-Jan	SUNDERLAND	HOME	2 - 1	CHARLTON & HUNTER	43,808
16-Jan	LEICESTER CITY	AWAY	2 - 2	CHARLTON & JOHNSON R	23,230
23-Jan	CHELSEA	HOME	2 - 2	STORRIE & GILES	47,109
06-Feb	NOTTINGHAM FOREST	AWAY	0 - 0		36,596
13-Feb	ARSENAL	AWAY	2 - 1	GILES & WESTON	32,132
27-Feb	TOTTENHAM HOTSPUR	AWAY	0 - 0		42,202
13-Mar	FULHAM	AWAY	2 - 2	PEACOCK & COLLINS	24,704
15-Mar	BURNLEY	HOME	5 - 1	COLLINS 2, CHARLTON 2 & JOHANNESON	38,506
20-Mar	EVERTON	HOME	4 - 1	JOHANNESON 2, BREMNER & PEACOCK	29,701
03-Apr	WEST HAM UNITED	HOME	2 - 1	PEACOCK & BREMNER	41,918
05-Apr	STOKE CITY	HOME	3 - 1	WESTON 2 & GREENHOFF J	38,133
12-Apr	WEST BROMWICH ALBION	AWAY	2 - 1	PEACOCK 2	20,007
17-Apr	MANCHESTER UNITED	HOME	0 - 1		52,368
19-Apr	SHEFFIELD WEDNESDAY	AWAY	0 - 3		39,054
20-Apr	SHEFFIELD WEDNESDAY	HOME	2 - 0	STORRIE & GILES (PEN)	45,065
24-Apr	SHEFFIELD UNITED	AWAY	3 - 0	STORRIE, BREMNER & PEACOCK	32,928
26-Apr	BIRMINGHAM CITY	AWAY	3 - 3	GILES (PEN), REANEY & CHARLTON	16,644

F. A. CUP

DATE	OPPONENTS	VENUE	SCORE	SCORERS	ATT.
09-Jan	SOUTHPORT (R3)	HOME	3 - 0	GREENHOFF J, JOHANNESON & JOHNSON R	31,297
30-Jan	EVERTON (R4)	HOME	1 - 1	STORRIE	50,051
02-Feb	EVERTON (R4R)	AWAY	2 - 1	CHARLTON & WESTON	65,940
20-Feb	SHREWSBURY TOWN (R5)	HOME	2 - 0	GILES (PEN) & JOHANNESON	47,740
10-Mar	CRYSTAL PALACE (R6)	AWAY	3 - 0	PEACOCK 2 & STORRIE	45,384
27-Mar	MANCHESTER UNITED (SF) $	NEUTRAL	0 - 0		65,000
31-Mar	MANCHESTER UNITED (SFR) <	NEUTRAL	1 - 0	BREMNER	46,300
01-May	LIVERPOOL (Fl) >	NEUTRAL	1 - 2	BREMNER	100,000

LEAGUE CUP

DATE	OPPONENTS	VENUE	SCORE	SCORERS	ATT.
23-Sep	HUDDERSFIELD TOWN (R2)	HOME	3 - 2	HUNTER, STORRIE & BELFITT	9,837
14-Oct	ASTON VILLA (R3)	HOME	2 - 3	JOHANNESON & COLLINS	10,656

LEAGUE AND CUP

APPEARANCES

PLAYER	LEAGUE	F. A. CUP	LEAGUE CUP	TOTAL
BELFITT	8		2	10
BELL W	35	7	2	44
BREMNER	40	8	1	49
CHARLTON	39	8	2	49
COLLINS	39	8	1	48
COOPER T	16	4	1	21
GILES	39	7		46
GREENHOFF J	9	1	1	11
HENDERSON T	2		2	4
HUNTER	41	8	2	51
JOHANNESON	30	5	1	36
JOHNSON R	9	1	1	11
LAWSON	3			3
LORIMER	1			1
MADELEY	6		1	7
PEACOCK	10	4		14
REANEY	41	8		49
SPRAKE	41	8		49
STORRIE	37	8	1	46
WESTON	15	3		18
WILLIAMSON	1		2	3
WRIGHT B			2	2

GOALSCORERS

PLAYER	LEAGUE	F. A. CUP	LEAGUE CUP	TOTAL
STORRIE	16	2	1	19
JOHANNESON	9	2	1	12
CHARLTON	9	1		10
COLLINS	9		1	10
BREMNER	6	2		8
GILES	7	1		8
PEACOCK	6	2		8
BELFITT	4		1	5
WESTON	4	1		5
BELL W	4			4
JOHNSON R	3	1		4
GREENHOFF J	2	1		3
HUNTER	2		1	3
REANEY	1			1
OWN GOALS	1			1

KEY :- $ = PLAYED AT HILLSBOROUGH, SHEFFIELD, < = PLAYED AT THE CITY GROUND, NOTTINGHAM, > = PLAYED AT WEMBLEY WITH RESULT BEING AFTER EXTRA TIME

As Don Revie began preparations for an assault on domestic and European honours, observers noted the miraculous turnaround of a club, who three years earlier had avoided relegation to Division 3 on the season's final day. If pundits wondered whether Revie's troops would continue to develop, they quickly got an answer as Leeds claimed six wins in the opening ten games, including a double over Aston Villa, veteran forward Alan Peacock scoring in both games.

Whilst Peacock and Don Weston were ending careers, more youngsters made a mark. Scoring his first senior goal in the 2-0 win against Villa was Terry Cooper, a deputy on the left flank for Albert Johanneson and Willie Bell. Striker Peter Lorimer notched the winner against Nottingham Forest and a brace in a 3-0 win against Blackburn Rovers, while Paul Madeley, a scorer in Leeds' 3-3 draw at Leicester City, seemed capable of playing anywhere, having filled in at full-back, centre-half and midfield.

Riding high in the league, Leeds held a slender advantage from their first Fairs Cup tie, having defeated Torino 2-1, Peacock heading the winner. However, heartbreak struck in the return when Bobby Collins suffered a broken thigh as United battled to an aggregate win. It effectively ended his Leeds career and signalled the beginning of the Giles-Bremner partnership in central midfield. Complementing each other perfectly, the duo would become the most feared domestically and in Europe.

Returning from injury, Jim Storrie scored in a 4-2 win over Harlepools United but Leeds quickly exited the League Cup. Whilst making progress in the Fairs Cup against SC Leipzig, in the league, United's form dipped before Christmas, though they enjoyed a 6-1 mauling of Northampton Town, Lorimer scoring a brace, and a 4-0 win over West Brom, Giles notching a double. A debutant against Town and scorer against Albion was new arrival Mike O'Grady from Huddersfield Town.

New Years Day saw teenager Eddie Gray score Leeds' third goal in a comfortable win. Left-footed, Gray's skill on the ball was exceptional. A Giles penalty secured a 2-1 win at West Brom, whilst a Lorimer spot kick formed part of his first hat-trick in a resounding 6-0 FA Cup win against Bury. A 1-0 defeat at Chelsea in round four was sandwiched between a 5-0 romp against West Ham and a 4-0 victory at Nottingham Forest, but the most impressive display was a 1-0 triumph in Valencia, O'Grady scoring the all-important goal to advance Leeds into the quarter-finals of their first European sojourn. With Peacock sidelined, Lorimer, Madeley, Storrie and Rod Belfitt led the line. Despite three defeats in March, 3-2 wins against Leicester and Blackburn kept Leeds in the title hunt. In Europe, a superb 4-1 home leg win against Ujpest Dozsa ended the tie as a contest, Bremner scoring his third goal of the competition.

Six victories during the run-in, four consecutively against Everton, Newcastle United, Arsenal and Burnley, Storrie scoring in three clashes, eventually resulted in a runners-up slot six points adrift of Liverpool. In the Fairs Cup, Leeds took Spanish giants Real Zaragoza to a semi-final play-off before going down 3-1 to end a remarkable campaign. Though no trophies arrived, Revie's charges had served notice they were now a major force. In an exhaustive season, Paul Reaney and Hunter made 55 appearances. Lorimer top scored with 19 goals.

1965 - 1966

DIVISION ONE (FINAL LEAGUE POSITION - 2ND)

PLD 42 W 23 D 9 L 10 F 79 A 38 PTS 55

DATE	OPPONENTS	VENUE	SCORE	SCORERS	ATT.
21-Aug	SUNDERLAND	HOME	1 - 0	HUNTER	36,348
23-Aug	ASTON VILLA	AWAY	2 - 0	PEACOCK & COOPER T	33,836
28-Aug	WEST HAM UNITED	AWAY	1 - 2	PEACOCK	27,995
01-Sep	ASTON VILLA	HOME	2 - 0	PEACOCK 2	33,575
04-Sep	NOTTINGHAM FOREST	HOME	2 - 1	BELL W & LORIMER	35,427
08-Sep	TOTTENHAM HOTSPUR	AWAY	2 - 3	LORIMER & O. G. (CLAYTON)	48,114
11-Sep	SHEFFIELD UNITED	HOME	2 - 2	BREMNER & HUNTER	33,249
15-Sep	TOTTENHAM HOTSPUR	HOME	2 - 0	BREMNER & CHARLTON	41,920
18-Sep	LEICESTER CITY	AWAY	3 - 3	PEACOCK 2 & MADELEY	23,276
25-Sep	BLACKBURN ROVERS	HOME	3 - 0	LORIMER 2 & COOPER T	31,098
09-Oct	SHEFFIELD WEDNESDAY	AWAY	0 - 0		35,105
16-Oct	NORTHAMPTON TOWN	HOME	6 - 1	LORIMER 2, BREMNER, CHARLTON, PEACOCK & STORRIE	33,748
23-Oct	STOKE CITY	AWAY	2 - 1	PEACOCK & O'GRADY M	30,093
30-Oct	BURNLEY	HOME	1 - 1	STORRIE	41,628
06-Nov	CHELSEA	AWAY	0 - 1		39,373
13-Nov	ARSENAL	HOME	2 - 0	BREMNER & GILES	36,383
20-Nov	EVERTON	AWAY	0 - 0		36,291
11-Dec	WEST BROMWICH ALBION	HOME	4 - 0	GILES 2, STORRIE & O'GRADY M	33,140
27-Dec	LIVERPOOL	AWAY	1 - 0	LORIMER	53,430
28-Dec	LIVERPOOL	HOME	0 - 1		49,192
01-Jan	SHEFFIELD WEDNESDAY	HOME	3 - 0	STORRIE, PEACOCK & GRAY E	34,841
08-Jan	WEST BROMWICH ALBION	AWAY	2 - 1	PEACOCK & GILES (PEN)	24,900
12-Jan	MANCHESTER UNITED	HOME	1 - 1	STORRIE	49,762
15-Jan	STOKE CITY	HOME	2 - 2	O'GRADY M & STORRIE	34,802
29-Jan	SUNDERLAND	AWAY	0 - 2		35,942
05-Feb	WEST HAM UNITED	HOME	5 - 0	HUNTER 2, LORIMER, BREMNER & STORRIE	33,312
19-Feb	NOTTINGHAM FOREST	AWAY	4 - 0	LORIMER 2, HIBBITT & GILES (PEN)	26,283
26-Feb	SHEFFIELD UNITED	AWAY	1 - 1	BELL W	35,682
05-Mar	NORTHAMPTON TOWN	AWAY	1 - 2	O'GRADY M	21,548
12-Mar	LEICESTER CITY	HOME	3 - 2	CHARLTON 2 & HUNTER	35,597
19-Mar	BLACKBURN ROVERS	AWAY	3 - 2	BREMNER, LORIMER & STORRIE	25,398
26-Mar	BLACKPOOL	HOME	1 - 2	CHARLTON	30,727
28-Mar	BLACKPOOL	AWAY	0 - 1		19,017
04-Apr	CHELSEA	HOME	2 - 0	BREMNER & O.G. (HINTON)	37,784
08-Apr	FULHAM	AWAY	3 - 1	BREMNER, JOHANNESON & STORRIE	38,960
12-Apr	FULHAM	HOME	0 - 1		33,968
16-Apr	EVERTON	HOME	4 - 1	CHARLTON, LORIMER, STORRIE & JOHANNESON	25,200
30-Apr	NEWCASTLE UNITED	HOME	3 - 0	LORIMER, STORRIE & O. G. (McGRATH)	29,531
05-May	ARSENAL	AWAY	3 - 0	STORRIE 2 & GREENHOFF J	4,554
07-May	BURNLEY	AWAY	1 - 0	O. G. (ELDER)	33,238
16-May	NEWCASTLE UNITED	AWAY	0 - 2		21,660
19-May	MANCHESTER UNITED	AWAY	1 - 1	REANEY	35,008

F. A. CUP

DATE	OPPONENTS	VENUE	SCORE	SCORERS	ATT.
22-Jan	BURY (R3)	HOME	6 - 0	LORIMER 3 (1 PEN), REANEY, GREENHOFF J & GILES	30,384
12-Feb	CHELSEA (R4)	AWAY	0 - 1		57,847

LEAGUE CUP

DATE	OPPONENTS	VENUE	SCORE	SCORERS	ATT.
22-Sep	HARTLEPOOLS UNITED (R2)	HOME	4 - 2	COOPER T, JOHNSON R, BELFITT & STORRIE	11,081
13-Oct	WEST BROMWICH ALBION (R3)	HOME	2 - 4	MADELEY & BELFITT	13,455

INTER - CITIES FAIRS CUP

DATE	OPPONENTS	VENUE	SCORE	SCORERS	ATT.
29-Sep	TORINO (R1-1)	HOME	2 - 1	BREMNER & PEACOCK	33,852
06-Oct	TORINO (R1-2)	AWAY	0 - 0		26,000
24-Nov	SC LEIPZIG (R2-1)	AWAY	2 - 1	LORIMER & BREMNER	8,000
01-Dec	SC LEIPZIG (R2-2)	HOME	0 - 0		32,111
02-Feb	VALENCIA (R3-1)	HOME	1 - 1	LORIMER	34,414
16-Feb	VALENCIA (R3-2)	AWAY	1 - 0	O'GRADY M	45,000
02-Mar	UJPEST DOZSA (QF4-1)	HOME	4 - 1	COOPER T, BELL W, STORRIE & BREMNER	40,462
09-Mar	UJPEST DOZSA (QF4-2)	AWAY	1 - 1	LORIMER	30,000
20-Apr	REAL ZARAGOZA (SF-1)	AWAY	0 - 1		35,000
27-Apr	REAL ZARAGOZA (SF-2)	HOME	2 - 1	JOHANNESON & CHARLTON	45,008
11-May	REAL ZARAGOZA (SF PLAY-OFF)	HOME	1 - 3	CHARLTON	43,046

LEAGUE AND CUP

APPEARANCES (SUBSTITUTE)

PLAYER	LEAGUE	F. A. CUP	LGE. CUP	I. C. F. CUP	TOTAL
BATES			1		1
BELFITT	3		2	1	6
BELL W	33	2	1	9	45
BREMNER	41	2		11	54
CHARLTON	40	2	1	11	54
COLLINS	10			2	12
COOPER T	15 (3)		2	4	21 (3)
DAVEY		1			1
GILES	40	2	1	11	54
GRAY E	3 (1)			2	5 (1)
GREENHOFF J	10 (2)	1		3	14 (2)
HARVEY	2		1		3
HAWKINS		1			1
HIBBITT	0 (1)				0 (1)
HUNTER	41	2	1	11	55
JOHANNESON	12	1		2	15
JOHNSON R	2 (3)		2		4 (3)
LORIMER	34	2		9	45
MADELEY	9 (4)	1	2	4	16 (4)
O'GRADY M	29	1		7	37
PEACOCK	24	1		3	28
REANEY	41	2	1	11	55
SPRAKE	40	1	1	11	53
STORRIE	30	1	2	9	42
WESTON	3		1		4
WILLIAMSON		1			1
WRIGHT B		1			1

GOALSCORERS

PLAYER	LEAGUE	F. A. CUP	LGE. CUP	I. C. F. CUP	TOTAL
LORIMER	13	3		3	19
STORRIE	13		1	1	15
BREMNER	8			3	11
PEACOCK	10			1	11
CHARLTON	6			2	8
GILES	5	1			6
HUNTER	5				5
O'GRADY M	4			1	5
COOPER T	2		1	1	4
BELL W	2			1	3
JOHANNESON	2			1	3
BELFITT			2		2
GREENHOFF J	1	1			2
MADELEY	1		1		2
REANEY	1	1			2
GRAY E	1				1
HIBBITT	1				1
JOHNSON R			1		1
OWN GOALS	4				4

Despite not winning any silverware since the beginning of a renaissance under Don Revie, Leeds United's success on the field had wiped out a £250,000 overdraft. With the departure of Ian Lawson, and soon Alan Peacock and Jim Storrie, Revie's top priority was a centre-forward. Rumours abounded as to likely targets and gossip increased when Leeds started the season poorly, despite Paul Madeley's efforts as a makeshift striker, scoring in 3-1 wins against Manchester United and Arsenal. Madeley would remarkably wear every shirt apart from the goalkeeper's and number 11 in the coming campaign!

Completing a double at the Gunners, Jack Charlton scoring, reserve striker Jimmy Greenhoff scored in a 3-1 win against Leicester City, but six victories in the opening 15 games was not championship material and increased Revie's determination to find a hitman. Sandwiched between the latter fixtures, Leeds interest ended in the League Cup following a 7-0 thrashing at West Ham. Twelve days later a 5-0 defeat at Liverpool, a clash when Gary Sprake's most embarrassing clanger; throwing the ball into his own net, had critics waxing lyrical as the Anfield Kop sang 'Careless Hands'.

Following Bobby Collins injury in Italy, Charlton had reluctantly taken up the mantle as captain before Revie handed the honour to Billy Bremner. It proved a brilliant decision. Ball winner one moment, goal scorer the next; Bremner had everything and despite a fiery temperament, his never-say-die attitude drove the team forward. After the Anfield shambles, Revie's players found form. Albert Johanesson sealed a 2-1 victory over West Ham before a Greenhoff brace and Eddie Gray strike saw Leeds home 3-2 against Tottenham Hotspur. Either side of Christmas Day, Revie's charges completed a double over Newcastle United, Johanesson notching the winner at St James Park, while a Lorimer brace was the highlight of a 5-0 Boxing Day win at Elland Road.

Johanesson was in dazzling form. Goals came in 3-1 wins against Burnley and Fulham, while another strike sparked an FA Cup run as Leeds brushed aside Crystal Palace. Goals by reserve forward Rod Belfitt aided a 5-0 triumph over West Brom and a 2-1 win against Sunderland; Giles notching the winner from the penalty spot in a second replay. Following victory over Manchester City in the quarter-finals, Charlton scoring the only goal, Leeds faced Chelsea for a place at Wembley. The clash against Tommy Docherty's side is one of the most infamous in United's history after Lorimer's last minute thunderbolt was disallowed.

In the league, one defeat in the final 13 games moved Leeds up the table but it was too late for a title charge. During a fine run, United claimed consecutive wins against Blackpool, an Easter double over Sheffield United, and Chelsea before a shadow team completed the league campaign against Sheffield Wednesday, Terry Hibbitt scoring the solitary goal as Leeds finished fourth.

One trophy now remained. Leeds' Fairs Cup campaign began with an easy passage past DWS Amsterdam, Johanesson notching a hat-trick, before titanic struggles against Valencia and Bologna, the latter clash won on the toss of a disc. A Belfitt treble secured a 4-2 aggregate win against Kilmarnock in the semi-finals. The club's first European final took place at the start of the 1967/68 season but Leeds' lack of cutting edge was acutely apparent as Dynamo Zagreb won on aggregate. In a season of ultimate disappointment, Paul Reaney made 61 appearances, Norman Hunter 60. Johnny Giles top scored with 18 goals. Capping a memorable season, Charlton was awarded the prestigious Football Writers Player of the Year award. Albert Morris succeeded Harry Reynolds as chairman.

1966 - 1967

DIVISION ONE (FINAL LEAGUE POSITION - 4TH)

PLD 42 W 22 D 11 L 9 F 62 A 42 PTS 55

DATE	OPPONENTS	VENUE	SCORE	SCORERS	ATT.
20-Aug	TOTTENHAM HOTSPUR	AWAY	1 - 3	GILES	43,844
24-Aug	WEST BROMWICH ALBION	HOME	2 - 1	BELL W & GILES	35,102
27-Aug	MANCHESTER UNITED	HOME	3 - 1	REANER, LORIMER & MADELEY	45,092
31-Aug	WEST BROMWICH ALBION	AWAY	0 - 2		22,303
03-Sep	BURNLEY	AWAY	1 - 1	GRAY E	30,757
07-Sep	SUNDERLAND	HOME	2 - 1	GILES (PEN) & JOHANNESON	37,646
10-Sep	NOTTINGHAM FOREST	HOME	1 - 1	GRAY E	35,634
17-Sep	FULHAM	AWAY	2 - 2	LORIMER & JOHANNESON	19,985
24-Sep	EVERTON	HOME	1 - 1	GILES (PEN)	38,486
01-Oct	STOKE CITY	AWAY	0 - 0		28,987
08-Oct	ASTON VILLA	AWAY	0 - 3		19,188
15-Oct	ARSENAL	HOME	3 - 1	BELL W, MADELEY & GILES	31,481
29-Oct	SOUTHAMPTON	HOME	0 - 1		32,232
05-Nov	ARSENAL	AWAY	1 - 0	CHARLTON	24,227
12-Nov	LEICESTER CITY	HOME	3 - 1	GILES 2 & GREENHOFF J	33,803
19-Nov	LIVERPOOL	AWAY	0 - 5		50,764
26-Nov	WEST HAM UNITED	HOME	2 - 1	GILES & JOHANNESON	37,382
03-Dec	SHEFFIELD WEDNESDAY	AWAY	0 - 0		35,264
10-Dec	BLACKPOOL	HOME	1 - 1	GREENHOFF J	28,466
17-Dec	TOTTENHAM HOTSPUR	HOME	3 - 2	GREENHOFF J 2 & GRAY E	29,853
24-Dec	NEWCASTLE UNITED	AWAY	2 - 1	O'GRADY M & JOHANNESON	29,160
26-Dec	NEWCASTLE UNITED	HOME	5 - 0	LORIMER 2, CHARLTON, STORRIE & COOPER T	40,680
31-Dec	MANCHESTER UNITED	AWAY	0 - 0		53,486
07-Jan	BURNLEY	HOME	3 - 1	GREENHOFF J & JOHANNESON 2	37,465
14-Jan	NOTTINGHAM FOREST	AWAY	0 - 1		43,899
21-Jan	FULHAM	HOME	3 - 1	GILES, GREENHOFF J & JOHANNESON	32,015
04-Feb	EVERTON	AWAY	0 - 2		48,738
11-Feb	STOKE CITY	HOME	3 - 0	BELL W, LORIMER & BELFITT	37,370
25-Feb	ASTON VILLA	HOME	0 - 2		34,398
04-Mar	SOUTHAMPTON	AWAY	2 - 0	CHARLTON & GILES	26,150
18-Mar	MANCHESTER CITY	HOME	0 - 0		34,366
25-Mar	BLACKPOOL	AWAY	2 - 0	BREMNER & CHARLTON	22,548
27-Mar	SHEFFIELD UNITED	AWAY	4 - 1	GILES (PEN), PEACOCK, BREMNER & O. G. (MATTHEWSON)	25,701
28-Mar	SHEFFIELD UNITED	HOME	2 - 0	CHARLTON & PEACOCK	38,755
01-Apr	CHELSEA	HOME	1 - 0	LORIMER	39,728
10-Apr	LEICESTER CITY	AWAY	0 - 0		15,437
22-Apr	WEST HAM UNITED	AWAY	1 - 0	LORIMER	25,500
03-May	LIVERPOOL	HOME	2 - 1	GILES (PEN) & GREENHOFF J	36,547
06-May	CHELSEA	AWAY	2 - 2	LORIMER & BELFITT	35,882
08-May	MANCHESTER CITY	AWAY	1 - 2	BELFITT	24,924
13-May	SUNDERLAND	AWAY	2 - 0	GRAY E & LORIMER	23,686
15-May	SHEFFIELD WEDNESDAY	HOME	1 - 0	HIBBITT	23,052

F. A. CUP

DATE	OPPONENTS	VENUE	SCORE	SCORERS	ATT.
28-Jan	CRYSTAL PALACE (R3)	HOME	3 - 0	O'GRADY M, BELL W & JOHANNESON	37,768
18-Feb	WEST BROMWICH ALBION (R4)	HOME	5 - 0	LORIMER 2, MADELEY & BELFITT 2	41,329
11-Mar	SUNDERLAND (R5)	AWAY	1 - 1	CHARLTON	55,763
15-Mar	SUNDERLAND (R5R) *	HOME	1 - 1	GILES	57,892
20-Mar	SUNDERLAND (R52R) <	NEUTRAL	2 - 1	BELFITT & GILES (PEN)	40,546
08-Apr	MANCHESTER CITY (R6)	HOME	1 - 0	CHARLTON	48,887
29-Apr	CHELSEA (SF) >	NEUTRAL	0 - 1		62,378

LEAGUE CUP

DATE	OPPONENTS	VENUE	SCORE	SCORERS	ATT.
13-Sep	NEWCASTLE UNITED (R2)	HOME	1 - 0	PEACOCK	18,131
04-Oct	PRESTON NORTH END (R3)	AWAY	1 - 1	STORRIE	15,049
12-Oct	PRESTON NORTH END (R3R)	HOME	3 - 0	LORIMER 2 (1 PEN) & GREENHOFF J	17,221
07-Nov	WEST HAM UNITED (R4)	AWAY	0 - 7		27,471

INTER - CITIES FAIRS CUP

DATE	OPPONENTS	VENUE	SCORE	SCORERS	ATT.
18-Oct	DWS AMSTERDAM (R2-1)	AWAY	3 - 1	BREMNER, JOHANNESON & GREENHOFF J	7,000
26-Oct	DWS AMSTERDAM (R2-2)	HOME	5 - 1	JOHANNESON 3, GILES (PEN) & MADELEY	27,096
18-Jan	VALENCIA (R3-1)	HOME	1 - 1	GREENHOFF J	40,644
08-Feb	VALENCIA (R3-2)	AWAY	2 - 0	GILES & LORIMER	45,000
22-Mar	BOLOGNA (QF4-1)	AWAY	0 - 1		18,000
19-Apr	BOLOGNA (QF4-2) $*	HOME	1 - 0	GILES (PEN)	42,126
19-May	KILMARNOCK (SF-1)	HOME	4 - 2	BELFITT 3 & GILES (PEN)	43,189
24-May	KILMARNOCK (SF-2)	AWAY	0 - 0		28,000
30-Aug	DYNAMO ZAGREB (Fi-1)	AWAY	0 - 2		40,000
06-Sep	DYNAMO ZAGREB (Fi-2)	HOME	0 - 0		35,604

LEAGUE AND CUP

APPEARANCES (SUBSTITUTE)

PLAYER	LEAGUE	F. A. CUP	LGE. CUP	I. C. F. CUP	TOTAL
BATES	8 (1)	0 (1)	0 (1)	1	9 (3)
BELFITT	10 (2)	5	1	7	23 (2)
BELL W	38	7	4	8	57
BREMNER	36 (1)	6	4	10	56 (1)
CHARLTON	28	6	4	7	45
COLLINS	7			1	8
COOPER T	20 (4)	2 (1)		6	28 (5)
GILES	29	7	3	9	48
GRAY E	29	4	1	6	40
GREENHOFF J	27 (2)	5 (1)	3	5	40 (3)
HARVEY	3	2			5
HAWKINS	1				1
HIBBITT	3 (1)			1	4 (1)
HUNTER	40	7	3	10	60
JOHANNESON	22	2	2	2	28
JOHNSON R	3				3
LORIMER	27 (2)	5 (1)	2	5	39 (3)
LUMSDEN	1				1
MADELEY	27 (1)	4 (1)	4	8	43 (2)
O'GRADY M	14	2	2	4	22
PEACOCK	6	1	2		9
REANEY	41	7	4	9	61
SIBBALD	0 (1)				0 (1)
SPRAKE	39	7	2	10	58
STORRIE	3 (3)		1	1	5 (3)

GOALSCORERS

PLAYER	LEAGUE	F. A. CUP	LGE. CUP	I. C. F. CUP	TOTAL
GILES	12	2		4	18
LORIMER	9	2	2	1	14
JOHANNESON	7	1		4	12
GREENHOFF J	7		1	2	10
BELFITT	3	3		3	9
CHARLTON	5	2			7
BELL W	3	1			4
GRAY E	4				4
MADELEY	2	1		1	4
BREMNER	2			1	3
PEACOCK	2		1		3
O'GRADY M	1	1			2
STORRIE	1		1		2
COOPER T	1				1
HIBBITT	1				1
REANEY	1				1
OWN GOALS	1				1

LEEDS ALSO PLAYED IN THE GLASGOW CHARITY CUP ON AUGUST 10TH 1966 VS. A GLASGOW SELECT XI AT HAMPDEN PARK AND DREW 1 - 1 (0 - 0) WITH GILES SCORING WITH AN ATTENDANCE OF 18,000. THE TEAM WAS SPRAKE, REANEY, BELL, BREMNER, CHARLTON (MADELEY), HUNTER, STORRIE, COLLINS, LORIMER, GILES & GRAY E.

KEY :- $ = WON ON TOSS OF DISC. * = AFTER EXTRA TIME. < = PLAYED AT BOOTHFERRY PARK, HULL & > = PLAYED AT VILLA PARK, BIRMINGHAM

Having gone close to honours, many pundits predicted success for Don Revie's charges but in a hectic opening, Leeds lost the delayed Fairs Cup final to Dynamo Zagreb and won only one of five opening league matches, scoring just four goals. Revie invested a club record £100,000 on Sheffield United centre-forward Mick Jones. Revie's line up also saw Terry Cooper replace Willie Bell at left-back, Bell joining Leicester City.

Results improved, the highlight a 7-0 win against Chelsea. Jones' first league goal came in a 3-1 win against Arsenal before a strike in a 2-1 victory over Wolves heralded six consecutive wins, including a double over Sheffield Wednesday and 5-0 romps against Fulham, Jimmy Greenhoff notching a hat-trick, and Southampton, Paul Madeley scoring a brace. At the turn of the year, Revie quashed rumours Madeley was the subject of a £100,000 bid from Arsenal.

Full of confidence, Leeds faced Derby County in the League Cup semi-finals, having disposed of Luton Town; Peter Lorimer notching a hat-trick, Bury, Sunderland and Stoke City. The cup run summed up Madeley's value to Leeds, filling in at left-back, centre-half and now centre-forward with Jones cup-tied and Rod Belfitt injured. Johnny Giles scored a penalty against Derby for an away win, before Belfitt's brace secured a 4-3 aggregate victory. The Wembley final against Arsenal was dour, but Cooper's controversial strike enabled Revie's team to claim a first major honour. Four weeks after Leeds' triumph, Percy Woodward began a 20-year term as chairman following the death of Albert Morris.

Back in the league, Leeds' unbeaten run continued but four draws in five games, including a 0-0 draw at Chelsea when Madeley become the first Leeds United player to wear every outfield shirt, dented title aspirations before five victories, including successive wins against Coventry City, Tottenham Hotspur and West Brom, saw Leeds head the table. Four games remained, but fixture congestion was biting as United chased more cup success. In the FA Cup, Leeds faced Everton in the semi-finals after overcoming Derby, Nottingham Forest, Bristol City and Sheffield United. Jones scored against Forest and City, clashes notable as Norman Hunter and Lorimer replaced Gary Sprake in goal! Leeds had an opportunity to be the first team to reach both domestic Wembley finals in a season but a Sprake gaffe ended the dream.

In the Fairs Cup, Leeds faced Dundee in the semi-finals after thrashing Spora Luxembourg by a club record 16-0 on aggregate; Lorimer notching four in the opening leg, Johanesson a treble in the return. Thereafter, it was tougher overcoming Partizan Belgrade; Lorimer scoring in both legs, Hibernian; Charlton claiming the clincher and Rangers; Giles and Lorimer coming up trumps in a humdinger of a tie. The final league games saw Leeds challenge Manchester City, Manchester United and Liverpool for the title but defeats against Stoke City and Liverpool meant a fourth place finish.

The semi-final first leg at Dundee saw Madeley score a crucial away goal and on a bone hard pitch Eddie Gray's strike squeezed Leeds through to a second European final, staged at the beginning of the 1968/69 campaign. Hungarian giants Ferencvaros packed their defence and relied on the counter-attack, but Jones scrambled a crucial goal at Elland Road and in front of a hostile 75,000 crowd, Leeds absorbed wave upon wave of attacks to record a magnificent triumph, Sprake the hero with a brilliant display. In a historic season, Paul Reaney made 65 appearances. Lorimer notched 30 goals, a total exceeded only by Tom Jennings, John Charles and latterly Lee Chapman in the club's history.

1967 - 1968

DIVISION ONE (FINAL LEAGUE POSITION - 4TH)

PLD 42 W 22 D 9 L 11 F 71 A 41 PTS 53

DATE	OPPONENTS	VENUE	SCORE	SCORERS	ATT.
19-Aug	SUNDERLAND	HOME	1 - 1	GREENHOFF J	36,252
23-Aug	MANCHESTER UNITED	AWAY	0 - 1		53,016
26-Aug	WOLVERHAMPTON WANDERERS	AWAY	0 - 2		35,368
02-Sep	FULHAM	HOME	2 - 0	BELFITT 2	25,760
09-Sep	SOUTHAMPTON	AWAY	1 - 1	LORIMER	25,522
16-Sep	EVERTON	AWAY	1 - 0	GRAY E	53,159
20-Sep	BURNLEY	HOME	2 - 1	LORIMER 2	32,944
23-Sep	LEICESTER CITY	HOME	3 - 2	LORIMER 2 (1 PEN) & GREENHOFF J	37,084
30-Sep	WEST HAM UNITED	AWAY	0 - 0		28,940
07-Oct	CHELSEA	HOME	7 - 0	JOHANNESON, GREENHOFF J, CHARLTON, GRAY E, LORIMER, BREMNER & O. G. (HINTON)	40,460
14-Oct	WEST BROMWICH ALBION	AWAY	0 - 2		21,300
25-Oct	NEWCASTLE UNITED	HOME	2 - 0	LORIMER & JOHANNESON	30,347
28-Oct	MANCHESTER CITY	AWAY	0 - 1		39,713
04-Nov	ARSENAL	HOME	3 - 1	LORIMER (PEN), JONES Mi. & GRAY E	31,632
08-Nov	MANCHESTER UNITED	HOME	1 - 0	GREENHOFF J	43,999
11-Nov	SHEFFIELD UNITED	AWAY	0 - 1		24,715
18-Nov	COVENTRY CITY	HOME	1 - 1	LORIMER	32,469
25-Nov	NOTTINGHAM FOREST	AWAY	2 - 0	GREENHOFF J & LORIMER	29,750
02-Dec	STOKE CITY	HOME	2 - 0	LORIMER & MADELEY	29,988
09-Dec	LIVERPOOL	AWAY	0 - 2		39,675
16-Dec	SUNDERLAND	AWAY	2 - 2	GREENHOFF J & GRAY E	21,189
23-Dec	WOLVERHAMPTON WANDERERS	HOME	2 - 1	JONES Mi. & CHARLTON	28,376
26-Dec	SHEFFIELD WEDNESDAY	AWAY	1 - 0	GILES (PEN)	51,055
30-Dec	SHEFFIELD WEDNESDAY	HOME	3 - 2	GREENHOFF J, GRAY E & HUNTER	36,409
06-Jan	FULHAM	AWAY	5 - 0	GREENHOFF J 3 & JONES Mi. 2	24,419
13-Jan	SOUTHAMPTON	HOME	5 - 0	MADELEY 2, LORIMER, JONES Mi. & HIBBITT	31,474
20-Jan	EVERTON	HOME	2 - 0	JONES Mi. & GILES (PEN)	44,119
03-Feb	LEICESTER CITY	AWAY	2 - 2	MADELEY & GILES	30,081
10-Feb	WEST HAM UNITED	HOME	2 - 1	LORIMER 2	41,814
13-Mar	NOTTINGHAM FOREST	HOME	1 - 1	BREMNER	32,508
16-Mar	NEWCASTLE UNITED	AWAY	1 - 1	HUNTER	45,190
20-Mar	CHELSEA	AWAY	0 - 0		47,470
23-Mar	MANCHESTER CITY	HOME	2 - 0	CHARLTON & GILES	51,818
06-Apr	SHEFFIELD UNITED	HOME	3 - 0	MADELEY & GILES 2 (2 PENS)	31,059
12-Apr	TOTTENHAM HOTSPUR	AWAY	1 - 2	MADELEY	56,597
13-Apr	COVENTRY CITY	AWAY	1 - 0	HIBBITT	38,778
17-Apr	TOTTENHAM HOTSPUR	HOME	1 - 0	LORIMER (PEN)	50,000
20-Apr	WEST BROMWICH ALBION	HOME	3 - 1	GRAY E (PEN), MADELEY & CHARLTON	38,334
23-Apr	STOKE CITY	AWAY	2 - 3	CHARLTON & GREENHOFF J	23,999
04-May	LIVERPOOL	HOME	1 - 2	JONES Mi.	44,553
07-May	ARSENAL	AWAY	3 - 4	LORIMER, JONES Mi. & GILES	25,043
11-May	BURNLEY	AWAY	0 - 3		13,247

F. A. CUP

DATE	OPPONENTS	VENUE	SCORE	SCORERS	ATT.
27-Jan	DERBY COUNTY (R3)	HOME	2 - 0	CHARLTON & LORIMER	39,735
17-Feb	NOTTINGHAM FOREST (R4)	HOME	2 - 1	JONES Mi. & GILES (PEN)	51,739
09-Mar	BRISTOL CITY (R5)	HOME	2 - 0	JONES Mi. & LORIMER	45,227
30-Mar	SHEFFIELD UNITED (R6)	HOME	1 - 0	MADELEY	48,322
27-Apr	EVERTON (SF) >	NEUTRAL	0 - 1		63,000

LEAGUE CUP

DATE	OPPONENTS	VENUE	SCORE	SCORERS	ATT.
13-Sep	LUTON TOWN (R2)	HOME	3 - 1	LORIMER 3 (1 PEN)	11,473
11-Oct	BURY (R3)	HOME	3 - 0	CHARLTON, JOHANNESON & GREENHOFF J	20,927
15-Nov	SUNDERLAND (R4)	AWAY	2 - 0	GREENHOFF J 2	29,536
13-Dec	STOKE CITY (R5)	HOME	2 - 0	BREMNER & LORIMER	24,556
17-Jan	DERBY COUNTY (SF-1)	AWAY	1 - 0	GILES (PEN)	31,904
07-Feb	DERBY COUNTY (SF-2)	HOME	3 - 2	BELFITT 2 & GRAY E	29,367
02-Mar	ARSENAL (FI) <	NEUTRAL	1 - 0	COOPER T	97,887

INTER - CITIES FAIRS CUP

DATE	OPPONENTS	VENUE	SCORE	SCORERS	ATT.
03-Oct	SPORA LUXEMBOURG (R1-1)	AWAY	9 - 0	LORIMER 4 (1 PEN), BREMNER, JONES Mi., GREENHOFF J 2 & MADELEY	2,500
17-Oct	SPORA LUXEMBOURG (R1-2)	HOME	7 - 0	JOHANNESON 3, GREENHOFF J 2, COOPER T & LORIMER	15,196
29-Nov	PARTIZAN BELGRADE (R2-1)	AWAY	2 - 1	LORIMER & BELFITT	8,000
06-Dec	PARTIZAN BELGRADE (R2-2)	HOME	1 - 1	LORIMER	34,258
20-Dec	HIBERNIAN (R3-1)	HOME	1 - 0	GRAY E	31,522
10-Jan	HIBERNIAN (R3-2)	AWAY	1 - 1	CHARLTON	40,503
26-Mar	RANGERS (QF4-1)	AWAY	0 - 0		60,000
09-Apr	RANGERS (QF4-2)	HOME	2 - 0	GILES (PEN) & LORIMER	50,498
01-May	DUNDEE (SF-1)	AWAY	1 - 1	MADELEY	30,000
15-May	DUNDEE (SF-2)	HOME	1 - 0	GRAY E	23,830
07-Aug	FERENCVAROS (FI-1)	HOME	1 - 0	JONES Mi.	25,268
11-Sep	FERENCVAROS (FI-2)	AWAY	0 - 0		75,000

LEAGUE AND CUP

APPEARANCES (SUBSTITUTE)

PLAYER	LEAGUE	F. A. CUP	LGE. CUP	I. C. F. CUP	TOTAL
BATES	6 (1)		0 (3)	0 (3)	6 (7)
BELFITT	11 (3)		5 (1)	2 (2)	18 (6)
BELL W	3		1		4
BREMNER	36	5	6	11	58
CHARLTON	34	4	5	11	54
COOPER T	37	5	6	12	60
DAVEY	2				2
GILES	20	5	3	7	35
GRAY E	32	3	7	8	50
GREENHOFF J	35 (2)	3	7	10 (1)	55 (3)
HARVEY	6			4	10
HAWKINS	1		1		2
HIBBITT	12 (4)	1	2	3	18 (4)
HUNTER	40	5	7	12	64
JOHANNESON	8 (1)		1	1 (1)	10 (2)
JOHNSON R	0 (1)		1 (1)		1 (2)
JONES Mi.	25	5		8	38
LORIMER	36 (1)	5	6	12	59 (1)
LUMSDEN	1				1
MADELEY	33 (3)	3 (2)	5	10 (1)	51 (6)
O'GRADY M	6	1		1	8
REANEY	40	5	7	12	64 (1)
SIBBALD	1				1
SPRAKE	36	5	7	8	56
YORATH	1				1

GOALSCORERS

PLAYER	LEAGUE	F. A. CUP	LGE. CUP	I. C. F. CUP	TOTAL
LORIMER	16	2	4	8	30
GREENHOFF J	11		3	4	18
JONES Mi.	8	2		2	12
GILES	7	1	1	1	10
MADELEY	7	1		2	10
GRAY E	6		1	2	9
CHARLTON	5	1	1	1	8
JOHANNESON	2		1	3	6
BELFITT	2		2	1	5
BREMNER	2		1	1	4
COOPER T			1	1	2
HIBBITT	2				2
HUNTER	2				2
OWN GOALS	1				1

KEY :- > = PLAYED AT OLD TRAFFORD, MANCHESTER & < = PLAYED AT WEMBLEY

Having removed the 'bridesmaid' tag, the club set its sights on the Division 1 crown and began well, winning the opening fixtures against Southampton, Queens Park Rangers, Stoke City and Ipswich Town; Mick Jones and Terry Hibbitt scoring in three games apiece. Further victories over Liverpool and Wolves; Jones and Jack Charlton notching winning goals, enhanced confidence prior to the delayed Fairs Cup final against Ferencvaros. Returning triumphantly, Leeds drew at Leicester City before defeating league-leaders Arsenal in an enthralling match. Undefeated, Revie's charges faced defending champions Manchester City but slipped to a 3-1 defeat. Undaunted, the players bounced back with three wins in a week before a crushing 5-1 defeat at Burnley.

The loss would be United's final defeat of the campaign. Following three goalless draws, a Paul Madeley strike settled a tight game at Coventry City. Recovering their poise, Peter Lorimer led the charge as Leeds hammered Burnley 6-1, which heralded 10 wins in 11 games as United's title challenge gathered pace. During a sensational run, after successive 2-1 wins against Newcastle United; Madeley striking a long-range winner, and Manchester United; Mike O'Grady slotting home a great goal, Revie's troops claimed seven successive wins; defeating Queens Park Rangers, Coventry City, Ipswich, Chelsea, Nottingham Forest, Southampton and Stoke City. Jones found a cutting edge; scoring in five games, whilst Billy Bremner notched braces against Coventry and Stoke. Leeds' 2-0 win at Ipswich finally overhauled Liverpool at the top of the table, having played the same number of games.

The major disappointments to date had been defeats to Crystal Palace in the League Cup and Sheffield Wednesday in an FA Cup third round replay, but the Fairs Cup defence was going well. The campaign began against Standard Liege where having drawn 0-0 in Belgium, Leeds, 2-0 behind in the return, came back in the last 20 minutes for a famous 3-2 win; Bremner notching the winner. The next round saw another remarkable win, when after winning the first leg against Napoli 2-0, the Italians levelled the tie, before Bremner claimed victory on the toss of a coin. The tie against Hannover 96 was all but over after a 5-1 defeat at Elland Road in the first leg before a fourth round clash against Ujpest Dozsa ended in defeat.

In pole position to clinch the Division 1 title, nine league games remained. Leeds appeared unstoppable and had one challenger, Liverpool. According to national papers the title race was over, but draws at Wolves, Sheffield Wednesday and West Brom, saw Bill Shankly's team edge back into the frame. Leeds, however, crucially defeated Arsenal 2-1 in a hard-fought Highbury clash; Giles notching the winner, and Leicester City 2-0; Jones and Eddie Gray scoring vital goals. A stalemate at Everton meant Leeds required a point against their great rivals, and in a nerve-jangling atmosphere, Revie's title pretenders secured the point necessary as Anfield's Kop acclaimed the new English champions.

Two days later, Johnny Giles late winner against Nottingham Forest at Elland Road created numerous records. Most points (67), most home points (39), most wins (27), most home wins (18), fewest defeats (2), fewest away defeats (2), goals conceded (26) and goals conceded at home (9). During an unforgettable campaign, Sprake, Reaney, Bremner and Hunter were ever-present in the league. Jones finished top scorer with 14 league goals. Revie collected the Manager of the Year award.

1968 - 1969

DIVISION ONE (FINAL LEAGUE POSITION - 1ST)

PLD 42 W 27 D 13 L 2 F 66 A 26 PTS 67

DATE	OPPONENTS	VENUE	SCORE	SCORERS	ATT.
10-Aug	SOUTHAMPTON	AWAY	3 - 1	LORIMER, JONES Mi. & HIBBITT	25,479
14-Aug	QUEENS PARK RANGERS	HOME	4 - 1	JONES Mi., GILES, REANEY & HIBBITT	31,612
17-Aug	STOKE CITY	HOME	2 - 0	JONES Mi. & JOHANNESON	30,383
20-Aug	IPSWICH TOWN	AWAY	3 - 2	O'GRADY M, BELFITT & HIBBITT	30,382
28-Aug	SUNDERLAND	HOME	1 - 1	BELFITT	37,797
31-Aug	LIVERPOOL	HOME	1 - 0	JONES Mi.	38,929
07-Sep	WOLVERHAMPTON WANDERERS	HOME	2 - 1	COOPER T & CHARLTON	31,227
14-Sep	LEICESTER CITY	AWAY	1 - 1	MADELEY	28,564
21-Sep	ARSENAL	HOME	2 - 0	CHARLTON & O'GRADY M	39,946
28-Sep	MANCHESTER CITY	AWAY	1 - 3	O'GRADY M	45,006
05-Oct	NEWCASTLE UNITED	AWAY	1 - 0	CHARLTON	41,915
09-Oct	SUNDERLAND	AWAY	1 - 0	JONES Mi.	33,853
12-Oct	WEST HAM UNITED	HOME	2 - 0	GILES (PEN) & LORIMER	40,786
19-Oct	BURNLEY	AWAY	1 - 5	BREMNER	26,423
26-Oct	WEST BROMWICH ALBION	HOME	0 - 0		33,926
02-Nov	MANCHESTER UNITED	AWAY	0 - 0		53,839
09-Nov	TOTTENHAM HOTSPUR	HOME	0 - 0		38,995
16-Nov	COVENTRY CITY	AWAY	1 - 0	MADELEY	33,224
23-Nov	EVERTON	HOME	2 - 1	GILES (PEN) & GRAY E	41,716
30-Nov	CHELSEA	AWAY	1 - 1	O'GRADY M	43,286
07-Dec	SHEFFIELD WEDNESDAY	HOME	2 - 0	LORIMER 2	32,718
14-Dec	WEST HAM UNITED	AWAY	1 - 1	GRAY E	27,418
21-Dec	BURNLEY	HOME	6 - 1	LORIMER 2, BREMNER, JONES Mi., GILES & GRAY E	31,409
26-Dec	NEWCASTLE UNITED	HOME	2 - 1	LORIMER (PEN) & MADELEY	42,000
11-Jan	MANCHESTER UNITED	HOME	2 - 1	JONES Mi. & O'GRADY M	48,145
18-Jan	TOTTENHAM HOTSPUR	AWAY	0 - 0		42,396
24-Jan	QUEENS PARK RANGERS	AWAY	1 - 0	JONES Mi.	26,163
01-Feb	COVENTRY CITY	HOME	3 - 0	O'GRADY M & BREMNER 2	32,314
12-Feb	IPSWICH TOWN	HOME	2 - 0	BELFITT & JONES Mi.	24,229
15-Feb	CHELSEA	HOME	1 - 0	LORIMER	35,789
25-Feb	NOTTINGHAM FOREST	AWAY	2 - 0	LORIMER & JONES Mi.	36,249
01-Mar	SOUTHAMPTON	HOME	3 - 2	GILES (PEN), JONES Mi. & O.G. (KIRKUP)	33,205
08-Mar	STOKE CITY	AWAY	5 - 1	JONES Mi., BREMNER 2 & O'GRADY M 2	24,327
29-Mar	WOLVERHAMPTON WANDERERS	AWAY	0 - 0		27,986
01-Apr	SHEFFIELD WEDNESDAY	AWAY	0 - 0		34,278
05-Apr	MANCHESTER CITY	HOME	1 - 0	GILES	43,176
09-Apr	WEST BROMWICH ALBION	AWAY	1 - 1	GRAY E	28,959
12-Apr	ARSENAL	AWAY	2 - 1	JONES Mi. & GILES	43,715
19-Apr	LEICESTER CITY	HOME	2 - 0	JONES Mi. & GRAY E	38,391
22-Apr	EVERTON	AWAY	0 - 0		59,000
28-Apr	LIVERPOOL	AWAY	0 - 0		53,750
30-Apr	NOTTINGHAM FOREST	HOME	1 - 0	GILES	46,508

F. A. CUP

DATE	OPPONENTS	VENUE	SCORE	SCORERS	ATT.
04-Jan	SHEFFIELD WEDNESDAY (R3)	AWAY	1 - 1	LORIMER (PEN)	52,111
06-Jan	SHEFFIELD WEDNESDAY (R3R)	HOME	1 - 3	JOHANNESON	48,234

LEAGUE CUP

DATE	OPPONENTS	VENUE	SCORE	SCORERS	ATT.
04-Sep	CHARLTON ATHLETIC (R2)	HOME	1 - 0	JONES Mi.	18,860
25-Sep	BRISTOL CITY (R3)	HOME	2 - 1	JOHANNESON & JONES Mi.	16,359
16-Oct	CRYSTAL PALACE (R4)	AWAY	1 - 2	MADELEY	25,937

INTER - CITIES FAIRS CUP

DATE	OPPONENTS	VENUE	SCORE	SCORERS	ATT.
18-Sep	STANDARD LIEGE (R1-1)	AWAY	0 - 0		35,000
23-Oct	STANDARD LIEGE (R1-2)	HOME	3 - 2	CHARLTON, LORIMER & BREMNER	24,178
13-Nov	NAPOLI (R2-1)	HOME	2 - 0	CHARLTON 2	26,967
27-Nov	NAPOLI (R2-2) > *	AWAY	0 - 2		15,000
13-Dec	HANNOVER 96 (R3-1)	HOME	5 - 1	O'GRADY M, HUNTER, LORIMER 2 & CHARLTON	25,162
04-Feb	HANNOVER 96 (R3-2)	AWAY	2 - 1	BELFITT & JONES Mi.	15,000
05-Mar	UJPEST DOZSA (QF4-1)	HOME	0 - 1		30,906
19-Mar	UJPEST DOZSA (QF4-2)	AWAY	0 - 2		40,000

LEAGUE AND CUP

APPEARANCES (SUBSTITUTE)

PLAYER	LEAGUE	F. A. CUP	LGE. CUP	I. C. F. CUP	TOTAL
BATES	3 (1)	2	0 (1)	1 (1)	6 (3)
BELFITT	6 (2)	0 (1)	1	4	11 (3)
BREMNER	42	2	2	8	54
CHARLTON	41	2	2	7	52
COOPER T	34 (1)		3	5	42 (1)
GILES	32		2	5	39
GRAY E	32 (1)	2	2	5 (1)	41 (2)
GREENHOFF J	3				3
HIBBITT	9 (3)		1	2 (2)	12 (5)
HUNTER	42	2	2	8	54
JOHANNESON	0 (1)	1	1		2 (1)
JONES Mi.	40	2	3	8	53
LORIMER	25 (4)	2	3	6 (1)	36 (5)
MADELEY	31	2	2	7	42
O'GRADY M	38	1	3	7	49
REANEY	42	2	3	7	54
SPRAKE	42	2	3	8	55
YORATH			0 (1)		0 (1)

GOALSCORERS

PLAYER	LEAGUE	F. A. CUP	LGE. CUP	I. C. F. CUP	TOTAL
JONES Mi.	14		2	1	17
LORIMER	9	1		3	13
O'GRADY M	8			1	9
GILES	8				8
BREMNER	6			1	7
CHARLTON	3			4	7
GRAY E	5				5
BELFITT	3			1	4
MADELEY	3		1		4
HIBBITT	3				3
JOHANNESON	1	1	1		3
COOPER T	1				1
HUNTER				1	1
REANEY	1				1
OWN GOALS	1				1

KEY :- > = WON ON TOSS OF DISC, * = AFTER EXTRA TIME

Although defending champions, Don Revie refused to rest. Signing Leicester City striker Allan Clarke for a £165,000 British record fee served notice that Leeds United would be the team to beat. Pairing Clarke with Mick Jones would prove a devastating partnership. The new strike-force appeared in a 2-1 Charity Shield victory against Manchester City, Jack Charlton heading the winner. The league campaign began with a 3-1 win over Tottenham Hotspur, Clarke striking his first goal, but Leeds claimed only two victories in the opening eight fixtures; a draw at Arsenal equalling Burnley's Division 1 record of 30 undefeated matches. Charlton became the first Leeds player to make 500 league appearances at Everton, who ended United's unbeaten run with a 3-2 triumph.

Stung into action, a 2-1 victory at Sheffield Wednesday heralded 12 wins in 17 matches. Back in the title-race, whilst Clarke notched braces in 2-0 wins against Derby County and Sheffield Wednesday, Peter Lorimer struck a hat-trick in a 6-1 thrashing over Nottingham Forest and a double in Leeds' 4-1 victory against West Ham. Knocked out by Chelsea in the League Cup, the European Cup campaign began well with a club-record 10-0 win, 16-0 on aggregate, against amateurs Lyn Oslo, Jones scoring a treble in the opening leg. The second round pitted Leeds against Ferencvaros. Pundits predicted a classic, but Leeds raced to a 6-0 aggregate win, Jones notching four goals in the tie.

Domestically, a Jones brace defeated league-leaders Everton, starting another unbeaten run that saw Chelsea 5-2 and West Brom 5-1 thrashed. Simultaneously, Leeds overcame Swansea Town, Sutton United; Clarke scoring four goals in a 6-0 rout, Mansfield Town and Swindon Town to reach the FA Cup quarter-finals. At the beginning of March, Leeds looked capable of claiming an unprecedented 'treble', but their European Cup quarter-final tie against Standard Leige; Lorimer and Johnny Giles securing a 2-0 aggregate win, coincided with fixture congestion due to a truncated season to accommodate the Mexico World Cup finals, and it took a cataclysmic toll.

When Leeds faced Celtic in the semi-final first leg at Elland Road, they'd played seven matches in 19 days, including an FA Cup trilogy against Manchester United, Billy Bremner claiming the vital strike in a second replay. Also, the Celtic clash came during a four-match sequence in seven days, and started a three-match sequence in four days! With players, mentally and physically fatigued, after a home defeat to Southampton, Revie fielded a reserve side at Derby County; the decision costing a £5,000 FA fine, and signalled the end to Leeds' title challenge. The final six games yielded a win over Burnley, when Eddie Gray scored a virtuoso 'goal in a million' in a 2-1 triumph. Finishing runners-up, Leeds focused on cup glory.

Recuperating for a week, Leeds outplayed Chelsea on an atrocious Wembley pitch but drew 2-2, Charlton and Jones scoring, resulting in a first replay for 58 years. From the twin towers, Leeds flew to Scotland, where in front of a European record attendance of 136,000, Bremner scored a scorcher, but two quick-fire Celtic goals left European Cup dreams in tatters. In the final phase of a doomed trilogy, Chelsea broke Leeds hearts, after Jones opened the scoring with a terrific strike; nevertheless despite the disappointments, the campaign is one of United's most memorable. Paul Madeley made 59 appearances, whilst Clarke and Jones top scored on 26 goals, Giles and Lorimer struck 19 goals apiece. Capping a remarkable season, Bremner claimed the Football Writers Player of the Year award, while Revie collected his second Manager of the Year trophy.

1969 - 1970

PLD 42 W 21 D 15 L 6 F 84 A 49 PTS 57

DATE	OPPONENTS	VENUE	SCORE	SCORERS	ATT.
09-Aug	TOTTENHAM HOTSPUR	HOME	3 - 1	BREMNER, CLARKE A & GILES (PEN)	35,804
13-Aug	ARSENAL	HOME	0 - 0		37,164
16-Aug	NOTTINGHAM FOREST	AWAY	4 - 1	CLARKE A, GILES (PEN), GRAY E & LORIMER	34,290
19-Aug	ARSENAL	AWAY	1 - 1	LORIMER	45,160
23-Aug	NEWCASTLE UNITED	HOME	1 - 1	JONES Mi.	40,403
26-Aug	BURNLEY	AWAY	1 - 1	JONES Mi.	28,000
30-Aug	EVERTON	AWAY	2 - 3	BREMNER & CLARKE A	51,797
06-Sep	MANCHESTER UNITED	HOME	2 - 2	O. G. (SADLER) & BREMNER	44,271
13-Sep	SHEFFIELD WEDNESDAY	AWAY	2 - 1	CLARKE A & GRAY E	31,998
20-Sep	CHELSEA	HOME	2 - 0	GILES (PEN) & LORIMER	33,130
27-Sep	COVENTRY CITY	AWAY	2 - 1	CLARKE A & GRAY E	36,091
04-Oct	STOKE CITY	HOME	2 - 1	GILES 2 (2 PENS)	35,860
11-Oct	WEST BROMWICH ALBION	AWAY	1 - 1	JONES Mi.	33,688
18-Oct	CRYSTAL PALACE	AWAY	1 - 1	LORIMER	31,910
25-Oct	DERBY COUNTY	HOME	2 - 0	CLARKE A 2	44,183
29-Oct	NOTTINGHAM FOREST	HOME	6 - 1	LORIMER 3, CHARLTON, BATES & HIBBITT	29,636
01-Nov	SUNDERLAND	AWAY	0 - 0		31,842
08-Nov	IPSWICH TOWN	HOME	4 - 0	GILES, JONES Mi., HUNTER & GRAY E	26,497
15-Nov	SOUTHAMPTON	AWAY	1 - 1	JONES Mi.	23,963
19-Nov	SUNDERLAND	HOME	2 - 0	JONES Mi. & LORIMER	25,890
22-Nov	LIVERPOOL	HOME	1 - 1	GILES (PEN)	43,293
29-Nov	MANCHESTER CITY	AWAY	2 - 1	GRAY E & JONES Mi.	44,590
06-Dec	WOLVERHAMPTON WANDERERS	HOME	3 - 1	O. G. (HOLSGROVE), CHARLTON & CLARKE A	33,090
13-Dec	SHEFFIELD WEDNESDAY	HOME	2 - 0	CLARKE A 2	31,114
17-Dec	WEST HAM UNITED	HOME	4 - 1	LORIMER 2, CLARKE A & GILES	30,699
26-Dec	NEWCASTLE UNITED	AWAY	1 - 2	GILES	54,527
27-Dec	EVERTON	HOME	2 - 1	JONES Mi. 2	46,770
10-Jan	CHELSEA	AWAY	5 - 2	CLARKE A, COOPER T, GILES (PEN), LORIMER & JONES Mi.	57,221
17-Jan	COVENTRY CITY	HOME	3 - 1	CLARKE A 2 & CHARLTON	34,295
26-Jan	MANCHESTER UNITED	AWAY	2 - 2	JONES Mi. & BREMNER	60,514
31-Jan	STOKE CITY	AWAY	1 - 1	GILES	35,908
10-Feb	WEST BROMWICH ALBION	HOME	5 - 1	GRAY E, JONES Mi., GILES 2 & LORIMER	31,515
14-Feb	TOTTENHAM HOTSPUR	AWAY	1 - 1	LORIMER	41,713
28-Feb	CRYSTAL PALACE	HOME	2 - 0	JONES Mi. 2	37,138
07-Mar	LIVERPOOL	AWAY	0 - 0		51,435
21-Mar	WOLVERHAMPTON WANDERERS	AWAY	2 - 1	JONES Mi. & CLARKE A	35,057
28-Mar	SOUTHAMPTON	HOME	1 - 3	LORIMER	38,370
30-Mar	DERBY COUNTY	AWAY	1 - 4	KENNEDY	41,011
02-Apr	WEST HAM UNITED	AWAY	2 - 2	CLARKE A 2	26,140
04-Apr	BURNLEY	HOME	2 - 1	GRAY E 2	24,691
18-Apr	MANCHESTER CITY	HOME	1 - 3	BELFITT	22,932
21-Apr	IPSWICH TOWN	AWAY	2 - 3	HIBBITT & GRAY E	16,875

F. A. CUP

DATE	OPPONENTS	VENUE	SCORE	SCORERS	ATT.
03-Jan	SWANSEA TOWN (R3)	HOME	2 - 1	GILES (PEN) & JONES Mi.	30,246
24-Jan	SUTTON UNITED (R4)	AWAY	6 - 0	CLARKE A 4 & LORIMER 2	14,000
07-Feb	MANSFIELD TOWN (R5)	HOME	2 - 0	GILES & CLARKE A	48,093
21-Feb	SWINDON TOWN (R6)	AWAY	2 - 0	CLARKE A 2	27,500
14-Mar	MANCHESTER UNITED (SF) $	NEUTRAL	0 - 0		55,000
23-Mar	MANCHESTER UNITED (SFR) ^*	NEUTRAL	0 - 0		62,500
26-Mar	MANCHESTER UNITED (SF2R) +	NEUTRAL	1 - 0	BREMNER	56,000
11-Apr	CHELSEA (FI) £*	NEUTRAL	2 - 2	CHARLTON & JONES Mi.	100,000
29-Apr	CHELSEA (R) #*	NEUTRAL	1 - 2	JONES Mi.	62,078

LEAGUE CUP

DATE	OPPONENTS	VENUE	SCORE	SCORERS	ATT.
03-Sep	FULHAM (R2)	AWAY	1 - 0	CHARLTON	22,446
24-Sep	CHELSEA (R3)	HOME	1 - 1	MADELEY	21,933
06-Oct	CHELSEA (R3R)	AWAY	0 - 2		38,485

F. A. CHARITY SHIELD

DATE	OPPONENTS	VENUE	SCORE	SCORERS	ATT.
02-Aug	MANCHESTER CITY	HOME	2 - 1	GRAY E & CHARLTON	39,835

EUROPEAN CUP

DATE	OPPONENTS	VENUE	SCORE	SCORERS	ATT.
17-Sep	LYN OSLO (R1-1)	HOME	10 - 0	O'GRADY M, JONES Mi. 3, CLARKE A 2, GILES 2 & BREMNER 2	25,979
01-Oct	LYN OSLO (R1-2)	AWAY	6 - 0	HIBBITT 2, BELFITT 2, JONES Mi. & LORIMER	7,595
12-Nov	FERENCVAROS (R2-1)	HOME	3 - 0	GILES & JONES Mi. 2	37,291
26-Nov	FERENCVAROS (R2-2)	AWAY	3 - 0	JONES Mi. 2 & LORIMER	5,400
04-Mar	STANDARD LIEGE (QF3-1)	AWAY	1 - 0	LORIMER	38,000
18-Mar	STANDARD LIEGE (QF3-2)	HOME	1 - 0	GILES (PEN)	48,775
01-Apr	GLASGOW CELTIC (SF-1)	HOME	0 - 1		45,505
15-Apr	GLASGOW CELTIC (SF-2)	AWAY	1 - 2	BREMNER	136,505

LEAGUE AND CUPS

APPEARANCES (SUBSTITUTE)

PLAYER	LEAGUE	F. A. CUP	LGE. CUP	EUR. CUP	CH. SHLD.	TOTAL
BATES	13 (3)	0 (1)	1 (1)	2 (3)		16 (8)
BELFITT	6 (1)		3	1		10 (1)
BREMNER	35	9	2	8	1	55
CHARLTON	32	9	2	7	1	51
CLARKE A	28	9		5	1	43
COOPER T	29 (1)	9	3	7	1	49 (1)
DAVEY	5					5
FAULKNER	2					2
GALVIN	3			0 (1)		3 (1)
GILES	32	9	1	7	1	50
GRAY E	30	6 (1)	2	5	1	44 (1)
HARVEY	5	2	2	0 (1)		9 (1)
HIBBITT	8 (3)		2	1		11 (3)
HUNTER	35	7	2	6	1	51
JOHANNESON	2					2
JONES Mi.	32	9	3	8	1	53
KENNEDY	2					2
LORIMER	36 (3)	8	3	7	0 (1)	54 (4)
LUMSDEN	1 (1)					1 (1)
MADELEY	39	8	3	8	1	59
O'GRADY M	3 (1)			1		4 (1)
PETERSON	3 (1)					3 (1)
REANEY	37	7	3	7	1	55
SPRAKE	37	7	1	8	1	54
YORATH	7 (4)					7 (4)

GOALSCORERS

PLAYER	LEAGUE	F. A. CUP	LGE. CUP	EUR. CUP	CH. SHLD.	TOTAL
CLARKE A	17	7		2		26
JONES Mi.	15	3		8		26
GILES	13	2		4		19
LORIMER	14	2		3		19
GRAY E	9				1	10
BREMNER	4	1		3		8
CHARLTON	3	1	1		1	6
HIBBITT	2			2		4
BELFITT	1			2		3
BATES	1					1
COOPER T	1					1
HUNTER	1					1
KENNEDY	1					1
MADELEY			1			1
O'GRADY M				1		1
OWN GOALS	2					2

KEY :- $ = PLAYED AT HILLSBOROUGH, SHEFFIELD, ^ = PLAYED AT VILLA PARK, BIRMINGHAM, + = PLAYED AT BURNDEN PARK, BOLTON, £ = PLAYED AT WEMBLEY STADIUM, LONDON, # = PLAYED AT OLD TRAFFORD, MANCHESTER, * = AFTER EXTRA TIME

Previous campaign disappointments were confined to history as Bremner and co began the season in scintillating fashion, winning their opening five fixtures against Manchester United, Tottenham Hotspur, Everton, West Ham and Burnley, before a stalemate against Arsenal ended a fine start. Consistent performances kept Leeds at the fore, despite a last gasp Sprake howler at Crystal Palace that cancelled out a brilliant Peter Lorimer strike.

The Selhurst Park clash came in the midst of a 16-match unbeaten run yielding 10 victories as Leeds turned on the style before Christmas and included successive wins against Blackpool, Stoke City, Wolves and Manchester City when Paul Madeley and Allan Clarke notched goals in three consecutive games. Clarke, dubbed 'Sniffer' due his clinical finishing was particularly on song and opened the scoring in a 3-0 Boxing Day win against Newcastle United; Johnny Giles converted two penalties. A defeat against Tottenham Hotspur in early January was Leeds' second of the league campaign. Although knocked out of the League Cup by Sheffield United, Revie's players made progress in the FA Cup.

A Lorimer brace accounted for Rotherham United in a hard-fought replay before Mick Jones scored a treble against Swindon Town, setting up a fifth round clash at Fourth Division Colchester United. However, in arguably the FA Cup's greatest upset the underdogs beat Don Revie's mighty Leeds United side 3-2. Leeds bounced back with wins over Wolves, Ipswich Town, Coventry City and Derby County, Lorimer scoring in the latter three clashes before extending his goal spree to seven games in a draw at Blackpool, a 2-1 win over Crystal Palace and both legs of a titanic Fairs Cup quarter-final tie against Vitoria Setubal.

Revie's team had reached the fourth round by overcoming Sarpsborg 6-0 over two legs, scraping past Dynamo Dresden courtesy of Jones' away goal and blitzing Sparta Prague 9-2 on aggregate. Challenging on two fronts, with eight league games remaining Leeds held a six-point lead over Arsenal, who had two games in hand. Following a 4-0 win at Burnley, Clarke notching all the goals, draws against Newcastle United and Huddersfield Town meant the players faced a crunch match at home to West Brom.

Leeds warmed up at Liverpool in the Fairs Cup semi-finals. Revie gambled on Billy Bremner's first start in three months, and playing as an auxiliary striker, United's skipper notched an away goal for a crucial first leg victory. The Scot lined up against Albion, without an away win in 16 months, but a controversial tap-in by Jeff Astle claimed a 2-1 win. Three decades on, Astle's goal is still one of the most talked about incidents of the era. Referee Ray Tinkler required a police escort and never officiated at Elland Road again.

Leeds won the final three league fixtures but Arsenal claimed the title by one point. The pitch invasion following Tinkler's decision brought an FA four-match ban from playing home games at Elland Road. Undaunted, Leeds reached a third Fairs Cup final following a 0-0 draw with Liverpool and in a sensational first leg display at Juventus gained a 2-2 draw, Madeley and Mick Bates scoring crucial away goals. A Clarke strike in the return was cancelled out by Pietro Anastasi, but proved sufficient for an 'away goals' triumph. In another exciting campaign, Norman Hunter and Paul Madeley made 58 appearances, Clarke top scored with 23 goals.

DIVISION ONE (FINAL LEAGUE POSITION - 2ND)

PLD 42 W 27 D 10 L 5 F 72 A 30 PTS 64

DATE	OPPONENTS	VENUE	SCORE	SCORERS	ATT.
15-Aug	MANCHESTER UNITED	AWAY	1 - 0	JONES Mi.	59,365
19-Aug	TOTTENHAM HOTSPUR	AWAY	2 - 0	GILES & GRAY E	39,927
22-Aug	EVERTON	HOME	3 - 2	BREMNER 2 & GILES	46,718
26-Aug	WEST HAM UNITED	HOME	3 - 0	JONES Mi., GILES (PEN) & BELFITT	42,677
29-Aug	BURNLEY	AWAY	3 - 0	CLARKE A 2 & JONES Mi.	26,006
01-Sep	ARSENAL	AWAY	0 - 0		47,749
05-Sep	CHELSEA	HOME	1 - 0	CLARKE A	47,662
12-Sep	STOKE CITY	AWAY	0 - 3		22,592
19-Sep	SOUTHAMPTON	HOME	1 - 0	GILES (PEN)	32,713
26-Sep	NOTTINGHAM FOREST	AWAY	0 - 0		31,537
03-Oct	HUDDERSFIELD TOWN	HOME	2 - 0	LORIMER 2 (1 PEN)	36,498
10-Oct	WEST BROMWICH ALBION	AWAY	2 - 2	CLARKE A & JONES Mi.	37,255
17-Oct	MANCHESTER UNITED	HOME	2 - 2	BELFITT & CHARLTON	50,190
24-Oct	DERBY COUNTY	AWAY	2 - 0	LORIMER & CLARKE A	32,797
31-Oct	COVENTRY CITY	HOME	2 - 0	CHARLTON & GILES	31,670
07-Nov	CRYSTAL PALACE	AWAY	1 - 1	LORIMER	37,963
14-Nov	BLACKPOOL	HOME	3 - 1	MADELEY, CHARLTON & GILES	32,921
18-Nov	STOKE CITY	HOME	4 - 1	MADELEY, CLARKE A, LORIMER & GILES (PEN)	30,549
21-Nov	WOLVERHAMPTON WANDERERS	AWAY	3 - 2	MADELEY, CLARKE A & O. G. (HOLSGROVE)	41,048
28-Nov	MANCHESTER CITY	HOME	1 - 0	CLARKE A	43,511
05-Dec	LIVERPOOL	AWAY	1 - 1	MADELEY	51,357
12-Dec	IPSWICH TOWN	HOME	0 - 0		29,675
19-Dec	EVERTON	AWAY	1 - 0	CHARLTON	47,393
26-Dec	NEWCASTLE UNITED	HOME	3 - 0	CLARKE A & GILES 2 (2 PENS)	46,758
09-Jan	TOTTENHAM HOTSPUR	HOME	1 - 2	CLARKE A	43,907
16-Jan	WEST HAM UNITED	AWAY	3 - 2	HUNTER, GILES & BELFITT	34,396
30-Jan	MANCHESTER CITY	AWAY	2 - 0	CLARKE A & CHARLTON	43,517
06-Feb	LIVERPOOL	HOME	0 - 1		48,425
20-Feb	WOLVERHAMPTON WANDERERS	HOME	3 - 0	MADELEY, CLARKE A & GILES (PEN)	37,273
23-Feb	IPSWICH TOWN	AWAY	4 - 2	LORIMER, CLARKE A 2 & GILES (PEN)	27,264
26-Feb	COVENTRY CITY	AWAY	1 - 0	LORIMER	40,012
06-Mar	DERBY COUNTY	HOME	1 - 0	LORIMER	36,467
13-Mar	BLACKPOOL	AWAY	1 - 1	LORIMER	27,401
20-Mar	CRYSTAL PALACE	HOME	2 - 1	LORIMER & GILES	31,876
27-Mar	CHELSEA	AWAY	1 - 3	COOPER T	58,462
03-Apr	BURNLEY	HOME	4 - 0	CLARKE A 4	31,192
10-Apr	NEWCASTLE UNITED	AWAY	1 - 1	LORIMER	49,640
12-Apr	HUDDERSFIELD TOWN	AWAY	0 - 0		43,011
17-Apr	WEST BROMWICH ALBION	HOME	1 - 2	CLARKE A	36,812
24-Apr	SOUTHAMPTON	AWAY	3 - 0	O. G. (HOLLYWOOD) & JONES Mi. 2	30,001
26-Apr	ARSENAL	HOME	1 - 0	CHARLTON	48,350
01-May	NOTTINGHAM FOREST	HOME	2 - 0	BREMNER & LORIMER	43,083

F. A. CUP

DATE	OPPONENTS	VENUE	SCORE	SCORERS	ATT.
11-Jan	ROTHERHAM UNITED (R3)	AWAY	0 - 0		24,000
18-Jan	ROTHERHAM UNITED (R3R)	HOME	3 - 2	LORIMER 2 & GILES	36,890
23-Jan	SWINDON TOWN (R4)	HOME	4 - 0	JONES Mi. 3 & CLARKE A	36,985
13-Feb	COLCHESTER UNITED (R5)	AWAY	2 - 3	HUNTER & GILES	16,000

LEAGUE CUP

DATE	OPPONENTS	VENUE	SCORE	SCORERS	ATT.
08-Sep	SHEFFIELD UNITED (R2)	AWAY	0 - 1		29,573

INTER - CITIES FAIRS CUP

DATE	OPPONENTS	VENUE	SCORE	SCORERS	ATT.
15-Sep	SARPSBORG (R1-1)	AWAY	1 - 0	LORIMER	8,769
29-Sep	SARPSBORG (R1-2)	HOME	5 - 0	CHARLTON 2, BREMNER 2 & LORIMER	19,283
21-Oct	DYNAMO DRESDEN (R2-1)	HOME	1 - 0	LORIMER (PEN)	21,292
04-Nov	DYNAMO DRESDEN (R2-2) ^	AWAY	1 - 2	JONES Mi.	35,000
02-Dec	SPARTA PRAGUE (R3-1)	HOME	6 - 0	CLARKE A, BREMNER, GRAY E 2, CHARLTON & O. G. (CHOVANEC)	25,843
09-Dec	SPARTA PRAGUE (R3-2)	AWAY	3 - 2	GRAY E, CLARKE A & BELFITT	30,000
10-Mar	VITORIA SETUBAL (QF-1)	HOME	2 - 1	LORIMER & GILES (PEN)	27,143
24-Mar	VITORIA SETUBAL (QF-2)	AWAY	1 - 1	LORIMER	30,000
14-Apr	LIVERPOOL (SF-1)	AWAY	1 - 0	BREMNER	52,877
28-Apr	LIVERPOOL (SF-2)	HOME	0 - 0		40,462
28-May	JUVENTUS (Fi-1)	AWAY	2 - 2	MADELEY & BATES	45,000
03-Jun	JUVENTUS (Fi-2) ^	HOME	1 - 1	CLARKE A	42,483

LEAGUE AND CUPS

APPEARANCES (SUBSTITUTE)

PLAYER	LEAGUE	F. A. CUP	LGE. CUP	I. C. F. CUP	TOTAL
BATES	29 (1)	2 (1)	1	8 (2)	40 (4)
BELFITT	3 (10)	1	0 (1)	6	10 (11)
BREMNER	26	2	1	10	39
CHARLTON	41	4	1	10	56
CLARKE A	41	4	1	10	56
COOPER T	41	3	1	10	55
DAVEY	6 (1)	1		3 (1)	10 (2)
GALVIN		0 (1)		0 (1)	0 (2)
GILES	34	4		8	46
GRAY E	18		1	5	24
HARVEY	8			3 (1)	11 (1)
HIBBITT	0 (3)			1	1 (3)
HUNTER	42	4	1	11	58
JONES Mi.	40	3	1	9	53
JORDAN				0 (2)	0 (2)
KENNEDY				1	1
LORIMER	37	4	1	10	52
MADELEY	41	4	1	12	58
REANEY	18 (1)	4		6 (3)	28 (4)
SPRAKE	34	4	1	9 (1)	48 (1)
YORATH	3			0 (2)	3 (2)

GOALSCORERS

PLAYER	LEAGUE	F. A. CUP	LGE. CUP	I. C. F. CUP	TOTAL
CLARKE A	19	1		3	23
LORIMER	12	2		5	19
GILES	13	2		1	16
JONES Mi.	6	3		1	10
CHARLTON	6			3	9
BREMNER	3			4	7
MADELEY	5			1	6
BELFITT	3			1	4
GRAY E	1			3	4
HUNTER	1	1			2
BATES				1	1
COOPER T	1				1
OWN GOALS	2			1	3

KEY :- ^ = WON ON AWAY GOALS

Close season media coverage concentrated on an FA four-match home ban following the previous season's crowd trouble against West Brom. Disadvantaged, Leeds began poorly, winning five of the opening dozen league fixtures, the most impressive, a 5-1 'home' rout against Newcastle United at Hillsborough. Compounding matters Allan Clarke and Mick Jones played only three games together. Peter Lorimer took up the mantle of main striker with winning strikes against Manchester City and Liverpool, but was thankful when Clarke and Jones returned against City at Elland Road, all three scoring; Lorimer's 30-yard dipping volley particularly special.

Surprisingly, Leeds exited the UEFA Cup to minnows Lierse SK and within weeks League Cup ambitions perished against West Ham. In the league, United quickly returned to form, Lorimer notching winners against Everton, Manchester United and Leicester City. Further joy for the Scot came in consecutive victories over Stoke City, Nottingham Forest and West Brom. Off the field, Terry Hibbitt and Rod Belfitt departed, whilst Asa Hartford's proposed £177,000 move to Elland Road collapsed when a medical noted a heart problem. By Christmas, Leeds sat five points adrift but a 2-0 New Years Day victory at Anfield, Clarke and Jones scoring, lifted Revie's team into the pack of title contenders.

The Liverpool win was a major turning point, not just because it inflicted a first home defeat on the Reds in 35 matches, but summed up the quality of recent performances. The coming weeks would produce dazzling football, in particular the destruction of Manchester United 5-1, Jones notching a hat-trick, and Southampton 7-0, Lorimer striking a treble. The clashes, televised on *Match of the Day*, earned acclaim. Prior to Easter, Leeds overcame Arsenal 3-0 and Nottingham Forest 6-1.

Back in the title race, Leeds battled to the FA Cup semi-finals, easily defeating Bristol Rovers, Giles and Lorimer grabbing braces, before a titanic battle against Liverpool, Clarke scoring a brilliant double in a home replay. Giles secured a win at Cardiff, before Leeds overcame a freak goal to defeat Tottenham Hotspur in the quarter-finals, Clarke and Jack Charlton claiming the goals. The game was also notable for Leeds' pre-match warm-up routine, and player's wearing named tracksuits and numbered stocking tabs. Despite media criticism, supporters loved the razzmatazz.

In the league, Leeds lost a crucial fixture at rivals Derby 2-0, but bounced back against Huddersfield Town and Stoke, although at a heavy price, as Terry Cooper broke a leg days before the semi-final clash with Birmingham City, effectively ending his United career. Undeterred, Leeds claimed an emphatic 3-0 win at Hillsborough, David Harvey succeeding Gary Sprake as number one keeper, whilst Jones and Lorimer booked a Wembley place. Back in the league, Leeds followed a defeat at Newcastle, with victories over West Brom and Chelsea, but though in pole position, an FA ruling switched the final clash at Wolves until 48 hours after the FA Cup final.

In the competition's Centenary year, Billy Bremner at last lifted the sole domestic honour to elude the club, Clarke's flying header from a pinpoint Jones cross securing the famous trophy against Arsenal. With no time to celebrate, Leeds travelled to Molineux, needing a point to clinch the Division 1 crown, but on a night of unbelievable tension, atrocious refereeing cost Revie's injury-hit team the dream double. Finishing runners-up for a third consecutive season, Hunter and Lorimer, who top scored with 29 goals, made 56 appearances. Revie collected the Manager of the Year award for a third time, while behind the scenes, Manny Cussins replaced Percy Woodward as chairman.

1971 - 1972

DIVISION ONE (FINAL LEAGUE POSITION - 2ND)
PLD 42 W 24 D 9 L 9 F 73 A 31 PTS 57

DATE	OPPONENTS	VENUE	SCORE	SCORERS	ATT.
14-Aug	MANCHESTER CITY	AWAY	1 - 0	LORIMER	38,566
17-Aug	SHEFFIELD UNITED	AWAY	0 - 3		40,725
21-Aug	WOLVERHAMPTON WANDERERS ^	HOME	0 - 0		20,686
25-Aug	TOTTENHAM HOTSPUR >	HOME	1 - 1	BREMNER	25,099
28-Aug	IPSWICH TOWN	AWAY	2 - 0	LORIMER & BELFITT	26,689
01-Sep	NEWCASTLE UNITED $	HOME	5 - 1	CHARLTON, LORIMER, GILES (PEN), YORATH & MADELEY	18,623
04-Sep	CRYSTAL PALACE ^	HOME	2 - 0	MADELEY & GILES (PEN)	18,715
11-Sep	ARSENAL	AWAY	0 - 2		51,196
18-Sep	LIVERPOOL	HOME	1 - 0	LORIMER	41,381
25-Sep	HUDDERSFIELD TOWN	AWAY	1 - 2	CHARLTON	26,340
02-Oct	WEST HAM UNITED	HOME	0 - 0		30,942
09-Oct	COVENTRY CITY	AWAY	1 - 3	O. G. (PARKER)	32,183
16-Oct	MANCHESTER CITY	HOME	3 - 0	CLARKE A, JONES Mi. & LORIMER	36,004
23-Oct	EVERTON	HOME	3 - 2	COOPER T, CHARLTON & LORIMER	34,208
30-Oct	MANCHESTER UNITED	AWAY	1 - 0	LORIMER	53,960
06-Nov	LEICESTER CITY	HOME	2 - 1	BREMNER & LORIMER	39,877
13-Nov	SOUTHAMPTON	AWAY	1 - 2	GILES	25,331
20-Nov	STOKE CITY	HOME	1 - 0	LORIMER	32,012
27-Nov	NOTTINGHAM FOREST	AWAY	2 - 0	LORIMER & CLARKE A	29,463
04-Dec	WEST BROMWICH ALBION	HOME	3 - 0	GILES 2 & LORIMER	32,521
11-Dec	CHELSEA	AWAY	0 - 0		45,867
18-Dec	CRYSTAL PALACE	AWAY	1 - 1	LORIMER	31,456
27-Dec	DERBY COUNTY	HOME	3 - 0	GRAY E & LORIMER 2	44,214
01-Jan	LIVERPOOL	AWAY	2 - 0	CLARKE A & JONES Mi	53,847
08-Jan	IPSWICH TOWN	HOME	2 - 2	BREMNER & CLARKE A	32,194
22-Jan	SHEFFIELD UNITED	HOME	1 - 0	CLARKE A	41,038
29-Jan	TOTTENHAM HOTSPUR	AWAY	0 - 1		46,774
12-Feb	EVERTON	AWAY	0 - 0		45,935
19-Feb	MANCHESTER UNITED	HOME	5 - 1	JONES Mi. 3, CLARKE A & LORIMER	45,399
04-Mar	SOUTHAMPTON	HOME	7 - 0	CLARKE A 2, LORIMER 3, CHARLTON & JONES Mi.	34,275
11-Mar	COVENTRY CITY	HOME	1 - 0	CHARLTON	43,154
22-Mar	LEICESTER CITY	AWAY	0 - 0		32,152
25-Mar	ARSENAL	HOME	3 - 0	CLARKE A, JONES Mi. & LORIMER	45,055
27-Mar	NOTTINGHAM FOREST	HOME	6 - 1	LORIMER 2, GRAY E 2 & CLARKE A 2	40,866
31-Mar	WEST HAM UNITED	AWAY	2 - 2	GRAY E 2	41,003
01-Apr	DERBY COUNTY	AWAY	0 - 2		39,450
05-Apr	HUDDERSFIELD TOWN	HOME	3 - 1	JONES Mi., LORIMER & GRAY E	46,148
08-Apr	STOKE CITY	AWAY	3 - 0	JONES Mi. 2 & LORIMER	35,123
19-Apr	NEWCASTLE UNITED	AWAY	0 - 1		42,006
22-Apr	WEST BROMWICH ALBION	AWAY	1 - 0	GILES (PEN)	39,724
01-May	CHELSEA	HOME	2 - 0	BREMNER & JONES Mi.	46,565
08-May	WOLVERHAMPTON WANDERERS	AWAY	1 - 2	BREMNER	53,379

F. A. CUP

DATE	OPPONENTS	VENUE	SCORE	SCORERS	ATT.
15-Jan	BRISTOL ROVERS (R3)	HOME	4 - 1	GILES 2 (1 PEN) & LORIMER 2	33,565
05-Feb	LIVERPOOL (R4)	AWAY	0 - 0		56,598
09-Feb	LIVERPOOL (R4R)	HOME	2 - 0	CLARKE A 2	45,821
26-Feb	CARDIFF CITY (R5)	AWAY	2 - 0	GILES 2	50,000
18-Mar	TOTTENHAM HOTSPUR (R6)	HOME	2 - 1	CLARKE A & CHARLTON	43,937
15-Apr	BIRMINGHAM CITY (SF) #	NEUTRAL	3 - 0	JONES Mi. 2 & LORIMER	55,000
06-May	ARSENAL (Fi) '	NEUTRAL	1 - 0	CLARKE A	100,000

LEAGUE CUP

DATE	OPPONENTS	VENUE	SCORE	SCORERS	ATT.
08-Sep	DERBY COUNTY (R2)	AWAY	0 - 0		34,023
27-Sep	DERBY COUNTY (R2R)	HOME	2 - 0	LORIMER 2	29,132
06-Oct	WEST HAM UNITED (R3)	AWAY	0 - 0		35,884
20-Oct	WEST HAM UNITED (R3R) '	HOME	0 - 1		26,504

INTER - CITIES FAIRS CUP PLAY - OFF

DATE	OPPONENTS	VENUE	SCORE	SCORERS	ATT.
22-Sep	BARCELONA @	AWAY	1 - 2	JORDAN	35,000

U. E. F. A. CUP

DATE	OPPONENTS	VENUE	SCORE	SCORERS	ATT.
15-Sep	LIERSE SK (R1-1)	AWAY	2 - 0	GALVIN & LORIMER	17,000
29-Sep	LIERSE SK (R1-2)	HOME	0 - 4		18,680

LEAGUE AND CUPS
APPEARANCES (SUBSTITUTE)

PLAYER	LEAGUE	F. A. CUP	LGE. CUP	U. E. F. A.	PLAY - OFF	TOTAL
BATES	6 (3)	2		2		10 (3)
BELFITT	10 (1)		3	2	1	16 (1)
BREMNER	41	7	4	1	1	54
CHARLTON	41	5	4		1	51
CLARKE A	35	6	2			43
COOPER T	34	5	3	1		43
DAVEY			1		1	2
EDWARDS M	0 (1)					0 (1)
FAULKNER			2			2
GALVIN	2 (1)	0 (1)		2	1	5 (2)
GILES	38	7	4	1	1	51
GRAY E	25 (1)	6	0 (1)			31 (2)
HARVEY	7	2	2			11
HUNTER	42	7	4	1 (1)	1	55 (1)
JONES MI.	24	5	1			30
JORDAN	5 (7)	1 (1)			1	7 (8)
LORIMER	42	7	4	2	1	56
MADELEY	42	7	4	1		54
MANN	1		0 (1)	1		2 (1)
REANEY	29 (4)	5 (1)	3	2	1	40 (5)
SHAW			1			1
SPRAKE	35	5	2	1 (1)	1	44 (1)
YORATH	3 (4)		3	2		8 (4)

GOALSCORERS

PLAYER	LEAGUE	F. A. CUP	LGE. CUP	U. E. F. A.	PLAY - OFF	TOTAL
LORIMER	23	3	2	1		29
CLARKE A	11	4				15
JONES MI.	11	2				13
GILES	6	4				10
CHARLTON	5	1				6
GRAY E	6					6
BREMNER	5					5
MADELEY	2					2
BELFITT	1					1
COOPER T	1					1
GALVIN				1		1
JORDAN				1		1
YORATH	1					1
OWN GOALS	1					1

KEY :- @ = PLAY OFF BETWEEN FIRST & LAST WINNERS OF THE COMPETITION FOR THE RETENTION OF THE TROPHY AT THE NOU CAMP STADIUM BARCELONA, # = PLAYED AT HILLSBOROUGH, SHEFFIELD, ' = PLAYED AT WEMBLEY STADIUM, LONDON, ^ = PLAYED AT LEEDS ROAD, HUDDERSFIELD, > = PLAYED AT BOOTHFERRY PARK, HULL, $ = PLAYED AT HILLSBOROUGH, SHEFFIELD BECAUSE ELLAND ROAD WAS CLOSED BY F. A. ORDER & ' = AFTER EXTRA TIME

Don Revie, sensing the future, signed Huddersfield Town utility defender Trevor Cherry for £100,000 and rookie St Mirren centre-half Gordon McQueen for £30,000. With Mick Jones sidelined in the opening weeks, Revie gave a run-out to reserve striker Joe Jordan, a £15,000 purchase from Morton. Leeds started indifferently, losing 4-0 at Chelsea, defeating Sheffield United and West Brom, prior to drawing 3-3 with Ipswich, Jordan notching a brace. On target in each game was Johnny Giles, becoming the second Leeds player to score three consecutive spot kicks in league games, matching Jack Milburn's feat in 1935/36.

A last minute Billy Bremner strike secured a win over Southampton before Jordan engineered a 2-0 win against Norwich City. Returning to the fray, Jones scored in wins against Leicester City and Everton, whilst helping Leeds advance in the League Cup against Burnley and Aston Villa. Jones also scored a spectacular overhead kick in a 2-1 defeat by Liverpool, but though results were encouraging, performances were workmanlike, apart from a 5-0 drubbing of defending champions Derby County, Giles notching two long-range strikes.

The result heralded a 16-match run, bringing a single defeat, Allan Clarke scoring a brace in wins against Sheffield United and Birmingham City. Four successive victories put Leeds among the pacemakers again, Jordan notching the winner against Newcastle United on Boxing Day, whilst Clarke settled clashes with Norwich and Stoke City. Liverpool ended League Cup hopes but in Europe, Leeds overcame an intimidating atmosphere in Ankara; squeezing home 2-1 on aggregate before being thankful for home form in a 2-0 aggregate win against Carl Zeiss Jena. The quarter-final against Rapid Bucharest however was far more comfortable; a 5-0 opening leg win making the return a formality.

The FA Cup campaign was torturous initially, Norwich particularly stubborn opponents before Clarke's treble wrapped up a 5-0 second replay. Thereafter wins over Plymouth Argyle and West Brom set up a quarter-final encounter with Brian Clough's Derby County, which a Peter Lorimer special settled. Facing Wolves in the semi-finals at Maine Road, Bremner scored the all-important goal. Four days on, Clarke edged Leeds ahead against crack Yugoslavian side Hajduk Split, prior to being sent off for retaliation. In the return, a 0-0 draw secured another European final, but Bremner's booking earned a suspension.

Reaching two finals however, caught up with the players. Three wins in 11 fixtures, including a 4-0 win against Crystal Palace that included a goal by Eddie Gray's younger brother Frank, brought a third place finish. Odds-on favourites to win the FA Cup, Sunderland created the biggest Wembley upset, winning 1-0, when Jim Montgomery pulled off a point-blank save of the century from Lorimer. Following the defeat, newspaper stories 24 hours before the European Cup Winners Final suggested Revie was to join Everton, but undaunted, Leeds performed heroically against AC Milan, falling to one goal, while Norman Hunter was dismissed after reacting to a cynical foul. Talk however surrounded a scandalous refereeing performance. Once again, a season of promise ended in heartache. David Harvey and Lorimer made 63 appearances, Clarke top scored with 26 goals.

1972 - 1973

DIVISION ONE (FINAL LEAGUE POSITION - 3RD)

PLD 42 W 21 D 11 L 10 F 71 A 45 PTS 53

DATE	OPPONENTS	VENUE	SCORE	SCORERS	ATT.
12-Aug	CHELSEA	AWAY	0 - 4		51,102
15-Aug	SHEFFIELD UNITED	AWAY	2 - 0	O. G. (COLQUHOUN) & GILES (PEN)	40,159
19-Aug	WEST BROMWICH ALBION	HOME	2 - 0	CLARKE A & GILES (PEN)	36,555
23-Aug	IPSWICH TOWN	HOME	3 - 3	JORDAN 2 & GILES (PEN)	32,461
26-Aug	TOTTENHAM HOTSPUR	AWAY	0 - 0		41,191
30-Aug	SOUTHAMPTON	HOME	1 - 0	BREMNER	31,401
02-Sep	NORWICH CITY	HOME	2 - 0	JORDAN & CHARLTON	34,261
09-Sep	STOKE CITY	AWAY	2 - 2	LORIMER & CLARKE A	26,705
16-Sep	LEICESTER CITY	HOME	3 - 1	CLARKE A, JONES MI. & BATES	33,930
23-Sep	NEWCASTLE UNITED	AWAY	2 - 3	CLARKE A & JONES MI.	38,962
30-Sep	LIVERPOOL	HOME	1 - 2	JONES MI.	46,468
07-Oct	DERBY COUNTY	HOME	5 - 0	GILES 2, CLARKE A, BREMNER & LORIMER	36,477
14-Oct	EVERTON	AWAY	2 - 1	JONES MI. & JORDAN	47,821
21-Oct	COVENTRY CITY	HOME	1 - 1	CHARLTON	36,240
28-Oct	WOLVERHAMPTON WANDERERS	AWAY	2 - 0	GRAY E & LORIMER	33,731
04-Nov	IPSWICH TOWN	AWAY	2 - 2	CHARLTON & LORIMER	27,566
11-Nov	SHEFFIELD UNITED	HOME	2 - 1	CLARKE A 2	31,600
18-Nov	CRYSTAL PALACE	AWAY	2 - 2	JONES MI. & GILES	30,107
25-Nov	MANCHESTER CITY	HOME	3 - 0	CHERRY, LORIMER & CLARKE A	39,879
02-Dec	ARSENAL	AWAY	1 - 2	LORIMER (PEN)	39,108
09-Dec	WEST HAM UNITED	HOME	1 - 0	JONES MI.	30,270
16-Dec	BIRMINGHAM CITY	HOME	4 - 0	CLARKE A 2, LORIMER & JONES MI.	25,285
23-Dec	MANCHESTER UNITED	AWAY	1 - 1	CLARKE A	46,382
26-Dec	NEWCASTLE UNITED	HOME	1 - 0	JORDAN	45,486
06-Jan	TOTTENHAM HOTSPUR	HOME	2 - 1	JONES MI. & LORIMER (PEN)	32,404
20-Jan	NORWICH CITY	AWAY	2 - 1	JORDAN & CLARKE A	27,447
27-Jan	STOKE CITY	HOME	1 - 0	CLARKE A	33,487
10-Feb	LEICESTER CITY	AWAY	0 - 2		35,976
17-Feb	CHELSEA	HOME	1 - 1	JONES MI.	41,781
03-Mar	DERBY COUNTY	AWAY	3 - 2	LORIMER 2 (2 PENS) & CLARKE A	38,100
10-Mar	EVERTON	HOME	2 - 1	CLARKE A & LORIMER	39,663
24-Mar	WOLVERHAMPTON WANDERERS	HOME	0 - 0		39,078
28-Mar	WEST BROMWICH ALBION	AWAY	1 - 1	CLARKE A	33,057
31-Mar	MANCHESTER CITY	AWAY	0 - 1		35,772
02-Apr	COVENTRY CITY	AWAY	1 - 0	REANEY	24,383
14-Apr	WEST HAM UNITED	AWAY	1 - 1	CLARKE A	38,804
18-Apr	MANCHESTER UNITED	HOME	0 - 1		45,450
21-Apr	CRYSTAL PALACE	HOME	4 - 0	BREMNER, LORIMER, GRAY F & CLARKE A	31,173
23-Apr	LIVERPOOL	AWAY	0 - 2		55,738
28-Apr	SOUTHAMPTON	AWAY	1 - 3	HUNTER	24,108
30-Apr	BIRMINGHAM CITY	AWAY	1 - 2	JORDAN	34,449
09-May	ARSENAL	HOME	6 - 1	LORIMER 3 (1 PEN), BREMNER & JORDAN 2	25,088

F. A. CUP

DATE	OPPONENTS	VENUE	SCORE	SCORERS	ATT.
13-Jan	NORWICH CITY (R3)	AWAY	1 - 1	LORIMER	32,310
17-Jan	NORWICH CITY (R3R) *	HOME	1 - 1	GILES	36,887
29-Jan	NORWICH CITY (R32R) $	NEUTRAL	5 - 0	CLARKE A 3, JONES MI. & LORIMER	33,275
03-Feb	PLYMOUTH ARGYLE (R4)	HOME	2 - 1	CLARKE A & BATES	38,374
24-Feb	WEST BROMWICH ALBION (R5)	HOME	2 - 0	CLARKE A 2	39,229
17-Mar	DERBY COUNTY (R6)	AWAY	1 - 0	LORIMER	38,670
07-Apr	WOLVERHAMPTON WANDERERS (SF) ^	NEUTRAL	1 - 0	BREMNER	52,505
05-May	SUNDERLAND (FI) <	NEUTRAL	0 - 1		100,000

LEAGUE CUP

DATE	OPPONENTS	VENUE	SCORE	SCORERS	ATT.
06-Sep	BURNLEY (R2)	HOME	4 - 0	LORIMER 2, JONES MI. & CHERRY	20,857
04-Oct	ASTON VILLA (R3)	AWAY	1 - 1	CHARLTON	46,185
11-Oct	ASTON VILLA (R3R)	HOME	2 - 0	O. G. (NICHOLL) & JONES MI.	28,894
31-Oct	LIVERPOOL (R4)	AWAY	2 - 2	JONES MI. & LORIMER	44,609
22-Nov	LIVERPOOL (R4R)	HOME	0 - 1		34,856

EUROPEAN CUP - WINNERS CUP

DATE	OPPONENTS	VENUE	SCORE	SCORERS	ATT.
13-Sep	ANKARAGUCU (R1-1)	AWAY	1 - 1	JORDAN	20,000
27-Sep	ANKARAGUCU (R1-2)	HOME	1 - 0	JONES MI.	22,411
25-Oct	CARL ZEISS JENA (R2-1)	AWAY	0 - 0		18,000
08-Nov	CARL ZEISS JENA (R2-2)	HOME	2 - 0	CHERRY & JONES MI.	26,885
07-Mar	RAPID BUCHAREST (QF-1)	HOME	5 - 0	GILES, CLARKE A, LORIMER 2 & JORDAN	25,702
21-Mar	RAPID BUCHAREST (QF-2)	AWAY	3 - 1	BATES, JONES MI. & JORDAN	25,000
11-Apr	HAJDUK SPLIT (SF-1)	HOME	1 - 0	CLARKE A	32,051
25-Apr	HAJDUK SPLIT (SF-2)	AWAY	0 - 0		30,000
16-May	A. C. MILAN (FI) >	NEUTRAL	0 - 1		40,154

LEAGUE AND CUPS

APPEARANCES (SUBSTITUTE)

PLAYER	LEAGUE	F. A. CUP	LGE. CUP	E. C. W. C.	TOTAL
BATES	26 (3)	4 (1)	4	6	40 (4)
BREMNER	38	7	5	7	57
CHARLTON	18	1	4	2	25
CHERRY	38 (1)	8	5	8	59 (1)
CLARKE A	36	8	4	5	53
ELLAM	6 (1)		1	2	9 (1)
GALVIN	1		1	1	3
GILES	33	8	1	6 (1)	48 (1)
GRAY E	16 (1)	3	3	2	24 (1)
GRAY F	3 (1)		1 (1)		4 (2)
HAMPTON	2				2
HARVEY	41	8	5	9	63
HUNTER	32	7	5	9	53
JONES MI.	27 (1)	8	4 (1)	6	45 (2)
JORDAN	16 (10)	0 (1)	1 (1)	6 (1)	23 (13)
LIDDELL	1				1
LORIMER	41	8	5	9	63
McGINLEY	0 (1)				0 (1)
McQUEEN	6			2 (1)	8 (1)
MADELEY	34	8	4	6	52
MANN	1				1
REANEY	29	8	2	8	47
SPRAKE	1				1
YORATH	16 (6)	2 (2)	1 (1)	4 (3)	23 (12)

GOALSCORERS

PLAYER	LEAGUE	F. A. CUP	LGE. CUP	E. C. W. C.	TOTAL
CLARKE A	18	6		2	26
LORIMER	15	3	3	2	23
JONES MI.	9	1	3	3	16
JORDAN	9			3	12
GILES	6	1		1	8
BREMNER	4	1			5
CHARLTON	3		1		4
BATES	1	1		1	3
CHERRY	1		1	1	3
GRAY E	1				1
GRAY F	1				1
HUNTER	1				1
REANEY	1				1
OWN GOALS	1	1			2

KEY :- * = AFTER EXTRA TIME, $ = PLAYED AT VILLA PARK, BIRMINGHAM, ^ = PLAYED AT MAINE ROAD, MANCHESTER, < = PLAYED AT WEMBLEY STADIUM, LONDON & > = PLAYED AT THE KAFTANTZOGLIO STADIUM, SALONIKA, GREECE

During the close season, following discussions with chairman Manny Cussins, Don Revie decided against joining Everton to stay at Elland Road. Nevertheless, media opinion believed Leeds United was a spent force, despite youngsters breaking through, including Gordon McQueen in the wake of Jack Charlton's retirement. Departing also was Gary Sprake as David Stewart arrived from Ayr United. Confounding critics, Revie's team began the campaign in sensational style, winning seven consecutive games. Billy Bremner set Leeds on the way to a 3-1 win against Everton and a 3-0 victory at Tottenham Hotspur, whilst Lorimer scored a brace in a 4-1 win over Wolves and a hat-trick to despatch Birmingham City 3-0.

Following a draw with Manchester United, the unbeaten run continued against Liverpool and Manchester City; Mick Jones and Mick Bates notching the winners, and in a 4-1 canter over West Ham, the pair scored again, taking Leeds six points clear. As Christmas approached, Leeds' interest in the League Cup and UEFA Cup was over, the highlight a 6-1 win against Stromsgodset; Jones and Allan Clarke notching a brace apiece. But consecutive wins over Ipswich Town, Chelsea, Norwich City (a clash that saw Bremner make his 500th full league appearance), and Newcastle United, extended the lead to nine points.

The 2-1 triumph at Stamford Bridge, Joe Jordan and Jones scoring, set a post-war record of 20 games unbeaten from the start of a Football League campaign, whilst Paul Madeley scored a Boxing Day winner at Newcastle. Following a draw at Birmingham, Jordan striking four minutes from time, bookmakers refused to take bets on Leeds winning the title, but offered 25-1 against United remaining undefeated for the season. Playing with panache and a swagger, the team deservedly received national acclaim.

With everyone desperate to beat Leeds, each match became more intense. The New Year began with one victory, 2-1 against Southampton, in four games, before consecutive wins over Arsenal and Manchester United, Jordan scoring in both clashes, took the undefeated run to 29 games, one shy of Burnley's all-time record from the start of a campaign in 1920/21. Favourites to complete the double, Leeds faced an FA Cup clash against Bristol City, and in the shock of the round, City claimed a replay win.

Suddenly doubts set in, Stoke City overcame a two-goal deficit to claim a 3-2 victory, ending United's unbeaten run, heralding one win in seven games, including successive defeats against Liverpool, Burnley and West Ham. Astonishingly, the Reds could mathematically overhaul Leeds. During a nerve-wracking few games, Lorimer and Bremner secured a dour win against Derby County while draws against Coventry City and Sheffield United left no room for manoeuvre. A Lorimer brace proved crucial in the return at Bramall Lane before Sniffer Clarke poached a late winner in the penultimate game of the season at home to Ipswich Town. Under intense pressure, Liverpool cracked, losing at home to Arsenal and handing Leeds the title. Clarke's clinical strike won the final match at Queens Park Rangers.

Bremner made 52 appearances, Jones top scored on 17 goals. During the close season, Revie became England manager after masterminding Leeds United's rise from oblivion to the summit of English football. Claiming two Division 1 crowns, two Fairs Cups, the FA Cup, League Cup and Charity Shield, Leeds also finished Division 1 runners-up on five occasions, reached three FA Cup finals and two European finals. Future Leeds teams have all faced comparison to Revie's legendary side in a golden era.

Mick Jones scores as Leeds defeat Hungarian Giants Ferencvaros in the 1968 Fairs Cup Final.

Leeds United Fairs Cup and League Cup winners 1967-68.

Leeds celebrate winning the Division One Championship in 1969.

Jack Charlton 1970.

1970 Peter Lorimer scores a cracker.

Allan Clarke's goal ensures victory in the 1971 Fairs Cup Final over Juventus.

Eddie Gray 1972.

Leeds United 1973-74.

1974 The Leeds team celebrate winning the Division One Championship with the Elland Road faithful.

Peter Lorimer's goal is disallowed in the controversial 1975 European Cup Final against Bayern Munich.

Leeds United 1977-78.

Leeds United 1983-84.

Gordon Strachan celebrates scoring against Leicester City 1990.

Lee Chapman scores in a 5 - 1 victory over Wimbledon as Leeds head towards the Division One title.

Division One Champions 1992

Gary McAllister 1992

Gary Kelly 1995

Lucas Radebe 2000

Nigel Martyn 2001

2000-01 Dominic Matteo scores a Champions League goal in a 6 - 0 victory over Besiktas.

1973 - 1974

DIVISION ONE (FINAL LEAGUE POSITION - 1ST)

PLD 42 W 24 D 14 L 4 F 66 A 31 PTS 62

DATE	OPPONENTS	VENUE	SCORE	SCORERS	ATT.
25-Aug	EVERTON	HOME	3 - 1	BREMNER, GILES & JONES Mi.	39,325
28-Aug	ARSENAL	AWAY	2 - 1	LORIMER & MADELEY	47,429
01-Sep	TOTTENHAM HOTSPUR	AWAY	3 - 0	BREMNER 2 & CLARKE A	42,801
05-Sep	WOLVERHAMPTON WANDERERS	HOME	4 - 1	LORIMER 2 (1 PEN), JONES Mi. & BREMNER	39,946
08-Sep	BIRMINGHAM CITY	HOME	3 - 0	LORIMER 3 (1 PEN)	39,736
11-Sep	WOLVERHAMPTON WANDERERS	AWAY	2 - 0	JONES Mi. & CLARKE A	36,980
15-Sep	SOUTHAMPTON	AWAY	2 - 1	CLARKE A 2	27,770
22-Sep	MANCHESTER UNITED	HOME	0 - 0		47,058
29-Sep	NORWICH CITY	AWAY	1 - 0	GILES	31,993
06-Oct	STOKE CITY	HOME	1 - 1	JONES Mi.	36,562
13-Oct	LEICESTER CITY	AWAY	2 - 2	JONES Mi. & BREMNER	36,978
20-Oct	LIVERPOOL	HOME	1 - 0	JONES Mi.	44,911
27-Oct	MANCHESTER CITY	AWAY	1 - 0	BATES	45,346
03-Nov	WEST HAM UNITED	HOME	4 - 1	BATES, JONES Mi. 2 & CLARKE A	36,869
10-Nov	BURNLEY	AWAY	0 - 0		37,894
17-Nov	COVENTRY CITY	HOME	3 - 0	CLARKE A, JORDAN & BREMNER	35,552
24-Nov	DERBY COUNTY	AWAY	0 - 0		36,003
01-Dec	QUEENS PARK RANGERS	HOME	2 - 2	BREMNER & JONES Mi.	32,194
08-Dec	IPSWICH TOWN	AWAY	3 - 0	YORATH, JONES Mi. & CLARKE A	27,110
15-Dec	CHELSEA	AWAY	2 - 1	JORDAN & JONES Mi.	40,768
22-Dec	NORWICH CITY	HOME	1 - 0	YORATH	34,747
26-Dec	NEWCASTLE UNITED	AWAY	1 - 0	MADELEY	54,474
29-Dec	BIRMINGHAM CITY	AWAY	1 - 1	JORDAN	50,451
01-Jan	TOTTENHAM HOTSPUR	HOME	1 - 1	JONES Mi.	46,545
12-Jan	SOUTHAMPTON	HOME	2 - 1	JONES Mi. & JORDAN	35,000
19-Jan	EVERTON	AWAY	0 - 0		55,811
02-Feb	CHELSEA	HOME	1 - 1	CHERRY	41,510
05-Feb	ARSENAL	HOME	3 - 1	O. G. (SIMPSON) & JORDAN 2	26,778
09-Feb	MANCHESTER UNITED	AWAY	2 - 0	JONES Mi. & JORDAN	60,025
23-Feb	STOKE CITY	AWAY	2 - 3	BREMNER & CLARKE A	39,598
26-Feb	LEICESTER CITY	HOME	1 - 1	LORIMER (PEN)	30,489
02-Mar	NEWCASTLE UNITED	HOME	1 - 1	CLARKE A	46,611
09-Mar	MANCHESTER CITY	HOME	1 - 0	LORIMER (PEN)	36,578
16-Mar	LIVERPOOL	AWAY	0 - 1		56,003
23-Mar	BURNLEY	HOME	1 - 4	CLARKE A	39,335
30-Mar	WEST HAM UNITED	AWAY	1 - 3	CLARKE A	37,480
06-Apr	DERBY COUNTY	HOME	2 - 0	LORIMER & BREMNER	37,838
13-Apr	COVENTRY CITY	AWAY	0 - 0		35,182
15-Apr	SHEFFIELD UNITED	HOME	0 - 0		41,140
16-Apr	SHEFFIELD UNITED	AWAY	2 - 0	LORIMER 2 (1 PEN)	39,972
20-Apr	IPSWICH TOWN	HOME	3 - 2	LORIMER, BREMNER & CLARKE A	44,015
27-Apr	QUEENS PARK RANGERS	AWAY	1 - 0	CLARKE A	35,353

F. A. CUP

05-Jan	WOLVERHAMPTON WANDERERS (R3)	AWAY	1 - 1	LORIMER (PEN)	38,132
09-Jan	WOLVERHAMPTON WANDERERS (R3R)	HOME	1 - 0	JONES Mi.	42,747
26-Jan	PETERBOROUGH UNITED (R4)	AWAY	4 - 1	LORIMER, JORDAN 2 & YORATH	28,000
16-Feb	BRISTOL CITY (R5)	AWAY	1 - 1	BREMNER	37,000
19-Feb	BRISTOL CITY (R5R)	HOME	0 - 1		47,182

LEAGUE CUP

08-Oct	IPSWICH TOWN (R2)	AWAY	0 - 2		26,379

U. E. F. A. CUP

19-Sep	STROMSGODSET (R1-1)	AWAY	1 - 1	CLARKE A	16,276
03-Oct	STROMSGODSET (R1-2)	HOME	6 - 1	CLARKE A 2, JONES Mi. 2, GRAY F & BATES	18,711
24-Oct	HIBERNIAN (R2-1)	HOME	0 - 0		27,145
07-Nov	HIBERNIAN (R2-2) *	AWAY	0 - 0		36,051
28-Nov	VITORIA SETUBAL (R3-1)	HOME	1 - 0	CHERRY	14,196
12-Dec	VITORIA SETUBAL (R3-2)	AWAY	1 - 3	LIDDELL	25,000

LEAGUE AND CUPS

APPEARANCES (SUBSTITUTE)

PLAYER	LEAGUE	F. A. CUP	LGE. CUP	U.E.F.A. CUP	TOTAL
BATES	9 (1)			5	14 (1)
BREMNER	42	5	1	4	52
CHERRY	37 (1)	5	1	6	49 (1)
CLARKE A	34	2 (1)		5	41 (1)
COOPER T	1 (1)	2			3 (1)
DAVEY			0 (1)		0 (1)
ELLAM	3 (1)	2	1	4	10 (1)
GILES	17	2			19
GRAY E	8			1	9
GRAY F	3 (3)	0 (1)	1	5 (1)	9 (5)
HAMPTON			1		1
HARVEY	39	4	1	4	48
HUNTER	42	5	1	1	49
JONES Mi.	28 (3)	4	1	3	36 (3)
JORDAN	25 (8)	4 (1)		3 (1)	32 (10)
LETHERAN			0 (1)		0 (1)
LIDDELL	0 (1)		1	1 (1)	2 (2)
LORIMER	37	5		5	47
McGINLEY			0 (1)		0 (1)
McQUEEN	36	3		3	42
MADELEY	39	5	1	2	47
MANN			1		1
O'NEILL		0 (1)	0 (2)		0 (3)
REANEY	36	3	1	4	44
SHAW			1		1
SPRAKE			1		1
STEWART D	3	1			4
YORATH	23 (5)	3 (1)	1	6	33 (6)

GOALSCORERS

PLAYER	LEAGUE	F. A. CUP	LGE. CUP	U.E.F.A. CUP	TOTAL
JONES Mi.	14	1		2	17
CLARKE A	13			3	16
LORIMER	12	2			14
BREMNER	10	1			11
JORDAN	7	2			9
BATES	2			1	3
YORATH	2	1			3
CHERRY	1			1	2
GILES	2				2
MADELEY	2				2
GRAY F				1	1
LIDDELL				1	1
OWN GOALS	1				1

KEY :- * = WON 5 - 4 ON PENALTIES AFTER EXTRA TIME

Throughout the summer, one story dominated Leeds United, Don Revie's replacement. When former Derby County boss Brian Clough got the job, it stunned players and supporters alike, as he had been such an outspoken critic of United. Leeds opened the season at Wembley in the Charity Shield, losing to Liverpool 6-5 in a penalty shoot-out after a 1-1 draw. One win in seven games, Allan Clarke striking the winner against Birmingham City, was the worst opening to a top-flight campaign for a decade. Amid 'player-power' rumours, Clough's tenure ended after 44 turbulent days.

Maurice Lindley as caretaker-boss oversaw a 5-1 win against Sheffield United, Clarke notching a brace during a blitz of nine goals in nine league and cup games, before the appointment of Jimmy Armfield, with Don Howe as first team coach. Altering little, apart from drafting in Clough's best signing Duncan McKenzie (Nottingham Forest) and giving Frank Gray a first extended first team run, Armfield stabilised the league campaign as Leeds climbed away from the relegation zone. The mercurial McKenzie quickly became a new cult hero, notching a brace in a 2-0 win over Arsenal, 2-2 draw with Middlesbrough and strikes in consecutive wins over the New Year against Leicester City, West Ham and Chelsea.

Although out of the League Cup, Clarke and McKenzie sparked an FA Cup run with a 4-1 win against Cardiff City. Own goals brought victories over non-league Wimbledon and Derby County, before McKenzie sent home supporters wild with a last gasp equaliser in a quarter-final replay with Ipswich Town. The Suffolk team claimed victory at the fourth attempt of a pulsating tie. Four draws in March, a month that saw Terry Cooper depart to Middlesbrough, ended any hopes of a top-four finish, but 2-1 wins at Arsenal, Norman Hunter notching the winner, and in the final home game of the season against Ipswich Town, winger Carl Harris securing the win, saw the defending champions finish in ninth spot.

Away from the domestic scene, Leeds played with confidence throughout the European Cup campaign. Years of experience helped United ease past FC Zurich 5-3 on aggregate, Clarke scoring in both legs, Ujpest Dozsa, McQueen scoring in both legs of a 5-1 aggregate win, and Anderlecht, Bremner notching a brilliant winner in the away leg after a 3-0 win at a fog-bound Elland Road. Drawn to play a Barcelona team that included Johann Cryuff and Johann Neeskens in its ranks, Bremner and Clarke secured a 2-1 victory, before Peter Lorimer notched a crucial away goal at the Nou Camp Stadium as Leeds clung to a 3-2 aggregate semi-final triumph. It was a glorious achievement despite McQueen's sending off.

Tragically, in the biggest game of Leeds United's history, refereeing decisions proved costly when a blatant foul by Beckenbauer on Clarke for a penalty was ignored, and Lorimer's sensational second half volley was ruled out when Bremner was adjudged to have strayed offside. Bayern, who had hardly threatened, grabbed two goals from counter-attacks. It was the end of an era as Bremner and co realised Leeds was about to enter a transitional phase. Paul Madeley made 60 appearances, Clarke top scored with 22 goals.

1974 - 1975

DIVISION ONE (FINAL LEAGUE POSITION - 9TH)
PLD 42 W 16 D 13 L 13 F 57 A 49 PTS 45

DATE	OPPONENTS	VENUE	SCORE	SCORERS	ATT.
17-Aug	STOKE CITY	AWAY	0 - 3		33,534
21-Aug	QUEENS PARK RANGERS	HOME	0 - 0		31,497
24-Aug	BIRMINGHAM CITY	HOME	1 - 0	CLARKE A	30,820
27-Aug	QUEENS PARK RANGERS	AWAY	1 - 1	YORATH	24,965
31-Aug	MANCHESTER CITY	AWAY	1 - 2	CLARKE A	37,919
07-Sep	LUTON TOWN	HOME	1 - 1	CLARKE A	26,450
14-Sep	BURNLEY	AWAY	1 - 2	LORIMER	25,122
21-Sep	SHEFFIELD UNITED	HOME	5 - 1	CLARKE A 2, McQUEEN, LORIMER (PEN) & YORATH	33,382
28-Sep	EVERTON	AWAY	2 - 3	CLARKE A & YORATH	41,824
05-Oct	ARSENAL	HOME	2 - 0	McKENZIE 2	32,784
12-Oct	IPSWICH TOWN	AWAY	0 - 0		29,815
15-Oct	BIRMINGHAM CITY	AWAY	0 - 1		36,513
19-Oct	WOLVERHAMPTON WANDERERS	HOME	2 - 0	CLARKE A & McKENZIE	31,224
26-Oct	LIVERPOOL	AWAY	0 - 1		54,996
02-Nov	DERBY COUNTY	HOME	0 - 1		33,551
09-Nov	COVENTRY CITY	AWAY	3 - 1	O'HARE, O. G. (HINDLEY) & BREMNER	25,414
16-Nov	MIDDLESBROUGH	HOME	2 - 2	McKENZIE 2	45,488
23-Nov	CARLISLE UNITED	AWAY	2 - 1	JORDAN & McKENZIE	19,975
30-Nov	CHELSEA	HOME	2 - 0	CHERRY & CLARKE A	30,441
04-Dec	TOTTENHAM HOTSPUR	HOME	2 - 1	McKENZIE & LORIMER (PEN)	25,832
07-Dec	WEST HAM UNITED	AWAY	1 - 2	McKENZIE	39,562
14-Dec	STOKE CITY	HOME	3 - 1	McQUEEN, LORIMER & YORATH	34,685
21-Dec	NEWCASTLE UNITED	AWAY	0 - 3		32,535
26-Dec	BURNLEY	HOME	2 - 2	JORDAN & LORIMER	34,724
28-Dec	LEICESTER CITY	AWAY	2 - 0	GRAY F & McKENZIE	29,699
11-Jan	WEST HAM UNITED	HOME	2 - 1	CLARKE A & McKENZIE	40,099
18-Jan	CHELSEA	AWAY	2 - 0	McKENZIE & YORATH	34,733
01-Feb	COVENTRY CITY	HOME	0 - 0		33,901
08-Feb	DERBY COUNTY	AWAY	0 - 0		33,641
22-Feb	MIDDLESBROUGH	AWAY	1 - 0	CLARKE A	39,500
25-Feb	CARLISLE UNITED	HOME	3 - 1	LORIMER, CLARKE A & GRAY E	32,346
01-Mar	MANCHESTER CITY	HOME	2 - 2	LORIMER 2	47,489
15-Mar	EVERTON	HOME	0 - 0		50,084
22-Mar	LUTON TOWN	AWAY	1 - 2	JORDAN	23,048
29-Mar	NEWCASTLE UNITED	HOME	1 - 1	CLARKE A	40,994
31-Mar	LEICESTER CITY	HOME	2 - 2	CLARKE A & GILES	29,898
01-Apr	SHEFFIELD UNITED	AWAY	1 - 1	MADELEY	38,442
05-Apr	LIVERPOOL	HOME	0 - 2		34,971
12-Apr	ARSENAL	AWAY	2 - 1	CLARKE A & HUNTER	36,619
19-Apr	IPSWICH TOWN	HOME	2 - 1	CHERRY & HARRIS C	30,174
26-Apr	WOLVERHAMPTON WANDERERS	AWAY	1 - 1	GRAY F	34,875
28-Apr	TOTTENHAM HOTSPUR	AWAY	2 - 4	JORDAN & LORIMER	49,886

F. A. CUP

04-Jan	CARDIFF CITY (R3)	HOME	4 - 1	GRAY E, CLARKE A 2 & McKENZIE	31,572
25-Jan	WIMBLEDON (R4)	HOME	0 - 0		46,230
10-Feb	WIMBLEDON (R4R) +	AWAY	1 - 0	O. G. (BASSETT)	45,701
18-Feb	DERBY COUNTY (R5)	AWAY	1 - 0	O. G. (NISH)	35,298
08-Mar	IPSWICH TOWN (R6)	AWAY	0 - 0		38,010
11-Mar	IPSWICH TOWN (R6R) *	HOME	1 - 1	McKENZIE	50,074
25-Mar	IPSWICH TOWN (R62R) *^	NEUTRAL	0 - 0		35,195
27-Mar	IPSWICH TOWN (R63R) ^	NEUTRAL	2 - 3	CLARKE A & GILES	19,510

LEAGUE CUP

10-Sep	HUDDERSFIELD TOWN (R2)	AWAY	1 - 1	LORIMER	15,013
24-Sep	HUDDERSFIELD TOWN (R2R) *	HOME	1 - 1	CLARKE A	18,496
07-Oct	HUDDERSFIELD TOWN (R22R)	HOME	2 - 1	BATES & LORIMER (PEN)	14,599
09-Oct	BURY (R3)	AWAY	2 - 1	LORIMER & CHERRY	16,354
13-Nov	CHESTER (R4)	AWAY	0 - 3		18,451

F. A. CHARITY SHIELD

10-Aug	LIVERPOOL $	NEUTRAL	1 - 1	CHERRY	67,000

EUROPEAN CUP

18-Sep	FC ZURICH (R1-1)	HOME	4 - 1	CLARKE A 2, LORIMER (PEN) & JORDAN	20,012
02-Oct	FC ZURICH (R1-2)	AWAY	1 - 2	CLARKE A	16,500
23-Oct	UJPEST DOZSA (R2-1)	AWAY	2 - 1	LORIMER & McQUEEN	20,000
06-Nov	UJPEST DOZSA (R2-2)	HOME	3 - 0	McQUEEN, BREMNER & YORATH	28,091
05-Mar	ANDERLECHT (QF-1)	HOME	3 - 0	JORDAN, McQUEEN & LORIMER	43,195
19-Mar	ANDERLECHT (QF-2)	AWAY	1 - 0	BREMNER	29,091
09-Apr	BARCELONA (SF-1)	HOME	2 - 1	BREMNER & CLARKE A	50,393
23-Apr	BARCELONA (SF-2)	AWAY	1 - 1	LORIMER	110,000
28-May	BAYERN MUNICH (Fi) >	NEUTRAL	0 - 2		48,374

LEAGUE AND CUPS
APPEARANCES (SUBSTITUTE)

PLAYER	LEAGUE	F. A. CUP	LGE. CUP	EUR. CUP	CH. SHLD.	TOTAL
BATES	2 (1)		2 (2)	1		5 (3)
BREMNER	27	8	2	6	1	44
CHERRY	24 (3)	0 (1)	5	2 (1)	1	32 (5)
CLARKE A	33 (1)	7	3	8	1	52 (1)
COOPER T	11		2	3		16
GILES	26 (3)	7	2	6	1	42 (3)
GRAY E	12	6		2 (1)	1	21 (1)
GRAY F	18	8	0 (1)	6		32 (1)
HAMPTON	0 (2)			0 (1)		0 (3)
HARRIS C	1 (2)			0 (1)		1 (3)
HARVEY	27	3	4	4	1	39
HUNTER	25	4	4	8	1	42
JORDAN	26 (3)	6	4	8	1	45 (3)
LETHERAN	1					1
LIDDELL	1					1
LORIMER	35 (1)	4	5	8	1	53 (1)
McGOVERN	4					4
McKENZIE	26 (1)	4 (3)	3	1	0 (1)	34 (5)
McQUEEN	33	4	4	7	1	49
MADELEY	38	8	4 (1)	9		59 (1)
O'HARE	6		1			7
REANEY	39	7	5	7	1	59
STEVENSON W	1					1
STEWART D	14	5	1	5		25
THOMAS G	0 (1)					0 (1)
YORATH	32 (1)	7	4	8 (1)		51 (2)

GOALSCORERS

PLAYER	LEAGUE	F. A. CUP	LGE. CUP	EUR. CUP	CH. SHLD.	TOTAL
CLARKE A	14	3	1	4		22
LORIMER	9		3	4		16
McKENZIE	11	2				13
JORDAN	4			2		6
YORATH	5			1		6
McQUEEN	2			3		5
BREMNER	1			3		4
CHERRY	2		1		1	4
GILES	1	1				2
GRAY E	1	1				2
GRAY F	2					2
BATES			1			1
HARRIS C	1					1
HUNTER	1					1
MADELEY	1					1
O'HARE	1					1
OWN GOALS	1	2				3

KEY :- $ = PLAYED AT WEMBLEY AND LOST 5 - 6 ON PENALTIES, > = PLAYED AT PARC DES PRINCES STADIUM, PARIS. * = AFTER EXTRA TIME. + = PLAYED AT SELHURST PARK, LONDON & ^ PLAYED AT FILBERT STREET, LEICESTER

LEEDS ALSO PLAYED A CHALLENGE MATCH AGAINST REPRESENTATIVE OPPOSITION AS FOLLOWS :- ON MAY 19TH 1975 VS. SCOTLAND U - 23 AT HAMPDEN PARK AND LOST 2 - 3 WITH LORIMER SCORING TWICE WITH AN ATTENDANCE OF 9,978. THE TEAM WAS HARVEY (LETHERAN), REANEY (CHERRY), GRAY F, BREMNER, MADELEY, HUNTER, LORIMER, CLARKE, JORDAN (McKENZIE), YORATH & GRAY E.

Calm, dignified and possessing a first-rate footballing brain, Jimmy Armfield had a huge task of breaking up Don Revie's legendary squad. A monumental brief maybe, but undaunted Armfield took on the challenge systematically. During the close season, Johnny Giles joined West Brom as player-manager but as Revie's aces moved on, new heroes emerged. Duncan McKenzie and Frank Gray established themselves in the side, whilst Paul Madeley partnered Norman Hunter in central defence with Gordon McQueen out with a long-term injury. Trevor Cherry became the utility player, wearing every outfield shirt apart from number 9; filling in at fullback, centre-half, midfield and as an emergency striker.

Leeds began the season well. Lorimer opened his account with a brace at Aston Villa in the season's opener, whilst Allan Clarke and McKenzie struck in wins over Sheffield United and Wolves. Cherry also popped up with strikes as Leeds picked up points at Norwich City, Burnley and Birmingham City. Clarke and Lorimer secured a win over Queens Park Rangers before notching a brace apiece to shoot down Everton 5-2. Another scorer against Everton was Eddie Gray, injury free for the first time in three years.

Whilst experienced players were performing well, supporters gasped to the unpredictable skills of McKenzie. Blessed with incredible touch and technique, McKenzie revelled in entertaining supporters and hit a rich vain of form, scoring a brace in 3-0 wins over Newcastle United and Birmingham, whilst notching a double in a 2-1 victory at Arsenal. Further success came over the festive period as Leeds shot up the table. Clarke struck his 100th league goal for Leeds to defeat Aston Villa; against Manchester City Madeley scored his third Boxing Day winner; a McKenzie brace was the highlight of a 4-0 victory against Leicester City before the sharpshooter notched with Billy Bremner in a 2-0 win over Stoke City.

Playing with confidence, Leeds were a good outside bet for the FA Cup. After knocking out Notts County, avenging a League Cup defeat earlier in the season, Leeds faced Crystal Palace at Elland Road, but Malcolm Allison's team caused a major upset. The defeat was a setback for Armfield's team, and they suffered a dip in form, winning just one in nine outings, Frank Gray scoring the only goal at Coventry City.

Introducing a number of promising reserves, the run-in brought successive wins over Everton, Arsenal, Newcastle; winger Carl Harris claiming the winner in a 3-2 triumph, and Burnley; Peter Hampton the hero in a 2-1 victory. Leeds' final home fixture saw striker David McNiven score a debut goal against Manchester City, Harris notching the winner. Finishing creditably in fifth spot, the season saw the retirement through injury of Mick Jones and departure of Mick Bates. Frank Gray was the only ever-present with 46 appearances, McKenzie top-scored with 17 goals.

1975 - 1976

DIVISION ONE (FINAL LEAGUE POSITION - 5TH)

PLD 42 W 21 D 9 L 12 F 65 A 46 PTS 51

DATE	OPPONENTS	VENUE	SCORE	SCORERS	ATT.
16-Aug	ASTON VILLA	AWAY	2 - 1	LORIMER 2 (1 PEN)	46,026
20-Aug	NORWICH CITY	AWAY	1 - 1	CHERRY	25,301
23-Aug	IPSWICH TOWN	HOME	1 - 0	LORIMER	30,912
26-Aug	LIVERPOOL	HOME	0 - 3		36,186
30-Aug	SHEFFIELD UNITED	AWAY	2 - 0	McKENZIE & CLARKE A	29,996
06-Sep	WOLVERHAMPTON WANDERERS	HOME	3 - 0	McQUEEN, CLARKE A & McKENZIE	24,460
13-Sep	STOKE CITY	AWAY	2 - 3	LORIMER 2 (1 PEN)	23,139
20-Sep	TOTTENHAM HOTSPUR	HOME	1 - 1	LORIMER	27,372
27-Sep	BURNLEY	AWAY	1 - 0	CHERRY	23,190
04-Oct	QUEENS PARK RANGERS	HOME	2 - 1	CLARKE A & LORIMER	30,943
11-Oct	MANCHESTER UNITED	HOME	1 - 2	CLARKE A	40,264
18-Oct	BIRMINGHAM CITY	AWAY	2 - 2	CHERRY & HUNTER	33,775
25-Oct	COVENTRY CITY	HOME	2 - 0	YORATH & CLARKE A	25,946
01-Nov	DERBY COUNTY	AWAY	2 - 3	CHERRY & McKENZIE	33,107
08-Nov	NEWCASTLE UNITED	HOME	3 - 0	McKENZIE 2 & YORATH	39,304
15-Nov	MIDDLESBROUGH	AWAY	0 - 0		33,000
22-Nov	BIRMINGHAM CITY	HOME	3 - 0	BREMNER & McKENZIE 2	26,640
29-Nov	EVERTON	HOME	5 - 2	LORIMER 2 (1 PEN), GRAY E & CLARKE A 2	30,879
06-Dec	ARSENAL	AWAY	2 - 1	McKENZIE 2	36,003
13-Dec	IPSWICH TOWN	AWAY	1 - 2	McKENZIE	26,858
20-Dec	ASTON VILLA	HOME	1 - 0	CLARKE A	29,118
26-Dec	MANCHESTER CITY	AWAY	1 - 0	MADELEY	48,077
27-Dec	LEICESTER CITY	HOME	4 - 0	CLARKE A, McKENZIE 2 & LORIMER	45,139
10-Jan	STOKE CITY	HOME	2 - 0	McKENZIE & BREMNER	36,906
17-Jan	WOLVERHAMPTON WANDERERS	AWAY	1 - 1	O. G. (McALLE)	34,925
31-Jan	NORWICH CITY	HOME	0 - 3		27,254
07-Feb	LIVERPOOL	AWAY	0 - 2		54,525
21-Feb	MIDDLESBROUGH	HOME	0 - 2		32,994
23-Feb	WEST HAM UNITED	AWAY	1 - 1	McKENZIE	28,025
28-Feb	COVENTRY CITY	AWAY	1 - 0	GRAY F	25,563
02-Mar	DERBY COUNTY	HOME	1 - 1	GRAY F (PEN)	40,608
09-Mar	WEST HAM UNITED	HOME	1 - 1	JORDAN	28,453
13-Mar	MANCHESTER UNITED	AWAY	2 - 3	CHERRY & BREMNER	59,429
20-Mar	EVERTON	AWAY	3 - 1	BREMNER, JORDAN & HARRIS C	28,566
27-Mar	ARSENAL	HOME	3 - 0	CLARKE A 2 & BREMNER	26,657
31-Mar	NEWCASTLE UNITED	AWAY	3 - 2	O. G. (OATES), CHERRY & HARRIS C	32,685
03-Apr	BURNLEY	HOME	2 - 1	McKENZIE & HAMPTON	25,384
10-Apr	TOTTENHAM HOTSPUR	AWAY	0 - 0		40,359
14-Apr	SHEFFIELD UNITED	HOME	0 - 1		22,799
17-Apr	MANCHESTER CITY	HOME	2 - 1	McNIVEN & HARRIS C	33,514
20-Apr	LEICESTER CITY	AWAY	1 - 2	McKENZIE	24,240
24-Apr	QUEENS PARK RANGERS	AWAY	0 - 2		31,002

F. A. CUP

DATE	OPPONENTS	VENUE	SCORE	SCORERS	ATT.
03-Jan	NOTTS COUNTY (R3)	AWAY	1 - 0	CLARKE A	31,129
24-Jan	CRYSTAL PALACE (R4)	HOME	0 - 1		43,116

LEAGUE CUP

DATE	OPPONENTS	VENUE	SCORE	SCORERS	ATT.
09-Sep	IPSWICH TOWN (R2)	HOME	3 - 2	McKENZIE, LORIMER & CLARKE A	15,318
08-Oct	NOTTS COUNTY (R3)	HOME	0 - 1		19,122

LEAGUE AND CUP
APPEARANCES (SUBSTITUTE)

PLAYER	LEAGUE	F. A. CUP	LEAGUE CUP	TOTAL
BATES	4			4
BREMNER	34	2	2	38
CHERRY	40	2	2	44
CLARKE A	35 (1)	2	1	38 (1)
GRAY E	27 (2)	1	2	30 (2)
GRAY F	42	2	2	46
HAMPTON	0 (1)			0 (1)
HARRIS C	9 (5)		0 (1)	9 (6)
HARVEY	40	2	2	44
HUNTER	31	1 (1)	2	34 (1)
JORDAN	15 (2)			15 (2)
LORIMER	27 (2)	2	2	31 (2)
McKENZIE	38 (1)	2	2	42 (1)
McNIVEN	0 (2)		1	1 (2)
McQUEEN	10			10
MADELEY	39	2	2	43
PARKINSON	3 (1)			3 (1)
REANEY	31 (1)	2	1	34 (1)
STEVENSON W	0 (1)			0 (1)
STEWART D	2			2
YORATH	35	2	1	38

GOALSCORERS

PLAYER	LEAGUE	F. A. CUP	LEAGUE CUP	TOTAL
McKENZIE	16		1	17
CLARKE A	11	1	1	13
LORIMER	10		1	11
CHERRY	6			6
BREMNER	5			5
HARRIS C	3			3
GRAY F	2			2
JORDAN	2			2
YORATH	2			2
GRAY E	1			1
HAMPTON	1			1
HUNTER	1			1
McNIVEN	1			1
McQUEEN	1			1
MADELEY	1			1
OWN GOALS	2			2

Jimmy Armfield splashed out £240,000 on flamboyant midfielder Tony Currie (Sheffield United) during the close season. Possessing panache, first class ball control, accurate passing and a venomous shot, Currie was seen as the long-term replacement for Johnny Giles. Moving out of Elland Road was Terry Yorath to Coventry City, and to many supporters disappointment, Anderlecht had a £200,000 bid for Duncan McKenzie accepted.

Currie's debut coincided with an entertaining 2-2 draw against Johnny Giles' West Brom team, Carl Harris and Allan Clarke scoring for Leeds, but the opening weeks brought only one victory, 2-0 against Derby County; Eddie Gray and Trevor Cherry hitting the target. Youngsters David McNiven and Harris earned another 2-2 draw, at home to Newcastle United, a game that brought an end to Billy Bremner's remarkable career at Elland Road. Harris was again on the scoresheet in Leeds' next triumph at West Ham, a clash that saw another legend, Norman Hunter, depart. The win sparked a mini-revival, Frank and Eddie Gray scoring in a 2-1 victory at Norwich City, the first occasion brothers had found the target in a first team clash.

With Allan Clarke sidelined, Armfield looked again to the future by signing Ray Hankin (Burnley) for £172,000, but an injury after just four games curtailed his season. Returning from a period out however were Scots Gordon McQueen and Joe Jordan, and Jordan came up trumps with winning strikes against Arsenal and Everton. With all the changes, form was inconsistent. Jordan secured a victory before the New Year at Sunderland and January signalled an improvement in form with both Jordan and McQueen making a major impact. The tall centre-back always looked dangerous at set pieces and made his presence tell with winning goals against West Brom, Birmingham City and Middlesbrough, whilst Jordan continued his good form securing wins over Derby, Tottenham and Norwich.

Although goal-shy, Leeds sat comfortably in mid-table and progressed in the FA Cup. Armfield brought Clarke back and United's goal poacher repaid the manager's faith with a goal against Norwich and the winner at Birmingham City. Cherry popped up with a last gasp 'toe poke' during a superb tie against Manchester City before Eddie Gray saw Leeds through an awkward quarter-final clash at Wolves. In the semi-finals against Manchester United, two quick-fire goals proved too much as Tommy Docherty's team won 2-1.

Finishing tenth, a number of fringe players made their bow, including Byron Stevenson, Gywn Thomas, Billy McGhie and David Whyte. While Stevenson and Thomas would make an impression in due course, neither McGhie nor Whyte would feature in the first team again as Armfield's search for talent continued. Frank Gray and Cherry, appointed club captain following Bremner's departure, made 47 appearances. Jordan top scored with 12 goals, the lowest total since the club's formation.

DIVISION ONE (FINAL LEAGUE POSITION - 10TH)				
PLD 42 W 15 D 12 L 15 F 48 A 51 PTS 42				
DATE	OPPONENTS	VENUE	SCORE SCORERS	ATT.
21-Aug	WEST BROMWICH ALBION	HOME	2 - 2 HARRIS C & CLARKE A	40,248
24-Aug	BIRMINGHAM CITY	AWAY	0 - 0	35,399
28-Aug	COVENTRY CITY	AWAY	2 - 4 GRAY F & CURRIE	18,227
04-Sep	DERBY COUNTY	HOME	2 - 0 GRAY E & CHERRY	33,352
11-Sep	TOTTENHAM HOTSPUR	AWAY	0 - 1	35,525
18-Sep	NEWCASTLE UNITED	HOME	2 - 2 McNIVEN & HARRIS C	35,089
25-Sep	MIDDLESBROUGH	AWAY	0 - 1	25,000
02-Oct	MANCHESTER UNITED	HOME	0 - 2	44,512
06-Oct	WEST HAM UNITED	AWAY	3 - 1 GRAY E, LORIMER & HARRIS C	21,909
16-Oct	NORWICH CITY	AWAY	2 - 1 GRAY F & GRAY E	25,217
23-Oct	LIVERPOOL	HOME	1 - 1 McNIVEN	44,696
30-Oct	ARSENAL	HOME	2 - 1 CHERRY & JORDAN	33,566
06-Nov	EVERTON	AWAY	2 - 0 McQUEEN & JORDAN	32,618
10-Nov	STOKE CITY	HOME	1 - 1 LORIMER	29,199
20-Nov	IPSWICH TOWN	AWAY	1 - 1 McQUEEN	30,096
27-Nov	LEICESTER CITY	HOME	2 - 2 LORIMER & McNIVEN	29,713
11-Dec	ASTON VILLA	HOME	1 - 3 McNIVEN	31,232
27-Dec	MANCHESTER CITY	HOME	0 - 2	48,708
29-Dec	SUNDERLAND	AWAY	1 - 0 JORDAN	26,999
03-Jan	ARSENAL	AWAY	1 - 1 CLARKE A	44,090
22-Jan	WEST BROMWICH ALBION	AWAY	2 - 1 GRAY E & McQUEEN	25,958
02-Feb	BIRMINGHAM CITY	HOME	1 - 0 McQUEEN	22,805
05-Feb	COVENTRY CITY	HOME	1 - 2 JORDAN	26,058
12-Feb	DERBY COUNTY	AWAY	1 - 0 JORDAN	28,350
19-Feb	TOTTENHAM HOTSPUR	HOME	2 - 1 JORDAN & CLARKE A	26,858
02-Mar	NEWCASTLE UNITED	AWAY	0 - 3	31,995
05-Mar	MIDDLESBROUGH	HOME	2 - 1 McQUEEN 2	32,152
08-Mar	QUEENS PARK RANGERS	AWAY	0 - 0	20,386
12-Mar	MANCHESTER UNITED	AWAY	0 - 1	60,612
23-Mar	NORWICH CITY	HOME	3 - 2 REANEY, HAMPTON & JORDAN	18,700
02-Apr	LIVERPOOL	AWAY	1 - 3 McQUEEN	48,791
08-Apr	MANCHESTER CITY	AWAY	1 - 2 JORDAN	47,727
09-Apr	SUNDERLAND	HOME	1 - 1 CHERRY	32,996
12-Apr	STOKE CITY	AWAY	1 - 2 JORDAN	17,960
16-Apr	IPSWICH TOWN	HOME	2 - 1 McGHIE & CLARKE A (PEN)	28,578
26-Apr	WEST HAM UNITED	HOME	1 - 1 JORDAN	16,891
30-Apr	BRISTOL CITY	HOME	2 - 0 THOMAS G & GRAY E	21,461
04-May	EVERTON	HOME	0 - 0	22,175
07-May	ASTON VILLA	AWAY	1 - 2 McNIVEN	38,205
10-May	BRISTOL CITY	AWAY	0 - 1	23,587
14-May	QUEENS PARK RANGERS	HOME	0 - 1	22,226
16-May	LEICESTER CITY	AWAY	1 - 0 GRAY F	13,642

F. A. CUP				
08-Jan	NORWICH CITY (R3)	HOME	5 - 2 CLARKE A, REANEY, JORDAN, McQUEEN & HAMPTON	28,130
29-Jan	BIRMINGHAM CITY (R4)	AWAY	2 - 1 JORDAN & CLARKE A	38,000
26-Feb	MANCHESTER CITY (R5)	HOME	1 - 0 CHERRY	47,731
19-Mar	WOLVERHAMPTON WANDERERS (R6)	AWAY	1 - 0 GRAY E	50,000
23-Apr	MANCHESTER UNITED (SF) $	NEUTRAL	1 - 2 CLARKE A (PEN)	55,000

LEAGUE CUP				
01-Sep	STOKE CITY (R2)	AWAY	1 - 2 CURRIE	22,601

LEAGUE AND CUP				
APPEARANCES (SUBSTITUTE)				
PLAYER	LEAGUE	F. A. CUP	LEAGUE CUP	TOTAL
BREMNER	4		1	5
CHERRY	42	4	1	47
CLARKE A	20	5	1	26
CURRIE	35	5	1	41
GRAY E	37	5		42
GRAY F	41	5	1	47
HAMPTON	30 (1)	5		35 (1)
HANKIN	4			4
HARRIS C	7 (9)		1	8 (9)
HARVEY	26	3		29
HUNTER	9		1	10
JORDAN	32	5	1	38
LORIMER	21 (5)	1 (1)		22 (6)
McGHIE	2			2
McNIVEN	13 (5)			13 (5)
McQUEEN	34	5		39
MADELEY	38	5	1	44
REANEY	34	5	1	40
STEVENSON W	10			10
STEWART D	16	2	1	19
THOMAS G	5 (2)			5 (2)
WHYTE D	1 (1)			1 (1)
YORATH	1			1

GOALSCORERS				
PLAYER	LEAGUE	F. A. CUP	LEAGUE CUP	TOTAL
JORDAN	10	2		12
McQUEEN	7	1		8
CLARKE A	4	3		7
GRAY E	5	1		6
McNIVEN	5			5
CHERRY	3	1		4
GRAY F	3			3
HARRIS C	3			3
LORIMER	3			3
CURRIE	1		1	2
HAMPTON	1	1		2
REANEY	1	1		2
McGHIE	1			1
THOMAS G	1			1

KEY :- $ = PLAYED AT HILLSBOROUGH, SHEFFIELD

Continuing his rebuilding programme, Jimmy Armfield signed Aberdeen winger Arthur Graham. An industrious player, Graham could play on either flank and down the centre. With Allan Clarke sidelined, Armfield partnered Joe Jordan with a fit-again Ray Hankin, and the burly striker made an impressive start to the season with nine goals in 10 games, including winning strikes against Birmingham City, Ipswich Town and Chelsea. Unfortunately, these were Leeds' only victories in a poor 14-match run. Peter Lorimer was also on target in the 2-1 win at Stamford Bridge, and found the net in a 2-2 draw at Derby County, a clash that brought Graham's first Leeds goal.

With Eddie Gray picking up an injury, Armfield brought Carl Harris back into the fray and purchased Burnley's combative midfielder Brian Flynn for £175,000. Flynn made an immediate impression on his debut at home to Norwich City, Lorimer notching a brace in a 2-2 draw, and his bow coincided with a change in Leeds' fortunes as United racked up consecutive victories against Manchester City, Nottingham Forest, West Ham and Queens Park Rangers. Hankin rediscovered his early season form with the winner in a 3-2 victory at City and 1-0 triumphs against Forest and the Hammers.

Flynn and Tony Currie quickly established a rapport in midfield and found the target in a comfortable 3-0 win against Rangers, but the festive period brought little joy bar a 3-1 success against Everton, Hankin notching a brace in United's triumph, watched by Leeds' biggest home gate of the season. Defeats at the turn of the New Year against West Brom and Newcastle United and the shock transfer of Jordan to archrivals Manchester United for £300,000, preceded a bad-tempered FA Cup defeat to Manchester City, where home supporters attempted to get the match abandoned, and as tempers flared, David Harvey and Gordon McQueen exchanged punches. Disgraceful scenes saw fences erected, whilst the club received a three-year ban on staging home ties, a decision later reduced.

Within a few weeks, a British record £450,000 bid by Manchester United saw McQueen cross the Pennines. Supporters were angry, but their departures heralded a purple patch as Leeds enjoyed their best form of season. The run was sparked by a Graham hat-trick at Birmingham in a 3-2 win, Hankin and Harris earned a 2-0 win against Coventry City whilst Eddie Gray claimed the winning strike at Ipswich. Unfortunately, after comfortably defeating Rochdale, Colchester United, Bolton Wanderers and Everton, League Cup aspirations ended with a heavy semi-final defeat against Nottingham Forest, managed by Brian Clough.

Bouncing back, Frank Gray and Currie saw off Chelsea, before Clarke returned to notch a memorable win at Old Trafford. With Blackpool's Paul Hart settling in as McQueen's replacement, braces by Clarke and Graham inspired a 5-0 win against Middlesbrough, Hankin scoring Leeds fifth, and the club's sharpshooter cracked the winner against Wolves before an Eddie Gray hat-trick was the highlight of a 5-1 thumping of Leicester City. Disappointingly, a top-six finish vanished during the run-in that yielded one 2-0 win over Derby. Finishing ninth, Cherry and Frank Gray made 48 appearances; Hankin scored 21 goals.

1977 - 1978

DIVISION ONE (FINAL LEAGUE POSITION - 9TH)

PLD 42 W 18 D 10 L 14 F 63 A 53 PTS 46

DATE	OPPONENTS	VENUE	SCORE	SCORERS	ATT.
20-Aug	NEWCASTLE UNITED	AWAY	2 - 3	HANKIN & LORIMER (PEN)	36,491
24-Aug	WEST BROMWICH ALBION	HOME	2 - 2	JORDAN & McQUEEN	21,000
27-Aug	BIRMINGHAM CITY	HOME	1 - 0	HANKIN	24,551
03-Sep	COVENTRY CITY	AWAY	2 - 2	HANKIN & McQUEEN	21,479
10-Sep	IPSWICH TOWN	HOME	2 - 1	HANKIN 2	24,280
17-Sep	DERBY COUNTY	AWAY	2 - 2	LORIMER & GRAHAM	24,274
24-Sep	MANCHESTER UNITED	HOME	1 - 1	HANKIN	33,514
01-Oct	CHELSEA	AWAY	2 - 1	LORIMER & HANKIN	35,427
05-Oct	ASTON VILLA	HOME	1 - 1	McQUEEN	27,797
08-Oct	BRISTOL CITY	AWAY	2 - 3	HANKIN 2	26,215
15-Oct	LIVERPOOL	HOME	1 - 2	THOMAS G	45,500
22-Oct	MIDDLESBROUGH	AWAY	1 - 2	HARRIS C	27,516
29-Oct	LEICESTER CITY	AWAY	0 - 0		20,128
05-Nov	NORWICH CITY	HOME	2 - 2	LORIMER 2	24,345
12-Nov	MANCHESTER CITY	AWAY	3 - 2	JORDAN, GRAHAM & HANKIN	42,651
19-Nov	NOTTINGHAM FOREST	HOME	1 - 0	HANKIN	42,925
26-Nov	WEST HAM UNITED	AWAY	1 - 0	HANKIN	26,883
03-Dec	QUEENS PARK RANGERS	HOME	3 - 0	O. G. (NEEDHAM), FLYNN B & CURRIE	26,597
10-Dec	ARSENAL	AWAY	1 - 1	McQUEEN	40,162
17-Dec	MANCHESTER CITY	HOME	2 - 0	McQUEEN & CHERRY	37,380
26-Dec	WOLVERHAMPTON WANDERERS	AWAY	1 - 3	JORDAN	27,704
27-Dec	EVERTON	HOME	3 - 1	HANKIN 2 & LORIMER	45,560
31-Dec	WEST BROMWICH ALBION	AWAY	0 - 1		24,249
02-Jan	NEWCASTLE UNITED	HOME	0 - 2		36,643
14-Jan	BIRMINGHAM CITY	AWAY	3 - 2	GRAHAM 3	23,703
21-Jan	COVENTRY CITY	HOME	2 - 0	HANKIN & HARRIS C	27,062
04-Feb	IPSWICH TOWN	AWAY	1 - 0	GRAY E	24,023
25-Feb	CHELSEA	HOME	2 - 0	GRAY F & CURRIE	25,263
01-Mar	MANCHESTER UNITED	AWAY	1 - 0	CLARKE A	49,101
04-Mar	BRISTOL CITY	HOME	0 - 2		24,830
11-Mar	LIVERPOOL	AWAY	0 - 1		48,233
18-Mar	MIDDLESBROUGH	HOME	5 - 0	HANKIN, GRAHAM 2 & CLARKE A 2	25,158
25-Mar	EVERTON	AWAY	0 - 2		45,020
27-Mar	WOLVERHAMPTON WANDERERS	HOME	2 - 1	GRAHAM & HANKIN	24,440
28-Mar	LEICESTER CITY	HOME	5 - 1	HANKIN, GRAY F & GRAY E 3	21,145
01-Apr	NORWICH CITY	AWAY	0 - 3		19,615
08-Apr	WEST HAM UNITED	HOME	1 - 2	GRAHAM	22,953
12-Apr	DERBY COUNTY	HOME	2 - 0	GRAY E & HANKIN	16,531
15-Apr	NOTTINGHAM FOREST	AWAY	1 - 1	GRAY F (PEN)	38,662
22-Apr	ARSENAL	HOME	1 - 3	CURRIE	33,263
26-Apr	ASTON VILLA	AWAY	1 - 3	HANKIN	30,524
29-Apr	QUEENS PARK RANGERS	AWAY	0 - 0		23,993

F. A. CUP

07-Jan	MANCHESTER CITY (R3)	HOME	1 - 2	GRAY F (PEN)	38,317

LEAGUE CUP

31-Aug	ROCHDALE (R2)	AWAY	3 - 0	JORDAN, CHERRY & HARRIS C	8,664
26-Oct	COLCHESTER UNITED (R3)	HOME	4 - 0	JORDAN, GRAHAM, LORIMER & HANKIN	17,713
30-Nov	BOLTON WANDERERS (R4)	AWAY	3 - 1	GRAHAM, JORDAN & GRAY F	33,766
18-Jan	EVERTON (R5)	HOME	4 - 1	CURRIE, LORIMER 2 (1 PEN) & GRAY E	35,020
08-Feb	NOTTINGHAM FOREST (SF-1)	HOME	1 - 3	GRAY E	43,222
22-Feb	NOTTINGHAM FOREST (SF-2)	AWAY	2 - 4	GRAY F & GRAHAM	38,138

LEAGUE AND CUP

APPEARANCES (SUBSTITUTE)

PLAYER	LEAGUE	F. A. CUP	LEAGUE CUP	TOTAL
CHERRY	41	1	6	48
CLARKE A	8 (1)	0 (1)	1	9 (2)
CURRIE	35	1	5	41
FLYNN B	28 (1)	1		29 (1)
GRAHAM	40	1	6	47
GRAY E	24 (3)		4	28 (3)
GRAY F	40 (1)	1	6	47 (1)
HAMPTON	10 (1)		1 (1)	11 (2)
HANKIN	33	1	6	40
HARRIS C	16 (3)	1	2 (2)	19 (5)
HART P	12			12
HARVEY	25	1	4	30
JORDAN	20		3	23
LORIMER	26 (2)		4	30 (2)
McNIVEN	2			2
McQUEEN	21	1	1	23
MADELEY	38	1	6	45
PARKER	0 (1)			0 (1)
PARKINSON	6 (2)		4	10 (2)
REANEY	15	1	5	21
STEVENSON W	3 (2)			3 (2)
STEWART D	17		2	19
THOMAS G	2 (1)			2 (1)

GOALSCORERS

PLAYER	LEAGUE	F. A. CUP	LEAGUE CUP	TOTAL
HANKIN	20		1	21
GRAHAM	9		3	12
LORIMER	6		3	9
GRAY E	5		2	7
GRAY F	3	1	2	6
JORDAN	3		3	6
McQUEEN	5			5
CURRIE	3		1	4
CLARKE A	3			3
HARRIS C	2		1	3
CHERRY	1		1	2
FLYNN B	1			1
THOMAS G	1			1
OWN GOALS	1			1

Jimmy Armfield guided Leeds United to a European Cup final, and League Cup and FA Cup semi-finals, but the club's board grew impatient, dismissing him during the close season. Breaking up Revie's star-studded team was an arduous task and in trying circumstances, Armfield did a sound job. The summer saw Allan Clarke and Paul Reaney depart, while Hull City striker John Hawley arrived to partner Ray Hankin in attack. As United's board pondered on appointing a new manager, Maurice Lindley stepped into the breach as caretaker-boss while Leeds gained a 2-2 draw at Arsenal, Tony Currie and Trevor Cherry scoring.

By the next game, at home to Manchester United, legendary Celtic boss Jock Stein was at the helm. Leeds lost 3-2 to their Pennine rivals, but Stein did not have to wait long to witness 3-0 wins against Wolves, Currie completing a comfortable triumph, and Chelsea, Hawley notching a brace. With all the changes, results were mixed. Frank Gray slotted home a spot kick in another 3-0 victory to see off Birmingham City, but within days, Stein accepted the vacant Scotland job. Again, Lindley stepped into the hot seat, until the appointment of Burnley boss Jimmy Adamson.

The new manager quickly settled and to his credit made an immediate impact as Leeds made progress in both Division 1 and the League Cup. At the core of United's revival was Currie. Blessed with elegant skills and inventiveness, Currie was in sparkling form as Leeds embarked on a 16-match unbeaten league run, whilst progressing to the semi-finals of the League Cup. Earning a point at Wolves, Currie's superb 25-yard 'banana' shot in a 4-0 triumph against Southampton was sandwiched between wins over Chelsea, Hankin notching the winner, and Ipswich Town, Cherry proving the hero.

In the League Cup, after ousting West Brom at the third attempt, Paul Hart securing Leeds' passage, an Eddie Gray brace was the highlight of an imperious 4-1 win at Sheffield United before Hawley and Hankin accounted for Queens Park Rangers. With the festive games coming up, the Gray brothers sealed another 4-1 win as Leeds moved into the last four at the expense of Luton Town. Favourites to despatch Southampton, Hawley continued a mini-scoring spree in draws against Everton and Manchester City, a 3-1 win over Middlesbrough and a 4-1 canter at Queens Park Rangers. In the League Cup clash against the Saints, alas, the first leg at Elland Road proved traumatic as Leeds let slip a 2-0 lead, drawing 2-2, eventually losing on 3-2 aggregate.

The result was a crushing blow, but United kept the European dream alive with 1-0 victories over Midlands outfits Coventry City, Birmingham City and Derby County; Currie, Frank Gray and Hawley striking the all-important goals, aligned to a 2-1 win at West Brom; Graham notching a brace. Despite Albion knocking Leeds out of the FA Cup and a 4-1 loss at Manchester United, future Leeds star Andy Ritchie scoring a treble, Hart and Currie brought furthers victories against Aston Villa and Everton. A 5-1 win over Bolton Wanderers and a thrilling 4-3 triumph against Queens Park Rangers, Cherry notching the winner, secured a fifth place finish and UEFA Cup qualification. Frank Gray and Flynn made 52 appearances, Hawley top scored on 17 goals.

1978 - 1979

DIVISION ONE (FINAL LEAGUE POSITION - 5TH)

PLD 42 W 18 D 14 L 10 F 70 A 52 PTS 50

DATE	OPPONENTS	VENUE	SCORE	SCORERS	ATT.
19-Aug	ARSENAL	AWAY	2 - 2	CURRIE & CHERRY	42,057
23-Aug	MANCHESTER UNITED	HOME	2 - 3	HART P & GRAY F (PEN)	36,845
26-Aug	WOLVERHAMPTON WANDERERS	HOME	3 - 0	HANKIN, GRAY F (PEN) & CURRIE	26,267
02-Sep	CHELSEA	AWAY	3 - 0	GRAHAM & HAWLEY 2	30,099
09-Sep	MANCHESTER CITY	AWAY	0 - 3		40,125
16-Sep	TOTTENHAM HOTSPUR	HOME	1 - 2	GRAHAM	36,062
23-Sep	COVENTRY CITY	AWAY	0 - 0		27,365
30-Sep	BIRMINGHAM CITY	HOME	3 - 0	FLYNN B, GRAY F (PEN) & HANKIN	23,331
07-Oct	BOLTON WANDERERS	AWAY	1 - 3	GRAHAM	27,751
14-Oct	WEST BROMWICH ALBION	HOME	1 - 3	STEVENSON W	25,931
21-Oct	NORWICH CITY	AWAY	2 - 2	GRAY F & HAWLEY	19,981
28-Oct	DERBY COUNTY	HOME	4 - 0	FLYNN B, HART P, HANKIN & HAWLEY	25,449
04-Nov	LIVERPOOL	AWAY	1 - 1	HAWLEY	51,857
11-Nov	ARSENAL	HOME	0 - 1		33,961
18-Nov	WOLVERHAMPTON WANDERERS	AWAY	1 - 1	CURRIE	18,961
22-Nov	CHELSEA	HOME	2 - 1	GRAHAM & HANKIN	24,088
25-Nov	SOUTHAMPTON	HOME	4 - 0	GRAHAM, CURRIE, O. G. (GOLAC) & MADELEY	23,592
02-Dec	IPSWICH TOWN	AWAY	3 - 2	HANKIN, HARRIS C & CHERRY	22,526
09-Dec	BRISTOL CITY	HOME	1 - 1	FLYNN B	22,529
16-Dec	EVERTON	AWAY	1 - 1	HAWLEY	37,997
23-Dec	MIDDLESBROUGH	HOME	3 - 1	HAWLEY, GRAY E & CURRIE	27,146
26-Dec	ASTON VILLA	AWAY	2 - 2	GRAY E 2	40,973
30-Dec	QUEENS PARK RANGERS	AWAY	4 - 1	HAWLEY 2, HARRIS C & GRAY E	17,435
13-Jan	MANCHESTER CITY	HOME	1 - 1	HAWLEY	36,303
20-Jan	TOTTENHAM HOTSPUR	AWAY	2 - 1	HART P & HANKIN	36,828
03-Feb	COVENTRY CITY	HOME	1 - 0	CURRIE	22,928
10-Feb	BIRMINGHAM CITY	AWAY	1 - 0	GRAY F (PEN)	17,620
24-Feb	WEST BROMWICH ALBION	AWAY	2 - 1	GRAHAM 2	26,426
03-Mar	NORWICH CITY	HOME	2 - 2	HAWLEY 2	23,038
10-Mar	DERBY COUNTY	AWAY	1 - 0	HAWLEY	22,800
24-Mar	MANCHESTER UNITED	AWAY	1 - 4	HANKIN	51,191
31-Mar	SOUTHAMPTON	AWAY	2 - 2	HAWLEY 2	21,805
07-Apr	IPSWICH TOWN	HOME	1 - 1	CHERRY	24,153
10-Apr	MIDDLESBROUGH	AWAY	0 - 1		23,260
14-Apr	ASTON VILLA	HOME	1 - 0	HART P	24,281
16-Apr	NOTTINGHAM FOREST	AWAY	0 - 0		37,397
21-Apr	EVERTON	HOME	1 - 0	CURRIE	29,125
25-Apr	BOLTON WANDERERS	HOME	5 - 1	CHERRY, GRAY F (PEN), HART P, HARRIS C & HAWLEY	20,218
28-Apr	BRISTOL CITY	AWAY	0 - 0		25,388
04-May	QUEENS PARK RANGERS	HOME		GRAHAM, HANKIN 2 & CHERRY	20,121
15-May	NOTTINGHAM FOREST	HOME	1 - 2	CHERRY	33,544
17-May	LIVERPOOL	HOME	0 - 3		41,324

F. A. CUP

18-Jan	HARTLEPOOL UNITED (R3)	AWAY	6 - 2	HART P, GRAHAM, GRAY E 2, HARRIS C & GRAY F (PEN)	16,000
26-Feb	WEST BROMWICH ALBION (R4) $	AWAY	3 - 3	GRAY F, GRAHAM & HARRIS C	31,130
01-Mar	WEST BROMWICH ALBION (R4R) *	AWAY	0 - 2		31,103

LEAGUE CUP

29-Aug	WEST BROMWICH ALBION (R2)	AWAY	0 - 0		25,124
06-Sep	WEST BROMWICH ALBION (R2R) *	HOME	0 - 0		29,316
02-Oct	WEST BROMWICH ALBION (R22R) ^	NEUTRAL	1 - 0	HART P	8,164
10-Oct	SHEFFIELD UNITED (R3)	AWAY	4 - 1	CURRIE, GRAY F & GRAY E 2	39,614
07-Nov	QUEENS PARK RANGERS (R4)	AWAY	2 - 0	HAWLEY & HANKIN	22,769
13-Dec	LUTON TOWN (R5)	HOME	4 - 1	CHERRY, CURRIE, GRAY E & GRAY F (PEN)	28,177
24-Jan	SOUTHAMPTON (SF-1)	HOME	2 - 2	CURRIE & HANKIN	33,415
30-Jan	SOUTHAMPTON (SF-2)	AWAY	0 - 1		23,646

LEAGUE AND CUP

APPEARANCES (SUBSTITUTE)

PLAYER	LEAGUE	F. A. CUP	LEAGUE CUP	TOTAL
CHERRY	38	3	7	48
CURRIE	32	3	7	42
FLYNN B	41	3	8	52
GRAHAM	39	3	7	49
GRAY E	25 (3)	1	6 (1)	32 (4)
GRAY F	41	3	8	52
HAMPTON	4		2	6
HANKIN	29 (1)		8	37 (1)
HARRIS C	29 (2)	3	1 (2)	33 (4)
HART P	40	2	8	50
HARVEY	39	3	6	48
HAWLEY	29 (3)	3	6	38 (3)
HIRD	13 (1)			13 (1)
LORIMER	3		0 (1)	3 (1)
MADELEY	39	3	7	49
PARKINSON	3 (2)	1		4 (2)
STEVENSON W	14 (1)	2	4	20 (1)
STEWART D	3		2	5
THOMAS G	1 (1)	0 (1)	1	2 (2)

GOALSCORERS

PLAYER	LEAGUE	F. A. CUP	LEAGUE CUP	TOTAL
HAWLEY	16		1	17
HANKIN	9		2	11
CURRIE	7		3	10
GRAHAM	8	2		10
GRAY F	6	2	2	10
GRAY E	4	2	3	9
CHERRY	6		1	7
HART P	5	1	1	7
HARRIS C	3	2		5
FLYNN B	3			3
MADELEY	1			1
STEVENSON W	1			1
OWN GOALS	1			1

KEY :- $ = PLAYED AT THE HAWTHORNS, WEST BROMWICH DUE TO F. A. BAN (DRAWN AT HOME), * = AFTER EXTRA TIME & ^ = PLAYED AT MAINE ROAD, MANCHESTER

Back in European competition, the close season brought numerous changes in personnel. Jimmy Adamson raised £500,000 with the sale of Frank Gray to Nottingham Forest and a further £400,000 by transferring Tony Currie to Queens Park Rangers, Currie citing domestic reasons for his move south. Other players to depart included John Hawley, David Stewart and Peter Lorimer. New arrivals included striker Alan Curtis (Swansea City) for a club record £400,000, defender Brian Greenhoff (Manchester United) and midfielder Gary Hamson (Sheffield United).

Anticipation among fans was high but Adamson's side began slowly, winning three of their opening dozen matches against Everton, Ipswich Town and Southampton. Kevin Hird, the most expensive full-back when he signed in March 1979, scored against Everton and Ipswich, while Curtis began well with goals in draws against Bristol City and Liverpool, and the winner at Southampton, but goals soon dried up. In Europe, United disposed of Valetta 7-0 on aggregate in the opening round of the UEFA Cup, Arthur Graham notching a hat-trick in the opening leg. However, a 7-0 drubbing saw Leeds crash out of the League Cup at Arsenal, and soon Universitatea Craiova ended European aspirations.

With fading confidence, three consecutive losses included a 3-1 home defeat against Bristol City and a 5-1 mauling at Everton. Despite teenage keeper John Lukic succeeding David Harvey in goal and 17-year-old centre-forward Terry Connor marking his debut with a goal in front of the Kop to defeat West Brom, there was discontent amongst supporters and calls for Adamson's dismissal. In spite of murmurings, Connor sparked a mini-revival of six wins in 10 games. Hird's midfield move brought a winner against Crystal Palace, whilst Connor enhanced his reputation by earning a draw at Manchester United and victories over Wolves and Stoke City.

Hird scored again on New Years Day to defeat Derby County before Connor gained a terrific win at Arsenal, but improved optimism disappeared after a 4-1 defeat to Nottingham Forest in the FA Cup, a clash that saw the Kop closed for two games after missiles were thrown. Given a vote of confidence by the board, the coming weeks would be hard toil. In a bid to resurrect an unproductive attack, Adamson purchased Rangers striker Derek Parlane for £160,000 before the transfer deadline, and Parlane grabbed a debut goal in a home win over Southampton but this victory would be Leeds' sole triumph in 10 games.

With dwindling gates, fewer than 15,000 attended a 0-0 draw against Coventry City, United's lowest crowd for 17 years and where mounted police dispersed dissenting followers. These were dark days for Adamson, but the run-in finally brought joy, especially a 2-0 win over bitter rivals Manchester United to deny them any hope of winning the title, Parlane and Hird scoring. However, a near capacity crowd could not conceal the growing frustration amongst supporters and United's board. Finishing eleventh, in a disappointing campaign Trevor Cherry made 46 appearances. Hird's eight goals set a record low for a top scorer.

1979 - 1980

DIVISION ONE (FINAL LEAGUE POSITION - 11TH)
PLD 42 W 13 D 14 L 15 F 46 A 50 PTS 40

DATE	OPPONENTS	VENUE	SCORE	SCORERS	ATT.
18-Aug	BRISTOL CITY	AWAY	2 - 2	CURTIS 2	22,845
22-Aug	EVERTON	HOME	2 - 0	HIRD & HARRIS C	30,000
25-Aug	NORWICH CITY	AWAY	1 - 2	HART P	18,444
01-Sep	ARSENAL	HOME	1 - 1	HART P	23,245
08-Sep	NOTTINGHAM FOREST	AWAY	0 - 0		26,914
15-Sep	LIVERPOOL	HOME	1 - 1	CURTIS	39,779
22-Sep	BOLTON WANDERERS	AWAY	1 - 1	GRAY E (PEN)	21,724
29-Sep	MANCHESTER CITY	HOME	1 - 2	HANKIN	29,592
06-Oct	IPSWICH TOWN	HOME	2 - 1	CHERRY & HIRD (PEN)	19,342
13-Oct	BRIGHTON & HOVE ALBION	AWAY	0 - 0		27,002
20-Oct	TOTTENHAM HOTSPUR	HOME	1 - 2	HANKIN	25,203
27-Oct	SOUTHAMPTON	AWAY	2 - 1	ENTWISTLE & CURTIS	23,259
03-Nov	BRISTOL CITY	HOME	1 - 3	GRAY E	17,376
10-Nov	COVENTRY CITY	AWAY	0 - 3		19,402
13-Nov	EVERTON	AWAY	1 - 5	HIRD	23,000
17-Nov	WEST BROMWICH ALBION	HOME	1 - 0	CONNOR	17,481
24-Nov	ASTON VILLA	AWAY	0 - 0		29,376
01-Dec	CRYSTAL PALACE	HOME	1 - 0	HIRD	21,330
08-Dec	MANCHESTER UNITED	AWAY	1 - 1	CONNOR	57,478
15-Dec	WOLVERHAMPTON WANDERERS	HOME	3 - 0	CONNOR, GRAHAM & HAMSON	21,227
21-Dec	STOKE CITY	AWAY	2 - 0	CONNOR & HARRIS C	16,878
26-Dec	MIDDLESBROUGH	AWAY	1 - 3	ENTWISTLE	23,259
29-Dec	NORWICH CITY	HOME	2 - 2	HIRD & HANKIN	23,493
01-Jan	DERBY COUNTY	HOME	1 - 0	HIRD	24,271
12-Jan	ARSENAL	AWAY	1 - 0	CONNOR	32,799
19-Jan	NOTTINGHAM FOREST	HOME	1 - 2	CONNOR	29,816
09-Feb	BOLTON WANDERERS	HOME	2 - 2	HIRD (PEN) & GRAHAM	16,428
16-Feb	MANCHESTER CITY	AWAY	1 - 1	GRAHAM	34,392
23-Feb	BRIGHTON & HOVE ALBION	HOME	1 - 1	FLYNN B	17,216
01-Mar	TOTTENHAM HOTSPUR	AWAY	1 - 2	CHANDLER	35,331
08-Mar	SOUTHAMPTON	HOME	2 - 0	HART P & PARLANE	21,169
14-Mar	IPSWICH TOWN	AWAY	0 - 1		23,140
19-Mar	LIVERPOOL	AWAY	0 - 3		37,008
22-Mar	COVENTRY CITY	HOME	0 - 0		14,967
29-Mar	WEST BROMWICH ALBION	AWAY	1 - 2	CHANDLER	18,898
02-Apr	MIDDLESBROUGH	HOME	2 - 0	CHERRY & FLYNN B	17,906
05-Apr	DERBY COUNTY	AWAY	0 - 2		22,745
08-Apr	STOKE CITY	HOME	3 - 0	PARLANE & HARRIS C 2	15,541
12-Apr	CRYSTAL PALACE	AWAY	0 - 1		25,318
19-Apr	ASTON VILLA	HOME	0 - 0		15,840
26-Apr	WOLVERHAMPTON WANDERERS	AWAY	1 - 3	FLYNN B	22,746
03-May	MANCHESTER UNITED	HOME	2 - 0	PARLANE & HIRD (PEN)	39,625

F. A. CUP

DATE	OPPONENTS	VENUE	SCORE	SCORERS	ATT.
05-Jan	NOTTINGHAM FOREST (R3)	HOME	1 - 4	O. G. (LLOYD)	35,945

LEAGUE CUP

DATE	OPPONENTS	VENUE	SCORE	SCORERS	ATT.
29-Aug	ARSENAL (R2-1)	HOME	1 - 1	STEVENSON W (PEN)	23,421
04-Sep	ARSENAL (R2-2)	AWAY	0 - 7		35,129

U. E. F. A. CUP

DATE	OPPONENTS	VENUE	SCORE	SCORERS	ATT.
19-Sep	VALETTA (R1-1)	AWAY	4 - 0	GRAHAM 3 & HART P	18,000
03-Oct	VALETTA (R1-2)	HOME	3 - 0	CURTIS, HANKIN & HART P	13,628
24-Oct	UNIVERSITATEA CRAIOVA (R2-1)	AWAY	0 - 2		25,000
07-Nov	UNIVERSITATEA CRAIOVA (R2-2)	HOME	0 - 2		14,438

LEAGUE AND CUPS
APPEARANCES (SUBSTITUTE)

PLAYER	LEAGUE	F. A. CUP	LGE. CUP	U.E.F.A. CUP	TOTAL
CHANDLER	13 (4)				13 (4)
CHERRY	39	1	2	4	46
CONNOR	20 (3)	1			21 (3)
CURTIS	22	1	2	4	29
DICKINSON	6				6
ENTWISTLE	7 (4)	0 (1)			7 (5)
FIRM	3				3
FLYNN B	24		2	4	30
GRAHAM	26 (1)		2	3	31 (1)
GRAY E	30	1		3	34
GREENHOFF B	22 (2)		2		24 (2)
HAMPTON	17		2	2	21
HAMSON	18 (1)	1		1 (1)	20 (2)
HANKIN	16		1	4	21
HARRIS C	13 (2)	1	1 (1)	1 (2)	16 (5)
HART P	30	1	2	4	37
HARVEY	9		2	1	12
HAWLEY	1				1
HIRD	39	1	2	3	45
LUKIC	33	1		3	37
MADELEY	25	1		3	29
PARKINSON	10 (1)			2	12 (1)
PARLANE	11				11
STEVENSON W	25 (1)	1	2	2	30 (1)
THOMAS G	3				3

GOALSCORERS

PLAYER	LEAGUE	F. A. CUP	LGE. CUP	U.E.F.A. CUP	TOTAL
HIRD	8				8
CONNOR	6				6
GRAHAM	3			3	6
CURTIS	4			1	5
HART P	3			2	5
HANKIN	3			1	4
HARRIS C	4				4
FLYNN B	3				3
PARLANE	3				3
CHANDLER	2				2
CHERRY	2				2
ENTWISTLE	2				2
GRAY E	2				2
HAMSON	1				1
STEVENSON W			1		1
OWN GOALS		1			1

Under mounting pressure, manager Jimmy Adamson set about strengthening his squad pre-season with the purchase of £400,000 Argentinean playmaker Alex Sabella (Sheffield United). Seven defeats and just one victory however, in the opening 10 fixtures, including a League Cup exit to Aston Villa, made his position untenable and it came as no surprise when Adamson resigned. Terry Connor had delivered Leeds' sole win to date in a 3-2 triumph at Norwich City, Paul Hart and Arthur Graham also scoring.

Stepping into the breach once again was Maurice Lindley, but the caretaker-boss stepped aside when former legendary striker Allan Clarke was appointed as the new Leeds United manager. Receiving a hero's welcome on his first game in charge before a 0-0 draw at home to Manchester United, Clarke, who made an impact at Barnsley in the lower leagues, initially worked on a leaky defence by switching Eddie Gray to left-back in place of Byron Stevenson. Brian Greenhoff took up the right-back slot, while skipper Trevor Cherry partnered centre-half Hart.

Although gates remained poor, the changes saw results slowly pick up as Leeds eased clear of relegation with hard-fought victories over Manchester City, Everton and Crystal Palace; Carl Harris, Alan Curtis and Connor striking the winning goals. Entertainment was limited, but stability was crucial, and Kevin Hird edged Leeds closer to that objective with a brace in a 2-1 home win over Middlesbrough, the first time United had scored more than one goal for 15 matches. Tedious stuff maybe but consecutive wins in the Christmas build-up against Brighton; Harris notching the only goal, West Brom; Harris and Graham securing a 2-1 win, and Nottingham Forest; Greenhoff scoring his sole goal for the club, were welcome.

Despite being knocked out of the FA Cup by Coventry City in a third round replay, the New Year brought a big improvement in form with eight victories in 11 games. Among five 1-0 triumphs, Hart earned a win at Leicester City, Harris strikes accounted for Norwich City and Sunderland, Derek Parlane edged the points at Crystal Palace but the most popular result came when a Brian Flynn strike gained a win over Manchester United, Leeds' last success to date at Old Trafford.

Defensively, Leeds had improved enormously throughout the campaign. In the run-in, they outlined this newfound confidence, conceding just two goals in eight games. Winning three matches, Leeds finally found the target as an attacking force, claiming 3-0 home wins over Ipswich Town and Coventry City. A dour 0-0 draw completed a satisfactory season in the end, with supporter's hopeful United could push on from a ninth place finish. The campaign saw Curtis return to Swansea for £165,000, while veteran utility player Paul Madeley retired. Cherry and Flynn made 45 appearances, Harris top scored on 10 goals. Leeds' total of 39 goals was the lowest recorded in the club's history.

1980 - 1981

DIVISION ONE (FINAL LEAGUE POSITION - 9TH)

PLD 42 W 17 D 10 L 15 F 39 A 47 PTS 44

DATE	OPPONENTS	VENUE	SCORE	SCORERS	ATT.
16-Aug	ASTON VILLA	HOME	1 - 2	STEVENSON W (PEN)	23,401
19-Aug	MIDDLESBROUGH	AWAY	0 - 3		19,470
23-Aug	NORWICH CITY	AWAY	3 - 2	HART P, GRAHAM & CONNOR	17,890
30-Aug	LEICESTER CITY	HOME	1 - 2	HART P	18,530
06-Sep	STOKE CITY	AWAY	0 - 3		12,729
13-Sep	TOTTENHAM HOTSPUR	HOME	0 - 0		21,947
20-Sep	MANCHESTER UNITED	HOME	0 - 0		32,539
27-Sep	SUNDERLAND	AWAY	1 - 4	PARLANE	29,619
04-Oct	IPSWICH TOWN	AWAY	1 - 1	SABELLA	24,087
08-Oct	MANCHESTER CITY	HOME	1 - 0	HARRIS C	19,134
11-Oct	EVERTON	HOME	1 - 0	CURTIS	25,601
18-Oct	WOLVERHAMPTON WANDERERS	AWAY	1 - 2	CONNOR	20,699
22-Oct	NOTTINGHAM FOREST	AWAY	1 - 2	HARRIS C	25,033
25-Oct	CRYSTAL PALACE	HOME	1 - 0	CONNOR	19,208
01-Nov	COVENTRY CITY	AWAY	1 - 2	CONNOR	13,970
08-Nov	ARSENAL	HOME	0 - 5		20,855
12-Nov	MIDDLESBROUGH	HOME	2 - 1	HIRD 2 (1 PEN)	17,382
15-Nov	ASTON VILLA	AWAY	1 - 1	SABELLA	29,106
22-Nov	SOUTHAMPTON	AWAY	1 - 2	GRAHAM	20,278
29-Nov	BRIGHTON & HOVE ALBION	HOME	1 - 0	HARRIS C	14,333
06-Dec	WEST BROMWICH ALBION	AWAY	2 - 1	HARRIS C & GRAHAM	17,771
13-Dec	NOTTINGHAM FOREST	HOME	1 - 0	GREENHOFF B	21,882
20-Dec	MANCHESTER CITY	AWAY	0 - 1		31,866
26-Dec	BIRMINGHAM CITY	HOME	0 - 0		19,214
27-Dec	LIVERPOOL	AWAY	0 - 0		44,086
10-Jan	SOUTHAMPTON	HOME	0 - 3		21,007
17-Jan	LEICESTER CITY	AWAY	1 - 0	HART P	16,094
31-Jan	NORWICH CITY	HOME	1 - 0	HARRIS C	15,836
07-Feb	TOTTENHAM HOTSPUR	AWAY	1 - 1	HARRIS C	32,372
14-Feb	STOKE CITY	HOME	1 - 3	FLYNN B	16,530
21-Feb	SUNDERLAND	HOME	1 - 0	HARRIS C	23,236
28-Feb	MANCHESTER UNITED	AWAY	1 - 0	FLYNN B	45,733
14-Mar	EVERTON	AWAY	2 - 1	PARLANE & HARRIS C	23,014
21-Mar	WOLVERHAMPTON WANDERERS	HOME	1 - 3	HARRIS C	19,252
28-Mar	CRYSTAL PALACE	AWAY	1 - 0	PARLANE	15,053
31-Mar	IPSWICH TOWN	HOME	3 - 0	HIRD, HARRIS C & HART P	26,462
04-Apr	COVENTRY CITY	HOME	3 - 0	STEVENSON W, PARLANE & FLYNN B	15,882
11-Apr	ARSENAL	AWAY	0 - 0		29,339
18-Apr	LIVERPOOL	HOME	0 - 0		39,206
21-Apr	BIRMINGHAM CITY	AWAY	2 - 0	PARLANE & HIRD (PEN)	14,505
02-May	BRIGHTON & HOVE ALBION	AWAY	0 - 2		27,577
06-May	WEST BROMWICH ALBION	HOME	0 - 0		17,218

F. A. CUP

DATE	OPPONENTS	VENUE	SCORE	SCORERS	ATT.
03-Jan	COVENTRY CITY (R3)	HOME	1 - 1	HIRD (PEN)	24,523
06-Jan	COVENTRY CITY (R3R)	AWAY	0 - 1		22,057

LEAGUE CUP

DATE	OPPONENTS	VENUE	SCORE	SCORERS	ATT.
27-Aug	ASTON VILLA (R2-1)	AWAY	0 - 1		24,238
03-Sep	ASTON VILLA (R2-2)	HOME	1 - 3	GRAHAM	12,236

LEAGUE AND CUP

APPEARANCES (SUBSTITUTE)

PLAYER	LEAGUE	F. A. CUP	LEAGUE CUP	TOTAL
BUTTERWORTH A	0 (1)			0 (1)
CHANDLER	8 (1)	1	1	10 (1)
CHERRY	41	2	2	45
CONNOR	25 (2)	1	2	28 (2)
CURTIS	6			6
DICKINSON	0 (1)			0 (1)
FIRM	5 (1)			5 (1)
FLYNN B	41	2	2	45
GRAHAM	40	2	2	44
GRAY E	38	2		40
GREENHOFF B	36	1	2	39
HAMSON	7 (4)	1 (1)	1	9 (5)
HARRIS C	33 (4)		0 (1)	33 (5)
HART P	38	2	2	42
HIRD	32 (1)	2		34 (1)
LUKIC	42	2	2	46
MADELEY	6		2	8
PARKINSON	3			3
PARLANE	22 (4)	2	1	25 (4)
SABELLA	22 (1)	2	2	26 (1)
STEVENSON W	17 (1)			17 (1)
THOMAS G	0 (2)		1	1 (2)

GOALSCORERS

PLAYER	LEAGUE	F. A. CUP	LEAGUE CUP	TOTAL
HARRIS C	10			10
HIRD	4	1		5
PARLANE	5			5
CONNOR	4			4
GRAHAM	3		1	4
HART P	4			4
FLYNN B	3			3
SABELLA	2			2
STEVENSON W	2			2
CURTIS	1			1
GREENHOFF B	1			1

Leeds United's improved fortunes during the previous campaign resulted in cautious optimism during pre-season at Elland Road. Looking to add experience and competition for places within his first team squad, Allan Clarke splashed out £930,000 on Manchester City winger and former England international Peter Barnes. The Leeds boss also brought Nottingham Forest's Frank Gray back to Elland Road. United travelled to Wales for the season's opener at Swansea City, but left demoralised following a 5-1 defeat.

Arthur Graham scored in a 1-1 draw against Everton, and notched a hat-trick in a 3-0 victory over Wolves, but the early weeks of the new term proved traumatic for Clarke's team; winning just the one league clash in 10 games. In a bid to shore up a defence heavily beaten 4-0 at Coventry City and Manchester City, Clarke invested £400,000 in resolute Nottingham Forest defender Kenny Burns. Making Burns club skipper, Trevor Cherry reverted to right-back, enabling Burns to partner Paul Hart in central defence. Amongst players departing, Alex Sabella joined Estudiantes for £120,000.

The defensive changes coincided with a return to form as Leeds claimed three consecutive home wins against West Brom; Graham, Trevor Cherry and Terry Connor finding the target, before Eddie Gray and Aiden Butterworth secured welcome victories over Sunderland and Notts County. For local lad Butterworth, his elevation was a surprise, but with Barnes proving a huge disappointment and Derek Parlane injured, the youngster had a chance to shine.

The coming weeks would yield more success, despite Leeds losing 4-0 at Southampton and to Ipswich Town in the League Cup. Following an entertaining 3-3 draw against West Ham, Graham and Gary Hamson scored at Stoke City to get Leeds back on the winning trail, before Byron Stevenson and Butterworth gained revenge for United's thumping at Swansea. Already out of the FA Cup, Clarke had one target, survival. However, five defeats and a draw, with no goals scored, placed Leeds firmly in the relegation zone. Desperate to pep up an ailing attack, Clarke swapped Byron Stevenson for Birmingham journeyman Frank Worthington.

The veteran striker immediately repaid Clarke's faith by claiming a priceless win at relegation rivals Sunderland. Paul Hart scored the only goal at another rival for the drop, Birmingham City, before a Worthington brace secured a 4-1 win at Aston Villa. However, three wins in 11 games was relegation form. The final six games began badly with a draw against Stoke City, and defeats at Everton and Tottenham Hotspur, before another Worthington double earned a 3-3 draw against Birmingham.

In the penultimate game, Leeds trailed Brighton 1-0, but late goals by Hamson and Kevin Hird gained an unlikely victory and apparent safety. However, with Birmingham, Sunderland and West Brom winning, Leeds had to defeat Albion to ensure safety. Heartbreakingly, in a match dogged by crowd trouble Leeds lost 2-0. Stoke's subsequent 3-0 win over West Brom sealed United's fate, ending 18 years of top-flight football. Relegation resulted in the axe for Clarke, Eddie Gray replacing him. John Lukic was the only ever-present, Graham and Worthington top-scored with nine goals.

1981 - 1982

DIVISION ONE (FINAL LEAGUE POSITION - 20TH)
PLD 42 W 10 D 12 L 20 F 39 A 61 PTS 42

DATE	OPPONENTS	VENUE	SCORE	SCORERS	ATT.
29-Aug	SWANSEA CITY	AWAY	1 - 5	PARLANE	23,489
02-Sep	EVERTON	HOME	1 - 1	GRAHAM	26,502
05-Sep	WOLVERHAMPTON WANDERERS	HOME	3 - 0	GRAHAM 3	20,216
12-Sep	COVENTRY CITY	AWAY	0 - 4		13,065
19-Sep	ARSENAL	HOME	0 - 0		21,410
23-Sep	MANCHESTER CITY	AWAY	0 - 4		35,077
26-Sep	IPSWICH TOWN	AWAY	1 - 2	BARNES	22,319
30-Sep	MANCHESTER UNITED	AWAY	0 - 1		47,019
03-Oct	ASTON VILLA	HOME	1 - 1	BALCOMBE	21,065
10-Oct	LIVERPOOL	AWAY	0 - 3		35,840
17-Oct	WEST BROMWICH ALBION	HOME	3 - 1	GRAHAM, CHERRY & CONNOR	19,164
24-Oct	SUNDERLAND	HOME	1 - 0	GRAY E	25,220
31-Oct	NOTTINGHAM FOREST	AWAY	1 - 2	BUTTERWORTH A	25,272
07-Nov	NOTTS COUNTY	HOME	1 - 0	BUTTERWORTH A	19,552
21-Nov	SOUTHAMPTON	AWAY	0 - 4		21,127
28-Nov	WEST HAM UNITED	HOME	3 - 3	GRAHAM, HIRD (PEN) & CHERRY	25,637
05-Dec	STOKE CITY	AWAY	2 - 1	GRAHAM & HAMSON	13,901
12-Dec	TOTTENHAM HOTSPUR	HOME	0 - 0		28,780
16-Jan	SWANSEA CITY	HOME	2 - 0	STEVENSON W & BUTTERWORTH A	18,700
30-Jan	ARSENAL	AWAY	0 - 1		22,408
06-Feb	COVENTRY CITY	HOME	0 - 0		16,385
20-Feb	IPSWICH TOWN	HOME	0 - 2		20,287
27-Feb	LIVERPOOL	HOME	0 - 2		33,689
02-Mar	BRIGHTON & HOVE ALBION	AWAY	0 - 1		12,857
10-Mar	MANCHESTER CITY	HOME	0 - 1		20,797
13-Mar	SUNDERLAND	AWAY	1 - 0	WORTHINGTON F	20,285
16-Mar	WOLVERHAMPTON WANDERERS	AWAY	0 - 1		11,729
20-Mar	NOTTINGHAM FOREST	HOME	1 - 1	WORTHINGTON F (PEN)	18,036
27-Mar	NOTTS COUNTY	AWAY	1 - 2	WORTHINGTON F	13,316
03-Apr	MANCHESTER UNITED	HOME	0 - 0		31,118
06-Apr	MIDDLESBROUGH	AWAY	0 - 0		15,494
10-Apr	BIRMINGHAM CITY	AWAY	1 - 0	HART P	14,497
13-Apr	MIDDLESBROUGH	HOME	1 - 1	PARLANE	20,458
17-Apr	SOUTHAMPTON	HOME	1 - 3	WORTHINGTON F	21,353
24-Apr	WEST HAM UNITED	AWAY	3 - 4	CONNOR, GRAHAM & FLYNN B	24,748
28-Apr	ASTON VILLA	AWAY	4 - 1	GRAHAM, WORTHINGTON F 2 & CONNOR	20,566
01-May	STOKE CITY	HOME	0 - 0		17,775
04-May	EVERTON	AWAY	0 - 1		17,137
08-May	TOTTENHAM HOTSPUR	AWAY	1 - 2	WORTHINGTON F	35,020
12-May	BIRMINGHAM CITY	HOME	3 - 3	WORTHINGTON F 2 (1 PEN) & CONNOR	18,583
15-May	BRIGHTON & HOVE ALBION	HOME	2 - 1	HAMSON & HIRD	19,831
18-May	WEST BROMWICH ALBION	AWAY	0 - 2		23,118

F. A. CUP

DATE	OPPONENTS	VENUE	SCORE	SCORERS	ATT.
02-Jan	WOLVERHAMPTON WANDERERS (R3)	AWAY	3 - 1	HAMSON, HIRD & GRAY E	20,923
23-Jan	TOTTENHAM HOTSPUR (R4)	AWAY	0 - 1		46,126

LEAGUE CUP

DATE	OPPONENTS	VENUE	SCORE	SCORERS	ATT.
07-Oct	IPSWICH TOWN (R2-1)	HOME	0 - 1		16,994
27-Oct	IPSWICH TOWN (R2-2)	AWAY	0 - 3		16,316

LEAGUE AND CUP
APPEARANCES (SUBSTITUTE)

PLAYER	LEAGUE	F. A. CUP	LEAGUE CUP	TOTAL
ARINS	0 (1)			0 (1)
ASPIN	1			1
BALCOMBE	1		1	2
BARNES	31		2	33
BURNS K	22 (1)	2		24 (1)
BUTTERWORTH A	13 (1)	2		15 (1)
CHERRY	38	2	1	41
CONNOR	23 (4)		1	24 (4)
FIRM	3			3
FLYNN B	16 (1)	0 (1)		16 (2)
GRAHAM	38	2	2	42
GRAY E	31	2	2	35
GRAY F	34	2	2	38
GREENHOFF B	10 (2)		1	11 (2)
HAMSON	17 (1)	2	1	20 (1)
HARRIS C	15 (3)		2	17 (3)
HART P	32	2	2	36
HIRD	35 (3)	2	2	39 (3)
LUKIC	42	2	2	46
PARLANE	12			12
STEVENSON W	18 (1)	2	1 (1)	21 (2)
THOMAS G	13 (2)			13 (2)
WORTHINGTON F	17			17

GOALSCORERS

PLAYER	LEAGUE	F. A. CUP	LEAGUE CUP	TOTAL
GRAHAM	9			9
WORTHINGTON F	9			9
CONNOR	4			4
BUTTERWORTH A	3			3
HAMSON	2	1		3
HIRD	2	1		3
CHERRY	2			2
GRAY E	1	1		2
PARLANE	2			2
BALCOMBE	1			1
BARNES	1			1
FLYNN B	1			1
HART P	1			1
STEVENSON W	1			1

161

Almost two decades on from playing outside the top-flight, new boss Eddie Gray's task was to gain promotion quickly, but with dwindling crowds and a £1.5 million debt, Gray's mission was nigh on impossible. Unable to make wholesale changes, Peter Barnes departed on loan to Spanish club Real Betis, while Carl Harris joined Charlton Athletic. Nevertheless, pre-season favourites Leeds made a promising start defeating Leicester City courtesy of an Aiden Butterworth goal, before Frank Worthington sealed a 3-2 win against Sheffield Wednesday and a 2-1 victory over Derby County.

The coming weeks would bring success over Cambridge United, Burnley and Newcastle United, Butterworth finding the target in each game, but the 3-1 win over Newcastle received more publicity due to crowd trouble than the result. Although both sets of supporters were guilty of throwing missiles, a ball bearing thrown from the Kop hit Kevin Keegan. The referee had no alternative but to take the teams off the pitch as a precaution. Action was swift.

Leeds United's board stated in the Charlton match programme that the club's future was in danger, whilst the FA ruled home clashes against Queens Park Rangers and Shrewsbury Town would be all-ticket; the latter match attracting under 9,000 spectators. On the field, results dipped as Leeds gained three wins from 17 games; Mark Gavin and Butterworth securing wins at Rotherham United and Grimsby, while Kevin Hird earned a 2-1 triumph against Blackburn Rovers. Amazingly, 10 draws kept Leeds in promotion contention; Arthur Graham scoring in battling 3-3 draws against Derby and Chelsea.

Meanwhile, change in personnel was occurring. Departures included Trevor Cherry and Brian Flynn, and the Rovers result saw keeper John Lukic play his final game after submitting a transfer request. Eddie Gray turned to former teammate David Harvey. Gray also decided to introduce promising youngsters. Making an instant impression was teenager midfielder John Sheridan, who secured a win at Charlton. By Leeds' next outing, former Manchester United and Brighton striker Andy Ritchie made a scoring debut in a 2-1 win against Crystal Palace. Ritchie arrived in a swap deal with Terry Connor.

Paul Hart made it three consecutive wins with a winner at Bolton before Ritchie set Leeds on the way to a 2-1 win at Burnley, but aspirations of a late promotion charge vanished as Leeds finished eighth. A disappointing end to the season maybe, but with obstacles on and off the pitch, there could be few complaints. With numerous old guards moving on, and the likes of Sheridan, defender Neil Aspin, striker Tommy Wright, who made a scoring debut against Fulham, and winger Scott Sellars breaking through, optimism was again rising. Frank Gray made 48 appearances, Butterworth top scored with 13 goals.

1982 - 1983

DIVISION TWO (FINAL LEAGUE POSITION - 8TH)

PLD 42 W 13 D 21 L 8 F 51 A 46 PTS 60

DATE	OPPONENTS	VENUE	SCORE	SCORERS	ATT.
28-Aug	GRIMSBY TOWN	AWAY	1 - 1	CONNOR	16,137
04-Sep	WOLVERHAMPTON WANDERERS	HOME	0 - 0		16,462
08-Sep	LEICESTER CITY	AWAY	1 - 0	BUTTERWORTH A	12,963
11-Sep	SHEFFIELD WEDNESDAY	AWAY	3 - 2	WORTHINGTON F 2 & BUTTERWORTH A	29,050
18-Sep	DERBY COUNTY	HOME	2 - 1	GRAY F & WORTHINGTON F	16,889
25-Sep	FULHAM	AWAY	2 - 3	THOMAS G & GRAHAM	12,798
02-Oct	CAMBRIDGE UNITED	HOME	2 - 1	BUTTERWORTH A & HIRD	14,910
09-Oct	CHELSEA	AWAY	0 - 0		25,358
16-Oct	CARLISLE UNITED	HOME	1 - 1	HART P	14,141
20-Oct	BURNLEY	HOME	3 - 1	WORTHINGTON F, BUTTERWORTH A & HIRD	13,827
23-Oct	BLACKBURN ROVERS	AWAY	0 - 0		12,040
30-Oct	NEWCASTLE UNITED	HOME	3 - 1	WORTHINGTON F, BUTTERWORTH A & BURNS K	26,570
06-Nov	CHARLTON ATHLETIC	HOME	1 - 2	CONNOR	15,148
13-Nov	CRYSTAL PALACE	AWAY	1 - 1	CONNOR	11,673
20-Nov	MIDDLESBROUGH	HOME	0 - 0		18,482
27-Nov	BARNSLEY	AWAY	1 - 2	BUTTERWORTH A	21,530
04-Dec	QUEENS PARK RANGERS	HOME	0 - 1		11,528
11-Dec	ROTHERHAM UNITED	AWAY	1 - 0	GAVIN	13,034
18-Dec	SHREWSBURY TOWN	HOME	1 - 1	HIRD	8,741
26-Dec	OLDHAM ATHLETIC	AWAY	2 - 2	BURNS K & SHERIDAN	15,658
28-Dec	BOLTON WANDERERS	HOME	1 - 1	GRAHAM	16,180
01-Jan	MIDDLESBROUGH	AWAY	0 - 0		17,000
03-Jan	WOLVERHAMPTON WANDERERS	AWAY	0 - 3		22,567
15-Jan	GRIMSBY TOWN	HOME	1 - 0	BUTTERWORTH A	13,583
22-Jan	DERBY COUNTY	AWAY	3 - 3	GRAHAM 2 & HART P	17,005
12-Feb	CAMBRIDGE UNITED	AWAY	0 - 0		6,909
19-Feb	CHELSEA	HOME	3 - 3	BUTTERWORTH A, GRAY F (PEN) & GRAHAM	19,365
26-Feb	CARLISLE UNITED	AWAY	2 - 2	CONNOR & BUTTERWORTH A	6,419
05-Mar	BLACKBURN ROVERS	HOME	2 - 1	GRAY F (PEN) & HIRD	12,280
12-Mar	NEWCASTLE UNITED	AWAY	1 - 2	CONNOR	24,580
19-Mar	CHARLTON ATHLETIC	AWAY	1 - 0	SHERIDAN	8,229
26-Mar	CRYSTAL PALACE	HOME	2 - 1	RITCHIE & GRAY F (PEN)	13,973
02-Apr	BOLTON WANDERERS	AWAY	2 - 1	BUTTERWORTH A & HART P	10,784
05-Apr	OLDHAM ATHLETIC	HOME	0 - 0		18,442
09-Apr	BURNLEY	AWAY	2 - 1	RITCHIE & O. G. (SCOTT)	12,149
16-Apr	FULHAM	HOME	1 - 1	WRIGHT T	24,328
23-Apr	QUEENS PARK RANGERS	AWAY	0 - 1		19,573
27-Apr	SHEFFIELD WEDNESDAY	HOME	1 - 2	RITCHIE	16,591
30-Apr	BARNSLEY	HOME	0 - 0		15,344
02-May	LEICESTER CITY	HOME	2 - 2	O. G. (O'NEILL) & GRAY F (PEN)	14,442
07-May	SHREWSBURY TOWN	AWAY	0 - 0		6,052
14-May	ROTHERHAM UNITED	HOME	2 - 2	BUTTERWORTH A & DONNELLY	14,958

F. A. CUP

08-Jan	PRESTON NORTH END (R3)	HOME	3 - 0	SHERIDAN, CONNOR & GRAHAM	16,816
29-Jan	ARSENAL (R4)	AWAY	1 - 1	O. G. (NICHOLAS)	33,930
02-Feb	ARSENAL (R4R) *	HOME	1 - 1	BUTTERWORTH A	24,410
09-Feb	ARSENAL (R42R)	AWAY	1 - 2	CONNOR	26,802

LEAGUE CUP

06-Oct	NEWCASTLE UNITED (R2-1)	HOME	0 - 1		24,012
27-Oct	NEWCASTLE UNITED (R2-2) *	AWAY	4 - 1	O. G. (SAUNDERS), WORTHINGTON F, BUTTERWORTH A & CONNOR	24,948
10-Nov	HUDDERSFIELD TOWN (R3)	HOME	0 - 1		24,215

LEAGUE AND CUP

APPEARANCES (SUBSTITUTE)

PLAYER	LEAGUE	F. A. CUP	LEAGUE CUP	TOTAL
ASPIN	14 (1)	4		18 (1)
BROWN T	1			1
BURNS K	19 (1)	1	3	23 (1)
BUTTERWORTH A	37 (1)	4	3	44 (1)
CHERRY	15 (1)		3	18 (1)
CONNOR	15 (4)	4	1 (2)	20 (6)
DICKINSON	31	3		34
DONNELLY	13 (1)			13 (1)
FLYNN B	2			2
GAVIN	3 (4)			3 (4)
GRAHAM	39	4	3	46
GRAY E	20 (1)	4	3	27 (1)
GRAY F	42	3	3	48
HAMSON		1		1
HARVEY	13			13
HART P	39	4	3	46
HIRD	30 (9)	1 (2)	2 (1)	33 (12)
LUKIC	29	4	3	36
McNAB	5	1		6
PARLANE	0 (1)			0 (1)
RITCHIE	10			10
SELLARS	1			1
SHERIDAN	27	2		29
THOMAS G	39	4	3	46
WRIGHT T	3 (1)			3 (1)
WORTHINGTON F	15		3	18

GOALSCORERS

PLAYER	LEAGUE	F. A. CUP	LEAGUE CUP	TOTAL
BUTTERWORTH A	11	1	1	13
CONNOR	5	2	1	8
GRAHAM	5	1		6
WORTHINGTON F	5		1	6
GRAY F	5			5
HIRD	4			4
HART P	3			3
RITCHIE	3			3
SHERIDAN	2	1		3
BURNS K	2			2
DONNELLY	1			1
GAVIN	1			1
THOMAS G	1			1
WRIGHT T	1			1
OWN GOALS	2	1	1	4

KEY :- * = AFTER EXTRA TIME

A hive of activity took place at Elland Road during the summer as sales of John Lukic, Arthur Graham and Paul Hart enabled Eddie Gray to purchase Celtic striker George McCluskey and Aberdeen midfield man Andy Watson. Big-money transfers were over and it showed. Six defeats in the opening nine games included a 5-1 thumping at Shrewsbury Town, demonstrating the depths to which United had sunk. The only triumphs came against Brighton; John Sheridan edging an exciting encounter 3-2, and Cardiff City; McCluskey securing a win.

Back from a loan spell in Spain was Peter Barnes and following a brief period out through injury, his return coincided with an upturn in fortunes as Leeds enjoyed three consecutive wins. Watson was among the scorers in a 3-1 win over Cambridge United, but the victory was soured by midfield protégé Sheridan breaking a leg. Barnes found the target in victories against Barnsley and Portsmouth, but four draws and four defeats confirmed that consistency would be Gray's biggest problem.

With the likes of Chelsea visiting, attendances swelled, but the majority of a near 24,000 crowd went home disappointed following a 2-1 Boxing Day defeat to Huddersfield Town. The derby did, however, see the re-introduction of Scott Sellars and Tommy Wright, who scored his second senior goal, albeit a consolation as Leeds slid into the bottom four. For the duo, it would be a breakthrough into first team football and both prospered with goals in an impressive 4-1 win over Middlesbrough on New Years Eve. The clash saw legendary sharpshooter Peter Lorimer return; briefed to steer Leeds clear from relegation.

With renewed optimism, following a 1-1 draw at promotion hopefuls Manchester City, Leeds hosted Scunthorpe United, managed by former boss Allan Clarke in the FA Cup. Already out of the League Cup, hopes were high of a much-needed cup run, but the lower league side claimed victory in a second replay. The result however, proved a catalyst as Leeds claimed five consecutive wins. Watson's strike against Fulham sparked the run, before the midfielder scored a brace in a comfortable 3-0 win over Shrewsbury. McCluskey settled a tight encounter against Cardiff, while Lorimer, dictating from central midfield, found his scoring touch against Swansea City and Portsmouth.

With relegation fears banished, five triumphs in the remaining 15 games brought a tenth place finish but more important, Gray's youngsters had settled at this level. Sellars, who completed a 2-1 win against Grimsby Town, had exceptional ball skills, whilst Leeds' other scorer, Neil Aspin, looked solid in the centre of defence. The highlight of remaining games however, was 'Hotshot' Lorimer's form. Though his best days were behind him, strikes against Oldham Athletic and Swansea took him past John Charles all-time league mark. Setting the seal on a season of transition, Gray made his final first team appearance at home to Charlton Athletic when Wright edged ahead in the scoring stakes over Andy Ritchie in a 1-0 win. Skipper David Harvey was ever-present with 47 appearances, Wright top scored on 11 goals. Off the field, Leslie Silver replaced Manny Cussins as chairman.

1983 - 1984

DIVISION TWO (FINAL LEAGUE POSITION - 10TH)					
PLD 42 W 16 D 12 L 14 F 55 A 56 PTS 60					
DATE	OPPONENTS	VENUE	SCORE	SCORERS	ATT.
27-Aug	NEWCASTLE UNITED	HOME	0 - 1		30,806
29-Aug	BRIGHTON & HOVE ALBION	HOME	3 - 2	WATSON, GRAY F & SHERIDAN	13,303
03-Sep	MIDDLESBROUGH	AWAY	2 - 2	GRAY F (PEN) & McCLUSKEY	12,793
06-Sep	GRIMSBY TOWN	AWAY	0 - 2		8,000
10-Sep	CARDIFF CITY	HOME	1 - 0	McCLUSKEY	12,336
17-Sep	FULHAM	AWAY	1 - 2	RITCHIE	10,055
24-Sep	MANCHESTER CITY	HOME	1 - 2	RITCHIE	21,918
01-Oct	SHREWSBURY TOWN	AWAY	1 - 5	RITCHIE	6,289
08-Oct	SHEFFIELD WEDNESDAY	AWAY	1 - 3	GRAY F (PEN)	26,814
14-Oct	CAMBRIDGE UNITED	HOME	3 - 1	HIRD, WATSON & DONNELLY	9,923
22-Oct	BARNSLEY	AWAY	2 - 0	DONNELLY & BARNES	18,236
29-Oct	PORTSMOUTH	HOME	2 - 1	WATSON & BARNES	16,254
05-Nov	CRYSTAL PALACE	HOME	1 - 1	McCLUSKEY	14,847
12-Nov	BLACKBURN ROVERS	AWAY	1 - 1	DONNELLY	9,556
19-Nov	DERBY COUNTY	AWAY	1 - 1	RITCHIE	16,726
26-Nov	CHELSEA	HOME	1 - 1	McCLUSKEY	20,680
03-Dec	CARLISLE UNITED	AWAY	0 - 1		6,845
15-Dec	CHARLTON ATHLETIC	AWAY	0 - 2		6,285
26-Dec	HUDDERSFIELD TOWN	HOME	1 - 2	WRIGHT T	23,791
27-Dec	OLDHAM ATHLETIC	AWAY	2 - 3	WRIGHT T & GRAY F	8,393
31-Dec	MIDDLESBROUGH	HOME	4 - 1	SELLARS, McCLUSKEY 2 & WRIGHT T	14,215
02-Jan	MANCHESTER CITY	AWAY	1 - 1	O. G. (BOND)	34,441
21-Jan	FULHAM	HOME	1 - 0	WATSON	11,421
04-Feb	SHREWSBURY TOWN	HOME	3 - 0	WATSON 2 & BROWN T	10,628
11-Feb	CARDIFF CITY	AWAY	1 - 0	McCLUSKEY	9,407
15-Feb	SWANSEA CITY	HOME	1 - 0	LORIMER	10,031
18-Feb	PORTSMOUTH	AWAY	3 - 2	WRIGHT T, WATSON & LORIMER (PEN)	13,911
25-Feb	BARNSLEY	HOME	1 - 2	WRIGHT T	19,138
03-Mar	CRYSTAL PALACE	AWAY	0 - 0		8,077
10-Mar	BLACKBURN ROVERS	HOME	1 - 0	BUTTERWORTH A	12,857
17-Mar	GRIMSBY TOWN	HOME	2 - 1	ASPIN & SELLARS	14,412
24-Mar	BRIGHTON & HOVE ALBION	AWAY	0 - 3		12,605
28-Mar	NEWCASTLE UNITED	AWAY	0 - 1		30,877
31-Mar	SHEFFIELD WEDNESDAY	HOME	1 - 1	RITCHIE	25,343
07-Apr	CAMBRIDGE UNITED	AWAY	2 - 2	BARNES & SELLARS	4,700
14-Apr	DERBY COUNTY	HOME	0 - 0		12,549
21-Apr	HUDDERSFIELD TOWN	AWAY	2 - 2	WRIGHT T & BARNES	16,270
24-Apr	OLDHAM ATHLETIC	HOME	2 - 0	RITCHIE & LORIMER (PEN)	9,576
28-Apr	CHELSEA	AWAY	0 - 5		33,447
05-May	CARLISLE UNITED	HOME	3 - 0	GAVIN, RITCHIE & McCLUSKEY	8,278
07-May	SWANSEA CITY	AWAY	2 - 2	WRIGHT T & LORIMER	5,498
12-May	CHARLTON ATHLETIC	HOME	1 - 0	WRIGHT T	13,254

F. A. CUP					
07-Jan	SCUNTHORPE UNITED (R3)	HOME	1 - 1	WRIGHT T	17,130
10-Jan	SCUNTHORPE UNITED (R3R) *	AWAY	1 - 1	WRIGHT T	13,129
16-Jan	SCUNTHORPE UNITED (R32R)	AWAY	2 - 4	WRIGHT T & RITCHIE	13,312

LEAGUE CUP					
05-Oct	CHESTER CITY (R2-1)	HOME	0 - 1		8,106
26-Oct	CHESTER CITY (R2-2)	AWAY	4 - 1	RITCHIE 2, BURNS K & BARNES	8,044
09-Nov	OXFORD UNITED (R3)	HOME	1 - 1	McCLUSKEY	13,349
23-Nov	OXFORD UNITED (R3R)	AWAY	1 - 4	BURNS K	13,389

LEAGUE AND CUP

APPEARANCES (SUBSTITUTE)

PLAYER	LEAGUE	F. A. CUP	LEAGUE CUP	TOTAL
ASPIN	21	3	2	26
BARNES	25 (2)	1	3	29 (2)
BROWN T	22			22
BURNS K	13		4	17
BUTTERWORTH A	4 (7)		1	5 (7)
DICKINSON	34	2	4	40
DONNELLY	23 (2)	1	3	27 (2)
GAVIN	10 (2)		1 (1)	11 (3)
GRAY E	4			4
GRAY F	24	2	4	30
HAMSON	23 (2)	3		26 (2)
HARVEY	40	3	4	47
HIRD	16 (2)		1	17 (2)
HUGHES P	2			2
IRWIN	12	1		13
LORIMER	20 (2)	2 (1)		22 (3)
McCLUSKEY	24 (8)	3	3 (1)	30 (9)
McGOLDRICK	7	3	2	12
RITCHIE	38	3	4	45
SELLARS	19	2		21
SHERIDAN	11			11
THOMAS G	16 (1)		4	20 (1)
THOMPSON N	1			1
WATSON	30 (1)	1	4	35 (1)
WRIGHT T	23 (2)	3	0 (1)	26 (3)

GOALSCORERS

PLAYER	LEAGUE	F. A. CUP	LEAGUE CUP	TOTAL
WRIGHT T	8	3		11
RITCHIE	7	1	2	10
McCLUSKEY	8		1	9
WATSON	7			7
BARNES	4		1	5
GRAY F	4			4
LORIMER	4			4
DONNELLY	3			3
SELLARS	3			3
BURNS K			2	2
ASPIN	1			1
BROWN T	1			1
BUTTERWORTH A	1			1
GAVIN	1			1
HIRD	1			1
SHERIDAN	1			1
OWN GOALS	1			1

KEY :- * = AFTER EXTRA TIME

Without a transfer budget, Eddie Gray generated limited funds by selling Peter Barnes and Gwyn Thomas. Purchasing Andy Linighan (Hartlepool) for £20,000, Gray kept faith with his promising youngsters, though experience was still present via David Harvey, Peter Lorimer and Frank Gray. With John Sheridan recovered from a broken leg, media attention focused on the schemer, in addition to budding stars Denis Irwin, Neil Aspin, Tommy Wright, Scott Sellars and now Linighan.

Vibrant and committed, Gray's young charges stunned observers by winning their opening four fixtures. Wright gave his side the perfect start with a brace against Notts County before sealing a 2-0 win over Fulham. Another Wright double and a Lorimer strike edged a thriller against Wolves 3-2, before George McCluskey and Lorimer combined to defeat Grimsby Town. Suddenly, talk was of promotion, but three consecutive defeats quelled budding optimism.

Andy Ritchie returned to the fray after a spell out through injury and marked his first start with a hat-trick as Leeds demolished Oldham Athletic 6-0. The coming weeks would see Leeds at their most consistent, winning five of seven games, with Ritchie at the fore averaging a goal-a-game. For supporters it was hugely entertaining. Hammered 5-2 at promotion-bound Oxford United, Ritchie notched his second treble of the season in a 5-2 canter against Wimbledon, before a brace secured a 3-2 win at Shrewsbury Town.

The festive fixtures however, only brought a 2-0 victory at Wolves, Frank Gray and McCluskey scoring. Out of both cup competitions, United could be dazzling, as Notts County experienced in a 5-0 drubbing at Elland Road; Wright scoring a treble, but sandwiched between, four draws summed up Leeds' inconsistency, yet they were still within touching distance of promotion. Eddie Gray decided to strengthen his squad. Severing links with Harvey after some two decades bar a brief sojourn abroad, Gray signed Mervyn Day, a former England international prospect who was attempting to resurrect his career. Day would prove a sound investment, as would striker Ian Baird from Southampton for £75,000.

Lorimer strikes accounted for Charlton Athletic and Barnsley, whilst Baird made his mark in a 2-1 win at promotion-hopefuls Manchester City, before opening the scoring as Leeds crushed Crystal Palace 4-1; Sheridan notching a brace. Further goals by the burly forward sealed wins over Oxford and Shrewsbury Town, giving Gray's youngsters a slim chance of promotion going into the final game at Birmingham City, but against a backdrop of simmering violence, United lost the 'Battle of St Andrews' 1-0 as mounted police quashed a potential riot by Leeds fans.

Finishing seventh, Linighan, Sheridan and Wright; who finished top scorer with 15 goals, were ever-present, but media coverage surrounded the disorder at St Andrews when a supporting wall collapsed. One teenager died and dozens were injured. In a grim month when football mourned victims of the Bradford fire and Heysal Stadium disasters, the Home Secretary ordered an inquiry. During the season, Leeds had experienced unrest at Oxford, Huddersfield and Barnsley. So-called Leeds United supporters cost the club a £5,000 fine. In addition, forthcoming away games would be all-ticket. United's 'wilderness years' in Division 2 were becoming fraught with difficulty.

1984 - 1985

DIVISION TWO (FINAL LEAGUE POSITION - 7TH)

PLD 42 W 19 D 12 L 11 F 66 A 43 PTS 69

DATE	OPPONENTS	VENUE	SCORE	SCORERS	ATT.
25-Aug	NOTTS COUNTY	AWAY	2 - 1	WRIGHT T 2	12,196
27-Aug	FULHAM	HOME	2 - 0	McCLUSKEY & WRIGHT T	14,207
01-Sep	WOLVERHAMPTON WANDERERS	HOME	3 - 2	WRIGHT T 2 & LORIMER	17,843
08-Sep	GRIMSBY TOWN	AWAY	2 - 0	McCLUSKEY & LORIMER	13,290
12-Sep	CARDIFF CITY	AWAY	1 - 2	SELLARS	6,893
15-Sep	PORTSMOUTH	HOME	0 - 1		19,438
22-Sep	CRYSTAL PALACE	AWAY	1 - 3	SELLARS	19,460
29-Sep	OLDHAM ATHLETIC	HOME	6 - 0	WRIGHT T, RITCHIE 3 (1 PEN), SHERIDAN & LINIGHAN	14,290
06-Oct	SHEFFIELD UNITED	HOME	1 - 1	LORIMER (PEN)	25,547
13-Oct	BARNSLEY	AWAY	0 - 1		16,199
20-Oct	HUDDERSFIELD TOWN	AWAY	0 - 1		15,257
27-Oct	MIDDLESBROUGH	HOME	2 - 0	LORIMER (PEN) & RITCHIE	14,838
03-Nov	CHARLTON ATHLETIC	AWAY	3 - 2	SHERIDAN, McCLUSKEY & GAVIN	6,950
10-Nov	CARLISLE UNITED	HOME	1 - 1	DICKINSON	13,327
17-Nov	BRIGHTON & HOVE ALBION	HOME	1 - 0	RITCHIE	13,127
24-Nov	OXFORD UNITED	AWAY	2 - 5	WRIGHT T & LORIMER	12,192
01-Dec	WIMBLEDON	HOME	5 - 2	WRIGHT T, RITCHIE 3 & SELLARS	10,899
08-Dec	SHREWSBURY TOWN	AWAY	3 - 2	RITCHIE 2 & LINIGHAN	6,358
15-Dec	BIRMINGHAM CITY	HOME	0 - 1		15,584
22-Dec	WOLVERHAMPTON WANDERERS	AWAY	2 - 0	GRAY F & McCLUSKEY	9,259
26-Dec	BLACKBURN ROVERS	AWAY	1 - 2	McCLUSKEY	20,149
29-Dec	CARDIFF CITY	HOME	1 - 1	LORIMER (PEN)	11,798
01-Jan	MANCHESTER CITY	HOME	1 - 1	RITCHIE	22,626
19-Jan	NOTTS COUNTY	HOME	5 - 0	SHERIDAN, WRIGHT T 3 & IRWIN	11,369
02-Feb	OLDHAM ATHLETIC	AWAY	1 - 1	LORIMER (PEN)	8,824
09-Feb	GRIMSBY TOWN	HOME	0 - 0		12,517
23-Feb	CHARLTON ATHLETIC	HOME	1 - 0	LORIMER	10,644
26-Feb	CARLISLE UNITED	AWAY	2 - 2	WRIGHT T & ASPIN	5,484
02-Mar	MIDDLESBROUGH	AWAY	0 - 0		8,781
09-Mar	HUDDERSFIELD TOWN	HOME	0 - 0		18,607
12-Mar	PORTSMOUTH	AWAY	1 - 3	SHERIDAN	16,208
16-Mar	BARNSLEY	HOME	2 - 0	LORIMER & SELLARS	13,091
23-Mar	SHEFFIELD UNITED	AWAY	1 - 2	RITCHIE	21,468
30-Mar	FULHAM	AWAY	2 - 0	WRIGHT T 2	7,901
06-Apr	BLACKBURN ROVERS	HOME	0 - 0		15,829
08-Apr	MANCHESTER CITY	AWAY	2 - 1	BAIRD I & SELLARS	33,553
13-Apr	CRYSTAL PALACE	HOME	4 - 1	BAIRD I, SELLARS & SHERIDAN 2	12,286
20-Apr	BRIGHTON & HOVE ALBION	AWAY	1 - 1	SELLARS	17,279
27-Apr	OXFORD UNITED	HOME	1 - 0	BAIRD I	17,992
04-May	WIMBLEDON	AWAY	2 - 2	BAIRD I 2	6,638
06-May	SHREWSBURY TOWN	HOME	1 - 0	BAIRD I	12,423
11-May	BIRMINGHAM CITY	AWAY	0 - 1		24,847

F. A. CUP

DATE	OPPONENTS	VENUE	SCORE	SCORERS	ATT.
04-Jan	EVERTON (R3)	HOME	0 - 2		21,211

LEAGUE CUP

DATE	OPPONENTS	VENUE	SCORE	SCORERS	ATT.
25-Sep	GILLINGHAM (R2-1)	AWAY	2 - 1	WRIGHT T & RITCHIE	8,881
10-Oct	GILLINGHAM (R2-2)	HOME	3 - 2	GAVIN, SELLARS & LORIMER	11,094
31-Oct	WATFORD (R3)	HOME	0 - 4		21,221

LEAGUE AND CUP
APPEARANCES (SUBSTITUTE)

PLAYER	LEAGUE	F. A. CUP	LEAGUE CUP	TOTAL
ASPIN	32	1		33
BAIRD I	10			10
BROWN T	1			1
DAY	18			18
DICKINSON	12		3	15
DONNELLY	0 (1)			0 (1)
ELI	0 (1)			0 (1)
GAVIN	7 (4)	0 (1)	3	10 (5)
GRAY F	39	1	3	43
HAMSON	31	1		32
HARVEY	20		3	23
HUGHES P	4	1		5
IRWIN	41	1	3	45
LINIGHAN	42	1	3	46
LORIMER	40	1	3	44
McCLUSKEY	13 (6)	1	0 (1)	14 (7)
RITCHIE	22 (6)		3	25 (6)
SELLARS	39	1	3	43
SHERIDAN	42	1	3	46
SIMMONDS	0 (1)			0 (1)
STILES	1			1
WATSON	7			7
WRIGHT T	41 (1)	1	3	45 (1)

GOALSCORERS

PLAYER	LEAGUE	F. A. CUP	LEAGUE CUP	TOTAL
WRIGHT T	14		1	15
RITCHIE	12		1	13
LORIMER	9		1	10
SELLARS	7		1	8
BAIRD I	6			6
SHERIDAN	6			6
McCLUSKEY	5			5
GAVIN	1		1	2
LINIGHAN	2			2
ASPIN	1			1
DICKINSON	1			1
GRAY F	1			1
IRWIN	1			1

A summer of contemplation followed the disgraceful scenes during the 'Battle of St Andrews'. Frank Gray's departure to Sunderland for £100,000 and Ian Snodin's arrival from Doncaster Rovers at £250,000 was the main transfer news, but attention quickly focused on a dreadful opening month's results. Two draws from five matches, including a 6-2 thumping at Stoke City; Snodin scoring one of Leeds' consolation goals, put Eddie Gray under mounting pressure. However, one loss in the next eight games, including back-to-back wins at Brighton and Shrewsbury Town; McCluskey scoring in both clashes, and a 2-1 derby win over Bradford City; Sellars securing a triumph, demonstrated resolve.

The team's improved form continued when a Snodin brace saw Leeds edge past Walsall in the League Cup, but 72 hours later, United fans and players alike were stunned following the sacking of Gray. The Scot's association stretched back 22 years; Gray departed with dignity and with words of gratitude from United's board, but the decision enraged supporters who demonstrated their feelings verbally during a 1-0 home win over Middlesbrough; Peter Lorimer slotting home his fourth goal of the season.

Whilst one legend departed, club directors appointed another celebrated hero to the hot seat. Billy Bremner had enjoyed success at Doncaster Rovers, his appointment calmed tensions. Bremner's arrival also sparked decisions as Leeds City Council purchased Elland Road for £2.5m, granting Leeds United a 125-year lease in return, whilst record goalscorer Lorimer departed.

Appointing Snodin skipper, results were patchy. Among four wins before Christmas, Andy Ritchie sealed a 2-1 win at Carlisle. Snodin, Ian Baird and Martin Dickinson secured a comfortable 3-0 win at Wimbledon, whilst John Sheridan's strike brought victory over Fulham. Off the field, United's hooligan element was still causing problems, ignoring an FA all-ticket ruling on away games. When four policeman were injured during a 3-1 defeat at Millwall, football authorities ruled that Leeds fans should be banned from all away games, but the judgement was unenforceable. Reversing the decision after two games, the original all-ticket ban remained.

A Baird brace and Ritchie strike opened the New Year with a 3-1 win against Oldham Athletic, but an embarrassing FA Cup defeat at Peterborough resulted in Bremner promoting youngsters Peter Swan and John Stiles to the first team set-up. The duo found the target in Leeds' most comprehensive win of the campaign, 4-0 against Stoke, before Bremner enhanced his defence by signing Brendon Ormsby and David Rennie. Teaming up for the final 12 games of the season, Ormsby opened the scoring in a 2-0 win over Huddersfield Town before Rennie struck in draws against Middlesbrough and Shrewsbury.

Rediscovering his goal scoring touch during the run-in, Ritchie notched eight goals in as many games, including a brace in a 3-2 win at Portsmouth and Leeds' third goal to seal a 3-1 win over Millwall. Sandwiched between these triumphs, a rare Neil Aspin goal earned a 1-0 victory at neighbours Bradford. Ritchie's final goals of a personal scoring-blitz brought the curtain down at Elland Road with a 2-0 triumph against Carlisle United, however a 4-0 loss at champions Norwich City demonstrated the distance Bremner had to travel with his emerging charges. Finishing an emotionally charged campaign fourteenth, Day made 46 appearances, whilst Baird top scored with 12 goals; one ahead of Ritchie.

DIVISION TWO (FINAL LEAGUE POSITION - 14TH)
PLD 42 W 15 D 8 L 19 F 56 A 72 PTS 53

DATE	OPPONENTS	VENUE	SCORE	SCORERS	ATT.
17-Aug	FULHAM	AWAY	1 - 3	LORIMER	5,772
21-Aug	WIMBLEDON	HOME	0 - 0		12,426
24-Aug	HULL CITY	HOME	1 - 1	BAIRD I	16,689
26-Aug	STOKE CITY	AWAY	2 - 6	ASPIN & SNODIN I	7,047
31-Aug	CHARLTON ATHLETIC	HOME	1 - 2	LORIMER (PEN)	10,860
04-Sep	BRIGHTON & HOVE ALBION	AWAY	1 - 0	McCLUSKEY	9,798
07-Sep	SHREWSBURY TOWN	AWAY	3 - 1	WRIGHT T, McCLUSKEY & BAIRD I	4,168
14-Sep	SUNDERLAND	HOME	1 - 1	SHERIDAN	19,693
21-Sep	BRADFORD CITY	HOME	2 - 1	LORIMER & SELLARS	21,104
28-Sep	SHEFFIELD UNITED	HOME	1 - 1	BAIRD I	15,622
05-Oct	HUDDERSFIELD TOWN	AWAY	1 - 3	BAIRD I	9,983
12-Oct	MIDDLESBROUGH	HOME	1 - 0	LORIMER (PEN)	14,117
19-Oct	GRIMSBY TOWN	HOME	1 - 1	BAIRD I	11,244
27-Oct	BARNSLEY	AWAY	0 - 3		8,302
02-Nov	PORTSMOUTH	HOME	2 - 1	SIMMONDS 2 (1 PEN)	15,672
09-Nov	MILLWALL	AWAY	1 - 3	RITCHIE	9,158
16-Nov	CRYSTAL PALACE	HOME	1 - 3	McCLUSKEY	10,378
23-Nov	CARLISLE UNITED	AWAY	2 - 1	LINIGHAN & RITCHIE	3,504
30-Nov	NORWICH CITY	HOME	0 - 2		11,480
07-Dec	WIMBLEDON	AWAY	3 - 0	SNODIN I, BAIRD I & DICKINSON	3,492
14-Dec	FULHAM	HOME	1 - 0	SHERIDAN	9,998
22-Dec	HULL CITY	AWAY	1 - 2	SHERIDAN	11,852
26-Dec	BLACKBURN ROVERS	AWAY	0 - 2		8,666
28-Dec	BRIGHTON & HOVE ALBION	HOME	2 - 3	BAIRD I & SNODIN I	13,110
01-Jan	OLDHAM ATHLETIC	HOME	3 - 1	BAIRD I 2 & RITCHIE	10,830
11-Jan	SUNDERLAND	AWAY	2 - 4	BAIRD I & SHERIDAN	15,139
18-Jan	CHARLTON ATHLETIC	AWAY	0 - 4		4,333
01-Feb	STOKE CITY	HOME	4 - 0	STILES, BAIRD I & SWAN P 2	10,425
08-Feb	GRIMSBY TOWN	AWAY	0 - 1		6,382
15-Feb	BARNSLEY	HOME	0 - 2		11,765
08-Mar	HUDDERSFIELD TOWN	HOME	2 - 0	ORMSBY & SNODIN I	14,667
15-Mar	MIDDLESBROUGH	AWAY	2 - 2	SIMMONDS & RENNIE	6,889
22-Mar	SHREWSBURY TOWN	HOME	1 - 1	RENNIE	9,641
28-Mar	OLDHAM ATHLETIC	AWAY	1 - 3	RITCHIE	4,937
31-Mar	BLACKBURN ROVERS	HOME	1 - 1	RITCHIE	9,919
05-Apr	PORTSMOUTH	AWAY	3 - 2	RITCHIE 2 & BAIRD I	14,430
09-Apr	BRADFORD CITY	AWAY	1 - 0	ASPIN	10,751
12-Apr	MILLWALL	HOME	3 - 1	SELLARS, SWAN P & RITCHIE	15,067
19-Apr	CRYSTAL PALACE	AWAY	0 - 3		6,285
22-Apr	SHEFFIELD UNITED	AWAY	2 - 3	RITCHIE & SNODIN I	9,158
26-Apr	CARLISLE UNITED	HOME	2 - 0	RITCHIE 2	13,868
03-May	NORWICH CITY	AWAY	0 - 4		17,942

F. A. CUP

DATE	OPPONENTS	VENUE	SCORE	SCORERS	ATT.
04-Jan	PETERBOROUGH UNITED (R3)	AWAY	0 - 1		10,137

MILK CUP

DATE	OPPONENTS	VENUE	SCORE	SCORERS	ATT.
25-Sep	WALSALL (R2-1)	HOME	0 - 0		8,880
08-Oct	WALSALL (R2-2)	AWAY	3 - 0	LINIGHAN & SNODIN I 2	7,085
30-Oct	ASTON VILLA (R3)	HOME	0 - 3		15,396

FULL MEMBERS CUP

DATE	OPPONENTS	VENUE	SCORE	SCORERS	ATT.
14-Oct	MANCHESTER CITY (NTH. GROUP 3)	AWAY	1 - 6	LORIMER (PEN)	4,029
16-Oct	SHEFFIELD UNITED (NTH. GROUP 3)	HOME	1 - 1	SELLARS	2,274

LEAGUE AND CUPS
APPEARANCES (SUBSTITUTE)

PLAYER	LEAGUE	F. A. CUP	MILK CUP	F. M. CUP	TOTAL
ASPIN	38	1	1	2	42
BAIRD I	34 (1)	1	3	2	40 (1)
CASWELL	8				8
DAY	40	1	3	2	46
DICKINSON	17 (2)	1	3		21 (2)
ELI	1				1
HAMSON	30	1	2	1	34
HARLE	3				3
IRWIN	19	1	2	2	24
LINIGHAN	24	1	3	2	30
LORIMER	14		2	2	18
McCLUSKEY	20 (2)		2 (1)	1	23 (3)
McGREGOR	5				5
ORMSBY	12				12
PHELAN	12 (2)		3	2	17 (2)
RENNIE	16				16
RITCHIE	28 (1)	1	2		31 (1)
ROBINSON R	16				16
SELLARS	13 (4)	1	1	2	17 (4)
SHERIDAN	31 (1)	0 (1)	3	2	36 (2)
SIMMONDS	6 (2)			1 (1)	7 (3)
SNODIN I	37	1	3		41
STILES	11 (1)			0 (1)	11 (2)
SWAN P	16	1		0 (2)	17 (2)
SWINBURNE	2				2
TAYLOR B	2				2
THOMPSON N	1			1	2
WRIGHT T	6 (4)		0 (1)		6 (5)

GOALSCORERS

PLAYER	LEAGUE	F. A. CUP	MILK CUP	F. M. CUP	TOTAL
BAIRD I	12				12
RITCHIE	11				11
SNODIN I	5		2		7
LORIMER	4			1	5
SHERIDAN	4				4
McCLUSKEY	3				3
SIMMONDS	3				3
SWAN P	3				3
ASPIN	2				2
RENNIE	2				2
SELLARS	2			1	3
LINIGHAN	1		1		2
DICKINSON	1				1
ORMSBY	1				1
STILES	1				1
WRIGHT T	1				1

Planning his first full season at the helm, Billy Bremner embarked on a hectic summer sale, purchasing Keith Edwards (Sheffield United), Peter Haddock (Newcastle United) and Jack Ashurst (Carlisle United), whilst George McCluskey, Gary Hamson, Terry Phelan and Denis Irwin departed. In a campaign that included end-of-season promotion play offs for the first time, early results saw Ian Baird secure wins over Stoke City and Barnsley, whilst John Buckley edged a 3-2 thriller against Reading.

An FA all-ticket ruling on United away games was reversed when rival supporters clashed amid appalling scenes during a 2-0 defeat at Bradford City. Away from hooliganism, Mervyn Day and Brendon Ormsby's reintroduction coincided with four victories in six games. Ormsby scored in 3-0 wins over Hull City and Crystal Palace, while John Sheridan, who slotted home a penalty against Palace, converted another in a 3-1 triumph over Portsmouth. Neil Aspin's goal against Shrewsbury Town sealed a fifth successive home win, but five defeats before Christmas, including a 7-2 drubbing at Stoke City, kept Leeds outside the promotion mix, despite Sheridan strikes in wins against high-flying Derby County and strugglers Brighton.

A New Years Day defeat at Ipswich Town cancelled out Andy Ritchie's winner at Oldham Athletic. Baird earned draws against Huddersfield Town and Barnsley, whilst firing Leeds into the FA Cup fifth round for the first time in a decade following winning strikes against Telford United and Swindon Town. As cup fever gripped supporters for a home clash with top-flight Queens Park Rangers, Bremner strengthened his squad with the arrival of Micky Adams (Coventry City), Bobby McDonald (Oxford), Mark Aizlewood and John Pearson (Charlton Athletic) after selling skipper Ian Snodin to Everton for £800,000.

Baird and new skipper Ormsby settled a thrilling 2-1 win over Rangers, whilst John Stiles and Adams won a quarter-final tie at Wigan. Through to the semi-finals, a season going nowhere was suddenly ignited as United pushed for promotion. Edwards edged a derby against Bradford, Sheridan secured a win over Grimsby Town, and a Baird hat-trick was the highlight of a 4-0 win over Plymouth Argyle before the hit-man teamed up with Ritchie to defeat Millwall. Competing on two fronts, Bremner's underdogs battled heroically in an FA Cup semi-final clash against Coventry. During a titanic struggle, David Rennie and Edwards scored before the Sky Blues dashed United's Wembley dreams with an extra-time winner.

Heartbroken, the drive for top-flight football quickly recommenced with Sheridan at the fore, scoring in triumphs over Shrewsbury, Ipswich and Birmingham City; Baird notching a brace in the 4-0 win. A 2-1 defeat at champions-elect Derby was forgotten when Sheridan, Pearson and Ormsby sealed a 3-2 win over West Brom, in turn securing a play-off spot alongside Oldham, Ipswich and Division 1 Charlton.

Facing Oldham in the semi-finals, super-sub Keith Edwards scored a last minute winner at Elland Road. In a nail-biting return, Edwards notched a last gasp equaliser in normal time, before Leeds held on for an away-goals win in extra-time. A goal down from the first leg against Charlton, Ormsby touched home a Bob Taylor shot to set-up a play-off final replay at Birmingham's St Andrews ground. A sublime Sheridan free-kick in extra-time took Leeds to within seven minutes of a return to Division 1, before two Peter Shirtliff strikes dashed United's promotion dreams. In a pulsating season, Ashurst and Aspin made 54 appearances, Baird top scored on 19 goals.

DIVISION TWO (FINAL LEAGUE POSITION - 4TH)
PLD 42 W 19 D 11 L 12 F 58 A 44 PTS 68

DATE	OPPONENTS	VENUE	SCORE	SCORERS	ATT.
23-Aug	BLACKBURN ROVERS	AWAY	1 - 2	RITCHIE	8,346
25-Aug	STOKE CITY	HOME	2 - 1	SHERIDAN & BAIRD I	13,334
30-Aug	SHEFFIELD UNITED	HOME	0 - 1		18,294
02-Sep	BARNSLEY	AWAY	1 - 0	BAIRD I	6,839
06-Sep	HUDDERSFIELD TOWN	AWAY	1 - 1	SHERIDAN	9,306
13-Sep	READING	HOME	3 - 2	EDWARDS K, RITCHIE & BUCKLEY J	12,248
20-Sep	BRADFORD CITY	AWAY	0 - 2		13,525
27-Sep	HULL CITY	HOME	3 - 0	RITCHIE (PEN), BAIRD I & ORMSBY	13,551
04-Oct	PLYMOUTH ARGYLE	AWAY	1 - 1	BAIRD I	11,923
11-Oct	CRYSTAL PALACE	HOME	3 - 0	SHERIDAN (PEN), ORMSBY & EDWARDS K	14,316
18-Oct	PORTSMOUTH	HOME	3 - 1	SHERIDAN (PEN), RITCHIE & BAIRD I	21,361
25-Oct	GRIMSBY TOWN	AWAY	0 - 0		7,223
01-Nov	SHREWSBURY TOWN	HOME	1 - 0	ASPIN	14,966
08-Nov	MILLWALL	AWAY	0 - 1		6,869
15-Nov	OLDHAM ATHLETIC	HOME	0 - 2		21,052
21-Nov	BIRMINGHAM CITY	AWAY	1 - 2	SHERIDAN	7,836
29-Nov	DERBY COUNTY	HOME	2 - 0	SHERIDAN & EDWARDS K	19,129
06-Dec	WEST BROMWICH ALBION	AWAY	0 - 3		19,853
13-Dec	BRIGHTON & HOVE ALBION	HOME	3 - 1	SHERIDAN, SNODIN I & BAIRD I	12,014
21-Dec	STOKE CITY	AWAY	2 - 7	BAIRD I & SHERIDAN (PEN)	12,358
26-Dec	SUNDERLAND	HOME	1 - 1	O. G. (BENNETT)	21,286
27-Dec	OLDHAM ATHLETIC	AWAY	1 - 0	RITCHIE	8,477
01-Jan	IPSWICH TOWN	AWAY	0 - 2		14,125
03-Jan	HUDDERSFIELD TOWN	HOME	1 - 1	BAIRD I	17,983
24-Jan	BLACKBURN ROVERS	HOME	0 - 0		14,452
07-Feb	SHEFFIELD UNITED	AWAY	0 - 0		12,494
14-Feb	BARNSLEY	HOME	2 - 2	BAIRD I & SHERIDAN	14,216
28-Feb	BRADFORD CITY	HOME	1 - 0	EDWARDS K	21,802
07-Mar	GRIMSBY TOWN	HOME	2 - 0	RITCHIE & SHERIDAN (PEN)	14,270
10-Mar	PORTSMOUTH	AWAY	1 - 1	ADAMS	13,745
21-Mar	CRYSTAL PALACE	AWAY	0 - 1		8,781
28-Mar	PLYMOUTH ARGYLE	HOME	4 - 0	SHERIDAN (PEN) & BAIRD I 3	18,618
04-Apr	MILLWALL	HOME	2 - 0	BAIRD I & RITCHIE	18,304
08-Apr	HULL CITY	AWAY	0 - 0		9,531
14-Apr	SHREWSBURY TOWN	AWAY	2 - 0	SHERIDAN & PEARSON	4,186
18-Apr	IPSWICH TOWN	HOME	3 - 2	McDONALD, SHERIDAN & ORMSBY	24,839
20-Apr	SUNDERLAND	AWAY	1 - 1	PEARSON	14,725
22-Apr	READING	AWAY	1 - 2	PEARSON	7,415
25-Apr	BIRMINGHAM CITY	HOME	4 - 0	SHERIDAN, BAIRD I 2 & EDWARDS K	19,100
02-May	DERBY COUNTY	AWAY	1 - 2	ASHURST	20,087
04-May	WEST BROMWICH ALBION	HOME	3 - 2	SHERIDAN (PEN), PEARSON & ORMSBY	24,688
09-May	BRIGHTON & HOVE ALBION	AWAY	1 - 0	EDWARDS K	8,139
PLAY - OFFS					
14-May	OLDHAM ATHLETIC (SF-1)	HOME	1 - 0	EDWARDS K	29,472
17-May	OLDHAM ATHLETIC (SF-2) *>	AWAY	1 - 2	EDWARDS K	19,216
23-May	CHARLTON ATHLETIC (FI-1)	AWAY	0 - 1		16,680
25-May	CHARLTON ATHLETIC (FI-2)	HOME	1 - 0	ORMSBY	31,395
29-May	CHARLTON ATHLETIC (FR) *^	NEUTRAL	1 - 2	SHERIDAN	18,000
F. A. CUP					
11-Jan	TELFORD UNITED (R3) $	AWAY	2 - 1	BAIRD I 2	6,460
03-Feb	SWINDON TOWN (R4)	AWAY	2 - 1	O. G. (QUINN) & BAIRD I	14,031
21-Feb	QUEENS PARK RANGERS (R5)	HOME	2 - 1	BAIRD I & ORMSBY	31,324
15-Mar	WIGAN ATHLETIC (R6)	AWAY	2 - 0	STILES & ADAMS	12,479
12-Apr	COVENTRY CITY (SF) <*	NEUTRAL	2 - 3	RENNIE & EDWARDS K	51,372
LITTLEWOODS CUP					
23-Sep	OLDHAM ATHLETIC (R2-1)	AWAY	2 - 3	ASPIN & TAYLOR B	5,569
08-Oct	OLDHAM ATHLETIC (R2-2)	HOME	0 - 1		11,447
FULL MEMBERS CUP					
01-Oct	BRADFORD CITY (R1) *	HOME	0 - 1		3,959

LEAGUE AND CUPS
APPEARANCES (SUBSTITUTE)

PLAYER	LEAGUE	PLAY-OFFS	F. A. CUP	LITT. CUP	F. M. CUP	TOTAL
ADAMS	17	5	4			26
AIZLEWOOD	15	5				20
ASHURST	41	5	5	2	1	54
ASPIN	41	5	5	2	1	54
BAIRD I	40	5	4	1		50
BUCKLEY J	6 (3)		0 (1)		1	7 (4)
CASWELL	1					1
DAY	34	5	5	1	1	46
DOIG	2 (2)		1			3 (2)
EDWARDS K	24 (6)	1 (4)	2 (3)	2	1	30 (13)
HADDOCK	10 (1)		0 (1)		1	11 (2)
McDONALD	17	5				22
ORMSBY	33	5	4	1	1	44
PEARSON	18	4	4			26
RENNIE	24		5	2	1	32
RITCHIE	29 (2)	2 (1)	5	2		38 (3)
ROBINSON R	11					11
SHERIDAN	40	5	5	2	1	53
SNODIN I	14					14
STILES	26 (3)	2	5	2	1	36 (3)
SINCLAIR	8			1		9
SWAN P	5 (2)		1		1	7 (2)
TAYLOR B	2	1		1 (1)	1	5 (1)
THOMPSON N	4 (1)			2	0 (1)	6 (2)
WRIGHT T				0 (1)	0 (1)	0 (2)

GOALSCORERS

PLAYER	LEAGUE	PLAY-OFFS	F. A. CUP	LITT. CUP	F. M. CUP	TOTAL
BAIRD I	15		4			19
SHERIDAN	15	1				16
EDWARDS K	6	2	1			9
RITCHIE	7					7
ORMSBY	4	1	1			6
PEARSON	4					4
ADAMS	1		1			2
ASPIN	1			1		2
ASHURST	1					1
BUCKLEY J	1					1
McDONALD	1					1
RENNIE			1			1
SNODIN I	1					1
STILES			1			1
TAYLOR B				1		1
OWN GOALS	1		1			2

KEY :- $ = PLAYED AT THE HAWTHORNS, WEST BROMWICH, < = PLAYED AT HILLSBOROUGH, SHEFFIELD, * = AFTER EXTRA TIME, > = WON ON AWAY GOALS & ^ = PLAYED AT ST. ANDREWS, BIRMINGHAM

Leeds United's escapades during the previous campaign made them strong favourites to gain promotion. Billy Bremner had stirred supporters' emotions and there was a feel-good factor surrounding the club. Offered an extended contract, Bremner readily accepted. Adding to his squad with the arrival of Glynn Snodin (Sheffield Wednesday) and Gary Williams (Aston Villa), somewhat surprisingly Ian Baird and Andy Ritchie departed. With Brendan Ormsby sidelined, Mark Aizlewood took over the captaincy.

Far from looking promotion candidates, the opening weeks were tortuous. Scoring three goals in nine games was not the start supporters expected. Without Baird and Ritchie, John Pearson and Bob Taylor led the line but struggled to impose themselves on opponents. United were indebted to John Sheridan strikes, one a penalty, for victories over Leicester City and West Brom. Selling Keith Edwards to Aberdeen, Bremner purchased Charlton Athletic striker Jim Melrose and Liverpool reserve Ken de Mange. De Mange inspired a 2-0 win on his debut against Manchester City, Glynn Snodin also scoring, but both signings quickly disappeared from the first team set-up.

Following two draws, Snodin scored a brace as United went down 6-3 at Plymouth Argyle. With a third of the season gone and Leeds sliding towards relegation, Bremner sparked a mini-revival with the introduction of reserve striker Peter Swan following an injury to Pearson. Tall and powerful, Swan earned hard-fought draws at Oldham Athletic and Sheffield United, and scored in a 3-2 home victory against Bournemouth, David Rennie notching the winner. Goals by John Stiles and Taylor claimed a 2-1 win over Shrewsbury Town before Bremner altered the course of the season further with the introduction of Derby County striker Bobby Davison and rookie midfielder David Batty.

The pair made their bow in a 4-2 home win against Swindon Town, Davison notching Leeds' second goal. Despite a 3-0 loss at Crystal Palace, Bremner's team suddenly came to life throughout the festive period, winning six consecutive games. Sheridan strikes inspired victories over Birmingham City, Reading, and Huddersfield Town and Batty scored his first senior goal in a terrific 2-1 Boxing Day win at Manchester City, before near capacity crowds watched home triumphs over Middlesbrough and Bradford City. However, an FA Cup third round defeat to Aston Villa ended Leeds' interests in both domestic cup competitions and disappointingly, the coming weeks would see Bremner's charges slide back to patchy form.

Winning two of seven clashes, Pearson returned to partner Davison, scoring in a 4-1 win at West Brom and a 1-0 victory over Ipswich Town, but an injury to Davison, saw Pearson with another strike partner; Ian Baird, who had failed to settle at Portsmouth. Baird marked his return to Elland Road with a winning strike against Plymouth, Taylor sealed a 2-1 win at Aston Villa before a Pearson treble inspired Leeds' biggest victory of the season, 5-0 against Sheffield United. On the cusp of play-off contention, two victories in the final seven games; Baird notching a brace at Swindon and a Sheridan penalty securing a 1-0 win in the final home game against Crystal Palace, summed up an anti-climatic season. Finishing seventh, Mervyn Day made 51 appearances, Sheridan top scored on 14 goals.

1987 - 1988

DIVISION TWO (FINAL LEAGUE POSITION - 7TH)
PLD 44 W 19 D 12 L 13 F 61 A 51 PTS 69

DATE	OPPONENTS	VENUE	SCORE	SCORERS	ATT.
16-Aug	BARNSLEY	AWAY	1 - 1	TAYLOR B	9,778
19-Aug	LEICESTER CITY	HOME	1 - 0	SHERIDAN (PEN)	21,034
22-Aug	READING	HOME	0 - 0		19,286
29-Aug	BRADFORD CITY	AWAY	0 - 0		11,428
31-Aug	WEST BROMWICH ALBION	HOME	1 - 0	SHERIDAN	19,847
05-Sep	IPSWICH TOWN	AWAY	0 - 1		11,163
12-Sep	HULL CITY	HOME	0 - 2		18,205
15-Sep	HUDDERSFIELD TOWN	AWAY	0 - 0		9,085
19-Sep	MIDDLESBROUGH	AWAY	0 - 2		12,051
26-Sep	MANCHESTER CITY	HOME	2 - 0	DE MANGE & SNODIN G	25,358
30-Sep	STOKE CITY	HOME	0 - 0		17,208
03-Oct	BLACKBURN ROVERS	AWAY	1 - 1	TAYLOR B	7,675
10-Oct	ASTON VILLA	HOME	1 - 3	TAYLOR B	20,741
17-Oct	PLYMOUTH ARGYLE	AWAY	3 - 6	TAYLOR B & SNODIN G 2	9,358
20-Oct	OLDHAM ATHLETIC	AWAY	1 - 1	SWAN P	6,312
24-Oct	BOURNEMOUTH	HOME	3 - 2	TAYLOR B, SWAN P & RENNIE	15,253
31-Oct	SHEFFIELD UNITED	AWAY	2 - 1	SNODIN G & SWAN P	12,095
07-Nov	SHREWSBURY TOWN	HOME	2 - 1	STILES & TAYLOR B	13,760
14-Nov	MILLWALL	AWAY	1 - 3	O. G. (McLEARY)	8,014
21-Nov	SWINDON TOWN	HOME	4 - 2	RENNIE, TAYLOR B, DAVISON & HADDOCK	15,457
28-Nov	CRYSTAL PALACE	AWAY	0 - 3		8,749
05-Dec	BIRMINGHAM CITY	HOME	4 - 1	SHERIDAN (PEN), DAVISON, SWAN P & TAYLOR B	15,977
12-Dec	READING	AWAY	1 - 0	SHERIDAN (PEN)	6,505
19-Dec	HUDDERSFIELD TOWN	HOME	3 - 0	SHERIDAN 2 & DAVISON	20,111
26-Dec	MANCHESTER CITY	AWAY	2 - 1	O. G. (REDMOND) & BATTY	30,153
28-Dec	MIDDLESBROUGH	HOME	2 - 0	DAVISON & SWAN P	34,186
01-Jan	BRADFORD CITY	HOME	2 - 0	WILLIAMS G & SNODIN G	36,004
03-Jan	HULL CITY	AWAY	1 - 3	SWAN P	14,694
16-Jan	BARNSLEY	HOME	0 - 2		19,028
30-Jan	WEST BROMWICH ALBION	AWAY	4 - 1	SHERIDAN, WILLIAMS G, PEARSON & DAVISON	9,008
06-Feb	IPSWICH TOWN	HOME	1 - 0	PEARSON	19,564
13-Feb	LEICESTER CITY	AWAY	2 - 3	WILLIAMS G & SHERIDAN (PEN)	11,937
23-Feb	STOKE CITY	AWAY	1 - 2	PEARSON	10,129
27-Feb	BLACKBURN ROVERS	HOME	2 - 2	SHERIDAN (PEN) & SNODIN G	23,843
05-Mar	PLYMOUTH ARGYLE	HOME	1 - 0	BAIRD I	18,115
12-Mar	ASTON VILLA	AWAY	2 - 1	SWAN P & TAYLOR B	19,677
19-Mar	SHEFFIELD UNITED	HOME	5 - 0	SWAN P, PEARSON 3 & SHERIDAN	22,376
26-Mar	BOURNEMOUTH	AWAY	0 - 0		9,147
02-Apr	SHREWSBURY TOWN	AWAY	0 - 1		7,369
06-Apr	MILLWALL	HOME	1 - 2	SHERIDAN (PEN)	24,241
23-Apr	OLDHAM ATHLETIC	HOME	1 - 1	SNODIN G	13,442
30-Apr	SWINDON TOWN	AWAY	2 - 1	BAIRD I 2	8,299
02-May	CRYSTAL PALACE	HOME	1 - 0	SHERIDAN (PEN)	13,217
06-May	BIRMINGHAM CITY	AWAY	0 - 0		6,024

F. A. CUP

DATE	OPPONENTS	VENUE	SCORE	SCORERS	ATT.
09-Jan	ASTON VILLA (R3)	HOME	1 - 2	DAVISON	29,002

LITTLEWOODS CUP

DATE	OPPONENTS	VENUE	SCORE	SCORERS	ATT.
23-Sep	YORK CITY (R2-1)	HOME	1 - 1	SNODIN G	11,555
06-Oct	YORK CITY (R2-2)	AWAY	4 - 0	SHERIDAN 2, TAYLOR B & MUMBY	6,059
28-Oct	OLDHAM ATHLETIC (R3)	HOME	2 - 2	SWAN P 2	15,615
04-Nov	OLDHAM ATHLETIC (R3R) *	AWAY	2 - 4	SNODIN G & TAYLOR B	7,058

SIMOD CUP

DATE	OPPONENTS	VENUE	SCORE	SCORERS	ATT.
25-Nov	SHEFFIELD UNITED (R1)	HOME	3 - 0	TAYLOR B, NOTEMAN & RENNIE	4,425
08-Dec	MILLWALL (R2)	AWAY	0 - 2		5,034

LEAGUE AND CUPS
APPEARANCES (SUBSTITUTE)

PLAYER	LEAGUE	F. A. CUP	LITT. CUP	SIMOD CUP	TOTAL
ADAMS	40	1	3	1	45
AIZLEWOOD	16 (1)				16 (1)
ASHURST	41	1	4	2	48
ASPIN	25 (1)	1	2	1	29 (1)
BAIRD I	10				10
BATTY	22 (1)	1		2	25 (1)
BROCKIE	2				2
BUCKLEY J	0 (1)				0 (1)
DAVISON	15 (1)	1		2	18 (1)
DAY	44	1	4	2	51
DE MANGE	14 (1)		3	2	19 (1)
DOIG	1 (1)		1 (2)		2 (3)
EDWARDS K	4 (4)				4 (4)
GRAYSON	2			1	3
HADDOCK	38 (2)	1	3	2	44 (2)
McDONALD	1		1		2
MAGUIRE	2				2
MELROSE	3 (1)	0 (1)	0 (1)		3 (3)
MUMBY	3 (2)		0 (2)		3 (4)
NOTEMAN	0 (1)			1	1 (1)
PEARSON	21 (7)		2	0 (1)	23 (8)
RENNIE	25 (3)		2	1	28 (3)
SHERIDAN	36 (2)	1	4	1	42 (2)
SNODIN G	33 (2)	1	4	1	39 (2)
STILES	7 (6)		2 (2)	0 (1)	9 (9)
SWAN P	21 (4)		2	1	24 (4)
TAYLOR B	27 (5)	1	4	2	34 (5)
WILLIAMS G	31	1	3		35

GOALSCORERS

PLAYER	LEAGUE	F. A. CUP	LITT. CUP	SIMOD CUP	TOTAL
SHERIDAN	12		2		14
TAYLOR B	9		2	1	12
SWAN P	8		2		10
SNODIN G	7		2		9
DAVISON	5	1			6
PEARSON	6				6
BAIRD I	3				3
WILLIAMS G	3				3
RENNIE	2				2
BATTY	1				1
DE MANGE	1				1
HADDOCK	1				1
MUMBY			1		1
NOTEMAN				1	1
RENNIE				1	1
STILES	1				1
OWN GOALS	2				2

LEEDS PLAYED IN THE MERCANTILE CREDIT FOOTBALL FESTIVAL ON APR. 16TH 1988 AT WEMBLEY VS. NOTTINGHAM FOREST WHERE THEY LOST 0 - 3 (0 - 2). ATTENDANCE WAS MAXIMISED BY THE FOOTBALL LEAGUE AT 20,000. THE TEAM WAS DAY, WILLIAMS G, ADAMS (SNODIN G), AIZLEWOOD, ASHURST, RENNIE, BATTY, SHERIDAN, BAIRD, TAYLOR (PEARSON) & GRAYSON. SUBSTITUTES NOT USED WERE SWAN, STILES & SINCLAIR

KEY :- * = AFTER EXTRA TIME

There was little change in personnel at Elland Road during the close season apart from the arrival of Noel Blake and Vince Hilaire. Determined to start well, Leeds made a dreadful opening, claiming one victory from 12 league fixtures. Bobby Davison and Hilaire secured a 2-0 win against Barnsley, but it was insufficient to save Billy Bremner from the sack 24 hours after guiding his team past Peterborough United in the League Cup. United's greatest skipper had taken the club to within a whisker of top-flight football and an FA Cup final, but sitting second bottom of Division 2, Bremner's tenure was over.

After appointing three legends in the hot seat, board members opted for a manager with no connection to past glory. Sheffield Wednesday boss Howard Wilkinson had proven experience, having guided Notts County and the Owls to Division 2 promotion. His arrival was seen as a coup with Wednesday sitting in the top half of Division 1. An air of optimism filled the press conference announcing his appointment. Ultra-professional, organised, tactically astute and bold, Wilkinson controversially removed pictures of the Don Revie glory years from the club foyer, stating it was time present players made a mark.

Setting an initial objective of clearing the relegation zone, an impressive 10-game unbeaten league run began. Ian Baird secured 2-1 home wins over Hull City and West Brom, before notching a brace in a 4-0 triumph over Stoke City. Davison also found the target against Stoke prior to netting a double during a 3-0 win at Walsall. With confidence restored, despite a 3-2 defeat against Shrewsbury Town, spectators packed Elland Road to see Leeds despatch Blackburn Rovers and Plymouth Argyle 2-0, Baird scoring in both clashes during the festive period, while Hilaire sealed a win over Birmingham City.

A 3-2 defeat at Oxford United and exiting the FA Cup at Nottingham Forest failed to dampen supporters enthusiasm, as a near-capacity crowd watched Leeds' 2-0 home win over Sunderland, John Sheridan despatching his fifth penalty of the season to seal victory. Glynn Snodin's winner at Leicester City kept United climbing to safety, before a season-high 33,000 crowd witnessed a 3-3 thriller against Bradford City. Strikes by Davison and Baird brought a win over Hull City. Baird scored against Portsmouth, but Leeds' 1-0 win over Pompey was notable for the debuts of midfield maestro Gordan Strachan; a £300,000 purchase from Manchester United, and central-defender Chris Fairclough. Pundits questioned the sense in signing 32-year old Strachan, but Wilkinson's judgement would prove exemplary.

Building for the future, players departing included Micky Adams, Peter Swan and Jack Ashurst, whilst Bob Taylor's £200,000 transfer to Bristol City saw Carl Shutt arrive for £50,000 in an exchange deal. Shutt's entry would be explosive, notching a hat-trick against Bournemouth on his debut before an injury sidelined him for the run-in, where Strachan made an immediate impact in the 'Bobby Collins' mould, clinching a 3-2 win at Stoke City before notching a brace in a 3-3 draw at relegated Shrewsbury Town. Finishing tenth, Sergeant Wilko had negotiated phase one of his mission. The hard work would now begin with one objective, a return to top-flight football. Mervyn Day made 52 appearances, Bobby Davison top scored with 17 goals. During May, the city of Leeds mourned the death of Don Revie.

1988 - 1989

DIVISION TWO (FINAL LEAGUE POSITION - 10TH)
PLD 46 W 17 D 16 L 13 F 59 A 50 PTS 67

DATE	OPPONENTS	VENUE	SCORE	SCORERS	ATT.
27-Aug	OXFORD UNITED	HOME	1 - 1	SNODIN G	22,038
03-Sep	PORTSMOUTH	AWAY	0 - 4		15,263
10-Sep	MANCHESTER CITY	HOME	1 - 1	BLAKE No.	23,677
17-Sep	BOURNEMOUTH	AWAY	0 - 0		7,922
21-Sep	BARNSLEY	HOME	2 - 0	DAVISON & HILAIRE	17,370
24-Sep	CHELSEA	HOME	0 - 2		26,080
01-Oct	BRIGHTON & HOVE ALBION	AWAY	1 - 2	BAIRD I	7,109
04-Oct	SUNDERLAND	AWAY	1 - 2	DAVISON	12,671
08-Oct	WATFORD	HOME	0 - 1		15,657
16-Oct	SWINDON TOWN	AWAY	0 - 0		9,234
22-Oct	LEICESTER CITY	HOME	1 - 1	HILAIRE	17,263
26-Oct	BRADFORD CITY	AWAY	1 - 1	DAVISON	13,048
29-Oct	HULL CITY	HOME	2 - 1	SHERIDAN & BAIRD I	17,536
05-Nov	IPSWICH TOWN	AWAY	1 - 0	SHERIDAN (PEN)	11,750
12-Nov	WEST BROMWICH ALBION	HOME	2 - 1	AIZLEWOOD & BAIRD I	20,442
19-Nov	OLDHAM ATHLETIC	AWAY	2 - 2	DAVISON 2	8,824
22-Nov	BIRMINGHAM CITY	AWAY	0 - 0		6,168
26-Nov	STOKE CITY	HOME	4 - 0	BAIRD I 2, DAVISON & SHERIDAN (PEN)	19,933
03-Dec	WALSALL	AWAY	3 - 0	DAVISON 2 & WHITLOW	6,885
10-Dec	SHREWSBURY TOWN	HOME	2 - 3	SHERIDAN (PEN) & DAVISON	19,967
17-Dec	CRYSTAL PALACE	AWAY	0 - 0		9,847
26-Dec	BLACKBURN ROVERS	HOME	2 - 0	BAIRD I & DAVISON	31,622
31-Dec	PLMOUTH ARGYLE	HOME	2 - 0	BAIRD I & SNODIN G	24,043
02-Jan	MANCHESTER CITY	AWAY	0 - 0		33,034
14-Jan	BIRMINGHAM CITY	HOME	1 - 0	HILAIRE	21,937
21-Jan	OXFORD UNITED	AWAY	2 - 3	BLAKE No. & HILAIRE	7,928
04-Feb	SUNDERLAND	HOME	2 - 0	DAVISON & SHERIDAN (PEN)	31,985
11-Feb	WATFORD	AWAY	1 - 1	PEARSON	13,439
18-Feb	LEICESTER CITY	AWAY	2 - 1	DAVISON & SNODIN G	14,151
25-Feb	SWINDON TOWN	HOME	0 - 0		22,651
01-Mar	BRADFORD CITY	HOME	3 - 3	HILAIRE, BAIRD I & BLAKE No.	33,325
05-Mar	WEST BROMWICH ALBION	AWAY	1 - 2	ADAMS	15,914
11-Mar	IPSWICH TOWN	HOME	2 - 4	HILAIRE & BLAKE No.	19,639
14-Mar	HULL CITY	AWAY	2 - 1	BAIRD I & DAVISON	8,887
19-Mar	BARNSLEY	AWAY	2 - 2	AIZLEWOOD & SHERIDAN (PEN)	11,578
25-Mar	PORTSMOUTH	HOME	1 - 0	BAIRD I	27,049
27-Mar	BLACKBURN ROVERS	AWAY	0 - 2		11,533
01-Apr	BOURNEMOUTH	HOME	3 - 0	SHUTT 3	21,095
05-Apr	CRYSTAL PALACE	HOME	1 - 2	SHUTT	25,604
09-Apr	PLMOUTH ARGYLE	AWAY	0 - 1		9,365
15-Apr	BRIGHTON & HOVE ALBION	HOME	1 - 0	WILLIAMS A	14,915
22-Apr	CHELSEA	AWAY	0 - 1		30,337
29-Apr	STOKE CITY	AWAY	3 - 2	SHERIDAN (PEN), DAVISON & STRACHAN	9,051
01-May	WALSALL	HOME	1 - 0	AIZLEWOOD	13,280
06-May	OLDHAM ATHLETIC	HOME	0 - 0		14,459
13-May	SHREWSBURY TOWN	AWAY	3 - 3	STRACHAN 2 (1 PEN) & RENNIE	4,693

F. A. CUP

07-Jan	BRIGHTON & HOVE ALBION (R3)	AWAY	2 - 1	BAIRD I 2	10,900
28-Jan	NOTTINGHAM FOREST (R4)	AWAY	0 - 2		28,107

LITTLEWOODS CUP

27-Sep	PETERBOROUGH UNITED (R2-1)	AWAY	2 - 1	SNODIN G & BAIRD I	4,979
12-Oct	PETERBOROUGH UNITED (R2-2)	HOME	3 - 1	DAVISON, HILAIRE & SHERIDAN (PEN)	8,904
02-Nov	LUTON TOWN (R3)	HOME	0 - 2		19,447

SIMOD CUP

09-Nov	SHREWSBURY TOWN (R1)	HOME	3 - 1	AIZLEWOOD & DAVISON 2	3,220
29-Nov	MILLWALL (R2)	AWAY	0 - 2		4,242

LEAGUE AND CUPS
APPEARANCES (SUBSTITUTE)

PLAYER	LEAGUE	F. A. CUP	LITT. CUP	SIMOD CUP	TOTAL
ADAMS	15 (1)	1	1		17 (1)
AIZLEWOOD	34 (4)	1	3	2	40 (4)
ANDREWS	1				1
ASHURST	6 (1)				6 (1)
ASPIN	31 (2)	2	2	2	37 (2)
BAIRD I	43	2	3	2	50
BATTY	25 (5)	1	3	1	30 (5)
BLAKE No.	44	2	3	2	51
DAVISON	37 (2)	1 (1)	2	2	42 (3)
DAY	45	2	3	2	52
FAIRCLOUGH	11				11
HADDOCK	8 (4)	0 (1)	0 (1)		8 (6)
HILAIRE	42	2	3	2	49
KERR	1 (2)				1 (2)
MUMBY	0 (1)				0 (1)
ORMSBY	1				1
PEARSON	6 (27)	0 (1)	1 (1)	0 (1)	7 (30)
RENNIE	30 (3)	2	3	2	37 (3)
SHERIDAN	38 (2)	2	2	2	44 (2)
SHUTT	3				3
SNODIN G	33 (2)	2	3	1	39 (2)
SPEED	1				1
STILES	4 (6)				4 (6)
STRACHAN	11				11
SWAN P	1	1			2
TAYLOR B	2 (4)			0 (1)	2 (5)
WHITLOW	18 (2)			2	20 (2)
WILLIAMS A	7 (11)	1			8 (11)
WILLIAMS G	8	0 (1)	1		9 (1)

GOALSCORERS

PLAYER	LEAGUE	F. A. CUP	LITT. CUP	SIMOD CUP	TOTAL
DAVISON	14		1	2	17
BAIRD I	10	2	1		13
SHERIDAN	7		1		8
HILAIRE	6		1		7
AIZLEWOOD	3			1	4
BLAKE No.	4				4
SHUTT	4				4
SNODIN G	3		1		4
STRACHAN	3				3
ADAMS	1				1
PEARSON	1				1
RENNIE	1				1
WHITLOW	1				1
WILLIAMS A	1				1

A wind of change swept through Elland Road in a summer shake-up of Howard Wilkinson's squad. Investing £3 million, season ticket sales reflected United's promotion favourite tag. New arrivals included Vinnie Jones (Wimbledon), John Hendrie (Bradford City), Mel Sterland and John McClelland (Rangers). John Sheridan, Mark Aizlewood, Neil Aspin, David Rennie and John Stiles departed.

A high-risk strategy had been adopted, but Wilkinson's revamped side quickly settled after an opening day 5-2 defeat at Newcastle United. A fortuitous last minute own goal by Gary Parkinson brought a 2-1 win over Middlesbrough, heralding an unbeaten 15-match league run. Consecutive wins at Hull City; Davison scoring the only goal, Swindon Town; Gordon Strachan notching a hat-trick, and Oxford United; Sterland securing victory, was followed up with further success after Jones sealed a 1-0 win at West Ham.

Davison in particular was on fire, scoring in five straight games, including winning strikes against Wolves, Bradford City and Plymouth Argyle. On target with a penalty in the 2-1 win over Argyle was Strachan. The Scot converted a spot kick in a 3-0 canter against Bournemouth but a third penalty in as many games proved a consolation as Leeds' unbeaten run ended in a 4-3 thriller at Leicester City. Strachan's penalty treble matched Jack Milburn's feat in 1935/36 and Johnny Giles' in 1972/73.

Ten wins in 17 league games was an excellent start. Challenging at the top, Wilkinson was utilising his squad fully, midfielder Andy Williams coming up trumps with a winner against Watford. Losing at West Brom, Leeds bounced back during the Christmas build-up. Baird secured a hard-fought win over Newcastle, Carl Shutt, in his first start with Davison injured, opened the scoring in a win at Middlesbrough prior to John Hendrie striking in a comfortable 3-0 victory against Brighton, placing Leeds top for the first time.

A Boxing Day draw at Sheffield United a New Year Day stalemate against Oldham Athletic kept Leeds firmly in the frame, but out of both domestic cups, and with Baird scoring only four goals in 24 league appearances, Wilkinson re-entered the transfer market, signing prolific striker Lee Chapman from Nottingham Forest for £400,000. Chapman made a scoring debut in a 2-1 win at Blackburn Rovers, while Baird joined Middlesbrough in a £500,000 deal. The Leeds boss also acquired Imre Varadi and Chris Kamara while Noel Blake and Vince Hilaire departed. United's match winner at Rovers was Strachan, and the Leeds skipper found the target again in a 2-0 win over Stoke City, before settling a sensational 4-3 triumph against Hull City in the last minute.

Charging towards promotion, Chapman braces secured a 4-2 win at Oxford United and a 3-2 triumph over West Ham. Seven points clear of third placed Swindon, another Chapman strike brought a 2-0 win over Portsmouth but with nine games remaining, a dip in form saw a substantial point's lead eroded. Facing nearest challengers Sheffield United at Easter, a Strachan double set up a 4-0 triumph, rookie midfielder Gary Speed sealing a brilliant win, but dropped points against Brighton and Barnsley meant Leeds had to overcome the challenge of Sheffield and Newcastle United in a race for promotion.

Strachan had been the key player throughout a nerve-jangling campaign and if one moment typified his impact, it came in the closing minutes of Leeds' penultimate game at home to Leicester City. With the scores level and tension unbearable, Strachan's sensational 18-yard strike secured a 2-1 victory. Leeds clinched promotion and the Division 2 title at Bournemouth with a Chapman header. Eight seasons in the wilderness were over as top-flight football beckoned. In a memorable season, Strachan made 53 appearances and top scored with 18 goals.

1989 - 1990

DIVISION TWO (FINAL LEAGUE POSITION - 1ST)
PLD 46 W 24 D 13 L 9 F 79 A 52 PTS 85

DATE	OPPONENTS	VENUE	SCORE	SCORERS	ATT.
19-Aug	NEWCASTLE UNITED	AWAY	2 - 5	DAVISON & BAIRD I	24,482
23-Aug	MIDDLESBROUGH	HOME	2 - 1	DAVISON & O. G. (PARKINSON)	25,004
26-Aug	BLACKBURN ROVERS	HOME	1 - 1	FAIRCLOUGH	25,045
02-Sep	STOKE CITY	AWAY	1 - 1	STRACHAN	10,915
09-Sep	IPSWICH TOWN	HOME	1 - 1	JONES V	22,972
16-Sep	HULL CITY	AWAY	1 - 0	DAVISON	11,620
23-Sep	SWINDON TOWN	HOME	4 - 0	STRACHAN 3 (1 PEN) & DAVISON	21,694
27-Sep	OXFORD UNITED	HOME	2 - 1	DAVISON & STERLAND	24,097
30-Sep	PORT VALE	AWAY	0 - 0		11,156
07-Oct	WEST HAM UNITED	AWAY	1 - 0	JONES V	23,539
14-Oct	SUNDERLAND	HOME	2 - 0	DAVISON & FAIRCLOUGH	27,815
17-Oct	PORTSMOUTH	AWAY	3 - 3	DAVISON, WHITLOW & STERLAND	10,260
21-Oct	WOLVERHAMPTON WANDERERS	HOME	1 - 0	DAVISON	28,204
28-Oct	BRADFORD CITY	AWAY	1 - 0	DAVISON	12,527
01-Nov	PLYMOUTH ARGYLE	HOME	2 - 1	STRACHAN (PEN) & DAVISON	26,791
04-Nov	BOURNEMOUTH	HOME	3 - 0	BAIRD I, STRACHAN (PEN) & FAIRCLOUGH	26,484
11-Nov	LEICESTER CITY	AWAY	3 - 4	BAIRD I, WILLIAMS A & STRACHAN (PEN)	18,032
18-Nov	WATFORD	HOME	2 - 1	FAIRCLOUGH & WILLIAMS A	26,921
25-Nov	WEST BROMWICH ALBION	AWAY	1 - 2	FAIRCLOUGH	15,116
02-Dec	NEWCASTLE UNITED	HOME	1 - 0	BAIRD I	31,715
09-Dec	MIDDLESBROUGH	AWAY	2 - 0	SHUTT & FAIRCLOUGH	19,686
16-Dec	BRIGHTON & HOVE ALBION	HOME	3 - 0	STRACHAN, HENDRIE & JONES V	24,070
26-Dec	SHEFFIELD UNITED	AWAY	2 - 2	STERLAND & SHUTT	31,254
30-Dec	BARNSLEY	AWAY	0 - 1		14,481
01-Jan	OLDHAM ATHLETIC	HOME	1 - 1	HENDRIE	30,217
13-Jan	BLACKBURN ROVERS	AWAY	2 - 1	CHAPMAN & STRACHAN	14,485
20-Jan	STOKE CITY	HOME	2 - 0	STRACHAN (PEN) & HENDRIE	29,318
04-Feb	SWINDON TOWN	AWAY	2 - 3	STRACHAN (PEN) & HENDRIE	16,208
10-Feb	HULL CITY	HOME	4 - 3	HENDRIE, JONES V, VARADI & STRACHAN	29,977
17-Feb	IPSWICH TOWN	AWAY	2 - 2	CHAPMAN 2	17,102
24-Feb	WEST BROMWICH ALBION	HOME	2 - 2	KAMARA & CHAPMAN	30,004
03-Mar	WATFORD	AWAY	0 - 1		13,468
07-Mar	PORT VALE	HOME	0 - 0		28,756
10-Mar	OXFORD UNITED	AWAY	4 - 2	CHAPMAN 2, VARADI & FAIRCLOUGH	8,397
17-Mar	WEST HAM UNITED	HOME	3 - 2	CHAPMAN 2 & STRACHAN	32,536
20-Mar	SUNDERLAND	AWAY	1 - 0	STERLAND	17,851
24-Mar	PORTSMOUTH	HOME	2 - 0	JONES V & CHAPMAN	27,600
31-Mar	WOLVERHAMPTON WANDERERS	AWAY	0 - 1		22,419
07-Apr	BRADFORD CITY	HOME	1 - 1	SPEED	32,316
10-Apr	PLYMOUTH ARGYLE	AWAY	1 - 1	CHAPMAN	11,382
13-Apr	OLDHAM ATHLETIC	AWAY	1 - 3	DAVISON	16,292
16-Apr	SHEFFIELD UNITED	HOME	4 - 0	STRACHAN 2, CHAPMAN & SPEED	32,727
21-Apr	BRIGHTON & HOVE ALBION	AWAY	2 - 2	SPEED & O. G. (CHAPMAN I)	11,359
25-Apr	BARNSLEY	HOME	1 - 2	FAIRCLOUGH	31,700
28-Apr	LEICESTER CITY	HOME	2 - 1	STERLAND & STRACHAN	32,597
05-May	BOURNEMOUTH	AWAY	1 - 0	CHAPMAN	9,918

F. A. CUP

06-Jan	IPSWICH TOWN (R3)	HOME	0 - 1		26,766

LITTLEWOODS CUP

19-Sep	OLDHAM ATHLETIC (R2-1)	AWAY	1 - 2	STRACHAN	8,415
03-Oct	OLDHAM ATHLETIC (R2-2)	HOME	1 - 2	FAIRCLOUGH	18,092

ZENITH DATA SYSTEMS CUP

07-Nov	BLACKBURN ROVERS (R1)	HOME	1 - 0	DAVISON	5,070
28-Nov	BARNSLEY (R2)	AWAY	2 - 1	STRACHAN (PEN) & WILLIAMS A	6,136
19-Dec	STOKE CITY (R3) *	AWAY	2 - 2	SHUTT 2	5,792
17-Jan	ASTON VILLA (SF-NORTH)	AWAY	0 - 2		17,543

LEAGUE AND CUPS
APPEARANCES (SUBSTITUTE)

PLAYER	LEAGUE	F. A. CUP	LITT. CUP	ZEN. CUP	TOTAL
BAIRD I	23 (1)	1	2	4	30 (1)
BATTY	39 (3)	1	2	4	46 (3)
BEGLIN	18 (1)			1	19 (1)
BLAKE No.	7		1 (1)	2	10 (1)
CHAPMAN	21				21
DAVISON	25 (4)		2	2	29 (4)
DAY	44	1	2	3	50
EDWARDS N				1	1
FAIRCLOUGH	42	1	1 (1)	3	47 (1)
HADDOCK	40	1	2	4	47
HENDRIE	22 (5)	1	1	2	26 (5)
HILAIRE	0 (2)				0 (2)
JONES V	43 (2)	1	2	4	50 (2)
KAMARA	10 (1)				10 (1)
KERR	2 (3)	1		0 (3)	3 (6)
McCLELLAND	3				3
O'DONNELL	0 (1)				0 (1)
PEARSON	2 (5)	0 (1)		1 (1)	3 (7)
SHUTT	6 (15)	1		0 (2)	7 (17)
SNODIN G	3 (1)	0 (1)			3 (2)
SPEED	12 (12)		0 (1)	0 (1)	12 (14)
STERLAND	41 (1)	1	2	3	47 (1)
STRACHAN	46	1	2	4	53
THOMAS M	3				3
TURNER C	2				2
VARADI	12 (1)				12 (1)
WHITLOW	27 (2)		2	4	33 (2)
WILLIAMS A	13 (3)		1 (1)	2	16 (4)

GOALSCORERS

PLAYER	LEAGUE	F. A. CUP	LITT. CUP	ZEN. CUP	TOTAL
STRACHAN	16		1	1	18
CHAPMAN	12				12
DAVISON	11			1	12
FAIRCLOUGH	8		1		9
HENDRIE	5				5
JONES V	5				5
STERLAND	5				5
BAIRD I	4				4
SHUTT	2			2	4
SPEED	3				3
WILLIAMS A	2			1	3
VARADI	2				2
KAMARA	1				1
WHITLOW	1				1
OWN GOALS	2				2

KEY :- * = AFTER EXTRA TIME & WON 5 - 4 ON PENALTIES

Back among the elite, Howard Wilkinson strengthened his squad, adding John Lukic (Arsenal), Gary McAllister (Leicester City) and Chris Whyte (West Brom) to a growing array of talent including young midfielders David Batty and Gary Speed. With a total outlay of £6 million, Wilkinson had broken the club's transfer record by bringing back Lukic to Elland Road for £1 million. Departures included John Hendrie, Brendon Ormsby and cult hero Vinnie Jones, with McAllister slotting into a strong midfield quartet alongside Gordon Strachan, Batty and Speed.

United made a promising start despite the odd setback among the first 10 games. Imre Varadi edged an opening day 3-2 win at Everton and was on target again in Leeds' first win at Elland Road, 3-0 against Norwich City; Chapman grabbing a brace, whilst Strachan secured a 2-0 win at Sheffield United, ironically Jones debut for the Blades. Attacking from both flanks, Wilkinson's team gained acclaim for entertaining football that was bringing results.

Following a defeat at Queens Park Rangers, United were unbeaten until New Years Day, eight victories in 10 games moving Leeds up the table. Both Chapman and Strachan found the target in three-goal wins over Nottingham Forest, Manchester City and Derby County, and Shutt secured home triumphs against Southampton and Everton, before right-back Mel Sterland demonstrated his eye for goal in victories against Sunderland, Chelsea and Wimbledon. The Boxing Day win over Chelsea was particularly impressive, Chapman notching a brace in a 4-1 win.

Entering the New Year, despite defeats at Liverpool and Norwich City, United were still among the chasing pack and making progress in both cup competitions. Overcoming Barnsley in the FA Cup, they began a titanic battle against champions-elect Arsenal, whilst moving into the League Cup semi-finals for the first time since 1978/79. Speed strikes helped secure early round success against Leicester City and Oldham Athletic, before Chapman and McAllister eased Leeds past Queens Park Rangers and Aston Villa. Chapman's brace ensuring a 4-1 win over Villa and a semi-final clash with Manchester United.

Playing just one league clash in February, a 0-0 at Tottenham, for supporters, interest concentrated on cup battles as Wembley beckoned for the first time in nearly two decades. Disappointingly, both avenues closed when the Gunners claimed a 2-1 victory after four engrossing clashes, while Alex Ferguson's team won a hard-fought semi-final 3-1 on aggregate. Both match-ups however, proved that Leeds could compete with the best but the campaign had not been without problems; notably at left-back with Glynn Snodin, Mike Whitlow and Chris Kamara all suffering injury. The jinx continued against Manchester United for Peter Haddock, ending his career.

The season's final months saw rip-roaring action. Forming a solid backbone in defence were Chris Fairclough and Chris Whyte; both also found the target, Fairclough sealing 2-1 victories over Luton Town and Chelsea, while Whyte scored in a 2-0 win against Coventry City. United's leading striker Chapman grabbed the headlines in the closing nine games with 10 further goals, including a brace as Leeds defeated Sunderland 5-0 and a hat-trick in an astonishing clash at home to Liverpool when Leeds 4-0 behind, lost 5-4. Further doubles arrived in a 5-2 win against Aston Villa prior to a 4-3 defeat at Nottingham Forest in the final game.

Leeds had surpassed everyone's expectations, finishing fourth. It was an incredible renaissance. Capping a memorable season, Strachan won the Football Writers Player of the Year Award. Scoring 31 goals in all competitions made Chapman the leading Division 1 sharpshooter, and alongside McAllister and Sterland made 55 appearances. Placing Chapman's scoring exploits into context for Leeds United, only Tom Jennings and John Charles have exceeded his total.

DIVISION ONE (FINAL LEAGUE POSITION - 4TH)
PLD 38 W 19 D 7 L 12 F 65 A 47 PTS 64

DATE	OPPONENTS	VENUE	SCORE	SCORERS	ATT.
25-Aug	EVERTON	AWAY	3 - 2	FAIRCLOUGH, SPEED & VARADI	34,412
28-Aug	MANCHESTER UNITED	HOME	0 - 0		29,172
01-Sep	NORWICH CITY	HOME	3 - 0	CHAPMAN 2 & VARADI	25,684
08-Sep	LUTON TOWN	AWAY	0 - 1		10,185
15-Sep	TOTTENHAM HOTSPUR	HOME	0 - 2		31,342
23-Sep	SHEFFIELD UNITED	AWAY	2 - 0	PEARSON & STRACHAN	26,078
29-Sep	ARSENAL	HOME	2 - 2	CHAPMAN & STRACHAN (PEN)	30,085
06-Oct	CRYSTAL PALACE	AWAY	1 - 1	SPEED	21,676
20-Oct	QUEENS PARK RANGERS	HOME	2 - 3	CHAPMAN & WHYTE C	27,443
27-Oct	ASTON VILLA	AWAY	0 - 0		24,219
03-Nov	NOTTINGHAM FOREST	HOME	3 - 1	CHAPMAN, STRACHAN (PEN) & McALLISTER	30,409
11-Nov	MANCHESTER CITY	AWAY	3 - 2	CHAPMAN, SHUTT & STRACHAN	27,782
17-Nov	DERBY COUNTY	HOME	3 - 0	CHAPMAN, STRACHAN & SPEED	27,868
24-Nov	COVENTRY CITY	AWAY	1 - 1	CHAPMAN	16,183
01-Dec	SOUTHAMPTON	HOME	2 - 1	FAIRCLOUGH & SHUTT	29,341
08-Dec	MANCHESTER UNITED	AWAY	1 - 1	STERLAND	40,927
16-Dec	EVERTON	HOME	2 - 0	STRACHAN (PEN) & SHUTT	27,775
23-Dec	SUNDERLAND	AWAY	1 - 0	STERLAND	23,773
26-Dec	CHELSEA	HOME	4 - 1	STERLAND, CHAPMAN 2 & WHITLOW	30,893
29-Dec	WIMBLEDON	HOME	3 - 0	CHAPMAN, SPEED & STERLAND	29,292
01-Jan	LIVERPOOL	AWAY	0 - 3		36,975
12-Jan	NORWICH CITY	AWAY	0 - 2		17,786
19-Jan	LUTON TOWN	HOME	2 - 1	STRACHAN (PEN) & FAIRCLOUGH	27,010
02-Feb	TOTTENHAM HOTSPUR	AWAY	0 - 0		32,253
02-Mar	SOUTHAMPTON	AWAY	0 - 2		16,585
09-Mar	COVENTRY CITY	HOME	2 - 0	DAVISON & WHYTE C	28,880
17-Mar	ARSENAL	AWAY	0 - 2		26,218
23-Mar	CRYSTAL PALACE	HOME	1 - 2	SPEED	28,556
30-Mar	CHELSEA	AWAY	2 - 1	SHUTT & FAIRCLOUGH	17,585
02-Apr	SUNDERLAND	HOME	5 - 0	CHAPMAN 2, SPEED 2 & SHUTT	28,132
06-Apr	WIMBLEDON	AWAY	1 - 0	CHAPMAN	6,800
10-Apr	MANCHESTER CITY	HOME	1 - 2	McALLISTER	28,757
13-Apr	LIVERPOOL	HOME	4 - 5	CHAPMAN 3 & SHUTT	31,460
17-Apr	QUEENS PARK RANGERS	AWAY	1 - 0	SHUTT	10,998
23-Apr	DERBY COUNTY	AWAY	1 - 0	SHUTT	12,666
04-May	ASTON VILLA	HOME	5 - 2	O. G. (PRICE), CHAPMAN 2, WHYTE C & SHUTT	29,188
08-May	SHEFFIELD UNITED	HOME	2 - 1	STERLAND & SHUTT	28,978
11-May	NOTTINGHAM FOREST	AWAY	3 - 4	CHAPMAN 2 & SHUTT	25,067

F. A. CUP

DATE	OPPONENTS	VENUE	SCORE	SCORERS	ATT.
06-Jan	BARNSLEY (R3)	AWAY	1 - 1	STERLAND	22,424
09-Jan	BARNSLEY (R3R)	HOME	4 - 0	O. G. (SMITH), CHAPMAN, McALLISTER & STRACHAN (PEN)	19,773
27-Jan	ARSENAL (R4)	AWAY	0 - 0		30,905
30-Jan	ARSENAL (R4R) *	HOME	1 - 1	CHAPMAN	27,753
13-Feb	ARSENAL (R42R) *	AWAY	0 - 0		30,433
16-Feb	ARSENAL (R43R)	HOME	1 - 2	CHAPMAN	27,190

RUMBELOWS CUP

DATE	OPPONENTS	VENUE	SCORE	SCORERS	ATT.
26-Sep	LEICESTER CITY (R2-1)	AWAY	0 - 1		13,774
10-Oct	LEICESTER CITY (R2-2)	HOME	3 - 0	O. G. (WALSH), SPEED & STRACHAN	19,090
31-Oct	OLDHAM ATHLETIC (R3)	HOME	2 - 0	CHAPMAN & SPEED	26,327
27-Nov	QUEENS PARK RANGERS (R4)	AWAY	3 - 0	McALLISTER, FAIRCLOUGH & CHAPMAN	15,832
16-Jan	ASTON VILLA (R5)	HOME	4 - 1	CHAPMAN 2, McALLISTER & SPEED	28,176
10-Feb	MANCHESTER UNITED (SF-1)	AWAY	1 - 2	WHYTE C	34,050
24-Feb	MANCHESTER UNITED (SF-2)	HOME	0 - 1		32,014

ZENITH DATA SYSTEMS CUP

DATE	OPPONENTS	VENUE	SCORE	SCORERS	ATT.
19-Dec	WOLVERHAMPTON WANDERERS (R2)	AWAY	2 - 1	VARADI & McALLISTER	11,080
22-Jan	DERBY COUNTY (R3)	HOME	2 - 1	SHUTT & CHAPMAN	6,334
20-Feb	MANCHESTER CITY (SF-NORTH) *	HOME	2 - 0	WILLIAMS A & STRACHAN	11,898
19-Mar	EVERTON (FI-NORTH FIRST LEG) *	HOME	3 - 3	STERLAND & CHAPMAN 2	13,387
21-Mar	EVERTON (FI-NORTH SECOND LEG) *	AWAY	1 - 3	STERLAND	12,603

LEAGUE AND CUPS
APPEARANCES (SUBSTITUTE)

PLAYER	LEAGUE	F. A. CUP	RUMB. CUP	ZEN. CUP	TOTAL
BATTY	37	6	6	4	53
BEGLIN				1	1
CHAPMAN	38	6	7	4	55
DAVISON	2 (3)	0 (2)		1 (2)	3 (7)
DAY			1	1	2
FAIRCLOUGH	34	6	7	4	51
HADDOCK	10 (5)	3	4 (1)	2	19 (6)
JONES V	1				1
KAMARA	5 (2)		1 (1)		6 (3)
KERR				0 (1)	0 (1)
LUKIC	38	6	6	4	54
McALLISTER	38	6	7	4	55
McCLELLAND	3	2			5
PEARSON	4 (9)	1 (3)	2 (3)	1	8 (15)
SHUTT	25 (3)	5	3 (1)	3 (1)	36 (5)
SNODIN G	14 (6)	2 (1)	2 (1)	2	20 (8)
SPEED	35 (3)	6	7	3 (2)	51 (5)
STERLAND	38	6	6	5	55
STRACHAN	34	6	7	5	52
VARADI	5 (1)		1	1 (1)	7 (2)
WHITLOW	14 (4)	1 (3)	2 (1)	3	20 (8)
WHYTE C	38	4	7	4	53
WILLIAMS A	5 (7)		1 (1)	3 (2)	9 (10)

GOALSCORERS

PLAYER	LEAGUE	F. A. CUP	RUMB. CUP	ZEN. CUP	TOTAL
CHAPMAN	21	3	4	3	31
SHUTT	10			1	11
SPEED	7		3		10
STRACHAN	7	1	1	1	10
STERLAND	5	1		2	8
McALLISTER	2	1	2	1	6
FAIRCLOUGH	4		1		5
WHYTE C	3		1		4
VARADI	2			1	3
DAVISON	1				1
PEARSON	1				1
WHITLOW	1				1
WILLIAMS A				1	1
OWN GOALS	1	1	1		3

KEY :- * = AFTER EXTRA TIME

Building on a tremendous season back in top-flight football, Howard Wilkinson bolstered his squad with £4.2 million of talent, spending a club-record £1.6 million on Southampton striker Rod Wallace and £1.3 million on Chelsea defender Tony Dorigo. Other signings included Steve Hodge (Tottenham) and in a joint deal, Jon Newsome and David Wetherall (Sheffield Wednesday).

Dark horses for the championship, Leeds kicked off with a win against Nottingham Forest, courtesy of a Gary McAllister strike, heralding an unbeaten 10-game run. A Gary Speed special highlighted a 4-0 win at Southampton prior to Lee Chapman securing hard-fought draws against Manchester United and Arsenal. A spectacular Dorigo strike began a canter against Manchester City, while Hodge ended 18 years without a triumph against Liverpool. Though unbeaten, Leeds trailed Manchester United by six points, but after a last-gasp defeat at Crystal Palace, Hodge and Mel Sterland scored braces in a bizarre 4-3 win over Sheffield United, after leading 4-0. A McAllister rocket sealed a 4-2 victory at Notts County before an own goal by Oldham Athletic defender Brian Kilcline sent Leeds top for the first time since 1974.

Injured for seven matches, Wallace returned with a goal blitz in consecutive wins over Queens Park Rangers, Aston Villa, Everton and Luton Town. However, four draws during the festive fixtures saw Alex Ferguson's team, seeking a first title since 1966/67, ahead by two points with two games advantage, and the deficit could have been greater had Sterland not stroked home a late penalty in the first of a Roses trilogy. Following a 3-1 victory at West Ham, attention turned to cup action, but in a tale of woe for the Yorkshire side, the Red Devils won a League Cup quarter-final clash 3-1, before edging an FA Cup tie. Sandwiched between the Roses battles, Leeds enjoyed a dazzling televised triumph, thumping Sheffield Wednesday 6-1, Chapman notching a hat-trick. The result was Leeds' biggest away victory since defeating Blackpool 7-3 in 1930, a season when they suffered relegation!

Concentrating on the league, one victory in four games, against Notts County; a clash that included a rare David Batty goal, illustrated a lack of cutting edge as Oldham ended Leeds' 16-match unbeaten run, a game that saw Eric Cantona's debut. The mercurial Frenchman had signed on loan and inspired a 2-0 win over Luton before McAllister sealed a 3-1 victory at Tottenham. With 10 games to go, each match was getting more significant. Following a heavy defeat at Queens Park Rangers, Chapman's treble brought a 5-1 mauling against Wimbledon, but Manchester City delivered a crushing 4-0 defeat with five games remaining. Now Leeds were a point behind having played two games more, but the red-hot favourites faced four games in eight days.

During key Easter fixtures, Cantona's 'wonder goal' sealed a 3-0 win over Chelsea, before a tenacious draw at Liverpool and a 2-0 win against Coventry City, hours after Manchester United lost to Nottingham Forest, edged Leeds ahead having played an extra match. Astonishingly, relegation-bound West Ham defeated Ferguson's side, enabling Leeds to take the ascendancy with two games remaining. In a madcap clash at Sheffield United, Wallace, Newsome and a Brian Gayle own goal secured a 3-2 win and a third title with Liverpool defeating Manchester United.

Playing with panache and power, Leeds had doggedly hung in until the Old Trafford club cracked. Wallace claimed a win on a day of celebration at Elland Road to complete an astounding campaign when the lead between the top-two changed hands seven times before Wilkinson's team triumphed. John Lukic was the only ever-present in all competitions, Chapman top scored with 20 goals. Sergeant Wilko collected the Manager of the Year award.

1991 - 1992

DIVISION ONE (FINAL LEAGUE POSITION - 1ST)
PLD 42 W 22 D 16 L 4 F 74 A 37 PTS 82

DATE	OPPONENTS	VENUE	SCORE	SCORERS	ATT.
20-Aug	NOTTINGHAM FOREST	HOME	1 - 0	McALLISTER	29,457
24-Aug	SHEFFIELD WEDNESDAY	HOME	1 - 1	HODGE	30,260
28-Aug	SOUTHAMPTON	AWAY	4 - 0	SPEED 2, STRACHAN 2 (2 PENS)	15,862
31-Aug	MANCHESTER UNITED	AWAY	1 - 1	CHAPMAN	43,778
03-Sep	ARSENAL	HOME	2 - 2	STRACHAN (PEN) & CHAPMAN	29,396
07-Sep	MANCHESTER CITY	HOME	3 - 0	DORIGO, BATTY & STRACHAN (PEN)	29,986
14-Sep	CHELSEA	AWAY	1 - 0	SHUTT	23,439
18-Sep	COVENTRY CITY	AWAY	0 - 0		15,488
21-Sep	LIVERPOOL	HOME	1 - 0	HODGE	32,917
28-Sep	NORWICH CITY	AWAY	2 - 2	DORIGO & SPEED	15,828
01-Oct	CRYSTAL PALACE	AWAY	0 - 1		18,298
05-Oct	SHEFFIELD UNITED	HOME	4 - 3	HODGE 2 & STERLAND 2 (1 PEN)	28,362
19-Oct	NOTTS COUNTY	AWAY	4 - 2	CHAPMAN, HODGE, WHYTE C & McALLISTER	12,964
26-Oct	OLDHAM ATHLETIC	HOME	1 - 0	O. G. (KILCLINE)	28,199
02-Nov	WIMBLEDON	AWAY	0 - 0		7,025
16-Nov	QUEENS PARK RANGERS	HOME	2 - 0	STERLAND & WALLACE Ro.	27,087
24-Nov	ASTON VILLA	AWAY	4 - 1	WALLACE Ro., STERLAND & CHAPMAN 2	23,713
30-Nov	EVERTON	HOME	1 - 0	WALLACE Ro.	30,043
07-Dec	LUTON TOWN	AWAY	2 - 0	WALLACE Ro. & SPEED	11,550
14-Dec	TOTTENHAM HOTSPUR	HOME	1 - 1	SPEED	31,404
22-Dec	NOTTINGHAM FOREST	AWAY	0 - 0		27,170
26-Dec	SOUTHAMPTON	HOME	3 - 3	HODGE 2 & SPEED	29,053
29-Dec	MANCHESTER UNITED	HOME	1 - 1	STERLAND (PEN)	32,638
01-Jan	WEST HAM UNITED	AWAY	3 - 1	CHAPMAN 2 & McALLISTER	21,766
12-Jan	SHEFFIELD WEDNESDAY	AWAY	6 - 1	CHAPMAN 3, DORIGO, WHITLOW & WALLACE Ro.	32,228
18-Jan	CRYSTAL PALACE	HOME	1 - 1	FAIRCLOUGH	27,717
01-Feb	NOTTS COUNTY	HOME	3 - 0	STERLAND, BATTY & WALLACE Ro.	27,224
08-Feb	OLDHAM ATHLETIC	AWAY	0 - 2		18,409
23-Feb	EVERTON	AWAY	1 - 1	SHUTT	19,248
29-Feb	LUTON TOWN	HOME	2 - 0	CANTONA & CHAPMAN	28,231
03-Mar	ASTON VILLA	HOME	0 - 0		28,896
07-Mar	TOTTENHAM HOTSPUR	AWAY	3 - 1	WALLACE Ro., NEWSOME & McALLISTER	27,622
11-Mar	QUEENS PARK RANGERS	AWAY	1 - 4	SPEED	14,641
14-Mar	WIMBLEDON	HOME	5 - 1	WALLACE Ro., CHAPMAN 3 & CANTONA	26,760
22-Mar	ARSENAL	AWAY	1 - 1	CHAPMAN	27,844
28-Mar	WEST HAM UNITED	HOME	0 - 0		31,101
04-Apr	MANCHESTER CITY	AWAY	0 - 4		30,239
11-Apr	CHELSEA	HOME	3 - 0	WALLACE Ro., CHAPMAN & CANTONA	31,363
18-Apr	LIVERPOOL	AWAY	0 - 0		37,186
20-Apr	COVENTRY CITY	HOME	2 - 0	FAIRCLOUGH & McALLISTER (PEN)	26,582
26-Apr	SHEFFIELD UNITED	AWAY	3 - 2	WALLACE Ro., NEWSOME & O. G. (GAYLE)	32,000
02-May	NORWICH CITY	HOME	1 - 0	WALLACE Ro.	32,673

F. A. CUP

DATE	OPPONENTS	VENUE	SCORE	SCORERS	ATT.
15-Jan	MANCHESTER UNITED (R3)	HOME	0 - 1		31,819

RUMBELOWS CUP

DATE	OPPONENTS	VENUE	SCORE	SCORERS	ATT.
24-Sep	SCUNTHORPE UNITED (R2-1)	AWAY	0 - 0		8,392
08-Oct	SCUNTHORPE UNITED (R2-2)	HOME	3 - 0	STERLAND (PEN), CHAPMAN & SPEED	14,558
29-Oct	TRANMERE ROVERS (R3)	HOME	3 - 1	CHAPMAN 2 & SHUTT	18,266
04-Dec	EVERTON (R4)	AWAY	4 - 1	SPEED, CHAPMAN & WALLACE Ro. 2	25,467
08-Jan	MANCHESTER UNITED (R5)	HOME	1 - 3	SPEED	28,886

ZENITH DATA SYSTEMS CUP

DATE	OPPONENTS	VENUE	SCORE	SCORERS	ATT.
22-Oct	NOTTINGHAM FOREST (R2)	HOME	1 - 3	WALLACE Ro.	6,145

LEAGUE AND CUPS
APPEARANCES (SUBSTITUTE)

PLAYER	LEAGUE	F. A. CUP	RUMB. CUP	ZEN. CUP	TOTAL
AGANA	1 (1)				1 (1)
BATTY	40		4	1	45
CANTONA	6 (9)				6 (9)
CHAPMAN	38	1	5		44
DAVISON	0 (2)	0 (1)			0 (3)
DORIGO	38	1	5	1	45
FAIRCLOUGH	30 (1)	1	3 (1)	1	35 (2)
GRAYSON				0 (1)	0 (1)
HODGE	12 (11)	1	3 (2)		16 (13)
KAMARA	0 (2)		0 (1)	1	1 (3)
KELLY G	0 (2)		0 (1)		0 (3)
LUKIC	42	1	5	1	49
McALLISTER	41 (1)	1	4		46 (1)
McCLELLAND	16 (2)		2 (1)		18 (3)
NEWSOME	7 (3)			1	8 (3)
SHUTT	6 (8)		2 (1)	1	9 (9)
SNODIN G				1	1
SPEED	41	1	4	1	47
STERLAND	29 (2)	1	5	1	36 (2)
STRACHAN	35 (1)		4		39 (1)
VARADI	2 (1)				2 (1)
WALLACE Ro.	34	1	3	0 (1)	38 (1)
WETHERALL	0 (1)				0 (1)
WHITLOW	3 (7)	0 (1)			3 (8)
WHYTE C	41	1	5	1	48
WILLIAMS A		1	1 (1)		2 (1)

GOALSCORERS

PLAYER	LEAGUE	F. A. CUP	RUMB. CUP	ZEN. CUP	TOTAL
CHAPMAN	16		4		20
WALLACE Ro.	11		2	1	14
SPEED	7		3		10
HODGE	7				7
STERLAND	6		1		7
McALLISTER	5				5
STRACHAN	4				4
CANTONA	3				3
DORIGO	3				3
SHUTT	2		1		3
BATTY	2				2
FAIRCLOUGH	2				2
NEWSOME	2				2
WHITLOW	1				1
WHYTE C	1				1
OWN GOALS	2				2

Howard Wilkinson wasted no time in adding to his championship-winning squad, splashing out a club-record £2 million on David Rocastle (Arsenal), securing Eric Cantona's services in a £900,000 deal, (Arsenal) and bringing Scott Sellars (Blackburn Rovers) back to Elland Road.

In the season's curtain raiser, Cantona joined an elite band of footballers to score a Wembley hat-trick in a 4-3 Charity Shield victory over Liverpool. Leeds' only player to score a treble at the famous stadium, 'Ooh-ah Cantona' rocked around the Twin Towers. Immensely talented, Leeds fans had a new hero. Leeds began their title defence with a 2-1 win over Wimbledon, Lee Chapman notching a brace, before Cantona scored a superb hat-trick in a 5-0 triumph against Tottenham Hotspur, but three wins in 14 league matches saw Leeds struggling near the foot of Division 1.

The club's third European Cup sojourn began with a 3-0 loss at VFB Stuttgart before a magnificent 4-1 win at Elland Road saw Leeds exit Europe's premier competition on away goals. However, United received a lifeline when it emerged Stuttgart coaches fielded an ineligible player, resulting in UEFA awarding Leeds the tie 3-0 by default. Carl Shutt sealed a memorable 2-1 replay victory at Barcelona's Nou Camp Stadium. In a second round tie against Rangers, dubbed the 'Battle of Britain', Gary McAllister gave Leeds a dream first-minute lead at Ibrox, before losing both legs 2-1.

Out of Europe, Leeds endured further woe, crashing to a 4-0 defeat at Manchester City before an embarrassing League Cup exit at Watford. Dropping Cantona against Arsenal, within days of a 3-0 win against the Gunners, Chris Fairclough, Chapman and McAllister scoring, the petulant Frenchman joined Manchester United for £1.2m. His transfer to Leeds' archrivals angered supporters, though in reality the enfant terrible only demonstrated fleeting moments of genius, notably at Wembley.

These were difficult days for Wilkinson, with memories of his side's championship endeavours consigned to history. A 3-1 win over Sheffield Wednesday was Leeds' sole triumph before the halfway point in the league campaign, and among four defeats was a 4-1 home drubbing by Nottingham Forest. Without an away win all season, talk was incredibly of survival. The New Year would bring only brief respite against Southampton; Gary Speed securing a 2-1 win, and Middlesbrough; mid-term signing Frank Strandli notching a debut goal in a 3-0 victory.

Knocked out of the FA Cup by Arsenal and trounced 4-0 at North London neighbours Tottenham, Leeds had a battle on their hands to avoid being sucked into a relegation battle. Grinding out their only consecutive wins of the season against Ipswich Town and Manchester City, courtesy of a Dorigo penalty and Rocastle strike, Rod Wallace and David Wetherall earned draws against Nottingham Forest and Chelsea, but it was tedious entertainment. With seven games remaining, a Gordon Strachan hat-trick included two penalties in a welcome 5-2 win over Blackburn but it would prove to be Leeds; last victory of an eminently forgettable campaign.

Mathematically safe following a 1-1 draw in the penultimate match at Sheffield Wednesday, a Wallace treble in a 3-3 thriller at Coventry City meant Leeds had failed to win an away game all season. Notching 19 goals, Chapman was not only top scorer for a third consecutive season but also made the most appearances. Away from first team action, Leeds rookies claimed the FA Youth Cup for the first time, defeating favourites Manchester United 4-1 on aggregate, Jamie Forrester, scoring in both legs.

1992 - 1993

PREMIER LEAGUE (FINAL LEAGUE POSITION - 17TH)
PLD 42 W 12 D 15 L 15 F 57 A 62 PTS 51

DATE	OPPONENTS	VENUE	SCORE	SCORERS	ATT.
15-Aug	WIMBLEDON	HOME	2 - 1	CHAPMAN 2	25,795
19-Aug	ASTON VILLA	AWAY	1 - 1	SPEED	29,151
22-Aug	MIDDLESBROUGH	AWAY	1 - 4	CANTONA	18,649
25-Aug	TOTTENHAM HOTSPUR	HOME	5 - 0	WALLACE Ro., CANTONA 3 & CHAPMAN	28,218
29-Aug	LIVERPOOL	HOME	2 - 2	McALLISTER & CHAPMAN	29,597
01-Sep	OLDHAM ATHLETIC	AWAY	2 - 2	CANTONA 2	13,848
06-Sep	MANCHESTER UNITED	AWAY	0 - 2		31,296
13-Sep	ASTON VILLA	HOME	1 - 1	HODGE	27,815
19-Sep	SOUTHAMPTON	AWAY	1 - 1	SPEED	16,229
26-Sep	EVERTON	HOME	2 - 0	McALLISTER (PEN) & CHAPMAN	27,915
03-Oct	IPSWICH TOWN	AWAY	2 - 4	CHAPMAN & SPEED	21,200
17-Oct	SHEFFIELD UNITED	HOME	3 - 1	CHAPMAN, SPEED & WHYTE C	29,706
24-Oct	QUEENS PARK RANGERS	AWAY	1 - 2	STRACHAN	19,326
31-Oct	COVENTRY CITY	HOME	2 - 2	CHAPMAN & FAIRCLOUGH	28,018
07-Nov	MANCHESTER CITY	AWAY	0 - 4		27,255
21-Nov	ARSENAL	HOME	3 - 0	FAIRCLOUGH, CHAPMAN & McALLISTER	30,516
29-Nov	CHELSEA	AWAY	0 - 1		24,345
05-Dec	NOTTINGHAM FOREST	HOME	1 - 4	SPEED	29,364
12-Dec	SHEFFIELD WEDNESDAY	HOME	3 - 1	SPEED, CHAPMAN & VARADI	29,770
20-Dec	CRYSTAL PALACE	AWAY	0 - 1		14,462
26-Dec	BLACKBURN ROVERS	AWAY	1 - 3	McALLISTER	19,910
28-Dec	NORWICH CITY	HOME	0 - 0		30,282
09-Jan	SOUTHAMPTON	HOME	2 - 1	CHAPMAN & SPEED	26,071
16-Jan	EVERTON	AWAY	0 - 2		21,031
30-Jan	MIDDLESBROUGH	HOME	3 - 0	STRANDLI, BATTY & FAIRCLOUGH	30,344
06-Feb	WIMBLEDON	AWAY	0 - 1		6,704
08-Feb	MANCHESTER UNITED	HOME	0 - 0		34,166
13-Feb	OLDHAM ATHLETIC	HOME	2 - 0	McALLISTER (PEN) & CHAPMAN	27,654
20-Feb	TOTTENHAM HOTSPUR	AWAY	0 - 4		32,040
24-Feb	ARSENAL	AWAY	0 - 0		21,061
27-Feb	IPSWICH TOWN	HOME	1 - 0	DORIGO (PEN)	28,848
13-Mar	MANCHESTER CITY	HOME	1 - 0	ROCASTLE	30,840
21-Mar	NOTTINGHAM FOREST	AWAY	1 - 1	WALLACE Ro.	25,148
24-Mar	CHELSEA	HOME	1 - 1	WETHERALL	28,135
06-Apr	SHEFFIELD UNITED	AWAY	1 - 2	STRANDLI	20,562
10-Apr	BLACKBURN ROVERS	HOME	5 - 2	STRACHAN 3 (2 PENS), WALLACE Ro. & CHAPMAN	31,789
14-Apr	NORWICH CITY	AWAY	2 - 4	CHAPMAN & WALLACE Ro.	18,613
17-Apr	CRYSTAL PALACE	HOME	0 - 0		27,545
21-Apr	LIVERPOOL	AWAY	0 - 2		34,992
01-May	QUEENS PARK RANGERS	HOME	1 - 1	HODGE	31,408
04-May	SHEFFIELD WEDNESDAY	AWAY	1 - 1	CHAPMAN	26,855
08-May	COVENTRY CITY	AWAY	3 - 3	WALLACE Ro. 3	19,591

F. A. CUP

DATE	OPPONENTS	VENUE	SCORE	SCORERS	ATT.
02-Jan	CHARLTON ATHLETIC (R3)	HOME	1 - 1	SPEED	21,287
13-Jan	CHARLTON ATHLETIC (R3R)	AWAY	3 - 1	SPEED, O. G. (GARLAND) & McALLISTER	8,337
25-Jan	ARSENAL (R4)	AWAY	2 - 2	SPEED & CHAPMAN	26,516
03-Feb	ARSENAL (R4R) *	HOME	2 - 3	SHUTT & McALLISTER	26,449

COCA - COLA CUP

DATE	OPPONENTS	VENUE	SCORE	SCORERS	ATT.
22-Sep	SCUNTHORPE UNITED (R2-1)	HOME	4 - 1	STRACHAN, CHAPMAN, SPEED & SHUTT	10,113
27-Oct	SCUNTHORPE UNITED (R2-2)	AWAY	2 - 2	WALLACE Ro. & CHAPMAN	7,419
10-Nov	WATFORD (R3)	AWAY	1 - 2	McALLISTER	18,035

F. A. CHARITY SHIELD

DATE	OPPONENTS	VENUE	SCORE	SCORERS	ATT.
08-Aug	LIVERPOOL $	NEUTRAL	4 - 3	CANTONA 3 & DORIGO	61,291

EUROPEAN CUP

DATE	OPPONENTS	VENUE	SCORE	SCORERS	ATT.
16-Sep	VFB STUTTGART (R1-1)	AWAY	0 - 3		38,000
30-Sep	VFB STUTTGART (R1-2) +	HOME	4 - 1	SPEED, McALLISTER (PEN), CANTONA & CHAPMAN	20,457
09-Oct	VFB STUTTGART (R1-PLAY-OFF) ^	NEUTRAL	2 - 1	STRACHAN & SHUTT	7,400
21-Oct	GLASGOW RANGERS (R2-1)	AWAY	1 - 2	McALLISTER	43,251
04-Nov	GLASGOW RANGERS (R2-2)	HOME	1 - 2	CANTONA	25,118

LEAGUE AND CUPS
APPEARANCES (SUBSTITUTE)

PLAYER	LEAGUE	F. A. CUP	CO. CUP	EUR. CUP	CH. SHLD.	TOTAL
BATTY	30	3	2	4	1	40
BEENEY	1					1
BOWMAN	3 (1)					3 (1)
CANTONA	12 (1)		1	5	1	19 (1)
CHAPMAN	36 (4)	4	3	5	1	49 (4)
DAY	2	1				3
DORIGO	33	4	1	5	1	44
FAIRCLOUGH	29 (1)	3 (1)	2	5	1	40 (2)
FORRESTER	5 (1)					5 (1)
HODGE	9 (14)		0 (1)	0 (2)	0 (1)	9 (18)
KERR	3 (2)	2				5 (2)
KERSLAKE	8					8
LUKIC	39	4	3	5		51
McALLISTER	32	4	3	5	1	45
NEWSOME	30 (7)	0 (1)	2	3	1	36 (8)
ROCASTLE	11 (7)	0 (3)	0 (2)	2 (1)		13 (13)
SELLARS	6 (1)		1 (1)	1		8 (2)
SHARP K	4					4
SHUTT	6 (8)	4	1	0 (2)		11 (10)
SPEED	39	4	3	5	1	52
STERLAND	3	2				5
STRACHAN	25 (6)	4	3	5	0 (1)	37 (7)
STRANDLI	5 (5)					5 (5)
TINKLER	5 (2)					5 (2)
VARADI	2 (2)					2 (2)
WALLACE Ra.	5 (1)					5 (1)
WALLACE Ro.	31 (1)	1 (3)	2	0 (2)	1	35 (6)
WETHERALL	13	4	2			19
WHELAN	1					1
WHYTE C	34	3	2 (1)	5	1	45 (1)

GOALSCORERS

PLAYER	LEAGUE	F. A. CUP	CO. CUP	EUR. CUP	CH. SHLD.	TOTAL
CHAPMAN	15	1	2	1		19
SPEED	7	3	1	1		12
CANTONA	6			2	3	11
McALLISTER	5	2	1	2		10
WALLACE Ro.	7		1			8
STRACHAN	4		1	1		6
FAIRCLOUGH	3					3
SHUTT		1	1	1		3
DORIGO	1				1	2
HODGE	2					2
STRANDLI	2					2
BATTY	1					1
ROCASTLE	1					1
VARADI	1					1
WETHERALL	1					1
WHYTE C	1					1
OWN GOALS		1				1

KEY :- * = AFTER EXTRA TIME, $ = PLAYED AT WEMBLEY, + = MATCH AWARDED TO LEEDS 3 - 0 WHICH MADE SCORES LEVEL ON AGGREGATE, ^ = PLAY - OFF AS STUTTGART PLAYED AN INELIGIBLE PLAYER - MATCH WAS PLAYED AT THE NOU CAMP STADIUM, BARCELONA

LEEDS HOSTED AND PLAYED IN THE MAKITA TROPHY. ON AUG 1ST 1992 THEY PLAYED VFB STUTTGART AND WON 2 - 1 (0 - 1) WITH WALLACE Ro. AND ROCASTLE SCORING WITH AN ATTENDANCE OF 12,500. THE TEAM WAS LUKIC, NEWSOME, DORIGO, HODGE, SELLARS (BATTY), WHYTE C, ROCASTLE (CANTONA), WALLACE Ro., CHAPMAN, McALLISTER & SPEED. ON AUG 2ND 1992 THEY PLAYED SAMPDORIA IN THE FINAL AND LOST 0 - 1 (0 - 1) WITH AN ATTENDANCE OF 15,000. THE TEAM WAS LUKIC, NEWSOME (WHYTE C), DORIGO, BATTY, FAIRCLOUGH, HODGE, ROCASTLE (CANTONA), WALLACE RO., CHAPMAN, McALLISTER & SPEED

Leeds United's dismal performance defending their Division 1 crown signalled a rebuilding programme during the close season. Splitting up his title-winning squad, Lee Chapman and Chris Whyte departed for new challenges while Mel Sterland retired. New arrivals included striker Brian Deane (Sheffield United) for a club-record 2.7 million signing, veteran centre-back David O'Leary (Arsenal) and winger David White (Manchester City). Breaking into the first team from the opening game was right-back Gary Kelly, who began his Elland Road career as a striker!

Deane made the perfect start with a debut goal at Manchester City as Leeds began the new term with a 1-1 draw. Gary Speed settled an opening home clash with West Ham before three consecutive defeats, including a 4-0 drubbing by Norwich City at Elland Road, signalled Mark Beeney replacing John Lukic in goal. Slotting in immediately, United's defence looked more assured in a 14-match unbeaten run that saw David Wetherall replace centre-half O'Leary, injured after just three starts.

Reeling off five consecutive wins, skipper Gordon Strachan settled a tight clash with Oldham Athletic before Speed secured Leeds' first away victory since April 1992, at Southampton. Strachan again proved the match winner in a 2-1 win over Sheffield United before a Wallace brace accounted for Coventry City, while Speed and Gary McAllister doubles sealed a 4-0 canter against Wimbledon.

Although knocked out of the League Cup by Sunderland, Wilkinson's side was once again challenging the leading Division 1 teams and entertaining supporters to boot in a number of thrilling encounters. Following back-to-back 3-3 draws against Blackburn Rovers and Sheffield Wednesday, another Wallace brace was the highlight of a thrilling 4-1 triumph over Chelsea. Although delighted with the club's renaissance, supporters raged at the board's decision to accept an offer from Blackburn Rovers of £2.75 million for local hero David Batty.

Struggling since his arrival was Deane, but he found the target against Chelsea and enjoyed further success, scoring in a 3-0 win over Swindon Town and a rousing 3-2 triumph against Manchester City. Wallace however, was Leeds main hitman, and scoring in five consecutive games, struck the only goal at West Ham. Prior to the Christmas fixtures, McAllister kept Leeds' impressive form going with the opening strike in a 2-1 win over Arsenal, however, before securing a 2-0 victory over Liverpool, United endured a dreadful nine-match spell that saw them crash out of the FA Cup to minnows Oxford United.

The remainder of the season would bring an upturn in fortunes and a number of highlights; Wallace was on target in wins against Aston Villa, Coventry and Queens Park Rangers before scoring the 'Goal of the Season' during a 2-0 victory against Tottenham Hotspur. Ending the campaign on a high, White found the net in Leeds' last three games to confirm a fifth place finish, while Deane scored a brace as Leeds' signed off with a 5-0 canter at relegated Swindon. Kelly and McAllister were the only ever-present players, while Wallace top scored on 17 goals.

1993 - 1994

PREMIER LEAGUE (FINAL LEAGUE POSITION - 5TH)

PLD 42 W 18 D 16 L 8 F 65 A 39 PTS 70

DATE	OPPONENTS	VENUE	SCORE	SCORERS	ATT.
14-Aug	MANCHESTER CITY	AWAY	1 - 1	DEANE	32,366
17-Aug	WEST HAM UNITED	HOME	1 - 0	SPEED	34,588
21-Aug	NORWICH CITY	HOME	0 - 4		32,008
24-Aug	ARSENAL	AWAY	1 - 2	STRACHAN	29,042
28-Aug	LIVERPOOL	AWAY	0 - 2		44,068
30-Aug	OLDHAM ATHLETIC	HOME	1 - 0	STRACHAN	28,717
11-Sep	SOUTHAMPTON	AWAY	2 - 0	DEANE & SPEED	13,511
18-Sep	SHEFFIELD UNITED	HOME	2 - 1	McALLISTER & STRACHAN	33,892
25-Sep	COVENTRY CITY	AWAY	2 - 0	WALLACE Ro. 2	13,934
02-Oct	WIMBLEDON	HOME	4 - 0	SPEED 2 & McALLISTER 2	30,020
17-Oct	IPSWICH TOWN	AWAY	0 - 0		17,548
23-Oct	BLACKBURN ROVERS	HOME	3 - 3	McALLISTER (PEN), NEWSOME & O. G. (SHERWOOD)	37,827
30-Oct	SHEFFIELD WEDNESDAY	AWAY	3 - 3	FAIRCLOUGH, WALLACE Ro. & SPEED	31,892
06-Nov	CHELSEA	HOME	4 - 1	DEANE, WALLACE Ro. 2 & ROCASTLE	35,022
20-Nov	TOTTENHAM HOTSPUR	AWAY	1 - 1	DEANE	31,275
23-Nov	EVERTON	AWAY	1 - 1	WALLACE Ro.	17,066
27-Nov	SWINDON TOWN	HOME	3 - 0	DEANE, WALLACE Ro. & SPEED	32,630
04-Dec	MANCHESTER CITY	HOME	3 - 2	WALLACE Ro., SPEED & DEANE	33,821
08-Dec	WEST HAM UNITED	AWAY	1 - 0	WALLACE Ro.	20,468
13-Dec	NORWICH CITY	AWAY	1 - 2	WALLACE Ro.	16,586
18-Dec	ARSENAL	HOME	2 - 1	McALLISTER & O. G. (ADAMS)	37,515
22-Dec	NEWCASTLE UNITED	AWAY	1 - 1	FAIRCLOUGH	36,388
29-Dec	QUEENS PARK RANGERS	HOME	1 - 1	HODGE	39,106
01-Jan	MANCHESTER UNITED	AWAY	0 - 0		44,724
15-Jan	IPSWICH TOWN	HOME	0 - 0		31,317
23-Jan	BLACKBURN ROVERS	AWAY	1 - 2	SPEED	16,938
06-Feb	ASTON VILLA	AWAY	0 - 1		26,919
19-Feb	LIVERPOOL	HOME	2 - 0	WETHERALL & McALLISTER	40,053
28-Feb	OLDHAM ATHLETIC	AWAY	1 - 1	McALLISTER	11,136
05-Mar	SOUTHAMPTON	HOME	0 - 0		30,890
13-Mar	SHEFFIELD UNITED	AWAY	2 - 2	SPEED & DEANE	19,250
16-Mar	ASTON VILLA	HOME	2 - 0	WALLACE Ro. & DEANE	33,120
19-Mar	COVENTRY CITY	HOME	1 - 0	WALLACE Ro.	30,023
26-Mar	WIMBLEDON	AWAY	0 - 1		9,035
01-Apr	NEWCASTLE UNITED	HOME	1 - 1	FAIRCLOUGH	40,005
04-Apr	QUEENS PARK RANGERS	AWAY	4 - 0	DEANE, WALLACE Ro. & WHITE D 2	13,365
17-Apr	TOTTENHAM HOTSPUR	HOME	2 - 0	WALLACE Ro. 2	33,658
23-Apr	CHELSEA	AWAY	1 - 1	SPEED	18,544
27-Apr	MANCHESTER UNITED	HOME	0 - 2		41,125
30-Apr	EVERTON	HOME	3 - 0	McALLISTER, O. G. (WATSON) & WHITE D	35,487
03-May	SHEFFIELD WEDNESDAY	HOME	2 - 2	WHITE D & WALLACE Ro.	33,806
07-May	SWINDON TOWN	AWAY	5 - 0	DEANE 2, WHITE D, WALLACE Ro. & FAIRCLOUGH	17,539

F. A. CUP

08-Jan	CREWE ALEXANDRA (R3)	HOME	3 - 1	DEANE & FORRESTER 2	23,475
29-Jan	OXFORD UNITED (R4)	AWAY	2 - 2	SPEED & WETHERALL	11,029
09-Feb	OXFORD UNITED (R4R) *	HOME	2 - 3	STRACHAN & WHITE D	22,167

COCA - COLA CUP

21-Sep	SUNDERLAND (R2-1)	AWAY	1 - 2	SPEED	17,101
06-Oct	SUNDERLAND (R2-2)	HOME	1 - 2	WHELAN	22,265

LEAGUE AND CUP

APPEARANCES (SUBSTITUTE)

PLAYER	LEAGUE	F. A. CUP	CO. CUP	TOTAL
BATTY	8 (1)			8 (1)
BEENEY	22	3	2	27
DEANE	41	3	2	46
DORIGO	37	3	2	42
FAIRCLOUGH	40	3	2	45
FORD	0 (1)			0 (1)
FORRESTER	2 (1)	1 (1)		3 (2)
HODGE	7 (1)	1 (1)	1	9 (2)
KELLY G	42	3	2	47
LUKIC	20			20
McALLISTER	42	3	2	47
NEWSOME	25 (4)	3	1	29 (4)
O'LEARY	10			10
PEMBERTON	6 (3)			6 (3)
ROCASTLE	6 (1)		0 (1)	6 (2)
SHARP K	7 (3)			7 (3)
SPEED	35 (1)	2	2	39 (1)
STRACHAN	32 (1)	3	2	37 (1)
STRANDLI	0 (4)	1	0 (1)	1 (5)
TINKLER	0 (3)			0 (3)
WALLACE Ra.	0 (1)			0 (1)
WALLACE Ro.	34 (3)	1	1	36 (3)
WETHERALL	31 (1)	0 (2)	2	33 (3)
WHELAN	6 (10)		1	7 (10)
WHITE D	9 (6)	3		12 (6)

GOALSCORERS

PLAYER	LEAGUE	F. A. CUP	CO. CUP	TOTAL
WALLACE Ro.	17			17
DEANE	11	1		12
SPEED	10	1	1	12
McALLISTER	8			8
WHITE D	5	1		6
FAIRCLOUGH	4			4
STRACHAN	3	1		4
FORRESTER		2		2
WETHERALL	1	1		2
HODGE	1			1
NEWSOME	1			1
ROCASTLE	1			1
WHELAN			1	1
OWN GOALS	3			3

LEEDS ALSO PLAYED A CHALLENGE MATCH AGAINST REPRESENTATIVE OPPOSITION AS FOLLOWS :- ON JUL. 23RD 1993 VS. LEAGUE OF IRELAND AT TOLKA PARK AND DREW 2 - 2 WITH SHUTT AND SPEED SCORING WITH AN ATTENDANCE OF 7,000. THE TEAM WAS :- BEENEY. KELLY, DORIGO, BATTY, WETHERALL, NEWSOME, STRACHAN, WALLACE Ro., TOBIN (SHUTT), McALLISTER & SPEED. TOBIN (STEVE) DID NOT PLAY FOR THE FIRST TEAM.

LEEDS ALSO PLAYED IN THE TRANSPENNINE EXPRESS TROPHY. ON JUL. 27TH 1993 VS. LIVERPOOL AT QUEENSGATE, BRIDLINGTON AND WON 4 - 0 (3 - 0) WITH SHUTT, CHAPMAN 2 & FORD SCORING. THE TEAM WAS BEENEY, COUZENS, OLIVER, HODGE, WETHERALL, WHYTE C., SHUTT, WALLACE Ra., CHAPMAN, TOBIN & FORD AND ON JUL. 29TH 1993 VS. TOTTENHAM HOTSPUR AT QUEENSGATE, BRIDLINGTON AND LOST 0 - 2 (0 - 1). THE TEAM WAS BEENEY, COUZENS, SHARP K., HODGE, WETHERALL, WHYTE C., SHUTT, TINKLER, CHAPMAN, FORRESTER & FORD. OLIVER (SIMON) AND TOBIN (STEVE) DID NOT PLAY A FIRST TEAM GAME FOR LEEDS. KEY :- * AFTER EXTRA TIME

Confidence restored, Howard Wilkinson boosted his squad with the arrival of £2.6 million midfielder Carlton Palmer (Sheffield Wednesday) and South African duo Philomen Masinga and Lucas Radebe for a combined fee of £250,000. Whilst Palmer slotted into midfield and Masinga attack, Radebe would have to await his opportunity, unlike rookie forward Noel Whelan when Gordon Strachan picked up an injury in United's opening home game against Arsenal.

Grasping his opportunity with a last ditch winner against the Gunners, Whelan sealed a win at Crystal Palace, notched a brace in a 2-0 victory against Manchester City before securing a 2-1 triumph over Leicester City. It was some introduction during the opening 11 games, but supporters highlight was a 2-1 win against defending champions Manchester United, David Wetherall and Brian Deane sealing Leeds' first win against their Pennine rivals since 1981.

Wilkinson's team was taking shape but with Deane struggling as target man, increased pressure was on fellow strikers Rod Wallace, Whelan and Masinga. Rising to the challenge, Wallace struck twice at former club Southampton in a 3-1 win, Whelan notched a winning goal against Nottingham Forest, while a Masinga brace settled a 3-1 triumph at Arsenal and a first double in almost two decades, but the festive period ended in defeat at Liverpool. The 2-0 loss at Anfield on New Years Eve marked Strachan's last game for Leeds. A stalwart in the club's renaissance, the Scot embarked on a managerial career as Ron Atkinson's assistant at Coventry City. Also moving on was Chris Fairclough and Jon Newsome, leaving only John Lukic, Wallace, Gary McAllister and Gary Speed from the title-winning team.

Bar an embarrassing League Cup defeat against Mansfield Town, the season had been encouraging, but without a cutting edge, the campaign was in danger of collapsing into mediocrity. Wilkinson acted decisively by signing prolific Bundesliga striker Tony Yeboah for a club record 3.4 million from Eintracht Frankfurt. Leeds followers had a new cult hero, but first Yeboah had to get match-fit while his teammates were goal-shy in five unbeaten league games that included three scoreless draws.

Masinga did notch a brace as Leeds dismantled Queens Park Rangers 4-0, before firing home a treble against Walsall and a winner against Oldham Athletic in the FA Cup, but draws at Blackburn and Wimbledon demonstrated United's deficiencies. A daunting sight when bearing down on goal, Yeboah scored in an FA Cup defeat at Manchester United. Handed a full debut against Everton, Yeboah scored the only goal with a predators strike, heralding a 16-match run that would yield two defeats. Scoring in three-goal wins against Chelsea, Leicester City and Coventry City, a sensational treble against Ipswich Town brought a new chant from the Elland Road faithful: 'Yeboah...Yeboah...Yeboah'.

With Yeboah leading the line, and on song, Wilkinson switched Deane to the flank, and profiting from the extra room, Deane rediscovered his scoring touch; securing Leeds' first win at Liverpool since 1972. Suddenly in UEFA Cup contention, McAllister sealed a win against European rivals Newcastle United, Palmer gained victories against Aston Villa and Norwich City, before a Yeboah brace set up a 3-1 triumph over Crystal Palace. Facing Tottenham Hotspur in the season's final game, Leeds pinched a UEFA Cup spot from Newcastle, courtesy of Deane. Finishing fifth, Lukic and Gary Kelly were ever-present. Yeboah top scored with 13 goals in 20 games. Supporters could not wait for the new season to come around.

PREMIER LEAGUE (FINAL LEAGUE POSITION - 5TH)

PLD 42 W 20 D 13 L 9 F 59 A 38 PTS 73

DATE	OPPONENTS	VENUE	SCORE	SCORERS	ATT.
20-Aug	WEST HAM UNITED	AWAY	0 - 0		18,610
23-Aug	ARSENAL	HOME	1 - 0	WHELAN	34,218
27-Aug	CHELSEA	HOME	2 - 3	WHELAN & MASINGA	32,212
30-Aug	CRYSTAL PALACE	AWAY	2 - 1	WHITE D & WHELAN	13,654
11-Sep	MANCHESTER UNITED	HOME	2 - 1	WETHERALL & DEANE	39,396
17-Sep	COVENTRY CITY	AWAY	1 - 2	SPEED	15,389
26-Sep	SHEFFIELD WEDNESDAY	AWAY	1 - 1	McALLISTER	23,227
01-Oct	MANCHESTER CITY	HOME	2 - 0	WHELAN 2	30,938
08-Oct	NORWICH CITY	AWAY	1 - 2	WALLACE Ro.	17,390
15-Oct	TOTTENHAM HOTSPUR	HOME	1 - 1	DEANE	39,224
24-Oct	LEICESTER CITY	HOME	2 - 1	McALLISTER & WHELAN	28,547
29-Oct	SOUTHAMPTON	AWAY	3 - 1	O. G. (MADDISON) & WALLACE Ro. 2	15,202
01-Nov	IPSWICH TOWN	AWAY	0 - 2		15,956
05-Nov	WIMBLEDON	HOME	3 - 1	WETHERALL, SPEED & WHITE D	27,284
19-Nov	QUEENS PARK RANGERS	AWAY	2 - 3	O. G. (McDONALD) & DEANE	17,416
26-Nov	NOTTINGHAM FOREST	HOME	1 - 0	WHELAN	38,191
05-Dec	EVERTON	AWAY	0 - 3		25,897
10-Dec	WEST HAM UNITED	HOME	2 - 2	WORTHINGTON N & DEANE	28,987
17-Dec	ARSENAL	AWAY	3 - 1	MASINGA 2 & DEANE	38,098
26-Dec	NEWCASTLE UNITED	HOME	0 - 0		39,337
31-Dec	LIVERPOOL	HOME	0 - 2		38,563
02-Jan	ASTON VILLA	AWAY	0 - 0		35,038
14-Jan	SOUTHAMPTON	HOME	0 - 0		28,953
24-Jan	QUEENS PARK RANGERS	HOME	4 - 0	MASINGA 2, WHITE D & DEANE	28,780
01-Feb	BLACKBURN ROVERS	AWAY	1 - 1	McALLISTER (PEN)	28,561
04-Feb	WIMBLEDON	AWAY	0 - 0		10,211
22-Feb	EVERTON	HOME	1 - 0	YEBOAH	30,793
25-Feb	MANCHESTER CITY	AWAY	0 - 0		22,892
04-Mar	SHEFFIELD WEDNESDAY	HOME	0 - 1		33,750
11-Mar	CHELSEA	AWAY	3 - 0	YEBOAH 2 & McALLISTER	20,174
15-Mar	LEICESTER CITY	AWAY	3 - 1	YEBOAH 2 & PALMER	20,068
18-Mar	COVENTRY CITY	HOME	3 - 1	YEBOAH, O. G. (GOULD) & WALLACE Ro.	29,179
22-Mar	NOTTINGHAM FOREST	AWAY	0 - 3		26,299
02-Apr	MANCHESTER UNITED	AWAY	0 - 0		43,712
05-Apr	IPSWICH TOWN	HOME	4 - 0	YEBOAH 3 & SPEED	28,600
09-Apr	LIVERPOOL	AWAY	1 - 0	DEANE	37,454
15-Apr	BLACKBURN ROVERS	HOME	1 - 1	DEANE	39,426
17-Apr	NEWCASTLE UNITED	AWAY	2 - 1	McALLISTER (PEN) & YEBOAH	35,626
29-Apr	ASTON VILLA	HOME	1 - 0	PALMER	32,955
06-May	NORWICH CITY	HOME	2 - 1	McALLISTER (PEN) & PALMER	31,981
09-May	CRYSTAL PALACE	HOME	3 - 1	YEBOAH 2 & WETHERALL	30,963
14-May	TOTTENHAM HOTSPUR	AWAY	1 - 1	DEANE	33,040

F. A. CUP

DATE	OPPONENTS	VENUE	SCORE	SCORERS	ATT.
07-Jan	WALSALL (R3)	AWAY	1 - 1	WETHERALL	8,619
17-Jan	WALSALL (R3R) *	HOME	5 - 2	DEANE, WETHERALL & MASINGA 3	17,881
28-Jan	OLDHAM ATHLETIC (R4)	HOME	3 - 2	WHITE D, PALMER & MASINGA	25,010
19-Feb	MANCHESTER UNITED (R5)	AWAY	1 - 3	YEBOAH	42,744

COCA - COLA CUP

DATE	OPPONENTS	VENUE	SCORE	SCORERS	ATT.
21-Sep	MANSFIELD TOWN (R2-1)	HOME	0 - 1		7,844
04-Oct	MANSFIELD TOWN (R2-2)	AWAY	0 - 0		7,227

LEAGUE AND CUP

APPEARANCES (SUBSTITUTE)

PLAYER	LEAGUE	F. A. CUP	CO. CUP	TOTAL
COUZENS	2 (2)			2 (2)
DEANE	33 (2)	3	1 (1)	37 (3)
DORIGO	28	1	0 (1)	29 (1)
FAIRCLOUGH	1 (4)		2	3 (4)
KELLY G	42	4	2	48
LUKIC	42	4	2	48
McALLISTER	41	4	2	47
MASINGA	15 (7)	2 (2)	1	18 (9)
PALMER	39	3	2	44
PEMBERTON	22 (5)	4	0 (1)	26 (6)
RADEBE	9 (3)	1 (1)	0 (1)	10 (5)
SHARP K	0 (2)			0 (2)
SPEED	39	4	2	45
STRACHAN	5 (1)		1	6 (1)
TINKLER	3			3
WALLACE Ro.	30 (2)	2 (1)	2	34 (3)
WETHERALL	38	4	1	43
WHELAN	18 (5)	2	2	22 (5)
WHITE D	18 (5)	3		21 (5)
WORTHINGTON N	21 (6)	3 (1)	2	26 (7)
YEBOAH	16 (2)	0 (2)		16 (4)

GOALSCORERS

PLAYER	LEAGUE	F. A. CUP	CO. CUP	TOTAL
YEBOAH	12	1		13
DEANE	9	1		10
MASINGA	5	4		9
WHELAN	7			7
McALLISTER	6			6
WETHERALL	3	2		5
PALMER	3	1		4
WALLACE Ro.	4			4
WHITE D	3	1		4
SPEED	3			3
WORTHINGTON N	1			1
OWN GOALS	3			3

KEY :- * AFTER EXTRA TIME

LEEDS ALSO PLAYED IN THE RYEDALE TROPHY. ON JUL. 30TH 1994 VS. SHEFFIELD WEDNESDAY AT THE RYEDALE STADIUM, YORK AND DREW 2 - 2 (1 - 1) WITH HODGE AND FORRESTER (PEN) SCORING. THE TEAM WAS PETTINGER, COUZENS, SHARP, FORD, WALLACE Ra., JACKSON, WHARTON, HODGE, BROWN A (GRAY A), FORRESTER & SMITHARD. ON JUL. 31ST 1994 VS. TOTTENHAM HOTSPUR AT THE RYEDALE STADIUM, YORK AND LOST 0 - 2 (0 - 0 AND 0 - 0 AT 90 MINUTES) AFTER EXTRA TIME. THE TEAM WAS PETTINGER, COUZENS, SHARP K., FORD, WALLACE Ra., JACKSON (O'SHEA), WHARTON, BLUNT, BROWN A (SHEPHERD), FORRESTER & SMITHARD. PETTINGER (PAUL), WHARTON (PAUL), BROWN (ANDREW), SMITHARD (MATTHEW) & O'SHEA (ALAN) DID NOT PLAY FOR THE FIRST TEAM.

With a balanced team emerging, hopes were high of a successful campaign at Leeds United. Howard Wilkinson's investment in Tony Yeboah had proved inspirational and his powerful sharpshooter began the new season in devastating fashion. Scoring a brace during a 2-1 win at West Ham in the opening clash, Yeboah posted a 'Goal of the Season' candidate against Liverpool with a spectacular strike. By the end of September, further contenders came with a stunning 30-yard thunderbolt in a 4-2 triumph at Wimbledon and a superb overhead kick in Leeds' 3-0 victory in Monaco on their return to European football.

Scoring hat-tricks in both games, Yeboah was the most talked about striker in Britain and had etched his name into club folklore. Scoring 10 goals in the opening 10 fixtures, Yeboah joined a select group, following in the footsteps of Tom Jennings (1926/27), Gordon Hodgson (1938/39) and John Charles (1953/54). A solo effort during a 2-0 victory over Sheffield Wednesday and a predatory strike against Chelsea had fans eulogising, however, apart from a Gary McAllister hat-trick in a 3-1 win over Coventry City, United endured an indifferent spell, winning three of 10 league encounters. In Europe, PSV Eindhoven won a second round UEFA Cup clash comprehensively 8-3 on aggregate.

Domestically, progress came in the League Cup after Gary Speed edged Leeds past Notts County 3-2 over two legs. Another Speed strike accounted for Derby County, whilst Yeboah notched the winner against Blackburn Rovers to see Leeds safely through to the quarter-finals. Leeds' dip in form brought movement in the transfer market, Wilkinson's highest profile signing, Swedish star Tomas Brolin from Parma. A debutante against Rovers, his first goal came in a 6-2 drubbing at Sheffield Wednesday.

Yeboah returned to form with a memorable goal in a 3-1 victory against Manchester United on Christmas Eve. Brolin sealed a 2-0 win at Bolton Wanderers, before Yeboah signed off, prior to representing Ghana in the African Nations Cup finals, with Leeds' final goal in a 4-2 FA Cup win at Derby. A Brolin brace secured a 2-0 win over West Ham, whilst a Speed effort edged Leeds past Reading in the League Cup, but without Yeboah, Leeds had little cutting edge and it coincided with a run of three consecutive league defeats.

Back early from the finals due to injury, Yeboah bounced back with goals in both legs of a comprehensive League Cup semi-final triumph against Birmingham City to book Leeds' first Wembley final for 23 years. Two days later, a McAllister brace at Port Vale in the FA Cup kept the dream of two Wembley appearances alive, but league form was abysmal; a Yeboah double securing a win at Queens Park Rangers, the only triumph in seven games leading up to United's big day at Wembley.

Leeds arrived at the twin towers to face Aston Villa low on confidence with injury worries to boot, and it showed in a harrowing 3-0 defeat. Crashing out of the FA Cup to Liverpool signalled a collapse in form, placing enormous pressure on Wilkinson. Six successive defeats equalled Leeds' worst run since 1946/47. Utilising 32 players, change was in the air both on and off the field as Bill Fotherby replaced Leslie Silver as chairman whilst new owners vied to purchase the club. In a season that turned into heartache, skipper McAllister made 54 appearances, Yeboah top scored with 19 goals.

PREMIER LEAGUE (FINAL LEAGUE POSITION - 13TH)

PLD 38 W 12 D 7 L 19 F 40 A 57 PTS 43

DATE	OPPONENTS	VENUE	SCORE	SCORERS	ATT.
19-Aug	WEST HAM UNITED	AWAY	2 - 1	YEBOAH 2	22,901
21-Aug	LIVERPOOL	HOME	1 - 0	YEBOAH	35,852
26-Aug	ASTON VILLA	HOME	2 - 0	SPEED & WHITE D	35,086
30-Aug	SOUTHAMPTON	AWAY	1 - 1	DORIGO	15,212
09-Sep	TOTTENHAM HOTSPUR	AWAY	1 - 2	YEBOAH	30,034
16-Sep	QUEENS PARK RANGERS	HOME	1 - 3	WETHERALL	31,504
23-Sep	WIMBLEDON	AWAY	4 - 2	PALMER & YEBOAH 3	13,307
30-Sep	SHEFFIELD WEDNESDAY	HOME	2 - 0	YEBOAH & SPEED	34,076
14-Oct	ARSENAL	HOME	0 - 3		38,552
21-Oct	MANCHESTER CITY	AWAY	0 - 0		26,390
28-Oct	COVENTRY CITY	HOME	3 - 1	McALLISTER 3	30,161
04-Nov	MIDDLESBROUGH	AWAY	1 - 1	DEANE	29,467
18-Nov	CHELSEA	HOME	1 - 0	YEBOAH	36,209
25-Nov	NEWCASTLE UNITED	AWAY	1 - 2	DEANE	36,572
02-Dec	MANCHESTER CITY	HOME	0 - 1		33,249
09-Dec	WIMBLEDON	HOME	1 - 1	JOBSON	27,984
16-Dec	SHEFFIELD WEDNESDAY	AWAY	2 - 6	BROLIN & WALLACE Ro.	24,573
24-Dec	MANCHESTER UNITED	HOME	3 - 1	McALLISTER (PEN), YEBOAH & DEANE	39,801
27-Dec	BOLTON WANDERERS	AWAY	2 - 0	BROLIN & WETHERALL	18,414
30-Dec	EVERTON	AWAY	0 - 2		40,009
01-Jan	BLACKBURN ROVERS	HOME	0 - 0		31,285
13-Jan	WEST HAM UNITED	HOME	2 - 0	BROLIN 2	30,658
20-Jan	LIVERPOOL	AWAY	0 - 5		40,254
31-Jan	NOTTINGHAM FOREST	AWAY	1 - 2	PALMER	24,465
03-Feb	ASTON VILLA	AWAY	0 - 3		35,982
02-Mar	BOLTON WANDERERS	HOME	0 - 1		30,106
06-Mar	QUEENS PARK RANGERS	AWAY	2 - 1	YEBOAH 2	13,991
13-Mar	BLACKBURN ROVERS	AWAY	0 - 1		23,358
17-Mar	EVERTON	HOME	2 - 2	DEANE 2	29,421
30-Mar	MIDDLESBROUGH	HOME	0 - 1		31,778
03-Apr	SOUTHAMPTON	HOME	1 - 0	DEANE	26,077
06-Apr	ARSENAL	AWAY	1 - 2	DEANE	37,619
08-Apr	NOTTINGHAM FOREST	HOME	1 - 3	WETHERALL	29,220
13-Apr	CHELSEA	AWAY	1 - 4	McALLISTER	22,131
17-Apr	MANCHESTER UNITED	AWAY	0 - 1		48,382
29-Apr	NEWCASTLE UNITED	HOME	0 - 1		38,862
02-May	TOTTENHAM HOTSPUR	HOME	1 - 3	WETHERALL	30,061
05-May	COVENTRY CITY	AWAY	0 - 0		22,769

F. A. CUP

DATE	OPPONENTS	VENUE	SCORE	SCORERS	ATT.
07-Jan	DERBY COUNTY (R3)	AWAY	4 - 2	SPEED, DEANE, McALLISTER & YEBOAH	16,155
14-Feb	BOLTON WANDERERS (R4)	AWAY	1 - 0	WALLACE Ro.	16,694
21-Feb	PORT VALE (R5)	HOME	0 - 0		18,607
27-Feb	PORT VALE (R5R)	AWAY	2 - 1	McALLISTER 2	14,023
10-Mar	LIVERPOOL (R6)	HOME	0 - 0		24,632
20-Mar	LIVERPOOL (R6R)	AWAY	0 - 3		30,812

COCA - COLA CUP

DATE	OPPONENTS	VENUE	SCORE	SCORERS	ATT.
19-Sep	NOTTS COUNTY (R2-1)	HOME	0 - 0		12,384
03-Oct	NOTTS COUNTY (R2-2)	AWAY	3 - 2	McALLISTER, COUZENS & SPEED	12,477
25-Oct	DERBY COUNTY (R3)	AWAY	1 - 0	SPEED	16,030
29-Nov	BLACKBURN ROVERS (R4)	HOME	2 - 1	DEANE & YEBOAH	26,006
10-Jan	READING (R5)	HOME	2 - 1	MASINGA & SPEED	21,023
11-Feb	BIRMINGHAM CITY (SF-1)	AWAY	2 - 1	YEBOAH & O. G. (WHITE)	24,781
25-Feb	BIRMINGHAM CITY (SF-2)	HOME	3 - 0	MASINGA, YEBOAH & DEANE	35,435
24-Mar	ASTON VILLA $ (Fi)	NEUTRAL	0 - 3		77,056

U. E. F. A. CUP

DATE	OPPONENTS	VENUE	SCORE	SCORERS	ATT.
12-Sep	MONACO (R1-1)	AWAY	3 - 0	YEBOAH 3	14,000
26-Sep	MONACO (R1-2)	HOME	0 - 1		24,501
17-Oct	PSV EINDHOVEN (R2-1)	HOME	3 - 5	SPEED, PALMER & McALLISTER	24,846
31-Oct	PSV EINDHOVEN (R2-2)	AWAY	0 - 3		25,750

LEAGUE AND CUPS

APPEARANCES (SUBSTITUTE)

PLAYER	LEAGUE	F. A. CUP	CO. CUP	U.E.F.A. CUP	TOTAL
BEENEY	10	1	1		12
BEESLEY	8 (2)	4	4 (1)	2 (2)	18 (5)
BLUNT	2 (1)				2 (1)
BOWMAN	1 (2)		0 (1)	1	2 (3)
BROLIN	17 (2)	1 (1)	2 (2)		20 (5)
CHAPMAN	2				2
COUZENS	8 (6)		1 (1)	0 (2)	9 (9)
DEANE	30 (4)	3 (3)	5 (2)	3	41 (9)
DORIGO	17	3	4	2	26
FORD	12	5	4	0 (1)	21 (1)
GRAY A	12 (3)	0 (2)	1 (1)		13 (6)
HARTE	2 (2)		0 (1)		2 (3)
JACKSON M	0 (1)				0 (1)
JOBSON	12	1			13
KELLY G	34	5	8	4	51
KEWELL	2				2
LUKIC	28	5	7	4	44
McALLISTER	36	6	8	4	54
MASINGA	5 (4)	1	2		8 (4)
MAYBURY	1				1
PALMER	35	6	8	4	53
PEMBERTON	16 (1)	1 (1)	3	4	24 (2)
RADEBE	10 (3)	3 (1)	1 (2)		14 (6)
SHARP K	0 (1)			0 (1)	0 (2)
SPEED	29	4	7	4	44
TINKLER	5 (4)		1	0 (1)	6 (5)
WALLACE Ro.	12 (12)	3 (1)	3 (1)	0 (1)	18 (15)
WETHERALL	34	5	8	4	51
WHELAN	3 (5)		0 (2)	3	6 (7)
WHITE D	1 (3)		1	1 (1)	3 (4)
WORTHINGTON N	12 (4)	3	2 (1)		17 (5)
YEBOAH	22	6	7	4	39

GOALSCORERS

PLAYER	LEAGUE	F. A. CUP	CO. CUP	U.E.F.A. CUP	TOTAL
YEBOAH	12	1	3	3	19
DEANE	7	1	2		10
McALLISTER	5	3	1	1	10
SPEED	2	1	3	1	7
BROLIN	4				4
WETHERALL	4				4
PALMER	2			1	3
MASINGA			2		2
WALLACE Ro.	1	1			2
COUZENS			1		1
DORIGO	1				1
JOBSON	1				1
WHITE D	1				1
OWN GOALS			1		1

LEEDS ALSO PLAYED IN THE RYEDALE TROPHY. ON AUG 5TH 1995 VS. TOTTENHAM HOTSPUR AT THE RYEDALE STADIUM, YORK AND LOST 1 - 4 (0 - 1) WITH FORD SCORING. THE TEAM WAS PETTINGER, MARKS, FIDLER, BOWMAN, O'SHEA, SMITHARD, WHARTON, BROWN A (MASINGA), FORRESTER & SHARP (BLUNT). ON AUG 6TH 1995 VS. SHEFFIELD WEDNESDAY AT THE RYEDALE STADIUM, YORK AND DREW 0 - 0 (0 - 0). THE TEAM WAS PETTINGER, SMITHARD, FIDLER (SHEPHERD), BLUNT, O'SHEA, JACKSON (MAYBURY), WHARTON, FORD, GRANT, LOWNDES (BROWN A) & GRAY A. PETTINGER (PAUL), WHARTON (PAUL), BROWN (ANDREW), SMITHARD (MATTHEW), O'SHEA (ALAN), FIDLER (RICHARD), GRANT (TONY) & LOWNDES (NATHAN) DID NOT PLAY FOR THE FIRST TEAM.

KEY :- $ = PLAYED AT WEMBLEY

During a frenzied close season, Caspian Group bought Leeds United for £35 million. Howard Wilkinson invested £12 million, new arrivals included £4.5 million winger Lee Sharpe (Manchester United), teenage midfielder Lee Bowyer (Charlton Athletic) for £2.6 million, goalkeeper Nigel Martyn (Crystal Palace) at £2.25 million and prolific Liverpool legend Ian Rush on a free transfer. Departures included Gary McAllister, Gary Speed and John Lukic. With brilliant players in the youth set-up, Wilkinson was building again but pressure was mounting amid rumours of a managerial change.

Bowyer made a scoring debut in a 3-3 thriller at Derby County before a 2-0 home defeat to Sheffield Wednesday sparked further gossip that Wilkinson would be the season's first managerial casualty. Sharpe and Ian Harte secured hard-fought wins over Wimbledon and Blackburn Rovers but a 4-0 mauling at the hands of Manchester United proved too much for United's new owners. Three days after the defeat at Elland Road, Caspian ended Wilkinson's eight-year association with the club. Many of his signings served the club with distinction, whilst his youth policy would eventually produce full internationals such as Harry Kewell, Alan Smith, Jonathon Woodgate and Paul Robinson. Numerous managers succeeded Don Revie; none enjoyed more success than Wilkinson did during his tenure.

Appointing former Arsenal manager George Graham as manager, a new era at Elland Road began. Graham, who guided the Gunners to numerous honours, named David O'Leary assistant-manager. Graham's tenure began inauspiciously as his new team racked up five defeats in six league games, a Rod Wallace brace in a 2-0 win against Nottingham Forest the only bright moment. Eliminated by Aston Villa in the League Cup, Graham concentrated on defence, and slowly Leeds began to grind out results to edge clear of relegation.

With Tony Yeboah injured and Ian Rush struggling as lone striker, Elland Road was not a place for entertainment, in spite of Sharpe scoring in wins over Sunderland and Southampton, and Rush notching his first goal in a 2-0 victory over Chelsea. Three goalless draws and three defeats through the festive period, culminating in a 3-0 loss at Newcastle United on New Year's Day, illustrated United followers' grim fare.

Bowyer scored in wins over Leicester City and West Ham, and introducing Robert Molenaar (Volendam) and Gunnar Halle (Oldham Athletic) brought more steel defensively. With increasing confidence, Wallace knocked Crystal Palace out of the FA Cup before claiming the prize scalp of Arsenal at Highbury to earn a fifth round tie against Portsmouth. A 3-2 defeat to Pompey though was a bitter blow for fans. Doggedly persevering, victories over fellow-strugglers Sunderland, West Ham and Everton, courtesy of Bowyer, Sharpe and Molenaar strikes, gave Leeds a cushion before seven draws in the final nine games achieved safety but summarised a desperate campaign in which United scored 28 league goals; a record low total.

Discontent had set in for a number of players, Tony Yeboah in particular, who failed to impress Graham. Frustrated at a lack of opportunities, Yeboah threw his shirt into the crowd after being substituted by Graham in a defeat at Tottenham. It was a sad end to his short-spell at Leeds. Martyn made 44 appearances, while Rod Wallace top scored with just eight goals, equalling Kevin Hird's total in 1979/80. Looking forward with optimism though, inspired by Harry Kewell, Jonathan Woodgate and Paul Robinson, United's youngsters again claimed the FA Youth Cup, defeating Crystal Palace.

PREMIER LEAGUE (FINAL LEAGUE POSITION - 11TH)

PLD 38 W 11 D 13 L 14 F 28 A 38 PTS 46

DATE	OPPONENTS	VENUE	SCORE	SCORERS	ATT.
17-Aug	DERBY COUNTY	AWAY	3 - 3	O. G. (LAURSEN), HARTE & BOWYER	17,927
20-Aug	SHEFFIELD WEDNESDAY	HOME	0 - 2		31,011
26-Aug	WIMBLEDON	HOME	1 - 0	SHARPE L	25,860
04-Sep	BLACKBURN ROVERS	AWAY	1 - 0	HARTE	23,226
07-Sep	MANCHESTER UNITED	HOME	0 - 4		39,694
14-Sep	COVENTRY CITY	AWAY	1 - 2	COUZENS	17,297
21-Sep	NEWCASTLE UNITED	HOME	0 - 1		36,070
28-Sep	LEICESTER CITY	AWAY	0 - 1		20,359
12-Oct	NOTTINGHAM FOREST	HOME	2 - 0	WALLACE Ro. 2	29,225
19-Oct	ASTON VILLA	AWAY	0 - 2		39,051
26-Oct	ARSENAL	AWAY	0 - 3		38,076
02-Nov	SUNDERLAND	HOME	3 - 0	FORD, SHARPE L & DEANE	31,667
16-Nov	LIVERPOOL	HOME	0 - 2		39,981
23-Nov	SOUTHAMPTON	AWAY	2 - 0	KELLY G & SHARPE L	15,241
01-Dec	CHELSEA	HOME	2 - 0	DEANE & RUSH	32,671
07-Dec	MIDDLESBROUGH	AWAY	0 - 0		30,018
14-Dec	TOTTENHAM HOTSPUR	HOME	0 - 0		33,783
21-Dec	EVERTON	AWAY	0 - 0		36,954
26-Dec	COVENTRY CITY	HOME	1 - 3	DEANE	36,465
28-Dec	MANCHESTER UNITED	AWAY	0 - 1		55,256
01-Jan	NEWCASTLE UNITED	AWAY	0 - 3		36,489
11-Jan	LEICESTER CITY	HOME	3 - 0	BOWYER & RUSH 2	29,486
20-Jan	WEST HAM UNITED	AWAY	2 - 0	KELLY G & BOWYER	19,441
29-Jan	DERBY COUNTY	HOME	0 - 0		27,549
01-Feb	ARSENAL	HOME	0 - 0		35,502
19-Feb	LIVERPOOL	AWAY	0 - 4		38,957
22-Feb	SUNDERLAND	AWAY	1 - 0	BOWYER	21,890
01-Mar	WEST HAM UNITED	HOME	1 - 0	SHARPE L	30,575
08-Mar	EVERTON	HOME	1 - 0	MOLENAAR	32,055
12-Mar	SOUTHAMPTON	HOME	0 - 0		25,913
15-Mar	TOTTENHAM HOTSPUR	AWAY	0 - 1		33,040
22-Mar	SHEFFIELD WEDNESDAY	AWAY	2 - 2	SHARPE L & WALLACE Ro.	30,373
07-Apr	BLACKBURN ROVERS	HOME	0 - 0		27,264
16-Apr	WIMBLEDON	AWAY	0 - 2		7,979
19-Apr	NOTTINGHAM FOREST	AWAY	1 - 1	DEANE	25,565
22-Apr	ASTON VILLA	HOME	0 - 0		26,897
03-May	CHELSEA	AWAY	0 - 0		28,277
11-May	MIDDLESBROUGH	HOME	1 - 1	DEANE	38,567

F. A. CUP

DATE	OPPONENTS	VENUE	SCORE	SCORERS	ATT.
14-Jan	CRYSTAL PALACE (R3)	AWAY	2 - 2	DEANE & O. G. (ANDERSEN)	21,052
25-Jan	CRYSTAL PALACE (R3R)	HOME	1 - 0	WALLACE Ro.	21,903
04-Feb	ARSENAL (R4)	AWAY	1 - 0	WALLACE Ro.	38,115
15-Feb	PORTSMOUTH (R5)	HOME	2 - 3	BOWYER 2	35,604

COCA - COLA CUP

DATE	OPPONENTS	VENUE	SCORE	SCORERS	ATT.
18-Sep	DARLINGTON (R2-1)	HOME	2 - 2	WALLACE Ro. 2	15,711
24-Sep	DARLINGTON (R2-2)	AWAY	2 - 0	WALLACE Ro. & HARTE	6,298
23-Oct	ASTON VILLA (R3)	HOME	1 - 2	SHARPE L	15,083

LEAGUE AND CUP

APPEARANCES (SUBSTITUTE)

PLAYER	LEAGUE	F. A. CUP	CO. CUP	TOTAL
BEENEY	1			1
BEESLEY	11 (1)	1	1	13 (1)
BLUNT	0 (1)		0 (1)	0 (2)
BOWYER	32	4		36
BOYLE	0 (1)			0 (1)
COUZENS	7 (3)		3	10 (3)
DEANE	27 (1)	4		31 (1)
DORIGO	15 (3)	4		19 (3)
FORD	15 (1)		3	18 (1)
GRAY A	1 (6)		2	3 (6)
HALLE	20	3		23
HARTE	10 (4)	1	2 (1)	13 (5)
HATELEY	5 (1)			5 (1)
JACKSON M	11 (6)	4		15 (6)
JOBSON	10		3	13
KELLY G	34 (2)	4	3	41 (2)
KEWELL	0 (1)			0 (1)
LAURENT	2 (2)			2 (2)
LILLEY	4 (2)			4 (2)
MARTYN	37	4	3	44
MOLENAAR	12	2		14
PALMER	26 (2)	3	2	31 (2)
RADEBE	28 (4)	3	1	32 (4)
RUSH	34 (2)	2 (2)	2	38 (4)
SHARPE L	26	0 (1)	3	29 (1)
SHEPHERD	1			1
TINKLER	1 (2)			1 (2)
WALLACE Ro.	17 (5)	4	3	24 (5)
WETHERALL	25 (4)	1 (1)	2 (1)	28 (6)
YEBOAH	6 (1)			6 (1)

GOALSCORERS

PLAYER	LEAGUE	F. A. CUP	CO. CUP	TOTAL
WALLACE Ro.	3	2	3	8
BOWYER	4	2		6
DEANE	5	1		6
SHARPE L	5		1	6
HARTE	2		1	3
RUSH	3			3
KELLY G	2			2
COUZENS	1			1
FORD	1			1
MOLENAAR	1			1
OWN GOALS	1	1		2

George Graham had stabilised Leeds United but was determined to bring fire back into the attack. New arrivals included Jimmy-Floyd Hasselbaink (Boavista) for £2 million, David Hopkin (Crystal Palace) for £3.25 million, Alf-Inge Haaland (Nottingham Forest) for £1.6 million and Bruno Ribeiro (Vitoria Setubal) for £500,000. Departures included Carlton Palmer, Tony Yeboah and Tony Dorigo.

Hasselbaink got off to a flyer with a debut strike against Arsenal but apart from a draw against the Gunners, Leeds claimed only a 3-1 win at Sheffield Wednesday from the opening five fixtures, Rod Wallace scoring two goals. Slowly but surely United improved. Another Wallace brace sealed a thrilling 4-3 win at Blackburn Rovers and a 2-0 triumph at Southampton before centre-back David Wetherall secured a 1-0 victory against Manchester United at Elland Road.

With Graham's new arrivals settling and the first graduate from the youth team, Harry Kewell, making his mark, Leeds had a refreshing look about them. Kewell and Wetherall both found the mark in a resounding 4-1 win against Newcastle United, before Wallace sparked a run of four consecutive wins. Notching the only goal at Tottenham Hotspur, Leeds suddenly became never-say-die specialists in a trio of classic encounters. Overturning a three-goal deficit to defeat Derby County 4-3, Bowyer scoring a last gasp winner, Hasselbaink inspired a comeback to beat West Ham 3-1 before Derek Lilley proved the hero in a 3-2 win over Barnsley after Leeds trailed the Tykes by two goals.

In the midst of these clashes, there was League Cup disappointment against lowly Reading prior to a dip in form; Leeds winning two of 11 league clashes, Hasselbaink scoring in 2-0 wins over Bolton Wanderers and Crystal Palace. Nevertheless, by Christmas Leeds had matched their total number of goals from the previous season and the New Year brought early success in the FA Cup. Facing lower league opposition, Leeds enjoyed comfortable wins over Oxford United and Grimsby Town before a 3-2 win against Birmingham City set up a quarter-final home clash versus Wolves.

With cup-fever building, Kewell secured a win over Tottenham Hotspur but Leeds failed to perform against Wolves in front of a full house at Elland Road, and to compound a hugely disappointing 1-0 defeat, Hasselbaink missed a late penalty. Credit to Graham's new-look team however, they bounced back with dazzling performances to beat Blackburn 4-0 and Derby 5-0, Hasselbaink and Bowyer scoring in both games, as Leeds chased a UEFA Cup spot. Following a 3-0 defeat at West Ham, tragedy almost hit the club on the return journey, but Captain John Hackett's' split second decision to abort the aeroplane's take off carrying United's squad saved the day; passengers escaping from the wreckage with only minor injuries.

Returning to action, further Hasselbaink strikes helped seal victories over Barnsley 2-1, Chelsea 3-1 and Bolton 3-2 before the sharpshooter's brace secured a 3-3 thriller against Coventry City. Graham's team had claimed a UEFA Cup spot with a fifth-place finish. Nigel Martyn made 45 appearances. Hasselbaink finished his debut season top scorer with 22 goals. United's youth policy continued to prosper with many of the FA Youth Cup side, nurtured by Eddie Gray, forming the backbone of the reserve team that claimed a first Division 1 crown in 61 years.

1997 - 1998

PREMIER LEAGUE (FINAL LEAGUE POSITION - 5TH)

PLD 38 W 17 D 8 L 13 F 57 A 46 PTS 59

DATE	OPPONENTS	VENUE	SCORE	SCORERS	ATT.
09-Aug	ARSENAL	HOME	1 - 1	HASSELBAINK	37,993
13-Aug	SHEFFIELD WEDNESDAY	AWAY	3 - 1	WALLACE Ro. 2 & RIBEIRO	31,520
23-Aug	CRYSTAL PALACE	HOME	0 - 2		29,076
26-Aug	LIVERPOOL	HOME	0 - 2		39,775
30-Aug	ASTON VILLA	AWAY	0 - 1		39,027
14-Sep	BLACKBURN ROVERS	AWAY	4 - 3	WALLACE Ro. 2, MOLENAAR & HOPKIN	21,956
20-Sep	LEICESTER CITY	HOME	0 - 1		29,620
24-Sep	SOUTHAMPTON	AWAY	2 - 0	MOLENAAR & WALLACE Ro.	15,102
27-Sep	MANCHESTER UNITED	HOME	1 - 0	WETHERALL	39,952
04-Oct	COVENTRY CITY	AWAY	0 - 0		17,770
18-Oct	NEWCASTLE UNITED	HOME	4 - 1	RIBEIRO, O. G. (BERESFORD), KEWELL & WETHERALL	39,834
25-Oct	WIMBLEDON	AWAY	0 - 1		15,718
01-Nov	TOTTENHAM HOTSPUR	AWAY	1 - 0	WALLACE Ro.	26,441
08-Nov	DERBY COUNTY	HOME	4 - 3	WALLACE Ro., KEWELL, HASSELBAINK (PEN) & BOWYER	33,572
23-Nov	WEST HAM UNITED	HOME	3 - 1	HASSELBAINK 2 & HAALAND	30,031
29-Nov	BARNSLEY	AWAY	3 - 2	HAALAND, WALLACE Ro. & LILLEY	18,690
06-Dec	EVERTON	HOME	0 - 0		34,869
13-Dec	CHELSEA	AWAY	0 - 0		34,690
20-Dec	BOLTON WANDERERS	HOME	2 - 0	RIBEIRO & HASSELBAINK	31,163
26-Dec	LIVERPOOL	AWAY	1 - 3	HAALAND	43,854
28-Dec	ASTON VILLA	HOME	1 - 1	HASSELBAINK	36,287
10-Jan	ARSENAL	AWAY	1 - 2	HASSELBAINK	38,018
17-Jan	SHEFFIELD WEDNESDAY	HOME	1 - 2	O. G. (PEMBRIDGE)	33,166
31-Jan	CRYSTAL PALACE	AWAY	2 - 0	WALLACE Ro. & HASSELBAINK	25,248
07-Feb	LEICESTER CITY	AWAY	0 - 1		21,244
22-Feb	NEWCASTLE UNITED	AWAY	1 - 1	WALLACE Ro.	36,511
28-Feb	SOUTHAMPTON	HOME	0 - 1		28,791
04-Mar	TOTTENHAM HOTSPUR	HOME	1 - 0	KEWELL	31,394
11-Mar	BLACKBURN ROVERS	HOME	4 - 0	BOWYER, HASSELBAINK & HAALAND 2	32,933
15-Mar	DERBY COUNTY	AWAY	5 - 0	HALLE, O.G. (LAURSEN), BOWYER, KEWELL & HASSELBAINK	30,217
30-Mar	WEST HAM UNITED	AWAY	0 - 3		24,107
04-Apr	BARNSLEY	HOME	2 - 1	HASSELBAINK & O. G. (MOSES)	37,749
08-Apr	CHELSEA	HOME	3 - 1	HASSELBAINK 2 & WETHERALL	37,276
11-Apr	EVERTON	AWAY	0 - 2		37,099
18-Apr	BOLTON WANDERERS	AWAY	3 - 2	HAALAND, HALLE & HASSELBAINK	25,000
25-Apr	COVENTRY CITY	HOME	3 - 3	HASSELBAINK 2 & KEWELL	36,522
04-May	MANCHESTER UNITED	AWAY	0 - 3		55,167
10-May	WIMBLEDON	HOME	1 - 1	HAALAND	38,172

F. A. CUP

DATE	OPPONENTS	VENUE	SCORE	SCORERS	ATT.
03-Jan	OXFORD UNITED (R3)	HOME	4 - 0	RADEBE, HASSELBAINK & KEWELL 2	20,568
24-Jan	GRIMSBY TOWN (R4)	HOME	2 - 0	MOLENAAR & HASSELBAINK	29,598
14-Feb	BIRMINGHAM CITY (R5)	HOME	3 - 2	WALLACE Ro. & HASSELBAINK 2	35,463
07-Mar	WOLVERHAMPTON WANDERERS (R6)	HOME	0 - 1		39,902

COCA - COLA CUP

DATE	OPPONENTS	VENUE	SCORE	SCORERS	ATT.
17-Sep	BRISTOL CITY (R2-1)	HOME	3 - 1	WETHERALL, HASSELBAINK & RIBEIRO	8,806
30-Sep	BRISTOL CITY (R2-2)	AWAY	1 - 2	HASSELBAINK	10,857
15-Oct	STOKE CITY (R3) *	AWAY	3 - 1	KEWELL & WALLACE Ro. 2	16,203
18-Nov	READING (R4)	HOME	2 - 3	WETHERALL & BOWYER	15,069

LEAGUE AND CUP

APPEARANCES (SUBSTITUTE)

PLAYER	LEAGUE	F. A. CUP	CO. CUP	TOTAL
BEENEY	1	0 (1)		1 (1)
BOWYER	21 (4)	3	2 (1)	26 (5)
HAALAND	26 (6)	2	3	31 (6)
HALLE	31 (2)	3	2 (1)	36 (3)
HARTE	12	1 (2)		13 (2)
HASSELBAINK	30 (3)	4	3	37 (3)
HIDEN	11	1		12
HOPKIN	22 (3)	1	4	27 (3)
JACKSON M	0 (1)			0 (1)
KELLY G	34	3 (1)	3	40 (1)
KEWELL	26 (3)	4	2	32 (3)
LILLEY	0 (12)	0 (1)	0 (3)	0 (16)
McPHAIL	0 (4)			0 (4)
MARTYN	37	4	4	45
MATTHEWS	0 (3)			0 (3)
MAYBURY	9 (3)	2	1	12 (3)
MOLENAAR	18 (4)	3	2 (1)	23 (5)
RADEBE	26 (1)	2	4	32 (1)
RIBEIRO	28 (1)	3	2 (1)	33 (2)
ROBERTSON	24 (2)	1	4	29 (2)
WALLACE Ro.	29 (2)	4	4	37 (2)
WETHERALL	33 (1)	3	4	40 (1)

GOALSCORERS

PLAYER	LEAGUE	F. A. CUP	CO. CUP	TOTAL
HASSELBAINK	16	4	2	22
WALLACE Ro.	10	1	2	13
KEWELL	5	2	1	8
HAALAND	7			7
WETHERALL	3		2	5
BOWYER	3		1	4
RIBEIRO	3		1	4
MOLENAAR	2	1		3
HALLE	2			2
HOPKIN	1			1
LILLEY	1			1
RADEBE		1		1
OWN GOALS	4			4

KEY :- * = AFTER EXTRA TIME

193

Cautious optimism was the watchword during pre-season training. Out of contract, Rod Wallace signed for Rangers, severing all links with Leeds United's 1992 title-winning squad, but new arrivals included Clyde Wijnhard, Martin Hiden and Danny Granville.

Early wins over Blackburn Rovers; Hasselbaink notching the only goal, and Southampton; Wijnhard scoring in a 3-0 victory, saw Leeds briefly top the table, however behind the scenes rumours were rife that George Graham was taking the reigns at Tottenham Hotspur. Uncertainty off the field spread to mediocrity on the pitch, save a thriller at White Hart Lane, where two injury time goals earned the hosts an unlikely 3-3 draw. The match proved to be Graham's swansong as his impending move quickly materialised.

Failing to persuade Martin O'Neill from Leicester City to become manager, assistant boss David O'Leary's appointment was soon ratified. Impressing immediately, O'Leary began blooding the club's promising youngsters. Harry Kewell had already made his mark, Ian Harte was claiming the left-back slot, now schemer Stephen McPhail and centre-back Jonathon Woodgate entered the fray and did not disappoint. In the UEFA Cup, Leeds edged past Maritimo before losing 1-0 on aggregate to Italian giants Roma, a tie that saw rookie keeper Paul Robinson make his bow with Nigel Martyn injured.

Although knocked out of the Worthington and UEFA Cups, an exciting era was dawning and game-by-game excitement was building. Woodgate scored the winner against Sheffield Wednesday before 17-year-old Alan Smith made an astonishing debut, scoring in Leeds' 3-1 win at Liverpool. The Anfield victory galvanised Leeds, aided by talented youngsters able to take their opportunity. Bowyer, Kewell and Smith all found the target in a 4-1 mauling of Charlton Athletic, prior to Bowyer's double sealing a 4-0 romp against West Ham; a match that saw seven Leeds players under 21 years of age.

Bowyer, the country's most expensive teenager on his arrival at Elland Road, secured a 2-0 win against Coventry City and a 3-0 Boxing Day triumph at Newcastle United. Combining with Smith, Leeds defeated Middlesbrough 2-0, but sandwiched between were two defeats; O'Leary needed experience. Amid rumours of David Batty's return to the club for £4.4 million from Newcastle United, Hasselbaink re-found his scoring touch, notching a brace in a 2-1 win at Aston Villa. Further victories over Everton, Leicester, Tottenham, Sheffield Wednesday, Derby County and Nottingham Forest equalled the club's all-time seven-game top-flight winning record set in 1973/74.

In a brilliant run, Kewell and Smith scored against Leicester, a clash that saw Batty's debut, while Hasselbaink notched against Wednesday, County and Forest. The only disappointment was an FA Cup defeat at Tottenham, but Leeds earned an impressive draw at Old Trafford and a 5-1 win at West Ham, Hasselbaink scoring in both games. As his first Leeds goal came against Arsenal so would Hasselbaink's last, in the final home game, to hand the championship to Manchester United. Finishing fourth, Leeds qualified for Europe, a wonderful achievement for such a young squad. With observers eulogising about the potential of O'Leary's side, the club's eightieth year could hardly have ended brighter. O'Leary justifiably received credit for the transformation, while Batty's homecoming re-established the link to United's '92 title-winning team. Kewell made 49 appearances, Hasselbaink top scored on 20 goals.

1998 - 1999

PREMIER LEAGUE (FINAL LEAGUE POSITION - 4TH)
PLD 38 W 18 D 13 L 7 F 62 A 34 PTS 67

DATE	OPPONENTS	VENUE	SCORE	SCORERS	ATT.
15-Aug	MIDDLESBROUGH	AWAY	0 - 0		34,162
24-Aug	BLACKBURN ROVERS	HOME	1 - 0	HASSELBAINK	30,652
29-Aug	WIMBLEDON	AWAY	1 - 1	BOWYER	16,437
08-Sep	SOUTHAMPTON	HOME	3 - 0	O. G. (MARSHALL) HARTE & WIJNHARD	30,637
12-Sep	EVERTON	AWAY	0 - 0		36,687
19-Sep	ASTON VILLA	HOME	0 - 0		33,446
26-Sep	TOTTENHAM HOTSPUR	AWAY	3 - 3	HALLE, HASSELBAINK & WIJNHARD	35,535
03-Oct	LEICESTER CITY	HOME	0 - 1		32,606
17-Oct	NOTTINGHAM FOREST	AWAY	1 - 1	HALLE	23,911
25-Oct	CHELSEA	HOME	0 - 0		36,292
31-Oct	DERBY COUNTY	AWAY	2 - 2	MOLENAAR & KEWELL	27,034
08-Nov	SHEFFIELD WEDNESDAY	HOME	2 - 1	HASSELBAINK & WOODGATE	30,012
14-Nov	LIVERPOOL	AWAY	3 - 1	SMITH A & HASSELBAINK 2	44,305
21-Nov	CHARLTON ATHLETIC	HOME	4 - 1	BOWYER, KEWELL, HASSELBAINK & SMITH A	32,487
29-Nov	MANCHESTER UNITED	AWAY	2 - 3	HASSELBAINK & KEWELL	55,172
05-Dec	WEST HAM UNITED	HOME	4 - 0	BOWYER 2, HASSELBAINK & MOLENAAR	36,320
14-Dec	COVENTRY CITY	HOME	2 - 0	HOPKIN & BOWYER	31,802
20-Dec	ARSENAL	AWAY	1 - 3	HASSELBAINK	38,025
26-Dec	NEWCASTLE UNITED	AWAY	3 - 0	KEWELL, HASSELBAINK & BOWYER	36,783
29-Dec	WIMBLEDON	HOME	2 - 2	RIBEIRO & HOPKIN	39,816
09-Jan	BLACKBURN ROVERS	AWAY	0 - 1		27,620
16-Jan	MIDDLESBROUGH	HOME	2 - 0	BOWYER & SMITH A	37,473
30-Jan	SOUTHAMPTON	AWAY	0 - 3		15,236
06-Feb	NEWCASTLE UNITED	HOME	0 - 1		40,202
17-Feb	ASTON VILLA	AWAY	2 - 1	HASSELBAINK 2	37,510
20-Feb	EVERTON	HOME	1 - 0	KORSTEN	36,344
01-Mar	LEICESTER CITY	AWAY	2 - 1	KEWELL & SMITH A	18,101
10-Mar	TOTTENHAM HOTSPUR	HOME	2 - 0	KEWELL & SMITH A	34,521
13-Mar	SHEFFIELD WEDNESDAY	AWAY	2 - 0	HASSELBAINK & HOPKIN	28,142
20-Mar	DERBY COUNTY	HOME	4 - 1	HARTE, BOWYER, KORSTEN & HASSELBAINK	38,971
03-Apr	NOTTINGHAM FOREST	HOME	3 - 1	HARTE, SMITH A & HASSELBAINK	39,645
12-Apr	LIVERPOOL	HOME	0 - 0		39,451
17-Apr	CHARLTON ATHLETIC	AWAY	1 - 1	WOODGATE	20,043
25-Apr	MANCHESTER UNITED	HOME	1 - 1	HASSELBAINK	40,255
01-May	WEST HAM UNITED	AWAY	5 - 1	HASSELBAINK, SMITH A., HARTE (PEN), BOWYER & HAALAND	25,997
05-May	CHELSEA	AWAY	0 - 1		34,762
11-May	ARSENAL	HOME	1 - 0	HASSELBAINK	40,124
16-May	COVENTRY CITY	AWAY	2 - 2	WIJNHARD & HOPKIN	23,049

F. A. CUP

DATE	OPPONENTS	VENUE	SCORE	SCORERS	ATT.
02-Jan	RUSHDEN & DIAMONDS (R3)	AWAY	0 - 0		6,431
13-Jan	RUSHDEN & DIAMONDS (R3R)	HOME	3 - 1	SMITH A 2 & HASSELBAINK	39,159
23-Jan	PORTSMOUTH (R4)	AWAY	5 - 1	HARTE, WETHERALL, RIBEIRO, KEWELL & WIJNHARD	18,864
13-Feb	TOTTENHAM HOTSPUR (R5)	HOME	1 - 1	HARTE	39,696
24-Feb	TOTTENHAM HOTSPUR (R5R)	AWAY	0 - 2		32,307

WORTHINGTON CUP

DATE	OPPONENTS	VENUE	SCORE	SCORERS	ATT.
28-Oct	BRADFORD CITY (R3)	HOME	1 - 0	KEWELL	27,561
11-Nov	LEICESTER CITY (R4)	AWAY	1 - 2	KEWELL	20,161

U. E. F. A. CUP

DATE	OPPONENTS	VENUE	SCORE	SCORERS	ATT.
15-Sep	CS MARITIMO (R1-1)	HOME	1 - 0	HASSELBAINK	38,033
29-Sep	CS MARITIMO (R1-2) *	AWAY	0 - 1		8,000
20-Oct	AS ROMA (R2-1)	AWAY	0 - 1		43,003
03-Nov	AS ROMA (R2-2)	HOME	0 - 0		39,161

LEAGUE AND CUPS
APPEARANCES (SUBSTITUTE)

PLAYER	LEAGUE	F. A. CUP	WORT. CUP	U.E.F.A. CUP	TOTAL
BATTY	10				10
BOWYER	35	4	2	4	45
GRANVILLE	7 (2)	3	1	0 (1)	11 (3)
HAALAND	24 (5)	3 (1)		2 (1)	29 (7)
HALLE	14 (3)	2 (1)	1	2	19 (4)
HARTE	34 (1)	5	1	3	43 (1)
HASSELBAINK	36	5	2	4	47
HIDEN	14		1	4	19
HOPKIN	32 (2)	5	2	4	43 (2)
JONES Ma.	3 (5)	0 (1)			3 (6)
KEWELL	36 (2)	5	2	4	47 (2)
KNARVIK		0 (1)			0 (1)
KORSTEN	4 (3)	2 (1)			6 (4)
LILLEY	0 (2)			0 (1)	0 (3)
McPHAIL	11 (6)		1	2	14 (6)
MARTYN	34	5	1	4	44
MOLENAAR	17		2	4	23
RADEBE	29	3	1	3	36
RIBEIRO	7 (6)	1	1	1 (1)	10 (7)
ROBINSON	4 (1)		1		5 (1)
SHARPE L	2 (2)			1 (2)	3 (4)
SMITH A	15 (7)	2 (2)			17 (9)
WETHERALL	14 (7)	4			18 (7)
WIJNHARD	11 (7)	1 (1)	1	1 (3)	14 (11)
WOODGATE	25	5	2	1	33

GOALSCORERS

PLAYER	LEAGUE	F. A. CUP	WORT. CUP	U.E.F.A. CUP	TOTAL
HASSELBAINK	18	1		1	20
BOWYER	9				9
KEWELL	6	1	2		9
SMITH A	7	2			9
HARTE	4	2			6
HOPKIN	4				4
WIJNHARD	3	1			4
HALLE	2				2
KORSTEN	2				2
MOLENAAR	2				2
RIBEIRO	1	1			2
WOODGATE	2				2
HAALAND	1				1
WETHERALL		1			1
OWN GOALS	1				1

KEY :- * = WON 4 - 1 ON PENALTIES AND AFTER EXTRA TIME

Throughout the summer Leeds boss David O'Leary and newly installed chairman Peter Ridsdale finalised contract talks with emerging youngsters but tying down Jimmy-Floyd Hasselbaink floundered. Despite attempts to pacify his salary expectations, Hasselbaink acrimoniously joined Atletico Madrid for £12m. Bolstering his squad with £20 million of talent, arrivals included Michael Bridges (Sunderland), Darren Huckerby (Coventry City), Danny Mills (Charlton Athletic), Michael Duberry (Chelsea) and Eirik Bakke (Sogndal). Departures included David Wetherall, Gunner Halle, Bruno Ribeiro and Danny Granville.

Early successes included a Bridges hat-trick in a 3-0 win at Southampton while Mills sealed a 2-1 triumph over Sunderland. With growing confidence, O'Leary's babes announced themselves with a stunning run, winning 10 consecutive games. Thrilling Premiership performances included victories over Tottenham Hotspur, Harte securing a 2-1 win, Coventry City, Bridges sealing a 4-3 triumph, and Newcastle United, Bridges settling a classic 3-2 encounter. A Harry Kewell strike at Watford sent Leeds top of the table.

United's UEFA Cup campaign began with comfortable wins over Partizan Belgrade and Lokomotiv Moscow, Lee Bowyer scoring in both ties, however following a win over Blackburn Rovers in the Worthington Cup, Leicester City ended United's first avenue to glory with a penalty shoot-out victory. Back in the Premiership, entertainment was overflowing during a 4-4 thriller at Everton before Leeds enjoyed another winning spell of five games, re-claiming top spot with a Bridges strike against Southampton. Harte kept Leeds at the helm, with spot kicks against Bradford City and Derby County.

Returning to Europe, Leeds' passage in round three against Spartak Moscow came courtesy of Kewell's 'away' goal in a 2-1 defeat coupled with Lucas Radebe's late strike at Elland Road, before O'Leary's youngsters focused again on domestic matters. In the FA Cup, unusually before Christmas, Bakke edged Leeds past Port Vale prior to another rookie, Stephen McPhail, making his mark in the Premiership with a brace at Chelsea, while Bowyer settled a Boxing Day clash against Leicester.

Competing on three fronts with New Year approaching, fatigue was O'Leary's biggest problem and it came as little surprise when Leeds lost top-spot, claiming two wins in seven league clashes; Bridges notching the winner at Sunderland, while Kewell sealed a tepid affair against Tottenham. In a depressing run, Aston Villa ended Leeds' FA Cup dreams after a tremendous 5-2 triumph at Manchester City, but European dreams still burned when Kewell came up trumps in round four with the only goal of a classic encounter against Roma to shoot Leeds into the quarter-finals.

Facing a packed run-in, Champions League football was the target. Leeds kept their ambitions alive with wins over Coventry, Bradford and Wimbledon prior to ousting Slavia Prague from the UEFA Cup, Kewell scoring in both legs. However, the season's complexion changed amid six Premiership and UEFA Cup defeats when two Leeds United supporters, Christopher Loftus and Kevin Speight, were stabbed to death in Istanbul on the eve of the club's first European semi-final for 25 years against Galatasaray.

Reluctantly agreeing to play, Leeds entered the stadium shielded by the Turkish Army. Galatasaray refused to wear black armbands and observe a minute's silence. Leeds lost 2-0 but the result was irrelevant as the football world in Britain grieved. On the field, Leeds went out 4-2 on aggregate before duly claiming a Champions League spot at West Ham on the final day of a campaign that encompassed many unforgettable moments as O'Leary's charges came of age. In a remarkable season, forever tinged with tragedy, Nigel Martyn made 55 appearances. Bridges top scored with 21 goals.

1999 - 2000

PREMIER LEAGUE (FINAL LEAGUE POSITION - 3RD)
PLD 38 W 21 D 6 L 11 F 58 A 43 PTS 69

DATE	OPPONENTS	VENUE	SCORE	SCORERS	ATT.
07-Aug	DERBY COUNTY	HOME	0 - 0		40,118
11-Aug	SOUTHAMPTON	AWAY	3 - 0	BRIDGES 3	15,206
14-Aug	MANCHESTER UNITED	AWAY	0 - 2		55,187
21-Aug	SUNDERLAND	HOME	2 - 1	BOWYER & MILLS Da.	39,064
23-Aug	LIVERPOOL	HOME	1 - 2	O. G. (SONG)	39,703
28-Aug	TOTTENHAM HOTSPUR	AWAY	2 - 1	SMITH A & HARTE	36,012
11-Sep	COVENTRY CITY	AWAY	4 - 1	BOWYER, HARTE (PEN), HUCKERBY & BRIDGES	21,532
19-Sep	MIDDLESBROUGH	HOME	2 - 0	BRIDGES & KEWELL	34,122
25-Sep	NEWCASTLE UNITED	HOME	3 - 2	BOWYER, KEWELL & BRIDGES	40,192
03-Oct	WATFORD	AWAY	2 - 1	BRIDGES & KEWELL	19,677
16-Oct	SHEFFIELD WEDNESDAY	HOME	2 - 0	SMITH A 2	39,437
24-Oct	EVERTON	AWAY	4 - 4	BRIDGES 2, KEWELL & WOODGATE	37,355
30-Oct	WEST HAM UNITED	HOME	1 - 0	HARTE	40,190
07-Nov	WIMBLEDON	AWAY	0 - 2		18,747
20-Nov	BRADFORD CITY	HOME	2 - 1	SMITH A & HARTE (PEN)	39,937
28-Nov	SOUTHAMPTON	HOME	1 - 0	BRIDGES	39,288
05-Dec	DERBY COUNTY	AWAY	1 - 0	HARTE (PEN)	29,455
19-Dec	CHELSEA	AWAY	2 - 0	McPHAIL 2	35,106
26-Dec	LEICESTER CITY	HOME	2 - 1	BRIDGES & BOWYER	40,105
28-Dec	ARSENAL	AWAY	0 - 2		38,096
03-Jan	ASTON VILLA	HOME	1 - 2	KEWELL	40,027
23-Jan	SUNDERLAND	AWAY	2 - 1	WILCOX & BRIDGES	41,947
05-Feb	LIVERPOOL	AWAY	1 - 3	BOWYER	44,793
12-Feb	TOTTENHAM HOTSPUR	HOME	1 - 0	KEWELL	40,127
20-Feb	MANCHESTER UNITED	HOME	0 - 1		40,160
26-Feb	MIDDLESBROUGH	AWAY	0 - 0		34,800
05-Mar	COVENTRY CITY	HOME	3 - 0	KEWELL, BRIDGES & WILCOX	38,710
12-Mar	BRADFORD CITY	AWAY	2 - 1	BRIDGES 2	18,276
19-Mar	WIMBLEDON	HOME	4 - 1	BAKKE 2, HARTE (PEN) & KEWELL	39,256
26-Mar	LEICESTER CITY	AWAY	1 - 2	KEWELL	21,095
01-Apr	CHELSEA	HOME	0 - 1		40,162
09-Apr	ASTON VILLA	AWAY	0 - 1		33,889
16-Apr	ARSENAL	HOME	0 - 4		39,307
23-Apr	NEWCASTLE UNITED	AWAY	2 - 2	BRIDGES & WILCOX	36,460
30-Apr	SHEFFIELD WEDNESDAY	AWAY	3 - 0	HOPKIN, BRIDGES & KEWELL	23,416
03-May	WATFORD	HOME	3 - 1	BRIDGES, DUBERRY & HUCKERBY	36,324
08-May	EVERTON	HOME	1 - 1	BRIDGES	37,713
14-May	WEST HAM UNITED	AWAY	0 - 0		26,044

F. A. CUP

DATE	OPPONENTS	VENUE	SCORE	SCORERS	ATT.
12-Dec	PORT VALE (R3)	HOME	2 - 0	BAKKE 2	11,912
09-Jan	MANCHESTER CITY (R4)	AWAY	5 - 2	BAKKE, SMITH A., KEWELL 2 & BOWYER	29,240
30-Jan	ASTON VILLA (R5)	AWAY	2 - 3	HARTE & BAKKE	30,026

WORTHINGTON CUP

DATE	OPPONENTS	VENUE	SCORE	SCORERS	ATT.
13-Oct	BLACKBURN ROVERS (R3)	HOME	1 - 0	MILLS Da.	24,353
15-Dec	LEICESTER CITY (R4) $	AWAY	0 - 0		16,125

U. E. F. A. CUP

DATE	OPPONENTS	VENUE	SCORE	SCORERS	ATT.
14-Sep	PARTIZAN BELGRADE (R1-1) ^	AWAY	3 - 1	BOWYER 2 & RADEBE	4,950
30-Sep	PARTIZAN BELGRADE (R1-2)	HOME	1 - 0	HUCKERBY	39,806
21-Oct	LOKOMOTIV MOSCOW (R2-1)	HOME	4 - 1	BOWYER 2, SMITH A & KEWELL	37,814
04-Nov	LOKOMOTIV MOSCOW (R2-2)	AWAY	3 - 0	HARTE (PEN) & BRIDGES 2	8,000
02-Dec	SPARTAK MOSCOW (R3-1) <	AWAY	1 - 2	KEWELL	5,485
09-Dec	SPARTAK MOSCOW (R3-2) >	HOME	1 - 0	RADEBE	39,732
02-Mar	AS ROMA (R4-1)	AWAY	0 - 0		37,726
09-Mar	AS ROMA (R4-2)	HOME	1 - 0	KEWELL	39,149
16-Mar	SLAVIA PRAGUE (QF-1)	HOME	3 - 0	WILCOX, KEWELL & BOWYER	39,519
23-Mar	SLAVIA PRAGUE (QF-2)	AWAY	1 - 2	KEWELL	13,460
06-Apr	GALATASARAY (SF-1)	AWAY	0 - 2		18,000
20-Apr	GALATASARAY (SF-2)	HOME	2 - 2	BAKKE 2	38,406

LEAGUE AND CUPS
APPEARANCES (SUBSTITUTE)

PLAYER	LEAGUE	F. A. CUP	WORT. CUP	U.E.F.A. CUP	TOTAL
BAKKE	24 (5)	3	2	9 (1)	38 (6)
BATTY	16		2	4	22
BOWYER	31 (2)	3	1	11	46 (2)
BRIDGES	32 (2)	1 (1)	2	12	47 (3)
DUBERRY	12 (1)	1	0 (1)	1	14 (2)
HAALAND	7 (6)			5 (1)	12 (7)
HARTE	33	3	1	12	49
HIDEN	0 (1)				0 (1)
HOPKIN	10 (4)		1	2 (1)	13 (5)
HUCKERBY	9 (24)	1 (2)	0 (1)	1 (8)	11 (35)
JONES Ma.	5 (6)	0 (1)	0 (1)	3 (2)	8 (10)
KELLY G	28 (3)	3	2	11	44 (3)
KEWELL	36	3	2	12	53
McPHAIL	23 (1)	3	1 (1)	9	36 (2)
MARTYN	38	3	2	12	55
MILLS Da.	16 (1)	0 (1)	1	2	19 (2)
RADEBE	31	2	2	11	46
SMITH A	20 (6)	2 (1)	1	2 (6)	25 (13)
WILCOX	15 (5)	2		3 (1)	20 (6)
WOODGATE	32 (2)	3	2	10	47 (2)

GOALSCORERS

PLAYER	LEAGUE	F. A. CUP	WORT. CUP	U.E.F.A. CUP	TOTAL
BRIDGES	19			2	21
KEWELL	10	2		5	17
BOWYER	5	1		5	11
BAKKE	2	4		2	8
HARTE	6	1		1	8
SMITH A	4	1		1	6
WILCOX	3			1	4
HUCKERBY	2			1	3
McPHAIL	2				2
MILLS Da.	1		1		2
RADEBE				2	2
DUBERRY	1				1
HOPKIN	1				1
WOODGATE	1				1
OWN GOALS	1				1

KEY :- $ = LOST 2 - 4 ON PENALTIES, ^ = PLAYED AT THE ABE LENSTRA STADIUM, HEERENVEEN, < = PLAYED AT THE GEORGI ASPARUCHOV STADIUM, SOFIA & > = WON ON AWAY GOALS

Against a growing backdrop of optimism, David O'Leary prepared his talented squad for a season of promise. Investing £18 million on Mark Viduka (Celtic), Olivier Dacourt (Lens) and Dominic Matteo (Liverpool), departures included David Hopkin, Robert Molenaar and Alf-Inge Haaland. With qualification to the Champions League group stages Leeds' initial target, Alan Smith saw Leeds past TSV 1860 Munich. Continuing his fine start, Smith notched goals in wins over Everton and Middlesbrough but injuries to David Batty, Harry Kewell, Jonathon Woodgate and Michael Bridges brought inconsistency. Viduka was struggling with injury too, but quickly teamed up with Smith to shoot down Tottenham Hotspur 4-3 and Charlton Athletic 3-1, before notching all four goals in another 4-3 thriller, to defeat Liverpool.

In Europe, United bounced back from a 4-0 thrashing in Barcelona to beat AC Milan, courtesy of a freak last minute goal by Lee Bowyer, and Besiktas, Bowyer scoring a brace in a 6-0 romp. Another Bowyer strike earned a creditable 1-1 draw with Barcelona, before Matteo's glancing header gained a 1-1 draw with AC Milan, guaranteeing a £10 million bonanza in the Champions League second phase with mouth-watering clashes against Real Madrid, Lazio and Anderlecht.

Despite Tranmere Rovers ending Worthington Cup aspirations, O'Leary brought West Ham star defender Rio Ferdinand to Elland Road for £18 million, a world record for a centre-half. Hot on Ferdinand's heels, Robbie Keane arrived from Inter Milan, for an agreed fee of £12 million due in the summer, while Darren Huckerby and Matthew Jones departed for a combined £6.7 million. For all Leeds' success in Europe, domestically two home victories in eight games, against Arsenal and Sunderland prior to the New Year, was not the form of aspiring champions.

However, with Ferdinand settling in defence alongside Woodgate, Matteo and Ian Harte, Leeds climbed the table as Keane secured away victories at Manchester City and Ipswich Town. Although knocked out of the FA Cup by Liverpool, O'Leary's troops struck a rich vain of form at home, and in Europe through February and March. Triumphing 1-0 in Italy against Lazio, courtesy of a Smith goal, Bowyer and Smith were the stars of a sensational double against Anderlecht to take United into the money-spinning Champions League knockout stages.

With confidence rising, Leeds claimed seven wins in eight Premiership games. Bowyer notched the winner against Tottenham before Viduka returned to form in a 1-1 draw against Manchester United; however, Leeds felt aggrieved over a late disallowed goal that would have brought victory. Nevertheless, Leeds' sharpshooter was on target in wins over Charlton and Sunderland, though revelations regarding Bowyer and Woodgate in a Sunday newspaper tempered supporter's joy. Showing character, Bowyer sealed a superb 2-1 win and double to boot at Liverpool, whilst Keane scored in victories against Southampton, West Ham and Chelsea.

Leeds had climbed into third spot and came through a nail biting Champions League quarter-final against Depotivo La Coruna 3-2 on aggregate; Harte, Smith and Ferdinand securing a 3-0 win at Elland Road, before valiant defending brought a semi-final berth against Valencia. In a quite amazing season, O'Leary's charges were defying all the odds but following a 0-0 draw against the Spanish giants, Leeds bowed out of Europe following a 3-0 defeat in Spain. The remaining games brought a 6-1 thumping of Bradford City and a 3-1 win over Leicester City, Smith scoring in both clashes, but a 2-1 defeat at Arsenal saw Leeds edged out of another Champions League campaign. Finishing fourth, Bowyer made 54 appearances. Viduka top scored with 22 goals.

2000 - 2001

PREMIER LEAGUE (FINAL LEAGUE POSITION - 4TH)
PLD 38 W 20 D 8 L 10 F 64 A 43 PTS 68

DATE	OPPONENTS	VENUE	SCORE	SCORERS	ATT.
19-Aug	EVERTON	HOME	2 - 0	SMITH A 2	40,010
26-Aug	MIDDLESBROUGH	AWAY	2 - 1	BOWYER & SMITH A	31,626
05-Sep	MANCHESTER CITY	HOME	1 - 2	BOWYER	40,055
09-Sep	COVENTRY CITY	AWAY	0 - 0		20,377
16-Sep	IPSWICH TOWN	HOME	1 - 2	BOWYER	35,552
23-Sep	DERBY COUNTY	AWAY	1 - 1	HARTE	26,248
30-Sep	TOTTENHAM HOTSPUR	HOME	4 - 3	VIDUKA 2 & SMITH A 2	37,562
14-Oct	CHARLTON ATHLETIC	HOME	3 - 1	SMITH A & VIDUKA 2	38,837
21-Oct	MANCHESTER UNITED	AWAY	0 - 3		67,525
29-Oct	BRADFORD CITY	AWAY	1 - 1	VIDUKA	17,364
04-Nov	LIVERPOOL	HOME	4 - 3	VIDUKA 4	40,055
12-Nov	CHELSEA	AWAY	1 - 1	VIDUKA	35,121
18-Nov	WEST HAM UNITED	HOME	0 - 1		40,005
26-Nov	ARSENAL	HOME	1 - 0	DACOURT	38,084
02-Dec	LEICESTER CITY	AWAY	1 - 3	VIDUKA	21,486
09-Dec	SOUTHAMPTON	AWAY	0 - 1		15,225
16-Dec	SUNDERLAND	HOME	2 - 0	BOWYER & VIDUKA	40,053
23-Dec	ASTON VILLA	HOME	1 - 2	WOODGATE	39,714
26-Dec	NEWCASTLE UNITED	AWAY	1 - 2	DACOURT	52,118
01-Jan	MIDDLESBROUGH	HOME	1 - 1	KEANE (PEN)	39,251
13-Jan	MANCHESTER CITY	AWAY	4 - 0	BAKKE, BOWYER & KEANE 2	34,288
20-Jan	NEWCASTLE UNITED	HOME	1 - 3	KEANE	40,005
24-Jan	ASTON VILLA	AWAY	2 - 1	BOWYER & HARTE (PEN)	29,335
31-Jan	COVENTRY CITY	HOME	1 - 0	KEANE	36,555
03-Feb	IPSWICH TOWN	AWAY	2 - 1	O. G. (VENUS) & KEANE	22,015
07-Feb	EVERTON	AWAY	2 - 2	HARTE & DACOURT	34,224
10-Feb	DERBY COUNTY	HOME	0 - 0		38,789
24-Feb	TOTTENHAM HOTSPUR	AWAY	2 - 1	HARTE (PEN) & BOWYER	36,070
03-Mar	MANCHESTER UNITED	HOME	1 - 1	VIDUKA	40,055
17-Mar	CHARLTON ATHLETIC	AWAY	2 - 1	VIDUKA & SMITH A	20,043
31-Mar	SUNDERLAND	AWAY	2 - 0	SMITH A & VIDUKA	48,285
07-Apr	SOUTHAMPTON	HOME	2 - 0	KEWELL & KEANE	39,267
13-Apr	LIVERPOOL	AWAY	2 - 1	FERDINAND & BOWYER	44,116
21-Apr	WEST HAM UNITED	AWAY	2 - 0	KEANE & FERDINAND	26,041
28-Apr	CHELSEA	HOME	2 - 0	KEANE & VIDUKA	39,253
05-May	ARSENAL	AWAY	1 - 2	HARTE	38,142
13-May	BRADFORD CITY	HOME	6 - 1	VIDUKA, HARTE, BAKKE, SMITH A., KEWELL & BOWYER	38,300
19-May	LEICESTER CITY	HOME	3 - 1	SMITH A 2 & HARTE	39,105

F. A. CUP

DATE	OPPONENTS	VENUE	SCORE	SCORERS	ATT.
06-Jan	BARNSLEY (R3)	HOME	1 - 0	VIDUKA	32,386
27-Jan	LIVERPOOL (R4)	HOME	0 - 2		37,108

WORTHINGTON CUP

DATE	OPPONENTS	VENUE	SCORE	SCORERS	ATT.
31-Oct	TRANMERE ROVERS (R3) *	AWAY	2 - 3	HUCKERBY 2	11,681

EUROPEAN CHAMPIONS LEAGUE

DATE	OPPONENTS	VENUE	SCORE	SCORERS	ATT.
09-Aug	TSV 1860 MUNICH (QR3-1)	HOME	2 - 1	SMITH A & HARTE (PEN)	33,769
23-Aug	TSV 1860 MUNICH (QR3-2)	AWAY	1 - 0	SMITH A	45,000
13-Sep	BARCELONA (FPGPH)	AWAY	0 - 4		85,000
19-Sep	AC MILAN (FPGPH)	HOME	1 - 0	BOWYER	35,398
26-Sep	BESIKTAS (FPGPH)	HOME	6 - 0	BOWYER 2, VIDUKA, MATTEO, BAKKE & HUCKERBY	34,485
18-Oct	BESIKTAS (FPGPH)	AWAY	0 - 0		20,000
24-Oct	BARCELONA (FPGPH)	HOME	1 - 1	BOWYER	36,721
08-Nov	AC MILAN (FPGPH)	AWAY	1 - 1	MATTEO	52,289
22-Nov	REAL MADRID (SPGPD)	HOME	0 - 2		36,794
05-Dec	LAZIO (SPGPD)	AWAY	1 - 0	SMITH A	42,450
13-Feb	ANDERLECHT (SPGPD)	HOME	2 - 1	HARTE & BOWYER	36,064
21-Feb	ANDERLECHT (SPGPD)	AWAY	4 - 1	SMITH A 2, VIDUKA & HARTE (PEN)	28,000
06-Mar	REAL MADRID (SPGPD)	AWAY	2 - 3	SMITH A & VIDUKA	39,460
14-Mar	LAZIO (SPGPD)	HOME	3 - 3	BOWYER, WILCOX & VIDUKA	36,741
04-Apr	DEPORTIVO LA CORUNA (QF-1)	HOME	3 - 0	HARTE, SMITH A & FERDINAND	35,508
17-Apr	DEPORTIVO LA CORUNA (QF-2)	AWAY	0 - 2		36,500
02-May	VALENCIA (SF-1)	HOME	0 - 0		36,437
08-May	VALENCIA (SF-2)	AWAY	0 - 3		53,000

LEAGUE AND CUPS
APPEARANCES (SUBSTITUTE)

PLAYER	LEAGUE	F. A. CUP	WORT. CUP	CHAMP. LG.	TOTAL
BAKKE	24 (5)	2	1	10 (2)	37 (7)
BATTY	13 (3)	2		7 (1)	22 (4)
BOWYER	38	1		15	54
BRIDGES	6 (1)			4	10 (1)
BURNS J	3 (1)		1	3 (1)	7 (2)
DACOURT	33	1		14	48
DUBERRY	5			4	9
EVANS	0 (1)			0 (1)	0 (2)
FERDINAND	23	2		7	32
HACKWORTH			0 (1)	0 (2)	0 (3)
HARTE	29	1	1	17	48
HAY	2 (2)		1	0 (1)	3 (3)
HUCKERBY	2 (5)		1	0 (2)	3 (7)
JONES Ma.	3 (1)		1	1	5 (1)
KEANE	12 (6)	2		14 (6)	
KELLY G	22 (2)	1	1	11 (1)	35 (3)
KEWELL	12 (5)			6 (3)	18 (8)
McPHAIL	3 (4)			1 (2)	4 (6)
MARTYN	23	1		12	36
MATTEO	30	2	1	15	48
MAYBURY				1	1
MILLS Da.	20 (3)	1		15 (1)	36 (4)
RADEBE	19 (1)	1	0 (1)	10	30 (2)
ROBINSON	15 (1)	1	1	6	23 (1)
SMITH A	26 (7)	1 (1)	0 (1)	16	43 (9)
VIDUKA	34	2	1	16	53
WILCOX	7 (10)	0 (1)		2 (3)	9 (14)
WOODGATE	14	1	1	5	21

GOALSCORERS

PLAYER	LEAGUE	F. A. CUP	WORT. CUP	CHAMP. LG.	TOTAL
VIDUKA	17	1		4	22
SMITH A	11			7	18
BOWYER	9			6	15
HARTE	7			4	11
KEANE	9				9
BAKKE	2			1	3
DACOURT	3				3
FERDINAND	2			1	3
HUCKERBY			2	1	3
KEWELL	2				2
MATTEO				2	2
WILCOX				1	1
WOODGATE	1				1
OWN GOALS	1				1

KEY :- * = AFTER EXTRA TIME, QR = QUALIFYING ROUND, FPGPH = FIRST PHASE, GROUP H, SPGPD = SECOND PHASE GROUP D, QF = QUARTER - FINAL & SF = SEMI - FINAL

With no Champions League football to cramp the fixture list, numerous pundits tipped Leeds United for Premiership success. No arrivals came in to Elland Road although as expected David O'Leary completed the £12 million purchase of Robbie Keane. With expectations high, Leeds began the campaign impressively. Unbeaten in 10 league games, O'Leary's charges claimed five wins to lead the way by the end of October.

Opening with a 2-0 win over Southampton, Lee Bowyer and Alan Smith scoring, Mark Viduka sealed an impressive win at Arsenal, despite Leeds having Bowyer and Danny Mills dismissed. Keane opened the scoring in away victories over Charlton Athletic and Ipswich Town, whilst a Harry Kewell brace secured a 3-0 triumph against Derby County. Imperious in defence, Rio Ferdinand and Nigel Martyn had been particularly impressive. Another Kewell strike secured a 2-1 win against Tottenham Hotspur before Sunderland inflicted Leeds' first defeat of the season. With Viduka struggling for goals and the Bowyer-Woodgate trial about to resume, the coming weeks would test United's resolve on and off the park.

Looking to boost his squad, O'Leary signed Seth Johnson (Derby) for £7 million before sealing the £11 million purchase of prolific striker Robbie Fowler (Liverpool). The new arrivals brought O'Leary's spending to around £100 million. To fund the purchases, United had taken a securitised 25-year £60 million loan. Results were imperative. The run up to Christmas brought a conclusion to the Bowyer-Woodgate trial; Bowyer acquitted; Woodgate guilty of affray, receiving 100 hours community service.

Fowler made an immediate impact with a brace in a 3-2 victory against Everton before notching a Boxing Day hat-trick at Bolton Wanders during a 3-0 triumph. A Bowyer strike at Southampton earned a hard-fought victory before Leeds turned on the style on New Years Day to defeat West Ham 3-0, Viduka returning to form with a brace while Fowler showed his class with another predatory strike. Top of the league, Leeds turned their attentions to the FA Cup, hoping for a good run after Chelsea had ended Worthington Cup aspirations; a Keane treble the highlight of 6-0 win at Leicester City in round three. Prior to Leeds' clash against Cardiff City, the publication of O'Leary's book *Leeds United On Trial* brought rancour and coincided with a calamitous loss of form starting with a shock FA Cup defeat.

Amongst a winless seven-game spell, Leeds suffered defeat against Newcastle, Chelsea and Liverpool, the latter a 4-0 thumping at Elland Road. In addition, after mediocre victories over Maritimo, Troyes and Grasshoppers of Zurich, PSV Eindhoven ended Leeds' UEFA Cup hopes and any chance of silverware. From Champions League certainties, qualification was now questionable. Fowler strikes kept Leeds in the frame with victories against Ipswich, Blackburn and Leicester, but defeats against Manchester United, Tottenham and Fulham ended all hope of competing in Europe's premier competition again. Viduka, Bowyer and Smith earned victories over Aston Villa, Derby and Middlesbrough to seal a UEFA Cup spot but for many it was scant consolation. Finishing fifth was a poor return for such a talented squad. Martyn made 49 appearances, Viduka top scored with 16 goals.

2001 - 2002

PREMIER LEAGUE (FINAL LEAGUE POSITION - 5TH)
PLD 38 W 18 D 12 L 8 F 53 A 37 PTS 66

DATE	OPPONENTS	VENUE	SCORE	SCORERS	ATT.
18-Aug	SOUTHAMPTON	HOME	2 - 0	BOWYER & SMITH A	39,715
21-Aug	ARSENAL	AWAY	2 - 1	HARTE & VIDUKA	38,062
25-Aug	WEST HAM UNITED	AWAY	0 - 0		24,517
08-Sep	BOLTON WANDERERS	HOME	0 - 0		40,153
16-Sep	CHARLTON ATHLETIC	AWAY	2 - 0	KEANE & MILLS Da.	20,451
23-Sep	DERBY COUNTY	HOME	3 - 0	BAKKE & KEWELL 2	39,155
30-Sep	IPSWICH TOWN	AWAY	2 - 1	KEANE & O. G. (VENUS)	22,643
13-Oct	LIVERPOOL	AWAY	1 - 1	KEWELL	44,352
21-Oct	CHELSEA	HOME	0 - 0		40,171
27-Oct	MANCHESTER UNITED	AWAY	1 - 1	VIDUKA	67,555
04-Nov	TOTTENHAM HOTSPUR	HOME	2 - 1	HARTE & KEWELL	40,203
18-Nov	SUNDERLAND	AWAY	0 - 2		48,005
25-Nov	ASTON VILLA	HOME	1 - 1	SMITH A	40,159
02-Dec	FULHAM	AWAY	0 - 0		20,918
09-Dec	BLACKBURN ROVERS	AWAY	2 - 1	KEWELL 2	28,309
16-Dec	LEICESTER CITY	HOME	2 - 2	KEWELL & VIDUKA	38,337
19-Dec	EVERTON	HOME	3 - 2	VIDUKA & FOWLER R 2	40,201
22-Dec	NEWCASTLE UNITED	HOME	3 - 4	BOWYER, VIDUKA & HARTE	40,287
26-Dec	BOLTON WANDERERS	AWAY	3 - 0	FOWLER R 3	27,060
29-Dec	SOUTHAMPTON	AWAY	1 - 0	BOWYER	31,622
01-Jan	WEST HAM UNITED	HOME	3 - 0	VIDUKA 2 & FOWLER R	39,320
12-Jan	NEWCASTLE UNITED	AWAY	1 - 3	SMITH A	52,130
20-Jan	ARSENAL	HOME	1 - 1	FOWLER R	40,143
30-Jan	CHELSEA	AWAY	0 - 2		40,614
03-Feb	LIVERPOOL	HOME	0 - 4		40,216
09-Feb	MIDDLESBROUGH	AWAY	2 - 2	BAKKE & FOWLER R	30,221
24-Feb	CHARLTON ATHLETIC	HOME	0 - 0		39,374
03-Mar	EVERTON	AWAY	0 - 0		33,226
06-Mar	IPSWICH TOWN	HOME	2 - 0	FOWLER R & HARTE (PEN)	39,414
17-Mar	BLACKBURN ROVERS	HOME	3 - 1	FOWLER R 2 & KEWELL	39,857
23-Mar	LEICESTER CITY	AWAY	2 - 0	VIDUKA & FOWLER R	18,976
30-Mar	MANCHESTER UNITED	HOME	3 - 4	VIDUKA, HARTE & BOWYER	40,058
01-Apr	TOTTENHAM HOTSPUR	AWAY	1 - 2	VIDUKA	35,167
07-Apr	SUNDERLAND	HOME	2 - 0	O. G. (CRADDOCK) & KEANE	39,195
13-Apr	ASTON VILLA	AWAY	1 - 0	VIDUKA	40,039
20-Apr	FULHAM	HOME	0 - 1		39,111
27-Apr	DERBY COUNTY	AWAY	1 - 0	BOWYER	30,705
11-May	MIDDLESBROUGH	HOME	1 - 0	SMITH A	40,218

F. A. CUP

DATE	OPPONENTS	VENUE	SCORE	SCORERS	ATT.
06-Jan	CARDIFF CITY	AWAY	1 - 2	VIDUKA	22,009

WORTHINGTON CUP

DATE	OPPONENTS	VENUE	SCORE	SCORERS	ATT.
09-Oct	LEICESTER CITY (R3)	AWAY	6 - 0	KEANE 3, BAKKE, VIDUKA & KEWELL	16,316
28-Nov	CHELSEA (R4)	HOME	0 - 2		33,841

U. E. F. A. CUP

DATE	OPPONENTS	VENUE	SCORE	SCORERS	ATT.
20-Sep	CS MARITIMO (R1-1)	AWAY	0 - 1		10,500
27-Sep	CS MARITIMO (R1-2)	HOME	3 - 0	KEANE, KEWELL & BAKKE	38,125
18-Oct	TROYES (R2-1)	HOME	4 - 2	VIDUKA 2 & BOWYER 2	40,015
01-Nov	TROYES (R2-2)	AWAY	2 - 3	VIDUKA & KEANE	14,500
22-Nov	GRASSHOPPER C. Z. (R3-1)	AWAY	2 - 1	HARTE & SMITH A	15,000
06-Dec	GRASSHOPPER C. Z. (R3-2)	HOME	2 - 2	KEWELL & KEANE	40,014
21-Feb	PSV EINDHOVEN (R4-1)	AWAY	0 - 0		32,000
28-Nov	PSV EINDHOVEN (R4-2)	HOME	0 - 1		39,775

LEAGUE AND CUPS
APPEARANCES (SUBSTITUTE)

PLAYER	LEAGUE	F. A. CUP	WORT. CUP	U.E.F.A. CUP	TOTAL
BAKKE	20 (7)		2	6	28 (7)
BATTY	30 (6)	1	1	5 (1)	37 (7)
BOWYER	24 (1)	1	1	3	29 (1)
DACOURT	16 (1)		2	6	24 (1)
DUBERRY	3	0 (1)	0 (2)	1	4 (3)
FERDINAND	31	1	2	7	41
FOWLER R	22	1			23
HARTE	34 (2)	1	2	8	45 (2)
JOHNSON Se.	12 (2)				12 (2)
KEANE	16 (9)		2	6	24 (9)
KELLY G	19 (1)	1	0 (1)	3	23 (2)
KEWELL	26 (1)		1	7	34 (1)
McPHAIL	0 (1)		0 (2)	1	1 (3)
MARTYN	38	1	2	8	49
MATTEO	32		1	7	40
MAYBURY	0 (1)				0 (1)
MILLS Da.	28	1	2	8	39
SMITH A	19 (4)	1	1 (1)	4 (1)	25 (6)
VIDUKA	33	1	1	7	42
WILCOX	4 (9)		1	1 (2)	6 (11)
WOODGATE	11 (2)	1	1		13 (2)

GOALSCORERS

PLAYER	LEAGUE	F. A. CUP	WORT. CUP	U.E.F.A. CUP	TOTAL
VIDUKA	11	1	1	3	16
FOWLER R	12				12
KEWELL	8		1	2	11
KEANE	3		3	3	9
BOWYER	5			2	7
HARTE	5			1	6
SMITH A	4			1	5
BAKKE	2		1	1	4
MILLS Da.	1				1
OWN GOALS	2				2

Throughout the summer, rumours circulated about players leaving Elland Road, however the first casualty was manager David O'Leary despite leading the club to two European semi-finals and four consecutive top-five finishes. Although Martin O'Neill again topped Leeds United's hit list, former England boss Terry Venables was appointed manager. With transfer speculation rife, Rio Ferdinand joined Manchester United in a world record £30 million deal for a defender but Lee Bowyer's £9 million move to Liverpool floundered.

With Paul Robinson selected ahead of stalwart keeper Nigel Martyn, Leeds kicked off the new term in fine style, winning four of the opening six games, Mark Viduka scoring in victories over Manchester City, West Brom and Newcastle United before a Harry Kewell strike sealed a 1-0 triumph over Manchester United. It was an impressive start but Venables honeymoon period evaporated following one victory, 4-3 at West Ham; Kewell notching a brace, in a dismal 11-game run. As Leeds plunged to the relegation zone, making his debut against the Hammers was talented teenager James Milner but with no Champions League football, financial reality saw Olivier Dacourt, Robbie Keane, and acrimoniously, Bowyer depart.

Sheffield United ended Worthington Cup hopes, whilst in Europe, Alan Smith provided the highlight with all four goals in a 4-1 second leg win over Hapoel Tel Aviv before UEFA Cup aspirations floundered against Malaga. With festive fixtures looming, Danny Mills, Robbie Fowler and Jason Wilcox boosted confidence in a 3-0 triumph at Bolton Wanderers before Milner, at 16 years 257 days, became the Premiership's youngest goalscorer during a 2-1 Boxing Day victory at Sunderland prior to a stunning effort to seal a 2-0 win over Chelsea. Milner's strike against Sunderland eclipsed Wayne Rooney's mark by 43 days. Another Everton youngster, James Vaughan, rewrote Milner's standard in April 2005. With optimism renewed, Viduka sealed a 2-0 victory over Birmingham City on New Years Day but a hard-fought win against West Ham, Seth Johnson scoring, would be the only bright note before April. To make matters worse, Jonathan Woodgate moved to Newcastle United while Fowler joined Manchester City amid speculation of financial meltdown at the club. On the park, Leeds crashed to another embarrassing defeat at Sheffield United in an FA Cup quarter-final clash, after hard-fought wins over Scunthorpe United, Gillingham and Crystal Palace; Kewell notching a cracker. Defeats against Manchester United and Middlesbrough ended Venables eight-month tenure, Peter Reid taking the helm as caretaker-boss.

With eight games remaining, Reid's task was simple, survival. By the end of the month, following a loss at Liverpool, Professor John McKenzie replaced Peter Ridsdale as chairman as the club announced debts of £79 million. Reid's arrival coincided with a return to form. Hammering Charlton Athletic 6-1, Viduka notching a hat-trick, braces by the Leeds hitman earned a 2-2 draw with Tottenham and a 2-0 win over Fulham, but defeats against Southampton and Blackburn saw United teetering on the edge of relegation with two games remaining.

Facing defending champions Arsenal, desperate for a victory to keep their title aspirations alive, supporters prepared themselves for a nerve-wracking final game at home to Aston Villa. However, in a major shock, Kewell, Ian Harte and Viduka clinched safety, handing Manchester United the title. It had been a helter-skelter season where there were more off-the-field stories than action on the pitch, but ending on a high, Viduka racked up his 14th goal in 10 games to seal a 3-1 win over Villa. Finishing fifteenth, Robinson was the only ever-present, making 50 appearances, Viduka top scored for a third successive year with 22 goals.

PREMIER LEAGUE (FINAL LEAGUE POSITION - 15TH)
PLD 38 W 14 D 5 L 19 F 58 A 57 PTS 47

DATE	OPPONENTS	VENUE	SCORE	SCORERS	ATT.
17-Aug	MANCHESTER CITY	HOME	3 - 0	BARMBY, VIDUKA & KEANE	40,195
24-Aug	WEST BROMWICH ALBION	AWAY	3 - 1	BOWYER, VIDUKA & KEWELL	26,618
28-Aug	SUNDERLAND	HOME	0 - 1		39,929
31-Aug	BIRMINGHAM CITY	AWAY	1 - 2	BOWYER	27,164
11-Sep	NEWCASTLE UNITED	AWAY	2 - 0	SMITH A & VIDUKA	51,730
14-Sep	MANCHESTER UNITED	HOME	1 - 0	KEWELL	39,662
22-Sep	BLACKBURN ROVERS	AWAY	0 - 1		25,145
28-Sep	ARSENAL	HOME	1 - 4	KEWELL	40,199
06-Oct	ASTON VILLA	AWAY	0 - 0		33,505
19-Oct	LIVERPOOL	HOME	0 - 1		40,187
26-Oct	MIDDLESBROUGH	AWAY	2 - 2	BOWYER & VIDUKA (PEN)	34,723
03-Nov	EVERTON	HOME	0 - 1		40,168
10-Nov	WEST HAM UNITED	AWAY	4 - 3	BARMBY, KEWELL 2 & VIDUKA	33,297
17-Nov	BOLTON WANDERERS	HOME	2 - 4	KEWELL & SMITH A	36,627
24-Nov	TOTTENHAM HOTSPUR	AWAY	0 - 2		35,718
01-Dec	CHARLTON ATHLETIC	HOME	1 - 2	KEWELL	35,547
07-Dec	FULHAM	AWAY	0 - 1		17,494
16-Dec	BOLTON WANDERERS	AWAY	3 - 0	MILLS Da., WILCOX & FOWLER R	23,378
21-Dec	SOUTHAMPTON	HOME	1 - 1	KEWELL	36,687
26-Dec	SUNDERLAND	AWAY	2 - 1	MILNER & FOWLER R	44,029
28-Dec	CHELSEA	HOME	2 - 0	MILNER & O. G. (DALLAS)	40,122
01-Jan	BIRMINGHAM CITY	HOME	2 - 0	BAKKE & VIDUKA	40,044
11-Jan	MANCHESTER CITY	AWAY	1 - 2	KEWELL	34,884
18-Jan	WEST BROMWICH ALBION	HOME	0 - 0		39,708
28-Jan	CHELSEA	AWAY	2 - 3	LUCIC & KEWELL	39,738
01-Feb	EVERTON	AWAY	0 - 2		40,153
08-Feb	WEST HAM UNITED	HOME	1 - 0	JOHNSON Se.	40,126
22-Feb	NEWCASTLE UNITED	HOME	0 - 3		40,025
05-Mar	MANCHESTER UNITED	AWAY	1 - 2	VIDUKA	67,135
15-Mar	MIDDLESBROUGH	HOME	2 - 3	VIDUKA 2	39,073
23-Mar	LIVERPOOL	AWAY	1 - 3	VIDUKA	43,021
05-Apr	CHARLTON ATHLETIC	AWAY	6 - 1	HARTE (PEN), KEWELL 2 & VIDUKA 3 (1 PEN)	26,274
12-Apr	TOTTENHAM HOTSPUR	HOME	2 - 2	VIDUKA 2 (1 PEN)	39,560
19-Apr	SOUTHAMPTON	AWAY	2 - 3	KEWELL & BARMBY	32,032
22-Apr	FULHAM	HOME	2 - 0	VIDUKA 2	37,220
26-Apr	BLACKBURN ROVERS	HOME	2 - 3	SMITH A & VIDUKA	38,122
04-May	ARSENAL	AWAY	3 - 2	HARTE, KEWELL & VIDUKA	38,127
11-May	ASTON VILLA	HOME	3 - 1	HARTE, VIDUKA & BARMBY	40,205

F. A. CUP

04-Jan	SCUNTHORPE UNITED (R3)	AWAY	2 - 0	BAKKE & VIDUKA (PEN)	8,329
25-Jan	GILLINGHAM (R4)	AWAY	1 - 1	SMITH A	11,093
04-Feb	GILLINGHAM (R4R)	HOME	2 - 1	BAKKE & VIDUKA	29,359
16-Feb	CRYSTAL PALCE (R5)	AWAY	2 - 1	KELLY G & KEWELL	24,512
09-Mar	SHEFFIELD UNITED (R6)	AWAY	0 - 1		24,633

WORTHINGTON CUP

06-Nov	SHEFFIELD UNITED (R3)	AWAY	1 - 2	O. G. (YATES)	26,663

U. E. F. A. CUP

19-Sep	METALURG ZAPORIZHIA (R1-1)	HOME	1 - 0	SMITH A	30,000
03-Oct	METALURG ZAPORIZHIA (R1-2)	AWAY	1 - 1	BARMBY	6,500
31-Oct	HAPOEL TEL - AVIV (R2-1)	HOME	1 - 0	KEWELL	31,867
14-Nov	HAPOEL TEL - AVIV (R2-2)	AWAY	4 - 1	SMITH A 4	4,000
28-Nov	MALAGA (R3-1)	AWAY	0 - 0		35,000
12-Dec	MALAGA (R3-2)	HOME	1 - 2	BAKKE	34,754

LEAGUE AND CUPS
APPEARANCES (SUBSTITUTE)

PLAYER	LEAGUE	F. A. CUP	WORT. CUP	U.E.F.A. CUP	TOTAL
BAKKE	31 (3)	3 (1)	1	6	41 (4)
BARMBY	16 (3)	0 (2)	1	3	20 (5)
BOWYER	15		1	5	21
BRAVO	5	1			6
BRIDGES	1 (4)		0 (1)	1 (2)	2 (7)
BURNS J	2				2
DACOURT	4 (3)			2	6 (3)
DUBERRY	11 (3)	1 (1)	0 (1)	3 (1)	15 (6)
FOWLER R	2 (6)	0 (1)		0 (1)	2 (8)
HARTE	24 (3)	3	1	5	33 (3)
JOHNSON Se.	3 (6)	3 (1)			6 (7)
JOHNSON Si.	1 (3)				1 (3)
KEANE	0 (3)				0 (3)
KELLY G	24 (1)	4		6	34 (1)
KEWELL	31	4	1	5	41
KILGALLON	0 (2)			0 (1)	0 (3)
LUCIC	16 (1)	2 (1)	1		19 (2)
McMASTER	0 (4)				0 (4)
McPHAIL	7 (6)		0 (1)	2 (3)	9 (10)
MATTEO	20	3		1	24
MILLS Da.	32 (1)	4	1	2 (1)	39 (2)
MILNER	1 (17)	0 (4)			1 (21)
OKON	15	5		1	21
RADEBE	16 (3)	4		3	23 (3)
RICHARDSON	0			0 (1)	0 (1)
ROBINSON P	38	5	1	6	50
SMITH A	33	4		6	43
VIDUKA	29 (4)	4	1	2	36 (4)
WILCOX	23 (2)	4	1	3	31 (2)
WOODGATE	18	1	1	4	24

GOALSCORERS

PLAYER	LEAGUE	F. A. CUP	WORT. CUP	U.E.F.A. CUP	TOTAL
VIDUKA	20	2			22
KEWELL	14	1		1	16
SMITH A	3	1		5	9
BARMBY	4			1	5
BAKKE	1	2		1	4
BOWYER	3				3
HARTE	3				3
FOWLER R	2				2
MILNER	2				2
JOHNSON Se.	1				1
KEANE	1				1
KELLY G		1			1
LUCIC	1				1
MILLS Da.	1				1
WILCOX	1				1
WOODGATE	1				1
OWN GOALS	1	1			2

Out of European football for the first time in five years, Peter Reid's squad was further ripped apart with the departure of Danny Mills to Middlesbrough. Bringing in a number of loan players including Jermaine Pennant (Arsenal), Leeds began the new term in reasonable fashion, Mark Viduka scoring in a 2-2 draw with Newcastle United and a 3-2 win at Middlesbrough. With no prospect of first team football, veteran keeper Nigel Martyn was allowed to join Everton, while 4-0 defeats at Leicester City and Everton demonstrated how far the club had fallen.

Peter Reid's wafer-thin squad was low on confidence, although they had squeezed past Swindon Town in the Coca Cola Cup on penalties after keeper Paul Robinson scored a last ditch equaliser in normal time, and claimed a 2-1 win against Blackburn Rovers courtesy of a Seth Johnson brace. However, Reid's position became untenable following five consecutive defeats, including a 6-1 drubbing at Portsmouth. Despatched from the Coca Cola Cup by Manchester United and bottom of the table after a third of the season, former legend Eddie Gray was given the unenviable task of trying to save the club from relegation.

Early indications appeared promising when James Milner clinched a 1-0 win at Charlton Athletic, while Pennant earned a draw against Chelsea. Viduka struck in a 3-2 win over Fulham before scoring in a 1-1 draw at Manchester City. A point gained against Aston Villa on Boxing Day demonstrated resolve, but supporters realised that the coming months would be hard grind when relegation candidates Wolves inflicted a 3-1 defeat to keep Leeds in the drop zone.

The New Year began with Arsenal cantering to a 4-1 win in the FA Cup before five consecutive league defeats, including a 3-0 loss to Middlesbrough, sent Leeds tumbling to the bottom once again. With rumours rampant about new owners, Gerald Krasner emerged as the club's new chairman. Looking forward with optimism, despite the club's crippling finances, the battle for survival continued. Viduka and Smith found the target in a 4-1 victory against Wolves before the duo struck again in hard-earned draws against Liverpool and Manchester United. Viduka sealed a 2-1 win against relegation rivals Manchester City either side of defeats against Fulham and Birmingham City, before striking again in crucial triumphs over Leicester City and Blackburn Rovers.

Leeds now had six games to save their Premiership status. Everton arrived at Elland Road on the edge of the relegation battle and somewhat fortuitously gained a point courtesy of a superb display by former keeper Martyn. With confidence draining away, champions-elect Arsenal demonstrated the gulf in class between the top and bottom teams by thumping Leeds 5-0 at Highbury, before further defeats against Portsmouth and Bolton confirmed relegation after 14 seasons of top-flight football.

In an emotionally charged final home game, Leeds drew against Charlton Athletic before Chelsea edged a win on the last day of a wretched campaign. Underperforming throughout the season, supporters were left to ponder how United had slipped from Champions League semi-finalists to relegation in just two years. Over-expenditure in pursuit of European glory was the ultimate failing, however, the new board had to prepare for a new era. Gary Kelly and Robinson made 39 appearances, Viduka top scored for an unprecedented fourth consecutive season with 12 goals.

2003 - 2004

PREMIER LEAGUE (FINAL LEAGUE POSITION - 19TH)				
PLD 38 W 8 D 9 L 21 F 40 A 79 PTS 33				
DATE	OPPONENTS	VENUE	SCORE	SCORERS	ATT.

DATE	OPPONENTS	VENUE	SCORE	SCORERS	ATT.
17-Aug	NEWCASTLE UNITED	HOME	2 - 2	VIDUKA & SMITH A	36,766
23-Aug	TOTTENHAM HOTSPUR	AWAY	1 - 2	SMITH A	34,354
26-Aug	SOUTHAMPTON	HOME	0 - 0		34,721
30-Aug	MIDDLESBROUGH	AWAY	3 - 2	CAMARA, SAKHO & VIDUKA	30,414
15-Sep	LEICESTER CITY	AWAY	0 - 4		30,480
20-Sep	BIRMINGHAM CITY	HOME	0 - 2		34,305
28-Sep	EVERTON	AWAY	0 - 4		39,151
04-Oct	BLACKBURN ROVERS	HOME	2 - 1	JOHNSON Se. 2	35,039
18-Oct	MANCHESTER UNITED	HOME	0 - 1		40,153
25-Oct	LIVERPOOL	AWAY	1 - 3	SMITH A	43,599
01-Nov	ARSENAL	HOME	1 - 4	SMITH A	36,491
08-Nov	PORTSMOUTH	AWAY	1 - 6	SMITH A	20,112
22-Nov	BOLTON WANDERERS	HOME	0 - 2		36,558
29-Nov	CHARLTON ATHLETIC	AWAY	1 - 0	MILNER	26,445
06-Dec	CHELSEA	HOME	1 - 1	PENNANT	36,305
14-Dec	FULHAM	HOME	3 - 2	DUBERRY, MATTEO & VIDUKA	30,544
22-Dec	MANCHESTER CITY	AWAY	1 - 1	VIDUKA	47,126
26-Dec	ASTON VILLA	HOME	0 - 0		38,513
28-Dec	WOLVERHAMPTON WANDERERS	AWAY	1 - 3	DUBERRY	29,139
07-Jan	NEWCASTLE UNITED	AWAY	0 - 1		52,130
10-Jan	TOTTENHAM HOTSPUR	HOME	0 - 1		35,365
17-Jan	SOUTHAMPTON	AWAY	1 - 2	KILGALLON	31,976
31-Jan	MIDDLESBROUGH	HOME	0 - 3		35,970
07-Feb	ASTON VILLA	AWAY	0 - 2		39,171
10-Feb	WOLVERHAMPTON WANDERERS	HOME	4 - 1	MATTEO, MILNER, SMITH A & VIDUKA	36,867
21-Feb	MANCHESTER UNITED	AWAY	1 - 1	SMITH A	67,744
29-Feb	LIVERPOOL	HOME	2 - 2	BAKKE & VIDUKA	39,932
13-Mar	FULHAM	AWAY	0 - 2		17,104
22-Mar	MANCHESTER CITY	HOME	2 - 1	McPHAIL & VIDUKA (PEN)	36,998
27-Mar	BIRMINGHAM CITY	AWAY	1 - 4	VIDUKA	39,690
05-Apr	LEICESTER CITY	HOME	3 - 2	DUBERRY, SMITH A & VIDUKA	34,036
10-Apr	BLACKBURN ROVERS	AWAY	2 - 1	CALDWELL S & VIDUKA	36,611
13-Apr	EVERTON	HOME	1 - 1	MILNER	39,835
16-Apr	ARSENAL	AWAY	0 - 5		38,094
25-Apr	PORTSMOUTH	HOME	1 - 2	HARTE (PEN)	39,273
02-May	BOLTON WANDERERS	AWAY	1 - 4	VIDUKA (PEN)	27,420
08-May	CHARLTON ATHLETIC	HOME	3 - 3	KILGALLON, PENNANT & SMITH A (PEN)	38,986
15-May	CHELSEA	AWAY	0 - 1		41,276

F. A. CUP					
04-Jan	ARSENAL (R3)	HOME	1 - 4	VIDUKA	30,207

CARLING CUP					
24-Sep	SWINDON TOWN (R2) $	HOME	2 - 2	HARTE & ROBINSON P	29,211
28-Oct	MANCHESTER UNITED (R3)	HOME	2 - 3	JUNIOR 2	37,546

KEY :- $ = WON 4 - 3 ON PENALTIES

LEAGUE AND CUP			
APPEARANCES (SUBSTITUTE)			
PLAYER	LEAGUE	F. A. CUP	CARLING CUP	TOTAL

PLAYER	LEAGUE	F. A. CUP	CARLING CUP	TOTAL
BAKKE	8 (2)	1		9 (2)
BARMBY	1 (5)			1 (5)
BATTY	10 (2)	1	1	12 (2)
BRIDGES	1 (9)		1 (1)	2 (10)
CALDWELL S	13			13
CAMARA	13		2	15
CARSON	2 (1)			2 (1)
CHAPUIS	0 (1)		1 (1)	1 (2)
DOMI	9 (3)		0 (2)	9 (5)
DUBERRY	19	1		20
HARTE	21 (2)	1	2	24 (2)
JOHNSON Se.	24 (1)		1	25 (1)
JOHNSON Si.	1 (4)			1 (4)
JUNIOR	5		2	7
KELLY G	37		2	39
KILGALLON	7 (1)	1		8 (1)
LENNON	0 (11)	0 (1)	1 (1)	1 (13)
McPHAIL	8 (4)			8 (4)
MATTEO	33	1		34
MILNER	27 (3)	1	1	29 (3)
MORRIS	11 (1)			11 (1)
OLEMBE	8 (4)		2	10 (4)
PENNANT	34 (2)			34 (2)
RADEBE	11 (3)		0 (1)	11 (4)
RICHARDSON	2 (2)	1		3 (2)
ROBINSON P	36	1	2	39
SAKHO	9 (8)	0 (1)	1	10 (9)
SMITH A	35	1	2	38
VIDUKA	30	1		31
WILCOX	3 (3)		1	4 (3)

GOALSCORERS			
PLAYER	LEAGUE	F. A. CUP	CARLING CUP	TOTAL
VIDUKA	11	1		12
SMITH A	9			9
DUBERRY	3			3
MILNER	3			3
HARTE	1		1	2
JOHNSON Se.	2			2
JUNIOR			2	2
KILGALLON	2			2
MATTEO	2			2
PENNANT	2			2
BAKKE	1			1
CALDWELL S	1			1
CAMARA	1			1
McPHAIL	1			1
ROBINSON P			1	1
SAKHO	1			1

Relegation resulted in a reality check during the close season at Elland Road. With Kevin Blackwell taking the helm, a cull of highly paid Premiership stars began as Paul Robinson (Tottenham Hotspur), Mark Viduka (Middlesbrough) and Dominic Matteo (Blackburn Rovers) departed. Reconciled to losing high earners, supporters watched on forlornly as one by one, former heroes moved on, but selling Alan Smith to bitter rivals Manchester United angered supporters, whilst accepting Newcastle United's offer for promising youngster James Milner bemused followers.

However, new players arrived including keeper Neil Sullivan, defenders Clark Carlisle and Paul Butler, midfielder Jermaine Wright, and former United favourite, striker Brian Deane. Raiding the club's bank of talent, Frazer Richardson, Matthew Kilgallon and Aaron Lennon supplemented a squad that included only Gary Kelly and Michael Duberry from the previous season's final game at Chelsea.

Bedding in a new team was no easy task for Blackwell and the opening months would be hard graft, facing teams desperate to beat the once proud club. Beginning with a victory against Derby County courtesy of a superb strike by Richardson, United claimed three further triumphs in the opening 16 games, defeating Coventry City, Plymouth Argyle and Preston North End. Lying sixth bottom, pressure was mounting on Blackwell, especially after a tepid 2-1 home defeat to Burnley, when Wright opened the scoring inside 10 seconds.

From adversity though came a morale boosting 4-2 win at Preston, new signing David Healy notching a brace, and a 6-1 drubbing of Queens Park Rangers, Deane joining a select band of players to score four goals in a match for United. Inconsistency however dominated the build up to Christmas but five games without a win was halted with a superb 3-2 Boxing Day triumph at promotion-bound Sunderland. Further 2-1 victories over Plymouth and Coventry followed.

With financial turmoil still afflicting the club, there was genuine relief for fans when former Chelsea chairman Ken Bates took the helm from Gerald Krasner early in the New Year. With finances stabilising, attention turned to matters on the field. Bates' arrival coincided with a 1-0 win at Stoke City, elevating Leeds to eleventh spot. Three victories in four fixtures over Burnley, Reading and West Ham followed, loan striker Rob Hulse scoring in the latter two triumphs. The Hammers win guaranteed safety but play-off talk disappeared with one victory in the final 10 games, 2-1 at Watford; Hulse again finding the target. Drawing seven matches during the run-in, United were no longer a soft touch and ended one of the club's most traumatic seasons fourteenth.

Thirty-seven players appeared, with United's bedrock in defence, Neil Sullivan, the only ever-present. History had also been made with Healy and Deane top scoring with seven goals in all competitions, an all-time low mark. Nevertheless, Blackwell deserves credit for leading Leeds through a turbulent campaign when the likes of Kilgallon and Richardson made their mark. Many pundits predicted doom and gloom, however, Leeds United survived and now enter a new dawn with genuine optimism.

CHAMPIONSHIP (FINAL LEAGUE POSITION - 14TH)
PLD 46 W 14 D 18 L 14 F 49 A 52 PTS 60

DATE	OPPONENTS	VENUE	SCORE	SCORERS	ATT.
07-Aug	DERBY COUNTY	HOME	1 - 0	RICHARDSON	30,459
10-Aug	GILLINGHAM	AWAY	1 - 2	PUGH	10,739
14-Aug	WOLVERHAMPTON WANDERERS	AWAY	0 - 0		28,397
21-Aug	NOTTINGHAM FOREST	HOME	1 - 1	GUPPY	31,808
29-Aug	SHEFFIELD UNITED	AWAY	0 - 2		22,959
11-Sep	COVENTRY CITY	HOME	3 - 0	CARLISLE, PUGH & JOACHIM	26,725
14-Sep	PLYMOUTH ARGYLE	AWAY	1 - 0	O. G. (KEITH)	20,555
18-Sep	CREWE ALEXANDRA	AWAY	2 - 2	PUGH 2	9,095
24-Sep	SUNDERLAND	HOME	0 - 1		28,926
28-Sep	STOKE CITY	HOME	0 - 0		25,759
02-Oct	CARDIFF CITY	AWAY	0 - 0		17,006
16-Oct	PRESTON NORTH END	HOME	1 - 1	PUGH	30,458
19-Oct	READING	AWAY	1 - 1	WALTON	22,230
23-Oct	BRIGHTON & HOVE ALBION	AWAY	0 - 1		6,716
31-Oct	WIGAN ATHLETIC	HOME	0 - 2		27,432
03-Nov	BURNLEY	HOME	1 - 2	WRIGHT	27,490
06-Nov	PRESTON NORTH END	AWAY	4 - 2	HEALY 2, WALTON & DEANE	18,531
13-Nov	IPSWICH TOWN	AWAY	0 - 1		29,995
20-Nov	QUEENS PARK RANGERS	HOME	6 - 1	DEANE 4, WRIGHT & HEALY	29,739
24-Nov	WATFORD	HOME	2 - 2	CARLISLE & WRIGHT	24,585
29-Nov	ROTHERHAM UNITED	AWAY	0 - 1		8,860
04-Dec	LEICESTER CITY	HOME	0 - 2		27,384
10-Dec	WEST HAM UNITED	AWAY	1 - 1	HEALY (PEN)	30,684
19-Dec	MILLWALL	HOME	1 - 1	OSTER	26,256
26-Dec	SUNDERLAND	AWAY	3 - 2	LENNON, DEANE & JOACHIM	43,253
28-Dec	PLYMOUTH ARGYLE	HOME	2 - 1	HEALY & O. G. (GILBERT)	34,496
01-Jan	CREWE ALEXANDRA	HOME	0 - 2		32,302
03-Jan	COVENTRY CITY	AWAY	2 - 1	HEALY & BLAKE Na.	19,084
15-Jan	CARDIFF CITY	HOME	1 - 1	WALTON	29,548
22-Jan	STOKE CITY	AWAY	1 - 0	O. G. (THOMAS)	18,372
26-Jan	DERBY COUNTY	AWAY	0 - 2		25,648
29-Jan	BRIGHTON & HOVE ALBION	HOME	1 - 1	CARLISLE	27,033
05-Feb	BURNLEY	AWAY	1 - 0	EINARSSON	17,789
12-Feb	READING	HOME	3 - 1	HEALY & HULSE 2	30,034
19-Feb	WIGAN ATHLETIC	AWAY	0 - 3		17,177
26-Feb	WEST HAM UNITED	HOME	2 - 1	HULSE & DERRY	34,115
06-Mar	MILLWALL	AWAY	1 - 1	HULSE	11,510
12-Mar	GILLINGHAM	HOME	1 - 1	HULSE	27,995
16-Mar	NOTTINGHAM FOREST	AWAY	0 - 0		25,101
02-Apr	WOLVERHAMPTON WANDERERS	HOME	1 - 1	DERRY	29,773
05-Apr	SHEFFIELD UNITED	HOME	0 - 4		28,936
09-Apr	WATFORD	AWAY	2 - 1	HULSE & CARLISLE	16,306
16-Apr	QUEENS PARK RANGERS	AWAY	1 - 1	JOHNSON Se.	18,182
23-Apr	IPSWICH TOWN	HOME	1 - 1	SPRING	29,607
30-Apr	LEICESTER CITY	AWAY	0 - 2		26,593
08-May	ROTHERHAM UNITED	HOME	0 - 0		30,900

F. A. CUP

DATE	OPPONENTS	VENUE	SCORE	SCORERS	ATT.
08-Jan	BIRMINGHAM CITY (R3)	AWAY	0 - 3		25,159

COCA - COLA CUP

DATE	OPPONENTS	VENUE	SCORE	SCORERS	ATT.
24-Aug	HUDDERSFIELD TOWN (R1)	HOME	1 - 0	PUGH	30,115
21-Sep	SWINDON TOWN (R2)	HOME	1 - 0	RICKETTS	18,476
26-Oct	PORTSMOUTH (R3)	AWAY	1 - 2	DEANE	15,215

LEAGUE AND CUP
APPEARANCES (SUBSTITUTE)

PLAYER	LEAGUE	F. A. CUP	CARLING CUP	TOTAL
BAKKE	0 (1)			0 (1)
BLAKE Na.	2	1		3
BUTLER P	39		2	41
CADAMARTERI	0		0 (1)	0 (1)
CARLISLE	29 (6)		3	32 (6)
CRAINEY	9		1	10
DEANE	23 (8)		1 (1)	24 (9)
DERRY	7			7
DUBERRY	4	1		5
EINARSSON	6 (2)			6 (2)
GRAY M	10			10
GREGAN	34 (1)	1	2	37 (1)
GRIFFIT	0 (1)			0 (1)
GUPPY	1 (2)		1	2 (2)
HEALY	27 (1)	1		28 (1)
HULSE	13			13
JOACHIM	10 (17)	0 (1)	3	13 (18)
JOHNSON Se.	4 (2)			4 (2)
JOHNSON Si.	1 (1)		1	2 (1)
KELLY G	43	1	3	47
KEOGH			0 (1)	0 (1)
KILGALLON	26	1	1	28
KING	4 (5)			4 (5)
LENNON	19 (8)	1	0 (1)	20 (9)
McMASTER	0 (7)		1 (1)	1 (8)
MOORE I	4 (2)			4 (2)
ORMEROD	6			6
OSTER	8			8
PUGH	33 (5)	0 (1)	3	36 (6)
RADEBE	1 (2)			1 (2)
RICHARDSON	28 (10)	1	2	31 (10)
RICKETTS	9 (12)		2 (1)	11 (13)
SPRING	4 (9)		2	6 (9)
SULLIVAN	46	1	3	50
WALTON S	23 (7)	1	1 (1)	25 (8)
WOODS	0 (1)			0 (1)
WRIGHT J	33 (2)	1	1	35 (2)

GOALSCORERS

PLAYER	LEAGUE	F. A. CUP	CARLING CUP	TOTAL
DEANE	6		1	7
HEALY	7			7
HULSE	6			6
PUGH	5		1	6
CARLISLE	4			4
WALTON S	3			3
WRIGHT J	3			3
DERRY	2			2
JOACHIM	2			2
BLAKE Na.	1			1
EINARSSON	1			1
GUPPY	1			1
JOHNSON Se.	1			1
LENNON	1			1
OSTER	1			1
RICHARDSON	1			1
RICKETTS			1	1
SPRING	1			1
OWN GOALS	3			3